21st Conference on Natural Language Processing/Konferenz zur Verarbeitung naturlicher Sprache (KONVENS 2025)

Volume 1 - Long and Short Papers

Hildesheim, Germany
9-12 September 2025

ISBN: 979-8-3313-2674-6

Printed from e-media with permission by:

Curran Associates, Inc.
57 Morehouse Lane
Red Hook, NY 12571

CURRAN ASSOCIATES INC. proceedings.com

Some format issues inherent in the e-media version may also appear in this print version.

Association for Computational Linguistics
209 N. Eighth Street
Stroudsburg, Pennsylvania 18360

Phone: 1-570-476-8006
Fax: 1-570-476-0860

acl@aclweb.org

Additional copies of this publication are available from:

Curran Associates, Inc.
57 Morehouse Lane
Red Hook, NY 12571 USA
Phone: 845-758-0400
Fax: 845-758-2633
Email: curran@proceedings.com
Web: www.proceedings.com

Imprint

Bibliographic Information of the German National Library

The German National Library lists this publication in the German National Bibliography. Detailed bibliographic data are available at `https://portal.dnb.de`.

HsH Applied Academics | Hannover 2025

Hochschule Hannover – University of Applied Sciences and Arts | Central Library
Ricklinger Stadtweg 118, 30459 Hannover, Germany
E-Mail: serwiss@hs-hannover.de
Website: `https://hs-h.de/bib`

BMFTR Project „DiamOnd@HsH – Towards a Science-Led Open Access Culture via Establishment of a Diamond Open Access University Press for the University of Applied Sciences and Arts Hannover" (16KOA042)

Cover Design: Lina Herschel (Hamburg, Germany), linaherschel.com

DOI: `https://doi.org/10.25968/opus-3678`
URN: urn:nbn:de:bsz:960-opus4-36787

KONVENS 2025 is hosted by the University of Hildesheim and chaired by Christian Wartena (DataIH Institute for Applied Data Science Hannover, Hochschule Hannover) and Ulrich Heid (Institut für Informationswissenschaft und Sprachtechnologie, Universität Hildesheim).

KONVENS was funded by the zukunft.niedersachsen program, in the program line 'Pro*Niedersachsen – Wissenschaftliche Veranstaltungen der Geistes-, Kultur- und Sozialwissenschaften in Niedersachsen'

Keynote speakers and tutorials were funded by the German Society for Computational Linguistics and Language Technology.

This publication was supported by the NiedersachsenOPEN publication fund, funded by zukunft.niedersachsen.

Preface

We are delighted to present the proceedings of the 21st edition of KONVENS (Konferenz zur Verarbeitung natürlicher Sprache / Conference on Natural Language Processing), held in Hildesheim from September 9 to 12, 2025. The conference was jointly organized by the University of Applied Sciences and Arts Hannover and the University of Hildesheim. KONVENS is a conference series on computational linguistics established in 1992 and is held annually in Germany, Austria, and Switzerland under the auspices of the German Society for Computational Linguistics and Language Technology, the Special Interest Group on Computational Linguistics of the German Linguistic Society, the Austrian Society for Artificial Intelligence, and SwissText.

This year, the main conference received 65 submissions, each reviewed by at least three program committee members. In total, 38 papers were accepted, of which 31 are included in these proceedings and 7 were presented as non-archival contributions. The accepted papers cover a wide range of subjects, including research on and with Large Language Models (LLMs), the development of new resources, discourse and semantics, the detection of hate speech, translation and multilinguality, and methods and applications with a particular focus on the German language. All authors were asked to indicate whether they would prefer an oral or poster presentation. In most cases, the preferred presentation form was honoured. Therefore, the presentation format is not an indicator of the quality of the paper. Both long and short papers were presented in oral and poster sessions.

The main program was complemented by six workshops, three tutorials, the GSCL award ceremony, and three keynote talks, offering a broad platform for exchange and discussion within the community. The workshops also addressed a wide variety of topics. KONVENS hosted the workshop KlarText on German Text Simplification and Readability Assessment, the 5th edition of the workshop on Computational Linguistics for the Political and Social Sciences (CPSS) and the Workshop on NLP for Sustainability (NLP4Sustain) conbined with the GermEval Shared Task on Understanding Sustainability Reports (SustainEval). There were three more workshops offering GermEval shared tasks: LLMs4Subjects (LLM-based Automated Subject Tagging for a National Technical Library's Open-Access Catalog), Candy Speech and Harmful Content Detection. Further details of the workshops, as well as all accepted workshop papers, are presented in the second volume of these proceedings. We would like to thank the organizers of all workshops and shared tasks for their great cooperation.

We would like to thank all authors for their submissions and the members of the program committee for their careful reviews. Our gratitude also goes to the local organizers in Hannover and Hildesheim and to all supporters who contributed to making KONVENS 2025 possible.

Christian Wartena
Ulrich Heid

KONVENS 2025
Conference on Natural Language Processing

KONVENS (Konferenz zur Verarbeitung natürlicher Sprache) is an annual conference series on computational linguistics (biennial until 2018) that started in 1992 and that is organized under the auspices of the German Society for Computational Linguistics and Language Technology, the Special Interest Group on Computational Linguistics of the German Linguistic Society, the Austrian Society for Artificial Intelligence and SwissNLP.

The conference takes place in Hildesheim, Germany, from September 9th to 12th, 2025

Event Website: https://konvens-2025.hs-hannover.de
E-Mail: info.konvens2025@gscl.org

ACL Anthology

The Proceedings of the 21th Conference on Natural Language Processing (KONVENS 2025) as well as the individual papers can also be found on ACL Anthology.

https://aclanthology.org/events/konvens-2025

Committees

Program Committee

Christian Wartena (Hochschule Hannover)
Ulrich Heid (Universität Hildesheim)

Local Organization

Gertrud Faaß (Universität Hildesheim)

Reviewing Board

Fernando Benites
Ostschweizer Fachhochschule

Joshua Berger
Hochschule Hannover

Maria Berger
Ruhr-Universität Bochum

Tobias Bocklet
TH Nürnberg

Peter Bourgonje
Universität Potsdam

Miriam Butt
Universität Konstanz

Erion Çano
Universität Paderborn

Yiyi Chen
Aalborg Universitet

Christian Chiarcos
Universität Augsburg

Stefanie Dipper
Ruhr-Universität Bochum

Luka Ebeling
Fides Technology GmbH

Nicolai Erbs
T-Systems International, Frankfurt

Kilian Evang
Heinrich-Heine-Universität Düsseldorf

Bernhard Fisseni
Universität Duisburg-Essen

Hamed Babaei Giglou
Tabriz University

Stefan Hillmann
TU Berlin

Anke Holler
Universität Göttingen

Andrea Horbach
IPN Kiel

Manuela Hürlimann
ZHAW, Zürich

Kerstin Jung
Universität Stuttgart

Casey Kennington
Boise State University

Fritz Kliche
Universität Hildesheim

Roman Klinger
Universität Bamberg

Thomas Kolb
TU Wien

Evangelia Kordoni
HU Berlin

Vasiliki Kougia
Universität Wien

Julia Krasselt
ZHAW, Zürich

Brigitte Krenn
OFAI Wien

Udo Kruschwitz
Universität Regensburg

Ekaterina Lapshinova-Koltunski
Universität Hildesheim

Pedro Henrique Luz de Araujo
Universität Wien

Thomas Mandl
Universität Hildesheim

Alexander Mehler
Universität Frankfurt

Margot Mieskes
Hochschule Darmstadt

Seid Muhie Yimam
Universität Hamburg

Friedrich Neubarth
OFAI Wien

Juri Opitz
Universität Zürich

Simon Ostermann
DFKI Saarbrücken

Simone Paolo Ponzetto
Universität Mannheim

Jakob Prange
Universität Augsburg

Michael Pucher
TU Graz

Michaela Regneri
Universität Hamburg

Georg Rehm
DFKI Berlin

Josef Ruppenhofer
FernUniversität in Hagen

Felix Sasaki
TH Brandenburg

Johannes Schäfer
Universität Bamberg

Yves Scherrer
University of Helsinki

David Schlangen
Universität Potsdam

Helmut Schmid
LMU München

Loris Schoenegger
Universität Wien

Marc Schulder
Universität Hamburg

Sabine Schulte im Walde
Universität Stuttgart

Barbara Schuppler
TU Graz

Rico Sennrich
Universität Zürich

Melanie Siegel
Hochschule Darmstadt

Michael Spranger
Hochschule Mittweida

Manfred Stede
Universität Potsdam

Julia Maria Struß
Fachhochschule Potsdam

Lukas Thoma
Universität Wien

Manfred Vogel
Fachhochschule Nordwestschweiz

Ahmadou Wagne
TU Wien

Yuxi Xia
Universität Wien

Sina Zarrieß
Universität Bielefeld

Torsten Zesch
FernUniversität in Hagen

Heike Zinsmeister
Universität Hamburg

Program

Tuesday, September 9, 2025

13:30 – 18:00 Klartext Workshop

13:30 – 15:30 GermEval Workshop: LLMs4Subj

13:30 – 18:00 Tutorials

- FlexiConc: Reading Concordances with Algorithms
- The 101 introduction explaining how to produce, publish, and use machine-readable scientific knowledge
- Fusing Vision and Language: A Tutorial on Vision-Language Models for Multimodal Content Analysis

Wednesday, September 10, 2025

9:00 – 12:30 CPSS Workshop

9:00 – 12:30 GermEval Workshops

- Sustaineval
- Harmful Content Detection
- Cabdy Speech

14:00 – 15:00 Keynote

Opening the Black Box of Language Models via Theory and Interpretability
Michael Hahn

14:00 – 15:00 Oral Session 1: Methods

1. Surprisal in Action: A Comparative Study of LDA and LSA for Keyword Extraction
   J. Nathanael Philipp, Max Kölbl, Michael Richter
2. Learn to pick the winner: Black-box ensembling for textual and visual question answering
   Yuxi Xia, Klim Zaporojets, Benjamin Roth
3. LRMs are not thinking straight: Unreliability of thinking trajectories
   Jhouben Cuesta-Ramirez, Samuel Beaussant, Mehdi Mounsif

Thursday, September 11, 2025

9:00 – 12:30 CPSS Workshop

9:00 – 10:00 Oral Session 2: Applications

1. Adaption and Evaluation of Generative Large Language Models for German Medical Information Extraction
   Sören Spiegel, Seid Muhie Yimam, Philipp Breitfeld, Frank Ückert
2. ZEFYS2025: A German Historical Newspaper Dataset for Named Entity Recognition and Entity Linking
   Sophie Schneider, Ulrike Förstel, Kai Labusch, Jörg Lehmann, Clemens Neudecker
3. Generating Search-Engine-Optimized Headlines for Sports News
   Frank Zalkow, Benedikt Schäfer, Thomas Moissl, Jonas Bücherl, Kerstin Markl, Sebastian Bothe, Francois Duchateau, Julia Dollase, Patric Kabus, Daniel Steinigen, Oliver Schmitt, Fabian Küch

10:30 – 11:30 Poster Session 1

1. German Aspect-based Sentiment Analysis in the Wild: B2B Dataset Creation and Cross-Domain Evaluation
   Jakob Fehle, Niklas Donhauser, Udo Kruschwitz, Nils Constantin Hellwig, Christian Wolff
2. Vague, Incomplete, Subjective, and Uncertain Information in Art Provenance
   Fabio Mariani
3. Automatic Creation of Marginalia
   Aaron Lang, Robin Jegan, Andreas Henrich
4. Localization of English Affective Narrative Generation to German
   Johannes Schäfer, Sabine Weber, Roman Klinger
5. Multimodal Docker Unified UIMA Interface: New Horizons for Distributed Microservice-Oriented Processing of Corpora using UIMA
   Daniel Bundan, Giuseppe Abrami, Alexander Mehler
6. Systematic Review of Linguistic Characteristics in Profiling and Automated Detection of Autistic Speech
   Charlotte Bellinghausen, Andreas Riedel
7. More than the Sum of Their Words: Generating and Contrasting Large Linguistic
   Hanna Schmück
8. Towards a Cross-Dialectal Dictionary for Low German (Low Saxon)
   Christian Chiarcos, Janine Siewert, Tabea Gröger, Christian Fäth
9. Rapid Text Segmentation: Crowd-sourcing Lay Intuition about Text Structure in the Browser
   Florian Frenken
10. Applying an Information-theoretic Approach for Automatic Identification of German Multi-word Expressions
    Sergei Bagdasarov, Elke Teich

11:30 – 12:30 Oral Session 3: New Resources

1. Predicting Functional Content Zones in German Source-Dependent Argumentative Essays: Experiments on a Novel Dataset
   Xiaoyu Bai, Manfred Stede
2. SocCor: A Multimodal-based Multilingual Soccer Corpus for Text Data Analytics
   Paul Löhr, Jannik Strötgen
3. A Survey of Idiom Datasets for Psycholinguistic and Computational Research
   Michael Flor, Xinyi Liu, Anna Feldman

12:30 – 13:30 Public Lecture

Smarte Technologie, bessere Bildung? KI in der Hochschule
Torsten Zesch

13:30 – 14:30 Keynote 2

What does it take to raise a BabyLM?
Sina Zarrieß

14:30 – 15:30 Oral Session 4: Discourse and Semantics

1. Function Words as Stable Features for German Opinion Articles Classification
   Amelie Schmidt-Colberg, Simon Burkard, Anne Grohnert, Michael John
2. LLM-based Classification of Grounding Acts in German
   Milena Belosevic, Hendrik Buschmeier
3. Efficient and Effective Coreference Resolution for German
   Fynn Petersen-Frey, Hans Ole Hatzel, Chris Biemann

16:00 – 17:00 BA/MA Award Presentations

1. Ranking for Abstract Screening in Systematic Literature Reviews using Large Language Models
   Christian Jaumann
2. Investigating Language Models for Classical Philology – Aspects of Morphology, Syntax, and Knowledge from a Multilingual Perspective
   Frederick Riemenschneider

Friday, September 12, 2025

9:00 – 10:00 Keynote 3

Dear XAI Community, We Need to Talk! Fundamental Misconceptions in Current XAI Research
Timo Freiesleben

10:30 – 11:30 Poster Session 2

1. Hit or Be Hit: Tests of (Pre)Compositional Abilities in Vision and Language Models
   Mădălina Zgreabăn, Albert Gatt, Pablo Mosteiro
2. Hybrid Feature-Embedding Models for Robust AI Text Detection
   Kasper Thomas Gartside Knudsen, Christian Hardmeier
3. Advancing German Language Modelling - Transparent Models and Comprehensive Benchmarks
   Jan Pfister, Julia Wunderle, Anton Ehrmanntraut, Fotis Jannidis, Andreas Hotho
4. Using LLMs for experimental stimulus pretests in linguistics. Evidence from semantic associations between words and social gender
   Christian Lang, Franziska Kretzschmar, Sandra Hansen
5. Developmentally plausible pretraining, now also auf Deutsch: a BabyLM Dataset for German
   Bastian Bunzeck, Daniel Duran, Sina Zarrieß
6. PETapter: Leveraging PET-style classification heads for modular few-shot parameter-efficient fine-tuning
   Jonas Rieger, Mattes Ruckdeschel, Gregor Wiedemann
7. Large Language Model Data Generation for Enhanced Intent Recognition in German Speech
   Theresa Pekarek Rosin, Burak Can Kaplan, Stefan Wermter
8. Detecting Sexism and Its Severity in German Online Comments: Modeling Annotation Subjectivity with BERT and mBERT
   Melanie Woodrow, Margot Mieskes

11:30 – 12:30 Oral Session 5: Hate Speech

1. FASCIST-O-METER: Classifier for Neo-fascist Discourse Online
   Rudy Alexandro Garrido Veliz, Martin Semmann, Chris Biemann, Seid Muhie Yimam
2. Conditioning Large Language Models on Legal Systems? Detecting Punishable Hate Speech
   Florian Ludwig, Frederike Zufall, Torsten Zesch
3. HICC: A Dataset for German Hate Speech in Conversational Context
   Lars Schmid, Pius von Däniken, Patrick Giedemann, Don Tuggener, Judith Bühler, Maria Kamenowski, Katja Girschick, Dirk Baier, Mark Cieliebak

11:30 – 12:30 Oral Session 6: Translation and Multilinguality

1. Evaluating the Feasibility of Using ChatGPT for Cross-cultural Survey Translation
   Danielly Sorato, Diana Zavala-Rojas
2. Information Divergence in Translation and Interpreting: Findings from Same-Source Texts
   Maria Kunilovskaya, Sharid Loáiciga, Ekaterina Lapshinova-Koltunski
3. SEAS: Sentence Extraction and Alignment from Subtitles
   Josh Stephenson, Libby Barak

Keynote Speakers

Opening the Black Box of Language Models via Theory and Interpretability

Michael Hahn
Saarland University

Abstract Recent progress in LLMs has rapidly outpaced our ability to understand their inner workings. This talk describes our work aiming towards such understanding. First, we mechanistically reverse-engineer transformers' solutions to tasks such as arithmetic and in-context learning. Second, we develop rigorous results describing the abilities (and limitations) of transformers and other architectures in performing reasoning. We show that this can help us understand abilities and limitations of LLMs on practically-relevant tasks, and even point to possible improvements. I will close with directions for future research.

Bio Michael Hahn is a Tenure-Track Professor (W2) at Saarland Informatics Campus at Saarland University, where he directs the Language, Computation, and Cognition Lab (LaCoCo). He is affiliated with the Departments of Language Science and Technology and Computer Science. Michael Hahn received his PhD from Stanford University in 2022, advised by Judith Degen and Dan Jurafsky.

What does it take to raise a BabyLM?

Sina Zarrieß
Bielefeld University

Abstract The current landscape of CL research is dominated by language models that are too large to be designed and built from scratch by most researchers. This radically limits the possibilities for scientific experimentation and thus our understanding of how these models work. In this talk, I will argue for research on small language models, trained from scratch, on orders of magnitude less data than LLMs. I will present evidence that basic linguistic abilities emerge in small language models in a very similar way to much larger models. I will also show how experimenting with modelling choices in small language models can help us understand the limitations of LLMs.

Bio Sina Zarrieß is a professor for Computational Linguistics at Bielefeld University. Previously, she held a junior professorship for Digital Humanities, Language Technology and Machine Learning at the University of Jena. She obtained her PhD at the Institute for Natural Language Processing at Stuttgart University and spent her post-doc at the University of Bielefeld as a member of the Excellence Cluster for Cognitive Interaction Technology. Her research focuses on computational models of language use in text and dialogue, with applications in natural language generation, dialogue systems, language & vision.

Dear XAI Community, We Need to Talk! Fundamental Misconceptions in Current XAI Research

Timo Freiesleben
University of Tübingen

Abstract Despite progress in the field, significant parts of current XAI research are still not on solid conceptual, ethical, or methodological grounds. Unfortunately, these unfounded parts are not on the decline but continue to grow. Many explanation techniques are still proposed without clarifying their purpose. Instead, they are advertised with ever more fancy-looking heatmaps or only seemingly relevant benchmarks. Moreover, explanation techniques are motivated with questionable goals, such as building trust, or rely on strong assumptions about the 'concepts' that deep learning algorithms learn. In this talk, I will highlight and discuss these and other misconceptions in current XAI research. Moreover, I will suggest steps to make XAI a more substantive area of research.

Bio Timo Freiesleben is a postdoctoral fellow at the Cluster of Excellence Machine Learning for Science at the University of Tübingen. His research explores how concepts from the philosophy of science — such as explanation, representation, and robustness — can inform and enhance both theoretical and practical aspects of machine learning. His work focuses particularly on how machine learning can contribute to generating new scientific insights. Prior to his position in Tübingen, he completed his PhD at the Munich Center for Mathematical Philosophy at LMU Munich, where he investigated the question of what explainable artificial intelligence actually explains.

Public Lecture

Smarte Technologie, bessere Bildung? KI in der Hochschule

Torsten Zesch
University of Tübingen

Abstract Der Vortrag beleuchtet die vielversprechenden Möglichkeiten und kritischen Herausforderungen beim Einsatz von KI-Technologien in der Lehre. Von personalisierten Lernplattformen über automatisierte Bewertungssysteme bis hin zu intelligenten Tutoren: KI verspricht individuellere Betreuung, effizientere Prozesse und neue Lernwege. Doch was bedeutet das für die Rolle der Lehrenden? Verbessern sich wirklich die Lernergebnisse? Und welche technischen Fragen stellen sich beim Umgang mit Daten und Algorithmen im Bildungsbereich? Anhand konkreter Beispiele aus dem Reallabor der FernUniversität in Hagen diskutieren wir Chancen und Risiken des digitalen Wandels an Hochschulen. Dabei wird deutlich: Technologie allein macht noch keine bessere Bildung – entscheidend ist, wie wir sie gestalten und einsetzen. Ein Ausblick auf mögliche Zukunftsszenarien rundet den Vortrag ab und lädt zur kritischen Reflexion über die Bildung von morgen ein.

Bio Torsten Zesch is a full professor of Computational Linguistics at CATALPA (Center of Advanced Technology for Assisted Learning and Predictive Analytics), FernUniversität in Hagen, Germany. He holds a doctoral degree in computer science from Technische Universität Darmstadt and was the president of the German Society for Computational Linguistics and Language Technology (GSCL) from 2017 to 2023. His main research interests are in educational natural language processing, in particular the ways in which teaching and learning processes can be supported by language technology. For this purpose, he develops methods for the automatic analysis of textual and multimodal language data, with a focus on robust and explainable models.

Contents

Translation and Multilinguality

Methods and Applications for German and English

KONVENS

21st Conference on Natural Language Processing (KONVENS 2025)

Proceedings of the Conference
9. – 12. September 2025

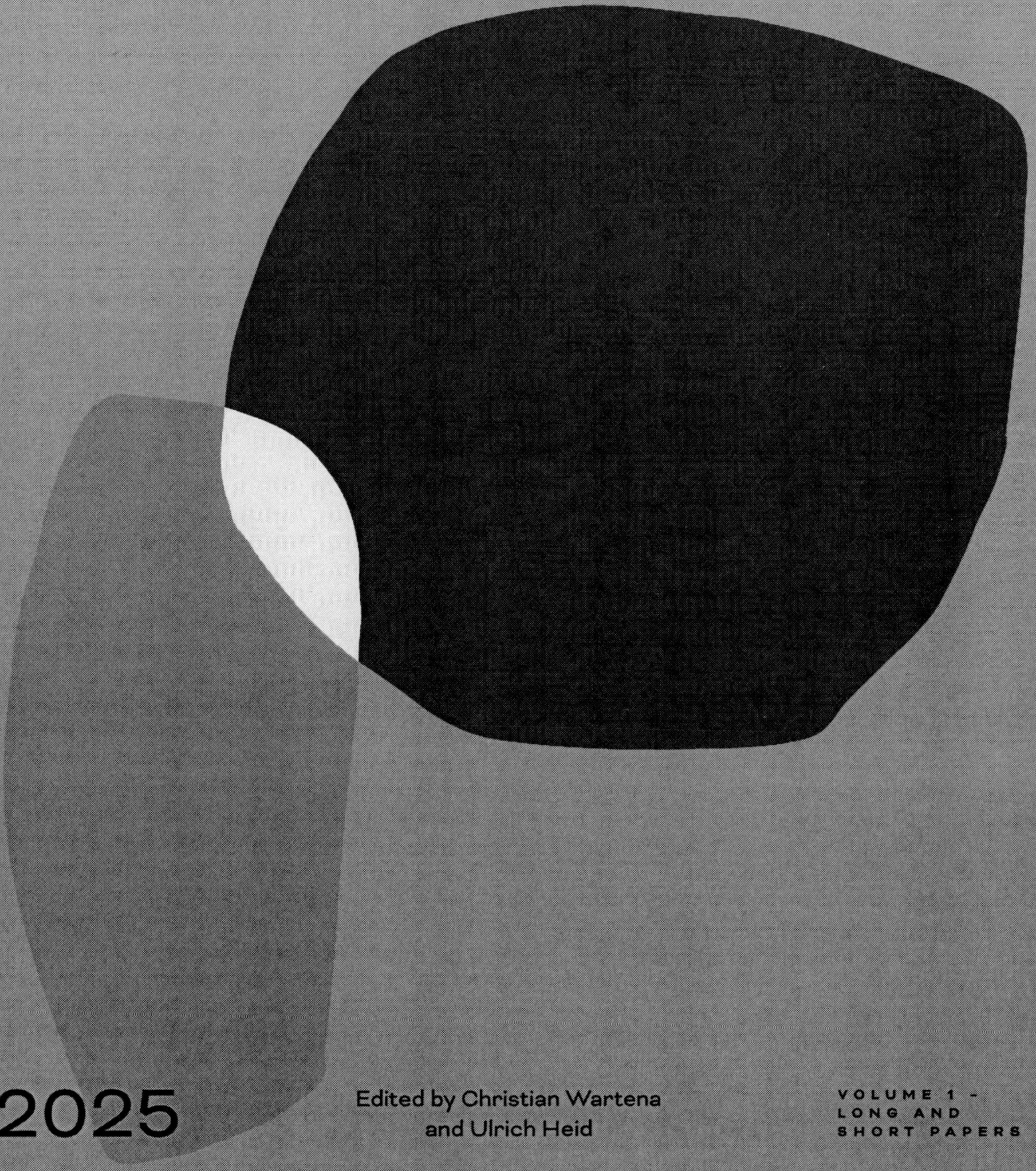

2025

Edited by Christian Wartena and Ulrich Heid

VOLUME 1 - LONG AND SHORT PAPERS

VOLUME 1 – LONG AND SHORT PAPERS

KONVENS (Konferenz zur Verarbeitung natürlicher Sprache, Conference on Natural Language Processing) is an annual conference series on computational linguistics first held in 1992. Originally biennial until 2018, the conference is organized under the auspices of the German Society for Computational Linguistics and Language Technology, the Special Interest Group on Computational Linguistics of the German Linguistic Society, the Austrian Society for Artificial Intelligence, and SwissNLP. The 21st edition of KONVENS took place in Hildesheim, Germany, from September 9 – 12, 2025, and was jointly organized by the University of Hildesheim and the University of Applied Sciences and Arts Hannover.

This year's conference centered on artificial intelligence and large language models (LLMs), reflecting the scientific community's efforts to better understand and optimize the properties of LLMs. These topics were addressed in three plenary lectures, a lecture session on methodological issues, and a poster session on LLMs, as well as in sessions on other topics such as methods based on LLMs, discourse and semantics, multilinguality and translation, new language resources, applications of language technology beyond linguistics, and the identification of hate speech on social media.

The proceedings are published in two volumes. The first volume contains all the peer-reviewed papers from the main conference, and the second volume contains the papers from the six workshops and shared tasks organised as part of the conference.

HOCHSCHULE HANNOVER
UNIVERSITY OF APPLIED SCIENCES AND ARTS

Stiftung Universität Hildesheim 2003

HsH Applied Academics

Surprisal in Action: A Comparative Study of LDA and LSA for Keyword Extraction

J. Nathanael Philipp
Sächsische Akademie der Wissenschaften zu Leipzig
Karl-Tauchnitz-Str. 1
04107 Leipzig, Germany
nathanael@philipp.land

Max Kölbl
Osaka University
1-5 Yamadaoka, Suita
565-0871 Osaka, Japan
max.w.koelbl@gmail.com

Michael Richter
Leipzig University
Augustusplatz 10
04109 Leipzig, Germany
mprrichter@gmail.com

Abstract

This study compares two methods of topic detection, *Latent Dirichlet Allocation* (LDA) and *Latent Semantic Analysis* (LSA), by using it in conjuction with the *Topic Context Model* (TCM) on the task of keyword extraction. The surprisal values that TCM outputs based on LDA and LSA are compared, both, directly and as inputs to a Recurrent Neural Network (RNN). While in the direct comparison LSA slightly outperforms LDA, LDA and LSA perform on a par when a Recurrent Neural Network (RNN) is trained with surprisal values. In general: semantic surprisal as input of an RNN improves its performance.

1 Introduction

Keywords serve as classification features of texts and play a crucial role in search engines and natural language understanding (Bharti and Babu, 2017; Karttunen, 1974; Stalnaker, 1977). Following (Çano and Bojar, 2019) and (Tomokiyo and Hurst, 2003), we follow the definition in (Kölbl et al., 2022) and define keywords as nouns or noun phrases, i.e., proper names that can be used as classification features of texts.

This study compares the performance for keyword extraction (KE) of two topic models: *Latent Dirichlet Allocation* (LDA) (Blei et al., 2003) against *Latent Semantic Analysis* (LSA) (Deerwester et al., 1990). These two topic models are applied within the framework of *Information Theory* (Shannon, 1948) and *Surprisal Theory* (Tribus, 1961; Hale, 2001; Jaeger and Levy, 2007) by which operationalisation is carried out using the Topic Context Model (TCM) (Kölbl et al., 2020, 2021; Philipp et al., 2022). TCM has been empirically tested in studies of (Kölbl et al., 2020, 2021) and (Philipp et al., 2022) and allows the calculation of *semantic surprisal*, that is, the degree to which a word is informative in a semantic context.

Following (Kölbl et al., 2021; Philipp et al., 2022), we assume that words with high surprisal values are strong keyword candidates, as they are both unexpected and semantically informative. TCM derives surprisal from topic distributions within a text, necessitating a topic model, LDA or LSA, whose different underlying principles warrant a systematic comparison. The comparison of LDA and LSA is therefore based on the criterion of which of the two topic models the TCM uses to generate the better keywords. Why is it interesting to compare the two topic models? While LDA is probabilistic and assumes a generative process where words are drawn from topics, LSA is deterministic and represents texts as points in a high-dimensional topic space based on word cooccurrences. Both methods have been widely used in information retrieval, yet their respective advantages for KE remain an open question. Our study integrates a Recurrent Neural Network (RNN) with TCM by using *semantic surprisal* as an input feature, allowing us to assess whether this additional information improves keyword prediction while maintaining interpretability. Our research question is: which topic model enables TCM to estimate surprisal more effectively for identifying keywords? While prior studies suggest LDA often outperforms LSA in text mining, the impact of these models on KE within the TCM framework remains unexplored. Since no general benchmark exists for comparing topic models in this regard, we focus on evaluating their KE performance. The structure of the article is as follows: first, we introduce the concept of *surprisal* and outline the theoretical foundation of TCM. This is followed by sections on related work, data resources, and the implementation of LDA and LSA in TCM. Finally, we present our results, followed by a discussion and conclusion.

Proceedings of the 21st Conference on Natural Language Processing (KONVENS), Volume 1: Long and Short Papers, pages 1–11, 2025

2 Surprisal and TCM

Surprisal is equivalent to information (Hale, 2001; Levy, 2008): the surprisal of a lingustic unit is estimated from the context of that unit and is thus based on conditional probabilities. In psycholinguistics, the amount of surprisal of a linguisitc unit and the mental effort to process it, are proportional to each other.

Surprisal is interwoven with predictive language processing: given for example a sentence-initial word, a language processor intuitively builds up a prediction what the next word will be (Venhuizen et al., 2019) which is accompanied by a mental *anticipatory pre-activation of information* (Heilbron, 2022). So, if the stimulus word is followed by an expected word, both the surprisal and the processing effort are small, if, in constrast, the stimulus word is followed by an unexpected word, the surprisal is high which requires more processing effort.

The idea of TCM is quite intuitive: the semantic surprisal of a linguistic unit is estimated from the distribution of topics in the environment of that unit. To give a simple but intuitive example, if the word *electric engine* appears in the context of the topics *chocolate* and *caries*, the semantic surprisal of this word is likely to be high and should cause a high processing effort. TCM can consider topics both in an non-local environment of a target word (a corpus, for instance) and topics in local environments (for instance, paragraphs, documents or even sentences).

Why do we utilise surprisal, i.e, information for KE? Our point of departure is Dretske's work (Dretske, 1981) on the flow of information and language comprehension: *Shannon information* is, according to Dretske, the 'raw material' necessary to convey meaning and to build knowledge.

Empirical evidence for a link between Shannon information and meaning comes, in addition to the above mentioned studies of Kölbl et al. (2021) and Philipp et al. (2022), among others from (Melamed, 1997) on semantic entropy, (Aji and Kaimal, 2012; Ravindra et al., 2004) on automatic summarisation, and from (Rubino et al., 2016; Bizzoni and Lapshinova-Koltunski, 2021) on classification of translations.

How can surprisal be defined? The surprisal of a linguistic unit w is proportional to the difficulty or mental effort to process w (Levy, 2008): the smaller the probability of a unit w given a context is, the more surprising and the more informative is w, and the greater the effort is that a language processor needs to process w. This is corroborated through empirical evidence (Brennan et al., 2016; Hale et al., 2015) for lexical surprisal (see amongst others (DeLong et al., 2005; Frank et al., 2015; Smith and Levy, 2008; Szewczyk and Schriefers, 2018; Goodkind and Bicknell, 2018)), for syntactic surprisal (Hagoort et al., 1993; Henderson et al., 2016), and for semantic surprisal (Rabovsky et al., 2018). The surprisal model (Hale, 2001; Levy, 2008) is given in Formula 1:

$$\text{difficulty} \propto \text{surprisal} = -\log_2 P(w_i | w_1 \dots w_{i-1}, \text{CONTEXT}) \quad (1)$$

In Formula 1, $w_1 \dots w_{i-1}$ as contexts of w can be n-grams of tokens or n-grams of part-of-speech tags. The former are the basis for the estimation of lexical surprisal, the latter are the basis for the estimation of grammatical surprisal. The variable CONTEXT represents some extra-sentential context, such as sentence structures for syntactic surprisal, or topics, world knowledge, or representation of the discourse for semantic surprisal.

3 Related work

Even though there has been no research comparing LSA and LDA in terms of KE, there are comparative studies from theoretical and empirical points of view. Some of these studies (Griffiths et al., 2007; Niraula et al., 2013) point out the incapability of LSA to grasp polysemy since words are represented as fixed Euclidean points. On the other hand, LDA is based on a generative probabilistic model which follows the Dirichlet multinomial distribution and thus can handle multiple meanings of a word. Based on these distinctive characteristics, (Griffiths et al., 2007) assert that LDA outperforms LSA in predicting associations between words. The most recent experimental research has indeed confirmed the superiority of LDA over LSA, for instance in classifying e-books (Mohammed and Al-augby, 2020; Kalepalli et al., 2020) and on detecting polysemy (Griffiths et al., 2007; Niraula et al., 2013).

Despite these drawbacks of LSA, the empirical study by Bergamaschi and Po (2015) shows that LSA achieves a better performance on movie recommendation than LDA. Papadimitriou et al. (2000) propose three conditions under which LSA, referred to as *Latent Semantic Indexing* (LSI), is capable of capturing the underlying semantics of the corpus, summarised by Anaya (2011, 16-17), i.e., (i) the documents should have an identical or at least very similar writing style, (ii) each document should have a clearly recognisable 'main' topic, and (iii) words should have only a high probability in one topic but a low probability in other topics.

With regard to the theoretical framework of our study, so far, information theory is almost completely disregarded for KE. To the best of our knowledge, only Herrera and Pury (2008) present a model based on information theory. Upon detecting keywords, they assume that highly relevant words should be concentrated in some portions of the text. Their model incorporates the distribution of occurrences of a word in the corpus. However, the calculation of entropy is not based on the semantic model, as in our study by LDA / LSA within the TCM.

With regard to the technique, the application of neural networks to KE achieves successful outcomes, and is state of the art, see for instance (Zhang et al., 2020) who propose the deep neural network model 'target centred LSTM model', which is trained as a binary classifier to determine whether a given word is a keyword or not, and (Grootendorst, 2020) who implemented a BERT-based model capable of KE.

4 Data and Methods

4.1 Text Corpus

As our data resource, we exploit the *Heise*[1] corpus (Philipp et al., 2022). The corpus comprises $100,673$ texts on a variety of topics, often related to technology and telecommunication, with a total of $38,633$ keywords. Each text is prefixed with a set of keywords that we use as a reference set. We assume that thematic diversity will be an advantage for the use of *TCM* since this means a high variety of topics and is expected to optimise the performance of the model. An additional advantage of the *Heise* corpus is that it includes numerous short texts as local environments for the TCM, this is, small environments of target words. In order to avoid memory limits in the case of LDA we use the same subset as Philipp et al. (2022) which consists of randomly drawn samples with a total of $30,284$ texts with $239,065$ words (lemmas, determined by spaCy[2]), and $7,347$ keywords. A randomly chosen sample of 10% of the texts is used as our validation set, the remaining 90% is the training set.

Each text is preceded by a headline, and for $15,454$ of the texts also a short summary, i.e., a *lead* is given, with a average length of one or two sentences.

We treat multiword expressions of named entities as single words and possible keyword candidates. In Philipp et al. (2022), the named-entity recogniser (NER) from *spaCy* classified 122 named entities as specifications of place (LOC), 288 as mixed specifications (MISC), 23 as specifications of organisations (ORG), 40 as specifications of persons (PER), and 6775 were not assigned to any of these categories.

The performance of the NER on the training is given in Philipp et al. (2022, Table 1). The results disclose that the accuracy positively correlates with complexity of the NER models, but all NER models have extremely weak precision and F1 values but better recall. The most complex NER model achieves only a precision of 0.1259. That is to say, only 12.6% of the predicted keywords are real keywords, and the model predicts a large set of keywords whereby the hit rate is relatively low. Recall is 0.3785, which says that almost 38 percent of the keywords are recognised.

4.2 Baselines

NER (Kölbl et al., 2021; Philipp et al., 2022), *TextRank* (Mihalcea and Tarau, 2004) and RNNs without surprisal as input are used as baselines. All named entities that NER identifies, are regarded as keywords. A detailed description of the RNNs can be found in Section 4.4.

TextRank (TR) (Mihalcea and Tarau, 2004) is a modification of Google's *PageRank*-algorithm (Brin and Page, 1998) and performs i.a. summarisation and KE[3]. TR models an entire text as a graph, whereby neighbourhood in the graph and a high weight of the link indicate semantic relatedness.

4.3 Topic Context Model

TCM is an extended topic model: it calculates semantic surprisal based on the output of genuine topic models.

[1] `https://heise.de`

[2] `https://spacy.io`

[3] `https://github.com/jnphilipp/TextRank`

When LDA is employed, TCM calculates surprisal based on probabilities of w in a topic weighted by the probability of that topic in a document. In LSA, only the log-likelihood of w in the main topic in a document is considered. LDA learns the relationship between words and topics in its training phase, while LSA establishes a relationship between documents through the cosine distance.

Figure 1 illustrates TCM, with either LDA or LSA as topic model for the topic distribution.

4.3.1 How LSA works in TCM

LSA reduces the dimension of a text using *Singular Value Decomposition* (SVD). Steinberger et al. (2004) pointed out that SVD "[...] reflects a breakdown of the original document into r linearly-independent base vectors or concepts."

Formula 2 says that, as a first step, the term by sentence-matrix A is decomposed into the three matrices U, Σ and V^T. The columns in U represent the concepts in the Steinberger's quote above (Steinberger et al., 2004):

$$A = U\Sigma V^T \tag{2}$$

The entries of matrix A are the weighted frequencies of terms (rows) in sentences (columns). The number of diagonal elements in Σ is the number of singular vectors representing the semantic dimensions of a text. Following Steinberger et al. (2004), the leftmost column vector in matrix U can be interpreted as the main topic of a document.

Given a finite set M of documents, we can relate the texts semantically by embedding their respective topic vectors into a vector space. (Steinberger et al., 2004) recommend cosine similarity as a measure of similarity of two documents. Since U is unitary, the length of each topic vector is 1, reducing the cosine to a simple scalar product. For a document d with topic vector v_d, we compute the likelihood $P(w_d)$ of a word w_d to appear in d by checking its appearance in other texts, see Formula 3.

$$P(w_d) = \frac{\sum\limits_{s \in M} \delta(w_d, s)\,(1 + \cos\langle v_s, v_d \rangle)}{\sum\limits_{s \in M} 1 + \cos\langle v_s, v_d \rangle} \tag{3}$$

Here, $\delta(w_d, s)$ is 1 if w_d appears in s or 0 if it does not. The corresponding surprisal is then given in Formula 4.

$$surprisal(w_d) = -\log_2 P(w_d|d) \tag{4}$$

We use a scoring function for the RNN, see Formula 5, in order for $surprisal$ values to be between -1 and 1, which we refer to as $\widehat{surprisal}$.

$$\widehat{surprisal}(w_d) = \tanh \frac{surprisal(w_d) - \mu_d}{\sqrt{\sigma_d^2 + \epsilon}} \tag{5}$$

In Formula 5, μ_d is the mean of the $surprisal$ for all the words w in a document d, and σ_d^2 is the variance. To ensure that the standard deviation is not zero we add $\epsilon = 1e^{-7}$.

4.3.2 How LDA works in TCM

LDA is a statistical topic model that tries through a generative process to detect and identify the topics that appear in a document and which words belong to them (Blei et al., 2003). LDA is based on the Dirichlet Distribution with two priors, i.e., *hyperparamaters*: η, the distribution of words in a topic and α, the topic distribution in a document d. The values of these parameters can be chosen deliberately. The only observable phenomena are words w in d, everything else are hidden variables. In d, a word $w_{d,n}$ occurs, given the non-observable assignment of a topic for the n-th word w in d, i.e., $z_{d,n}$, and given the complete set of k topics $\beta_{1:k}$ where β is a distribution of words in a topic k. There is a conditional probability of $z_{d,n}$ given θ_d, i.e., the distribution of topics in document d. The values for β and θ are determined in an iterative process. Let us illustrate this in a fictitious example: The distribution in an (abstract) topic, which is interpreted as 'food', could look as follows (the probability that a word with its meaning is assigned to a topic is given after the comma in each case): topic 'food': chocolate 0.02, butter 0.019, soup 0.021, bicycle 0.00001. 'Bicycle' is thus assigned to the topic 'food' with some much lower probability than 'chocolate', 'butter' and 'soup'.

We define the context as a topic calculated by LDA and calculate the average surprisal $\overline{surprisal}$ for each word, see Formula 6, where n is the number of topics of the LDA. We fixed this at 1000 topics. The calculation is given in Formula 6.

$$\overline{surprisal}(w_d) = -\frac{1}{n}\sum_{i=1}^{n} \log_2 P(w_d|t_i) \tag{6}$$

The term $P(w_d|t_i)$ is the probability of a word w_d given a topic t_i in a document d, which is calculated according to Formula 7. $c_d(w)$ is the frequency of a word w given a document d, $|d|$ is

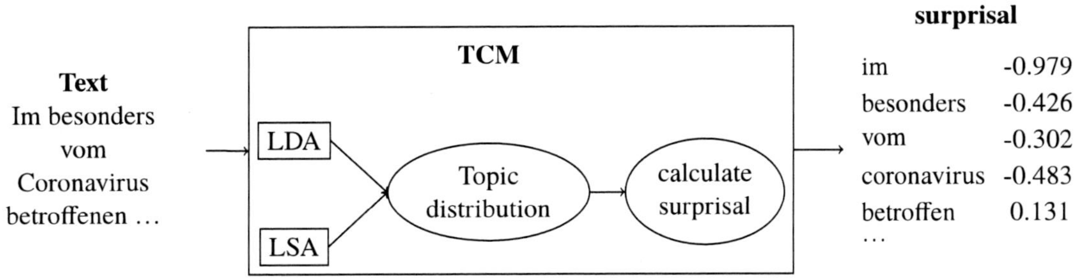

Figure 1: Illustration of the Topic Context Model.

the total number of words in the document d, WT is the normalised word topic distribution of the LDA[4], and $P(t_i|d)$ is probability of a topic t and a document d given by the LDA.

$$P(w_d|t_i) = \frac{c_d(w_d)}{|d|} WT_{w_d,t_i} P(t_i|d) \quad (7)$$

For LDA, we use the same scoring function as for LSA (see Formula 5) except using the $\overline{surprisal}$ instead of $surprisal$ values.

4.4 Recurrent Neural Network

The RNNs in our study carry out the binary classification whether a word in the input sequence is a keyword or not (see Zhang et al. (2016), Kölbl et al. (2020),Kölbl et al. (2021) and Philipp et al. (2022)).

The architectures of the RNNs in this study is identical to the ones in Philipp et al. (2022). That is to say, for each of the input parts of the texts, namely *headline*, *lead*, and *text*, the RNN has a separate in- and output. In between, one or two bidirectional *Gated Recurrent Units* (GRU) for processing are located. We use identical embeddings and bidirectional GRU(s) for all input types. The architecture of the RNNs is given in Figure 2 that illustrates also the classification-process: when a respective input-word is classified as a keyword, the output is 1, while the output 0 means that the respective word is not classified as a keyword.

Five different input types can be distinguished: (i) text only, (ii) text and information of words $\widehat{surprisal}$ from the topic model LDA, (iii) text and $\widehat{surprisal}$ from the topic model LSA, (iv) – (v) only the $\widehat{surprisal}$ from the TCM model, either from LDA or LSA, respectably. That is to say, the latter two models (iv) – (v) are exclusively trained on the surprisal of words and not on any text. In model (i), each word is represented as a vector with 128 entries from an embedding layer. In the models (ii) – (v), the $\widehat{surprisal}$ values from LDA / LSA in (ii) – (v) are used directly, and in (ii) and (iii) the original embedding vector is concatenated with the $\widehat{surprisal}$ value, resulting in a vector of size 129.

Following in Philipp et al. (2022), for each of the five input types, three configurations with one bidirectional GRU of sizes $(256, 512, 1024)$ and two configurations with two bidirectional GRUs of sizes $(256, 512)$ were trained.

For the input types (i), (ii) and (iv) we report the results from Philipp et al. (2022). We trained, in total, 10 different RNNs ((iii), (v)), each for 15 epochs.

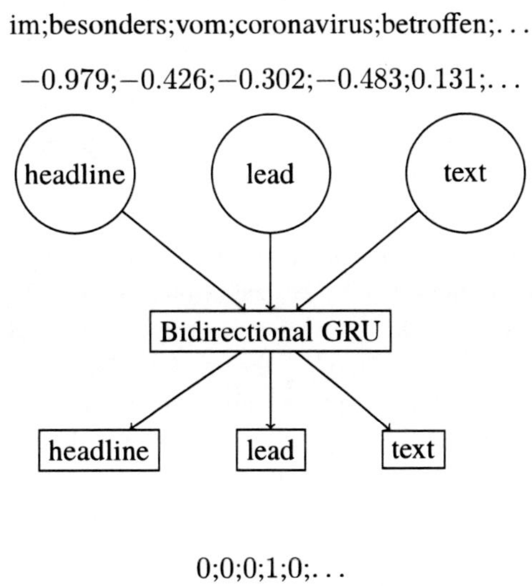

Figure 2: Schematic of the RNN architectures with text and $\widehat{surprisal}$ as input. (Philipp et al., 2022)

[4] `model.components_ / model.components_.sum(axis=1)[:, np.newaxis]` as suggested by `https://scikit-learn.org/stable/modules/generated/sklearn.decomposition.LatentDirichletAllocation.html`

5 Results

Table 1 gives the results of the baseline models on the validation set from (Philipp et al., 2022), and Table 2 displays the results of the recent study that employs LSA in addition to LDA as part of the TCM.

As in (Philipp et al., 2022), accuracy 1 to 5, precision, recall, and F1-measure are reported, whereby accuracy n means how often at least n keywords are correctly predicted. The F1 score is a measure of the accuracy of a test and is calculated as the harmonic mean of precision and recall. The baselines are NER, TR and RNNs without $surprisal$ as input. For LDA and LSA, the evaluation covers the most informative words of a text, either absolute, e.g., LDA_5 means the top 5 most informative words, or as percentage, e.g., $LDA_{10\%}$ means that the 10% most informative words were selected as keyword candidates. With TR we have the levels TR_5 and TR_{10}, respectively.

Regarding the RNN models, the index refers to, firstly, the input type, e.g., T if it is trained on texts and LDA / LSA means that $surprisal$ from LDA / LSA is part of the input, and secondly, it refers to the layer-sizes of the GRU, i.e., 256, 512, and 1024 respectively.

When no RNN is employed, i.e., with 'pure' TCM, LSA outperforms LDA in direct comparison, in all measures and all rankings. This means that the words with a high $surprisal$ from LSA are more likely keywords than words from the LDA. Further we observe, that neither the top 5 nor the top 10 informative words are better than the 10% most informative words which means that for both LDA and LSA, the most informative words are not necessarily *good* keywords. In general, the 'pure' TCM performs poorly, and is outperformed by other models.

Training the RNNs on both text and $surprisal$ yields the overall best performances in recall, although NER achieves relatively high recall as well. For $a4$ and $a5$ the model $\text{RNN}_{T,LDA,512}$ has the overall best results, for recall it is the model $\text{RNN}_{T,LSA,1024}$, and for F1 the model $\text{RNN}_{LDA,2\times256}$ outperforms the remaining models. However, the differences are small: when training with the $surprisal$ from LDA, the improvement of F1 is about 0.01. The baseline RNN, i.e., trained only on texts, achieves a paper-thin lead in precision of all models - closely followed by the neural networks with $surprisal$ of LDA and LSA.

The model $\text{RNN}_{T,LDA,1024}$ performs surprisingly poorly, and we attribute this outcome to a slower learning process compared to the other models. The RNNs trained solely on $surprisal$ from LDA perform in general better than the baseline model 'TR top 5' but not better than 'TR top 10'. This indicates that the $surprisal$ alone performs on the same level as the baselines. In general, we observe that the performance of RNN is improved when the input is supplemented by the input of surprisal values. There is no correlation between performance and the complexity of the network.

Apart from the $a1$ - $a3$ values, where the baselines NER ($a1$) and TextRank ($a2$ and $a3$) achieve the highest values, the RNNs yield the best results in F1 values, which can still be improved by using $surprisal$ as input. NER is the winner in $a1$-accuracy which is probably due to the fact, that most keywords are names. This also explains the *pure* performes for the NER, i.e., the NER is not a very reliable in recognizing the names in the data, which is due to the nature of the data, see (Kölbl et al., 2021; Philipp et al., 2022; Kölbl et al., 2022)

The accuracy values can be interpreted as follows: for about 88% of texts, at least one keyword is a named entity, as far as the spaCy model is concerned. All RNNs trained on $surprisal$ have at some point the same accuracy values, showing that here is their limit, i.e., the RNNs can only learn a certain amount of the pure $surprisal$. TR_{10} achieves high accuracy values $a1 - a3$ and the second highest recall of all models, but only weak precision and a low F1 value. This means that the model fails to detect a satisfactory percentage of keywords from an existing set of keywords. TextRank with the five highest ranked words (TR_5) achieves slightly higher F1 and precision values than when ten hightest ranked words are considered (TR_{10}).

6 Discussion and conclusion

Acceptable results for KE are obtained when $surprisal$ is the input of a recurrent neural network whereby it does almost not matter whether LDA and LSA is employed in the TCM.

So, the first finding of our study is that semantic surprisal improves the performance of RNN, and LDA and LSA are on a par here. In order to recognise the relevance of a word for a text, it is therefore in general beneficial to know the semantic context

Model	a1	a2	a3	a4	a5	Precision	Recall	F1
Baselines								
NER	**0.8771**	0.4528	0.1896	0.0918	0.0558	0.1249	0.3808	0.1784
TR_5	0.7781	0.3633	0.1998	0.1724	0.1707	0.2161	0.4341	0.2725
TR_{10}	0.8606	**0.5112**	**0.3078**	0.2550	0.2398	0.1371	<u>0.5351</u>	0.2094
$RNN_{T,256}$	0.6902	0.3636	0.2919	0.2847	0.2840	0.5363	0.4669	0.4638
$RNN_{T,512}$	0.6989	0.3795	0.3012	<u>0.2936</u>	<u>0.2926</u>	0.5544	0.4772	<u>0.4773</u>
$RNN_{T,1024}$	0.6929	0.3702	0.2926	0.2853	0.2847	0.5562	0.4697	0.4759
$RNN_{T,2\times256}$	0.6764	0.3557	0.2734	0.2678	0.2672	0.5416	0.4531	0.4622
$RNN_{T,2\times512}$	0.6635	0.3504	0.2751	0.2698	0.2692	**0.5615**	0.4471	0.4660

Table 1: Precision, recall, F1-measure, and the accuracy-values ($a1 - a5$) of the baseline models. The best results in for the baselines are underlined and the overall best results in both tables are bold faced. For the RNN models, the subscript first refer to the input and second the model used. T means that the RNN was trained on text, and LDA / LSA refers to what $\widehat{surprisal}$ was part of the input. The numbers refer to the size of the GRU and the number of GRUs. For LDA / LSA / $TextRank$ the subscript refers either to the highest ranked words used, or the percentage of words used.

of this word.

Second, in a direct comparison without a neural network, LSA outperforms LDA. This result is somewhat surprising because, as we mentioned in the introduction, the performance of LDA in practical applications is considered a bit better than that of LSA. We explain this finding that obviously at least one of the three conditions for a good performance of LSA (Papadimitriou et al., 2000; Anaya, 2011) (see 3), i.e., similar writing style ands a clearly recognisable 'main' topic in the documents and high probability in one topic but a low probability in other, have been met in our corpus. But it is hard to say which of the three conditions applies.

Besides the better performance of LSA in KE in direct comparison, an additional argument in favour of LSA is that it is 'nicer' and more economical in its mathematical computability than LDA. With all due caution, this study provides preliminary evidence that the proposed linear model of topics as vectors in LSA works successfully as part of TCM for KE.

Among the baselines, TR's performance is very strong in accuracy and recall but the model has shortcomings. The poor performance in precision and the resulting low F1 value can, in our opinion, be explained by TR's well known weakness that semantic contexts are not considered (Yu et al., 2016).

In general, we observe that the results of our study are mediocre. Why is that the case? The explanation is, as we presume, that semantic surprisal from TCM is derived only from a singular type of context, i.e., topics. Consequently the aim of future research is to build a more complex context model which outputs combined lexical, syntactic and semantic surprisal, and, in addition, situational and knowledge of the world-surprisal (Venhuizen et al., 2019). While the situational and knowledge of the world-surprisal is possibly hard to derive, estimating lexical, syntactic and semantic surprisal should be a realistic goal. We expect that a more complex context model will output better keywords. In addition, it could be tested how LDA and LSA work together in TCM. The conclusions of our study on KE are:

(i) surprisal computed by TCM, improves the performance of RNN, (ii) LSA is slightly superior to LDA, (iii) semantic surprisal alone as features of words provides mediocre results yet, (iv) TCM with both with LDA and LSA is a promising tool for keyword extraction when it enriches the 'knowledge' of a neural network.

Limitations

(i) Theoretical: Our work deals only peripherally with mathematical aspects of the comparison between LDA and LSA. We briefly explain the basics of both techniques based on the fundamental distinction that LDA is probabilistic and LSA deterministic.

(ii) Methodological: We have limited ourselves to keyword extraction as an empirical testing procedure of our research question. Other techniques for checking the quality of the ke-

Model	a1	a2	a3	a4	a5	Precision	Recall	F1
Topic Context Models with LDA and LSA								
LDA$_5$	0.0281	0.0043	0.0036	0.0033	0.0033	0.0059	0.0126	0.0076
LDA$_{10}$	0.0888	0.0185	0.0135	0.0135	0.0132	0.0096	0.0427	0.0152
LDA$_{10\%}$	0.1219	0.0228	0.0162	0.0162	0.0159	0.0107	0.0552	0.0173
LDA$_{20\%}$	0.2665	0.0816	0.0532	0.0479	0.0476	0.0128	0.1371	0.0228
LDA$_{30\%}$	0.3653	0.1374	0.0869	0.0766	0.0753	0.0124	0.2018	0.0230
LSA$_5$	0.0535	0.0149	0.0132	0.0129	0.0129	0.0113	0.0290	0.0154
LSA$_{10}$	0.1433	0.0469	0.0370	0.0363	0.0363	0.0160	0.0799	0.0256
LSA$_{10\%}$	0.1780	0.0528	0.0376	0.0367	0.0363	0.0171	0.0948	0.0279
LSA$_{20\%}$	0.4326	0.2057	0.1526	0.1410	0.1404	0.0228	0.2725	0.0411
LSA$_{30\%}$	0.6380	0.3785	0.2949	0.2711	0.2682	0.0246	0.4465	0.0459
Recurrent Neural Networks with LDA								
RNN$_{LDA,256}$	0.3362	0.1159	0.1143	0.1143	0.1143	0.3249	0.2038	0.2355
RNN$_{T,LDA,256}$	0.7028	0.3768	0.3015	0.2933	0.2929	0.5571	0.4785	0.4798
RNN$_{LDA,512}$	0.2645	0.0908	0.0888	0.0888	0.0888	0.2518	0.1605	0.1845
RNN$_{T,LDA,512}$	0.7028	0.3768	0.3048	**0.2959**	**0.2952**	0.5576	0.4792	0.4812
RNN$_{LDA,1024}$	0.3445	0.1159	0.1133	0.1133	0.1133	0.3245	0.2069	0.2371
RNN$_{T,LDA,1024}$	0.6767	0.3639	0.2860	0.2807	0.2801	0.5423	0.4602	0.4645
RNN$_{LDA,2\times256}$	0.3554	0.1219	0.1189	0.1189	0.1189	0.3349	0.2144	0.2455
RNN$_{T,LDA,2\times256}$	0.6988	0.3791	0.3025	0.2932	0.2926	0.5586	0.4775	**0.4817**
RNN$_{LDA,2\times512}$	0.3326	0.1169	0.1139	0.1139	0.1139	0.2299	0.3094	0.2031
RNN$_{T,LDA,2\times512}$	0.6929	0.3686	0.2933	0.2853	0.2847	0.5527	0.4696	0.4751
Recurrent Neural Networks with LSA								
RNN$_{LSA,256}$	0.2503	0.0803	0.0803	0.0803	0.0803	0.25	0.1491	0.1767
RNN$_{T,LSA,256}$	0.6823	0.3613	0.2870	0.2810	0.2804	0.5461	0.4620	0.4680
RNN$_{LSA,512}$	0.2345	0.0836	0.0822	0.0822	0.0822	0.2282	0.1446	0.1669
RNN$_{T,LSA,512}$	0.6879	0.3771	0.2966	0.2906	0.2900	0.5510	0.4708	0.4745
RNN$_{LSA,1024}$	0.4128	0.1404	0.1328	0.1328	0.1328	0.2774	0.3722	0.2472
RNN$_{T,LSA,1024}$	0.6952	0.3748	0.2962	0.2900	0.2890	0.4739	**0.5483**	0.4731
RNN$_{LSA,2\times256}$	0.2490	0.0925	0.0908	0.0908	0.0908	0.2389	0.1552	0.1768
RNN$_{T,LSA,2\times256}$	0.6863	0.3616	0.2906	0.2837	0.2834	0.5591	0.4638	0.4721
RNN$_{LSA,2\times512}$	0.1156	0.0423	0.0423	0.0423	0.0423	0.1151	0.0723	0.0842
RNN$_{T,LSA,2\times512}$	0.7034	0.3699	0.2949	0.2867	0.2863	0.5313	0.4756	0.4671

Table 2: Precision, recall, F1-measure, and the accuracy-values ($a1 - a5$) of TCMs and RNNs. The best results in the respective blocks are underlined and the overall best esults in both tables are bold faced. For the RNN models, the subscript first refer to the input and second the model used. T means that the RNN was trained on text, and LDA / LSA refers to what $\widehat{surprisal}$ was part of the input. The numbers refer to the size of the GRU and the number of GRUs. For LDA / LSA / $TextRank$ the supscript refers either to the highest ranked words used, or the percentage of words used.

words are conceivable such as experiments with raters or experiments on language generation based on the keywords by LLM, as are other techniques for answering our research question from text mining and information extraction such as summarisation. These are tasks of future work and were beyond the scope of this work.

(iii) Empirical: Our study is based on a single corpus that tends to contain texts on the topic of 'computer technology'. In future, corpora with mixed thematic orientations would be desirable in order to avoid bias.

References

Subhanpurno Aji and Ramachandra Kaimal. 2012. Document summarization using positive pointwise mutual information. *International Journal of Computer Science & Information Technology*, 4(2):47.

Leticia H. Anaya. 2011. *Comparing Latent Dirichlet Allocation and Latent Semantic Analysis as Classifiers*. ProQuest LLC. Publication Title: ProQuest LLC.

Sonia Bergamaschi and Laura Po. 2015. Comparing LDA and LSA Topic Models for Content-Based Movie Recommendation Systems. In *Web Information Systems and Technologies*, Lecture Notes in Business Information Processing, pages 247–263, Cham. Springer International Publishing.

Santosh Kumar Bharti and Korra Sathya Babu. 2017. Automatic keyword extraction for text summarization: A survey. *arXiv preprint arXiv:1704.03242*.

Yuri Bizzoni and Ekaterina Lapshinova-Koltunski. 2021. Measuring translationese across levels of expertise: Are professionals more surprising than students? In *Proceedings of the 23rd Nordic Conference on Computational Linguistics (NoDaLiDa)*, pages 53–63, Reykjavik, Iceland (Online). Linköping University Electronic Press, Sweden.

David M. Blei, Andrew Y. Ng, and Michael I. Jordan. 2003. Latent dirichlet allocation. *Journal of machine Learning research*, 3(Jan):993–1022.

Jonathan R Brennan, Edward P Stabler, Sarah E Van Wagenen, Wen-Ming Luh, and John T Hale. 2016. Abstract linguistic structure correlates with temporal activity during naturalistic comprehension. *Brain and language*, 157:81–94.

Sergey Brin and Lawrence Page. 1998. The anatomy of a large-scale hypertextual web search engine. *Computer networks and ISDN systems*, 30(1-7):107–117.

Erion Çano and Ondřej Bojar. 2019. Keyphrase generation: A multi-aspect survey. In *2019 25th Conference of Open Innovations Association (FRUCT)*, pages 85–94. IEEE.

Scott Deerwester, Susan T Dumais, George W Furnas, Thomas K Landauer, and Richard Harshman. 1990. Indexing by latent semantic analysis. *Journal of the American society for information science*, 41(6):391–407.

Katherine A DeLong, Thomas P Urbach, and Marta Kutas. 2005. Probabilistic word pre-activation during language comprehension inferred from electrical brain activity. *Nature neuroscience*, 8(8):1117–1121.

Fred Dretske. 1981. *Knowledge and the Flow of Information*. MIT Press.

Stefan L Frank, Leun J Otten, Giulia Galli, and Gabriella Vigliocco. 2015. The erp response to the amount of information conveyed by words in sentences. *Brain and language*, 140:1–11.

Adam Goodkind and Klinton Bicknell. 2018. Predictive power of word surprisal for reading times is a linear function of language model quality. In *Proceedings of the 8th workshop on cognitive modeling and computational linguistics (CMCL 2018)*, pages 10–18.

Thomas L. Griffiths, Mark Steyvers, and Joshua B. Tenenbaum. 2007. Topics in semantic representation. *Psychological Review*, 114(2):211–244.

Maarten Grootendorst. 2020. Keybert: Minimal keyword extraction with bert.

Peter Hagoort, Colin Brown, and Jolanda Groothusen. 1993. The syntactic positive shift (sps) as an erp measure of syntactic processing. *Language and cognitive processes*, 8(4):439–483.

John Hale. 2001. A probabilistic earley parser as a psycholinguistic model. In *Proceedings of the second meeting of the North American Chapter of the Association for Computational Linguistics on Language technologies*, pages 1–8. Association for Computational Linguistics.

John Hale, David Lutz, Wen-Ming Luh, and Jonathan Brennan. 2015. Modeling fmri time courses with linguistic structure at various grain sizes. In *Proceedings of the 6th workshop on cognitive modeling and computational linguistics*, pages 89–97.

Micha Heilbron. 2022. *Getting ahead: Prediction as a window into language, and language as a window into the predictive brain*. Ph.D. thesis, [Sl]:[Sn].

John M Henderson, Wonil Choi, Matthew W Lowder, and Fernanda Ferreira. 2016. Language structure in the brain: A fixation-related fmri study of syntactic surprisal in reading. *Neuroimage*, 132:293–300.

Juan P. Herrera and Pedro A. Pury. 2008. Statistical keyword detection in literary corpora. *The European Physical Journal B*, 63(1):135–146. ArXiv: cs/0701028.

T Florian Jaeger and Roger P Levy. 2007. Speakers optimize information density through syntactic reduction. In *Advances in neural information processing systems*, pages 849–856.

Yaswanth Kalepalli, Shaik Tasneem, Pasupuleti Durga Phani Teja, and Suneetha Manne. 2020. Effective Comparison of LDA with LSA for Topic Modelling. In *2020 4th International Conference on Intelligent Computing and Control Systems (ICICCS)*, pages 1245–1250.

Lauri Karttunen. 1974. Presupposition and linguistic context. *Theoretical linguistics*, 1(1-3):181–194.

Max Kölbl, Yuki Kyogoku, J. Nathanael Philipp, Michael Richter, Clemens Rietdorf, and Tariq Yousef. 2020. Keyword Extraction in German: Information-theory vs. Deep Learning. In *Proceedings of the 12th International Conference on Agents and Artificial Intelligence - Volume 1: NLPinAI*, pages 459–464. INSTICC, SciTePress.

Max Kölbl, Yuki Kyogoku, J. Nathanael Philipp, Michael Richter, Clemens Rietdorf, and Tariq Yousef. 2021. The semantic level of shannon information: Are highly informative words good keywords? a study on german. In Roussanka Loukanova, editor, *Natural Language Processing in Artificial Intelligence - NLPinAI 2020*, volume 939 of *Studies in Computational Intelligence (SCI)*, pages 139–161. Springer International Publishing.

Max Kölbl, Yuki Kyogoku, J. Nathanael Philipp, Michael Richter, Clements Rietdorf, and Tariq Yousef. 2022. Beyond the failure of direct-matching in keyword evaluation: A sketch of a graph based solution. *Frontiers in Artificial Intelligence*, 5.

Roger Levy. 2008. Expectation-based syntactic comprehension. *Cognition*, 106(3):1126–1177.

I Dan Melamed. 1997. Measuring semantic entropy. In *Tagging Text with Lexical Semantics: Why, What, and How?*

Rada Mihalcea and Paul Tarau. 2004. Textrank: Bringing order into text. In *Proceedings of the 2004 conference on empirical methods in natural language processing*, pages 404–411.

Shaymaa H. Mohammed and Salam Al-augby. 2020. LSA & LDA topic modeling classification: comparison study on e-books. *Indonesian Journal of Electrical Engineering and Computer Science*, 19(1):353–362. Number: 1.

Nobal Niraula, Rajendra Banjade, Dan Ştefănescu, and Vasile Rus. 2013. Experiments with Semantic Similarity Measures Based on LDA and LSA. In *Statistical Language and Speech Processing*, Lecture Notes in Computer Science, pages 188–199, Berlin, Heidelberg. Springer.

Christos H. Papadimitriou, Prabhakar Raghavan, Hisao Tamaki, and Santosh Vempala. 2000. Latent Semantic Indexing: A Probabilistic Analysis. *Journal of Computer and System Sciences*, 61(2):217–235.

J. Nathanael Philipp, Max Kölbl, Yuki Kyogoku, Tariq Yousef, and Michael Richter. 2022. One step beyond: Keyword extraction in german utilising surprisal from topic contexts. In *Intelligent Computing*, pages 774–786, Cham. Springer International Publishing.

Milena Rabovsky, Steven S Hansen, and James L McClelland. 2018. Modelling the n400 brain potential as change in a probabilistic representation of meaning. *Nature Human Behaviour*, 2(9):693–705.

G Ravindra, N Balakrishnan, and KR Ramakrishnan. 2004. Multi-document automatic text summarization using entropy estimates. In *International Conference on Current Trends in Theory and Practice of Computer Science*, pages 289–300. Springer.

Raphael Rubino, Ekaterina Lapshinova-Koltunski, and Josef van Genabith. 2016. Information density and quality estimation features as translationese indicators for human translation classification. In *Proceedings of the 2016 Conference of the North American Chapter of the Association for Computational Linguistics: Human Language Technologies*, pages 960–970, San Diego, California. Association for Computational Linguistics.

Claude Elwood Shannon. 1948. A mathematical theory of communication. *The Bell system technical journal*, 27(3):379–423.

Nathaniel J Smith and Roger Levy. 2008. Optimal processing times in reading: a formal model and empirical investigation. In *Proceedings of the Annual Meeting of the Cognitive Science Society*, volume 30.

Robert Stalnaker. 1977. Pragmatic presuppositions. In *Proceedings of the Texas conference on per~ formatives, presuppositions, and implicatures. Arlington, VA: Center for Applied Linguistics*, pages 135–148. ERIC.

Josef Steinberger, Karel Jezek, and 1 others. 2004. Using latent semantic analysis in text summarization and summary evaluation. *Proc. ISIM*, 4:93–100.

Jakub M Szewczyk and Herbert Schriefers. 2018. The n400 as an index of lexical preactivation and its implications for prediction in language comprehension. *Language, Cognition and Neuroscience*, 33(6):665–686.

Takashi Tomokiyo and Matthew Hurst. 2003. A language model approach to keyphrase extraction. In *Proceedings of the ACL 2003 workshop on Multiword expressions: analysis, acquisition and treatment*, pages 33–40.

Myron Tribus. 1961. Information theory as the basis for thermostatics and thermodynamics. *Journal of Applied Mechanics*, 28(1):1–8.

Noortje J Venhuizen, Matthew W Crocker, and Harm Brouwer. 2019. Expectation-based comprehension: Modeling the interaction of world knowledge and linguistic experience. *Discourse Processes*, 56(3):229–255.

Shan-shan Yu, Jin-dian Su, and Peng-fei Li. 2016. Improved textrank-based method for automatic summarization. *Computer Science*, 43(6):240–247.

Qi Zhang, Yang Wang, Yeyun Gong, and Xuan-Jing Huang. 2016. Keyphrase extraction using deep recurrent neural networks on Twitter. In *Proceedings of the 2016 conference on empirical methods in natural language processing*, pages 836–845.

Yu Zhang, Mingxiang Tuo, Qingyu Yin, Le Qi, Xuxiang Wang, and Ting Liu. 2020. Keywords extraction with deep neural network model. *Neurocomputing*, 383:113–121.

Learn to pick the winner: Black-box ensembling for textual and visual question answering

Yuxi Xia [1,2*], Klim Zaporojets[3], Benjamin Roth[1,4],

[1]Faculty of Computer Science, University of Vienna,
[2] UniVie Doctoral School Computer Science, University of Vienna,
[3]Department of Computer Science, Aarhus University,
[4]Faculty of Philological and Cultural Studies, University of Vienna,
***Correspondence:** yuxi.xia@univie.ac.at

Abstract

A diverse range of large language models (LLMs), e.g., ChatGPT, and visual question answering (VQA) models, e.g., BLIP, have been developed for solving textual and visual question answering tasks. However, fine-tuning these models is either difficult, as it requires access via APIs, rendering them as black-boxes, or costly due to the need to tune a large number of parameters. To address this, we introduce ***InfoSel***, a data-efficient ensemble method that learns to dynamically pick the winner from existing black-box models for predictions on both textual and multimodal visual question answering tasks. Unlike traditional ensemble models, ***InfoSel*** does not rely on prediction probabilities or confidences, which typically are not available in black-box models. Experimental results on four datasets demonstrate that our approach achieves an absolute increase of up to +5% in the F1-score compared to standalone LLMs using only 1K training instances.

1 Introduction

Large language models (LLMs) have demonstrated remarkable proficiency across a wide range of tasks (Laskar et al., 2023; Yuan et al., 2024). For example, ChatGPT finds extensive utilization in daily textual question answering (TQA) tasks, rendering substantial convenience to a myriad of users (OpenAI, 2024). Furthermore, for visual question answering (VQA) tasks, VQA models have exhibited exceptional versatility, primarily due to their capability to comprehend both visual and textual context (Gong et al., 2023).

However, recent work (Mao et al., 2024; Laskar et al., 2023) indicates that LLMs, such as ChatGPT, fall short of state-of-the-art performance on task-specific datasets such as question answering. Similarly, VQA models (Li et al., 2022, 2021b; Bao et al., 2022) face challenges when applied to specialized datasets due to the idiosyncrasies in the content, format or structure of these datasets (Arora et al., 2018). Unfortunately, fine-tuning LLMs (e.g., LLaMA 70b model (Touvron et al., 2023)) on task-specific data requires a large number of GPU hours. Alternatively, training smaller, task-specific models from scratch requires a large amount of labeled data to achieve comparable performance (Tajbakhsh et al., 2016). Furthermore, fine-tuning LLMs through proprietary APIs with self-uploaded labeled training data not only requires LLM experts' knowledge but is also expensive.[1] These fine-tuned models further remain black-box, with restricted access to details regarding architectural intricacies, model weights, training data, and even prediction confidences.

In order to address these computational and accessibility challenges associated with fine-tuning, we introduce a scalable ensemble method called ***InfoSel*** (*Informed Selection*), which trains a small-sized selection model with just a few labeled task-specific samples. Unlike current ensemble methods (e.g., MetaQA (Puerto et al., 2023)), which depend on the confidence scores and thus can not be applied to black-box models like GPT3.5 text-davinci, *InfoSel* does not rely on such information and offers black-box ensembling. While traditional ensemble methods such as OLA (Woods et al., 1997) and PageRank (Brin and Page, 2012) are not adapted to task-specific particularities (e.g., different features) of different datasets. *InfoSel* incorporates *task-specific* optimization by considering variations of both the inputs and predicted answers from the ensembled LLMs/VQA models (*base models*), which allows it to be easily adapted to different datasets. Finally, our method efficiently deals with *multi-modal* inputs. We showcase the adaptability and effectiveness of the method by testing it on textual and visual question answering tasks. Concretely,

[1]`https://platform.openai.com/docs/guides/fine-tuning/`

Proceedings of the 21st Conference on Natural Language Processing (KONVENS), Volume 1: Long and Short Papers, pages 12–26, 2025

our results exhibit superior performance on multi-modal VQA inputs compared to the state-of-the-art PairRanker (Jiang et al., 2023) ensemble method that is designed to work exclusively with text. Table 1 compares our method with alternatives.

	FT	Pair-Ranker	OLA/PageRank	*InfoSel*
Task-specific	✓	✓	✗	✓
Data-efficient	✗	✗	✓	✓
Black-box	✗	✓	✓	✓
Multimodal	✗	✗	✓	✓
Ensemble	✗	✓	✓	✓

Table 1: Our method (*InfoSel*) aims to optimize ***task-specific*** ensembling of ***black-box*** models, where confidences and parameters can not be accessed. We use only a small portion of training data (***data-efficient***). We optimize the performance of the ***ensemble*** instead of standalone fine-tuned (FT) models. Finally, our method is ***multimodal***, and applicable to VQA task.

At its core, *InfoSel* (see Figure 1) trains a small-size ensemble model to dynamically identify the most accurate base model (i.e., LLM or VQA model) for a given input, which we refer to as the *winner*. This is achieved by designing a meta-level classification task considering all the base models as labels for every input. We designed and implemented two ensemble architectures for textual and visual QA tasks. Our first proposed architecture, *InfoSel*-TT, uses a textual transformer (TT, 110M parameters) (Devlin et al., 2019) as the backbone to generate a textual representation of the question with the predicted answers by base models. Although *InfoSel*-TT is straightforward and effective, it cannot handle multimodal data. To address this, we propose a second architecture named *InfoSel*-MT, where we incorporate a multimodal transformer (MT, 115M parameters) (Li et al., 2020) to generate fused contextual representations of a multimodal input (image, question, and the predicted answers). These fused representations are used to train a dense layer for selecting the winning model. The challenge with this approach is the lack of exposure of the base models to new (unseen) labels appearing in the task-specific datasets. To address this, we fine-tune TT and MT models (FT-TT and FT-MT) separately to learn these new labels. The predictions of these fine-tuned models are fused with the output from *InfoSel* using a second, separately trained ***InfoSel**** ensemble model. We experiment with and without *InfoSel**, as this component is considered optional when *InfoSel* is already performing well.

To demonstrate the effectiveness of our method with limited resources. We selects three less costly LLMs (GPT-3.5-turbo (OpenAI, 2023), LLaMA-2-70b-chat (Touvron et al., 2023) and GPT3.5 text-davinci-003) and three local VQA models (ALBEF (Li et al., 2021a), BLIP (Li et al., 2022) and VLMo (Bao et al., 2022)). These models are used as base models to provide answers for textual and visual QA ensemble tasks respectively. For showing the *data efficiency* of the proposed architectures, we train them on a subsample of training data from public benchmark datasets and test on the corresponding full test data. Experimental results showcase improvements in the performance up to +5% on TQA tasks and +31% on VQA tasks when compared to the ensembled base models.

In summary, our contributions are: (1) *InfoSel*, a novel data-efficient approach to ensemble black-box models without relying on access to model architecture, weights or prediction confidences for optimizing on task-specific datasets; (2) Assessment of the performance on textual and multimodal visual QA tasks, demonstrating gains of up to +5% with *InfoSel* and up to +31% with *InfoSel**compared to ensembled base models on four benchmark datasets; (3) A detailed analysis of data efficiency, demonstrating that *InfoSel* surpasses the performance of the leading base models with as few as 10 training samples. [2]

2 Related Work

Domain Adaptation. These methods aim to improve the performance of a model on a task-specific domain by leveraging knowledge from other domains (Zhou et al., 2022). Methods such as fine-tuning (Yosinski et al., 2014), feature adaptation (Long et al., 2015) and data augmentation (Choi et al., 2019) aim to improve the performance of standalone models and thus typically require large amounts of labeled training data or access to the model architecture and weights.

Ensemble Learning. Ensemble methods generate and combine multiple learners (ML models) to address a particular ML task (Sagi and Rokach, 2018). Classical ensembling approaches like boosting (Schapire, 2013) and bagging (Breiman, 1996) are designed to train and combine a large number of individual models and are thus computationally

[2]Code and data are available at: `https://github.com/Yuuxii/Black-box-QA-Ensemling`.

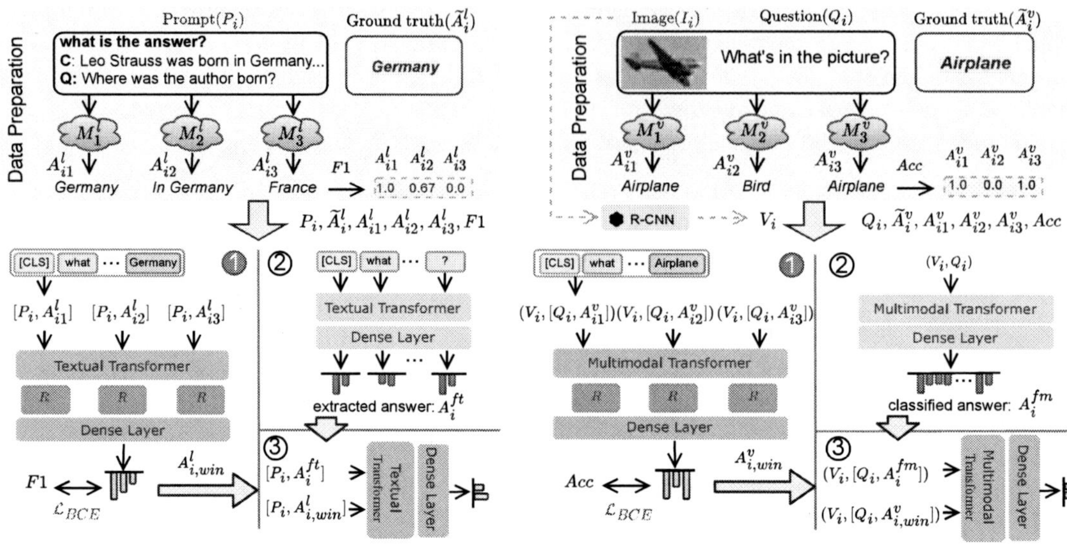

Figure 1: Architecture of our ***InfoSel*** (step ①) , FT (step ②) and ***InfoSel**** (step ③) models. M_*^l and M_*^v refer to black-box LLMs and VQA base models respectively, which are not trainable. The number of these base models is flexible and is not restricted to 3 as in the figure. The models on the left are trained for the TQA tasks, while the models on the right are trained for the VQA tasks. All our models are trained independently. Note that FT and *InfoSel** (step ② and ③) are optional and are best suited for datasets that contain a high percentage of labels that the base models have not been exposed to.

expensive. Stacking (Wolpert, 1992) uses a meta-learner to integrate the probabilities of the predictions from base models for the final output. Recent methods proposed by Jitkrittum et al. (2024); Puerto et al. (2023) require either the knowledge of confidence score or the base model's training data. Other methods train their base models to avoid dataset biases (Han et al., 2021), while Xu et al. (2020) aim to learn joint feature embeddings across different domains. However, these methods require at least one piece of knowledge that the black-box models can not provide, including base models' confidence scores or training data (not available for ChatGPT).

Multimodal Black-box Models Ensembling. Dynamic classifier selection methods, most notably OLA (Woods et al., 1997), can be applied to black-box models by ranking the best-performed local classifier dynamically in the nearest region of the input. Alternatively, majority voting (Chan and van der Schaar, 2022) and PageRank (Brin and Page, 2012) weight the predictions by their internal agreements. Yet, these methods are not designed for task-specific optimization. Pair-Ranker (Jiang et al., 2023) is task-specific but not designed for handling multimodal inputs. To address this, *InfoSel* proposes a transformer-based setup that utilizes multimodal information in the black-box setting to enhance task-specific performance.

3 InfoSel Ensemble Training

Figure 1 illustrates the proposed *InfoSel* and *InfoSel** frameworks to ensemble LLMs for TQA tasks (left), and VQA models for VQA tasks (right). We differentiate TQA components using LLMs and VQA components using VQA models by denoting them with superscripts l and v respectively. Similarly, to distinguish models used in TQA and VQA tasks, we add suffixes "-TT" and "-MT" respectively. For example, the *InfoSel*-MT model, refers to the *InfoSel* for the VQA task.

3.1 InfoSel Training for TQA

Before training *InfoSel*, we first perform the *data preparation* (top of Figure 1) for both training and testing. Next, we train *InfoSel* (step ①). Training FT models (step ②) and *InfoSel** (step ③) is optional, but can significantly improve performance for datasets that contain a high percentage of labels that the base models have not been exposed to.

Data Preparation. First, we randomly sample N content-question pairs $\{(C_i, Q_i)\}_{i=1}^N$ and the corresponding ground truth answers $\{\widetilde{A}_i^l\}_{i=1}^N$ from various benchmark datasets (refer to Section

4.1). Next, we build prompts P_i following specific prompt rules $P_i = R(C_i, Q_i)$ (refer to Section 4.1). Using these prompts instead of plain (C_i, Q_i) text improves the LLMs' answer quality (Bach et al., 2022). We select K (K=3) black-box LLMs $\{M_j^l\}_{j=1}^K$ to generate answers on the N prompts. The answer generated by M_j^l on P_i is denoted as A_{ij}^l ($A_{ij}^l = M_j^l(P_i)$). Thereby, K LLMs provide $N * K$ candidate answers for N prompts. We calculate the word-level $F1$-scores (Rajpurkar et al., 2018) of all the candidate answers $\{A_{ij}^l\}_{j=1}^K$ respectively for P_i. These $F1$-scores serve as target Y_i^l to optimize the ensemble model:

$$Y_i^l = \{F1(A_{ij}^l, \widetilde{A}_i^l)\}_{j=1}^K, Y_i^l \in \mathbb{R}^K.$$

The input for the ensemble training consists of K texts. Each text is formed by concatenating P_i with each individual answer predicted by a base model j, A_{ij}^l. More formally, the input X_i^l is:

$$X_i^l = \{[P_i, A_{ij}^l]\}_{j=1}^K, |X_i^l| = K.$$

The inputs $\{X_i^l\}_{i=1}^N$ and the corresponding target labels $\{Y_i^l\}_{i=1}^N$ are used for ensemble training.

***InfoSel*-TT.** We use a textual BERT-base (Devlin et al., 2019) transformer f_θ^t, (θ denote trainable model parameters) as the backbone of *InfoSel*-TT. To achieve faster convergence, we load the pre-trained weights of *bert-base-uncased* model. The input vector X_i^l is passed to f_θ^t to generate K sentence representations for each value in X_i^l respectively. Thus, the sentence representation R_{ij}^t of $[P_i, A_{ij}^l]$ from f_θ^t is:

$$R_{ij}^t = f_\theta^t([P_i, A_{ij}^l]), R_{ij}^t \in \mathbb{R}^{768}.$$

A dense layer (f_θ^d) is followed to classify $\{R_{ij}^t\}_{j=1}^K$, and is trained to match the target label Y_i^l using binary cross entropy loss $\mathcal{L}_{BCE}$. More formally, the training objective of *InfoSel*-TT is:

$$\min_\theta \sum_{i=1}^N \mathcal{L}_{BCE}(f_\theta^d([f_\theta^t([P_i, A_{ij}^l])]_{j=1}^K), Y_i^l).$$

Finally, the trained *InfoSel*-TT model (M^{it}) selects the winner model $M_{i,win}^l$ from $\{M_j^l\}_{j=1}^K$ for the input P_i with the highest probability score based on the selection logits produced by f_θ^d. $A_{i,win}^l$ denotes the answer provided by $M_{i,win}^l$.

FT-TT. Using only the *InfoSel*-TT model may limit performance due to the base models' lack of exposure to new (unseen) labels in the task-specific datasets. To address this, we fine-tune a separate lightweight TT model directly on the TQA datasets to learn these new labels. Specifically, the training objective is to locate the start and end token position of the answer from the context C_i. We provide the token positions of $\widetilde{A}_i^l$ as the target label, such that the model is optimized to classify each token in two classes (start/end token). This fine-tuned textual transformer model is referred to as FT-TT (M^{ft}).[3] We denote the answer predicted by M^{ft} on P_i as A_i^{ft}.

***InfoSel**-TT.** This model performs a further ensemble training of FT-TT and *InfoSel*-TT models with the same training scheme and labeled training data as *InfoSel*-TT. We anticipate that the thus trained *InfoSel**-TT model on the output of *InfoSel*-TT and the label finetuned FT-TT, will improve the ability to handle labels unseen by base models. As a result, we expect an improvement in the overall task-specific performance. The winner model selected by *InfoSel**-TT belong to $\{M^{it}, M^{ft}\}$.

3.2 InfoSel Training for VQA

Data Preparation. Given N image-question pairs $\{(I_i, Q_i)\}_{i=1}^N$ from dev data of VQA benchmark datasets, we use K (K=3) pre-trained VQA models to predict answers A_{ij}^v as follows: $\{M_j^v((I_i, Q_i)) \rightarrow A_{ij}^v\}_{j=1}^K$. We denote the ground truth answer for image-question pair (I_i, Q_i) as $\widetilde{A}_i^v$. Target labels Y_i^v for ensemble training are given by the accuracy scores of the K candidate answers evaluated on $\widetilde{A}_i^v$:

$$Y_i^v = \{Acc(A_{ij}^v, \widetilde{A}_i^v)\}_{j=1}^K, Y_i^v \in \mathbb{R}^K.$$

The concatenation of question (Q_i) with each of the candidate answers (A_{ij}^v) obtained from the base models and the corresponding image (I_i) serves the input to our ensemble model *InfoSel*-MT:

$$X_i^v = \{(I_i, [Q_i, A_{ij}^v])\}_{j=1}^K, |X_i^v| = K.$$

***InfoSel*-MT.** A Multimodal Transformer (MT, f_θ^m) (Li et al., 2021b) is employed as the backbone for *InfoSel*-MT. Specifically, we first generate visual features V_i of I_i using a pre-trained R-CNN model (M_r) (Anderson et al., 2018). V_i is composed of a vector of the image region features v_i

[3]The training scheme is adapted from https://huggingface.co/learn/nlp-course/chapter7/7?fw=pt with the additional option to allow the model to return empty answers for unanswerable questions.

and the detected *tags* (i.e., object labels of the image) (Li et al., 2021b). The concatenated question-answer pair $[Q_i, A^v_{ij}]$ and V_i is then passed together to MT (f^m_θ) to generate a fused contextual representation R^m_{ij}:

$$V_i = (v_i, tags) = M^r(I_i),$$

$$R^m_{ij} = f^m_\theta(V_i, [Q_i, A^v_{ij}]), R^m_{ij} \in \mathbb{R}^{768}.$$

Finally, we use an additional dense layer (f^d_θ) to map R^m_{ij} to the target label Y^v_i. The training is optimized using binary cross-entropy loss:

$$\min_\theta \sum_{i=1}^{N} \mathcal{L}_{BCE}(f^d_\theta([f^m_\theta(V_i, [Q_i, A^v_{ij}])]^K_{j=1}), Y^v_i).$$

We denote M^{im} to the trained *InfoSel*-MT model, M^{im} selects the winner model $M^v_{i,win}$ from $\{M^v_j\}^K_{j=1}$ to predict answer $A^v_{i,win}$ for the image-question pair (I_i, Q_i) based on the selection logits produced by f^d_θ.

FT-MT. Similar to FT-TT, FT-MT composed of a trainable MT and a Multilayer Perceptron (MLP) is fine-tuned with the same training data as *InfoSel*-MT. Differently, FT-MT solves a multi-label classification task by classifying the fused contextual representation of Q_i (instead of $[Q_i, A^v_{ij}]$ like *InfoSel*-MT) and V_i to a predefined answer list (labels). This list contains frequent answers from the training data. As a result, a trained FT-MT model (M^{fm}) can learn to predict the unseen (new) labels (answers) contained in the task-specific datasets, but not in the pre-training data of the base models. A^{fm}_i denotes the answer predicted by M^{fm} over (I_i, Q_i). The training scheme is adapted from (Li et al., 2021b).

InfoSel*-MT. Similar to *InfoSel**-TT, *InfoSel**-MT model ensembles the FT-MT and *InfoSel*-MT models using the same training scheme as in *InfoSel*-MT. The winner model selected by *InfoSel**-MT belong to $\{M^{im}, M^{fm}\}$.

4 Experiments and Analysis

We first introduce the setup of our experiments, followed by detailed results and analysis.

4.1 Datasets

To demonstrate the *data efficiency* of our approach, we subsampled four publicly available benchmark datasets. This resulted in four *Mini* datasets, the train set amounts to ~1% of the TQA datasets' and ~10% of the VQA datasets' original full size. Table 2 presents the details of these datasets.

Mini Dataset	Source Dataset	Num.	%
Mini-SDv2 train	SQuAD-V2 train	800	0.56
Mini-SDv2 val	SQuAD-V2 train	200	0.14
Mini-SDv2 test	SQuAD-V2 dev	11,873	8.39
Mini-NQ train	NQ-Open train	800	0.87
Mini-NQ val	NQ-Open train	200	0.22
Mini-NQ test	NQ-Open dev	3,499	3.83
Mini-GQA train	GQA dev	105,640	9.80
Mini-GQA val	GQA dev	26,422	2.45
Mini-GQA test	GQA test	12,578	1.17
Mini-Viz train	VizWiz dev	3,456	10.5
Mini-Viz val	VizWiz dev	863	2.63
Mini-Viz test	VizWiz test	8,000	24.39

Table 2: Details of the *Mini* datasets used for *InfoSel* ensemble training and testing. % stands for the percentage of the original full dataset.

TQA datasets. We generated two *Mini* datasets, Mini-SDv2 and Mini-NQ, consisting of 1,000 randomly sampled instances from SQuAD-V2 (Rajpurkar et al., 2018) and NQ-Open (Kwiatkowski et al., 2019) train splits, respectively. Details of the datasets are shown in Appendix A.1.

VQA datasets. Our results (Figure 2) reveal that VQA tasks demand a greater quantity of training samples compared to TQA tasks. Therefore, we constructed Mini-GQA and Mini-Viz datasets using a larger fraction (the dev data) of GQA (Hudson and Manning, 2019) and VizWiz (Gurari et al., 2018) datasets compared to TQA datasets.

4.2 Base Models

We experiment with ensembling GPT-3.5-turbo-0613 (ChatGPT), LLaMA-2-70b-chat (hereinafter referred to as "LLaMA") (Touvron et al., 2023) and GPT-3.5 text-davinci-003 (hereinafter referred to as "Davinci") to generate answers for TQA tasks.[4] To tackle VQA tasks, we employ three local VQA models (VLMo (Bao et al., 2022), ALBEF (Li et al., 2021a) and BLIP (Li et al., 2022)), which are pre-trained on VQA v2 dataset (Antol et al., 2015). Note that we use less costly and publicly accessible VQA models to save experimental costs.

Evaluation Metric. LLMs tend to generate contextual answers that lead to lower scores in the exact match (EM). Therefore, we mainly use the (per-answer) token-level F1-score from the official evaluation guidance of the datasets as the main evaluation metric for TQA performance. Our re-

[4] GPT3.5 text-davinci-003 is deprecated after our experiments, but this does not influence the effectiveness of our method.

Textual Question Answering				
Model	**Mini-SDv2**		**Mini-NQ**	
	EM	**F1**	**EM**	**F1**
LLaMA-2-70b-chat	0.24	11.34	28.07	46.47
text-davinci-003	52.37	58.44	52.24	69.44
ChatGPT	30.89	44.95	57.53	71.54
Oracle	58.61	66.20	64.02	79.21
MV	26.95	37.75	46.07	62.43
WV	52.37	58.44	57.53	71.54
PageRank	25.39	37.31	51.76	68.53
OLA	47.90	55.59	54.70	70.05
PairRanker	57.28	63.33	57.96	72.21
(0-shot) LLM-Blender	4.90	21.20	1.03	25.06
FT-TT	46.80	47.68	36.52	40.60
***InfoSel*-TT (ours)**	**57.74**	**63.63**	**58.45**	**73.37**
***InfoSel**-TT (ours)**	49.09	49.85	48.16	53.70

Visual Question Answering		
Model	**Mini-GQA**	**Mini-Viz**
	Acc	**Acc**
ALBEF	50.60	21.28
BLIP	48.08	20.80
VLMo	48.21	19.77
Oracle	65.03	-
MV	51.05	21.47
WV	52.10	19.43
PageRank	51.47	21.66
OLA	48.65	20.32
PairRanker	52.05	22.42
(0-shot) LLM-Blender	0.0	0.0
FT-MT	50.48	51.76
***InfoSel*-MT (ours)**	**55.16**	23.16
***InfoSel**-MT (ours)**	52.54	**52.91**

Table 3: Test performance comparison on textual and visual QA datasets. The overall best results are highlighted in bold, and the best results of base models are underlined. The test data of Mini-Viz is not publicly accessible and thus the Oracle cannot be reported.

sults differ from the ones reported in (Laskar et al., 2023; Kocoń et al., 2023) because we do not apply any post-processing, human evaluation or output constraints for the generated answers.

Finally, we use **Oracle** to represent the maximum capability of a combination of base models. Specifically, for each input, the Oracle selects the answer with the highest agreement to the ground truth among all the answers predicted by the base models. Thus, the Oracle score represents the performance of an ideal ensemble model.

4.3 Baselines

We use Majority Voting (MV), Weighted Voting (WV) (Schick and Schütze, 2021), PageRank (Brin and Page, 2012), Overall Local Accuracy (OLA) (Woods et al., 1997), PairRanker and LLM-Blender (Jiang et al., 2023) as baselines.

Majority Voting (MV). MV makes a collective decision by considering the predicted answers as a group of individuals voting on a particular input. The answer that receives the most votes is the winner; otherwise, ties are broken randomly.

Weighted Voting (WV). We adopt a strategy similar to Schick and Schütze (2021), where the model accuracy of the train data before training is used as the weight for average weighting. In our case, we use the corresponding accuracy of the base models as the weight for voting.

PageRank (Brin and Page, 2012). We adapt PageRank as a baseline to determine the most suitable answer in a graph where all the answers to one question are connected by their BLEURT (Sellam et al., 2020) similarities.

Overall Local Accuracy (OLA) (Woods et al., 1997). Following (Cruz et al., 2018), we use the k-nearest neighbors algorithm to divide the input space (representations of prompts for TQA, representations of images and questions for VQA) of training data into 7 regions. The overall local accuracy of each base model in different regions is computed as its region competence. The model presenting the highest competence level is selected to predict the label of inputs that fall in the same region.

PairRanker and LLM-Blender (Jiang et al., 2023). The PairRanker model is trained to rank a pair of candidate predictions from two LLMs using multiple optimizing objectives (i.e., EM, F1). The logits of the LLMs produced by the trained model are sorted to get the top k (we use k=2) predictions among multiple pairwise comparison results for a GENFUSER model (Flan-T5-XL (Chung et al., 2022), 3B parameters) to generate the final fused prediction. LLM-Blender is a composite of the PairRanker and the GENFUSER model. We train PairRanker using the same textual transformer backbone as *InfoSel* for comparison, and we use 0-shot LLM-Blender models which have been trained over massive data (105k), including TQA data to test on our data.

4.4 Performance Comparison

In this section, we analyze the performance of our method, taking into account its distinctive characteristics as described in Table 1. Concretely, we focus on comparing our models in terms of *task-specific* performance, *data efficiency*, and *multi-*

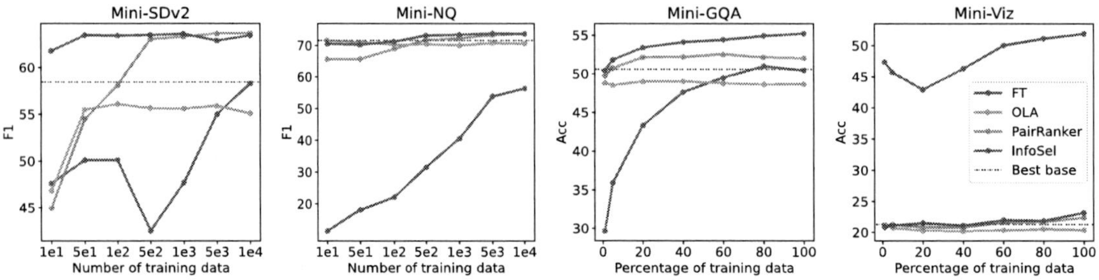

Figure 2: Test performance of *InfoSel* compared to baselines over increasing size of training data for TQA (left two figures) and VQA (right two figures). *Best base* represented the best performance of the base models.

modal capabilities.

4.4.1 Task-specific Performance

Table 3 demonstrates the *task-specific* performance of *InfoSel*, base models and ensemble baselines on textual and visual QA datasets. For TQA, we observe that LLaMA underperforms other base models. Upon closer examination, we found that LLaMA generates longer explanation text which, although often accurate, decreases the EM and F1-score values. Conversely, a more consistent performance of base models is observed for VQA. Mini-Viz contains 28% of unanswerable questions, and the label "unanswerable" has never been seen by base models. Consequently, this lack of exposure leads to significantly lower performance scores.

Baseline ensemble methods such as WV, PageRank and OLA achieve only marginal improvements compared to base models ($\leq$+1.5%) on VQA datasets. These results highlight the limitations of these methods when applied to *task-specific* datasets (see also Table 1). PairRanker underperformed *InfoSel* even though it has been trained with the same data. 0-shot LLM-Blender tends to generate longer answers compared to PairRanker which leads to a low score especially when evaluated in the exact-match settings (EM, ACC).

For TQA tasks, *InfoSel*-TT achieves 5.19% (63.63-58.44) improvement compared to individual base models, and reaches 96.12% (63.63/66.20) of the Oracle on Mini-SDv2. Similarly, the corresponding improvement in Mini-NQ performance is 1.83%, reaching 93.06% of the performance achieved by the Oracle. In contrast, FT-TT, despite its superior performance over two base models on Mini-SDv2, underperforms *InfoSel*-TT by more than 15% due to the small-size training data (refer to Figure 2). This low performance of FT-TT models negatively impacts the performance of *InfoSel**. As a result, we conclude that while *InfoSel** can exhibit superior performance (see further for VQA tasks), it also requires more training data.

For VQA tasks, the results in Table 3 showcase an improvement of 4.56% in the accuracy score of *InfoSel*-MT compared to the base models (55.16-50.60) on Mini-GQA. Furthermore, FT-MT improves 30.48% (51.76-21.28) accuracy on Mini-Viz due to a high percentage of unseen labels (e.g., "unanswerable") introduced during fine-tuning. Finally, the superior performance of *InfoSel**-MT model on Mini-Viz dataset demonstrates the effectiveness of the proposed blending approach, which improves 31.63% (52.91-21.28) accuracy upon the *InfoSel*-MT model.

4.4.2 Data Efficiency

The experimental results shown in Figure 2 demonstrate the *data efficiency* of our method by evaluating the model's performance across varying training data sizes. We observe that *InfoSel*-TT achieves a higher F1-score compared to the best base model when trained on as few as 10 samples from Mini-SDv2. This result has been further verified with the mean F1-score of 10 test results using different seed variations for sampling the training data (shown in Figure 5 in Appendix). Conversely, the number of training samples needed to surpass the performance of base models is higher for VQA datasets: 5% (6,603 samples) for Mini-GQA and 20% (864 samples) for Mini-Viz. We hypothesize that this is due to the inherent complexity of the VQA task.

PairRanker is less data-efficient than *InfoSel* as it only achieves close performance when the training samples are more than 500 on both Mini-SDv2 and Mini-NQ. Additionally, we find that a larger training data size benefits FT-TT more than *InfoSel*-TT and OLA. For example, the F1-score of FT-TT increases ~200% and ~500% from 10 to 10,000 training samples on Mini-SDv2 and Mini-

NQ respectively, while *InfoSel*-TT only increases by ~3% and ~4%. However, FT-TT still underperforms the best base model, which suggests that fine-tuning a small-sized model requires larger training data for getting a comparable performance with LLMs or *InfoSel*. Finally, we observe that a larger training data size does not necessarily lead to improved performance for the fine-tuned FT-TT model (e.g., when increasing from 80% to 100% the training data size on Mini-GQA). In contrast, OLA does not benefit as much as *InfoSel* and FT from a larger size of training data, only outperforming *InfoSel*-TT on Mini-NQ when 10 and 20 training samples are used.

4.4.3 Multimodal Data

InfoSel is able to utilize multimodal data (image and text) for VQA tasks, and thus outperform the latest text-exclusive LLM ensemble methods (PairRanker and LLM-Blender) as evidenced in Table 3. In contrast, PairRanker and LLM-Blender cannot process image features, thereby lacking crucial information in the multimodal setting, leading to a low accuracy on VQA datasets.[5] Further insights into the significance of modality information are elaborated in Section A.8 and Table 4.

4.4.4 Lightweight Model

Table 7 (Appendix) reports the parameter size of the base models and their ensemble models (*InfoSel*-TT and *InfoSel*-MT). *InfoSel* provides an efficient method for ensembling large LLMs such as ChatGPT (175B parameters) using only 110M trainable parameters. Even though only 37% ((182M-115M)/182M) trainable parameters are saved for the VQA task, we still demonstrate that *InfoSel* can effectively enhance the task-specific performance of small-size black-box VQA models, offering a lightweight solution.

4.5 Ablation Studies

Is *InfoSel* robust to the base models' individual performances? We carry out this study to assess whether *InfoSel* can effectively utilize the predictions obtained from various base models, regardless of their individual performance levels. In Figure 3, we observe a minor F1-score difference (0.15%) on the Mini-SDv2 dataset between the *InfoSel* model ensembled with and without the lowest performing

[5]The most frequent answer of LLM-Blender on VQA datasets is *"I'm sorry, I don't have enough context to answer that question."*

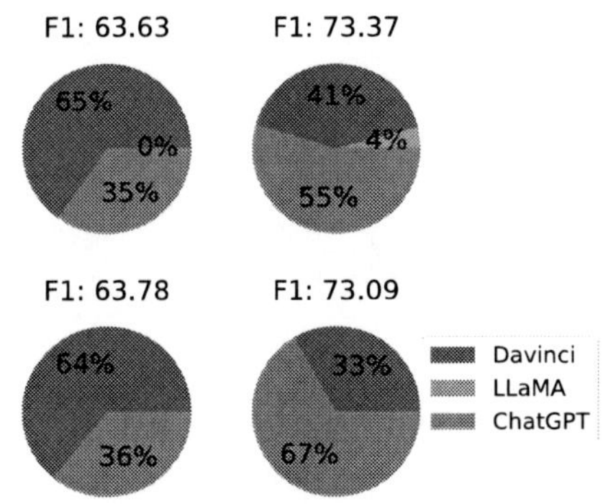

Figure 3: The portions of answers selected from different base models by *InfoSel* models on Mini-SDv2 (right column) and Mini-NQ (left column). The upper row represents the results of the *InfoSel* model ensembled with all three LLMs, and the model in the lower row excluded the worst base model (LLaMA).

base model (LLaMA). This finding suggests that *InfoSel* is robust, and not significantly affected by the individual model's performance. In a more detailed analysis, we observe that *InfoSel* selects 4% of answers from LLaMA, resulting in an overall gain of +0.28% of the F1-score. This observation highlights the effectiveness of *InfoSel*, as it can leverage the knowledge contained in the answers provided even by the lowest performing base model to some extent.

Which modality information helps the most for ensembling? In Table 4, we compare the effect of providing different modality information to *InfoSel*-MT during ensemble training. Notice that even with just the question and answer (Q+A) information, our model surpasses the performance of the PairRanker. The setting that yields the lowest accuracy solely utilizes the image (V) as the signal. This can be explained by the fact that a single image often corresponds to multiple questions in VQA datasets, making it challenging for the model to acquire discriminative features. Furthermore, we conclude that the superior performance of our model when utilizing image, question, and answer (V+Q+A) data demonstrates the effectiveness of our model in *multimodal* setting.

4.6 Case Study

The first case of Table 5 indicates that *InfoSel* captures the only correct answer ("toaster") from base models. The second case demonstrates the ability of *InfoSel** to recognize a task-specific label (i.e., "unanswerable") introduced by FT-MT. *InfoSel*-MT

Model	Mini-GQA	Mini-Viz
PairRanker(Q+A)	52.05	22.42
InfoSel-MT(V)	50.56	20.79
InfoSel-MT(Q)	51.11	21.21
InfoSel-MT(V+Q)	50.83	20.06
InfoSel-MT(V+A)	52.38	22.66
InfoSel-MT(Q+A)	54.76	22.89
***InfoSel*-MT(V+Q+A)**	**55.16**	**23.16**

Table 4: Accuracy of ***InfoSel***-MT models when using different input information for training compared to baseline models. V, Q, and A represent visual, question, and answer information respectively.

	Mini-GQA	Mini-Viz
Image:		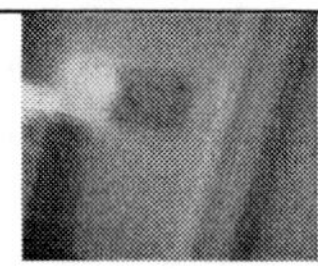
Question:	What appliance is it?	What is this product?
ALBEF	blender	refrigerator
BLIP	**toaster**	toilet
VLMo	microwave	door
FT-MT	coffee maker	**unanswerable**
***InfoSel*-MT**	**toaster**	toilet
***InfoSel**-MT**	coffee maker	**unanswerable**

Table 5: Case study of our models on Mini-GQA test and Mini-Viz validation data. Ground truth answers are bolded.

struggles with such labels as they are unseen to the base models. This showcases the benefits of training *InfoSel** models on datasets containing a high percentage of task-specific unseen labels. The corresponding case study of TQA is shown in Table 9 (Appendix).

5 Conclusion

In this paper, we propose *InfoSel*, a novel lightweight and task-specific ensemble method designed to learn the dynamic selection of the optimal model from a range of distinct black-box base LLMs. We find that using only 110M trainable parameters, our method is able to substantially increase the performance upon the best performing base LLM. Additionally, our analysis reveals that *InfoSel* remains robust regardless the incorrect predictions of the lowest performing LLM. Our findings also show that our solution is highly data-efficient. Concretely, it requires only a fraction of instances (as few as 10) from the training set to outperform base LLMs. Finally, our experimental results reveal the ability of *InfoSel* to be adapted to multimodal setting, showing a substantial increase in performance compared to state-of-the-art alternatives.

6 Limitations

InfoSel offers an effective approach to enhancing out-domain black-box model performance and addressing answer selection. However, it is important to acknowledge certain limitations that come with its application:

Dependency on Annotated Data: *InfoSel*, like many machine learning techniques, relies on a small amount of annotated training and development data specific to the new domain. While this requirement is relatively modest, and *InfoSel*'s strength is it's data efficiency (as demonstrated in the experiments), this may still pose a limitation in scenarios where obtaining such data is challenging or costly.

Limited Applicability to Open-Ended Text Generation: *InfoSel*'s primary strength lies in its ability to select the best answer from a set of base models, making it particularly valuable in question-answering scenarios. However, for more open-ended text-generation tasks, where it may be beneficial to combine multiple answers, *InfoSel*'s single-answer selection mechanism may not be the ideal choice, and future research directions may include approaches for combining several long-form answers.

API Fine-Tuning Availability: At the time of this study, *InfoSel* operates based on the assumption that many APIs do not offer the ability to fine-tune models, which is a constraint driven by the current landscape of AI services. However, since the field of AI is rapidly evolving, API providers may potentially introduce fine-tuning as a standard feature in the future. However, our experiments show that selection may still help even when one (and potentially more) of the answer models are fine-tuned.

Transparency and Explainability: *InfoSel*, like other machine learning models, which selects answers from black-box models may itself operate as a "black box". This means its decision-making process might not be readily interpretable or explainable to end-users. Pairing *InfoSel* with explainability techniques may give users a clearer understanding of how the model makes its selections.

References

Peter Anderson, Xiaodong He, Chris Buehler, Damien Teney, Mark Johnson, Stephen Gould, and Lei Zhang. 2018. Bottom-up and top-down attention for image captioning and visual question answering. In *Proceedings of the IEEE conference on computer vision and pattern recognition*, pages 6077–6086.

Stanislaw Antol, Aishwarya Agrawal, Jiasen Lu, Margaret Mitchell, Dhruv Batra, C Lawrence Zitnick, and Devi Parikh. 2015. Vqa: Visual question answering. In *Proceedings of the IEEE international conference on computer vision*, pages 2425–2433.

Sanjeev Arora, Rong Ge, Behnam Neyshabur, and Yi Zhang. 2018. Stronger generalization bounds for deep nets via a compression approach. In *International Conference on Machine Learning*, pages 254–263. PMLR.

Stephen Bach, Victor Sanh, Zheng Xin Yong, Albert Webson, Colin Raffel, Nihal V. Nayak, Abheesht Sharma, Taewoon Kim, M Saiful Bari, Thibault Fevry, Zaid Alyafeai, Manan Dey, Andrea Santilli, Zhiqing Sun, Srulik Ben-david, Canwen Xu, Gunjan Chhablani, Han Wang, Jason Fries, Maged Alshaibani, Shanya Sharma, Urmish Thakker, Khalid Almubarak, Xiangru Tang, Dragomir Radev, Mike Tian-jian Jiang, and Alexander Rush. 2022. PromptSource: An integrated development environment and repository for natural language prompts. In *Proceedings of the 60th Annual Meeting of the Association for Computational Linguistics: System Demonstrations*, pages 93–104, Dublin, Ireland. Association for Computational Linguistics.

Hangbo Bao, Wenhui Wang, Li Dong, Qiang Liu, Owais Khan Mohammed, Kriti Aggarwal, Subhojit Som, Songhao Piao, and Furu Wei. 2022. Vlmo: Unified vision-language pre-training with mixture-of-modality-experts. *Advances in Neural Information Processing Systems*, 35:32897–32912.

Leo Breiman. 1996. Bagging predictors. *Machine learning*, 24:123–140.

Sergey Brin and Lawrence Page. 2012. Reprint of: The anatomy of a large-scale hypertextual web search engine. *Comput. Networks*, 56:3825–3833.

Alex Chan and Mihaela van der Schaar. 2022. Synthetic model combination: an instance-wise approach to unsupervised ensemble learning. *Advances in Neural Information Processing Systems*, 35:27797–27809.

Jaehoon Choi, Taekyung Kim, and Changick Kim. 2019. Self-ensembling with gan-based data augmentation for domain adaptation in semantic segmentation. In *Proceedings of the IEEE/CVF International Conference on Computer Vision*, pages 6830–6840.

Hyung Won Chung, Le Hou, Shayne Longpre, Barret Zoph, Yi Tay, William Fedus, Yunxuan Li, Xuezhi Wang, Mostafa Dehghani, Siddhartha Brahma, Albert Webson, Shixiang Shane Gu, Zhuyun Dai, Mirac Suzgun, Xinyun Chen, Aakanksha Chowdhery, Alex Castro-Ros, Marie Pellat, Kevin Robinson, Dasha Valter, Sharan Narang, Gaurav Mishra, Adams Yu, Vincent Zhao, Yanping Huang, Andrew Dai, Hongkun Yu, Slav Petrov, Ed H. Chi, Jeff Dean, Jacob Devlin, Adam Roberts, Denny Zhou, Quoc V. Le, and Jason Wei. 2022. Scaling instruction-finetuned language models. *Journal of Machine Learning Research 25 (2024) 1-53.*

Rafael MO Cruz, Robert Sabourin, and George DC Cavalcanti. 2018. Dynamic classifier selection: Recent advances and perspectives. *Information Fusion*, 41:195–216.

Jacob Devlin, Ming-Wei Chang, Kenton Lee, and Kristina Toutanova. 2019. BERT: Pre-training of deep bidirectional transformers for language understanding. In *Proceedings of the 2019 Conference of the North American Chapter of the Association for Computational Linguistics: Human Language Technologies, Volume 1 (Long and Short Papers)*, pages 4171–4186, Minneapolis, Minnesota. Association for Computational Linguistics.

Alexey Dosovitskiy, Lucas Beyer, Alexander Kolesnikov, Dirk Weissenborn, Xiaohua Zhai, Thomas Unterthiner, Mostafa Dehghani, Matthias Minderer, Georg Heigold, Sylvain Gelly, et al. 2021. An image is worth 16x16 words: Transformers for image recognition at scale. In *International Conference on Learning Representations*.

Adam Fisch, Alon Talmor, Robin Jia, Minjoon Seo, Eunsol Choi, and Danqi Chen. 2019. MRQA 2019 shared task: Evaluating generalization in reading comprehension. In *Proceedings of 2nd Machine Reading for Reading Comprehension (MRQA) Workshop at EMNLP*.

Tao Gong, Chengqi Lyu, Shilong Zhang, Yudong Wang, Miao Zheng, Qian Zhao, Kuikun Liu, Wenwei Zhang, Ping Luo, and Kai Chen. 2023. Multimodal-gpt: A vision and language model for dialogue with humans. *arXiv preprint arXiv:2305.04790*.

Danna Gurari, Qing Li, Abigale J Stangl, Anhong Guo, Chi Lin, Kristen Grauman, Jiebo Luo, and Jeffrey P Bigham. 2018. Vizwiz grand challenge: Answering visual questions from blind people. In *Proceedings of the IEEE conference on computer vision and pattern recognition*, pages 3608–3617.

Xinzhe Han, Shuhui Wang, Chi Su, Qingming Huang, and Qi Tian. 2021. Greedy gradient ensemble for robust visual question answering. In *Proceedings of the IEEE/CVF International Conference on Computer Vision*, pages 1584–1593.

Drew A Hudson and Christopher D Manning. 2019. Gqa: A new dataset for real-world visual reasoning and compositional question answering. In *Proceedings of the IEEE/CVF conference on computer vision and pattern recognition*, pages 6700–6709.

Dongfu Jiang, Xiang Ren, and Bill Yuchen Lin. 2023. LLM-blender: Ensembling large language models with pairwise ranking and generative fusion. In *Proceedings of the 61st Annual Meeting of the Association for Computational Linguistics (Volume 1: Long Papers)*, pages 14165–14178, Toronto, Canada. Association for Computational Linguistics.

Wittawat Jitkrittum, Neha Gupta, Aditya Krishna Menon, Harikrishna Narasimhan, Ankit Singh Rawat, and Sanjiv Kumar. 2024. When does confidence-based cascade deferral suffice? In *Advances in Neural Information Processing Systems 36 (NeurIPS 2023)*.

Jan Kocoń, Igor Cichecki, Oliwier Kaszyca, Mateusz Kochanek, Dominika Szydło, Joanna Baran, Julita Bielaniewicz, Marcin Gruza, Arkadiusz Janz, Kamil Kanclerz, Anna Kocoń, Bartłomiej Koptyra, Wiktoria Mieleszczenko-Kowszewicz, Piotr Miłkowski, Marcin Oleksy, Maciej Piasecki, Łukasz Radliński, Konrad Wojtasik, Stanisław Woźniak, and Przemysław Kazienko. 2023. ChatGPT: Jack of all trades, master of none. *Information Fusion*, 99:101861.

Tom Kwiatkowski, Jennimaria Palomaki, Olivia Redfield, Michael Collins, Ankur Parikh, Chris Alberti, Danielle Epstein, Illia Polosukhin, Jacob Devlin, Kenton Lee, Kristina Toutanova, Llion Jones, Matthew Kelcey, Ming-Wei Chang, Andrew M. Dai, Jakob Uszkoreit, Quoc Le, and Slav Petrov. 2019. Natural questions: A benchmark for question answering research. *Transactions of the Association for Computational Linguistics*, 7:452–466.

Md Tahmid Rahman Laskar, M Saiful Bari, Mizanur Rahman, Md Amran Hossen Bhuiyan, Shafiq Joty, and Jimmy Huang. 2023. A systematic study and comprehensive evaluation of ChatGPT on benchmark datasets. In *Findings of the Association for Computational Linguistics: ACL 2023*, pages 431–469, Toronto, Canada. Association for Computational Linguistics.

Junnan Li, Dongxu Li, Caiming Xiong, and Steven Hoi. 2022. BLIP: Bootstrapping language-image pre-training for unified vision-language understanding and generation. In *Proceedings of the 39th International Conference on Machine Learning*, volume 162 of *Proceedings of Machine Learning Research*, pages 12888–12900. PMLR.

Junnan Li, Ramprasaath Selvaraju, Akhilesh Gotmare, Shafiq Joty, Caiming Xiong, and Steven Chu Hong Hoi. 2021a. Align before fuse: Vision and language representation learning with momentum distillation. In *Advances in Neural Information Processing Systems*, volume 34, pages 9694–9705. Curran Associates, Inc.

Liunian Harold Li, Mark Yatskar, Da Yin, Cho-Jui Hsieh, and Kai-Wei Chang. 2020. What does BERT with vision look at? In *Proceedings of the 58th Annual Meeting of the Association for Computational Linguistics*, pages 5265–5275, Online. Association for Computational Linguistics.

Liunian Harold Li, Haoxuan You, Zhecan Wang, Alireza Zareian, Shih-Fu Chang, and Kai-Wei Chang. 2021b. Unsupervised vision-and-language pre-training without parallel images and captions. In *Proceedings of the 2021 Conference of the North American Chapter of the Association for Computational Linguistics: Human Language Technologies*, pages 5339–5350, Online. Association for Computational Linguistics.

Mingsheng Long, Yue Cao, Jianmin Wang, and Michael Jordan. 2015. Learning transferable features with deep adaptation networks. In *Proceedings of the 32nd International Conference on Machine Learning*, volume 37 of *Proceedings of Machine Learning Research*, pages 97–105, Lille, France. PMLR.

Rui Mao, Guanyi Chen, Xulang Zhang, Frank Guerin, and Erik Cambria. 2024. GPTEval: A survey on assessments of ChatGPT and GPT-4. In *Proceedings of the 2024 Joint International Conference on Computational Linguistics, Language Resources and Evaluation (LREC-COLING 2024)*, pages 7844–7866, Torino, Italia. ELRA and ICCL.

OpenAI. 2023. Chatgpt. `https://chat.openai.com/`. Mar 14 version.

OpenAI. 2024. Hello gpt-4o. Accessed: 2025-05-01.

Haritz Puerto, Gözde Şahin, and Iryna Gurevych. 2023. MetaQA: Combining expert agents for multi-skill question answering. In *Proceedings of the 17th Conference of the European Chapter of the Association for Computational Linguistics*, pages 3566–3580, Dubrovnik, Croatia. Association for Computational Linguistics.

Pranav Rajpurkar, Robin Jia, and Percy Liang. 2018. Know what you don't know: Unanswerable questions for SQuAD. In *Proceedings of the 56th Annual Meeting of the Association for Computational Linguistics (Volume 2: Short Papers)*, pages 784–789, Melbourne, Australia. Association for Computational Linguistics.

Nils Reimers and Iryna Gurevych. 2019. Sentence-BERT: Sentence embeddings using Siamese BERT-networks. In *Proceedings of the 2019 Conference on Empirical Methods in Natural Language Processing and the 9th International Joint Conference on Natural Language Processing (EMNLP-IJCNLP)*, pages 3982–3992, Hong Kong, China. Association for Computational Linguistics.

Omer Sagi and Lior Rokach. 2018. Ensemble learning: A survey. *Wiley Interdisciplinary Reviews: Data Mining and Knowledge Discovery*, 8(4):e1249.

Robert E Schapire. 2013. Explaining adaboost. In *Empirical Inference: Festschrift in Honor of Vladimir N. Vapnik*, pages 37–52. Springer.

Timo Schick and Hinrich Schütze. 2021. Exploiting cloze-questions for few-shot text classification and natural language inference. In *Proceedings of the*

16th Conference of the European Chapter of the Association for Computational Linguistics: Main Volume, pages 255–269, Online. Association for Computational Linguistics.

Thibault Sellam, Dipanjan Das, and Ankur Parikh. 2020. BLEURT: Learning robust metrics for text generation. In *Proceedings of the 58th Annual Meeting of the Association for Computational Linguistics*, pages 7881–7892, Online. Association for Computational Linguistics.

Nima Tajbakhsh, Jae Y Shin, Suryakanth R Gurudu, R Todd Hurst, Christopher B Kendall, Michael B Gotway, and Jianming Liang. 2016. Convolutional neural networks for medical image analysis: Full training or fine tuning? *IEEE transactions on medical imaging*, 35(5):1299–1312.

Hugo Touvron, Louis Martin, Kevin Stone, Peter Albert, Amjad Almahairi, Yasmine Babaei, Nikolay Bashlykov, Soumya Batra, Prajjwal Bhargava, Shruti Bhosale, Dan Bikel, Lukas Blecher, Cristian Canton Ferrer, Moya Chen, Guillem Cucurull, David Esiobu, Jude Fernandes, Jeremy Fu, Wenyin Fu, Brian Fuller, Cynthia Gao, Vedanuj Goswami, Naman Goyal, Anthony Hartshorn, Saghar Hosseini, Rui Hou, Hakan Inan, Marcin Kardas, Viktor Kerkez, Madian Khabsa, Isabel Kloumann, Artem Korenev, Punit Singh Koura, Marie-Anne Lachaux, Thibaut Lavril, Jenya Lee, Diana Liskovich, Yinghai Lu, Yuning Mao, Xavier Martinet, Todor Mihaylov, Pushkar Mishra, Igor Molybog, Yixin Nie, Andrew Poulton, Jeremy Reizenstein, Rashi Rungta, Kalyan Saladi, Alan Schelten, Ruan Silva, Eric Michael Smith, Ranjan Subramanian, Xiaoqing Ellen Tan, Binh Tang, Ross Taylor, Adina Williams, Jian Xiang Kuan, Puxin Xu, Zheng Yan, Iliyan Zarov, Yuchen Zhang, Angela Fan, Melanie Kambadur, Sharan Narang, Aurelien Rodriguez, Robert Stojnic, Sergey Edunov, and Thomas Scialom. 2023. Llama 2: Open foundation and fine-tuned chat models. *Preprint*, arXiv:2307.09288.

David H Wolpert. 1992. Stacked generalization. *Neural networks*, 5(2):241–259.

Kevin Woods, W. Philip Kegelmeyer, and Kevin Bowyer. 1997. Combination of multiple classifiers using local accuracy estimates. *IEEE transactions on pattern analysis and machine intelligence*, 19(4):405–410.

Yiming Xu, Lin Chen, Zhongwei Cheng, Lixin Duan, and Jiebo Luo. 2020. Open-ended visual question answering by multi-modal domain adaptation. In *Findings of the Association for Computational Linguistics: EMNLP 2020*, pages 367–376, Online. Association for Computational Linguistics.

Jason Yosinski, Jeff Clune, Yoshua Bengio, and Hod Lipson. 2014. How transferable are features in deep neural networks? *Advances in neural information processing systems*, 27.

M. Yuan, P. Bao, J. Yuan, Y. Shen, Z. Chen, Y. Xie, J. Zhao, Q. Li, Y. Chen, L. Zhang, L. Shen, and B. Dong. 2024. Large language models illuminate a progressive pathway to artificial intelligent healthcare assistant. *Medicine Plus*, 1(2):100030.

Kaiyang Zhou, Ziwei Liu, Yu Qiao, Tao Xiang, and Chen Change Loy. 2022. Domain generalization: A survey. *IEEE Transactions on Pattern Analysis and Machine Intelligence*.

A Appendix

A.1 TQA Datasets

SQuAD-V2 (Rajpurkar et al., 2018) stands for Stanford Question Answering Dataset 2.0, a dataset designed for the task of question answering. It is an extension of the original SQuAD dataset by including over 50,000 unanswerable questions written adversarially by crowdworkers. The dataset is widely used in natural language understanding research.

NQ-Open (Kwiatkowski et al., 2019) is derived from Natural Questions and serves as an open-domain question-answering evaluation. The entirety of the questions can be addressed using the information found in the English Wikipedia. It was created for research purposes.

For Mini-NQ, we followed (Fisch et al., 2019) to use long answers as the context, and short answers as the ground truth answers. The 1,000 samples are divided into train and validation data using an 8:2 ratio, while the trained models are tested on the dev data of the original datasets due to the unavailability of original test data. We use the setup proposed in (Laskar et al., 2023) to generate the answers from LLMs.

Note that the answers of LLMs can be greatly influenced by some factors such as the use of different prompts or temperatures. However, our study does not focus on prompt engineering but rather on selecting the optimal base model to generate an answer. We will publicly release our prompts as well as the answers from LLMs for reproducibility.

A.2 VQA Datasets

GQA (Hudson and Manning, 2019) is a large-scale dataset for visual reasoning and compositional question answering research. The dataset contains over 113k images collected from a diverse set of sources and over 22 million questions. Only one ground-truth answer is provided for each image-question pair.

VizWiz (Gurari et al., 2018) is a benchmark dataset for visual question answering. It includes

Dataset	Sample Prompts
Mini-SDv2	What is the answer? Context:[context]; Question:[question]; If you can't find the answer, please respond "unanswerable". Answer:
	Answer the question depending on the context. Context: [context]; Question: [question]; If you can't find the answer, please respond "unanswerable". Answer:
Mini-NQ	Answer the question depending on the context without explanation. Context: [context]; Question: [question]; Answer:

Table 6: Our sample prompts in QA datasets. SQuAD-V2 were available in PromptSource (Bach et al., 2022) for prompt generation, we selected the prompt from PromptSource for Mini-SDv2, which contains two forms of prompts.

31K images, 250K questions, and answers collected through a mobile app for visually impaired users. 10 ground-truth answers are provided for each image-question pair.

Additionally, we compare the label differences of the pre-trained dataset (VQA v2 (Antol et al., 2015)) of VQA base models with task-specific datasets (GQA, VizWiz) for ensemble training. Figure 4 shows the top 7 most frequent answers and their percentages of GQA, VQA v2 and VizWiz. Four answers in GQA do not appear in the top list of VQA v2 and three for VizWiz (including the top frequent answer "unanswerable"). We also sample 3k most frequent answers from each dataset and calculate their percentage of overlapping, which is reported on the intersection in the figure. GQA and VizWiz have 32.9 % and 21.6% of overlap with VQA v2 respectively, showcasing significant differences between the pre-trained dataset and task-specific datasets.

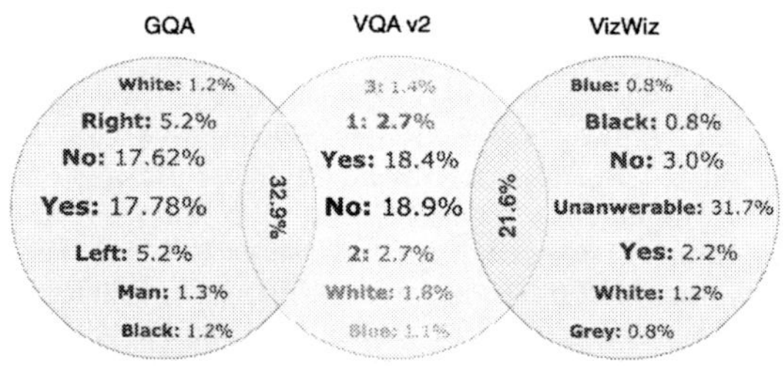

Figure 4: Top 7 most frequent answers of VQA v2 (pre-trained dataset of VQA base models), GQA and VizWiz (task-specific datasets for ensemble training). This explains why *InfoSel* performs poorly in Mini-Viz, as the new label "unanswerable" is the top frequent answer in VizWiz, but this new label has been exposed to base models that are pre-trained on VQA v2.

A.3 Base Models

LLMs		VQA Models	
Model	**#Param**	**Model**	**#Param**
LLaMA-2-70b-chat	70B	ALBEF	290M
text-davinci-003	175B	BLIP	361M
ChatGPT	175B	VLMo	182M
PairRanker	110M	PairRanker	110M
InfoSel-TT	110M	*InfoSel*-MT	115M
*InfoSel**-TT	110M	*InfoSel**-MT	115M

Table 7: Parameter size of the models used in our experiments.

ChatGPT is a large language model with 175B parameters, it allows you to have human-like conversations and much more with the chatbot. ChatGPT can generate context-based responses to user prompts (questions). However, this model is currently only accessible by cloud APIs.

GPT 3.5 text-davinci-003 is similar to ChatGPT but designed specifically for instruction-following tasks which enables it to respond concisely and more accurately. This model is deprecated after our experiments.

LLaMA-2-70b-chat (Touvron et al., 2023) is a large language model with 70B parameters. It is fine-tuned on LLaMA 2 with publicly available instruction datasets and over 1 million human annotations, while Llama 2 models are trained on 2 trillion tokens from publicly available online data sources. LLaMA 2 models are currently publicly accessible.

ALBEF (Li et al., 2021a)[6] first encodes the image and text with an image encoder (visual trans-

[6]https://github.com/salesforce/ALBEF

former (Dosovitskiy et al., 2021)) and a text encoder respectively. Then a multimodal encoder is used to fuse the image features with the text features through cross-modal attention. The V&L representation is trained with objectives of image-text contrastive learning, masked language modeling and image-text matching. Different from U-VisualBERT, ALBEF uses a 6-layer transformer decoder to generate answers for VQA tasks.

BLIP (Li et al., 2022)[7] uses a visual transformer as the image encoder, and a multi-task model (multimodal mixture of encoder-decoder) as a unified model with both understanding and generation capabilities. The model is jointly pre-trained with three vision-language objectives: image-text contrastive learning, image-text matching, and image-conditioned language modeling. Similarly to ALBEF, the VQA task is considered an answer generation task in this method.

VLMo (Bao et al., 2022)[8] is a unified vision-language pre-training method with Mixture-of-Modality-Experts. VLMO leverages large-scale image and text data to learn joint representations of vision and language. It employs a mixture model to capture diverse interactions between visual and textual information, achieving state-of-the-art performance on various vision-language tasks.

A.4 Experiment Setup

We fixed the batch size to the upper limit of the server capacity, while the learning rates and epochs are selected after a grid search on a set of values (learning rates: {e3, 5e4, e4, 5e5, e5, 5e6, e6}, epochs: {3, 5, 10, 15, 20}). Models for TQA are trained for 5 epochs using a learning rate of 5×10^{-5} and batch size of 4. Models for VQA use the same learning rate but a batch size of 16 for 20 epochs. We spent ~74 and ~290 seconds training 1 epoch on 1,000 samples for TQA and 4,319 samples for VQA respectively. The training was performed on 1 GPU with 16GB memory of a DGX1 server ((Pascal) Tesla P100).

A.5 Multi-modal Information Concatenation or Fusion?

We studied the impact of concatenating and fusing multi-modal input information for the VQA task. *InfoSel*-MLP is an alternative model type for *InfoSel* which processes all the input information separately with a simple Multilayer perceptron (MLP) instead of MT. A pre-trained Sentence-BERT (Reimers and Gurevych, 2019) [9] M_{qa} is used for generating question embedding R^q and answer embeddings R^a.

$$R_i^q = M^{qa}(Q_i), R^q \in \mathbb{R}^{768}$$
$$R_{ij}^a = M^{qa}(A_{ij}^v), R_{ij}^a \in \mathbb{R}^{768}$$

MLP takes the concatenated representation of question, answer, and visual embeddings R_i^v as input and maps it to the label space. The objective function of *InfoSel*-MLP is formalized as:

$$\min_{\theta} \sum_{i=1}^{N} \mathcal{L}_{BCE}(MLP_\theta(\{R_i^v, [R_i^q, R_{ij}^a]\}_{j=1}^{K}), Y_i^v) \quad (1)$$

The input layer of the MLP maps the concatenated representations to a hidden layer with a size equal to 300, followed by a ReLU activation layer and then an output layer with an output size equal to the number of models.

Model	Mini-GQA	Mini-Viz
	ACC	
InfoSel-MLP	52.35	21.12
***InfoSel*-MT**	**55.16**	**23.16**

Table 8: Comparison of using different architecture for processing input information differently. Input concatenation result is demonstrated by *InfoSel*-MLP and the fusion result is shown by *InfoSel*-MT.

Table 8 demonstrates the performance of the input concatenation result (*InfoSel*-MLP) and fusion result (*InfoSel*-MT). We observe that *InfoSel*-MT achieves ~3% and ~2% higher accuracy than *InfoSel*-MLP in Mini-GQA and Mini-Viz respectively, which proves that a fused contextual representation of inputs provides more discriminative information than a concatenation of input embeddings.

A.6 Case Study for TQA

Table 9 illustrates two insightful cases from the predictions of different models on textual Mini-SDv2 and Mini-NQ QA datasets. The first case showcases the ability of *InfoSel*-TT to select the right model (Davinci) when the rest of the models is incorrect. However, *InfoSel**-TT selects the wrong answers from the FT-TT model and underperforms

[7] https://github.com/salesforce/BLIP

[8] https://github.com/microsoft/unilm/tree/master/vlmo

[9] https://huggingface.co/sentence-transformers/multi-qa-mpnet-base-dot-v1

	Mini-SDv2	Mini-NQ
Context:	...Derrick Norman Lehmer's list of primes up to 10,006,721...	...in 2005 and the release of her eponymous debut album the following year...
Question:	How many primes were included in Derrick Norman Lehmer's list of prime numbers?	When did Taylor Swift 's first album release?
LLaMA	unanswerable	2006
Davinci	**10,006,721**	2006
ChatGPT	unanswerable	2006
FT-TT	unanswerable	2005
***InfoSel*-TT**	**10,006,721**	2006
***InfoSel**-TT**	unanswerable	2005

Table 9: Case study of our models on Mini-SDv2 and Mini-NQ test data. Answers of LLMs are shortened to keywords for better demonstration. Ground truth answers are bolded, and one incorrect ground truth answer is colored red.

InfoSel-TT. The second case illustrates the ability of LLMs to generate correct answer ("2006") despite the ground truth annotation error ("2005"). This demonstrates the advantage of ensembling highly expressive LLMs instead of relying only on fine-tuning small-size models such as FT-TT.

A.7 Robustness Analysis.

We analyze the robustness of the data efficiency property of *InfoSel* by training *InfoSel*-TT with 10 different sets of randomly sampled train data. Figure 5 demonstrates the mean and standard deviation of these 10 sets of results on Mini-SDv2 and Mini-NQ. We observe that the deviation decreases as the number of training data increases, and the deviation is less than 0.5 when using 1,000 training samples (0.29 for Mini-SDv2, 0.40 for Mini-NQ). The mean value (61.12%) when using 10 samples from Mini-SDv2 is still better than the F1-score of the best base model, while the mean (71.60%) when using 100 samples from Mini-NQ is already higher than the F1-score of the best base model which is fewer samples than the result reported in the main paper (500 samples).

A.8 Ablation Studies

Figure 6 shows the results when removing ChatGPT and Davinci models respectively. It is not recommended to use *InfoSel* to ensemble only two base models where one of the base models performs significantly worse than the other one.

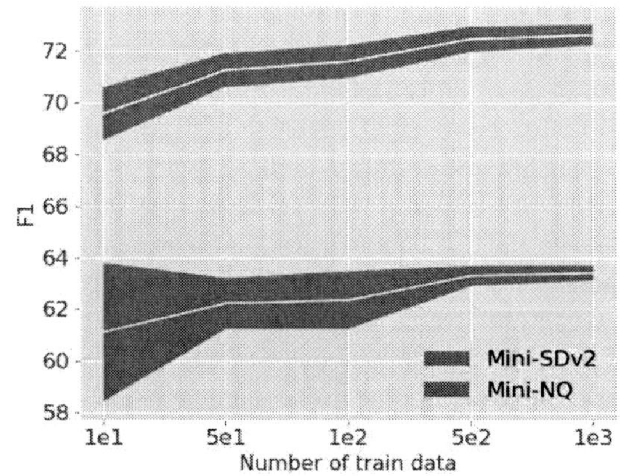

Figure 5: Mean and standard deviation of results on Mini-SDv2 and Mini-NQ when training *InfoSel*-TT with 10 sets of randomly sampled training data.

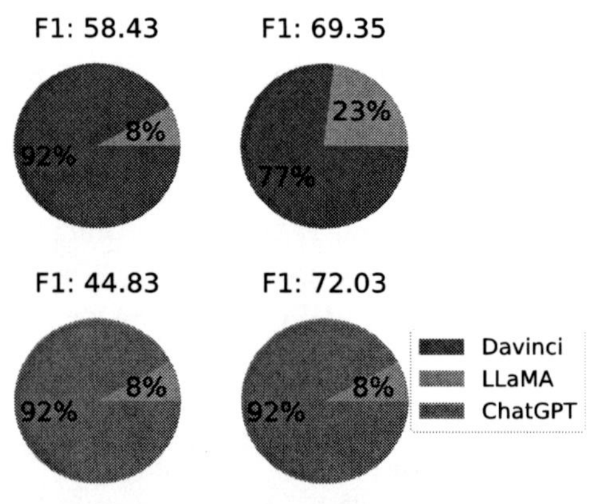

Figure 6: The portions of answers selected from different base models by *InfoSel* models on Mini-SDv2 and Mini-NQ test data. The upper row represents the results of the *InfoSel* model ensembled with Davinci and LLaMA, and the model in the lower row ensembled with ChatGPT and LLaMA.

Large Reasoning Models are not thinking straight: on the unreliability of thinking trajectories

Jhouben Cuesta-Ramirez[1*], **Samuel Beaussant**[1*], **Mehdi Mounsif**[1*]
[1]Akkodis Research
[*]Equal contributions
{Jhouben-Janyk.CUESTA-RAMIREZ, samuel.beaussant, mehdi.mounsif}@akkodis.com

Abstract

Large Language Models (LLMs) trained via Reinforcement Learning (RL) have recently achieved impressive results on reasoning benchmarks. Yet, growing evidence shows that these models often generate longer but ineffective chains of thought (CoTs), calling into question whether benchmark gains reflect real reasoning improvements. We present new evidence of **overthinking**, where models disregard correct solutions even when explicitly provided, instead continuing to generate unnecessary reasoning steps that often lead to incorrect conclusions. Experiments on three state-of-the-art models using the AIME2024 math benchmark reveal critical limitations in these models' ability to integrate corrective information, posing new challenges for achieving robust and interpretable reasoning.

1 Introduction

Recent advancements have seen LLMs achieve impressive scores on diverse linguistic and cognitive benchmarks, suggesting significant progress in their reasoning capabilities (Arora and Singh, 2023). However, this performance often degrades substantially when encountering out-of-distribution (OOD) tasks revealing limitations in their reliability and adaptive reasoning (Wang et al., 2022).

Strategies such as enhanced test-time inference budgets offer potential mitigation for OOD challenges (Hou et al., 2025) but a more focused approach involves specialized reasoning models trained via reinforcement learning (RL) with verifiable rewards (Ankner et al., 2023). This enables backtracking and self-revision, significantly outperforming standard LLMs. The CoT embodying these strategies are themselves a subject of intense study, offering potential blueprints for enhancing reasoning in smaller models (Yao et al., 2023).

Nevertheless, concerns remain regarding the authenticity of these CoTs. Prior work (Wang et al., 2023) has shown that cold-start RL can produce unconventional CoTs (often with unusual syntax or mixed languages) that still lead to correct answers. This raises doubts about whether these CoTs represent genuine reasoning or merely environment-specific artifacts anthropomorphized by researchers (Gao et al., 2023). Such phenomena may result from RL incentives that encourage retrieving known solutions from the base model, rather than fostering new cognitive skills (Yue et al., 2025). Recent evidence even suggests that disabling explicit reasoning processes in LRMs can still achieve state-of-the-art results if sampling budgets are sufficiently increased (Ma et al., 2025a).

We present new evidence suggesting that CoTs may not meaningfully support models' reasoning processes. Extending prior work (Wang et al., 2025), we explore the **underthinking** phenomenon, where models prematurely abandon promising reasoning paths maybe due to inability to correctly identify a valid solution. We find that even explicitly injecting ground-truth solutions into reasoning sequences often fails, with models instead pursuing incorrect reasoning. This issue closely relates to **overthinking** (Chen et al., 2025), where models generate excessive, unproductive reasoning tokens. In this preliminary work, we demonstrate empirically that even state-of-the-art reasoning models are not apart from this issue with two main contributions: Demonstrating that LLMs often disregard externally provided correct solutions, producing redundant reasoning steps and Highlighting fundamental limitations in the integration of corrective information by models, revealing critical flaws in current reasoning dynamics.

2 Related Work

Following the seminal work of (Wei et al., 2022), suggesting that LLM's reasoning capabilities can be enhanced *via* Chain-of-Thought (CoT), numer-

Proceedings of the 21st Conference on Natural Language Processing (KONVENS), Volume 1: Long and Short Papers, pages 27–32, 2025

ous works have explored prompt augmentations (Yao et al., 2023; Wang et al., 2022), specific scaffolding (Bairi et al., 2023; Cheng et al., 2024; Zheng et al., 2025). Concurrently, research has also highlighted that expanding the sampling budget can lead to further performance gains (Wang et al., 2024; Tian et al., 2024). For instance, (Brown et al., 2025) observed a strong correlation between sampling budget and benchmark performance, indicating that models may have internalized much more knowledge than what is revealed through single-shot forward pass. However, while these methods can enhance performance, their reliability often rests on the capabilities of the verifier. This challenge aligns naturally with the reinforcement learning (RL) framework, where algorithms such as (Schulman et al., 2017; Ramesh et al., 2024) leverage ground truth rewards as training signals to optimize LLMs (OpenAI, 2024, 2025; DeepSeek-AI, 2025; Lambert et al., 2025).

Despite initial competitive metrics and hill-climbing trends (Luo et al., 2025), fundamental questions about LLMs' planning capabilities persist (Kambhampati et al., 2024; Valmeekam et al., 2024), prompting skepticism about their CoTs' relevance (Wang et al., 2025; Chen et al., 2025). RL optimization often leads to overfitting, unreadable CoTs, or anthropomorphic strategies (Qwen-Team, 2024), emphasizing the need for robust reasoning and interpretability (Dunefsky et al., 2024; Cunningham et al., 2023) to handle shifted distributions in inference (Andriushchenko et al., 2025). Recent works (Ameisen et al., 2025; Lindsey et al., 2025) have identified interpretable internal circuits within transformer models, but scaling these insights remains challenging (Lieberum et al., 2024). Evidence of sycophancy and divergence between textual outputs and internal activations further complicates system trustworthiness. Our work fundamentally challenges the assumed relationship between CoT length and performance by demonstrating multiple models' inability to recognize correct answers even when explicitly presented. Along with recent studies (Muennighoff et al., 2025; Yeo et al., 2025; Ma et al., 2025b; Tang et al., 2025) these results reveal a more complex dynamic influenced by training dynamics and task complexity, underscoring the need for a deeper understanding of LLM reasoning processes.

3 Results and Discussion

We conduct our experiments on three different models. LLaMA 70B and Qwen7B were distilled from R1 (DeepSeek-AI, 2025), while DeepScalR1.5B (Luo et al., 2025) was trained via RL. Our reasoning analysis focus on the AIME2024 dataset, a challenging set of mathematical problems.

3.1 Baseline Thoughts Generation

Baseline solutions are generated by providing the models with a standard system prompt and problem statement. The LLM then produces CoTs enclosed in <think> tags before delivering a final answer, spontaneously exploring multiple hypotheses and engaging in self-reflection. Individual reasoning thoughts are identified using a simple heuristic based on specific keywords, with *Alternatively* and *Wait* serving as thought separators. We denote the reasoning trace up to the tth thought as $\mathcal{R}[:t]$, which includes the system prompt and problem statement. For $t = 0$, $\mathcal{R}[:0]$ contains only the prompt and statement; for $t = T$, $\mathcal{R}_{[:T]}$ represents the full reasoning trajectory. This notation enables the analysis of reasoning at any intermediate step t, supporting counterfactual studies.

3.2 Ground Truth Integration

We investigate the impact of integrating the ground truth solution (reasoning + answer) after each baseline thoughts, assessing whether models recognize and integrate correct answers. For each problem, we concatenate the solution $\mathcal{Y}$ to the already generated thinking trace $\mathcal{R}_{[:t]}$ as if it was generated by the model itself during its reasoning process. This achieved by prefixing the solution with the relevant set of tokens $\mathcal{V}$ to mimic the model's writing style. More formally, the prompt P_t sent to the model is: $P_t = \mathcal{R}_{[:t]} \oplus \mathcal{V} \oplus \mathcal{Y}$ (1), where $\oplus$ denotes concatenation and with $\mathcal{V} =$ "<think> Okay, so " if $t = 0$ and "Alternatively, " otherwise. Given P_t for each $t \in [0, T]$, the model continues the reasoning trajectory without additional prompts or guidance. We expect the model to pick-up the ground truth solution and use it as its final answer. However, models often generate excessive additional tokens, frequently doubting or even discarding the correct solution, as illustrated in Figure 2b. Surprisingly, in this pathological case the model almost always commits to a wrong answer despite the given solution. However, this illustrative example is not an isolated case as shown In Figure 1. This phe-

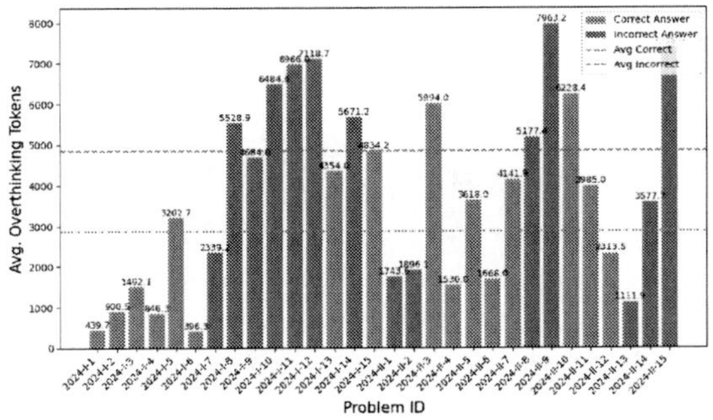

(a) Llama-70b

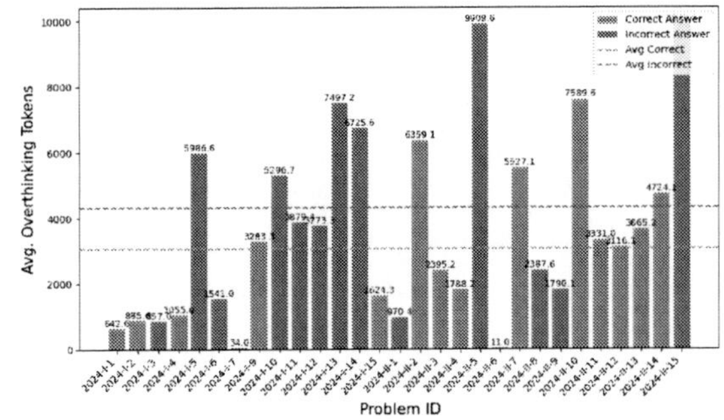

(b) Qwen-7b

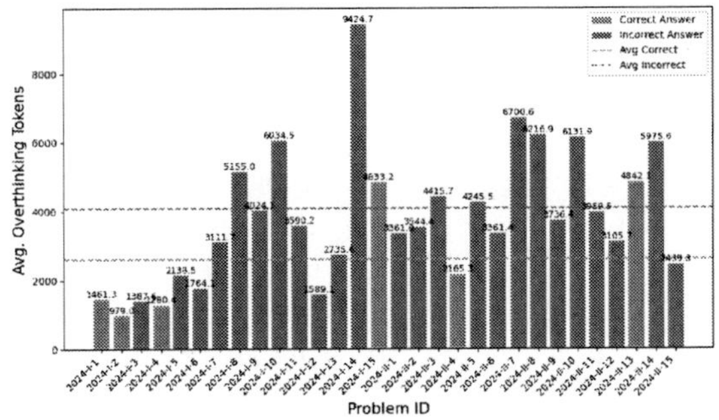

(c) DeepScalR-1.5b

Figure 1: Averaged number of *overthinking* tokens generated for each problem from AIME2024. Amount of *overthinking* tokens is problem-dependent but all four models overthink. The correct/incorrect coloring is based on whether the problem was successfully solved on the first try.

nomenon emerges in all models regardless of their size and post-training method. The amount of overthinking tokens however is largely problem-dependent, with some specific problems creating more overthinking tokens than others (e.g. problem I-14 on Figure 1).

A rare positive case, observed only twice, is shown in Figure 2a. Here, after $t = 17$, the model consistently accepted the injected solution, producing a reduced and stable number of tokens. The reasoning reflected diverse yet coherent strategies, such as applying cyclic quadrilaterals, similar triangles, and the British flag theorem which suggests that the model could have required a number of thoughts (Wei et al., 2022) before being able to understand and accept the injected truth. This is represented in the figure as a big reduction in the number of tokens generated and the completion ratio suggesting a *converging number* of generated tokens, after a spiky, iterative and often *divergent behavior* employing an excessive amount of tokens.

We found that this divergent behavior is common in most of the problems, with an example represented in Figure 3 where for the first four of them, the number of overthinking tokens in order to provide a bad answer is close to 0 and to provide / accept the correct answer is lower than 2000. Then for the rest things went out of control as this grew considerably even while accepting the truth. Which to our point of view could correspond to a clear prioritization on self-generated tokens, lack of capabilities of comprehension or simply randomly divergent CoTs.

These results reveal that reasoning models often struggle to identify valid solutions, relying on complex but fragile heuristics that do not reflect genuine reasoning. For instance, in a particularly challenging problem (II-15), none of the models confidently arrived at the correct solution, even when provided with the ground truth (Figure 2). When models did accept the correct answer, it was typically out of resignation or time pressure rather than true understanding, as shown by statements like, "But perhaps given the time I have, I think the initial calculation of 315 might be correct," which appeared nearly 3000 tokens after the ground truth. This shows that in some cases, the correct answer may not even exist within the model's solution space, making it unattainable through further sampling or prompting.

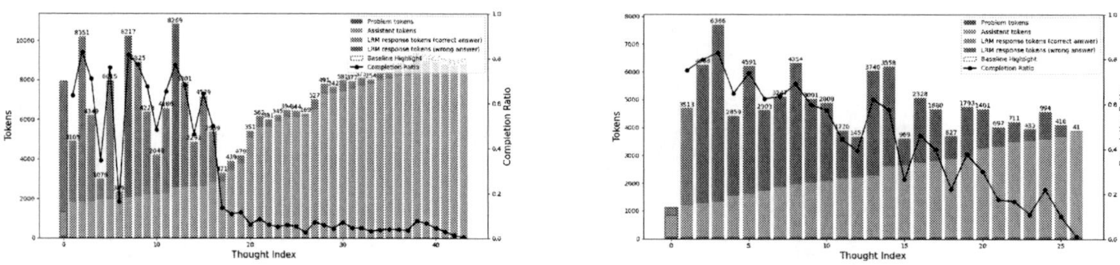

(a) 2024-I-5

(b) 2024-II-5

Figure 2: Illustration of the *overthinking* issue on two problems from AIME2024 with DeepScalR1.5B. P_t is pictured in orange (assistant tokens) while "LRM response" represents the completion tokens with the coloring indicating wether the model predicted the correct answer or not. The completion ratio indicates the amount of completion tokens generated in proportion to the total amount of tokens.

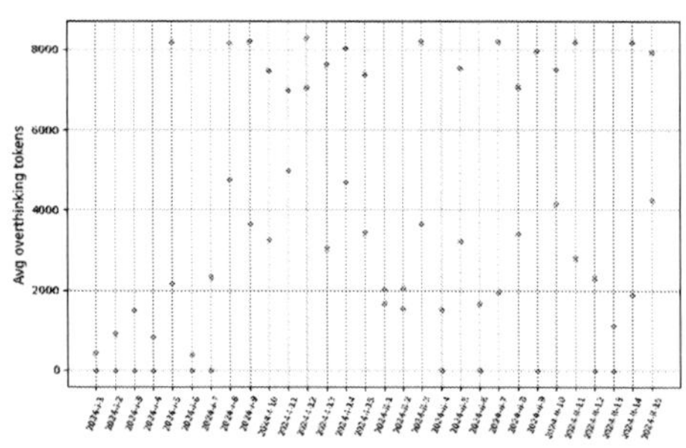

Figure 3: Averaged number of *overthinking* tokens generated for each problem from AIME2024 with model LLaMA 70B. The average is conditioned to the model providing a correct answer(green) or not(purple) at the end of its reasoning.

This behavior likely stems from overfitting to specific patterns and spurious correlations that do not generalize. As shown in Figure 2, the number of overthinking tokens often decreases in proportion to the total tokens generated, though this relationship sometimes appears thresholded. Models tend to delay committing to an answer until reaching a predefined token count or detecting unknown patterns. These tendencies likely arise from RL training dynamics and poor credit assignment, where correct answers reached through faulty CoTs are mistakenly rewarded and associated with the CoT's length or other irrelevant features. This mirrors reward hacking seen in smaller RL tasks, where optimization exploits shortcuts that maximize rewards but fail to generalize.

4 Conclusion and Future work

While recent advances in reasoning models have generated significant interest, their evaluation often relies on anthropomorphizing behavior, treating CoTs as reflections of human reasoning. Our findings reveal a critical limitation: current LRMs lack robust mechanisms to integrate external corrective signals. This challenges assumptions about their coherence and questions the reliability of CoTs as transparent indicators of cognition. Proxy metrics like completion length also fail to consistently reflect reasoning quality, as models frequently display both underthinking and overthinking. Our analysis shows that models often ignore provided ground-truth solutions, raising key questions: What truly drives the reasoning process, and can it be effectively guided? Models that reject external solutions are also prone to disregarding guidance, feedback, or human intervention.

Building on these insights our future work will focus on developing heuristics to improve model receptiveness to external suggestions or corrections. By leveraging recent advances in understanding interpretable circuits within transformer models, we aim to uncover why models tend to doubt or even reject correct answers during reasoning. This deeper understanding will inform the development of more reliable and efficient reasoning models.

Limitations

Our study focuses solely on mathematical reasoning tasks (AIME2024), so the findings may not generalize to other domains. The set of models tested is also limited and may not capture the full diversity of training paradigms. Additionally, our method of injecting ground-truth solutions relies on heuristics that might not fully align with the models' internal reasoning dynamics. Finally, while we provide behavioral analysis, deeper interpretability work remains for future research.

References

Emmanuel Ameisen, Jack Lindsey, Adam Pearce, Wes Gurnee, Nicholas L. Turner, Brian Chen, Craig Citro, David Abrahams, Shan Carter, Basil Hosmer, Jonathan Marcus, Michael Sklar, Adly Templeton, Trenton Bricken, Callum McDougall, Hoagy Cunningham, Thomas Henighan, Adam Jermyn, Andy Jones, and 8 others. 2025. Circuit tracing: Revealing computational graphs in language models. *Transformer Circuits Thread.*

Maksym Andriushchenko, Francesco Croce, and Nicolas Flammarion. 2025. Jailbreaking Leading Safety-Aligned LLMs with Simple Adaptive Attacks. *Preprint*, arXiv:2404.02151.

Zachary Ankner, Mansheej Paul Brandon Cui, Jonathan D. Chang, and Prithviraj Ammanabrolu. 2023. Critique-out-loud reward models. *arXiv preprint arXiv:2408.11791.*

Daman Arora and Himanshu Gaurav Singh. 2023. Have llms advanced enough? a challenging problem solving benchmark for large language models. *arXiv preprint arXiv:2305.15074.*

Ramakrishna Bairi, Atharv Sonwane, Aditya Kanade, Vageesh D C, Arun Iyer, Suresh Parthasarathy, Sriram Rajamani, B. Ashok, and Shashank Shet. 2023. CodePlan: Repository-level Coding using LLMs and Planning. *Preprint*, arXiv:2309.12499.

Bradley Brown, Jordan Juravsky, Ryan Saul Ehrlich, Ronald Clark, Quoc V Le, Christopher Re, and Azalia Mirhoseini. 2025. Large Language Monkeys: Scaling Inference Compute with Repeated Sampling.

Xingyu Chen, Jiahao Xu, Tian Liang, Zhiwei He, Jianhui Pang, Dian Yu, Linfeng Song, Qiuzhi Liu, Mengfei Zhou, Zhuosheng Zhang, Rui Wang, Zhaopeng Tu, Haitao Mi, and Dong Yu. 2025. Do not think that much for 2+3=? on the overthinking of o1-like llms. *Preprint*, arXiv:2412.21187.

Kewei Cheng, Jingfeng Yang, Haoming Jiang, Zhengyang Wang, Binxuan Huang, Ruirui Li, Shiyang Li, Zheng Li, Yifan Gao, Xian Li, Bing Yin, and Yizhou Sun. 2024. Inductive or Deductive? Rethinking the Fundamental Reasoning Abilities of LLMs. *Preprint*, arXiv:2408.00114.

Hoagy Cunningham, Aidan Ewart, Logan Riggs, Robert Huben, and Lee Sharkey. 2023. Sparse autoencoders find highly interpretable features in language models. *Preprint*, arXiv:2309.08600.

DeepSeek-AI. 2025. Deepseek-r1: Incentivizing reasoning capability in llms via reinforcement learning. *Preprint*, arXiv:2501.12948.

Jacob Dunefsky, Philippe Chlenski, and Neel Nanda. 2024. Transcoders find interpretable llm feature circuits. *Preprint*, arXiv:2406.11944.

Zitian Gao, Boye Niu, Xuzheng He, Haotian Xu, Hongzhang Liu, Aiwei Liu, Xuming Hu, and Lijie Wen. 2023. Interpretable contrastive monte carlo tree search reasoning. *arXiv preprint arXiv:2410.01707.*

Zhenyu Hou, Xin Lv, Rui Lu, Jiajie Zhang, Yujiang Li, Zijun Yao, Juanzi Li, Jie Tang, and Yuxiao Dong. 2025. Advancing language model reasoning through reinforcement learning and inference scaling. *arXiv preprint arXiv:2501.11651.*

Subbarao Kambhampati, Karthik Valmeekam, Lin Guan, Mudit Verma, Kaya Stechly, Siddhant Bhambri, Lucas Saldyt, and Anil Murthy. 2024. Llms can't plan, but can help planning in llm-modulo frameworks. *Preprint*, arXiv:2402.01817.

Nathan Lambert, Jacob Morrison, Valentina Pyatkin, Shengyi Huang, Hamish Ivison, Faeze Brahman, Lester James V. Miranda, Alisa Liu, Nouha Dziri, Shane Lyu, Yuling Gu, Saumya Malik, Victoria Graf, Jena D. Hwang, Jiangjiang Yang, Ronan Le Bras, Oyvind Tafjord, Chris Wilhelm, Luca Soldaini, and 4 others. 2025. Tulu 3: Pushing frontiers in open language model post-training. *Preprint*, arXiv:2411.15124.

Tom Lieberum, Senthooran Rajamanoharan, Arthur Conmy, Lewis Smith, Nicolas Sonnerat, Vikrant Varma, János Kramár, Anca Dragan, Rohin Shah, and Neel Nanda. 2024. Gemma scope: Open sparse autoencoders everywhere all at once on gemma 2. *Preprint*, arXiv:2408.05147.

Jack Lindsey, Wes Gurnee, Emmanuel Ameisen, Brian Chen, Adam Pearce, Nicholas L. Turner, Craig Citro, David Abrahams, Shan Carter, Basil Hosmer, Jonathan Marcus, Michael Sklar, Adly Templeton, Trenton Bricken, Callum McDougall, Hoagy Cunningham, Thomas Henighan, Adam Jermyn, Andy Jones, and 8 others. 2025. On the biology of a large language model. *Transformer Circuits Thread.*

Michael Luo, Sijun Tan, Justin Wong, Xiaoxiang Shi, William Y. Tang, Manan Roongta, Colin Cai, Jeffrey Luo, Li Erran Li, Raluca Ada Popa, and Ion Stoica. 2025. Deepscaler: Surpassing o1-preview with a 1.5b model by scaling rl. https://pretty-radio-b75.notion.site/DeepScaleR-Surpassing-O1-Preview-with-a-1-5B-Model-by-Scaling-RL-19681902c1468005bed8ca303013a4e2. Notion Blog.

Wenjie Ma, Jingxuan He, Charlie Snell, Tyler Griggs, Sewon Min, and Matei Zaharia. 2025a. Reasoning models can be effective without thinking. *arXiv preprint arXiv:2504.09858.*

Wenjie Ma, Jingxuan He, Charlie Snell, Tyler Griggs, Sewon Min, and Matei Zaharia. 2025b. Reasoning models can be effective without thinking. *Preprint*, arXiv:2504.09858.

Niklas Muennighoff, Zitong Yang, Weijia Shi, Xiang Lisa Li, Li Fei-Fei, Hannaneh Hajishirzi, Luke Zettlemoyer, Percy Liang, Emmanuel Candès, and Tatsunori Hashimoto. 2025. s1: Simple test-time scaling. *Preprint*, arXiv:2501.19393.

OpenAI. 2024. Openai o1 system card.

OpenAI. 2025. Openai o3 and o4-mini system card.

Qwen-Team. 2024. Qwq: Reflect deeply on the boundaries of the unknown.

Shyam Sundhar Ramesh, Yifan Hu, Iason Chaimalas, Viraj Mehta, Pier Giuseppe Sessa, Haitham Bou Ammar, and Ilija Bogunovic. 2024. Group robust preference optimization in reward-free rlhf. *Preprint*, arXiv:2405.20304.

John Schulman, Filip Wolski, Prafulla Dhariwal, Alec Radford, and Oleg Klimov. 2017. Proximal policy optimization algorithms. *CoRR*, abs/1707.06347.

Yunhao Tang, Kunhao Zheng, Gabriel Synnaeve, and Rémi Munos. 2025. Optimizing language models for inference time objectives using reinforcement learning. *Preprint*, arXiv:2503.19595.

Ye Tian, Baolin Peng, Linfeng Song, Lifeng Jin, Dian Yu, Haitao Mi, and Dong Yu. 2024. Toward Self-Improvement of LLMs via Imagination, Searching, and Criticizing. *Preprint*, arXiv:2404.12253.

Karthik Valmeekam, Kaya Stechly, and Subbarao Kambhampati. 2024. Llms still can't plan; can lrms? a preliminary evaluation of openai's o1 on planbench. *Preprint*, arXiv:2409.13373.

Junlin Wang, Jue Wang, Ben Athiwaratkun, Ce Zhang, and James Zou. 2024. Mixture-of-Agents Enhances Large Language Model Capabilities. *Preprint*, arXiv:2406.04692.

Lei Wang, Wanyu Xu, Yihuai Lan, Zhiqiang Hu, Yunshi Lan, Roy Ka-Wei Lee, and Ee-Peng Lim. 2023. Plan-and-solve prompting: Improving zero-shot chain-of-thought reasoning by large language models. *arXiv preprint arXiv:2305.04091*.

Xuezhi Wang, Jason Wei, Dale Schuurmans, Quoc Le, Ed H. Chi, Sharan Narang, Aakanksha Chowdhery, and Denny Zhou. 2022. Self-consistency improves chain of thought reasoning in language models. *arXiv preprint arXiv:2203.11171*.

Yue Wang, Qiuzhi Liu, Jiahao Xu, Tian Liang, Xingyu Chen, Zhiwei He, Linfeng Song, Dian Yu, Juntao Li, Zhuosheng Zhang, Rui Wang, Zhaopeng Tu, Haitao Mi, and Dong Yu. 2025. Thoughts are all over the place: On the underthinking of o1-like llms. *Preprint*, arXiv:2501.18585.

Jason Wei, Xuezhi Wang, Dale Schuurmans, Maarten Bosma, brian ichter, Fei Xia, Ed H. Chi, Quoc V Le, and Denny Zhou. 2022. Chain of Thought Prompting Elicits Reasoning in Large Language Models. In *Advances in Neural Information Processing Systems*.

Shunyu Yao, Dian Yu, Jeffrey Zhao, Izhak Shafran, Tom Griffiths, Yuan Cao, and Karthik Narasimhan. 2023. Tree of Thoughts: Deliberate Problem Solving with Large Language Models. In *Advances in Neural Information Processing Systems*, volume 36, pages 11809–11822. Curran Associates, Inc.

Edward Yeo, Yuxuan Tong, Morry Niu, Graham Neubig, and Xiang Yue. 2025. Demystifying long chain-of-thought reasoning in llms. *Preprint*, arXiv:2502.03373.

Yang Yue, Zhiqi Chen, Rui Lu, Andrew Zhao, Zhaokai Wang, Shiji Song, and Gao Huang. 2025. Does reinforcement learning really incentivize reasoning capacity in llms beyond the base model? *arXiv preprint arXiv:2504.13837*.

Zhi Zheng, Zhuoliang Xie, Zhenkun Wang, and Bryan Hooi. 2025. Monte Carlo Tree Search for Comprehensive Exploration in LLM-Based Automatic Heuristic Design. *Preprint*, arXiv:2501.08603.

Adaption and Evaluation of Generative Large Language Models for German Medical Information Extraction

Sören Spiegel[1], Seid Muhie Yimam[2], Philipp Breitfeld[1], Frank Ückert[1]

[1]Institute for Applied Medical Informatics, University Medical Center Hamburg-Eppendorf,
[2]University of Hamburg

Correspondence: Sören Spiegel s.spiegel@uke.de

Abstract

Analyzing unstructured patient data from electronic health records can improve clinical decision-making. However, the standard approach for medical information extraction (IE) that relies on fine-tuning foundation models for specific tasks faces several challenges, especially in German where training data availability is very scarce. This work investigates the feasibility of large language models (LLMs) equipped with 7 billion parameters for clinical IE in the German medical domain, evaluating their performance on all three publicly available German gold-standard datasets. The results show that LLMs achieve strong performance in drug extraction (F1: 0.71–0.87) but struggle with diagnoses and treatments (F1: 0.44–0.71). Instruction tuning with QLoRA improves performance and reduces hallucinations. While baseline models outperform LLMs on dataset-specific tasks, instruction-tuned LLMs excel on out-of-distribution data, making them a viable option when training data is scarce and detailed accuracy is less critical.

1 Introduction

The widespread adoption of electronic health records has led to the collection of extensive patient data, including family history, symptoms, diagnostic results, and treatments. Effectively analyzing this vast amount of data has the potential to enhance clinical care and support clinical decision-making (Jensen et al., 2012). As most documentation exists in text form, automated information extraction (IE) plays a crucial role in enabling comprehensive analysis of healthcare data (Lentzen et al., 2022).

The potential applications are manifold, one plausible area of application for IE from free written text is premedication in anesthesia. Each patient is examined and assessed preoperatively by an anesthetist to minimize perioperative risk and prepare the patient medically and psychologically for anesthesia (Larsen, 2016). Before the preoperative visit, the anesthetist reviews the patients medical history, focusing on prior diseases, surgeries, allergies, medications, and lab results. This typically involves manually examining physician notes from various sources, such as hospital units or external providers, without any tool to assist in generating premedication reports. This time-consuming process is further complicated by duplicated text in clinical notes (Steinkamp et al., 2022).

Physicians can leverage natural language processing (NLP) methods, such as fine-tuning foundation models, to analyze clinical notes. While current state-of-the-art (SOTA) fine-tuned transformer models achieve remarkable results in clinical named entity recognition (NER), their performance often declines significantly when applied to other datasets (Kühnel and Fluck, 2022). Furthermore, medical IE in Germany faces challenges due to data protection laws, limited annotated datasets, and less research activity in German compared to English (Lentzen et al., 2022; Roller et al., 2022; Richter-Pechanski et al., 2023). Generative large language models (LLMs) offer a promising solution, achieving strong results in various NLP tasks without task-specific fine-tuning (Touvron et al., 2023; Jiang et al., 2024). This paper aims to answer the following research questions: (**RQ1**) Which LLM performs best for medical information extraction in German? (**RQ2**) Which approach yields the highest performance for medical IE: few-shot prompting, instruction fine-tuning or retrieval-augmented generation (RAG)? (**RQ3**) Can generative LLMs with 7 billion parameters compete with smaller task specific fine-tuned models (SLMs) in German clinical IE?

The main **Contributions** of this work include: (1) We present a comprehensive analysis of 7B LLMs for IE in the German medical domain, evaluating their strengths and limitations across multiple datasets. (2) We assess the generalizability of transformer-based NER models by testing models

Proceedings of the 21st Conference on Natural Language Processing (KONVENS), Volume 1: Long and Short Papers, pages 33–47, 2025

on several datasets. (3) We establish a benchmark for LLM performance in German clinical IE.

2 Related Works

2.1 Medical Information Extraction

With the rise of electronic health records, extracting structured information from clinical text has become a key research area (Jensen et al., 2012). NER and relation extraction (RE) are central to this task (Landolsi et al., 2023), with early rule-based methods achieving strong results but requiring extensive manual effort. The introduction of transformer-based models like BERT (Devlin et al., 2019) shifted the focus toward machine learning approaches, leading to specialized biomedical models such as BioBERT and ClinicalBERT (Lee et al., 2020; Huang et al., 2020). While these models achieve SOTA performance in shared tasks like CLEF eHealth and n2c2 (Henry et al., 2020), their success relies on well-annotated training data, which is costly to produce and limits generalizability across datasets (Kühnel and Fluck, 2022; Lentzen et al., 2022; Llorca et al., 2023).
German medical IE research lags behind English due to commercialization and data protection constraints (Lentzen et al., 2022; Roller et al., 2022; Richter-Pechanski et al., 2023). Despite these challenges, five annotated German NER datasets have been released: BRONCO (Kittner et al., 2021), CARDIO:DE (Richter-Pechanski et al., 2023), GGPONC2 (Borchert et al., 2022), GERNERMED (Frei and Kramer, 2023) and GPTNERMED (Frei and Kramer, 2023). Note that the latter two are not gold-standard, GERNERMED is an automatically translated subset of n2c2 2018, while GPTNERMED is a synthetic dataset created with GPT NeoX (Black et al., 2022). Studies on token classification models highlight performance disparities across entity types. Early baselines, such as CRF and LSTM on BRONCO (Kittner et al., 2021), showed moderate results (F1: 0.71–0.90), with dictionary-based normalization yielding inconsistent scores. Transformer-based models, including fine-tuned BERT variants on GGPONC2 and CARDIO:DE (Borchert et al., 2022; Richter-Pechanski et al., 2023), consistently outperformed CRF, especially in drug extraction. The work by Frei et al., 2022 demonstrated advancements from CNNs (F1: 0.67) to transformers (F1: 0.91) on GERNERMED, though generalizability remained an issue. Recent efforts, like GPTNERMED (Frei and Frank, 2023), leveraged synthetic data to enhance entity recognition but struggled on external datasets. While progress has been made, the field remains focused on dataset creation and model improvements, with gaps in generalization and broader application.
Beyond pre-trained language models, NLP frameworks like Apache cTakes (Savova et al., 2010) and MetaMap (Aronson, 2001) provide medical IE tools but are optimized for English. Attempts to adapt them to German, such as mapping UMLS concepts from translated clinical notes, resulted in low F1 scores due to linguistic and dataset limitations (Becker and Böckmann, 2016). This highlights a major challenge in clinical NLP: the dominance of English resources, which restricts research in other languages.

2.2 Usage of LLMs for Information Extraction

With the public release of models like LLAMA2 (Touvron et al., 2023), researchers began adapting LLMs for medical tasks, primarily focusing on text summarization and question answering (QA) (Li et al., 2023; Singhal et al., 2023). Notable advancements include Med-PaLM 2, which achieved 86.5% on USMLE-style questions and outperformed physician-written answers on consumer medical questions (Singhal et al., 2023). Similarly, LLMs have shown promise in clinical text summarization and outperforming baseline models in various NLP tasks, such as ICD-9 classification and entity normalization (Van Veen et al., 2023; Gema et al., 2023). Studies also highlight their robustness in low-resource scenarios and generalizability to unseen entities (Wang et al., 2025; Peeters and Bizer, 2024). However, challenges remain in using generative LLMs for token-level tasks like NER, as their architectures are optimized for text generation (Wang et al., 2025).
While initial studies explore LLMs for IE (Agrawal et al., 2022; Wang et al., 2025; Wu et al., 2023), their performance on German medical text remains unexplored. Furthermore, existing research predominantly utilizes LLMs exceeding 70B parameters, making them impractical for users lacking specialized hardware or substantial computational resources.

3 Methods

In this work a mixed method approach is used to explore the applicability of generative LLMs in the realm of German clinical IE tasks. Traditional NER treats entity recognition as a multiclass classification task, where token classifiers assign labels (e.g., drug, diagnosis, treatment or none often defined as O) to each token. In contrast, generative LLMs are designed to generate text based on a given input, which adds an additional layer of complexity to the task, as the model must not only recognize entities but also generate them correctly in a structured format, ensuring that the output can be processed automatically (Wang et al., 2025). Our study evaluates chat and further instruction-tuned versions of the following LLMs to baseline NER token-classifiers: LLAMA2 7B (Touvron et al., 2023), Mistral 7B (Jiang et al., 2023), Meditron 7B (Chen et al., 2023), Leo hessianai 7B and Leo hessianai Mistral 7B (Plüster, 2023). While Meditron is specifically trained for the medical domain, the latter two are trained for German.

3.1 Few-shot Prompting

When given a few demonstrations, a generative LLM can achieve performance comparable to fine-tuned models specifically trained on one task (Brown et al., 2020). To standardize output and reduce post-processing, we use a few-shot approach, as shown in Figure 1. The LLM is guided to produce structured lists for each entity class. Special instruction tokens *[INST]* within the prompt, used in Mistral 7B Instruct, help distinguish user input from generated content. These tokens vary across models. Following Agrawal et al., 2022, our

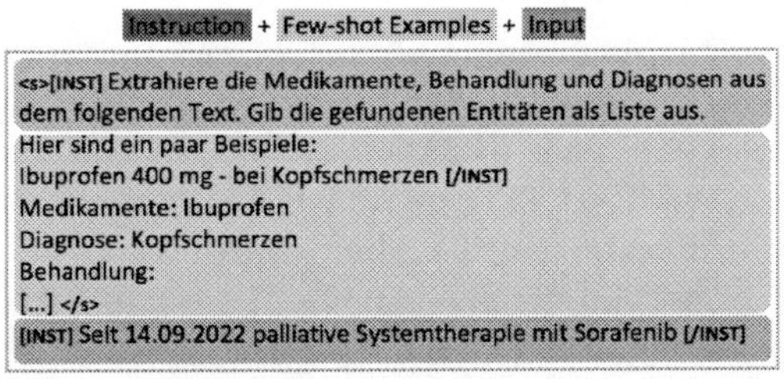

Figure 1: Few-shot approach to extract named entities from input

prompt includes all entity classes, with eight examples covering different entity combinations and a negative case resulting in 8 few-shot examples. To enhance consistency, the inference temperature is set to 0.1. Entity span boundaries are excluded, as even SOTA models like ChatGPT struggle with accurate character counts (OpenAI, 2022).

3.2 QLoRA Instruction Fine-tuning

To enhance LLMs ability to extract instructed medical entities from clinical text, we fine-tune the models on a custom instruction-tuning dataset. The training data comprises four NER datasets described in Section 4. The heterogeneous data formats were harmonized to the Alpaca instruction template (Taori et al., 2023) as illustrated in Figure 2. Each of the 34,096 training records includes an

```
### Instruction:
Extract all medications and diagnoses from the
following text.
Output the found entities as a list.
### Input:
0.4 Diuretics 0.25 1x/week
### Output:
Medication: Diuretics
Diagnosis:
```

Figure 2: Alpaca based schema for instruction fine-tuning.

instruction, input, and output. The instruction specifies dataset-specific entities in either German or English. The input contains the clinical sentence, and the output lists extracted entities by type. Given the LLMs 7B parameters, full fine-tuning is infeasible within this work. Instead, we employ QLoRA (Dettmers et al., 2023), a parameter-efficient fine-tuning (peft) method. The model is first quantized, after which the *LoRA* adapter is added, freezing the base model while enabling fine-tuning. The LoRA configuration follows Dettmers et al., 2023 with (r=64) and (lora_alpha=16). Fine-tuning is conducted using the *Supervised Fine-tuning Trainer* (Wolf et al., 2020), optimizing the model to predict training records.

3.3 RAG Enhanced Information Extraction

Researchers have shown that Retrieval-Augmented Generation (RAG) improves LLM performance by incorporating relevant information from domain-specific knowledge bases (Lewis et al., 2020; Jadhav et al., 2024). Given that BRONCOs diagnosis annotations are based on the German-modified International Statistical Classification Of Diseases (ICD-10-GM) and treatment annotations originate from the German procedure classification (OPS), this approach aims to enrich few-shot prompts with relevant domain knowledge. The retriever model is designed to suggest relevant ICD-10-GM diagnoses for a given input text. To achieve this, a vector database of the ICD-10-GM classification catalog is constructed using the danielheinz/e5-base-sts-en-de[1] model, which is trained for German semantic textual similarity. Similarly, the model is used to generate a vector database from the OPS procedure catalog to retrieve matching treatments. We chunk the ICD-10-GM data at the category level, including all associated subcategories, ensuring seamless integration of the retriever models output into the few-shot prompt. Notably, all code IDs are removed from the chunks before embedding, enhancing similarity between the vector embeddings and input text, as clinical documents rarely contain ICD-10-GM codes. The Mistral 7B Instruct LLM acts as the generator model, which processes the input sentence with instructions to extract medical entities while incorporating contextual information from the retriever model in the form of ICD-10-GM diagnoses or OPS procedures.

3.4 Information Extraction Evaluation

To compare the NER performance of generative LLMs with SLMs, this study uses three gold-standard annotated German datasets: BRONCO (Kittner et al., 2021), GGPONC2 (Borchert et al., 2022) and CARDIO:DE (Richter-Pechanski et al., 2023). Drug, diagnosis, and treatment extraction is evaluated using SemEval'13 metrics (Segura-Bedmar et al., 2013) on single runs, which also account for partial entity matches, relevant for multi-token entities like diagnoses, where annotation guidelines vary. Following Dror et al., 2018, we assess statistical significance using McNemar's test (McNemar, 1947). The SLMs are fine-tuned versions of medBert.de (Bressem et al., 2024), a SOTA 109M-parameter German medical language model. The different LLMs, in contrast, are tested without prior exposure to the datasets to assess their generalizability. Reference models include GERNERMED by Frei et al., 2022 for drug extraction, and GPTNERMED by Frei and Frank, 2023.

4 Datasets

Instruction Tuning Data. The custom instruction tuning dataset is a collection of the following four NER datasets: GERNERMED (Frei et al., 2022), GPTNERMED (Frei and Frank, 2023), i2b2 (Uzuner et al., 2011), and n2c2 (Henry et al., 2020).

Dataset	Train	Validation	Test
BRONCO	6,279	1,346	1,346
GGPONC2	59,515	12,770	3,000
CARDIO:DE	67,062	14,370	8,969

Table 1: Dataset splits used to train baseline NER tagger and compare LLMs to baseline.

A detailed overview of the datasets and their medical entities can be found in the Appendix A Table 5.

Evaluation Data. We evaluate our approach using the BRONCO, GGPONC2, and CARDIO:DE gold-standard datasets. While BRONCO and CARDIO:DE consist of pseudonymized clinical documents, GGPONC2 is a collection of annotated guidelines, resulting in a larger corpus. As shown in Table 5 in Appendix A, the annotated entity types vary greatly across these datasets. Since the CARDIO:DE annotations do not follow the IOB schema, this test split cannot be evaluated on entity type level but on strict spans only. The dataset splits used for training the baseline model medBert.de are detailed in Table 1, with the test split serving as the evaluation set.

5 Experimentation

All experiments were executed on the same server with the following specifications: NVIDIA RTX A5000 with 24564MiB, Cuda version 11. The source code to reproduce the experiments is available online[2].

5.1 LLM Comparison

Before turning to the LLM comparison to baseline token classifiers, Figure 3 shows the evaluation of instruction-tuned LLMs on the BRONCO test set to answer **RQ1** and explore **RQ2**. All models performed best on medication extraction and worst on identifying treatments, with F1 ranging from 0.88 for medication to 0.14 for treatments. The QLoRA instruction-tuning consistently improved performance, especially for Meditron, while Mistral LLMs outperformed other models across all entity types. We also observed a drastic decline in hallucinations for our instruction fine-tuned LLMs. While the chat-based LLMs generated up to 156 entities that could not be matched to the input text, the instruction-tuned models produced only 0 to 3 hallucinated entities on the BRONCO test sample (Ap-

[1] https://huggingface.co/danielheinz/e5-base-sts-en-de

[2] https://github.com/IAMspiegel/LLMGerMedIE

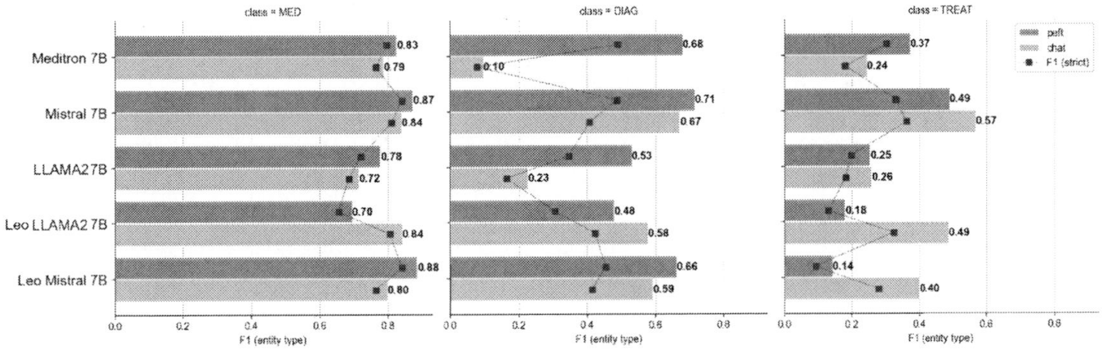

Figure 3: NER results for the BRONCO test sample on entity type level for different versions of LLMs. Compared is the publicly available chat version with instruction tuned (peft) models. Note that the Meditron 7B chat version is not publicly available, thus the base version was used.

Level	Model (Train Data)	Medication			Diagnosis			Treatment			Micro Avg.
		P	R	F1	P	R	F1	P	R	F1	F1
Entity Type	medBert.de (BRONCO)	.95	.96	**.96**	.84	.94	**.89**	.86	.94	**.90**	**.90**
	medBert.de (GGPONC2)	.75	.85	.80	.63	.84	.72	.44	.88	.59	.69
	medBert.de (CARDIO:DE)	.81	.81	.81	.0	.0	.0	.0	.0	.0	.27
	GermanBERT (GERNERMED)	.39	.92	.55	.0	.0	.0	.0	.0	.0	.28
	GermanMedBERT (GPTNERMED)	.51	.88	.64	.44	.62	.51	.0	.0	.0	.55
	Mistral 7B Instruct (8-shot)	.86	.82	.84	.70	.64	.67	.48	.71	.57	.66
	peft Mistral 7B	.86	.88	.87	.67	.77	.71	.61	.41	.49	.69
Token	medBert.de (BRONCO)	.90	.91	**.91**	.73	.81	**.77**	.75	.82	**.79**	**.80**
	medBert.de (GGPONC2)	.70	.80	.75	.38	.51	.44	.33	.64	.43	.48
	medBert.de (CARDIO:DE)	.81	.81	.81	.0	.0	.0	.0	.0	.0	.27
	GermanBERT (GERNERMED)	.37	.92	.52	.0	.0	.0	.0	.0	.0	.26
	GermanMedBERT (GPTNERMED)	.48	.85	.62	.29	.41	.34	.0	.0	.0	.55
	Mistral 7B Instruct (8-shot)	.83	.80	.81	.43	.39	.41	.30	.45	.36	.46
	peft Mistral 7B	.83	.85	.84	.45	.52	.49	.41	.27	.33	.51

Table 2: Results (precision, recall, F1) of BRONCO test sample. Comparison of best fine-tuned LLM, chat Mistral-7B to the BRONCO baseline model and BERT based models trained on other datasets. The displayed scores are calculated on entity type basis and strict span evaluation (token). The reported scores for medBert.de (GGPONC2) follow the mapping: Clinical_Drug → Medication, Diagnosis_or_Pathology → Diagnosis, Therapeutic and Diagnostic → Treatment. Alternative mappings result in a lower performance.

pendix B.1 Table 6). LLMs tended to over-tag diagnoses, likely due to broader concept recognition beyond ICD-10-GM. In contrast, they struggled with identifying cancer-related treatments, showing high precision but low recall. Overall, LLMs excelled in drug extraction but underperformed in recognizing OPS treatments. An additional analysis of medical abbreviations further confirmed a performance drop for previously unseen diagnosis and treatment phrases, highlighting the models limitations in generalizing to less common or implicitly expressed entities. Since both Mistral versions perform best in their category, we use these LLMs in the following comparison to baseline NER models.

5.2 LLMs Compared to Baseline

5.2.1 BRONCO

The results of the baseline SLMs and top-performing LLMs on the BRONCO test set to answer **RQ2** and **RQ3** are shown in Table 2. As expected, medBert.de fine-tuned on BRONCO achieves the best overall F1 (0.9). Its performance surpasses the baseline of Kittner et al., 2021 but remains below the top-performing model on the BRONCO leaderboard[3]. Notably, GERNERMED and GPTNERMED perform poorly, over-generating medication entities with low precision and failing to capture treatments.

Our fine-tuned peft Mistral 7B model achieves the best F1 for medication and diagnosis second

[3]https://www2.informatik.hu-berlin.de/~leser/bronco/index.html

to medBert.de (BRONCO). However, not significantly better than medBert.de (GGPONC2), which outperforms the LLMs in identifying treatments, although its performance remains significantly below the BRONCO-trained baseline as illustrated in Appendix B.3. Interestingly, Mistral-7B Instruct achieves slightly better results in extracting medications compared to most NER models, reinforcing the strengths of LLM transfer learning over dataset-specific fine-tuning.

5.2.2 GGPONC2

The NER results for the GGPONC2 test sample are presented in Table 3. Its annotation guidelines differ from BRONCO, leading to variations in entity types. The diagnosis class includes pathology related entities, and previous analysis found that mapping GGPONC2s therapeutic class to BRONCOs treatment class yields the highest extraction scores. Since therapeutic entities dominate this category, it serves as the test datasets equivalent to the treatment entity type. As expected, medBert.de (GGPONC2) achieves the highest F1 (0.92) across all entities, slightly surpassing the performance of the BERT based NER model reported by Borchert et al., 2022. While medBert.de (CARDIO:DE) performed reasonably well on BRONCO medications, it struggles on GGPONC2 drugs (F1: 0.57). Both Mistral 7B Instruct and our instruction-tuned peft variant outperform three reference token classifiers across all entities, excelling in the drug class but performing worst in therapeutic. A closer look reveals that medBert.de (BRONCO) and both Mistral LLMs exhibit higher precision than recall for the diagnosis/pathology class, likely because the token classifier was trained for diagnoses only, while the LLMs were prompted for diagnoses but not pathology or symptoms. Our fine-tuned peft Mistral 7B LLM outperforms Mistral-7B Instruct across all entities, with the largest gap in the diagnosis/pathology class. However, it marginally surpasses medBert.de (BRONCO) only in the drug category. While the F1 difference for diagnosis/-pathology is notable, results for therapeutic are comparable.

5.2.3 CARDIO:DE

As the CARDIO:DE annotations distinguish between active ingredients and drug entities but BRONCO and GGPONC2 do not, the entity classes were combined into one single class. The results in Table 4 show that the medBert.de model trained on CARDIO:DE achieves the highest F1 score, with a notable gap between recall and precision. Its performance also exceeds that of the BERT transformer presented in the original CARDIO:DE study by Richter-Pechanski et al., 2023. Other models exhibit comparable trends, while medBert.de (BRONCO) and our peft Mistral 7B have recall scores close to medBert.de (CARDIO:DE), their precision is noticeably lower. GERNERMED and GPTNERMED again show strikingly low precision, suggesting excessive entity tagging. The instruction fine-tuned Mistral 7B achieves the second-best F1 score, outperforming medBert.de models trained on BRONCO and GGPONC2. Notably, Mistral 7B Instruct, with just eight few-shot examples, surpasses medBert.de (BRONCO) in F1, making it the only model with higher precision than recall. Its precision matches the best baseline model, likely because it was not influenced by fine-tuning on datasets where active ingredients were tagged as drugs.

5.3 RAG Information Extraction

To further investigate **RQ2** and to enhance the IE performance of LLMs for diagnosis and treatment entities, we tested a RAG approach, which provides the LLM with additional context, including relevant ICD-10-GM codes or OPS procedures. However, our experiment did not result in an improvement in NER scores on the BRONCO test sample. The embedding model evaluation, shown in Figure 4, reveals that diagnoses were better recognized, with higher similarity scores between the retrieved code categories and input sentences. In contrast, treatment entities did not exhibit the same clear pattern. Despite using optimized prompts, the F1 scores for both diagnosis and treatment entities decreased drastically, as shown in Figure 6 in Appendix B.2, with treatment entities experiencing a more substantial decline due to insufficient context generation and limitations of the OPS knowledge source. Several factors likely contributed to this decline in performance. First, the OPS catalog proved suboptimal for retrieval, often returning context with high lexical similarity but low semantic relevance. Second, the German embedding model may luck sufficient domain coverage, reducing retrieval accuracy. Third, the Mistral 7B chat model struggled to process single-phrase inputs effectively, highlighting limitations in contextual understanding compared to larger models.

Level	Model (Train Data)	Drug			Diagnosis/Pathology			Therapeutic			Micro Avg.
		P	R	F1	P	R	F1	P	R	F1	F1
Entity Type	medBert.de (BRONCO)	.77	.70	.74	.84	.59	.69	.65	.38	.48	.62
	medBert.de (GGPONC2)	.91	.94	**.93**	.91	.94	**.92**	.91	.93	**.92**	**.92**
	medBert.de (CARDIO:DE)	.58	.55	.57	.0	.0	.0	.0	.0	.0	.19
	GermanBERT (GERNERMED)	.45	.70	.55	.0	.0	.0	.0	.0	.0	.12
	GermanMedBERT (GPTNERMED)	.35	.69	.47	.39	.46	.42	.0	.0	.0	.32
	Mistral 7B Instruct (8-shot)	.78	.62	.70	.71	.34	.46	.52	.37	.43	.48
	peft Mistral 7B	.77	.73	.75	.73	.48	.58	.65	.33	.44	.55
Token	medBert.de (BRONCO)	.73	.67	.70	.64	.45	.53	.47	.27	.35	.48
	medBert.de (GGPONC2)	.88	.90	**.89**	.90	.92	**.91**	.90	.92	**.91**	**.91**
	medBert.de (CARDIO:DE)	.58	.55	.57	.0	.0	.0	.0	.0	.0	.19
	GermanBERT (GERNERMED)	.41	.64	.50	.0	.0	.0	.0	.0	.0	.11
	GermanMedBERT (GPTNERMED)	.34	.67	.45	.31	.37	.34	.0	.0	.0	.27
	Mistral 7B Instruct (8-shot)	.73	.58	.65	.58	.28	.37	.42	.30	.35	.40
	peft Mistral 7B	.71	.68	.70	.51	.34	.41	.45	.23	.31	.41

Table 3: Results (precision, recall, F1) of GGPONC2 test sample. Comparison of best fine-tuned LLM, chat Mistral 7B to the baseline model and BERT based models trained on other datasets. The displayed scores are calculated on entity type basis and strict span evaluation (token).

Model (Train Data)	Precision	Recall	F1
medBert.de			
- (BRONCO)	.43	.89	.58
- (GGPONC2)	.61	.83	.70
- (CARDIO:DE)	**.84**	**.93**	**.88**
GermanBERT - (GERNERMED)	.20	.89	.32
GermanMedBERT - (GPTNERMED)	.24	.85	.37
Mistral 7B Instruct (8-shot)	.81	.54	.64
peft Mistral 7B	.59	.88	.71

Table 4: Results of CARDIO:DE test sample. Comparison of best fine-tuned LLM, chat Mistral-7B to the baseline models. The displayed scores are calculated on token level.

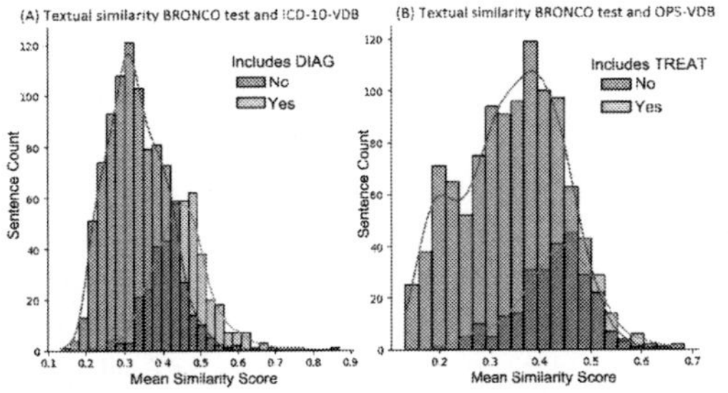

Figure 4: Textual similarity between BRONCO test data and vector databases. (A) Similarity distribution between BRONCO test sentences and the ICD-10-GM vector database (VDB), categorized by whether the sentence contains a diagnosis entity. (B) Similarity distribution between BRONCO test sentences and the OPS VDB, categorized by whether the sentence includes a treatment entity.

5.4 Out-of-Distribution Analysis

To address **RQ3** and assess generalizability, an additional analysis of the datasets reveals that the strong performance of medBert.de (GGPONC2) across all three evaluation datasets, including BRONCO, can be attributed to a high proportion of shared entities between the GGPONC2 training and BRONCO test data. 58% of BRONCOs test treatment entities and 51% of diagnoses appear in GGPONC2, while the overlap with LLM instruction data is remarkably lower (31% for diagnoses, 28% for treatments). Figure 5 further illustrates how models perform on out-of-distribution (OOD) entities. medBert.de (GGPONC2) exhibits a sharp performance drop in the OOD (GGPONC2) dataset, in which all overlapping entities between BRONCO and GGPONC2 were removed. This highlights the models strong reliance training data. Conversely, our instruction fine-tuned peft Mistral 7B maintains more stable performance across OOD datasets, even surpassing medBert.de (GGPONC2) on OOD drugs and diagnoses. Additionally, Mistral 7B Instruct achieves an F1 score for treatment concepts comparable to medBert.de (GGPONC2).

These findings underscore the advantages of domain overlap in training data for token classifiers while demonstrating LLMs greater adaptability to unseen entities.

6 Discussion

The presented work was designed to test 7B LLMs for German medical IE on unseen datasets and compare their performance with the baseline SLMs. We found that LLMs exhibit strong generalizability on unseen data due to their extensive pre-training on large corpora and vast parameter size. However, their limited domain-specific knowledge pre-

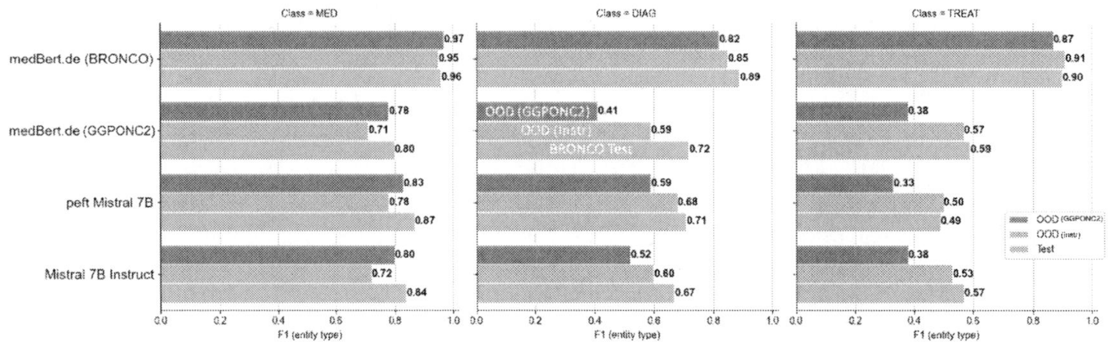

Figure 5: F1 scores for entity type classification on different subsets of the BRONCO test dataset. Each model is evaluated on the full test set (Test) and two OOD subsets: (1) OOD (GGPONC2), where entities present in the GGPONC2 training data are removed, and (2) OOD (Instr), where entities overlapping with the instruction fine-tuning dataset are excluded.

vents them from reaching the F1 scores above 0.90 needed for reliable, production-level applications. While QLoRA instruction tuning enables effective 7B LLM fine-tuning on a single GPU and has demonstrated strong IE performance, this study also identified drawbacks. The trained adapters can reduce generalizability and multitask ability, as noted by Van Veen et al., 2023, who observed worsened text summarization after QLoRA fine-tuning. Similarly, our findings show a considerable drop in treatment extraction performance, likely due to the instruction datasets lack of treatment examples. Despite this, LLMs offer greater flexibility, making them more adaptable to various tasks and domains than SLMs. However, post-processing may be more challenging. As a result, they can be a viable option for extracting medical information from unstructured text when top-tier performance is not essential.

While SOTA commercial LLMs, such as GPT-4, perform well on multilingual clinical tasks (Qiu et al., 2024), we observe that this is not the case for smaller 7B models like Meditron. Despite additional training in the medical domain on English data, Meditron failed to reliably extract German medical terms. Domain-specific terminology and abbreviations may therefore pose a greater challenge for cross-lingual transfer in smaller LLMs.

Computational Resources. LLMs incur higher CPU and GPU costs compared to baseline SLMs, but using the vLLM package (Kwon et al., 2023) significantly reduces inference time, making it comparable to that of baseline SLMs, despite requiring around 24GB of VRAM. Without vLLM, inference times can stretch for hours with just a few thousand samples, underscoring the importance of frameworks like vLLM for optimizing LLM performance and managing resource demands.

Future Work. This paper shows that 7B LLMs lack the medical expertise needed for accurate diagnosis and treatment extraction. To address this, future work could explore larger LLMs, such as the Mixtral 8x7B, which has 47 billion parameters and outperforms 70B models while being manageable during inference. Although our RAG setup did not improve IE performance for several factors, it remains a promising strategy for boosting LLMs capabilities in extracting information (Vithanage et al., 2025; Bartels and Carus, 2025). Another potential approach is integrating medical knowledge via knowledge graphs, as outlined by Pan et al., 2024.

Instead of solely adapting LLMs, future research could focus on disambiguating clinical text to enhance model understanding, as demonstrated by Agrawal et al., 2022.

7 Conclusion

This work explored the ability of 7B LLMs for German medical IE across multiple datasets. Key findings include: **(1)** Mistral 7B outperforms other LLMs, including German trained models, in extracting medications, diagnoses and treatments. **(2)** Instruction tuning via QLoRA improves IE performance but may reduce treatment recognition due to imbalanced training data. **(3)** While LLMs do not surpass SLMs on their domain, they achieve strong medication extraction results (F1: 0.87–0.71) and remain competitive in diagnosis and treatment extraction. **(4)** When comparing LLMs to baseline

SLMs on out-of-domain datasets, the instruction-tuned peft Mistral 7B outperformed four of the five baseline models. Additionally, the Mistral LLMs surpassed the baseline models on out-of-distribution data.

These findings highlight the ongoing challenges in German medical IE and emphasize the need for diverse, high-quality, language-specific datasets for fine-tuning models, particularly in specialized domains like medical NLP. While 7B LLMs are less suited for tasks requiring precise information extraction, they can still be valuable in situations where training data is limited, and the primary objective is to gain a broader understanding of unstructured text rather than achieving excellent accuracy.

8 Limitations

The scarcity of publicly available gold-standard medical datasets in Germany hinders both NER model development and cross-dataset validation. The evaluation datasets BRONCO, GGPONC2, and CARDIO:DE differ in size, origin, document type, and annotation style, making general conclusions about cross-domain performance difficult. BRONCO and GGPONC2 stem from oncology, while CARDIO:DE, from cardiology, lacks annotated diagnoses and treatments. Annotation inconsistencies further impact performance, as BRONCO follows structured classification catalogs (ATC, ICD-10-GM, OPS), whereas GGPONC2 does not. Document-level differences also introduce ambiguity, affecting entity classification. Additionally, BRONCOs shuffled sentence structure disrupts context, potentially impairing LLM performance. While the three German datasets used for evaluation in this study are publicly available only upon request and are stored in CoNLL-style or other structured annotation formats, we cannot rule out the possibility that portions of them were included in the pretraining corpora of the evaluated LLMs. Given that most LLM training data sources are undisclosed, this remains a general limitation in LLM evaluation.

References

Monica Agrawal, Stefan Hegselmann, Hunter Lang, Yoon Kim, and David Sontag. 2022. Large language models are few-shot clinical information extractors. In *Proceedings of the 2022 Conference on Empirical Methods in Natural Language Processing*, pages 1998–2022. Association for Computational Linguistics.

Alan R Aronson. 2001. Effective mapping of biomedical text to the umls metathesaurus: the metamap program. In *Proceedings of the AMIA Symposium*, page 17. American Medical Informatics Association.

Stefan Bartels and Jasmin Carus. 2025. From text to data: Open-source large language models in extracting cancer related medical attributes from german pathology reports. *International Journal of Medical Informatics*, 203:106022.

Matthias Becker and Britta Böckmann. 2016. Extraction of umls® concepts using apache ctakes™ for german language. In *Health Informatics Meets Ehealth*, pages 71–76. IOS Press.

Sidney Black, Stella Biderman, Eric Hallahan, Quentin Anthony, Leo Gao, Laurence Golding, Horace He, Connor Leahy, Kyle McDonell, Jason Phang, Michael Pieler, Usvsn Sai Prashanth, Shivanshu Purohit, Laria Reynolds, Jonathan Tow, Ben Wang, and Samuel Weinbach. 2022. GPT-NeoX-20b: An open-source autoregressive language model. In *Proceedings of BigScience Episode #5 – Workshop on Challenges & Perspectives in Creating Large Language Models*, pages 95–136. Association for Computational Linguistics.

Florian Borchert, Christina Lohr, Luise Modersohn, Jonas Witt, Thomas Langer, Markus Follmann, Matthias Gietzelt, Bert Arnrich, Udo Hahn, and Matthieu-P. Schapranow. 2022. GGPONC 2.0 - the german clinical guideline corpus for oncology: Curation workflow, annotation policy, baseline NER taggers. In *Proceedings of the Thirteenth Language Resources and Evaluation Conference*, pages 3650–3660. European Language Resources Association.

Keno K. Bressem, Jens-Michalis Papaioannou, Paul Grundmann, Florian Borchert, Lisa C. Adams, Leonhard Liu, Felix Busch, Lina Xu, Jan P. Loyen, Stefan M. Niehues, Moritz Augustin, Lennart Grosser, Marcus R. Makowski, Hugo J. W. L. Aerts, and Alexander Löser. 2024. medBERT.de: A comprehensive german BERT model for the medical domain. *Expert Systems with Applications*, 237:121598.

Tom B. Brown, Benjamin Mann, Nick Ryder, Melanie Subbiah, Jared Kaplan, Prafulla Dhariwal, Arvind Neelakantan, Pranav Shyam, Girish Sastry, Amanda Askell, Sandhini Agarwal, Ariel Herbert-Voss, Gretchen Krueger, Tom Henighan, Rewon Child, Aditya Ramesh, Daniel M. Ziegler, Jeffrey Wu, Clemens Winter, Christopher Hesse, Mark Chen, Eric Sigler, Mateusz Litwin, Scott Gray, Benjamin

Chess, Jack Clark, Christopher Berner, Sam McCandlish, Alec Radford, Ilya Sutskever, and Dario Amodei. 2020. Language models are few-shot learners. *Preprint*, arxiv:2005.14165 [cs].

Zeming Chen, Alejandro Hernández Cano, Angelika Romanou, Antoine Bonnet, Kyle Matoba, Francesco Salvi, Matteo Pagliardini, Simin Fan, Andreas Köpf, Amirkeivan Mohtashami, Alexandre Sallinen, Alireza Sakhaeirad, Vinitra Swamy, Igor Krawczuk, Deniz Bayazit, Axel Marmet, Syrielle Montariol, Mary-Anne Hartley, Martin Jaggi, and Antoine Bosselut. 2023. MEDITRON-70b: Scaling medical pretraining for large language models. *Preprint*, arxiv:2311.16079 [cs].

Tim Dettmers, Artidoro Pagnoni, Ari Holtzman, and Luke Zettlemoyer. 2023. QLoRA: Efficient finetuning of quantized LLMs. *Preprint*, arxiv:2305.14314 [cs].

Jacob Devlin, Ming-Wei Chang, Kenton Lee, and Kristina Toutanova. 2019. BERT: Pre-training of deep bidirectional transformers for language understanding. In *Proceedings of the 2019 Conference of the North American Chapter of the Association for Computational Linguistics: Human Language Technologies, Volume 1 (Long and Short Papers)*, pages 4171–4186. Association for Computational Linguistics.

Rotem Dror, Gili Baumer, Segev Shlomov, and Roi Reichart. 2018. The hitchhiker's guide to testing statistical significance in natural language processing. In *Proceedings of the 56th Annual Meeting of the Association for Computational Linguistics (Volume 1: Long Papers)*, pages 1383–1392. Association for Computational Linguistics.

Johann Frei and Kramer Frank. 2023. Annotated dataset creation through large language models for non-english medical NLP. *Journal of Biomedical Informatics*, 145:104478.

Johann Frei, Ludwig Frei-Stuber, and Frank Kramer. 2022. GERNERMED++: Transfer learning in german medical NLP. *Preprint*, arxiv:2206.14504 [cs].

Johann Frei and Frank Kramer. 2023. German medical named entity recognition model and data set creation using machine translation and word alignment: Algorithm development and validation. *JMIR Formative Research*, 7(1):e39077.

Aryo Pradipta Gema, Luke Daines, Pasquale Minervini, and Beatrice Alex. 2023. Parameter-efficient finetuning of LLaMA for the clinical domain. *Preprint*, arxiv:2307.03042 [cs].

Sam Henry, Kevin Buchan, Michele Filannino, Amber Stubbs, and Ozlem Uzuner. 2020. 2018 n2c2 shared task on adverse drug events and medication extraction in electronic health records. *Journal of the American Medical Informatics Association*, 27(1):3–12.

Kexin Huang, Jaan Altosaar, and Rajesh Ranganath. 2020. ClinicalBERT: Modeling clinical notes and predicting hospital readmission. *Preprint*, arxiv:1904.05342 [cs].

Suramya Jadhav, Abhay Shanbhag, Sumedh Joshi, Atharva Date, and Sheetal Sonawane. 2024. Maven at MEDIQA-CORR 2024: Leveraging RAG and medical LLM for error detection and correction in medical notes. In *Proceedings of the 6th Clinical Natural Language Processing Workshop*, pages 374–381. Association for Computational Linguistics.

Peter B. Jensen, Lars J. Jensen, and Søren Brunak. 2012. Mining electronic health records: towards better research applications and clinical care. *Nature Reviews Genetics*, 13(6):395–405.

Albert Q. Jiang, Alexandre Sablayrolles, Arthur Mensch, Chris Bamford, Devendra Singh Chaplot, Diego de las Casas, Florian Bressand, Gianna Lengyel, Guillaume Lample, Lucile Saulnier, Lélio Renard Lavaud, Marie-Anne Lachaux, Pierre Stock, Teven Le Scao, Thibaut Lavril, Thomas Wang, Timothée Lacroix, and William El Sayed. 2023. Mistral 7b. *Preprint*, arxiv:2310.06825 [cs].

Albert Q. Jiang, Alexandre Sablayrolles, Antoine Roux, Arthur Mensch, Blanche Savary, Chris Bamford, Devendra Singh Chaplot, Diego de las Casas, Emma Bou Hanna, Florian Bressand, Gianna Lengyel, Guillaume Bour, Guillaume Lample, Lélio Renard Lavaud, Lucile Saulnier, Marie-Anne Lachaux, Pierre Stock, Sandeep Subramanian, Sophia Yang, Szymon Antoniak, Teven Le Scao, Théophile Gervet, Thibaut Lavril, Thomas Wang, Timothée Lacroix, and William El Sayed. 2024. Mixtral of experts. *Preprint*, arxiv:2401.04088 [cs].

Madeleine Kittner, Mario Lamping, Damian T Rieke, Julian Götze, Bariya Bajwa, Ivan Jelas, Gina Rüter, Hanjo Hautow, Mario Sänger, Maryam Habibi, Marit Zettwitz, Till de Bortoli, Leonie Ostermann, Jurica Ševa, Johannes Starlinger, Oliver Kohlbacher, Nisar P Malek, Ulrich Keilholz, and Ulf Leser. 2021. Annotation and initial evaluation of a large annotated german oncological corpus. *JAMIA Open*, 4(2):ooab025.

Woosuk Kwon, Zhuohan Li, Siyuan Zhuang, Ying Sheng, Lianmin Zheng, Cody Hao Yu, Joseph E. Gonzalez, Hao Zhang, and Ion Stoica. 2023. Efficient memory management for large language model serving with PagedAttention. *Preprint*, arxiv:2309.06180 [cs].

Lisa Kühnel and Juliane Fluck. 2022. We are not ready yet: limitations of state-of-the-art disease named entity recognizers. *Journal of Biomedical Semantics*, 13(1):26.

Mohamed Yassine Landolsi, Lobna Hlaoua, and Lotfi Ben Romdhane. 2023. Information extraction from electronic medical documents: state of the art and future research directions. *Knowledge and Information Systems*, 65(2):463–516.

Reinhard Larsen. 2016. Präoperative Einschätzung und Prämedikation. *Anästhesie und Intensivmedizin für die Fachpflege*, pages 26–35.

Jinhyuk Lee, Wonjin Yoon, Sungdong Kim, Donghyeon Kim, Sunkyu Kim, Chan Ho So, and Jaewoo Kang. 2020. BioBERT: a pre-trained biomedical language representation model for biomedical text mining. *Bioinformatics*, 36(4):1234–1240.

Manuel Lentzen, Sumit Madan, Vanessa Lage-Rupprecht, Lisa Kühnel, Juliane Fluck, Marc Jacobs, Mirja Mittermaier, Martin Witzenrath, Peter Brunecker, Martin Hofmann-Apitius, Joachim Weber, and Holger Fröhlich. 2022. Critical assessment of transformer-based AI models for german clinical notes. *JAMIA Open*, 5(4):ooac087.

Patrick Lewis, Ethan Perez, Aleksandra Piktus, Fabio Petroni, Vladimir Karpukhin, Naman Goyal, Heinrich Küttler, Mike Lewis, Wen-tau Yih, Tim Rocktäschel, Sebastian Riedel, and Douwe Kiela. 2020. Retrieval-augmented generation for knowledge-intensive NLP tasks. In *Advances in Neural Information Processing Systems*, volume 33, pages 9459–9474. Curran Associates, Inc.

Yunxiang Li, Zihan Li, Kai Zhang, Ruilong Dan, Steve Jiang, and You Zhang. 2023. ChatDoctor: A medical chat model fine-tuned on a large language model meta-AI (LLaMA) using medical domain knowledge. *Preprint*, arxiv:2303.14070 [cs].

Ignacio Llorca, Florian Borchert, and Matthieu-P. Schapranow. 2023. A meta-dataset of german medical corpora: Harmonization of annotations and cross-corpus NER evaluation. In *Proceedings of the 5th Clinical Natural Language Processing Workshop*, pages 171–181. Association for Computational Linguistics.

Quinn McNemar. 1947. Note on the sampling error of the difference between correlated proportions or percentages. *Psychometrika*, 12(2):153–157.

OpenAI. 2022. Introducing ChatGPT. https://openai.com/index/chatgpt/.

Shirui Pan, Linhao Luo, Yufei Wang, Chen Chen, Jiapu Wang, and Xindong Wu. 2024. Unifying large language models and knowledge graphs: A roadmap. *IEEE Transactions on Knowledge and Data Engineering*, 36(7):3580–3599.

Ralph Peeters and Christian Bizer. 2024. Entity matching using large language models. *Preprint*, arxiv:2310.11244 [cs].

Björn Plüster. 2023. LeoLM: Igniting german-language LLM research | LAION. https://laion.ai/blog/leo-lm.

Pengcheng Qiu, Chaoyi Wu, Xiaoman Zhang, Weixiong Lin, Haicheng Wang, Ya Zhang, Yanfeng Wang, and Weidi Xie. 2024. Towards building multilingual language model for medicine. *Nature Communications*, 15(1):8384. Publisher: Nature Publishing Group.

Phillip Richter-Pechanski, Philipp Wiesenbach, Dominic M. Schwab, Christina Kiriakou, Mingyang He, Michael M. Allers, Anna S. Tiefenbacher, Nicola Kunz, Anna Martynova, Noemie Spiller, Julian Mierisch, Florian Borchert, Charlotte Schwind, Norbert Frey, Christoph Dieterich, and Nicolas A. Geis. 2023. A distributable german clinical corpus containing cardiovascular clinical routine doctor's letters. *Scientific Data*, 10(1):207.

Roland Roller, Laura Seiffe, Ammer Ayach, Sebastian Möller, Oliver Marten, Michael Mikhailov, Christoph Alt, Danilo Schmidt, Fabian Halleck, Marcel Naik, Wiebke Duettmann, and Klemens Budde. 2022. A medical information extraction workbench to process german clinical text. *Preprint*, arxiv:2207.03885 [cs].

Guergana K Savova, James J Masanz, Philip V Ogren, Jiaping Zheng, Sunghwan Sohn, Karin C Kipper-Schuler, and Christopher G Chute. 2010. Mayo clinical text analysis and knowledge extraction system (cTAKES): architecture, component evaluation and applications. *Journal of the American Medical Informatics Association*, 17(5):507–513.

Isabel Segura-Bedmar, Paloma Martínez, and María Herrero-Zazo. 2013. SemEval-2013 task 9 : Extraction of drug-drug interactions from biomedical texts (DDIExtraction 2013). In *Second Joint Conference on Lexical and Computational Semantics (*SEM), Volume 2: Proceedings of the Seventh International Workshop on Semantic Evaluation (SemEval 2013)*, pages 341–350. Association for Computational Linguistics.

Karan Singhal, Tao Tu, Juraj Gottweis, Rory Sayres, Ellery Wulczyn, Le Hou, Kevin Clark, Stephen Pfohl, Heather Cole-Lewis, Darlene Neal, Mike Schaekermann, Amy Wang, Mohamed Amin, Sami Lachgar, Philip Mansfield, Sushant Prakash, Bradley Green, Ewa Dominowska, Blaise Aguera y Arcas, Nenad Tomasev, Yun Liu, Renee Wong, Christopher Semturs, S. Sara Mahdavi, Joelle Barral, Dale Webster, Greg S. Corrado, Yossi Matias, Shekoofeh Azizi, Alan Karthikesalingam, and Vivek Natarajan. 2023. Towards expert-level medical question answering with large language models. *Preprint*, arxiv:2305.09617 [cs].

Jackson Steinkamp, Jacob J. Kantrowitz, and Subha Airan-Javia. 2022. Prevalence and sources of duplicate information in the electronic medical record. *JAMA network open*, 5(9):e2233348.

Rohan Taori, Ishaan Gulrajani, Tianyi Zhang, Yann Dubois, Xuechen Li, Carlos Guestrin, Percy Liang, and Tatsunori B. Hashimoto. 2023. Stanford alpaca: An instruction-following llama model. `https://github.com/tatsu-lab/stanford_alpaca`.

Hugo Touvron, Louis Martin, Kevin Stone, Peter Albert, Amjad Almahairi, Yasmine Babaei, Nikolay Bashlykov, Soumya Batra, Prajjwal Bhargava, Shruti Bhosale, Dan Bikel, Lukas Blecher, Cristian Canton

Ferrer, Moya Chen, Guillem Cucurull, David Esiobu, Jude Fernandes, Jeremy Fu, Wenyin Fu, Brian Fuller, Cynthia Gao, Vedanuj Goswami, Naman Goyal, Anthony Hartshorn, Saghar Hosseini, Rui Hou, Hakan Inan, Marcin Kardas, Viktor Kerkez, Madian Khabsa, Isabel Kloumann, Artem Korenev, Punit Singh Koura, Marie-Anne Lachaux, Thibaut Lavril, Jenya Lee, Diana Liskovich, Yinghai Lu, Yuning Mao, Xavier Martinet, Todor Mihaylov, Pushkar Mishra, Igor Molybog, Yixin Nie, Andrew Poulton, Jeremy Reizenstein, Rashi Rungta, Kalyan Saladi, Alan Schelten, Ruan Silva, Eric Michael Smith, Ranjan Subramanian, Xiaoqing Ellen Tan, Binh Tang, Ross Taylor, Adina Williams, Jian Xiang Kuan, Puxin Xu, Zheng Yan, Iliyan Zarov, Yuchen Zhang, Angela Fan, Melanie Kambadur, Sharan Narang, Aurelien Rodriguez, Robert Stojnic, Sergey Edunov, and Thomas Scialom. 2023. Llama 2: Open foundation and fine-tuned chat models. *Preprint*, arxiv:2307.09288 [cs].

Özlem Uzuner, Brett R South, Shuying Shen, and Scott L DuVall. 2011. 2010 i2b2/VA challenge on concepts, assertions, and relations in clinical text. *Journal of the American Medical Informatics Association*, 18(5):552–556.

Dave Van Veen, Cara Van Uden, Louis Blankemeier, Jean-Benoit Delbrouck, Asad Aali, Christian Bluethgen, Anuj Pareek, Malgorzata Polacin, Eduardo Pontes Reis, Anna Seehofnerova, Nidhi Rohatgi, Poonam Hosamani, William Collins, Neera Ahuja, Curtis P. Langlotz, Jason Hom, Sergios Gatidis, John Pauly, and Akshay S. Chaudhari. 2023. Clinical text summarization: Adapting large language models can outperform human experts. *Preprint*, arxiv:2309.07430 [cs].

Dinithi Vithanage, Chao Deng, Lei Wang, Mengyang Yin, Mohammad Alkhalaf, Zhenyu Zhang, Yunshu Zhu, and Ping Yu. 2025. Adapting generative large language models for information extraction from unstructured electronic health records in residential aged care: A comparative analysis of training approaches. *Journal of Healthcare Informatics Research*, 9(2):191–219.

Shuhe Wang, Xiaofei Sun, Xiaoya Li, Rongbin Ouyang, Fei Wu, Tianwei Zhang, Jiwei Li, Guoyin Wang, and Chen Guo. 2025. GPT-NER: Named entity recognition via large language models. In *Findings of the Association for Computational Linguistics: NAACL 2025*, pages 4257–4275. Association for Computational Linguistics.

Thomas Wolf, Lysandre Debut, Victor Sanh, Julien Chaumond, Clement Delangue, Anthony Moi, Pierric Cistac, Tim Rault, Remi Louf, Morgan Funtowicz, Joe Davison, Sam Shleifer, Patrick von Platen, Clara Ma, Yacine Jernite, Julien Plu, Canwen Xu, Teven Le Scao, Sylvain Gugger, Mariama Drame, Quentin Lhoest, and Alexander Rush. 2020. Transformers: State-of-the-art natural language processing. In *Proceedings of the 2020 Conference on Empirical Methods in Natural Language Processing: System Demonstrations*, pages 38–45. Association for Computational Linguistics.

Chaoyi Wu, Weixiong Lin, Xiaoman Zhang, Ya Zhang, Yanfeng Wang, and Weidi Xie. 2023. PMC-LLaMA: Towards building open-source language models for medicine. *Preprint*, arxiv:2304.14454 [cs].

A Dataset Descriptions

Instruction Data

	GPTNERMED (Frei and Frank, 2023)	**GERNERMED** (Frei et al., 2022)	**i2b2 2010** (Uzuner et al., 2011)	**n2c2 2018** (Henry et al., 2020)
Textual Elements				
Language	GER	GER	EN	EN
Segments	18,683	24,091	16,701	19,276
Tokens	76,347	109,011	133,799	516,723
Entities				
Diagnosis	4,756	-	-	-
ADE	-	-	-	867
Drug	7,889	6,633	-	14,617
Problem	-	-	6,327	-
Reason for Drug	-	-	-	3,457
Treatment	-	-	4,368	-

Evaluation Data

	BRONCO (Kittner et al., 2021)	**GGPONC2** (Borchert et al., 2022)	**CARDIO:DE** (Richter-Pechanski et al., 2023)
Document Type	Discharge Summaries	Guidelines	Doctor Letters
Textual Elements			
Documents	200	30	500
Sentences	11,434	78,090	
Tokens	89,942	1877,100	993,143
Entities			
ActiveIng	-	-	7,580
Diagnosis	5,245	-	-
Diagnostic	-	27,829	-
Diagnosis|Pathology	-	81,380	-
Drug	2,013	19,478	2,093
Other Finding	-	51,376	-
Therapeutic	-	61,034	-
Treatment	2,013	-	-

Table 5: Overview of datasets and entities used for instruction fine-tuning, training baseline models and evaluation. ADE is short for Adverse Drug Events.

B Additional Analysis

B.1 Hallucinations

Model	Match	Fuzzy Match	Hallucination
peft Mistral 7B	1178	2	0
peft LLAMA2 7B	613	6	0
peft Meditron 7B	1248	6	1
peft Leo LLAMA2 7B	1120	5	3
Leo LLAMA2 7B chat	846	16	36
Mistral 7B Instruct	1186	27	76
LLAMA2 7B chat	596	43	151

Table 6: Count of entities generated by the LLMs when prompted to extract diagnoses, medications and treatments for the BRONCO test samples. An entity is categorized as a match if it is identical to a phrase in the input. If no exact match is found but the entity has a low Levenshtein distance to an input phrase, it is counted as a fuzzy match. Entities that cannot be matched to any input phrase are categorized as hallucinations

B.2 RAG Information Extraction

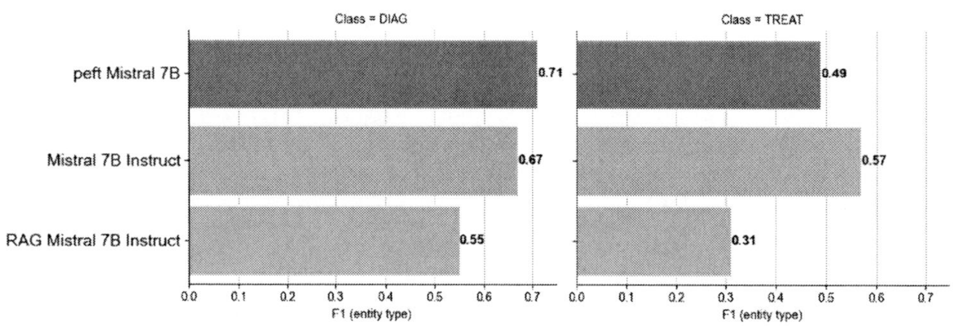

Figure 6: Results on the test BRONCO dataset for different versions of the Mistral 7B LLM. The chat version Mistral 7B Instruct and the fine-tuned peft Mistral 7B are compared to the retrieval-augmented generation approach RAG Mistral 7B Instruct. The F1 score is presented on entity type level.

B.3 Significance Tests

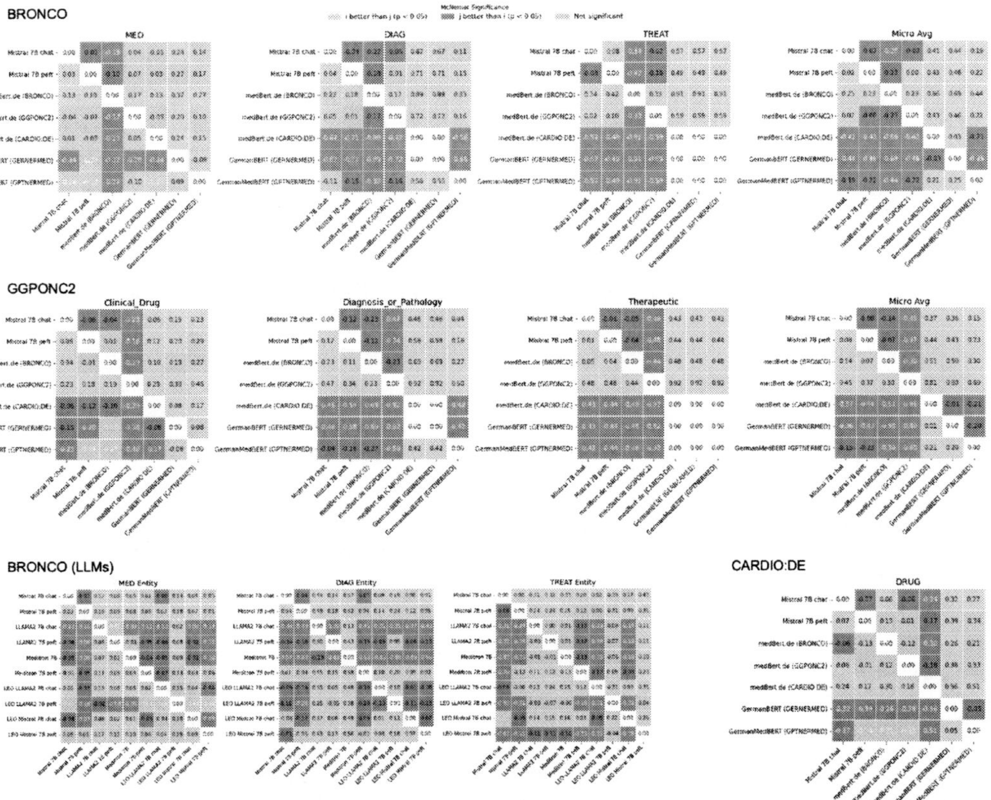

Figure 7: Pairwise McNemar significance heatmaps for entity-level F1 scores across all test datasets and entities, as well as micro-average. Each cell shows the F1-score difference between model i (row) and model j (column). Colors indicate statistical significance based on McNemar's test ($p < 0.05$) based on span-level entity comparisons using strict matching criteria. Green: model i significantly better than j, Red: model j significantly better than i, Gray: no significant difference.

ZEFYS2025: A German Historical Newspaper Dataset for Named Entity Recognition and Entity Linking

Sophie Schneider, Ulrike Förstel, Kai Labusch, Jörg Lehmann, Clemens Neudecker
Staatsbibliothek zu Berlin – Preußischer Kulturbesitz, Berlin, Germany
Correspondence: clemens.neudecker@sbb.spk-berlin.de

Abstract

We present ZEFYS2025, a dataset for named entity recognition and entity linking that comprises 100 annotated German historical newspaper pages covering the time period from 1837 to 1940. We describe the data selection and annotation processes and evaluate various models fine-tuned on the NER downstream task using ZEFYS2025 as well as additional historical and contemporary German NER datasets. Our findings show that the recognition performance on ZEFYS2025 is on par or better than on other historical newspaper datasets while pretraining on ZEFYS2025 improves NER performance in most cases.

1 Introduction

The concept of a named entity (NE) can be defined by drawing upon the notion of a rigid designator (Kripke, 1980). It implies that many of the NE instances in texts equal proper names, although theoretically other units are encompassed in this definition as well. While named entity recognition (NER) aims at detecting and classifying NEs within a text into predefined classes (e.g., person, location and organisation), entity linking (EL) concerns their disambiguation and linking to corresponding entries in a database. Information extraction techniques such as NER and EL can support the semantic indexing and enrichment of historical documents (Ehrmann et al., 2019). Digital cultural heritage collections are often queried for NEs (Sumikawa et al., 2019), and information retrieval applications such as semantic search, cross-document contextualisation or automatic text summarisation can be improved through NER and EL.

Due to numerous mentions of people, places and events contained in them, historical newspapers are a rich source for NEs. Furthermore, historical newspapers are frequently used by scholars in the digital humanities, as their broad coverage and mix of content supports diverse research use cases, often in combination with NEs. This makes historical newspapers particularly valuable for NER and EL processing and large historical newspaper corpora with annotated NEs highly desirable.

The introduction of the Transformer (Vaswani et al., 2017) led to the emergence of numerous pretrained models, including various downstream language modeling tasks, one of which is NER (Wolf et al., 2020). However, historical sources present these models with a wide variety of specific challenges (Ehrmann et al., 2023). Texts obtained by optical character recognition (OCR) of historical documents inevitably exhibit noise leading to a drop in NER accuracy (Hamdi et al., 2020, Hamdi et al., 2019), and spelling conventions have undergone significant changes over time (Provatorova et al., 2024). Variations in orthography and language usage are complemented by changes in how persons, organisations, or places are addressed. Thus, the application of generic NE processing tools to historical sources does not achieve the same quality as for contemporary texts; resources derived from modern perspectives such as benchmark datasets or knowledge bases do not include domain-specific entities or information (Dereza et al., 2023). Establishing large, annotated corpora is a cumbersome and costly endeavour, although they are indispensable to facilitate sound performances of NER and EL systems or to precisely measure the performance of NER and EL methods. With ZEFYS2025, we contribute a consistently annotated, comprehensive dataset for NE processing of historical German texts.

2 Related Work

Historical German-language datasets for NER and EL with more than 100,000 tokens are only sparsely available. In our experiments, we focused on contemporary (CoNLL-2003, GermEval 2014) as well as historical corpora (e.g., HIPE 2020, Europeana) and also included smaller datasets (such as NEISS-Sturm and HisGermaNER). We considered

Proceedings of the 21st Conference on Natural Language Processing (KONVENS), Volume 1: Long and Short Papers, pages 48–58, 2025

adding the German subset of the NewsEye dataset (Hamdi et al., 2021) which comprises 527,756 tokens derived from historical newspapers. However, as our initial test results indicated that prediction on this specific subset is challenging (in line with those of previous examinations, (Schweter et al., 2022)), we excluded it from further experiments and evaluations. We still included the NewsEye dataset statistics in our dataset overview for comparison (see tables 1 and 2). Except for HIPE 2020 and NewsEye, the datasets discussed here contain NE tags, but no EL information.

2.1 CoNLL-2003

The CoNLL-2003 shared task (Tjong Kim Sang and De Meulder, 2003) introduced datasets for contemporary English and German NER. The German part of CoNLL-2003 contains 310,318 tokens and was extracted from articles published in the German newspaper *Frankfurter Rundschau* in August 1992. The CoNLL-2003 data includes miscellaneous names (MISC) as an additional entity type besides persons (PER), locations (LOC) and organizations (ORG). Nested entities are not considered, only the surface level is annotated.

2.2 GermEval 2014

GermEval 2014 (Benikova et al., 2014) is a contemporary German NER corpus consisting of 591,006 tokens. It was sampled from German Wikipedia articles and online newspapers. NEs are tagged with four main types: PER, LOC, ORG and other (OTH). GermEval 2014 annotations can occur as nested, partly or derived NEs. The annotation guidelines aim at capturing semantically relevant information within a text rather than restricting it to its syntactic functionality.

2.3 HIPE 2020

The HIPE-2020 shared task (Ehrmann et al., 2020a) resulted in a dataset for evaluating NE processing tasks on French, German and English historical newspapers. Its German subset includes 153,875 tokens from historical newspapers up to 1950. HIPE annotation guidelines (Ehrmann et al., 2020b) contain several entity types and subtypes/components, while nested annotations were only carried out for PER, LOC and ORG entities. The dataset includes links to Wikidata identifiers (QIDs) as well.

2.4 NEISS

The NER datasets developed in the NEISS project (Zöllner et al., 2021) are built from existing digital editions. More precisely, the NEISS corpus consists of two different German datasets. The "Essays from H. Arendt" dataset is constructed from 23 documents published between 1932 and 1976 and comprises 157,637 tokens. NEs have been tagged intellectually and entity types were primarily revised/mapped, for instance to resolve ambiguities between tag type definitions. Besides PER, LOC and ORG, ethnicity, event and language are kept as NE types. By contrast, the "Sturm Edition" contains 174 letters from 1914 to 1922. It includes only the entity types PER, LOC and date, but not ORG. Its size is limited to 35,953 tokens.

2.5 HisGermaNER

The HisGermaNER dataset[1] is compiled from 100 newspaper pages from the Austrian National Library (ÖNB), covering a time span from 1710 to 1840. NE types are identical to those in our ZEFYS2025 dataset and the dataset format is derived from the HIPE-2022 shared task. According to our calculations performed after preprocessing this dataset, it comprises roughly 72,000 tokens.

2.6 Europeana

In the context of the Europeana Newspapers project, a multilingual resource for NER on the basis of Dutch, French and German newspapers has been created (Neudecker, 2016). The German part of this dataset consists of 100 newspaper pages and 96,735 tokens in total, compiled from the Dr Friedrich Teßmann Library (LFT) and the Austrian National Library (ÖNB). A later addition to the dataset included newspaper pages by the Berlin State Library (SBB).[2] However, we refrained from including the SBB material, since a significantly modified version of it is already contained in the ZEFYS2025 dataset. The classes used for annotating NEs are PER, LOC and ORG.

3 The ZEFYS2025 dataset

3.1 Data selection

With ZEFYS2025, we present a German dataset for historical NER and EL consisting of 100 an-

[1] https://huggingface.co/datasets/stefan-it/HisGermaNER

[2] https://github.com/EuropeanaNewspapers/ner-corpora

notated newspaper pages, totaling approximately 350,000 tokens. All newspaper pages were extracted from the Berlin State Library's newspaper system ZEFYS (an abbreviation of ZEitungsinFormationssYStem),[3] preprocessed and annotated with a predefined set of NE types and links to Wikidata identifiers. The pages included in ZEFYS2025 stem from 20 newspaper titles, all of which were published between 1837 and 1940, such as the *Berliner Börsen-Zeitung*, the *Berliner Tageblatt und Handels-Zeitung* and *Berliner Volkszeitung*.

A key objective in establishing ZEFYS2025 was the creation of a dataset that is both sufficiently sized and homogeneously annotated. Frequently, datasets for historical NE processing are tailored to a particular project or task, resulting in incompatible and segmented resources due to differences in annotation. Accordingly, HIPE-2022 included a task specifically addressing heterogeneous annotation tag sets and guidelines (Ehrmann et al., 2022). For ZEFYS2025, we combine pre-existing NE datasets, originally produced in two distinct projects over a time period of 10 years, with additional, newly annotated newspaper pages into a single coherent resource. Existing annotations were harmonized to a common standard (cf. 3.2) and annotations for all pages were carefully checked in iterations to ensure consistency. In order to facilitate the comparison and analysis of the effects of OCR errors, the final dataset comprises full texts which were produced automatically by OCR (84 pages) and also 16 pages with manually transcribed text (i.e. ground truth).

3.2 Annotation guidelines and NE tagset

We refer to the Impresso guidelines (Ehrmann et al., 2020b) as a starting point, from which an adapted version was developed. Impresso defines five named entity types (persons, locations, organisations, human products and time) and includes 23 fine-grained subtypes. We restrict our NE tag set to the three entity types PER, LOC and ORG originally included in the ENAMEX tag types defined for the MUC-7 Named Entity Task (Chinchor and Robinson, 1998). Furthermore, we generally did not consider components such as the title or function of a person to be part of a NE, with the exception of them being regarded as inseparable from the remaining entity token sequence. Most other datasets discussed here describe additional NE types, for instance a class for other or miscellaneous entities. In some cases also derived or partial entities were tagged, and even instructions themselves can lead to NEs being treated differently. To achieve as much interoperability as possible, we deliberately focused on a minimalist tag set and preferably annotated the literal instead of a metonymic or similar figurative meaning when in doubt. By discarding the individual tag classes, all specialized NE tag sets from the presented datasets can be mapped to our broader tag set and therefore merged with the ZEFYS2025 dataset (Palladino and Yousef, 2024). We also emphasize the demand for more generalizable and compatible historical NER/EL datasets (Ehrmann et al., 2023, Hamdi et al., 2021) and point towards the limitations of such mapping approaches (e.g., loss of very specific information incorporated in annotations). Nonetheless, from a pragmatic point of view we consider this a useful strategy for dealing with differently annotated datasets.

Concerning the annotation of NEs, we allow nesting up to a depth of one, resulting in NEs on a higher (NE-TAG) and second, lower level (NE-EMB). Only the higher level NEs were considered for the EL annotations. Ideally, each recognized NE is linked to one definite Wikidata identifier (QID[4]) in our dataset. This is challenging due to innumerable factors, for instance the evolution of entities and their meaning (entity drift) or domain and time shifts between historical resources and the modern knowledge bases used for linking (Munnelly and Lawless, 2018, Linhares Pontes et al., 2020). The links added should describe a certain entity as specifically as possible – in particular with regard to the (spatio-)temporal dimension and historical correctness. This can result in multiple entries of an entity in the database being (correctly) linked to the same token sequence.

How NEs are tagged and linked to entries in a contemporary knowledge base does not only depend on the context in which they appear, but also requires attentiveness to the rhetorical use of language. We linked immediately recognizable entities on a literal basis and did not strive for resolving any intended meaning. An exception to this rule are the numerous company names listed within historical financial newspapers. These companies are tagged as ORG at the highest level in spite of them being often abbreviated to the persons or places

[3] https://zefys.staatsbibliothek-berlin.de/?lang=en

[4] https://www.wikidata.org/wiki/Q43649390

after which they are named (e.g. *Baltimore and Ohio* instead of *Baltimore and Ohio Railroad*).

3.3 Annotation tool

A browser-based tool[5] has been developed for the manual annotation and correction of NEs, tokens and segmentation. The tool is a simple HTML-/JS-based web application and can be run locally. It accepts tab-separated value (TSV) files in the data format described in 3.5 as input and returns similar TSV files when saving the results after editing. Several functionalities are implemented for ease of use when annotating NEs. In additional columns, a IIIF Image API URL and image region coordinates can be specified to display image snippets from a scanned newspaper page on hovering. Shortcuts for all NE tagging and further options were included to speed up the annotation and correction process. OCR corrections are facilitated by the integration of a virtual keyboard offering a variety of specific Unicode characters occurring in historical documents.

3.4 Annotation process

Automatic annotation. As a starting point to the entire processing chain, OCR has been applied to 84 out of 100 newspaper pages, with 16 pages being manually transcribed to ground truth, resulting in either ALTO-XML or PAGE-XML files. The OCR output and ground truth were then converted into our TSV format with the help of TSV tools[6]. This data conversion included preprocessing steps such as tokenization and sentence splitting with SoMaJo.[7] The resulting files were automatically enriched with NER by applying a BERT-based system presented at KONVENS 2019 (Labusch et al., 2019). In a second step, recognized NEs have been disambiguated and linked to Wikidata entries using an EL system presented at HIPE-2020 (Labusch and Neudecker, 2020) and HIPE-2022 (Labusch and Neudecker, 2022).

Intellectual revision. Using the annotation tool, all automatically generated annotations have been intellectually checked and revised by a group of German native speakers. This included the verification of the NE tags assigned previously as well as the addition or deletion of tags if needed. For NEs confirmed in this step, existing links were checked for the most precise and correct option for linking, and missing links to entities were inserted when available. To flag ambiguous or uncertain cases arising during annotation for later discussion, an extra NE-TAG class *TODO* was used during this process. Consensus about challenging cases collected throughout the annotation was reached in regular discussion meetings, and the set of instructions was expanded iteratively, adding further rules or examples when necessary. Since the revision was carried out by one expert per page only, it was not possible to calculate inter-annotator agreement or similar measures to assess consistency between multiple annotators. Instead, we employed computational methods to assist in localizing and reducing inconsistencies within extensively annotated datasets (Rücker and Akbik, 2023, Reiss et al., 2020). The automated analyses identified reappearing tokens throughout our dataset with a high divergence in how they were transcribed, tagged or linked. In additional correction loops, these inconsistencies were systematically reviewed once again by the annotators.

3.5 Dataset characteristics and format

The resulting ZEFYS2025 dataset presented here comprises 100 newspaper pages totaling 348,307 tokens, 16,727 sentences, 14,072 entities (~3% of which are nested) and 10,341 links. Locations are not only the most frequently occurring entity type within our dataset, they also seem to be by far the most straightforward to disambiguate and link to Wikidata (less than 5% NIL fraction for LOC, whilst ~31% and ~47% NIL fractions for ORG and PER entities). Using the train_test_split function provided by the Hugging Face datasets library (Lhoest et al., 2021), the ZEFYS2025 dataset was sampled and divided into a 80%/10%/10% train-validation-test split. See tables 1 (overall dataset statistics) and 2 (PER, LOC and ORG statistics) for more detailed information on ZEFYS2025 in comparison to other datasets described here. In these tables, we present the numbers as stated in the corresponding original publications referenced here. For the sake of completeness, we also calculated missing values afterwards. The results of these calculations might slightly deviate from the statistics taken from a publication, as we might have used a newer dataset version than the one decribed originally, and file preprocessing was performed prior to the calculations.

We release ZEFYS2025 in a file format based on the GermEval TSV format (Benikova et al.,

[5]https://github.com/qurator-spk/neat

[6]https://github.com/qurator-spk/page2tsv

[7]https://github.com/tsproisl/SoMaJo

dataset	sentences	tokens
ZEFYS2025	16,727	348,307
CoNLL-2003	18,933	310,318
GermEval 2014	31,300	591,006
HIPE 2020	5,887*	153,875
NewsEye	26,826*	527,756
NEISS-Arendt	10,731*	157,647
NEISS-Sturm	3,250*	35,953
HisGermaNER	2,345	72,430*
Europeana-LFT	2,768*	70,254*
Europeana-ÖNB	976*	28,012*
	entities	**links**
ZEFYS2025	14,072	10,341
CoNLL-2003	20,357	-
GermEval2014	41,005	-
HIPE 2020	6,584	5,066
NewsEye	13,786	2,279
NEISS-Arendt	4,424	-
NEISS-Sturm	2,144	-
HisGermaNER	2,700	-
Europeana-LFT	7,350*	-
Europeana-ÖNB	3,302*	-

Table 1: Description of the ZEFYS2025 dataset in comparison to other German NER datasets. *These data have been calculated on our final, preprocessed versions.

dataset	PER	LOC	ORG
		simple	
ZEFYS2025	4,389	6,049	3,223
train	3,476	4,771	2,592
validation	432	616	310
test	481	662	321
CoNLL-2003	5,369	6,579	4,441
GermEval 2014	10,500	12,165	7,175
HIPE 2020	1,910	3,006	660
NewsEye	3,500	5,904	3,370
NEISS-Arendt	1,702	1,087	455
NEISS-Sturm	930	492	-
HisGermaNER	1,488	1,182	30
Europeana-LFT	2,797*	3,433*	1,120*
Europeana-ÖNB	1,589*	1,618*	95*
		nested	
ZEFYS2025	207	203	1
GermEval 2014	488	1,452	281
HIPE 2020	29	209	61
NewsEye	246	544	176
		links	
ZEFYS2025	2,329	5,775	2,237
HIPE 2020	1,332	2,883	458
NewsEye	685	610	967

Table 2: Amount of named entity annotations per class across different datasets. *These data have been calculated on our final, preprocessed version.

2014), which in turn is derived from the widely used CoNLL data format (Tjong Kim Sang and De Meulder, 2003). Further columns were added containing links to Wikidata entries and token coordinates from the corresponding scanned page images. Annotations comply with the IOB scheme (Ramshaw and Marcus, 1999), more specifically IOB2, in which the position of the tags at the beginning (B-) or inside (I-) an entity is determined more precisely by means of a prefix. Tokens that do not constitute a NE (chunk) receive an outside (O) tag.

4 Experiments

4.1 Data preprocessing

The CoNLL-2003[8] and GermEval 2014[9] datasets have been retrieved directly via the Hugging Face API as they did not require extensive preprocessing from our side. We downloaded the HIPE 2020,[10] NEISS,[11] HisGermaNER[12] and Europeana[13] datasets directly from the corresponding repositories. Comments and other metadata, mostly indicating the beginning of a document and its provenance, were removed at this stage. Train-validation-test splits and sentence splitting have been reused for all historical and contemporary datasets from the original publications. For Europeana, we refer to the German subset in the latest dataset version, from which we extracted the ÖNB/LFT parts and added train-validation-test plus sentence splits in the same way as in ZEFYS2025. With regard to our second and third experiment, all NE tags were matched with their tag names from ZEFYS2025 (*B-pers* was changed to *B-PER* etc.). Similarly, subtypes and components were ignored to fit the broader class names from our selection. We created an new version of each dataset on the basis of the updated labels from the coarse (upper level) NE annotations.

4.2 Model training

Building upon the Hugging Face Transformers library (Wolf et al., 2020), we implemented a pipeline to read and transform datasets, load models from Hugging Face and train and evaluate var-

[8] https://huggingface.co/datasets/eriktks/conll2003

[9] https://huggingface.co/datasets/GermanEval/germeval_14

[10] https://github.com/hipe-eval/HIPE-2022-data/tree/main/data/v2.1/hipe2020/de

[11] https://github.com/NEISSproject

[12] https://huggingface.co/datasets/stefan-it/HisGermaNER

[13] https://github.com/cneud/ner-corpora

ious dataset-model combinations.[14] Prior to the actual training process, we filtered the NER labels of the corresponding datasets to only contain the classes PER, LOC and ORG that are also present in ZEFYS2025. In other words, NE tags describing entities other than persons, places or organisations were replaced with an outside (O) tag. All models were trained until the F_1-score on the validation split did not improve further for two consecutive epochs. We optimized over different batch sizes and learning rates, selected the results with the best F_1-score on the validation split and then tested on the test split. All reported global F_1-scores summarize the class-specific F_1-scores for PER, LOC and ORG by weighing them according to their support in the dataset.

4.3 Model selection

In our choice of models for the experiments, we focus on BERT-based models (Devlin et al., 2019) that have been obtained using different pretraining strategies (GermanBERT, RoBERTa, Electra, GBERT), are either optimized for contemporary (GermanBERT, GBERT) or historical German (hmBERT, Europeana ELECTRA), or are multilingual (hmBERT, Roberta, XLM-Roberta). We consider distilled or smaller model variants (DistilBERT, hmBERT-mini, hmBERT-tiny, comp. Zöllner et al., 2021) as well as larger architectures (GermanBERT, GBERT, hmBERT, Europeana-ELECTRA, RoBERTa, XLM-RoBERTa).

- DISTILBERT (Sanh et al., 2019) constitutes a version of the original BERT reduced through knowledge distillation. It is 40% lighter and 60% smaller while sacrificing only little performance in general language understanding as well as on several downstream tasks.

- ROBERTA (Liu et al., 2019) originates from a replication study of BERT and introduces an optimized approach with several changes in hyperparameter settings and strategies employed during pretraining procedure.

- XLM-ROBERTA (Conneau et al., 2020) is a multilingual masked language model, pretrained with texts in 100 different languages. Besides its multilingual approach, XLM-RoBERTa still performs well on monolingual and low-resource language modeling tasks.

model	F_1^{TE}	F_1^{VAL}	F_1^{PER}	F_1^{LOC}	F_1^{ORG}
CoNLL-2003					
RoBERTa	0.94	0.97	0.96	0.93	0.92
XLM-RoBERTa	0.93	0.96	0.96	0.92	0.90
GermanBERT	0.90	0.94	0.91	0.91	0.88
DistilBERT	0.92	0.94	0.96	0.91	0.88
GBERT	0.90	0.94	0.92	0.90	0.88
hmBERT	0.89	0.93	0.92	0.90	0.84
Europ-ELECTRA	0.88	0.91	0.90	0.90	0.84
hmBERT-mini	0.84	0.89	0.86	0.86	0.80
hmBERT-tiny	0.77	0.84	0.80	0.79	0.72
GermEval					
GermanBERT	0.88	0.89	0.93	0.90	0.79
GBERT	0.88	0.89	0.94	0.89	0.78
XLM-RoBERTa	0.86	0.87	0.91	0.88	0.76
Europ-ELECTRA	0.84	0.84	0.90	0.87	0.73
hmBERT	0.82	0.83	0.88	0.86	0.69
RoBERTa	0.81	0.83	0.87	0.83	0.71
DistilBERT	0.76	0.77	0.80	0.80	0.66
hmBERT-mini	0.72	0.75	0.78	0.76	0.59
hmBERT-tiny	0.63	0.66	0.66	0.69	0.50

Table 3: Results on contemporary datasets. F_1^{TE}: F_1-score on test split. F_1^{VAL}: early stopping F_1-score on validation split. F_1^{PER},F_1^{LOC},F_1^{ORG}: Class-specific F_1-scores on test split.

- GBERT (Chan et al., 2020) is a BERT-based model, pretrained with different German datasets and applying Whole Word Masking (WWM). WWM ensures that all subword tokens of a word are masked simultaneously.

- HMBERT (Schweter et al., 2022) is a historical multilingual BERT-based model which is pretrained on historical German, English, French, Swedish and Finnish corpora from Europeana and the British Library. By filtering these data based on OCR confidence scores and creating domain-specific vocabulary, the particular challenges associated with historical language were considered.

- Additionally, we included the GermanBERT[15] and Europeana-ELECTRA[16] models published by DBMDZ on Hugging Face. GermanBERT has been pretrained on contemporary German text. ELECTRA is an alternative BERT pretraining approach that relies on a classification task rather than on token prediction (Clark et al., 2020).

[14] https://github.com/qurator-spk/sbb_ner_hf

[15] https://huggingface.co/dbmdz/bert-base-german-cased

[16] https://huggingface.co/dbmdz/electra-base-german-europeana-cased-discriminator

model	F_1^{TE}	$F_{1_{PH}}^{TE}$	F_1^{PER}	F_1^{LOC}	F_1^{ORG}
Europ-ELECTRA	0.83	**0.84**	0.84	0.89	0.70
hmBERT	**0.83**	**0.83**	0.85	0.88	0.71
GermanBERT	0.82	**0.83**	0.84	0.89	0.70
GBERT	**0.82**	0.81	0.83	0.88	0.67
XLM-RoBERTa	0.80	**0.81**	0.82	0.87	0.67
RoBERTa	0.78	**0.80**	0.80	0.87	0.69
DistilBERT	**0.75**	**0.75**	0.74	0.82	0.64
hmBERT-mini	**0.72**	**0.72**	0.70	0.80	0.57
hmBERT-tiny	0.60	**0.64**	0.61	0.74	0.46

Table 4: Results on the new ZEFYS2025 dataset. F_1^{TE}: F_1-score on test split. $F_{1_{PH}}^{TE}$: F_1-score on test split when model is pretrained on the joined training splits of all historical NER datasets. F_1^{PER},F_1^{LOC},F_1^{ORG}: Class-specific F_1-scores of best configuration on test split, i.e., either with pretraining on joined historical NER datasets or without.

4.4 Baseline results

In a first experiment, we establish baseline results for the contemporary and historical German NER ground truth datasets in section 2. We fine-tune the state-of-the-art Transformer models listed in 4.3 with respect to the NER task. Table 3 shows the results for the contemporary datasets CoNLL-2003 and GermEval 2014. Column F_1^{TE} of table 4 presents the respective results on our ZEFYS2025 dataset for the same models. Column F_1^{TE} of table 5 lists the respective results for the other historical NER ground truth datasets listed in section 2.

4.5 Two-stage fine-tuning

In a second and third experiment, we investigate to which degree ZEFYS2025 is compatible with other historical datasets. We study whether the results improve when models are either previously fine-tuned on the ZEFYS2025 dataset or on the joined historical datasets mentioned in section 2 including ZEFYS2025. Final training is performed in a second stage with respect to the target dataset.

In the second experiment, we use the ZEFYS2025 training split for the first of the two consecutive NER fine-tunings. The training iteration was stopped if the F_1-score on the ZEFYS2025 validation split did not increase any longer for two consecutive epochs. Then we perform the second fine-tuning with the training split of the final target dataset, for instance HIPE 2020, until the F_1-score on the validation split of the final target dataset did not increase any more for two consecutive epochs. We report the resulting F_1-scores on the test split of the target dataset in table 5 in the $F_{1_{PZ}}^{TE}$ column.

In the third experiment we use the same setup as in the second one, but for the first fine-tuning stage we train on the joined training splits of all the historical datasets listed in section 2 including ZEFYS2025. We use the F_1-score on joined validation splits of all these datasets as early stopping criterion. The second fine-tuning stage is performed exactly as in the second experiment. The columns $F_{1_{PH}}^{TE}$ in table 4 and table 5 report the resulting F_1-score on the test splits of the respective datasets.

For all experiments we also provide the class-specific F_1-scores F_1^{PER}, F_1^{LOC} and F_1^{ORG} in table 3, table 4 and table 5. The class-specific scores presented in these tables relate in each row to the best-performing run, i.e., baseline, pretraining on ZEFYS2025 (PZ) or pretraining on joined historical ground truth (PH).

5 Discussion

Generally speaking, models pretrained with contemporary data perform best on contemporary datasets (RoBERTa, XLM-RoBERTa, GBERT, GermanBERT), whereas models pretrained with historical German perform better on the historical datasets (Europeana-ELECTRA, hmBERT). With respect to the GermEval 2014 dataset, German models (GermanBERT, GBERT) perform best, while multi-lingual models (RoBERTa, XLM-RoBERTa) perform best on the CoNLL-2003 dataset. On all tested datasets, smaller models (DistilBERT, hmBERT-mini, hmBERT-tiny) perform worse than larger models.

Throughout all experiments, the recognition performance for PER and LOC is significantly better than for ORG. This might be due to PER and LOC being relatively unambiguous entity classes, whereas ORG always has the smallest support and overlaps with LOC depending on the annotation guidelines. It might therefore be the most difficult class to learn. The only exception to the general rule is CoNLL-2003, where recognition performance for ORG is similar to PER and LOC. CoNLL-2003 has a strong support of the ORG class and is not affected by OCR errors, which might explain the observed high recognition performance of many models.

model	F_1^{TE}	$F_{1_{PZ}}^{TE}$	$F_{1_{PH}}^{TE}$	F_1^{PER}	F_1^{LOC}	F_1^{ORG}
HisGermanNER						
hmBERT	0.80	0.82	**0.84**	0.88	0.84	0.21
Europ-ELECTRA	0.80	**0.84**	0.81	0.86	0.86	0.15
GBERT	0.78	0.80	**0.81**	0.84	0.84	0.00
GermanBERT	0.77	0.79	**0.82**	0.81	0.87	0.16
XLM-RoBERTa	0.74	0.79	**0.82**	0.82	0.85	0.17
RoBERTa	0.71	0.76	**0.79**	0.81	0.82	0.00
DistilBERT	0.61	0.67	**0.74**	0.72	0.78	0.10
hmBERT-mini	0.60	0.68	**0.72**	0.73	0.76	0.00
hmBERT-tiny	0.30	0.51	**0.58**	0.51	0.67	0.00
Europeana-LFT						
Europ-ELECTRA	0.79	**0.80**	0.79	0.83	0.81	0.67
XLM-RoBERTa	**0.78**	**0.78**	**0.78**	0.80	0.80	0.68
hmBERT	0.76	0.76	**0.77**	0.79	0.79	0.68
RoBERTa	**0.76**	0.75	**0.76**	0.76	0.78	0.69
GermanBERT	0.73	0.73	**0.74**	0.77	0.75	0.62
GBERT	**0.74**	0.73	0.73	0.77	0.75	0.63
DistilBERT	0.65	**0.67**	0.66	0.63	0.73	0.59
hmBERT-mini	0.63	**0.67**	0.65	0.66	0.72	0.53
hmBERT-tiny	0.50	0.55	**0.58**	0.57	0.64	0.44
Europeana-ÖNB						
Europ-ELECTRA	0.84	0.86	**0.88**	0.82	0.94	0.44
XLM-RoBERTa	0.84	**0.88**	0.86	0.85	0.92	0.13
hmBERT	0.84	**0.86**	**0.86**	0.78	0.92	0.50
RoBERTa	0.81	0.84	**0.87**	0.81	0.92	0.20
GBERT	0.83	**0.84**	0.83	0.75	0.92	0.40
GermanBERT	0.82	0.83	**0.84**	0.73	0.92	0.53
hmBERT-mini	0.70	0.76	**0.78**	0.68	0.86	0.28
DistilBERT	0.70	0.74	**0.75**	0.61	0.86	0.15
hmBERT-tiny	0.50	0.63	**0.65**	0.48	0.78	0.38
HIPE 2020						
Europ-ELECTRA	0.76	**0.78**	0.75	0.75	0.84	0.57
GermanBERT	0.73	**0.76**	0.74	0.75	0.81	0.60
hmBERT	0.73	**0.75**	**0.75**	0.72	0.82	0.54
GBERT	**0.74**	**0.74**	**0.74**	0.72	0.81	0.48
XLM-RoBERTa	0.73	**0.74**	**0.74**	0.71	0.82	0.50
RoBERTa	0.67	**0.70**	**0.70**	0.68	0.77	0.50
DistilBERT	0.60	**0.62**	**0.62**	0.52	0.74	0.33
hmBERT-mini	0.57	0.58	**0.62**	0.50	0.74	0.38
hmBERT-tiny	0.40	0.48	**0.51**	0.36	0.64	0.31
Neiss-Arendt						
GermanBERT	**0.88**	**0.88**	**0.88**	0.94	0.83	0.74
hmBERT	0.87	**0.88**	0.87	0.94	0.85	0.71
GBERT	0.87	0.87	**0.88**	0.95	0.81	0.71
RoBERTa	0.86	**0.87**	**0.87**	0.92	0.83	0.72
DistilBERT	0.85	**0.87**	**0.87**	0.92	0.80	0.72
XLM-RoBERTa	0.86	0.86	**0.87**	0.93	0.85	0.69
Europ-ELECTRA	**0.86**	**0.86**	**0.86**	0.93	0.80	0.75
hmBERT-mini	0.85	**0.86**	0.84	0.91	0.84	0.70
hmBERT-tiny	0.79	**0.83**	**0.83**	0.89	0.82	0.64
Neiss-Sturm						
XLM-RoBERTa	0.90	**0.93**	**0.93**	0.95	0.88	-
hmBERT	**0.91**	**0.91**	**0.91**	0.94	0.83	-
Europ-ELECTRA	0.89	**0.92**	**0.92**	0.92	0.90	-
GermanBERT	**0.91**	**0.91**	0.90	0.93	0.86	-
GBERT	0.89	**0.91**	**0.91**	0.95	0.84	-
RoBERTa	0.88	**0.91**	**0.91**	0.95	0.86	-
DistilBERT	0.85	0.88	**0.90**	0.92	0.86	-
hmBERT-mini	0.82	**0.86**	**0.86**	0.90	0.79	-
hmBERT-tiny	0.71	0.75	**0.78**	0.79	0.74	-

Table 5: Comparison on different historical NER datasets. Column descriptions see table 4. PZ: Pretraining on ZEFYS2025. PH: Pretraining on joined historical NER datasets.

In the ZEFYS2025, Europeana-ÖNB and HIPE 2020 datasets, performance for LOC is significantly better than for PER, while performance for PER and LOC is similar in HisGermanNER and Europeana-LFT. NEISS-Arendt, NEISS-Sturm, CoNLL-2003 and GermEval 2014 exhibit a better performance for PER than for LOC. NEISS-Sturm is the only dataset that does not contain ORG labels, hence we did not report any results for this class there.

In most cases pretraining on ZEFYS2025 improves the results in comparison to a training that is only performed on a single dataset. The impact of pretraining with ZEFYS2025 is especially significant for smaller models, i.e., hmBERT-mini, hmBERT-tiny, DistilBERT. The datasets that benefit most from pretraining with ZEFYS2025 are HisGermanNER, Europeana-ÖNB and HIPE 2020. On Europeana-LFT, NEISS-Arendt and NEISS-Sturm, there are only minor improvements observable; the latter two have not been derived from historical newspapers.

The impact of pretraining on joined historical datasets including ZEFYS2025 is again most significant for smaller models, i.e., hmBERT-mini, hmBERT-tiny, DistilBERT. For all models, it is most beneficial on the HisGermanNER, Europeana-ÖNB and HIPE 2020 datasets. In most cases, the improvement is similar when training is performed on a single, combined dataset as compared to pretraining with ZEFYS2025. In some cases the results are even better than pretraining only with ZEFYS2025, in particular for small models (hmBERT-mini, hmBERT-tiny, DistilBERT).

6 Conclusion

We present a comprehensively annotated German NER and EL dataset created from historical newspapers. The ZEFYS2025 dataset exceeds the size of previously published historical German NER/EL datasets concerning the number of entities and links included. The contemporary datasets CoNLL-2003 and GermEval 2014 are larger, but do not contain EL information. We described the dataset creation and annotation processes in depth and explained how we reached annotation quantity *and* quality through a combination of computational methods and iterative intellectual revisions. By focusing on a core tag set supported by clear guidelines, we aimed at achieving maximum interoperability with similar resources.

In several experiments and dataset evaluations we were able to show the following contributions:

- NER results on ZEFYS2025 indicate data consistency for a broad range of models that is on par with or higher than that of the other historical datasets.
- ZEFYS2025 can in many cases successfully be used as pretraining data to improve the recognition performance for historical NER on other datasets.
- ZEFYS2025 is particularly useful for NER and EL in historical source material that is affected by OCR artefacts.

We believe that this dataset constitutes a valuable resource for a wide variety of information extraction tasks on German-language historical material, concerning not only NER, but also EL due to the large number of manually verified links to Wikidata. As a future research direction, ZEFYS2025 will allow us to conduct further analyses and evaluations of the previously developed system for historical EL, e.g. in a similar way to the HIPE Shared Tasks of 2020 and 2022. It is probably also of use to others in terms of benchmarking comparable systems in this specific domain, since the inadequacy or simply absence of resources has constituted an obstacle so far.

The ZEFYS2025 dataset and associated resources have been published under a CC-BY-4.0 licence on Zenodo[17] and GitHub.[18] We also release an open source tool for fine-tuning and evaluating NER models for German historical newspaper contents with the help of the Hugging Face Transformers library.[19]

Acknowledgments

The dataset was annotated by all authors; we acknowledge contributions by Markus Bierkoch (annotations) and Knut Lohse (provision of ground truth), both Staatsbibliothek zu Berlin – Berlin State Library.

Funding statement

This work was partially supported by the German Federal Government Commissioner for Culture and the Media (BKM), project grant no. 2522DIG002.

[17]https://doi.org/10.5281/zenodo.15771823

[18]https://github.com/qurator-spk/ZEFYS2025

[19]https://github.com/qurator-spk/sbb_ner_hf

References

Darina Benikova, Chris Biemann, and Marc Reznicek. 2014. NoSta-D Named Entity Annotation for German: Guidelines and Dataset. In *Proceedings of the Ninth International Conference on Language Resources and Evaluation (LREC'14)*, pages 2524–2531, Reykjavik, Iceland. European Language Resources Association (ELRA).

Branden Chan, Stefan Schweter, and Timo Möller. 2020. German's next language model. In *Proceedings of the 28th International Conference on Computational Linguistics*, pages 6788–6796, Barcelona, Spain (Online). International Committee on Computational Linguistics.

Nancy Chinchor and Patricia Robinson. 1998. Appendix E: MUC-7 Named Entity Task Definition (version 3.5). In *Seventh Message Understanding Conference (MUC-7): Proceedings of a Conference Held in Fairfax, Virginia, April 29 – May 1, 1998.*

Kevin Clark, Minh-Thang Luong, Quoc V. Le, and Christopher D. Manning. 2020. ELECTRA: Pre-training text encoders as discriminators rather than generators. *Preprint*, arXiv:2003.10555.

Alexis Conneau, Kartikay Khandelwal, Naman Goyal, Vishrav Chaudhary, Guillaume Wenzek, Francisco Guzmán, Edouard Grave, Myle Ott, Luke Zettlemoyer, and Veselin Stoyanov. 2020. Unsupervised cross-lingual representation learning at scale. In *Proceedings of the 58th Annual Meeting of the Association for Computational Linguistics*, pages 8440–8451, Online. Association for Computational Linguistics.

Oksana Dereza, Theodorus Fransen, and John P. Mccrae. 2023. Do not Trust the Experts - How the Lack of Standard Complicates NLP for Historical Irish. In *Proceedings of the Fourth Workshop on Insights from Negative Results in NLP*, pages 82–87, Dubrovnik, Croatia. Association for Computational Linguistics.

Jacob Devlin, Ming-Wei Chang, Kenton Lee, and Kristina Toutanova. 2019. BERT: Pre-training of Deep Bidirectional Transformers for Language Understanding. In *Proceedings of the 2019 Conference of the North*, pages 4171–4186, Minneapolis, Minnesota. Association for Computational Linguistics.

Maud Ehrmann, Estelle Bunout, and Marten Düring. 2019. Historical Newspaper User Interfaces: A Review. In *Proceedings of the 85th IFLA General Conference and Assembly*, pages 1–24.

Maud Ehrmann, Ahmed Hamdi, Elvys Linhares Pontes, Matteo Romanello, and Antoine Doucet. 2023. Named Entity Recognition and Classification in Historical Documents: A Survey. *ACM Computing Surveys*, 56(2):1–47.

Maud Ehrmann, Matteo Romanello, Stefan Bircher, and Simon Clematide. 2020a. Introducing the CLEF 2020 HIPE Shared Task: Named Entity Recognition and Linking on Historical Newspapers. In Joemon M. Jose, Emine Yilmaz, João Magalhães, Pablo Castells, Nicola Ferro, Mário J. Silva, and Flávio Martins, editors, *Advances in Information Retrieval*, volume 12036, pages 524–532. Springer International Publishing, Cham. Series Title: Lecture Notes in Computer Science.

Maud Ehrmann, Matteo Romanello, Sven Najem-Meyer, Antoine Doucet, and Simon Clematide. 2022. Extended Overview of HIPE-2022: Named Entity Recognition and Linking in Multilingual Historical Documents. Publisher: CEUR-WS.

Maud Ehrmann, Camille Watter, Matteo Romanello, Simon Clematide, and Alex Flückiger. 2020b. Impresso Named Entity Annotation Guidelines. Publisher: Zenodo Version Number: 2.2.0.

Ahmed Hamdi, Axel Jean-Caurant, Nicolas Sidere, Mickael Coustaty, and Antoine Doucet. 2019. An Analysis of the Performance of Named Entity Recognition over OCRed Documents. In *2019 ACM/IEEE Joint Conference on Digital Libraries (JCDL)*, pages 333–334, Champaign, IL, USA. IEEE.

Ahmed Hamdi, Axel Jean-Caurant, Nicolas Sidère, Mickaël Coustaty, and Antoine Doucet. 2020. Assessing and Minimizing the Impact of OCR Quality on Named Entity Recognition. In *Digital Libraries for Open Knowledge*, pages 87–101, Cham. Springer International Publishing.

Ahmed Hamdi, Elvys Linhares Pontes, Emanuela Boros, Thi Tuyet Hai Nguyen, Günter Hackl, Jose G. Moreno, and Antoine Doucet. 2021. A Multilingual Dataset for Named Entity Recognition, Entity Linking and Stance Detection in Historical Newspapers. In *Proceedings of the 44th International ACM SIGIR Conference on Research and Development in Information Retrieval*, pages 2328–2334, Virtual Event Canada. ACM.

Saul A. Kripke. 1980. *Naming and necessity*, rev. and enl. edition. Library of philosophy and logic. Blackwell, Oxford.

Kai Labusch and Clemens Neudecker. 2020. Named Entity Disambiguation and Linking on Historic Newspaper OCR with BERT. In *CLEF 2020*, pages 1–14.

Kai Labusch and Clemens Neudecker. 2022. Entity Linking in Multilingual Newspapers and Classical Commentaries with BERT. In *CLEF 2022*, pages 1–11.

Kai Labusch, Clemens Neudecker, and David Zellhöfer. 2019. BERT for Named Entity Recognition in Contemporary and Historical German. In *KONVENS. Conference on Natural Language Processing*, pages 1–9.

Quentin Lhoest, Albert Villanova Del Moral, Yacine Jernite, Abhishek Thakur, Patrick Von Platen, Suraj Patil, Julien Chaumond, Mariama Drame, Julien Plu, Lewis Tunstall, Joe Davison, Mario Šaško, Gunjan Chhablani, Bhavitvya Malik, Simon Brandeis, Teven Le Scao, Victor Sanh, Canwen Xu, Nicolas Patry, Angelina McMillan-Major, Philipp Schmid, Sylvain Gugger, Clément Delangue, Théo Matussière, Lysandre Debut, Stas Bekman, Pierric Cistac, Thibault Goehringer, Victor Mustar, François Lagunas, Alexander Rush, and Thomas Wolf. 2021. Datasets: A Community Library for Natural Language Processing. In *Proceedings of the 2021 Conference on Empirical Methods in Natural Language Processing: System Demonstrations*, pages 175–184, Online and Punta Cana, Dominican Republic. Association for Computational Linguistics.

Elvys Linhares Pontes, Luis Adrián Cabrera-Diego, Jose G. Moreno, Emanuela Boros, Ahmed Hamdi, Nicolas Sidère, Mickaël Coustaty, and Antoine Doucet. 2020. Entity Linking for Historical Documents: Challenges and Solutions. In Emi Ishita, Natalie Lee San Pang, and Lihong Zhou, editors, *Digital Libraries at Times of Massive Societal Transition*, volume 12504, pages 215–231. Springer International Publishing, Cham.

Yinhan Liu, Myle Ott, Naman Goyal, Jingfei Du, Mandar Joshi, Danqi Chen, Omer Levy, Mike Lewis, Luke Zettlemoyer, and Veselin Stoyanov. 2019. RoBERTa: A Robustly Optimized BERT Pretraining Approach. *Preprint*, arXiv:1907.11692.

Gary Munnelly and Seamus Lawless. 2018. Investigating entity linking in early english legal documents. In *Proceedings of the 18th ACM/IEEE on Joint Conference on Digital Libraries*, JCDL '18, page 59–68, New York, NY, USA. Association for Computing Machinery.

Clemens Neudecker. 2016. An open corpus for named entity recognition in historic newspapers. In *Proceedings of the Tenth International Conference on Language Resources and Evaluation (LREC 2016)*, pages 4348–4352, Paris, France. European Language Resources Association (ELRA).

Chiara Palladino and Tariq Yousef. 2024. Development of robust NER models and named entity tagsets for Ancient Greek. In *Proceedings of the Third Workshop on Language Technologies for Historical and Ancient Languages (LT4HALA) @ LREC-COLING-2024*, pages 89–97, Torino, Italia. ELRA and ICCL.

Vera Provatorova, Marieke van Erp, and Evangelos Kanoulas. 2024. Too Young to NER: Improving Entity Recognition on Dutch Historical Documents. In *Proceedings of the Third Workshop on Language Technologies for Historical and Ancient Languages (LT4HALA) @ LREC-COLING-2024*, pages 30–35, Torino, Italia. ELRA and ICCL.

Lance A. Ramshaw and Mitchell P. Marcus. 1999. Text Chunking Using Transformation-Based Learning. In Nancy Ide, Jean Véronis, Susan Armstrong, Kenneth Church, Pierre Isabelle, Sandra Manzi, Evelyne Tzoukermann, and David Yarowsky, editors, *Natural Language Processing Using Very Large Corpora*, volume 11, pages 157–176. Springer Netherlands, Dordrecht. Series Title: Text, Speech and Language Technology.

Frederick Reiss, Hong Xu, Bryan Cutler, Karthik Muthuraman, and Zachary Eichenberger. 2020. Identifying Incorrect Labels in the CoNLL-2003 Corpus. In *Proceedings of the 24th Conference on Computational Natural Language Learning*, pages 215–226, Online. Association for Computational Linguistics.

Susanna Rücker and Alan Akbik. 2023. CleanCoNLL: A Nearly Noise-Free Named Entity Recognition Dataset. In *Proceedings of the 2023 Conference on Empirical Methods in Natural Language Processing*, pages 8628–8645, Singapore. Association for Computational Linguistics.

Victor Sanh, Lysandre Debut, Julien Chaumond, and Thomas Wolf. 2019. DistilBERT, a distilled version of BERT: smaller, faster, cheaper and lighter. In *Proceedings of the 5th Workshop on Energy Efficient Machine Learning and Cognitive Computing – NeurIPS 2019*, pages 1–5, Vancouver BC, Canada.

Stefan Schweter, Luisa März, Katharina Schmid, and Erion Çano. 2022. hmbert: Historical multilingual language models for named entity recognition. In *Proceedings of the Working Notes of CLEF 2022 - Conference and Labs of the Evaluation Forum, Bologna, Italy, September 5th - to - 8th, 2022*, volume 3180 of *CEUR Workshop Proceedings*, pages 1109–1129. CEUR-WS.org.

Yasunobu Sumikawa, Adam Jatowt, Antoine Doucet, and Jean-Philippe Moreux. 2019. Large Scale Analysis of Semantic and Temporal Aspects in Cultural Heritage Collection's Search. In *2019 ACM/IEEE Joint Conference on Digital Libraries (JCDL)*, pages 77–86, Champaign, IL, USA. IEEE.

Erik F. Tjong Kim Sang and Fien De Meulder. 2003. Introduction to the CoNLL-2003 Shared Task: Language-Independent Named Entity Recognition. In *Proceedings of the Seventh Conference on Natural Language Learning at HLT-NAACL 2003*, pages 142–147.

Ashish Vaswani, Noam Shazeer, Niki Parmar, Jakob Uszkoreit, Llion Jones, Aidan N. Gomez, Łukasz Kaiser, and Illia Polosukhin. 2017. Attention is All you Need. In *Advances in Neural Information Processing Systems*, volume 30, pages 1–11. Curran Associates, Inc.

Thomas Wolf, Lysandre Debut, Victor Sanh, Julien Chaumond, Clement Delangue, Anthony Moi, Pierric Cistac, Tim Rault, Remi Louf, Morgan Funtowicz, Joe Davison, Sam Shleifer, Patrick Von Platen, Clara Ma, Yacine Jernite, Julien Plu, Canwen Xu, Teven Le Scao, Sylvain Gugger, Mariama Drame, Quentin Lhoest, and Alexander Rush. 2020. Transformers: State-of-the-Art Natural Language Processing. In *Proceedings of the 2020 Conference on Empirical Methods in Natural Language Processing: System Demonstrations*, pages 38–45, Online. Association for Computational Linguistics.

Jochen Zöllner, Konrad Sperfeld, Christoph Wick, and Roger Labahn. 2021. Optimizing Small BERTs Trained for German NER. *Information*, 12(11):443.

Generating Search-Engine-Optimized Headlines for Sports News

Frank Zalkow[1], Benedikt Schäfer[2], Thomas Moissl[1], Jonas Bücherl[1], Kerstin Markl[1], Sebastian Bothe[2], Francois Duchateau[2], Julia Dollase[2], Patric Kabus[3], Daniel Steinigen[4], Oliver Schmitt[5], Fabian Küch[1]

[1] Fraunhofer IIS, Erlangen, Germany, [2] Westdeutscher Rundfunk, Cologne, Germany,
[3] Hessischer Rundfunk, Frankfurt am Main, Germany,
[4] Fraunhofer IAIS, Sankt Augustin, Germany, [5] Südwestrundfunk, Stuttgart, Germany

Correspondence: frank.zalkow@iis.fraunhofer.de

Abstract

Search engines rank websites based on various features, such as headline wording, keyword usage, links, and site structure. Achieving a high rank is crucial for increasing website traffic, a key goal of search engine optimization (SEO). Automating content adjustments for improved SEO can significantly enhance workflows in media publishing. In this paper, we explore the use of large language models (LLMs) to automatically generate SEO-optimized headlines and toplines for German sports news articles. We compare the results from medium- and large-sized LLMs, both finetuned and non-finetuned, against headlines crafted by journalists. Our evaluation, based on a survey with SEO experts, reveals that finetuning is crucial for effectiveness and that medium-sized LLMs perform well in this task. These findings suggest promising opportunities for optimizing workflows in online media publishing.

1 Introduction

Search engine optimization (SEO) is a critical strategy for enhancing a website's visibility and increasing traffic by improving its ranking in search engine results. Search engines use various features of a website to rank it, given a relevant search query, including headline wording, keyword usage, links, and site structure.

Automatically adjusting a website's content for better SEO suitability presents an excellent opportunity to improve the workflows within media publishing houses for three reasons. First, not all editorial departments employ SEO specialists who can revise the journalistic output for the target publication medium. Second, the increasing demand for SEO expertise can overwhelm existing specialists, especially during peak content production periods. Third, optimizing content for SEO can be regarded as a initial step toward automatic content adaptation, which may lead to adapting content for different target audiences, potentially tailoring content for diverse audiences and further boosting website traffic.

In this paper, we explore the application of large language models (LLMs) to automatically generate SEO-optimized head- and toplines for German sports news articles. We assess several models, including large, closed-source models not specifically finetuned for this task, such as Gemini (Gemini Team Google et al., 2024), GPT-4 (OpenAI et al., 2023), and GPT-4o (OpenAI et al., 2024). We also evaluate a version of GPT-4o finetuned for the specific task, and two different task-specific finetuned versions of the medium-sized, open-source Teuken-7B-Instruct model (Ali et al., 2024). The results generated from these models are compared against human-written head- and toplines created by journalists and SEO experts.

Our application scenario focuses on the German sports website Sportschau[1], where SEO is a key growth factor since a significant portion of their reach comes from users who discover the content through search engines. We conduct a survey with SEO experts from the Sportschau department to assess the models' effectiveness for the given task. Our results indicate that task-specific finetuning is essential and that medium-sized LLMs are well-suited for this task. These findings open up possibilities for improved workflows in online media publishing houses, enabling editors to automatically select SEO-optimized headlines, regardless of their depth of SEO knowledge.

While several studies have adressed the generation of headlines (Ding et al., 2023; Gu et al., 2020) and related tasks like extreme summarization (Narayan et al., 2018), only few works expicitely focused on the SEO-compatibility of generated headlines. Unlike our research, machine learning has been previously applied in the SEO domain for tasks such as web page classification (Shaffi

[1] `https://www.sportschau.de`

Proceedings of the 21st Conference on Natural Language Processing (KONVENS), Volume 1: Long and Short Papers, pages 59–65, 2025

and Muthulakshmi, 2022; Matošević et al., 2021) or analysis (Roumeliotis and Tselikas, 2023), content optimization through commercial tools like Clearscope[2] or MarketMuse[3], automatic page creation (Jie et al., 2022), and enhancing search engine functionality (Xiong et al., 2024). More related to our work, a few previous studies have explored the generation of SEO-optimized titles for web pages. For instance, Mathur et al. (2018) focused on the large-scale production of headlines in the e-commerce sector, where manually crafting titles is impracticale for quantitative reasons. In contrast to their approach, our goal is to generate high-quality headlines that closely resemble those written by human SEO experts. Anastasiu et al. (2021) pursued a similar objective to ours but employed a multi-step process. They used a BERT-based model to create a one-sentence summary of an article, followed by generating a list of potential keywords, and finally combining these elements. In contrast, our approach is a data-driven, end-to-end method that leverages the capabilities of modern pre-trained LLMs. Some preliminary steps of our experiments have been described in a Master's thesis (Moissl, 2024).

The rest of the paper is structured as follows. In Section 2, we detail the task addressed in our paper. Next, we explain how we used and finetuned the models in Section 3. Then, we describe how we set up the survey in Section 4. Next, in Section 5, we discuss our results. Finally, we close with a short summary in Section 6.

2 Task

The task approached in this paper is to generate SEO-optimized headlines and toplines for German sports news articles. The headline serves as the primary entry point for an article, designed to convey the article's key message and integrate relevant keywords to maximize visibility for both readers and search engines. The topline, positioned above the headline, provides additional context and plays a crucial role in helping both users and search engines in understanding the article's relevance, often by including the competition name, event, or sport category. Together, the topline and headline form the technical headline used by search engines for indexing.

The key challenge of the task is to craft concise, informative, truthful, and engaging headlines that achieve high search engine rankings, without resorting to clickbait or sensationalism. At the same time, they should capture user interest and encourage readership. Specifically, the objective of SEO is to ensure that a user can immediately discern whether their search intent is met by a given search result. Unlike print headlines, which can rely on accompanying images and layout to attract attention, digital headlines must function independently in search results, mobile news feeds, and app notifications.

An essential consideration is the target tone of the publication medium. In our case study, we aim to meet the tone of the German sports news website Sportschau, known for its reputable style with high linguistic and journalistic standards, as opposed to more tabloid-style sports websites, which presents a challenge: On the one hand, the content needs to remain discoverable and competitive in search rankings. On the other hand, the aim is to maintain quality-driven, fact-based, and serious journalism, rather than being led by short-term SEO trends or sensational language.

Character count limitations are also a critical aspect for SEO headlines. While we acknowledge this factor, we do not address it beyond prompting (see Appendix A) and the typical lengths in our training corpus. Although we conducted internal experiments to shorten the generated LLM outputs with an additional postprocessing step utilizing another LLM call, this aspect is not the focus of our paper.

3 Models

In this section, we present the models employed in our experiments, with an overview provided in Table 1.

It is well-known that modern state-of-the-art LLMs exhibit robust performance on unseen tasks and are well-suited for zero-shot inference (Bubeck et al., 2023). Therefore, we utilize such large commercial models in a zero-shot setting, specifically Gemini, GPT-4, and GPT-4o. The simple prompts used for these models are given in Appendix A.

To tailor the models for our specific task, we compiled a dataset comprising 3576 web articles from the German sports news website Sportschau[4], covering diverse sports genres such as soccer, cricket, and tennis. During dataset curation, we

[2]https://www.clearscope.io

[3]https://www.marketmuse.com

[4]https://www.sportschau.de

Short Name	Model	Version	Open Source	Finetuned
Gemini_Orig	Gemini	gemini-1.5-pro-001	✗	✗
GPT-4_Orig	GPT-4	0613	✗	✗
GPT-4o_Orig	GPT-4o	2024-05-13	✗	✗
GPT-4o_Tuned	GPT-4o	2024-08-06	✗	✓ (API)
Teuken_LoRA	Teuken-7B-Instruct	commercial-v0.4	✓	✓ (LoRA)
Teuken_Full	Teuken-7B-Instruct	commercial-v0.4	✓	✓ (Full)

Table 1: Models used in the experiments of this paper.

ensured only articles with headlines reviewed or revised by SEO experts were included (having internal advice from the Sportschau department).

The collected articles serve as training data for finetuning. First, we employ OpenAI's commercial finetuning API to develop a finetuned version of GPT-4o. While some specifications of the finetuning procedure remain undisclosed, the documentation and job task description indicate that the training is conducted over three epochs using a LoRA-based approach (Hu et al., 2022) with a batch size of three.

In addition to large commercial models, we use a medium-sized open-source model, which is convenient for local experimentation, on-premise deployment, and guarantueed data security. We decided on the recently published Teuken model (Ali et al., 2024) that has a multilingual focus on Europe's linguistic diversity and particularly strong performance in the German language. We use two different finetuning procedures: a full finetuning of all model parameters and a parameter-efficient LoRA approach (Hu et al., 2022). Both finetunings are conducted in an instruction-tuning setting, where the task description and the provided article (i.e., the instruction) serve as context, and only the expected outputs from the models (i.e., the headline) are used for computing the loss (Zhang et al., 2023). In both cases, we train for 100 epochs, using a linear learning rate schedule with warmup, an initial learning rate of 10^{-5}, an effective batch size of 512, and the AdamW optimizer (Loshchilov and Hutter, 2019). For our LoRA finetuning, we use a rank of 32 (corresponding to roughly 0.17 % of the parameters, equating approximately to 12.8 M), an α value of 32, and a LoRA dropout rate of 0.05.

4 Survey

We conducted a survey, where we asked members from the Sportschau team to rate several top- and headline pairs for a given sports news article, which was excluded from the training set used for finetuning. In particular, we asked the participants to rate each pair on a discrete scale from 1 (very poor) to 5 (very good), where the primary focus should be on the SEO quality. Additionally, they were instructed to also consider other factors such as the journalistic alignment with the article and the seriousness and orientation of their publication medium. In cases where these criteria conflicted, the participants were encouraged to rely on their subjective judgment to assign an appropriate score. We are aware that this rating task is multi-dimensional and challenging. However, since the participants were experts who actually had a real use case for the system, we believe they could provide meaningful scores that reflect real-life usefulness overall. To give a better impression of the survey content, we show one entry in Appendix B.

Nine Sportschau members participated in the survey. Among them, five self-described as having deep SEO knowledge, three as having basic SEO knowledge, and one as having no SEO knowledge. Each participant reviewed ten articles of representative sports genres, where the distribution of sports genres was determined in collaboration with the Sportschau department. Specifically, the survey included articles on basketball, cycle sport, European handball (two articles), Formula One, Olympic Games, and soccer (four articles). For each article, the participants rated seven top- and headline pairs. Six of them were generated by the models (see Section 3) and one served as a reference, which was human-written and reviewed or revised by an expert on SEO. The participants were not informed about which pair was the reference or which pairs were generated by the models.

5 Results

Figure 1 presents boxplots along with corresponding raw histograms for the scores obtained from our survey. The reference obtained an average score of 3.533, positioned between "fair" and "good." In contrast, the commercial non-finetuned mod-

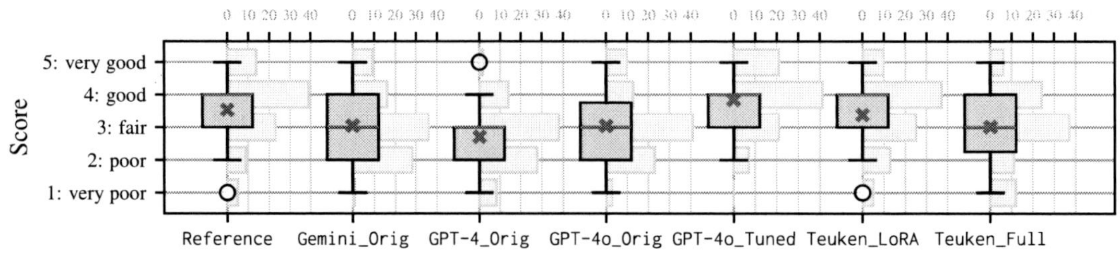

Figure 1: Visualization of the score distributions obtained in our survey: boxplots (gray boxes) with median values (red lines), mean values (dark blue crosses), and underlying raw scores (vertical histograms in light blue).

els Gemini (Gemini_Orig), GPT-4 (GPT-4_Orig), and GPT-4o (GPT-4o_Tuned) received lower average scores of 3.044, 2.711, and 3.044, respectively. The finetuned version of GPT-4o (GPT-4o_Tuned) obtained an excellent average score of 3.844, which is even better than that of the reference. Among the finetuned versions of the Teuken model, the LoRA-finetuned variant (Teuken_LoRA) yielded a good score of 3.378, and the full finetuning (Teuken_Full) scored 3.011. These results suggest that our approach to the task is promising since several models received scores close to the reference's scores, where the output of the finetuned version of GPT-4o was rated even better than the human-written headlines. It is also noteworthy that one finetuned version of the medium-sized Teuken model outperformed all non-finetuned commercial models. A potential reason for the superior performance of the LoRA finetuning compared to the full finetuning of the Teuken model is that our dataset's size was insufficient for a full finetuning.

We conducted a significance test to further analyze the relevance of the differences among the scores. Since the scores are non-normally distributed, we conducted pairwise comparisons using the Wilcoxon signed-rank test with Bonferroni correction. Specifically, we applied the correction by adjusting the p-values ($p_{\text{Bonferroni}} = k \cdot p_{\text{orig}}$, where $k = 21$ is the number of comparisons). The test evaluates the null hypothesis that two pairs of ratings come from the same distribution. Table 2 presents the adjusted p-values, where low values indicate pairs of significantly different score distributions. The most critical entries of the table are in the first row, comparing the scores produced by the models with those by the reference. Using a standard significance threshold of $p \leq 0.05$, the scores for Gemini, GPT-4, GPT-4o, and the fully finetuned version of Teuken are considered significantly different from the scores of the reference. Conversely, the scores of the finetuned version of GPT-4o and the LoRA-finetuned version of Teuken are both considered to be not significantly different from the scores of the reference, suggesting that these models produce headlines perceived as comparable to human-written ones by our expert evaluators.

6 Summary

In this paper, we explored the non-standard task of generating SEO-optimized head- and toplines for journalistic web articles. We conducted a case study where we utilized various large language models, including some that were finetuned with use-case-specific data, to generate such headlines. To assess the models' performance, we conducted a survey in which expert participants rated both the model-generated and human-written headlines. Our results show that finetuning is essential for achieving optimal performance. Furthermore, both large commercial models and medium-sized open-

	Reference	Gemini_Orig	GPT-4_Orig	GPT-4o_Orig	GPT-4o_Tuned	Teuken_LoRA	Teuken_Full
Reference	1.000	0.026	0.000	0.033	0.305	1.000	0.011
Gemini_Orig		1.000	0.058	1.000	0.000	0.578	1.000
GPT-4_Orig			1.000	0.124	0.000	0.000	0.841
GPT-4o_Orig				1.000	0.000	0.402	1.000
GPT-4o_Tuned					1.000	0.018	0.000
Teuken_LoRA						1.000	1.000
Teuken_Full							1.000

Table 2: p-values obtained by our significance test. Cells with $p \leq 0.05$. are highlighted.

source models can achieve a strong performance level producing headlines comparable to those written by human experts.

Acknowledgments

This work was funded by the German Federal Ministry for Economic Affairs and Climate Action (BMWK) through the project OpenGPT-X (project no. 68GX21007D). The authors gratefully acknowledge the scientific support and HPC resources provided by the Erlangen National High Performance Computing Center (NHR@FAU) of the Friedrich-Alexander-Universität Erlangen-Nürnberg (FAU) and the NHR Center of TU Dresden (NHR@TUD). The hardware by NHR@FAU is funded by the German Research Foundation (DFG) and the NHR@TUD is supported by the Federal Ministry of Education and Research and the state governments participating in the NHR. Furthermore, we thank all participants of our survey.

References

M. Ali, M. Fromm, K. Thellmann, J. Ebert, A. A. Weber, R. Rutmann, C. Jain, M. Lübbering, D. Steinigen, J. Leveling, K. Klug, J. S. Buschhoff, L. Jurkschat, H. Abdelwahab, B. J. Stein, et al. 2024. Teuken-7B-Base & Teuken-7B-Instruct: Towards European LLMs. *arXiv CoRR*, abs/2410.03730.

C. Anastasiu, H. Behnke, S. Lück, V. Malesevic, A. Najmi, and J. Poveda-Panter. 2021. DeepTitle – leveraging BERT to generate search engine optimized headlines. *arXiv CoRR*, abs/2107.10935.

S. Bubeck, V. Chandrasekaran, R. Eldan, J. Gehrke, E. Horvitz, E. Kamar, P. Lee, Y. T. Lee, Y. Li, S. M. Lundberg, H. Nori, H. Palangi, M. T. Ribeiro, and Y. Zhang. 2023. Sparks of artificial general intelligence: Early experiments with GPT-4. *arXiv CoRR*, abs/2303.12712.

Z. Ding, A. Smith-Renner, W. Zhang, J. R. Tetreault, and A. Jaimes. 2023. Harnessing the power of LLMs: Evaluating human-AI text co-creation through the lens of news headline generation. In *Proceedings of the Conference on Empirical Methods in Natural Language Processing (EMNLP)*, pages 3321–3339, Singapore.

Gemini Team Google, P. Georgiev, V. I. Lei, R. Burnell, L. Bai, A. Gulati, G. Tanzer, D. Vincent, Z. Pan, S. Wang, S. Mariooryad, Y. Ding, X. Geng, F. Alcober, R. Frostig, et al. 2024. Gemini 1.5: Unlocking multimodal understanding across millions of tokens of context. *arXiv CoRR*, abs/2403.05530.

X. Gu, Y. Mao, J. Han, J. Liu, Y. Wu, C. Yu, D. Finnie, H. Yu, J. Zhai, and N. Zukoski. 2020. Generating representative headlines for news stories. In *Proceedings of the Web Conference (WWW)*, pages 1773–1784, Taipei, Taiwan.

E. J. Hu, Y. Shen, P. Wallis, Z. Allen-Zhu, Y. Li, S. Wang, L. Wang, and W. Chen. 2022. LoRA: Low-rank adaptation of large language models. In *Proceedings of the International Conference on Learning Representations (ICLR)*, virtual.

C. Jie, D. Xu, Z. Wang, and W. Shen. 2022. Deep learning based page creation for improving e-commerce organic search traffic. *arXiv CoRR*, abs/2209.10792.

I. Loshchilov and F. Hutter. 2019. Decoupled weight decay regularization. In *Proceedings of the International Conference on Learning Representations (ICLR)*, New Orleans, LA, USA.

P. Mathur, N. Ueffing, and G. Leusch. 2018. Multilingual neural title generation for e-commerce browse pages. In *Proceedings of the Conference of the North American Chapter of the Association for Computational Linguistics: Human Language Technologies (NAACL-HLT)*, pages 162–169, New Orleans, LA, USA.

G. Matošević, J. Dobša, and D. Mladenić. 2021. Using machine learning for web page classification in search engine optimization. *Future Internet*, 13(1).

T. Moissl. 2024. Adapting large language models for the application in media use cases. Master's thesis, Technical University of Darmstadt.

S. Narayan, S. B. Cohen, and M. Lapata. 2018. Don't give me the details, just the summary! Topic-aware convolutional neural networks for extreme summarization. In *Proceedings of the Conference on Empirical Methods in Natural Language Processing (EMNLP)*, pages 1797–1807, Brussels, Belgium.

OpenAI, J. Achiam, S. Adler, S. Agarwal, L. Ahmad, I. Akkaya, F. L. Aleman, D. Almeida, J. Altenschmidt, S. Altman, S. Anadkat, R. Avila, I. Babuschkin, S. Balaji, V. Balcom, et al. 2023. GPT-4 technical report. *arXiv CoRR*, abs/2303.08774.

OpenAI, A. Hurst, A. Lerer, A. P. Goucher, A. Perelman, A. Ramesh, A. Clark, A. Ostrow, A. Welihinda, A. Hayes, A. Radford, A. Mądry, A. Baker-Whitcomb, A. Beutel, A. Borzunov, et al. 2024. GPT-4o system card. *arXiv CoRR*, abs/2410.21276.

K. I. Roumeliotis and N. D. Tselikas. 2023. A machine learning Python-based search engine optimization audit software. *Informatics*, 10(3).

S. S. Shaffi and I. Muthulakshmi. 2022. Search engine optimization by using machine learning for web page classification. In *Proceedings of the International Conference on Augmented Intelligence and Sustainable Systems (ICAISS)*, pages 342–349, Trichy, India.

H. Xiong, J. Bian, Y. Li, X. Li, M. Du, S. Wang, D. Yin, and S. Helal. 2024. When search engine services meet large language models: Visions and challenges. *IEEE Transactions on Services Computing*, 17(6):4558–4577.

S. Zhang, L. Dong, X. Li, S. Zhang, X. Sun, S. Wang, J. Li, R. Hu, T. Zhang, F. Wu, and G. Wang. 2023. Instruction tuning for large language models: A survey. *arXiv CoRR*, abs/2308.10792.

A Prompts

Here, we briefly list the prompts used in our experiments. Note that the string "`{input_txt}`" is to be replaced by the article for which the head- and topline is going to be generated.

The following prompt was used for `Gemini_Orig`, `GPT-4_Orig`, `GPT-4o_Orig`, and `GPT-4o_Tuned`.

```
Verfassen Sie eine suchmaschinenoptimierte Dachzeile und Überschrift für den folgenden Artikel. Nutzen Sie dabei maximal 25 Zeichen für die Dachzeile und 45 Zeichen für die Überschrift. Verwenden Sie das Format
Dachzeile: <Dachzeile hier>
SEO-Überschrift: <Überschrift hier>

Artikel:

{input_txt}
```

The following prompt was used for `Teuken_LoRA` and `Teuken_Full`.

```
System: Ein Gespräch zwischen einem Menschen und einem Assistenten mit künstlicher Intelligenz. Der Assistent gibt hilfreiche und höfliche Antworten auf die Fragen des Menschen.
User: Schreibe eine SEO-optimierte Dachzeile und Überschrift für folgenden Artikel.

{input_txt}
Assistant:<s>
```

B Survey Example

In this appendix section, we provide an example entry from the survey. Each survey page included an article, a task description (identical across all pages), and the top- and headline pairs to rate.

Below is an example of an article:

```
[Dachzeile]
[Überschrift]

Der 1. FC Heidenheim hat seine Aufstiegsambitionen im letzten Hinrundenspiel der 2. Fußball-Bundesliga mit einem glücklichen Sieg gegen Jahn Regensburg nach einer wilden Schlussphase untermauert.

Das Team von Trainer Frank Schmidt gewann in einem höchst unterhaltsamen Spiel gegen Regensburg mit 5:4 (3:2) und geht als Tabellendritter in die lange WM- und Winterpause.

Spektakel in der Nachspielzeit

Stefan Schimmer (90.+4) setzte in der Nachspielzeit den Schlusspunkt, zwei Minuten zuvor hatte Regensburgs Aygün Yildirim (90.+2) das 4:4 erzielt. Zuvor hatten Tim Kleindienst (21./39.), Adrian Beck (36.) und Denis Thomalla (76.) für Heidenheim sowie Prince Osei Owusu (14.), Charalambos Makridis (45.+1) und Nicklas Shipnoski (55.) für den Jahn getroffen.

In einem Duell mit vielen Chancen auf beiden Seiten waren die Gastgeber die etwas effektivere Mannschaft und hatten das glückliche Ende auf ihrer Seite. Die Regensburger von Trainer Mersad Selimbegovic verpassten es, ihre Negativbilanz gegen Heidenheim aufzubessern. Regensburg hatte vor 9.695 Zuschauern einige große Chancen: Doch Blendi Idrizi (60.) traf nur den Pfosten. Makridis schoss aus sechs Metern am leeren Tor vorbei.
```

Model	Top- and Headline	Average Score
`Gemini_Orig`	Heidenheim siegt im Spektakel 5:4! Heidenheim dreht nach Rückstand auf und feiert Sieg im Krimi	3.000
`GPT-4_Orig`	Sieg für Heidenheim 1. FC Heidenheim untermauert Aufstiegsambitionen mit Sieg	2.889
`GPT-4o_Orig`	2. Bundesliga Heidenheim siegt dramatisch 5:4 gegen Regensburg	3.889
`GPT-4o_Tuned`	Neun Tore Heidenheim gewinnt turbulentes Spiel gegen Regensburg	4.333
`Teuken_LoRA`	2. Bundesliga Heidenheim besiegt Regensburg in wilder Schlussphase	3.778
`Teuken_Full`	Sieg gegen Jahn Heidenheim mit Happy End gegen Regensburg	3.222
`Reference`	Siegtor in der Nachspielzeit Heidenheim entscheidet Spektakel gegen Regensburg für sich	3.667

Table 3: Example top- and headlines from our survey.

```
Heidenheim nach der Pause gegen Rostock

Am 18. Spieltag geht es für Heidenheim zu Hause gegen Rostock um wichtige Punkte im Aufstiegskampf (Samstag, 28.01.2023 um 13.00 Uhr). Regensburg ist zum Auftakt der Rückrunde in Darmstadt gefordert.
```

Following the article, participants received the task description:

```
Bitte bewerten Sie die Qualität folgender Dachzeilen und Überschriften auf einer Skala von 1 bis 5. Dabei steht 1 für "sehr mangelhaft" und 5 für "sehr gut". Im Zentrum Ihrer Bewertung sollte die Suchmaschinenoptimierung stehen, allerdings ohne Beachtung der typischen Längenbeschränkungen für die Textelemente. Beziehen Sie auch weitere Kriterien, wie die journalistische Passgenauigkeit zum Artikel sowie die Seriösität und Ausrichtung Ihres Publikationsmediums ein. Sollten sich diese Kriterien widersprechen, verlassen Sie sich auf Ihr subjektives Empfinden, um eine angemessene Punktzahl zu vergeben.
```

Finally, the pairs of top- and headline pairs for rating was shown to the participants. The order of these pairs was randomized, and the models used to generate them was not disclosed to the participants. In Table 3, we present these pairs along with the average scores these particular entries received in our survey.

Predicting Functional Content Zones in German Source-Dependent Argumentative Essays: Experiments on a Novel Dataset

Xiaoyu Bai and Manfred Stede
Applied Computational Linguistics
University of Potsdam
Karl-Liebknecht-Straße 24-25
14476, Potsdam, Germany
{xiaoyu.bai|stede}@uni-potsdam.de

Abstract

We present a crowdsourced corpus of German-language essays that addresses a middle-school level argumentative writing task. The essays have been composed in response to news articles as reading material, with instructions for the writer to make reference to arguments in the source text in a structured way. The essays were then annotated with fine-grained sentence-level content zones that reflect sentences' functional roles in the essay. Our long-term goal is training a tutoring tool to automatically predict such content zones in unseen essays and to generate helpful feedback on them. To this end we experimented with a range of machine learning models for the prediction task, including a large language model. We obtained the best performance from an ensemble model.

1 Introduction

A common argumentative essay writing exercise in German secondary school is known as *textgebundene Erörterung*[1] (TE), roughly "text-bound argumentation". Students are asked to read an article that discusses a social topic and subsequently to write an essay in which they introduce the topic, summarise and analyse the article author's argumentation and conclude with thoughts of their own. In the long term, we aim to create an intelligent tutoring system (ITS) that supports students in this exercise by providing formative feedback on their essay drafts. Specifically, the system will check whether or not an essay contains the core components of a typical TE-like essay, such as an introduction, paraphrases of arguments from the article, novel arguments of one's own etc. and will point out their absence to the student writer and recommend a revision in a targeted way.

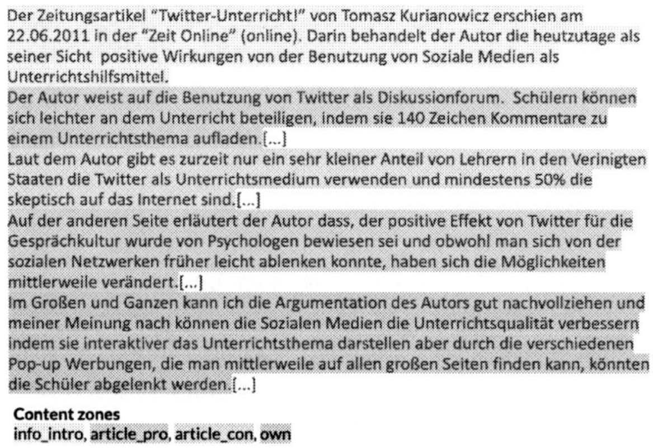
Der Zeitungsartikel "Twitter-Unterricht!" von Tomasz Kurianowicz erschien am 22.06.2011 in der "Zeit Online" (online). Darin behandelt der Autor die heutzutage als seiner Sicht positive Wirkungen von der Benutzung von Soziale Medien als Unterrichtshilfsmittel.
Der Autor weist auf die Benutzung von Twitter als Diskussionforum. Schülern können sich leichter an dem Unterricht beteiligen, indem sie 140 Zeichen Kommentare zu einem Unterrichtsthema aufladen.[...]
Laut dem Autor gibt es zurzeit nur ein sehr kleiner Anteil von Lehrern in den Verinigten Staaten die Twitter als Unterrichtsmedium verwenden und mindestens 50% die skeptisch auf das Internet sind.[...]
Auf der anderen Seite erläutert der Autor dass, der positive Effekt von Twitter für die Gesprächkultur wurde von Psychologen bewiesen sei und obwohl man sich von der sozialen Netzwerken früher leicht ablenken konnte, haben sich die Möglichkeiten mittlerweile verändert.[...]
Im Großen und Ganzen kann ich die Argumentation des Autors gut nachvollziehen und meiner Meinung nach können die Sozialen Medien die Unterrichtsqualität verbessern indem sie interaktiver das Unterrichtsthema darstellen aber durch die verschiedenen Pop-up Werbungen, die man mittlerweile auf allen großen Seiten finden kann, könnten die Schüler abgelenkt werden.[...]

Content zones
info_intro, article_pro, article_con, own

Figure 1: Partly shortened example essay from our corpus with content zone annotations. Labels used in the annotation are explained in the text.

For this purpose, our present work presents a novel, crowdsourced dataset consisting of TE-like essays that have been written on three discussion topics, based on three news articles as source text. To our knowledge, it is the first openly available dataset of German-language argumentative essays that are source-dependent, i.e. written in response to and with reference to a source text. Following existing work which have annotated scientific papers (Teufel and Moens, 2002), parliamentary speeches (Peldszus and Stede, 2016) and student essays (Schaller et al., 2024) with rhetorical or content zones, we annotated our essays with a fine-grained set of content zones, where each zone reflects a functional component of TE-like essays. To illustrate, Figure 1 shows an authentic, albeit partly shortened example essay from our corpus. The essay on the topic of whether or not social media should be used as a tool in schools has been annotated with the following content zones which

[1]See for instance the following prominent tutoring websites: https://www.schuelerhilfe.de/online-lernen/2-deutsch/976-textgebundene-eroerterung and https://www.studienkreis.de/deutsch/textgebundene-eroerterung-schreiben/

Proceedings of the 21st Conference on Natural Language Processing (KONVENS), Volume 1: Long and Short Papers, pages 66–79, 2025

denote the respective functional components:

- **info_intro**: Introductory statement presenting the topic and/or providing (publication) information on the source article
- **article_pro**: Arguments from the source text in support of a given position
- **article_con**: Arguments from the source text against a given position
- **own**: Writer's own argument or viewpoint

For the full dataset, we defined a total of eight content zone labels, which are described in detail in Section 3. Based on our annotated data, we trained machine learning models to automatically predict content zones in unseen essays. Given the source-dependent nature of our task, recognising similarities between arguments in the essays and those in the source text is a particular challenge in our task that sets it apart from the analysis of stand-alone essays.

Overall, the contributions of our present work are the following:

- Through crowdsourcing, we collected a set of 117 German source-dependent argumentative essays written in reference to three news articles.
- We annotated these essays with a pre-defined set of functional content zones.
- We present a series of machine learning experiments for the automatic prediction of these content zones, including using large language models (LLMs). We show that ensembling different classifiers is most successful by a sizeable margin, whereas (smaller) LLMs do not excel.

We make our annotated data and code openly available.[2] Our dataset is referred to as *GerTE* (**Ger**man **T**extgebundene **E**rörterung).

2 Related Work

2.1 Content Zone Recognition

Earlier work on content zone recognition has largely been on domains other than student essays: Working on German parliamentary speeches that argue either in favour of or against a political action, Peldszus and Stede (2016) assign each discourse segment in a speech to one of a pre-defined set of functional building blocks (*content zones*) for the text genre, such as "central thesis" or "pro argument". An older but related approach is taken by Teufel and Moens (2002), who work on scientific papers and annotate them with so-called *rhetorical zones*. They assign each sentence in a given scientific paper to a set of rhetorical classes that are typically found in academic papers, such as research aims or methodology descriptions.

The German-language DARIUS corpus (Schaller et al., 2024) is the only work we know of to apply content zone annotations to student essays. The corpus comprises over 4500 argumentative essays by secondary school students and is annotated with multiple layers of information, most of which target argumentation mining. Content zone annotations for DARIUS use three coarse-grained labels: *Introduction*, *Main Part* and *Conclusion*. Unlike DARIUS, our essays are source-dependent; our content zone labels, which are more fine-grained, target making adequate reference to the argumentative source text rather than independent argumentation.

2.2 Source-Dependent Student Essays

Among the most prominent work addressing source-dependent essays is eRevise (Zhang et al., 2019; Zhang and Litman, 2020, 2021), a tutoring system that assesses secondary student essays' explicit reference to relevant passages from the source text and gives feedback on them. Other than that, the highly popular Kaggle ASAP-AES dataset[3], which has been used in a vast amount of automated essay scoring research (Bai and Stede, 2023), also features source-dependent essays (Mathias and Bhattacharyya, 2018). However, they are labelled for holistic scoring, which does not specifically target reference to the source text.

For German, accessible datasets of school-level essays are scarce. In addition to DARIUS (Schaller et al., 2024), Stahl et al. (2024) have released a dataset of secondary-level students' persuasive essays with argumentation annotations. However, neither corpus contains source-based essays. Horbach et al. (2017) have scored source-based, German-language summary essays, yet the dataset is drawn from university students and is not publicly available. We are not aware of work on

[2] https://github.com/XYB1001/GerTE-Konvens-25

[3] https://www.kaggle.com/competitions/asap-aes

German that addresses source-dependent secondary school-level essays similar to eRevise (Zhang et al., 2019) for English. We address this gap by releasing our present dataset.

3 Data

3.1 Data Collection

Data collection from real school students is difficult due to legal and ethical concerns. Therefore, as a second-best solution for starting the new task, we used crowdsourcing to collect essays in response to our TE exercise. We chose three news articles that deal with the following easily accessible discussion topics, each with a short-hand name given in brackets:

1. Should Twitter be integrated into school classes as a tool?[4] (*Twitter*)
2. Should climate change be taught at school in a subject of its own?[5] (*Climate*)
3. Should school start later in the morning?[6] (*LateSchool*)

The articles are openly accessible and approximately 600 - 700 words in length. Along with a link to the article and an example essay, an instruction with approximately the following wording (albeit in German) is given to the crowd workers: *Read this news article. Write a "textgebundene Erörterung" (TE) of approximately 300 to 350 words, using the example essay as an orientation if needed. Summarise the topic and the arguments given by the author in a structured way and conclude with your own viewpoint on the topic*. The example essay deals with a fourth topic that is not one of the three topics listed above and was written by the first author of the present paper.

The data collection process took place in April 2021 on the Prolific[7] crowdsourcing platform. We hired workers above the age of 18 who reported a good level of general education and sufficient proficiency in German. Overall, we obtained 117 essays, 50 each for the topics of *Twitter* and *LateSchool* and 17 for the topic of *Climate*, which was considered a less straightforward topic. All submissions were rigorously checked for quality, and those of low quality were replaced with new submissions. The essays range between 210 to 445 words, with an average length of 267.6 words. Statistics divided by topic are shown in Table 1. For illustration, one of the essays for the topic of *Twitter* is shown in full in Figure 5 in the Appendix.

Topic	Twitter	LateSchool	Climate	Total
Range	210 - 313	215 - 445	230 - 395	210 - 445
Mean	249.5	268.8	317.7	267.6
SD	25.5	39.8	40.8	41.0

Table 1: Word count statistics for the essays on each topic in our collected dataset.

3.2 Data Annotation

In our approach to recognising core components of a TE-like essay, we follow Teufel and Moens (2002) and work on the sentence level, assigning each sentence in an essay to a single functional content zone (cz). We define a total of eight fine-grained cz-labels, which are summarised in Table 2. The example sentences shown in the table are based on authentic data from our dataset (translated and in part shortened).

With regard to the *LateSchool* topic, where no clear stance is put forward by the article's author, the label *article_pro* is used for sentences which support starting school later and *article_con* for sentences arguing against it. We consider every token to be part of a sentence (whether well-formed or not) and therefore as belonging to one of these cz classes. Hence, the label *other* is introduced as a fall-back class for any chunk of text that cannot be assigned to any of the other seven classes, including badly-formed and/or incomprehensible pieces of text.

Spacy (Honnibal and Montani, 2017) was used to perform sentence segmentation. Two annotators – the first author of the present work and a research assistant – each independently annotated all 117 essays and achieved a good inter-annotator agreement of 0.78 (Cohen's Kappa). In an adjudication process, all annotations showing disagreement were discussed and a single annotation agreed on.

Out of the 1682 essay sentences, 64 (3.8 %) were temporarily assigned to two different cz-classes as

[4]From Zeit-Online, at https://www.zeit.de/digital/internet/2011-06/twitter-unterricht/komplettansicht, last access on 30.04.2025

[5]From Zeit-Online, at https://www.zeit.de/gesellschaft/schule/2020-01/klimawandel-schulfach-bildung-unterricht-konkurrenz, last access on 30.04.2025

[6]From ÄrzteZeitung Online, at https://www.aerztezeitung.de/Panorama/Ist-es-vernuenftig-die-Schule-um-8-zu-beginnen-402238.html, last access on 30.04.2025

[7]https://www.prolific.co/

Cz-label	Description	Example
info_article	Sentences presenting information on the source article, such as author, publication date etc.	The news article "Twitter-Unterricht" was published on 22nd of June, 2011 in "Zeit" (online).
topic_intro	Sentences which introduce the discussion topic	In the article, the author discusses whether it makes sense that school starts as early as 8:00 in the morning.
article_pro	Sentences from the article that *support* the author's side of the argumentation	The author believes that Twitter allows students to better get in touch with their teachers.
article_con	Sentences from the article that *undermine* the author's viewpoint	The authors sees the only counter-argument in old fashioned teachers who are sceptical towards new media.
own	Sentences which present the student writer's own position or thoughts on the discussion topic	I believe the author's suggestion is a good idea and would really help the educational system.
meta	Sentences that the writer uses to structure the essay	Now I turn to the arguments against this idea.
off_topic	Sentences that are comprehensible but do not relate to the discussion topic and feel "off topic"	Recently young people have forgotten the past, which has given rise to issues like racism [found in an essay on the Climate topic] .
other	Fall-back class for sentences for which none of the above content zone labels apply	Also the news from the world, and it's the last minute [found in an essay on the Twitter topic].

Table 2: Content zones used in our annotation scheme

neither can be said to be more significant:

- 33 sentences were labelled with both *info_article* and *topic_intro* and are of the form *The article, which was published in ... deals with the question of ....* Since both content zones form introductory statements for our essays and often can be expressed by a single sentence, we chose to conflate the two classes into a single class *info_intro*.

- The remaining cases of double labelling are of the form *Although [pro/con argument from article], [pro/con argument from article or own argument].* An authentic (but translated) example from our data reads *Although children would like to sleep longer and go to school later, they also like it when school finishes earlier, which gives them much free time in the afternoon.*. We manually split these sentences into sentential clauses such that each clause could be annotated with a single cz-label. They were thus treated as separate single-label sentences.

After these steps, our overall dataset for content zone recognition consists of 1713 sentences from 117 essays, each sentence being labelled with exactly one out of seven possible cz-labels. The distribution among the seven classes is shown in Figure 6 in the Appendix.

4 Classification Experiments

In our dataset, samples for the classes *meta*, *off-topic* and *other* are significantly less frequent than the remaining classes, with less than 100 samples for each of them in the full dataset. Moreover, sentences of these classes are less relevant to our prospective use case where we wish to draw attention to missing core components of an TE-like essay, which these classes do not count among. Due to these reasons, in our current classification experiments we conflated the classes *meta*, *off-topic* and *other* into a single class *other*. The resulting cz label distribution based on five classes in total is as shown in Figure 2. This is the data basis for our classification experiments.

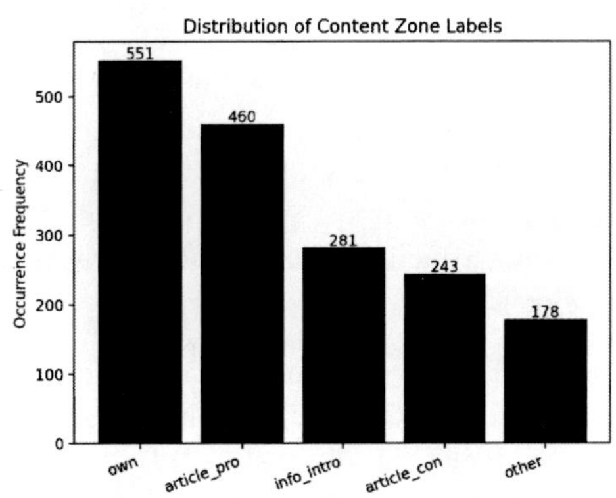

Figure 2: Distribution of content zone labels in our data in the conflated 5-class setting.

With the exception of the experiments based on

LLMs, all of our experiments were carried out in 5-fold cross-validation. In each fold, the models were trained on roughly 80% of the essays (93 or 94 out of 117) and tested on the held-out 20%.

4.1 Preprocessing

Apart from sentence segmentation, which had already been done prior to annotation, we did not undertake any preprocessing steps.

4.2 Basic Feature-Based Models

We experimented with a combination of feature-based and neural, representation-based models. All feature-based machine learning models used implementations by scikit-learn (Pedregosa et al., 2011). Our baseline was either a linear SVM or a random forest classifier using only TF-IDF-weighted word unigrams and bigrams. Additional hand-crafted features we experimented with are the following:

Surface character features A straight-forward addition to the baseline is the addition of character n-grams in the range [3,4].

Position features We defined position features to encode the relative position of a given sentence in the essay that it was drawn from. For this, we split each essay into four parts, where all parts have approximately the same number of sentences. The position feature is defined as 4 binary features with values 1 or 0, where each represents one of the four quarters of the essay and 1 indicates that a given sentence occurs in the corresponding quarter. This feature aims at capturing the intuition that some content zones (e.g. introduction statements) tend to occur at specific positions within the essay. For instance, in our dataset, 252 out of the 281 instances (89.7%) of *info_intro*-labelled sentences occur within the first three sentences of the essay; 104 out of the 117 essays (88.9%) end in a sentence labelled as *own* as most writers concluded their essays with a final verdict of their own on the discussion topic.

Static BERT embedding features We experimented with static embeddings from pre-trained BERT (Devlin et al., 2019), specifically the German model "bert-base-german-cased"[8], released by deepset.ai[9]. For each sentence, we took the representation of the special `[CLS]` token as its embedding.

SBERT article similarity features We used sentence-BERT (SBERT) (Reimers and Gurevych, 2019) to encode the amount of similarity between a target sentence and each sentence in the corresponding source article. The motivation here is that sentences labelled as *article_pro* or *article_con* reproduce arguments from the source article and therefore can be expected to be near-paraphrases of and show high similarity scores with specific sentences in the article that introduce those arguments. For instance, for *LateSchool*, a translated essay sentence labelled *article_pro* is: *They have more time for sleep*, which we expect to exhibit a higher similarity score with the article sentence *On average, students slept 34 minutes longer* than with other sentences in the article. SBERT is known to perform well in paraphrase detection tasks (Khairova et al., 2022; Peng et al., 2022) and therefore chosen for this feature. We used the pre-trained multilingual model "sentence-transformers/paraphrase-multilingual-MiniLM-L12-v2"[10], and the cosine measure to encode the similarity between target sentences and each corresponding article sentence.

4.3 Fine-tuning a BERT Model

Alongside feature-based models, we also tested the same BERT-based neural model in the fine-tuning scenario. That is, we again fed each target sentence to BERT and extracted the embedding of the `[CLS]` token. To inject information on the relative position of a sentence within an essay, we concatenated this sentence embedding with our position features as detailed above. The resulting representation was then passed to an output layer with logged softmax for classification.

The model was implemented with PyTorch (Paszke et al., 2019) and Hugging Face (Wolf et al., 2020). We used the PyTorch implementation of the weighted Adam optimiser (Loshchilov and Hutter, 2017) with default parameters and the negative log likelihood loss as our loss function. Based on a preliminary examination using 10 essays (4 from *Twitter* and *LateSchool* and 2 from *Climate*) as validation data, we decided to fine-tune the model for 4 epochs, with a batch size of 16 and a learning

[8] `https://huggingface.co/bert-base-german-cased`

[9] `https://www.deepset.ai/german-bert`

[10] Available through the Hugging Face Hub at `https://huggingface.co/sentence-transformers/paraphrase-multilingual-MiniLM-L12-v2`

rate of $1e^{-5}$. The final fine-tuning experiment was again carried out in 5-fold cross-validation.

4.4 Ensemble Modelling

As an alternative to using n-grams and embeddings as different feature sets in order to exploit both surface-level and deep representational information, we experimented with combining them through ensemble modelling. In this approach, multiple base models learned to output probability values for each cz class, and a meta model predicted the final cz label based on these probability features. We chose the following three base models, which used different features that have already been described above:

- Model 1: linear SVM with static BERT embeddings, SBERT article similarity and position features
- Model 2: linear SVM with word and character ngrams, SBERT article similarity and position features
- Model 3: Random Forest with word and character ngrams, SBERT article similarity and position features

At training time, we used 10-fold cross-validation within the training partition of the overall 5-fold cross-validation scheme to obtain content zone predictions by the three models on the training partition[11]. Each prediction is a probability distribution among the 5 possible content zone labels. This gave us a set of base model predictions on each sentence in the training partition.

At the meta level, we used a logistic regression model which took the base predictions for each sentence as its sole feature, i.e. a vector of 15 components (5 probability values from each of the 3 base models), and finally produced a label for the sentence. At training time, the meta-model trained on the base model predictions for the sentences in the full training partition, paired with the true content zone labels in the annotations. At test time, we retrained each of the three base models on the full training partition and applied them to the test data. Their probability predictions for the test sentences were then fed to the trained meta-model to obtain the final labels for the test partition.

[11]That is, rotating through 10 folds, they repeatedly trained on 90% of the training partition and made predictions for the remaining 10%.

4.5 Prompting an LLM

As a final approach, we experimented with prompting an LLM to output cz labels. We chose Meta's instruction fine-tuned Llama3.1 model with 8 billion parameters[12] (Grattafiori et al., 2024) as it is an openly available, state-of-the-art multilingual LLM that is still easy to use in terms of hardware requirements. Access to the model was through its integration with the Groq[13] framework. We examined three prompting scenarios:

- **Zero-shot**: We treated all of our data as test data and prompted Llama to output content zone labels for each essay in a single run. The prompt did not include the source article text.
- **Zero-shot with article**: Same as *zero-shot*, but we included the article text which the target essay references in the prompt.
- **One-shot**: We manually inspected the labelled essays and chose a single essay[14] to include in the prompt as a demonstration for in-context learning. The chosen essay deals with the *Twitter* topic and well exemplifies each of the five content zone labels. We then used this one-shot prompt to ask Llama to produce labels for all other essays in the dataset; the article text was not included in this setting.

A gloss of the system prompt we used is: *You are a middle-school German teacher who checks whether a student's essay contains all the expected essay components.* The user prompt approximately reads: *Here is an argumentative essay written by a student in response to reading a text. The essay is split into sentences. Each sentence is numbered and follows this format [...]. Each sentence can be paired with one of the following five functions.* Following a concise description of each content zone label using one sentence, the prompt concludes with *Assign each sentence to one of these five functions. The output should follow this format [...]* before displaying the target essay in the format promised. In the *zero-shot with article* scenario, we appended the system prompt with the sentence *Here is the article to*

[12]https://huggingface.co/meta-llama/Llama-3.1-8B-Instruct

[13]https://groq.com/

[14]The essay chosen to serve as demonstration and its gold content zone labelling are given in the Appendix.

which the essay refers and the full article text. In the prompt texts, we gave the content zone labels meaningful German names, such as *Einleitung* or *Pro_aus_Lesetext* for *info_intro* and *article_pro*, respectively. An example of our original German-language prompts is provided in the Appendix.

In its output, Llama was prompted to reference each sentence by its number and pair it with a cz label. This allowed us to extract the labels from the output text using simple Regex-based rules. If the number of labels extracted matched the number of sentences in the essay (and thus the number of gold labels), we could apply the same evaluation procedure as for all the other classification models.

4.6 Sentence-Level Sequence Classification

Apart from the LLM-based approach, all of the models described above cast the task as a sentence classification task[15] where a single sentence is independently labelled with a single content zone. The handcrafted position feature detailed above is the only indication concerning a sentence's relative position to other sentences from the same essay.

As an alternative, we also experimented with casting our task as a sequence labelling task on the sentence level. In this case, each essay is represented as a sequence of sentence representations and labelled with a corresponding sequence of content zones. We experimented with a BiLSTM-CRF model architecture (Huang et al., 2015) with different sentence embeddings. However, our initial experiments showed very poor classification results; we therefore did not further pursue this approach. Since this approach works on the essay instead of the sentence level, we suspect that our dataset of 117 essays (of which less than 100 are used for training) is too small to perform efficient training on.

5 Results

We evaluated our models in terms of the common classification metrics accuracy, precision, recall and F1. For the latter three, we report the weighted macro average across the five classes. The most frequent classes in our dataset, viz. those with the labels *article_pro*, *article_con* and *own*, are also those of the most interest to our intended use case of recognising central components of a TE-like essay. It therefore appears plausible to weigh the classes by their frequency. Table 3 shows the results in terms of these metrics. With the exception of the Llama models, the scores for all models are averaged across the five folds in cross-validation.

Regarding the Llama models, in the two zero-shot scenarios, 12 (without the article in the prompt) and 8 (with the article) essays, respectively, led to output in which the numbers of output labels and sentences did not match and which were therefore excluded from evaluation. In the one-shot scenario, 10 essays produced invalid output. For each prompt scenario, we report the single set of metrics as evaluated on all the essays in the respective scenario that produced valid output and were considered in evaluation. In line with expectations, both the addition of the source article and of an appropriate demonstration essay boosts the LLM's performance (though the improvement from the one-shot scenario is minor).

6 Discussion and Future Directions

Overall, the ensemble model clearly produced the best results. The fine-tuned BERT model and the hybrid model using an SVM with both surface features and static BERT embeddings also achieved competitive results. Moreover, the simple and fast approach of feeding word and character ngrams with position features to an SVM turned out to be remarkably successful, achieving comparable performance with fine-tuned BERT.

To further analyse the results, we show in Figure 3 the by-class F1 metric of the following three models, as averaged across five folds: the baseline SVM, the SVM with surface and static BERT features (*Hybrid*) and the best-performing ensemble model. The class *other* clearly stands out as the worst-performing class across the board and the only class on which the overall best-performing ensemble model does *not* achieve the highest F1 score. The low performance is expected since the class is both heavily under-represented and fuzzily defined since it serves as a fall-back class for sentences that do not fit elsewhere. However, with respect to our designated use case, it is also the least relevant class. The easiest class to recognise is clearly *info_article*. This is also unsurprising; not only are certain phrases such as *the article deals with...* or *the article was published in...* highly indicative of the class, sentences of this class also almost exclusively occur at the beginning of an essay, which is captured by the position feature.

[15]The LLM-based approach treats the task as a chat-completion task.

	Accuracy	P (weighted)	R (weighted)	F1 (weighted)
SVM + word ngrams (baseline)	0.653	0.683	0.653	0.634
SVM + w&c ngrams + position	0.680	0.679	0.680	0.674
RF + w&c ngrams + position	0.671	0.725	0.671	0.641
SVM + w&c ngram + BERT (static) + position + article	0.686	0.685	0.688	0.682
RF + w&c ngram + BERT (static) + position + article	0.646	0.66	0.646	0.61
BERT (fine-tuned) + position	0.686	0.686	0.686	0.674
Ensemble model	**0.728**	**0.723**	**0.728**	**0.713**
Llama (zero-shot)	0.654	0.636	0.654	0.641
Llama (zero-shot with article)	0.673	0.659	0.673	0.661
Llama (one-shot)	0.661	0.639	0.661	0.649

Table 3: Evaluation results for selected models; *P* and *R* refer to precision and recall, *RF* denotes the random forest classifier, *w&c ngrams* refers to word and character ngrams, *position* denotes position features and *article* denotes article similarity features. Values for all but the Llama models are averaged across five folds.

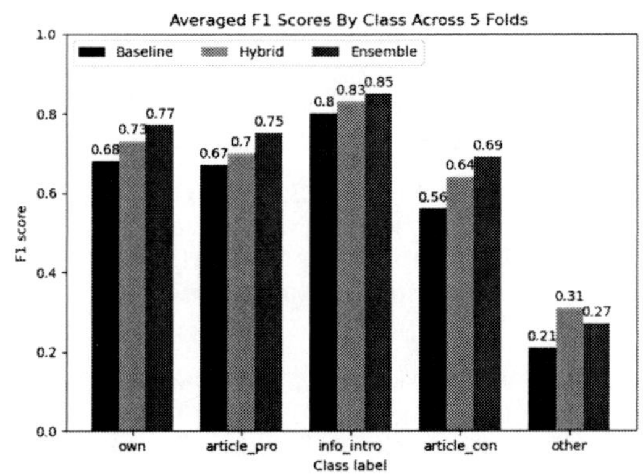

Figure 3: Averaged F1 scores by class for three selected models.

The success of the ensemble model could be attributed to performance behaviour of the different base models that complement each other to some degree, which can be seen in the confusion matrices shown in Figure 4. For instance, Plot b) suggests that the random forest model with n-gram and position features has a bias towards the class *own* such that it correctly recognises the large majority (86%) of them but also overpredicts over 30% of *article_con* and nearly 60% of *other* sentences as *own*. This tendency is not shared by the hybrid SVM with surface and BERT embeddings (Plot a)); in contrast, it predicts (and overpredicts) *article_con* far more often than the random forest model, which often misses this class. The ensemble model (Plot c)) seems to build on the strengths of its base models, both achieving high recall on *own* (comparable to the random forest) while reducing misclassification of *article_con* samples as *own* (comparable to the SVM).

With respect to the performance by Llama, we examined the output texts that we had to discard from evaluation and made the following observation: In many of these cases, Llama generated more pairs of sentence number and content zone labels than there were sentences in the input essay, which seems to indicate model hallucination. To illustrate this, an example output along with the corresponding prompt is given in the Appendix.

It should be noted, however, that our Llama experiments are only a first step. Future work could investigate the performance of the larger versions of Llama and of other LLMs such as DeepSeek-R1 (Guo et al., 2025) or commercial ones like GPT-4 (Achiam et al., 2023). Moreover, the fact that classification has benefitted both from the addition of the source article and from the one-shot prompt scenario is in line with expectations and indicates that in the given task, the LLM can successfully exploit additional information in the prompt to increase its performance. Thus, focus on further prompt engineering efforts will likely yield better classification results. For instance, we plan to look into improved and automatic ways to select demonstration essays for in-context learning in a few-shot prompting scenario.

7 Conclusion

In this work, we have presented a novel German dataset consisting of 117 middle-school level, source-dependent argumentative essays and their annotations with fine-grained, sentence-level content zones. While the essays were collected through crowdsourcing, we examined them closely to ensure their quality. Based on this dataset, we trained different machine learning models, including LLMs, to predict content zones in the essays. Our best-performing model is an ensemble model that combines an SVM and

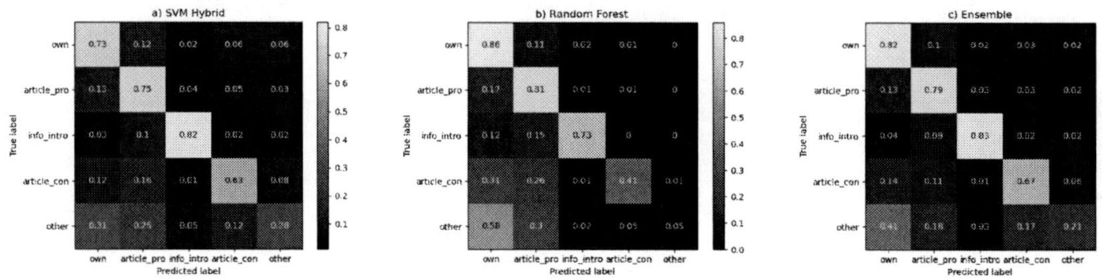

Figure 4: Normalised confusion matrices for three selected models. All values are as averaged across five folds.

a random forest model with both hand-crafted features and static BERT embeddings. We believe further investigation of LLMs can be a promising direction, although we also believe that practical advantages of more lightweight classification approaches remain an important consideration in terms of computation power needed, runtime, energy consumption etc. As the next step, we plan to continue our work by presenting our exercise to real students from schools and collecting authentic data. In the long term, we hope to incorporate our analysis into a tutoring system that generates formative feedback to support students' in their essay writing in TE-like exercises.

Limitations

We point out and acknowledge two limitations with regard to our current dataset: First, with 117 essays it is a fairly small dataset. Second, it has been collected by means of crowdsourcing from adult workers whose essay writing skills are not necessarily representative of middle-school students. We plan to address both limitations in the future by presenting our exercise in schools to extend our dataset with essays from real students.

Ethical Considerations

We do not foresee significant ethical risks in relation to our work. The nature of our exercise and our manual validation of the essays ensure that no personal information is disclosed through the essays. However, since our crowdsourcing data collection was anonymous, we could not ensure that writers of different population groups in terms of gender, ethnicity, socio-economic background etc. were adequately represented. Possible bias in classification models that disadvantage certain population groups should therefore be kept in mind.

References

Josh Achiam, Steven Adler, Sandhini Agarwal, Lama Ahmad, Ilge Akkaya, Florencia Leoni Aleman, Diogo Almeida, Janko Altenschmidt, Sam Altman, Shyamal Anadkat, et al. 2023. Gpt-4 technical report. *arXiv preprint arXiv:2303.08774*.

Xiaoyu Bai and Manfred Stede. 2023. A survey of current machine learning approaches to student free-text evaluation for intelligent tutoring. *International Journal of Artificial Intelligence in Education*, 33(4):992–1030.

Jacob Devlin, Ming-Wei Chang, Kenton Lee, and Kristina Toutanova. 2019. BERT: Pre-training of Deep Bidirectional Transformers for Language Understanding. *arXiv:1810.04805 [cs]*. ArXiv: 1810.04805.

Aaron Grattafiori, Abhimanyu Dubey, Abhinav Jauhri, Abhinav Pandey, Abhishek Kadian, Ahmad Al-Dahle, Aiesha Letman, Akhil Mathur, Alan Schelten, Alex Vaughan, et al. 2024. The llama 3 herd of models. *arXiv preprint arXiv:2407.21783*.

Daya Guo, Dejian Yang, Haowei Zhang, Junxiao Song, Ruoyu Zhang, Runxin Xu, Qihao Zhu, Shirong Ma, Peiyi Wang, Xiao Bi, et al. 2025. Deepseek-r1: Incentivizing reasoning capability in llms via reinforcement learning. *arXiv preprint arXiv:2501.12948*.

Matthew Honnibal and Ines Montani. 2017. spaCy 2: Natural language understanding with Bloom embeddings, convolutional neural networks and incremental parsing.

Andrea Horbach, Dirk Scholten-Akoun, Yuning Ding, and Torsten Zesch. 2017. Fine-grained essay scoring of a complex writing task for native speakers. In *Proceedings of the 12th Workshop on Innovative Use of NLP for Building Educational Applications*, pages 357–366, Copenhagen, Denmark. Association for Computational Linguistics.

Zhiheng Huang, Wei Xu, and Kai Yu. 2015. Bidirectional lstm-crf models for sequence tagging. *arXiv preprint arXiv:1508.01991*.

Nina Khairova, Anastasiia Shapovalova, Orken Mamyrbayev, Nataliia Sharonova, and Kuralay

Mukhsina. 2022. Using bert model to identify sentences paraphrase in the news corpus. In *COLINS*, pages 38–48.

Ilya Loshchilov and Frank Hutter. 2017. Decoupled weight decay regularization. *arXiv preprint arXiv:1711.05101*.

Sandeep Mathias and Pushpak Bhattacharyya. 2018. Asap++: Enriching the asap automated essay grading dataset with essay attribute scores. In *Proceedings of the eleventh international conference on language resources and evaluation (LREC 2018)*.

Adam Paszke, Sam Gross, Francisco Massa, Adam Lerer, James Bradbury, Gregory Chanan, Trevor Killeen, Zeming Lin, Natalia Gimelshein, Luca Antiga, et al. 2019. Pytorch: An imperative style, high-performance deep learning library. *Advances in neural information processing systems*, 32:8026–8037.

Fabian Pedregosa, Gaël Varoquaux, Alexandre Gramfort, Vincent Michel, Bertrand Thirion, Olivier Grisel, Mathieu Blondel, Peter Prettenhofer, Ron Weiss, Vincent Dubourg, et al. 2011. Scikit-learn: Machine learning in python. *the Journal of machine Learning research*, 12:2825–2830.

Andreas Peldszus and Manfred Stede. 2016. Inhaltszonen. In Manfred Stede, editor, *Handbuch Textannotation: Potsdamer Kommentarkorpus 2.0*, pages 133–144. Universitätsverlag Potsdam.

Qiwei Peng, David Weir, Julie Weeds, and Yekun Chai. 2022. Predicate-Argument Based Bi-Encoder for Paraphrase Identification. In *Proceedings of the 60th Annual Meeting of the Association for Computational Linguistics (Volume 1: Long Papers)*, pages 5579–5589, Dublin, Ireland. Association for Computational Linguistics.

Nils Reimers and Iryna Gurevych. 2019. Sentence-BERT: Sentence Embeddings using Siamese BERT-Networks. *arXiv:1908.10084 [cs]*. ArXiv: 1908.10084.

Nils-Jonathan Schaller, Andrea Horbach, Lars Höft, Yuning Ding, Jan Luca Bahr, Jennifer Meyer, and Thorben Jansen. 2024. DARIUS: A Comprehensive Learner Corpus for Argument Mining in German-Language Essays.

Maja Stahl, Nadine Michel, Sebastian Kilsbach, Julian Schmidtke, Sara Rezat, and Henning Wachsmuth. 2024. A School Student Essay Corpus for Analyzing Interactions of Argumentative Structure and Quality. In *Proceedings of the 2024 Conference of the North American Chapter of the Association for Computational Linguistics: Human Language Technologies (Volume 1: Long Papers)*, pages 2661–2674, Mexico City, Mexico. Association for Computational Linguistics.

Simone Teufel and Marc Moens. 2002. Summarizing scientific articles: experiments with relevance and rhetorical status. *Computational linguistics*, 28(4):409–445.

Thomas Wolf, Lysandre Debut, Victor Sanh, Julien Chaumond, Clement Delangue, Anthony Moi, Pierric Cistac, Tim Rault, Rémi Louf, Morgan Funtowicz, Joe Davison, Sam Shleifer, Patrick von Platen, Clara Ma, Yacine Jernite, Julien Plu, Canwen Xu, Teven Le Scao, Sylvain Gugger, Mariama Drame, Quentin Lhoest, and Alexander M. Rush. 2020. Transformers: State-of-the-art natural language processing. In *Proceedings of the 2020 Conference on Empirical Methods in Natural Language Processing: System Demonstrations*, pages 38–45, Online. Association for Computational Linguistics.

Haoran Zhang and Diane Litman. 2020. Automated Topical Component Extraction Using Neural Network Attention Scores from Source-based Essay Scoring. In *Proceedings of the 58th Annual Meeting of the Association for Computational Linguistics*, pages 8569–8584, Online. Association for Computational Linguistics.

Haoran Zhang and Diane Litman. 2021. Essay Quality Signals as Weak Supervision for Source-based Essay Scoring. In *Proceedings of the 16th Workshop on Innovative Use of NLP for Building Educational Applications*, pages 85–96, Online. Association for Computational Linguistics.

Haoran Zhang, Ahmed Magooda, Diane Litman, Richard Correnti, Elaine Wang, LC Matsmura, Emily Howe, and Rafael Quintana. 2019. erevise: Using natural language processing to provide formative feedback on text evidence usage in student writing. In *Proceedings of the AAAI Conference on Artificial Intelligence*, volume 33, pages 9619–9625.

A Example Essay Sample

The shortened and annotated essay shown in Figure 1 of the main text is shown in full in Figure 5, without annotations.

B Content Zone Distribution With Seven Classes

The content zone label distribution with seven class labels, before mapping *meta* and *off-topic* to *other*, is shown in Figure 6.

C Example LLM Prompts and Outputs

An example prompt fed to Llama in the zero-shot scenario with an input essay on the *LateSchool* topic is given in Table 4. Table 5 shows the demo essay on the *Twitter* topic and the demo output that we used as our example in the one-shot prompting scenario. Table 6 shows an example of an invalid output on the same topic in the one-shot

Der Zeitungsartikel "Twitter-Unterricht!" von Tomasz Kurianowicz erschien am 22.06.2011 in der "Zeit Online" (online). Darin behandelt der Autor die heutzutage als seiner Sicht positive Wirkungen von der Benutzung von Soziale Medien als Unterrichtshilfsmittel.
Der Autor weist auf die Benutzung von Twitter als Diskussionforum. Schülern können sich leichter an dem Unterricht beteiligen, indem sie 140 Zeichen Kommentare zu einem Unterrichtsthema aufladen. Die niedrige Schwelle, ermöglicht es den Schülern, die normalerweise schweigen würden, am Unterricht Teil zu nehmen.
Laut dem Autor gibt es zurzeit nur ein sehr kleiner Anteil von Lehrern in den Verinigten Staaten die Twitter als Unterrichtsmedium verwenden und mindestens 50% die skeptisch auf das Internet sind. Das passiert wegen der Angst vor Zerstreuung die immer noch sehr groß ist.
Auf der anderen Seite erläutert der Autor dass, der positive Effekt von Twitter für die Gesprächkultur wurde von Psychologen bewiesen sei und obwohl man sich von der sozialen Netzwerken früher leicht ablenken konnte, haben sich die Möglichkeiten mittlerweile verändert.
Der Autor meint dass, die Informationen im Digitalformat besser im Gedächtnis gespeichert werden und die Schüler auch von einem interessanten und abwechslungreichen Unterricht profitieren können und die Einführung des Social Web der Erfindung des Buchdrucks ähnelt und es irgendwann im Unterricht als selbstverständlich betrachten wird.
Im Großen und Ganzen kann ich die Argumentation des Autors gut nachvollziehen und meiner Meinung nach können die Sozialen Medien die Unterrichtsqualität verbessern indem sie interaktiver das Unterrichtsthema darstellen aber durch die verschiedenen Pop-up Werbungen, die man mittlerweile auf allen großen Seiten finden kann, könnten die Schüler abgelenkt werden. Es gibt auch das Problem der immer sinkenden Aufmerksamkeitsspanne die durch Soziale Medien beeinträchtigt wird.

Figure 5: Example essay in full on the *Twitter* topic.

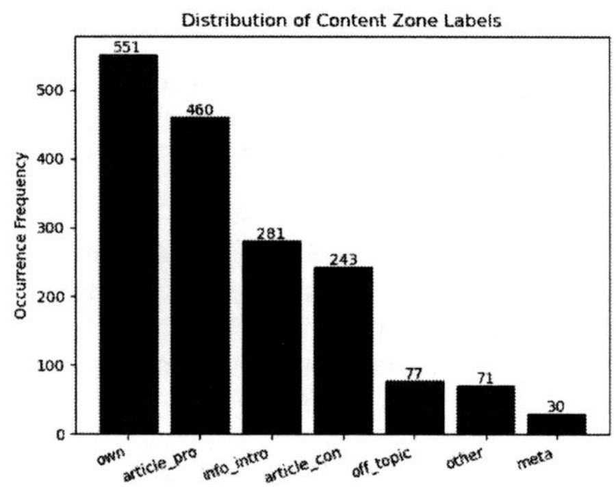

Figure 6: Distribution of our content zone labels in the 7-class setting.

scenario. This output produces 13 pairs of sentence numbers and content zone labels when the essay only consists of 9 sentences. It is therefore not valid and was excluded from evaluation.

Du bist ein Deutschlehrer der 9. Klasse und analysierst Aufsätze deiner Schüler. Du überprüfst dabei, ob die Aufsätze alle zu erwartenden Bestandteile enthält.

Hier liegt ein argumentativer Aufsatz vor, den ein Schüler mit Bezug auf einen Lesetext geschrieben hat. Der Aufsatz wurde in Sätzen unterteilt. Die Sätze sind nummeriert. Das Format dabei is "Satznummer: Satz".
Jeder Satz wird einer der folgenden 5 Funktionen zugeordnet:
"_Einleitung" bedeutet: Der Satz leitet den Aufsatz ein und gibt evtl. Informationen zum Lesetext und zum Thema des Aufsatzes.
"_Pro_aus_Lesetext" bedeutet: Der Satz gibt ein Pro-Argument aus dem Lesetext wider.
"_Con_aus_Lesetext" bedeutet: Der Satz gibt ein Kontra-Argument aus dem Lesetext wider.
"_Eigen" bedeutet: Der Satz gibt eigene Meinungen und Argumente des Schülers wider.
"_Sonstiges" bedeutet: Der Satz kann keiner der vorherigen 4 Funktionen zugeordnet werden.
Werte den Schüleraufsatz aus und ordne jeden Satz einer der genannten 5 Funktionen zu. Das Format des Outputs soll ausschließlich wie folgt sein: "Satznummer: Funktion", zum Beispiel "1: _Einleitung" oder "8: _Eigen".

Schüleraufsatz

1: In dem Text von Cornelia Dieckmann aus dem Jahr 2019 wird die Frage gestellt, ob der "Schulbeginn um 8 Uhr sinnvoll" ist.
2: Dieser Artikel ist in dem Magazin "Ärzte Zeitung" zu lesen.
3: <PB> Sie greift auf Schlafforschungen zurück, um ein klareres Bild der Vor - und Nachteile zu schaffen.
4: <PB> Laut einer US-amerikanischen Studie werden die Leistungsfähigkeit und die Konzentration der Schüler:innen deutlich verbessert und außerdem schlafen sie ca 30 Minuten länger, wenn der Unterricht um 8:45 beginnnt und nicht um 8:00 Uhr.
5: <PB> Dies bedeutet jedoch auch, dass der Schultag später endet, was Eltern und Schülern nicht gefällt.
6: Denn im Ende geht es um die Freizeit die man am Tag noch hat.
7: Würden die Schulen später anfangen, gäbe es auch mehr Busverbindungs-Probleme, da nun Schulen unterschiedlich beginnen und man trotzdem noch zum pünktlich zum Unterricht muss.
8: <PB> Tageslicht spielt dabei auch eine große Rollle, denn wenn man morgens wenn es noch dunkel ist in die Schule kommt und abend wieder die Schule verlässt, beinträchtigt das zum Ersten die Konzentration und Leistungsfähigkeit der Schüler:innen, und zum Zweiten auch deren Laune.
9: <PB> Zusammenfassend ausgedrückt geht es um den Schüler:innen mehr um den Rest des Tages den sie übrig haben.
10: Denn wenn man eine Stunde mehr draußen,, zum Beispiel am See sein kann, dann nimmt man die frühe Stunde der Schule in Kauf.
11: Die Organisation eines späteren Schulbeginns hört sich am Anfang leicht an, ist aber komplizierter als erwartet was ein Grund dafür ist, die Zeiten beizubehalten.
12: Allerdings darf man die positiven Auswirkungen auf die Schüler:innen nicht ignorieren, denn nur 30 Minuten mehr schlaf führen zu besseren Ergebnissen.

Table 4: Example prompt fed to Llama in the zero-shot scenario. The top part is the system prompt, the lower part the user prompt.

1: Der Zeitungsartikel "Twitter-Untericht" von Tomasz Kurianowicz erschien am 22.
2: Juni 2011 in der "Zeit Online".
3: Dahin behandler der Autor eine neue Lehrmethode - nutzung der sozial Netzwerken im Unterrichten.
4: Es ist sehr wichtig, dass die Lehrer ihre Studenten zuzugehehen und heutzutage gibt es keine bessere Methode Schülern zu erreichen, als durch sozial Netzwerken.
5: Es ist auch ein guten Trick die Jugendliche in der Unterricht zu angarieren, weil Mehrheit der jungen Leute jeden Tag mehrere sozial Netzwerke nutzt und deswegen ist das spannend für ihnen.
6: Wie alles, hat diese Methode nicht nur Vorteile aber auch Nachteile.
7: Obwohl positive Effekt für die Gesprächskultur durch Psychologen bewiesen sei,
8: viele Lehrer auf diese Method mit skepsis reagieren und nicht verwenden im ihren Unterrichten.
9: Der Grund dafür ist höchstwahrscheinlich die Angst vor Zerstreuung.
10: Tradizionell, können die Schülern während des Unterrichts nicht benutzen, früher Lehrer sogar sammelten die Handys vor dem Unterricht ein, um Ablenkungen zu vermeiden.
11: Für diesen Lehrer ist also twittern im Unterricht fast unvorstellbar.
12: <PB> Persönlich glaube ich, dass heutzutage ist die virtuelle wert gleichermaßen wichtig wie die Realität ist.
13: Manche Leute interagieren mit anderen Persönen durch das Internet sogar mehr, als im Realität.
14: Scheuen sich davon das Internet zu nutzen ist also sinnlos und kann sozial Fähigkeiten der Studenten schaden.
15: Meine Meinung nach, wir sollen neue Lösungen verwenden und nicht nur verlassen sich auf die Tradizion.

1: _Einleitung
2: _Einleitung
3: _Einleitung
4: _Pro_aus_Lesetext
5: _Pro_aus_Lesetext
6: _Sonstiges
7: _Pro_aus_Lesetext
8: _Con_aus_Lesetext
9: _Con_aus_Lesetext
10: _Con_aus_Lesetext
11: _Con_aus_Lesetext
12: _Eigen
13: _Eigen
14: _Eigen
15: _Eigen

Table 5: The example essay and output given to Llama as demonstration in the one-shot scenario. The top part is the input essay, the lower part the demo output.

[Removed for brevity: System prompt, example essay and example output for in-context learning]

Hier liegt ein argumentativer Aufsatz vor, den ein Schüler mit Bezug auf einen Lesetext geschrieben hat. Der Aufsatz wurde in Sätzen unterteilt. Die Sätze sind nummeriert. Das Format dabei is "Satznummer: Satz". Jeder Satz wird einer der folgenden 5 Funktionen zugeordnet:
"_Einleitung" bedeutet: Der Satz leitet den Aufsatz ein und gibt evtl. Informationen zum Lesetext und zum Thema des Aufsatzes.
"_Pro_aus_Lesetext" bedeutet: Der Satz gibt ein Pro-Argument aus dem Lesetext wider.
"_Con_aus_Lesetext" bedeutet: Der Satz gibt ein Kontra-Argument aus dem Lesetext wider.
"_Eigen" bedeutet: Der Satz gibt eigene Meinungen und Argumente des Schülers wider.
"_Sonstiges" bedeutet: Der Satz kann keiner der vorherigen 4 Funktionen zugeordnet werden.
Werte den Aufsatz aus und ordne jeden Satz einer dieser 5 Funktionen zu. Das Format des Outputs soll ausschließlich wie folgt sein: "Satznummer: Funktion", zum Beispiel "1: _Einleitung" oder "8: _Eigen".

Schüleraufsatz

1: Im Artikel von Cordula Dieckmann geht es darum, ob ein späterer Schulbeginn nicht sinnvoller wäre als die aktuelle Form.
2: <PB> Für eine Verschiebung des Beginns spricht, dass den Schülern dadurch mehr Schlafzeit zustehen würde, und somit können sie ausgeschlafen zum Unterricht erscheinen.
3: Da während der Pubertät viele Jugendliche eher dazu neigen, erst später ins Bett zu gehen und aufzustehen, wäre dies eine Möglichkeit, die fehlende Schlafzeit auszugleichen.
4: <PB> Dagegen spricht allerdings, dass die Umsetzung nicht reibungslos erfolgen würde.
5: Zum einen müssen sämtliche Verkehrsdienste wie Schulbusse umstrukturiert werden, um Schulen mit abweichenden Uhrzeiten zu bedienen, zum anderen wäre in so einem Fall zusätzliche Unterrichtsblöcke erforderlich, die den Nachmittag belegen würde.
6: Dies sei unter vielen eine unbeliebte Idee, da sie u.a. im Winter im Dunkel zur Schule gehen und sie auch im Dunkel verlassen würden -
7: Kontakt zum Sonnenlicht regelt nämlich die innere Uhr und ist vor allem in der Entwicklungsphase unverzichtbar.
8: <PB> Ein späterer Schulbeginn ist eine interessante Idee, dessen Umsetzung jedoch nur unter einem Kompromiss möglich ist - dass es unbedingt mit einem Riesenaufwand verbunden ist, was den Schulbusbetrieb oder auch Verpflegung von Schülern angeht, macht sie aber nicht attraktiver.
9: Würde ein Teilverzicht auf sie allerdings eine Verbesserung der Lernbedingungen für Schüler bedeuten, wäre das Gesamtkonzept nicht unwägbar - wichtig ist dabei nur, dass die Schüler eine bessere Schulerfahrung genießen können.

1: _Einleitung
2: _Pro_aus_Lesetext
3: _Pro_aus_Lesetext
4: _Con_aus_Lesetext
5: _Con_aus_Lesetext
6: _Sonstiges
7: _Con_aus_Lesetext
8: _Eigen
9: _Eigen
10: _Sonstiges
11: _Eigen
12: _Sonstiges
13: _Eigen

Table 6: Example invalid output by Llama in the one-shot scenario. Upper part contains the (shortened) prompt containing the input essay, lower part the output by Llama.

SocCor: A Multimodal-based Multilingual Soccer Corpus for Text Data Analytics

Paul Löhr and Jannik Strötgen
Karlsruhe University of Applied Sciences, Karlsruhe, Germany
{paul.loehr,jannik.stroetgen}@h-ka.de

Abstract

In this paper, we present SocCor, a novel dataset containing multimodal-based, multilingual media coverage of the UEFA EURO 2024. SocCor contains transcribed live commentary and video highlights as well as livetickers and reports in multiple European languages, with a total of more than 1.7 million tokens and 92,421 player mentions. By enriching SocCor with metadata about the games and curating it with normalized entity mentions based on a well-performing, tailored entity normalization approach, we provide the basis for sophisticated soccer-related text data analysis studies. Due to its multilingual nature and covering audio and text, real-time and post-game descriptions, SocCor opens ample opportunities for various types of analysis in multiple dimensions.

We demonstrate the value of SocCor by conducting and describing exploratory studies, which reveal sentiment variations, media biases, and opportunities to create player embeddings capturing soccer-specific relationships. Thus, this work provides a solid foundation for multilingual sports media research.

1 Introduction

Media coverage analyses can reveal interesting insights about events and how it is reported about them. For instance, there have been several media coverage studies on COVID-related topics (e.g., Hart et al., 2020; Mach et al., 2021). A sports domain of great interest to people is soccer. While there have been a few linguistic-centric studies in the past about this sports domain (e.g., Meier-Vieracker, 2017), there is only little work on soccer-related news media coverage analysis. One reason for this is probably the lack of well-curated datasets that allow for sophisticated studies.

In this paper, we present SocCor, a novel soccer news dataset containing multilingual media coverage of the UEFA EURO 2024. A key feature of SocCor is that it is multimodal-based: it consists of transcribed live commentary and video highlights as well as text data in the form of livetickers and reports. SocCor covers seven European languages, totaling to more than 1.7 million tokens with data from 20 sources, e.g., Kicker (Germany), BBC (England), L'Equipe (France), and Marca (Spain).

By enriching SocCor with metadata about the games, we increase the value of the data set for sophisticated multilingual sports media research. In addition, we increase SocCor's quality by tackling spelling mistakes from the original data and in particular mistakes from the transcription process, by developing a well-performing, tailored entity normalization approach to normalize entity mentions referring to players and coaches.

Due to its multilingual nature and covering audio and text, real-time and post-game descriptions, SocCor opens ample opportunities for various types of analysis across multiple dimensions. For instance, studies could be cross-language / cross-culture (e.g., are there differences regarding the sentiment of the reporting across languages and countries and does it depend on which teams are playing?) or cross-modality (e.g., is there a difference in live commenting in video vs. live commenting in "ticker"-style reports? Are ticker reports more descriptive to compensate for the missing image data?). By conducting and describing exploratory sample studies, we demonstrate the broad opportunities of SocCor-based data analysis, revealing, for instance, sentiment variations across media types and languages, country-specific media biases, and opportunities to create player embeddings capturing soccer-specific relationships.

In summary, this work provides a solid foundation for future research on diverse multilingual sports media.[1]

[1] SocCor and further resources related to this paper can be found at https://github.com/PaulLoehr/SocCor.

Proceedings of the 21st Conference on Natural Language Processing (KONVENS), Volume 1: Long and Short Papers, pages 80–89, 2025

2 Related Work

Soccer datasets can be of different nature: text-based, statistical, and about tracking information. We develop a dataset for natural language processing (NLP) and text data analytics and thus focus on text-based data. This type of data conveys the emotional, linguistic, and cultural facets of soccer discourse. However, statistical data, when used as metadata (e.g., lineups, possession, results, and goals), are valuable for providing contextual match information that enriches text-based analyses.

This section reviews existing datasets, emphasizing the limitations of text-based resources and the absence of integrated statistical metadata, to highlight the gaps addressed by our work.

Text-Based Datasets Text-based datasets about soccer are rare. However, they are critical for NLP and text data analytics, enabling the analysis of language use, sentiment, and cultural dimensions. One dataset is the soccer linguistics corpus by Meier-Vieracker (2017), a multilingual dataset designed for studying soccer journalism. Covering 13 languages (e.g., English, Spanish, German, Portuguese) and with approximately 75 million words, it contains reports, livetickers, and live commentary transcripts. Reports offer detailed game analyses, covering team performances and tactical aspects. Livetickers provide real-time updates with spontaneous reactions to events like goals or fouls, while live commentary transcripts from radio broadcasts combine objective descriptions with subjective assessments, enhancing emotional engagement.

Despite its strengths, the soccer linguistics corpus has significant limitations. It does not focus on a specific tournament, instead aggregating texts across various matches and seasons. This lack of tournament-specific coverage prevents comprehensive analysis of all reports, livetickers, and commentary for individual games within a single tournament, limiting its utility for tasks like comparative sentiment analysis or event detection across multiple sources for the same match. Crucially, it does not include statistical metadata, such as lineups, possession statistics, or match results, which are essential for contextualizing textual analyses with general match information. With SocCor, we focus on one tournament (the UEFA Euro 2024).

Statistical and Tracking Data While text-based data are the focus of this work, statistical and tracking datasets provide complementary numerical insights that are particularly relevant as metadata. Statistical datasets, such as those on Kaggle by Sekhri (2024) and Dizdarevic (2024) for UEFA Euro 2024, offer match and player statistics, including goals, assists, and team performance metrics. FBref (2024)'s UEFA Euro 2024 dataset provides comprehensive data on results and player contributions. Tracking data from StatsBomb (2024), including event and tactical data for UEFA Euro 2024, enable detailed analyses of player movements and strategies. These datasets are valuable for objective analysis and can serve as metadata to contextualize text-based data, providing details like lineups, possession percentages, or substitutions that enhance NLP tasks, such as linking sentiment to specific game events.

However, existing statistical and tracking datasets are typically standalone and not integrated with text-based corpora. To bridge this gap, we release SocCor and provide a unified resource, which allows a variety of analytics tasks to be performed on a single resource covering linguistic aspects as well as metadata.

3 SocCor

The main contribution of this work is SocCor, a novel dataset designed for text data analytics with a focus on the UEFA Euro 2024 tournament. SocCor comprises multilingual text and transcribed audio data from diverse sources, including livetickers, match reports, video highlights, and complete game commentaries, complemented by statistical metadata (e.g., lineups, results) and automatically annotated player mentions.

The sources differ in various aspects: real-time (livetickers, complete game commentaries) vs. post-hoc (match reports, video highlights), as well as text-based (livetickers, match reports) vs. speech-based (complete game commentaries, video highlights) data. Furthermore, data are collected from sources in seven major European countries (Germany, France, Spain, England, Italy, the Netherlands, and Turkey) and thus multilingual (see Figure 1 for an overview of the distribution by language and media type). This heterogeneity of the data provides a comprehensive representation of soccer discourse, capturing linguistic, emotional, and cultural nuances, which allows for a huge diversity of analysis tasks.

In the following, we describe the collection of the data (Section 3.1), the preprocessing (Section 3.2), the automatic annotation processes (Section 3.3), and dataset statistics (Section 3.4).

3.1 Data Collection

SocCor aggregates multimodal data from media coverage of the UEFA Euro 2024 for all 51 matches. The dataset includes four primary data types and statistical metadata, collected to capture diverse textual and audio narratives of the tournament and its individual matches. To address the heterogeneity of sources, tailored Python scripts were developed for automated data acquisition, ensuring consistent and structured storage across text, audio, and metadata.

Livetickers Real-time text updates with minute-by-minute event descriptions and spontaneous reactions to goals, fouls, and other match events. Stored as `.json` files with event timestamps.

Reports Detailed journalistic analyses, offering summaries of team performances, key moments, and tactical insights, reflecting diverse linguistic and cultural perspectives. Stored as `.json` files.

Video Highlights Extracted audio tracks, capturing live commentary and crowd reactions. Initially stored as .mp3 files, with transcriptions to be stored as `.json` files, consistent with the liveticker format.

Game Commentaries Audio recordings of full matches, representing the most restricted data due to limited availability. Initially stored as .mp3 files, with transcriptions to be stored as `.json` files, mirroring the liveticker structure.

Metadata Match details (location, date, teams, lineups, results and goals) to contextualize textual and audio data. Stored as `.csv` files.

Data collection targeted comprehensive coverage from major soccer nations, leveraging their robust media ecosystems to ensure multiple perspectives on each match. Python scripts systematically scraped and processed data, transforming heterogeneous inputs into a unified format. All data are organized by unique match identifiers, enabling efficient retrieval for NLP and analytics tasks.

3.2 Preprocessing

Preprocessing SocCor's audio data is essential to convert spoken commentary into a text format suitable for analysis. Here, we describe the transcription of audio files from video highlights and complete game commentaries, ensuring consistency with the `.json` storage format for text data.

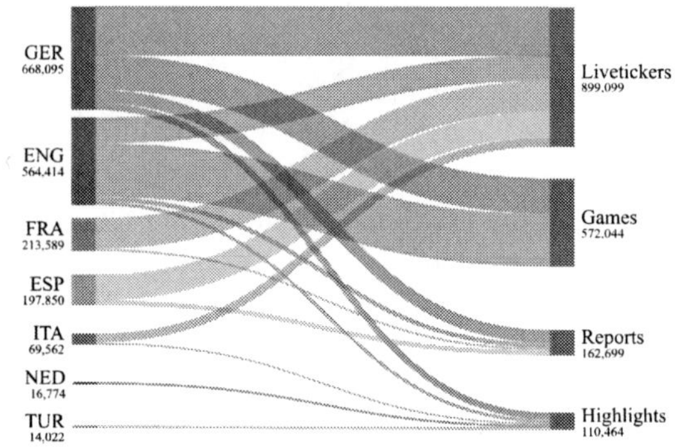

Figure 1: Sankey diagram of the SocCor dataset, showing the distribution of token counts across languages and media types.

Transcription of Audio Files Due to its robustness across multiple languages, we use the Whisper automatic speech recognition (ASR) model (Radford et al., 2023). However, technical limitations of Whisper require that the audio is segmented prior to transcription. To preserve contextual coherence, a pause-based segmentation strategy is employed, leveraging natural breaks in the commentary.

Audio files are initially stored as .mp3, with transcriptions saved as `.json` files, consistent with liveticker data, including timestamps and match IDs (e.g., "51_ENG_ESP") for event alignment.

However, the transcription of such sports commentary audio files faces several challenges:

- **Background Noise**: Stadium sounds and crowd noise, varying by broadcaster, reduce transcription accuracy, especially in high-volume segments.
- **Artifacts**: Unclear audio segments produce repeated (partially strange) text passages, necessitating post-processing to remove redundant (and incorrect) content – as detailed below.
- **Pronunciation Variations**: Inconsistent transcriptions of player names (e.g., "Füllkrug" in German vs. various misspellings in other languages) due to language-specific phonetics complicate entity normalization.

To address artifacts, a frequency-based detection system filters unwanted elements, including recognition failures (e.g., repetitive text due to noise), model hallucinations (e.g., "Das war ein guter Treffer" not present in audio), and broadcaster elements (e.g., jingles mistranscribed as "Subtitles by ZDF

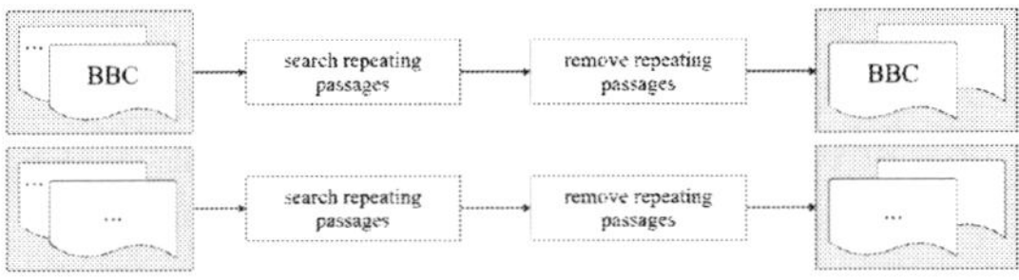

Figure 2: Artifact identification and removal workflow for systematic transcription refinement.

for funk, 2017"). Broadcaster-specific artifact inventories are compiled, capturing recurring phrases' frequency distributions. Figure 2 shows the workflow in which a filtering algorithm refines the segmented transcriptions into clean `.json` outputs.

A critical example from *Sportschau*, a German broadcaster, involves the phrase "Sieg Heil! Sieg Heil! Sieg Heil!" appearing six times across two match transcriptions. This error arose due to the Whisper model misinterpreting loud, euphoric fan chants in the stadium as spoken words during commentary. Manual audio verification confirms that no Nazi salutations were sung in the stadium; the chants were enthusiastic but indistinct crowd noise. This demonstrates the need for careful verification to avoid misrepresentation in noisy environments.

Pronunciation variations and entity normalization challenges are addressed in subsequent processing steps, ensuring high-quality data for downstream NLP and analytics tasks.

3.3 Automatic Annotation

The main goal of the automatic annotation of the data in SocCor is to enrich the corpus with metadata about entity mentions. By normalizing player and coach names across multilingual text data from transcribed audio, livetickers, and match reports, the automatic annotation of SocCor enhances its utility for analytics tasks.

This subsection details the use of spaCy models for named entity recognition and our normalization approach against match-specific player lineups to resolve entity ambiguities, addressing challenges like pronunciation variations, spelling errors, and transcription errors.

Named Entity Recognition To extract named entities, we employ spaCy's pre-trained large NER models (Honnibal and Montani, 2023) for each of SocCor's language (English, German, Spanish, French, Italian, Dutch, and Turkish). These models, trained on general-domain corpora, effectively recognize PERSON entities in the sports media context of SocCor, offering consistency and com-

	# entities	prec	rec	f-score
German	528	0.89	0.79	0.84
English	852	0.92	0.74	0.82
Italian	99	0.87	0.59	0.70

Table 1: NER performance on a subset of SocCor for three languages using spaCy's large NER models. 2 English and 2 German full match transcripts, and 2 highlight summaries for all three languages, respectively.

putational efficiency.

For each input document $d \in D$ (e.g., a transcribed audio segment, liveticker entry, or match report), the pipeline extracts entities, retaining only those classified as PERSON, as only these are relevant for player and coach identification. This results in a set of entities $E_d = \{e_1, \ldots, e_n\}$.

To evaluate NER performance, a subset of SocCor was manually annotated using INCEpTION (Klie et al., 2018), creating a ground truth for PERSON entities. Despite differences in ASR transcription quality across broadcasters and languages, the evaluation results shown in Table 1 demonstrate robust performance across languages.

Pattern Matching with Match Lineups To normalize PERSON entities as specific players or coaches, extracted names are matched against match-specific lists from the dataset's metadata. For each match, identified by unique IDs, the system loads the lineups of the two competing teams. This context-aware approach results in a high-quality corpus with player and coach names relevant to each match.

The system employs two complementary matching approaches to handle orthographic and phonetic variations in extracted entity mentions.

1. **Levenshtein-based Fuzzy Matching**: This method quantifies orthographic similarity using Levenshtein distance (Navarro, 2001), accounting for minor variations such as accents, spacing, or misspellings (e.g., *Fullkrug* vs. *Füllkrug*).

2. **Soundex-based Matching**: To address transcription errors, names are encoded using the Soundex algorithm (Zobel and Dart, 1996), generating 4-character codes that represent phonological patterns. These codes are compared using Levenshtein distance to identify matches despite incorrect transcriptions (e.g., *Tchouaméni* as *Schuamanni*).

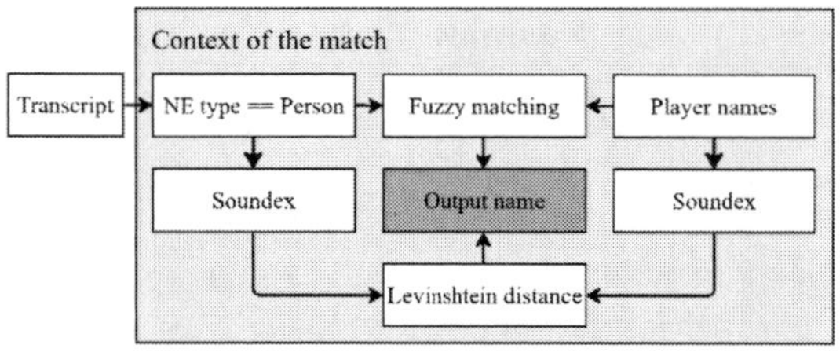

Figure 3: Our approach to perform player name normalization in multilingual transcriptions.

Figure 3 depicts our name correction pipeline to normalize entity mentions in multilingual transcriptions. The system evaluates three outcomes for each PERSON entity: retaining the original name, replacing it with the best Levenshtein fuzzy match, or replacing it with the best Soundex-based match. Levenshtein distance quantifies orthographic similarity (δ_f), while Soundex code comparisons (using Levenshtein distance) identify phonological correlations (δ_s), each producing a similarity coefficient as a confidence metric. If either method yields a high-confidence match (i.e., above a predefined threshold), the entity is corrected to the corresponding player name from the lineup, linking to the metadata. If both methods agree on the same match, the confidence is reinforced. Entities with insufficient confidence (i.e., low similarity scores) are kept unchanged, preserving potential non-player references (i.e., other persons). The output name is chosen based on similarity thresholds and the agreement between methods formalized as follows:

$$\text{name} = \begin{cases} n, & \text{if } \delta_f = 100\% \\ m_f, & \text{if } m_f = m_s \\ m_f, & \text{if } \delta_f \geq 80\% \wedge \delta_f \geq \delta_s \\ m_s, & \text{if } \delta_s \geq 85\% \wedge \delta_s > \delta_f \\ n, & \text{otherwise} \end{cases} \quad (1)$$

where m_f, m_s are best matches from fuzzy and Soundex methods, respectively, δ_f, δ_s are similarity scores (0–100%) for fuzzy and Soundex methods, respectively, and n is the original input name. Some sample corrections are shown in Table 2.

To evaluate our entity normalization approach, 10 transcription documents in German, English, and Italian are manually verified. Our approach achieves a 92% normalization accuracy (726/791 entities resolved), a 24 percentage point improvement over the 68% baseline ASR accuracy (539/791), correcting 74.4% of errors (189/254 discrepancies), as shown in Figure 4.

ASR output	Harbertz	Schumanni
Best Fuzzy	Havertz	Muani
Best Soundex	Havertz	Tchouaméni
Combined	Havertz	Tchouaméni
Ground Truth	Havertz	Tchouaméni

Table 2: Sample corrections of ASR-induced errors: orthographic and morphological variations.

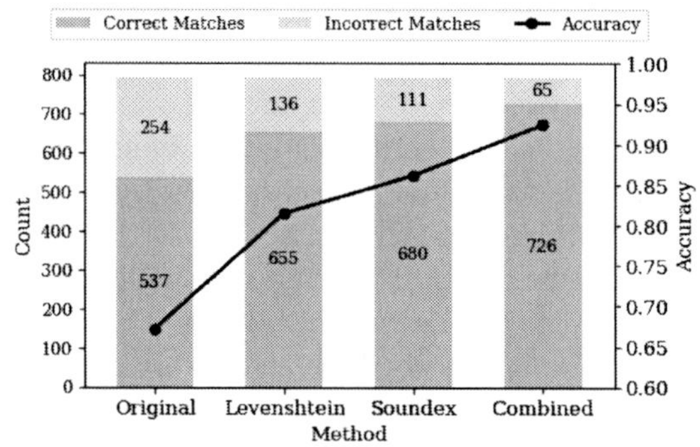

Figure 4: Comparative player name correction performance across methodologies.

Player Token Generation To normalize player and coach mentions across multilingual text data in SocCor, we implement a standardized tokenization approach that transforms names into consistent structured tokens. Full names, official roles (e.g., playing position or coach), and team identifiers are extracted from the metadata, filtered by match-specific identifiers derived from filename conventions. A rule-based text substitution pipeline applies Unicode normalization to convert text to ASCII, removing diacritical marks, followed by lexical pattern matching to detect complete names (e.g., *Harry Kane*) or surnames (e.g., *Kane*). Detected mentions are replaced with tokens in the format <NAME_POSITION_TEAM> (e.g., <KANE_CENTRE-FORWARD_ENG>), preserving positional context and team affiliation. This process addresses cross-lingual name variations, ensures consistent player references, and supports downstream NLP and analytics tasks.

3.4 SocCor Statistics

The SocCor dataset, sourced from UEFA Euro 2024 media coverage, consists of 1,180 files with a total storage size of 20.3 MB. It contains livetickers, game commentaries, written re-

Media	Initial Modality	Tokens
Livetickers	text	899,099
Games	audio	572,044
Reports	text	162,699
Highlights	audio	110,464
Sum		1,744.306

Table 3: Distribution of tokens across source types of different modalities in the SocCor dataset.

Media	Tokens	Player	Ratio [%]
Games	7,221.5	226	3.13
Highlights	332	23	6.93
Livetickers	1,661	112	6.74
Reports	586	26	4.43

Table 4: Median token and player mention counts, and player-to-token ratios across media types, showing denser player references in highlights and livetickers.

ports, and video highlights, all processed into text. Text-based sources (livetickers and reports) are scraped, with player names replaced by standardized tokens (e.g., *Kylian Mbappé* as <MBAPPE_CENTRE-FORWARD_FRA>). Audio sources (video highlights and game commentary) are transcribed using Whisper, with various player-related transcription errors corrected via the above-described named entity recognition and name normalization. The distribution of tokens across the four data sources in SocCor is summarized in Table 3.

On average, each match contains 34,202 tokens. Token counts range from approximately 19,548 (Slovenia vs. Serbia) to 58,853 (England vs. Switzerland, quarterfinal with extra time and penalties). In addition to the varying number of sources per match, this range indicates that token counts are also influenced by match duration and notable in-game events.

For all 51 matches of the UEFA Euro 2024, data is available across media types to ensure comprehensive coverage. Some game commentary files are missing either from *Sportschau* (German) or *BBC* (English), as these broadcasters did not provide data for all matches. *AS English* has incomplete livetickers due to scraping challenges with dynamic website structures. Written reports are also missing for some games due to minor scraping inconsistencies. However, a multi-source approach mitigates these gaps by leveraging complete data from alternative broadcasters' livetickers, game commentaries, and highlights, ensuring that every match is represented with adequate data for analysis.[2]

4 Sample Analytics Tasks on SocCor

To demonstrate the value of our novel SocCor dataset, we now present a series of text data analytics tasks conducted on SocCor. We apply NLP techniques to analyze player mentions, sentiment distributions, and player embeddings, addressing the research goal of understanding cross-modality and language-specific differences in soccer media narratives. This analysis reveals several sample findings: patterns in player prominence, sentiment variations across media types, and semantic relationships encoded in domain-specific embeddings. Thus, first insights into the representation of players and teams in the UEFA Euro 2024 media landscape can be gained.

4.1 Modality-based Player Mentions Analysis

Among the 92,421 player mentions in SocCor, *Kylian Mbappé* leads with 1,408 mentions, followed by *Harry Kane* (1,177), *Cristiano Ronaldo* (1,075), *Jude Bellingham* (1,020), and *Phil Foden* (1,003). This distribution reflects the media's emphasis on high-profile players during UEFA Euro 2024, with stars from prominent teams like France, England, and Spain dominating coverage due to their on-field impact and public recognition.

Variation Across Media Types Player mentions vary significantly across media types, influenced by the format and purpose of each modality. Table 4 presents the median word counts, player mention counts, and player-to-token ratios for each media type. Game commentaries exhibit the highest median player mentions (226), driven by comprehensive match coverage, but their large word count (7,221.5) results in the lowest player-to-token ratio (3.13%). Livetickers, with a median of 112 mentions and a ratio of 6.74%, and highlights, with 23 mentions and a ratio of 6.93%, show denser player references, reflecting their focus on key events. Reports, with 26 mentions and a ratio of 4.43%, balance player focus with tactical analysis, indicating modality-specific reporting styles.

Match-specific Mention Disparities Analysis of specific matches highlights disparities in player

[2]Further details about sources will be provided on the SocCor website.

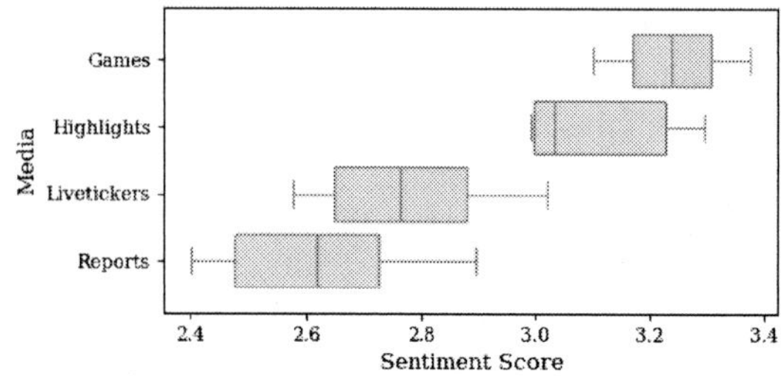

Figure 5: Boxplot of sentiment score distributions across media types in SocCor.

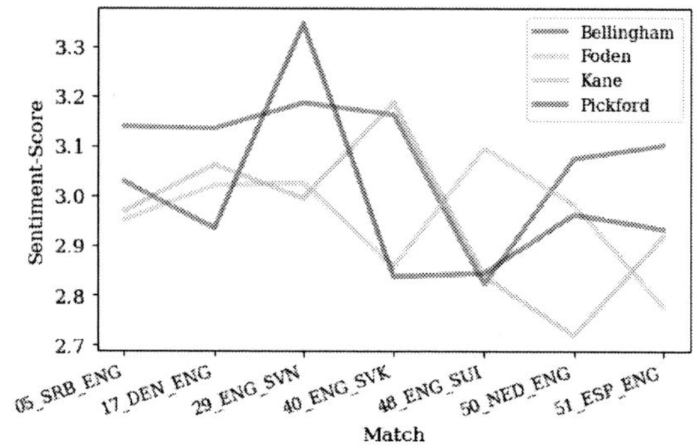

Figure 6: Mean sentiment scores of four players, reflecting media perceptions of performance per match.

mentions, reflecting match outcomes and media focus. In the opening match between Germany and Scotland, which Germany won 5-1, the corpus records 1,333 mentions of German players compared to 566 for Scottish players across all broadcasters. This imbalance aligns with Germany's dominance, suggesting that media attention amplifies the winning team's players.

In the final match between Spain and England, where Spain secured a 2-1 victory, mentions are more balanced, with 1,145 for English players and 1,047 for Spanish players. However, broadcaster-specific patterns emerge: the BBC reports 299 English player mentions versus 208 Spanish in game coverage and 29 versus 19 in post-match reports, indicating a preference for the home team, while livetickers show near parity. These findings underscore how match context and broadcaster perspective shape player mention patterns across modalities.

4.2 Sentiment-based Analysis

We also split SocCor into individual sentences to perform a sentence-based sentiment analysis. Each sentence is processed using a pre-trained multilingual BERT-based (Devlin et al., 2019) sentiment model, which assigns a sentiment score on a scale from 1 (negative) to 5 (positive) (Hugging Face, 2020). When a sentence contains a player token, such as <KANE_CENTRE-FORWARD_ENG>, the sentiment score is assigned to multiple entities: the player, his team, the game, the broadcasting organization, and the media type (e.g., game commentaries, video highlights, livetickers and reports). This multi-level assignment enables detailed sentiment analysis across dataset dimensions.

Two sample sentences mentioning *Harry Kane* demonstrate the model's ability to capture tonal differences: "Brilliant work by Kane." (positive sentiment, 5) and "And Bjorn's not letting Kane go anywhere." (negative sentiment, 1). These corpus-derived examples highlight the model's sensitivity to sentiment variations in soccer media.

Media Type Sentiment Distribution Mean sentiment scores across media types, visualized in Figure 5, reveal tonal differences. Game commentaries exhibit the highest mean score at 3.2, followed by highlights at 3.1, suggesting more positive coverage in these formats. Livetickers have a mean score of 2.7, while reports are lowest at 2.5, indicating more neutral or critical tones, likely due to their focus on continuous real-time updates (e.g., without slow motions of highlights in contrast to game commentaries) or rather objective post-game analysis. The boxplot illustrates the spread and variability of sentiment scores, highlighting modality-specific narrative styles in the UEFA Euro 2024 coverage.

Temporal Per-Game Sentiment Analysis Mean sentiment scores for selected English players are aggregated per game and analyzed across the tournament's matches, ordered chronologically, as visualized in Figure 6. This analysis reveals variations in media portrayal, reflecting perceived performance in individual matches.

For instance, goalkeeper *Jordan Pickford* achieves his highest sentiment score in the Slovenia match, a 0-0 draw, likely due to consistent positive coverage of his defensive actions that contributed to a clean sheet. In contrast, *Harry Kane* records his lowest sentiment score in the semi-final against the Netherlands, where, despite scoring a penalty, critical commentary on missed opportunities during regular play time lowers his aggregated score.

These per-game and temporal trends, supported by the visualization, highlight how match-specific events shape sentiment-based player ratings, of-

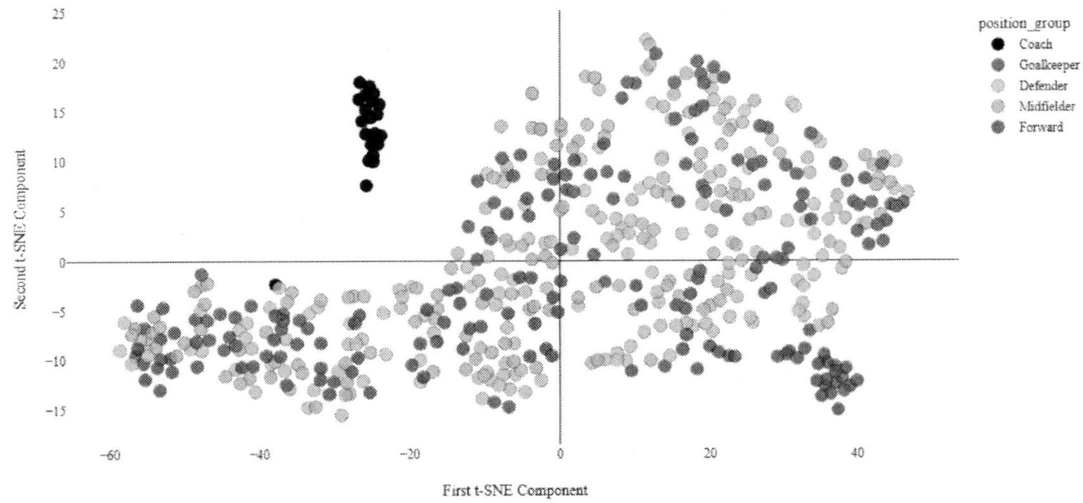

Figure 7: t-SNE visualization of German player embeddings in SocCor, colored by position group, showing clustering based on textual references.

fering a nuanced view of performance across the tournament.

4.3 SocCor-based Player Embeddings

To further demonstrate the value of SocCor, we generate static word embeddings for the German corpus of SocCor (650,000 tokens) using the Word2Vec CBOW model (Mikolov et al., 2013). Interesting future work opportunities could be, for instance, to create word embeddings for all languages and perform a detailed player analysis.

CBOW is chosen for its efficiency in capturing stable representations of domain-specific soccer terminology on a small corpus. Training uses a minimum token frequency of 5, filtering infrequent terms to ensure reliable vector representations while retaining relevant vocabulary. The resulting 300-dimensional embeddings encode semantic and syntactic relationships among players and soccer concepts, enabling downstream tasks like similarity analysis and visualizations.

t-SNE Visualization To explore the spatial structure of player embeddings, we project the 300-dimensional vectors into a two-dimensional space using t-SNE (van der Maaten and Hinton, 2008). Figure 7 illustrates this visualization, with players colored by position as one sample dimension.

Coaches form a distinct cluster (top left), reflecting their unique textual references, while goalkeepers cluster separately (lower-right), indicating distinct roles. Outfield players (defenders, midfielders, forwards) show overlapping distributions, suggesting textual similarity across these positions. Notably, the lower-left region includes players with limited playing time, hinting that the horizontal axis may capture match involvement. While t-SNE reduces complexity and may distort high-dimensional relationships, it reveals positional patterns and role distinctions.

Again, we expect that future work could perform much more detailed analyses on SocCor across various dimensions, e.g., to identify most similar players across countries.

Kroos Case Study A case study of *Toni Kroos*, frequently nicknamed in a negative manner as *Querpass Toni* for his horizontal passing, exemplifies the embeddings' insights. *Kroos*' vector (<KROOS_MIDFIELDER_GER>) has a cosine similarity of 0.86 to *querpass* (sideways pass), ranking him 234th among players for this term. Centerbacks *Faes* (0.96), *Vestergaard* (0.96), and *Christensen* (0.95) show much stronger associations with *querpass*, reflecting defensive passing patterns.

Kroos' embedding aligns more closely with technical passing terms: *steckpass* (one-touch pass, 0.92), *steilpass* (through ball, 0.92), *verlagern* (lateral distribution, 0.92), and *doppelpass* (give-and-go, 0.89). This suggests a versatile passing profile, contrasting with past media narratives emphasizing horizontal passes. The discrepancy highlights the embeddings' ability to uncover nuanced player roles, potentially limited by corpus coverage of stylistic nuances, and underscores their value for analyzing soccer media discourse.

Obviously, SocCor-based embeddings offer ample opportunities to perform person-centric analyses highlighting its value for future research.

5 Conclusion

In this paper, we presented SocCor, a novel dataset containing multimodal-based, multilingual media coverage of the UEFA EURO 2024. With its multilingual content covering audio and text as well as real-time and post-game descriptions, SocCor allows for various types of analysis across multiple dimensions, e.g., cross-language, cross-modality, and time-centric analyses.

By enriching SocCor with normalized player and coach mentions using a tailored, well-performing entity normalization approach, we provide the basis for future sophisticated text data analysis tasks. We exemplified this opportunity by performing and describing several sample analyses such as a player-centric sentiment analysis and SocCor-based player embeddings which can reveal interesting insights as we demonstrated about a sample player.

Limitations

Despite SocCor being a multilingual dataset, it covers only seven languages – and some of them do not cover all media types. Obviously, it would be nice if further languages and more languages across all media types were covered in the dataset. In addition, the data is not equally distributed across all covered languages so that language comparisons should probably be made with subsets of the dataset only. Despite covering multimodal-based sources, SocCor contains only a limited number of different news outlets and broadcasters due to difficulties in accessing additional sources.

Regarding the analysis performed on SocCor, we only present several sample analysis results and many further analyses could be performed. However, we want to emphasize that our sample analyses shall mainly demonstrate the value of SocCor besides providing interesting insights.

Finally, for generating word embeddings more sophisticated methods could be used, and embeddings could be generated on more than one language. However, again, we mainly aim at demonstrating opportunities to perform a variety of analysis tasks on SocCor, and leave more sophisticated approaches for future work.

References

Jacob Devlin, Ming-Wei Chang, Kenton Lee, and Kristina Toutanova. 2019. Bert: Pre-training of deep bidirectional transformers for language understanding. In *Proceedings of the 2019 Conference of the North American Chapter of the Association for Computational Linguistics: Human Language Technologies, Volume 1 (Long and Short Papers)*, pages 4171–4186.

Damir Dizdarevic. 2024. UEFA EURO 2024 - players. `https://www.kaggle.com/datasets/damirdizdarevic/uefa-euro-2024-players`.

FBref. 2024. UEFA Euro 2024 stats. `https://fbref.com/en/comps/676/UEFA-Euro-Stats`.

P. Sol Hart, Sedona Chinn, and Stuart Soroka. 2020. Politicization and polarization in covid-19 news coverage. *Science Communication*, 42(5):679–697.

Matthew Honnibal and Ines Montani. 2023. spaCy: Industrial-strength Natural Language Processing in Python. Version 3.7.2.

Hugging Face. 2020. nlptown/bert-base-multilingual-uncased-sentiment. Accessed: 2025-05-06.

Jan-Christoph Klie, Michael Bugert, Beto Boullosa, Richard Eckart de Castilho, and Iryna Gurevych. 2018. The inception platform: Machine-assisted and knowledge-oriented interactive annotation. In *Proceedings of the 27th International Conference on Computational Linguistics: System Demonstrations*, pages 5–9. Association for Computational Linguistics.

Katharine J. Mach, Raúl Salas Reyes, Brian Pentz, Jennifer Taylor, Clarissa A. Costa, Sandip G. Cruz, Kerronia E. Thomas, James C. Arnott, Rosalind Donald, Kripa Jagannathan, Christine J. Kirchhoff, Laura C. Rosella, and Nicole Klenk. 2021. News media coverage of covid-19 public health and policy information. *Humanities and Social Sciences Communications*, 8(1).

Simon Meier-Vieracker. 2017. Korpora zur Fußballlinguistik – eine mehrsprachige Forschungsressource zur Sprache der Fußballberichterstattung. In *Zeitschrift für germanistische Linguistik*, volume 45, pages 374–381.

Tomas Mikolov, Kai Chen, Greg Corrado, and Jeffrey Dean. 2013. Efficient estimation of word representations in vector space. *Preprint*, arXiv:1301.3781.

Gonzalo Navarro. 2001. A guided tour to approximate string matching. *ACM Computing Surveys (CSUR)*, 33(1):31–88.

Alec Radford, Jong Wook Kim, Tao Xu, Greg Brockman, Christine McLeavey, and Ilya Sutskever. 2023. Robust speech recognition via large-scale weak supervision. In *Proceedings of the 40th International Conference on Machine Learning*, ICML'23, pages 28492 – 28518. JMLR.org.

Thamer Sekhri. 2024. Euro 2024 matches stats. https://www.kaggle.com/datasets/thamersekhri/euro-2024-matches.

StatsBomb. 2024. StatsBomb release free Euro 2024 data. https://statsbomb.com/news/statsbomb-release-free-euro-2024-data/.

Laurens van der Maaten and Geoffrey Hinton. 2008. Visualizing data using t-SNE. *Journal of Machine Learning Research*, 9(86):2579–2605.

Justin Zobel and Philip Dart. 1996. Phonetic string matching: lessons from information retrieval. In *Proceedings of the 19th Annual International ACM SIGIR Conference on Research and Development in Information Retrieval*, SIGIR '96, page 166–172, New York, NY, USA. Association for Computing Machinery.

A Survey of Idiom Datasets for Psycholinguistic and Computational Research

Michael Flor
Educational Testing Service
Princeton, New Jersey, USA
mflor@ets.org

Xinyi Liu
Montclair State University
Montclair, New Jersey, USA
liux2@montclair.edu

Anna Feldman
Montclair State University, Montclair, New Jersey, USA
feldmana@montclair.edu

Abstract

Idioms are figurative expressions whose meanings often cannot be inferred from their individual words, making them difficult to process computationally and posing challenges for human experimental studies. This survey reviews datasets developed in psycholinguistics and computational linguistics for studying idioms, focusing on their content, form, and intended use. Psycholinguistic resources typically contain normed ratings along dimensions such as familiarity, transparency, and compositionality, while computational datasets support tasks like idiomaticity detection/classification, paraphrasing, and cross-lingual modeling. We present trends in annotation practices, coverage, and task framing across 53 datasets. Although recent efforts expanded language coverage and task diversity, there seems to be no relation yet between psycholinguistic and computational research on idioms.

1 Introduction

Idioms are conventional expressions whose meanings cannot be reliably inferred from the meanings of their individual words. Phrases such as *kick the bucket* or *spill the beans* demonstrate how idioms often convey figurative meanings that diverge from literal interpretations. Because of their semantic opacity and syntactic variability, idioms present persistent challenges for natural language processing (NLP) systems.

Recognizing and interpreting idiomatic expressions is essential for a range of NLP applications, including machine translation, dialogue systems, and sentiment analysis. However, automatic idiom processing remains difficult. The same expression can be used literally or figuratively depending on context, and idioms vary in their degree of flexibility, compositionality, and transparency. Addressing these challenges requires high-quality datasets that capture the complexities of idiomatic language in realistic contexts.

Over the past two decades, a number of datasets for idiom processing have been created, often as part of individual research projects. However, these resources are highly heterogeneous: they differ in their annotation schemes, languages covered, idiom types included, and dataset sizes. There is currently no standard benchmark, no unified annotation framework, and limited cross-dataset compatibility, making it difficult to compare methods or advance the field systematically.

This paper surveys the available datasets for idiom analysis and processing. Those come from two different disciplines - psycholinguistics and computational linguistics. We provide an overview of their properties, including language coverage, annotation strategies, intended tasks, and dataset sizes. We highlight the strengths and limitations of existing resources and identify areas where further development is needed to support progress in idiom-aware NLP. A continuously updated list of idiom datasets, with links to datasets and publications, is maintained at `https://github.com/maafiah/IdiomsResearch`.

2 Idiom datasets in psycholinguistic research

In psycholinguistics, research on idioms has been largely focused on the immediate processing of idioms, such as reading time, most notably the comprehension of idioms in (and out of) context. The motivations for specific hypotheses in such research are often related to the linguistically-informed theories or models of idiom processing (Cacciari, 2014; Espinal and Mateu, 2019).

The time-course of idiom processing by human subjects is influenced by a variety of variables, such as idiom familiarity. Controlling for such variables is an important feature of psycholinguistic experiments. Some of those variables are motivated by linguistic theories, other variables are motivated

Proceedings of the 21st Conference on Natural Language Processing (KONVENS), Volume 1: Long and Short Papers, pages 90–100, 2025

by psychological considerations. Norming studies allow researchers to collect subjective individual ratings for a variety of postulated dimensions and aggregate them across respondents (Winter, 2022). Idiom norming studies use Likert scales to rate idiomatic expressions on various dimensions. However, the constructs are not always the same across studies. Table 1 in the appendix lists 16 public datasets dedicated to psycholinguistic aspects of idiomatic expressions. Most of those datasets are publicly available. The aspects/dimensions are described below.

Familiarity of an idiom has been construed as the frequency with which a person has been exposed to a given expression in their everyday life. However, since such frequency cannot be measured objectively, the standard approach is to ask raters for a subjective estimation (*subjective frequency*), explained as 'familiarity'. Several studies demonstrated that familiar idioms are processed faster than less familiar ones (Schweigert, 1986; Schweigert and Moates, 1988).

Knowledge of meaning. A notion related to familiarity is knowledge, the degree to which a person thinks they know the meaning of an idiom, and can explain what the expression means (Li et al., 2016). This also sometimes serves as a control on the adequacy of participant ratings (Pagliai, 2023).

The notion of **literality** (also called literalness or ambiguity) concerns whether the idiom has a plausible literal interpretation. For example, *break the ice* has a literal interpretation, but *shoot the breeze* is semantically anomalous because a breeze is not something that can be shot. Literality is usually measured by asking participants to rate whether the phrase could be used literally in addition to its figurative meaning (Libben and Titone, 2008; Caillies, 2009; Tabossi et al., 2011). While literality could be conceived as a dichotomous variable, it is usually measured on a scale.

Compositionality and **decomposability**. This dimension estimates the degree to which the idiom's component words contribute to its idiomatic interpretation. This is based on the notion that some idioms can be compositionally analyzed (Nunberg et al., 1994). For example, for *spill the beans*, meaning 'reveal secrets', the verb 'spill' corresponds to 'reveal', 'beans' corresponds to 'secrets', showing some composition of the whole figurative meaning. No such composition occurs in e.g. *kick the bucket*, that idiom is not decomposable. Hamblin and Gibbs (1999) suggested that the degree to which the meaning of idiom parts contributes to idiom interpretation can be classified on a continuum, calling it *degree of analyzability*. Experimental studies have found mixed effects of idiom analyzability on processing time (Titone and Libben, 2014; Tabossi et al., 2008).

Transparency is defined as the ease by which the motivation for the structure of an idiomatic expression can be deduced (Nunberg et al., 1994), or how easy it is to recognize why an idiom means what it means. Such motivation can be a metaphorical relation (e.g., the idiom *flip one's lid* might be based on a metaphor that anger is like steam), or a historical remnant (e.g., '*carry coals to Newcastle*'), etc. The reciprocal notion for transparency is *opacity*. Semantic (or conceptual) transparency of idioms is not the same notion as compositionality, but they are related as the ratings are often highly correlated. According to Citron et al. (2016), transparency is a problematic measure since participant ratings are based on intuitions and guesses, and highly dependent on the knowledge of the correct idiomatic meaning.

Age of acquisition (AoA) is the estimated age at which a word (or expression) and its meaning were first learned (Johnston and Barry, 2006). AoA is typically measured in years and months. While AoA for words has been a common measure in psycholinguistics (Morrison et al., 1997), norming AoA estimations for idiomatic expressions was introduced by Tabossi et al. (2011). AoA was found to correlate with knowledge, familiarity, and subjective frequency for idioms (Bonin et al., 2013, 2018; Li et al., 2016). Li et al. (2016) suggested that the earlier an idiom is learned, the more frequently it might be encountered, and thus become more familiar. Bonin et al. (2013) found that AoA was predictive for idiom reading times. Bonin et al. (2018) suggested that AoA norms might be useful for studying idiom processing in children.

Predictability of idioms is defined as the probability of completing an incomplete string to a full idiomatic expression, for example completing *'be in seventh....'* with *'heaven'*. For measuring predictability, participants are asked to read incomplete sentences with idioms and provide the last word of the idiom (that is blanked out).

Syntactic flexibility refers to the notion that idiomatic expressions are often not entirely frozen and allow some degrees of syntactic variability, such as inflection of verbs, insertions of adjective or adverbs, sometimes passivization, etc., (Fraser, 1970; Moon, 1998). As noted by Gibbs and Gonzales (1985), this can have psychological implications. For example, flexible idioms can easily undergo transformations, e.g., for *throw in the towel*, the passive form *the towel was thrown in by him* retains the idiomatic meaning *he gave up*. Less flexible expressions are less likely to be interpreted figuratively, e.g., *the bucket was kicked by him* is less likely to be interpreted as *he died*. For norming studies, idiomatic expressions are presented in various forms and participants are asked to rate their idiomaticity (Tabossi et al., 2011).

The notion of **concreteness** describes the extent to which the meaning of a word refers to a state or event that can be experienced via one or more sensory modalities (Paivio et al., 1968). In experiments, participants process concrete words faster and more accurately than abstract words (the so called *concreteness effect*, Paivio 1991). Two studies collected concreteness ratings for idiomatic phrases, as opposed to concreteness of constituent words (Citron et al., 2016; Morid and Sabourin, 2024). Whether concreteness of idioms might be related to idiom processing or representation is yet unknown.

Imageability refers to the ability to create a mental image of a word. Generally, imageability enhances word recognition (Connell and Lynott, 2012). Imageability is often highly correlated with concreteness. Mental imagery has been linked to idiom comprehension (Gibbs and O'Brien, 1990), and norming imageability of idioms is a new research trend.

In psycholinguistics, three important non-cognitive aspects are known to have influence on representation and meaning of individual words (Osgood et al., 1957; Russell, 2003), known collectively as VAD: **valence** (affective value, sentiment, positiveness–negativeness, or pleasantness of a stimulus), **arousal** (feeling active or passive, or intensity associated with the stimulus), and **dominance** (dominant–submissive, degree of control). VAD norms for individual words are well known in psycholinguistic research (e.g. Warriner et al. 2013), and also in computational linguistics research (Mohammad, 2018). Nunberg et al. (1994) stated that "idioms are typically used to imply a certain evaluation or affective stance toward the things they denote". Peng et al. (2014) used the rated valence of idiom component words for automated detection of idioms in texts. Obtaining valence and arousal ratings of whole idiomatic expressions is a recent trend in norming studies (Gavilán et al., 2021; Morid and Sabourin, 2024).

3 Idiom datasets in computational linguistic research

Computational linguistics research on idioms has produced a wide range of datasets designed for classification, disambiguation, paraphrasing, and multilingual modeling. Unlike psycholinguistic norming studies, which focus on controlled ratings of idiom properties, these resources are typically drawn from real-world corpora and are suited for NLP tasks. Table 2 in the appendix lists the datasets published in computational-linguistics literature. Most of those datasets are publicly available.

3.1 Classification and Disambiguation

A significant portion of computational idiom datasets focus on binary classification – distinguishing idiomatic from literal uses of the same expression in context. The VNC-Tokens dataset (Fazly et al., 2009) includes nearly 3,000 usages of verb-noun combinations in English, annotated as idiomatic or literal. Similarly, the IDIX corpus (Sporleder et al., 2010) collected over 5,800 English sentences labeled for idiomaticity, though it is not publicly available.

Several benchmark datasets have been created in the context of shared tasks. SemEval-2013 Task 5b (Korkontzelos et al., 2013) presents 85 ambiguous idioms with over 4,000 instances, each provided with a five-sentence context for disambiguation. The RU Idioms dataset (Aharodnik et al., 2018) includes 2,420 idiomatic instances and 3,027 literal ones, drawn from Classical and Modern Russian literature and Wikipedia texts. Designed to support supervised classification of idiomaticity in Russian, the corpus provides richly contextualized examples in paragraph-level texts. The MAGPIE dataset (Haagsma et al., 2020) introduced 56,622 instances of potential idioms in short textual context, for 1,756 different English idioms.

3.2 Paraphrase, Sentiment, and Substitution

Beyond disambiguation, idiom paraphrasing has been a central task. Pershina et al. (2015) collected over 2,400 English idioms with associated paraphrases and 1,400 idiom-idiom pairs annotated for mutual paraphrasability. The Idiom Substitution dataset (Liu and Hwa, 2016) offers definitions and plausible substitutions for 172 English idioms, useful for generation tasks. The Parallel Idioms Corpus (Zhou et al., 2021) presented 823 English-language idioms with 5,170 sentence-pairs, where a sentence contains an idiom or its literal paraphrase.

Sentiment-oriented datasets such as IDIOMENT (Williams et al., 2015) and SLIDE (Jochim et al., 2018) capture affective dimensions. IDIOMENT includes 580 idioms with both idiomatic and sentence-level sentiment annotations, while SLIDE contains sentiment scores for over 5,000 idioms. IDEM (Prochnow et al., 2024) has about 9685 sentences with idioms and labels for expressed emotion in each sentence. These resources are especially relevant for tasks like figurative sentiment classification and sentiment-aware generation.

3.3 Multilingual Resources

Recent efforts have addressed the lack of multilingual idiom data. The LIdioms dataset (Moussallem et al., 2018) provides 815 idioms across five languages (English, German, Italian, Portuguese, and Russian) in RDF format, linking semantically equivalent expressions. The IMIL corpus (Agrawal et al., 2018) contains over 2,200 English idioms and their translations in seven Indian languages, annotated across 250K sentences. PETCI (Tang, 2022) includes 4,310 Chinese idioms with 29,936 English translations, capturing diverse translation errors and paraphrase strategies.

SemEval-2022 Task 2 (Tayyar Madabushi et al., 2022) extended idiomaticity detection to three languages – English, Portuguese, and Galician – by providing labeled training and development data for English and Portuguese, and zero-shot test data for Galician. While this marked a step toward multilingual idiom processing, the dataset does not include aligned idiom instances across languages or annotations for contextual factors such as register, familiarity, or cultural variation, limiting its utility for studying pragmatic differences.

IdiomKB (Li et al., 2024b) merged several previously published idiom datasets (for English, Chinese, and Japanese), with the purpose of improving cross-lingual LLM-based translation of texts with idiomatic expressions.

3.4 Model Probing and Representation Learning

Several datasets have been developed to probe and improve language models' handling of idioms. AStitchInLanguageModels (Tayyar Madabushi et al., 2021) comprises naturally occurring sentences containing potentially idiomatic multiword expressions (MWEs) in English and Portuguese, annotated with fine-grained meanings and paraphrases. This dataset supports tasks evaluating models' ability to detect idiom usage and generate effective representations of idiomaticity.

IDIOMEM (Haviv et al., 2023) is a probe dataset of English idioms used to analyze memorization behavior in transformer language models. It facilitates the study of when and how models recall memorized idiomatic sequences. CultureLLM (Li et al., 2024a) focuses on incorporating cultural differences into large language models (LLMs), generating semantically equivalent training data through semantic data augmentation, fine-tuning culture-specific LLMs for nine cultures. Liu et al. (2024) and Khoshtab et al. (2024) use proverbs and idioms to probe LLMs inference in processing figurative language across multiple languages.

3.5 Gaps and Future Directions

While these datasets have enabled significant progress in idiom-aware NLP, several limitations persist. Annotation schemes vary widely across datasets—some mark idiomaticity at the phrase level, others at the sentence level; some provide paraphrases or sentiment labels, others do not. This heterogeneity reflects the diversity of research goals, but it also makes cross-dataset evaluation difficult. Dataset sizes and scopes differ considerably: some focus on depth (many instances per idiom), others on breadth (many idioms with few examples). While multilingual coverage is growing, most datasets do not include semantically aligned idioms across languages or cultural contexts. In addition, idioms are drawn from limited domains, with little attention to genre, register, or discourse variation. Rather than imposing a single standard, future work could benefit from shared metadata conventions, interoperable formats, and more transparent documentation to support comparison, reuse, and integration across datasets. In addition, there seems to be no relation yet between psycholinguistic and computational research on idioms. This is not surprising, as those research domains traditionally had different orientations and research agendas. Notably, datasets from psycholinguistics focus on idioms as 'types', while computational datasets often work with idioms as 'tokens' (instances) in various textual contexts. One area where some cross-pollination between the fields may develop is the notion of valence (sentiment) of idioms. Another possible direction could be using computational methods to model/explain human ratings on various aspects of idioms.

4 Conclusion

This survey compares idioms datasets developed in psycholinguistics and computational linguistics, focusing on their design, intended use, and underlying assumptions. By examining both types, we highlight how methodological differences shape what each dataset can support.

Limitations

While we conducted an extensive search for various research-oriented datasets of idiomatic expressions, some resources might have been missed.

Acknowledgments

This material is partially based upon work supported by the U.S. National Science Foundation under Grant Numbers 2428506 and 2226006.

References

Tosin Adewumi, Roshanak Vadoodi, Aparajita Tripathy, Konstantina Nikolaido, Foteini Liwicki, and Marcus Liwicki. 2022. Potential idiomatic expression (PIE)-English: Corpus for classes of idioms. In *Proceedings of the Thirteenth Language Resources and Evaluation Conference*, pages 689–696, Marseille, France. European Language Resources Association.

Ruchit Agrawal, Vighnesh Chenthil Kumar, Vigneshwaran Muralidharan, and Dipti Sharma. 2018. No more beating about the bush : A step towards idiom handling for Indian language NLP. In *Proceedings of the Eleventh International Conference on Language Resources and Evaluation (LREC 2018)*, Miyazaki, Japan. European Language Resources Association (ELRA).

Katsiaryna Aharodnik, Anna Feldman, and Jing Peng. 2018. Designing a Russian idiom-annotated corpus. In *Proceedings of the Eleventh International Conference on Language Resources and Evaluation (LREC 2018)*, Miyazaki, Japan. European Language Resources Association (ELRA).

Sara D. Beck. 2020. *Native and Non-native Idiom Processing: Same Difference*. Ph.D. thesis, University of Tübingen.

Sara D. Beck and Andrea Weber. 2016. English-German Database of Idiom Norms. University of Tübingen.

Patrick Bonin, Alain Méot, Jean-Michel Boucheix, and Aurélia Bugaiska. 2018. Psycholinguistic norms for 320 fixed expressions (idioms and proverbs) in French. *Quarterly Journal of Experimental Psychology*, 71(5):1057–1069.

Patrick Bonin, Alain Méot, and Aurélia Bugaiska. 2013. Norms and comprehension times for 305 French idiomatic expressions. *Behavior Research Methods*, 45:1259–1271.

Nyssa Z. Bulkes and Darren Tanner. 2017. "Going to town": Large-scale norming and statistical analysis of 870 American English idioms. *Behavior Research Methods*, 49:772–783.

Cristina Cacciari. 2014. Processing multiword idiomatic strings: Many words in one? *The Mental Lexicon*, 9(2):267–293.

Stéphanie Caillies. 2009. Descriptions de 300 expressions idiomatiques: familiarité, connaissance de leur signification, plausibilité littérale, «décomposabilité» et «prédictibilité». *L'Année psychologique*, 109:463–508.

Tuhin Chakrabarty, Arkadiy Saakyan, Debanjan Ghosh, and Smaranda Muresan. 2022. FLUTE: Figurative language understanding through textual explanations. In *Proceedings of the 2022 Conference on Empirical Methods in Natural Language Processing*, pages 7139–7159, Abu Dhabi, United Arab Emirates. Association for Computational Linguistics.

Francesca M. M. Citron, Cristina Cacciari, Michael Kucharski, Luna Beck, Markus Conrad, and Arthur M. Jacobs. 2016. When emotions are expressed figuratively: Psycholinguistic and Affective Norms of 619 Idioms for German (PANIG). *Behavior Research Methods*, 48:91–111.

Louise Connell and Dermot Lynott. 2012. Strength of perceptual experience predicts word processing performance better than concreteness or imageability. *Cognition*, 125(3):452–465.

Paul Cook, Afsaneh Fazly, and Suzanne Stevenson. 2008. The vnc-tokens dataset. In *Proceedings of the LREC Workshop Towards a Shared Task for Multiword Expressions (MWE 2008)*, Marrakech, Morocco.

Silvio Cordeiro, Aline Villavicencio, Marco Idiart, and Carlos Ramisch. 2019. Unsupervised compositionality prediction of nominal compounds. *Computational Linguistics*, 45(1):1–57.

Ricarda Dormeyer and Ingrid Fischer. 1998. Building Lexicons out of a Database for Idioms. In *Proceedings of the First International Conference on Language Resources and Evaluation*, pages 833–838.

M. Teresa Espinal and Jaume Mateu. 2019. Idioms and Phraseology. In *Oxford Research Encyclopedia of Linguistics*. Oxford University Press.

Marzieh Fadaee, Arianna Bisazza, and Christof Monz. 2018. Examining the tip of the iceberg: A data set for idiom translation. In *Proceedings of the Eleventh International Conference on Language Resources and Evaluation (LREC 2018)*, Miyazaki, Japan. European Language Resources Association (ELRA).

Afsaneh Fazly, Paul Cook, and Suzanne Stevenson. 2009. Unsupervised type and token identification of idiomatic expressions. *Computational Linguistics*, 35(1):61–103.

Christiane Fellbaum and Alexander Geyken. 2005. Transforming a Corpus Into a Lexical Resource - the Berlin Idiom Project. *Revue française de linguistique appliquée*, X(2):49–62.

Fraser. 1970. Idioms within a transformational grammar. *Foundation of Language*, 6:22–42.

Marcos Garcia, Tiago Kramer Vieira, Carolina Scarton, Marco Idiart, and Aline Villavicencio. 2021. Probing for idiomaticity in vector space models. In *Proceedings of the 16th Conference of the European Chapter of the Association for Computational Linguistics: Main Volume*, pages 3551–3564, Online. Association for Computational Linguistics.

José M. Gavilán, Juan Haro, José Antonio Hinojosa, Isabel Fraga, and Pilar Ferré. 2021. Psycholinguistic and affective norms for 1,252 Spanish idiomatic expressions. *PLoS ONE*, 16(7).

Raymond W. Gibbs and Gayle P. Gonzales. 1985. Syntactic frozenness in processing and remembering idioms. *Cognition*, 20(3):243–259.

Raymond W. Gibbs and Jennifer E. O'Brien. 1990. Idioms and mental imagery: The metaphorical motivation for idiomatic meaning. *Cognition*, 36(1):35–68.

Begoña Góngora, Andre Gómez-Lombardi, and Alonso Ortega González. 2022. Descriptive Norms for 1,082 Chilean-Spanish Idiomatic Expressions. *Revista signos*, 55(110).

Hessel Haagsma, Johan Bos, and Malvina Nissim. 2020. MAGPIE: A large corpus of potentially idiomatic expressions. In *Proceedings of the Twelfth Language Resources and Evaluation Conference*, pages 279–287, Marseille, France. European Language Resources Association.

Jennifer L. Hamblin and Raymond W. Gibbs. 1999. Why You Can't Kick the Bucket as You Slowly Die: Verbs in Idiom Comprehension. *Journal of Psycholinguistic Research*, 28:25–39.

Chikara Hashimoto and Daisuke Kawahara. 2008. Construction of an idiom corpus and its application to idiom identification based on WSD incorporating idiom-specific features. In *Proceedings of the 2008 Conference on Empirical Methods in Natural Language Processing*, pages 992–1001, Honolulu, Hawaii. Association for Computational Linguistics.

Adi Haviv, Ido Cohen, Jacob Gidron, Roei Schuster, Yoav Goldberg, and Mor Geva. 2023. Understanding transformer memorization recall through idioms. In *Proceedings of the 17th Conference of the European Chapter of the Association for Computational Linguistics*, pages 248–264, Dubrovnik, Croatia. Association for Computational Linguistics.

Ferdy Hubers, Catia Cucchiarini, Helmer Strik, and Ton Dijkstra. 2019. Normative Data of Dutch Idiomatic Expressions: Subjective Judgments You Can Bank on. *Frontiers in Psychology*, 10:1075.

Zhiying Jiang, Boliang Zhang, Lifu Huang, and Heng Ji. 2018. Chengyu cloze test. In *Proceedings of the Thirteenth Workshop on Innovative Use of NLP for Building Educational Applications*, pages 154–158, New Orleans, Louisiana. Association for Computational Linguistics.

Charles Jochim, Francesca Bonin, Roy Bar-Haim, and Noam Slonim. 2018. SLIDE - a sentiment lexicon of common idioms. In *Proceedings of the Eleventh International Conference on Language Resources and Evaluation (LREC 2018)*, Miyazaki, Japan. European Language Resources Association (ELRA).

Robert A. Johnston and Christopher Barry. 2006. Age of acquisition and lexical processing. *Visual Cognition*, 13(7-8):789–845.

Paria Khoshtab, Danial Namazifard, Mostafa Masoudi, Ali Akhgary, Samin Mahdizadeh Sani, and Yadollah Yaghoobzadeh. 2024. Comparative study of multilingual idioms and similes in large language models. *Preprint*, arXiv:2410.16461.

Ioannis Korkontzelos, Torsten Zesch, Fabio Massimo Zanzotto, and Chris Biemann. 2013. SemEval-2013 task 5: Evaluating phrasal semantics. In *Second Joint Conference on Lexical and Computational Semantics (*SEM), Volume 2: Proceedings of the Seventh International Workshop on Semantic Evaluation (SemEval 2013)*, pages 39–47, Atlanta, Georgia, USA. Association for Computational Linguistics.

Murathan Kurfalı, Robert Östling, Johan Sjons, and Mats Wirén. 2020. A multi-word expression dataset for Swedish. In *Proceedings of the Twelfth Language Resources and Evaluation Conference*, pages 4402–4409, Marseille, France. European Language Resources Association.

Anastasia Lada, Philippe Paquier, Ifigenia Dosi, Christina Manouilidou, Simone Sprenger, and Stefanie Keulen. 2024. Four hundred Greek idiomatic expressions: Ratings for subjective frequency, ambiguity, and decomposability. *Behavior Research Methods*, 56:8181–8195.

Cheng Li, Mengzhou Chen, Jindong Wang, Sunayana Sitaram, and Xing Xie. 2024a. CultureLLM: Incorporating Cultural Differences into Large Language Models. *Preprint*, arXiv:2402.10946.

Degao Li, Yu Zhang, and Xiaolu Wang. 2016. Descriptive norms for 350 Chinese idioms with seven syntactic structures. *Behavior Research Methods*, 48:1678–1693.

Shuang Li, Jiangjie Chen, Siyu Yuan, Xinyi Wu, Hao Yang, Shimin Tao, and Yanghua Xiao. 2024b. Translate meanings, not just words: IdiomKB's role in optimizing idiomatic translation with language models. In *Proceedings of the Thirty-Eighth AAAI Conference on Artificial Intelligence and Thirty-Sixth Conference on Innovative Applications of Artificial Intelligence and Fourteenth Symposium on Educational Advances in Artificial Intelligence*, AAAI'24/IAAI'24/EAAI'24. AAAI Press.

Maya R. Libben and Debra A. Titone. 2008. The multi-determined nature of idiom processing. *Memory & Cognition*, 36(6):1103–1123.

Changsheng Liu and Rebecca Hwa. 2016. Phrasal substitution of idiomatic expressions. In *Proceedings of the 2016 Conference of the North American Chapter of the Association for Computational Linguistics: Human Language Technologies*, pages 363–373, San Diego, California. Association for Computational Linguistics.

Chen Liu, Fajri Koto, Timothy Baldwin, and Iryna Gurevych. 2024. Are multilingual LLMs culturally-diverse reasoners? an investigation into multicultural proverbs and sayings. In *Proceedings of the 2024 Conference of the North American Chapter of the Association for Computational Linguistics: Human Language Technologies (Volume 1: Long Papers)*, pages 2016–2039, Mexico City, Mexico. Association for Computational Linguistics.

Saif Mohammad. 2018. Obtaining reliable human ratings of valence, arousal, and dominance for 20,000 English words. In *Proceedings of the 56th Annual Meeting of the Association for Computational Linguistics (Volume 1: Long Papers)*, pages 174–184, Melbourne, Australia. Association for Computational Linguistics.

Rosamund Moon. 1998. *Fixed Expressions and Idioms in English: A Corpus-Based Approach*. Clarendon Press, Oxford.

Mahsa Morid and Laura Sabourin. 2024. Affective and sensory–motor norms for idioms by L1 and L2 English speakers. *Applied Psycholinguistics*, 45(1):138–155.

Catriona M. Morrison, Tameron D. Chappell, and Andrew W. Ellis. 1997. Age of Acquisition Norms for a Large Set of Object Names and Their Relation to Adult Estimates and Other Variables. *The Quarterly Journal of Experimental Psychology Section A*, 50(3):528–559.

Diego Moussallem, Mohamed Ahmed Sherif, Diego Esteves, Marcos Zampieri, and Axel-Cyrille Ngonga Ngomo. 2018. LIdioms: A multilingual linked idioms data set. In *Proceedings of the Eleventh International Conference on Language Resources and Evaluation (LREC 2018)*, Miyazaki, Japan. European Language Resources Association (ELRA).

Emily Nordmann and Antonia A. Jambazova. 2017. Normative data for idiomatic expressions. *Behavior Research Methods*, 49:198–215.

Geoffrey Nunberg, Ivan A. Sag, and Thomas Wasow. 1994. Idioms. *Language*, 70(3):491–538.

Charles E. Osgood, George J. Suci, and Percy H. Tannenbaum. 1957. *The measurement of meaning*. University of Illinois Press.

Irene Pagliai. 2023. Bridging the Gap: Creation of a Lexicon of 150 Pairs of English and Italian Idioms Including Normed Variables for the Exploration of Idiomatic Ambiguity. *Journal of Open Humanities data*, 9(1).

Allan Paivio. 1991. Dual coding theory: Retrospect and current status. *Canadian Journal of Psychology*, 45(3):255–287.

Allan Paivio, John C. Yuille, and Stephen A. Madigan. 1968. Concreteness, imagery, and meaningfulness values for 925 nouns. *Journal of Experimental Psychology*, 76(1):1–25.

Jing Peng, Anna Feldman, and Ekaterina Vylomova. 2014. Classifying idiomatic and literal expressions using topic models and intensity of emotions. In *Proceedings of the 2014 Conference on Empirical Methods in Natural Language Processing (EMNLP)*, pages 2019–2027, Doha, Qatar. Association for Computational Linguistics.

Maria Pershina, Yifan He, and Ralph Grishman. 2015. Idiom paraphrases: Seventh heaven vs cloud nine. In *Proceedings of the First Workshop on Linking Computational Models of Lexical, Sentential and Discourse-level Semantics*, pages 76–82, Lisbon, Portugal. Association for Computational Linguistics.

Alexander Prochnow, Johannes E. Bendler, Caroline Lange, Foivos Ioannis Tzavellos, Bas Marco Göritzer, Marijn ten Thij, and Riza Batista-Navarro. 2024. IDEM: The IDioms with EMotions dataset for emotion recognition. In *Proceedings of the 2024 Joint International Conference on Computational Linguistics, Language Resources and Evaluation (LREC-COLING 2024)*, pages 8569–8579, Torino, Italia. ELRA and ICCL.

Siva Reddy, Diana McCarthy, and Suresh Manandhar. 2011. An empirical study on compositionality in compound nouns. In *Proceedings of 5th International Joint Conference on Natural Language Processing*, pages 210–218, Chiang Mai, Thailand. Asian Federation of Natural Language Processing.

James A. Russell. 2003. Core affect and the psychological construction of emotio. *Psychological Review*, 110(1):145–172.

Prateek Saxena and Soma Paul. 2021. Labelled epie: A dataset for idiom sense disambiguation. In *Text, Speech, and Dialogue*, pages 210–221, Cham. Springer International Publishing.

Wendy A. Schweigert. 1986. The comprehension of familiar and less familiar idioms. *Journal of Psycholinguistic Research*, 15(1):33–45.

Wendy A. Schweigert and Danny R. Moates. 1988. Familiar idiom comprehension. *Journal of Psycholinguistic Research*, 17(4):281–296.

Marco Silvio Giuseppe Senaldi. 2019. *Working both sides of the street: computational and psycholinguistic investigations on idiomatic variability*. Ph.D. thesis, Scuola Normale Superiore, Pisa.

Caroline Sporleder, Linlin Li, Philip Gorinski, and Xaver Koch. 2010. Idioms in context: The IDIX corpus. In *Proceedings of the Seventh International Conference on Language Resources and Evaluation (LREC'10)*, Valletta, Malta. European Language Resources Association (ELRA).

Patrizia Tabossi, Lisa Arduino, and Rachele Fanari. 2011. Descriptive norms for 245 Italian idiomatic expressions. *Behavior Research Methods*, 43:110–123.

Patrizia Tabossi, Rachele Fanari, and Kinou Wolf. 2008. Processing idiomatic expressions: Effects of semantic compositionality. *Journal of Experimental Psychology: Learning, Memory, and Cognition*, 34(2):313–327.

Kenan Tang. 2022. Petci: A parallel english translation dataset of chinese idioms. *Preprint*, arXiv:2202.09509.

Harish Tayyar Madabushi, Edward Gow-Smith, Marcos Garcia, Carolina Scarton, Marco Idiart, and Aline Villavicencio. 2022. SemEval-2022 task 2: Multilingual idiomaticity detection and sentence embedding. In *Proceedings of the 16th International Workshop on Semantic Evaluation (SemEval-2022)*, pages 107–121, Seattle, United States. Association for Computational Linguistics.

Harish Tayyar Madabushi, Edward Gow-Smith, Carolina Scarton, and Aline Villavicencio. 2021. AStitchInLanguageModels: Dataset and methods for the exploration of idiomaticity in pre-trained language models. In *Findings of the Association for Computational Linguistics: EMNLP 2021*, pages 3464–3477, Punta Cana, Dominican Republic. Association for Computational Linguistics.

Simone Tedeschi, Federico Martelli, and Roberto Navigli. 2022. ID10M: Idiom identification in 10 languages. In *Findings of the Association for Computational Linguistics: NAACL 2022*, pages 2715–2726, Seattle, United States. Association for Computational Linguistics.

Debra Titone and Maya Libben. 2014. Time-dependent effects of decomposability, familiarity and literal plausibility on idiom priming: A cross-modal priming investigation. *The Mental Lexicon*, 9(3):473–496.

Lei Wang and Shiwen Yu. 2010. Construction of Chinese idiom knowledge-base and its applications. In *Proceedings of the 2010 Workshop on Multiword Expressions: from Theory to Applications*, pages 11–18, Beijing, China. Coling 2010 Organizing Committee.

Amy Beth Warriner, Victor Kuperman, and Marc Brysbaert. 2013. Norms of valence, arousal, and dominance for 13,915 english lemmas. *Behavior Research Methods*, 45(4):1191–1207.

Lowri Williams, Christian Bannister, Michael Arribas-Ayllon, Alun Preece, and Irena Spasić. 2015. The role of idioms in sentiment analysis. *Expert Systems with Applications*, 42(21):7375–7385.

Bodo Winter. 2022. Managing Semantic Norms for Cognitive Linguistics, Corpus Linguistics, and Lexicon Studies. In Andrea L. Berez-Kroeker, Bradley McDonnell, Eve Koller, and Lauren B. Collister, editors, *The Open Handbook of Linguistic Data Management*, pages 489–497. MIT Press.

Chujie Zheng, Minlie Huang, and Aixin Sun. 2019. ChID: A large-scale Chinese IDiom dataset for cloze test. In *Proceedings of the 57th Annual Meeting of the Association for Computational Linguistics*, pages 778–787, Florence, Italy. Association for Computational Linguistics.

Jianing Zhou, Hongyu Gong, and Suma Bhat. 2021. PIE: A parallel idiomatic expression corpus for idiomatic sentence generation and paraphrasing. In *Proceedings of the 17th Workshop on Multiword Expressions (MWE 2021)*, pages 33–48, Online. Association for Computational Linguistics.

A Appendix

In this appendix we list datasets from psycholinguistic research in Table 1, and datasets from computational linguistics research in Table 2.

Authors	Count	Language	Contents (rating dimensions)	Avail.
Libben and Titone (2008)	210	English	familiarity, meaningfulness, literal plausibility, decomposability	y
Caillies (2009)	300	French	familiarity, knowledge of meaning, literality, compositionality and predictability	y
Tabossi et al. (2011)	245	Italian	knowledge, familiarity, AoA, predictability, syntactic flexibility, compositionality	y
Bonin et al. (2013)	305	French	knowledge, familiarity, subjective and objective frequency, AoA, predictability, literality, compositionality, and length	y
Citron et al. (2016)	619	German	emotional valence, arousal, familiarity, semantic transparency, figurativeness, concreteness	y
Beck and Weber (2016) Beck (2020)	300	German English	meaningfulness, familiarity, literality, decomposability; ratings by L1 and L2 speakers	y
Li et al. (2016)	350	Chinese	knowledge, familiarity, subjective frequency, AoA, predictability, literality, compositionality	y
Bulkes and Tanner (2017)	870	English	familiarity, meaningfulness, literal plausibility, decomposability, predictability	y
Nordmann and Jambazova (2017)	90 100	Bulgarian English	familiarity, compositionality, literality, etc.	y
Bonin et al. (2018)	160+	French	knowledge, predictability, literality, compositionality, subjective and objective frequency, familiarity, AoA, length	y
Hubers et al. (2019)	374	Dutch	frequency of exposure, meaning familiarity, frequency of usage, transparency, imageability	y
Gavilán et al. (2021)	1252	Spanish	familiarity, knowledge, decomposability, literality, predictability, valence, arousal	y
Góngora et al. (2022)	1082	Chilean-Spanish	familiarity, ambiguity, compositionality, transparency	n
Pagliai (2023)	150 150	Italian English	familiarity, literality, decomposability, transparency, objective knowledge, meaningfulness	y
Lada et al. (2024)	400	Greek	subjective frequency, ambiguity, decomposability	y
Morid and Sabourin (2024)	210	English	arousal, valence, concreteness, imageability - from English L1 and L2 speakers	y

Table 1: Published datasets from psycholinguistic research, listed chronologically. The 'Avail.' column indicates dataset availability. 'Count' indicates number of idioms.

Dataset	Authors	Language	Contents	Avail.
Phraseo-Lex	Dormeyer and Fischer (1998)	German	verbal idioms (types), with linguistic annotations	n
Berlin Idiom Project	Fellbaum and Geyken (2005)	German	500 idioms (types) with linguistic annotations	n
VNC-Tokens	Cook et al. (2008) Fazly et al. (2009)	English	53 types, almost 3000 English verb-noun combination instances annotated as to whether they are literal or idiomatic	y
OpenMWE	Hashimoto and Kawahara (2008)	Japanese	146 ambiguous idioms (types), 102846 sentences, annotated literal/idiomatic	y
IDIX	Sporleder et al. (2010)	English	78 idioms (types), 5836 instances annotated as y/n idiomatic	n
CIKB	Wang and Yu (2010)	Chinese	38K idioms (types) with linguistic annotations	n
Reddy et al. 2011	Reddy et al. (2011)	English	90 nominal compounds with compositionality ratings	y
Semeval2013 Task 5b	Korkontzelos et al. (2013)	English	85 ambiguous idioms (types), 4350 instances, each in 5-sentences context, marked y/n idiomatic	y
IDIOMENT	Williams et al. (2015)	English	580 idioms (types) with sentiment ratings; 2521 instances in sentence context, with sentiment ratings	y
Idiom Paraphrases	Pershina et al. (2015)	English	2432 idioms (types) with paraphrases, 1400 pairs of idioms annotated as y/n mutual paraphrases	y
Idiom substitution	Liu and Hwa (2016)	English	172 idioms with definitions and substitution phrases	y
IMIL	Agrawal et al. (2018)		2208 English idioms in English with their translations in seven Indian languages, 250,815 sentences with idioms	y
Idiom Translation DS	Fadaee et al. (2018)	English, German	1500 parallel sentences whose German side contains an idiom, and 1500 parallel sentences whose English side contains an idiom	y
LIdioms	Moussallem et al. (2018)	English +4	815 idioms total, in English, German, Italian, Portuguese, and Russian, with links between idioms across languages (RDF format)	y
RU idioms	Aharodnik et al. (2018)	Russian	5.4K instances of 100 idiomatic expressions (3K literal, 2.4K idiomatic), each in paragraph context.	y
CCT	Jiang et al. (2018)	Chinese	7395 Chengyu form idioms (types) and 100K context sentences	y
SLIDE	Jochim et al. (2018)	English	5000 idioms (types) with sentiment annotations	y
Senaldi 2019	Senaldi (2019)	Italian	90 verb-noun and 24 adjective-noun expressions (types)	y
Composition. of Nominal Compounds	Cordeiro et al. (2019)	English, French, Portuguese	190/180/180 nominal compounds (types), rated for compositionality	y

Table 2: Published datasets from computational linguistics research, listed chronologically. The 'Avail.' column indicates dataset availability. Table continues on the next page.

Dataset	Authors	Language	Contents	Avail.
ChID	Zheng et al. (2019)	Chinese	3848 Chengyu form idioms (types) and 518K context paragraphs with cloze blanks and multiple options	y
Swedish MWEs	Kurfalı et al. (2020)	Swedish	96 Swedish multi-word expressions (types), annotated with degree of compositionality	y
MAGPIE	Haagsma et al. (2020)	English	56622 instances of idioms in short textual context (1756 different types)	y
NCS	Garcia et al. (2021)	English, Portuguese	280 and 180 noun compounds (NCs) in English and Portuguese, with 5620/3600 sentences, marked for compositionality	y
EPIE	Saxena and Paul (2021)	English	21891 static idiom instances in sentence context (359 types) and 3135 formal idiom instances in sentence context (358 types)	y
PIE	Zhou et al. (2021)	English	823 idioms (types) with 5170 sentence-pairs containing those idioms or their literal paraphrases.	y
AStitchIn Language-Models	Tayyar Madabushi et al. (2021)	English Portuguese	223/113 nominal compounds in sentence context (4558/1872 instances), annotated as literal, idiomatic, proper noun, or 'meta usage'	y
Semeval2022 Task 2	Tayyar Madabushi et al. (2022)	English, Portuguese, Galician	5352/2555/776 instances in sentence context, extends the AStitchInLanguageModels dataset	y
PIE-English	Adewumi et al. (2022)	English	20100 samples with almost 1,200 cases of idioms (with their meanings), classified into 10 types of figurative expressions	y
FLUTE	Chakrabarty et al. (2022)	English	Part of larger dataset on figurative language. Has 1000 idiomatic sentences paired with sentences that entail or contradict the focal sentence	y
PETCI	Tang (2022)	Chinese, English	4310 Chinese idioms with 29,936 English translations.	y
ID10M	Tedeschi et al. (2022)	multiple	Training data in 10 languages was autogenerated: 10K idioms (types) 262781 sentences (32% idioms); gold test data: only for English, German, Italian Spanish, 200 sentences each	y
IDIOMEM	Haviv et al. (2023)	English	814 idiom types	y
IDEM	Prochnow et al. (2024)	English	9685 idiom-containing sentences, labelled with emotions	y
CultureLLM	Li et al. (2024a)			y
IdiomKB	Li et al. (2024b)	multiple	A merger of several datasets in English, Chinese and Japanese	y
MAPS	(Liu et al., 2024)	6 languages	proverbs and sayings, in English, German, Russian, Bengali, Chinese, Indonesian (364 to 424 per language); with entailing and non-entailing continuations	y
Multilingual Idioms and Similes in LLMs	Khoshtab et al. (2024)	Persian, English (11 total)	316 instances of idioms in LLM-generated sentence context, with entailing and non-entailing continuations. English translations provided. Also used previous figurative language datasets	y

Table 2: Continued: Published datasets from computational linguistics research.

Function Words as Stable Features for German Opinion Articles Classification

Amelie Schmidt-Colberg[1], Simon Burkard[1], Anne Grohnert[1], Michael John[1]
[1]Fraunhofer Institute for Open Communication Systems (FOKUS)
Correspondence: <firstname>.<lastname>@fokus.fraunhofer.de

Abstract

The paper addresses the challenge of stable classification of neutral news reports and opinion articles under shifts in publisher and domain. We apply experiments using different lexical and grammatical word categories on a hand curated data set of German online news and opinion articles that are labeled in terms of topic and publisher trustworthiness. The findings demonstrate that function words, typically used as stop words, are effective markers for opinion article classification that provide stable predictions under domain shifts and across different publishers. The results can help with the development of suitable feature sets to distinguish between opinion-free news articles and opinion articles, for example as a tool to flag online articles with a high level of subjectivity.

1 Introduction

In the modern information society, it is sometimes difficult for consumers to assess the level of subjectivity of journalistic content. That's why a missing labeling of opinion articles can lead to disinformation (Molina et al., 2021). Analyzing the level of objectivity and subjectivity of a text is therefore a major challenge for reception of news articles. Tools for the automatic classification of online news articles can serve as an essential aid (Alhindi et al., 2020).

Regarding the objectivity of the articles, news pieces can be roughly divided into two types: 1) factual, opinion-neutral news reports and 2) subjectively composed opinion articles. News reports can be either - often short and precisely written - pieces from news agencies that are distributed to many publishers or news stories written by journalists especially for the respective publisher. Opinion articles, on the other hand, subjectively present the author's point of view trying to convince the reader of certain stance (e.g. editorials, columns or guest comments). Since both types of articles (news reports and opinion articles) have different functions (fact presentation vs. persuasion), they also differ in their linguistic form (McCabe and Heilman, 2007).

Related research on the classification between opinion pieces and factually neutral articles usually uses sets of various and complex linguistic features (Krüger et al., 2017). However, these approaches typically show a loss in accuracy when subject to publishers- or topic-related distribution shifts. Beyond the analysis of content words, which obviously are markers for different text types, our assumption is that opinion pieces and factually neutral articles also vary in terms of the sole use of content-independent function words, e.g. prepositions, conjunctions and auxiliary verbs.

We thus hypothesize that using function words as classification features we can achieve stable classification distinguishing neutral news articles from opinion articles with respect to changes in publisher and topic. Specifically, the main research question of this paper is: Can function words effectively be used as markers to distinguish between journalistic text types with high and low level of subjectivity, i.e. opinion articles and news reports?

In this paper, we therefore present the experimental results on the classification of online news articles using features constructed from function words compared to features from common part-of-speech tags like adverbs, adjectives, verbs or nouns. We apply the experiments on a hand curated data set of 600 German online news articles which were labeled regarding the reliability of the publisher (reliable vs. non-reliable), the article type (opinion vs. news report) and whether the article originates from a news agency. Hence, the contributions of our work are two-fold:

- Curation of a German-language dataset of 600 labelled news and opinion articles, from both reliable and unreliable news publishers

- Demonstration that function words can be used as markers to differentiate between factual news reports and opinion pieces, with stable predictions under domain shifts and across different data subsets depending on publisher reliability and news agencies

The results of this work should help to develop a better understanding of how objective and subjective news articles can be distinguished from each other. On this basis, algorithms for the stable recognition of opinions and factual news articles can be developed more effectively, for example as a tool for news consumers to specifically flag articles with a high level of subjectivity.

2 Related Work

Related work to our research task particularly includes other linguistic approaches to classifying news genres as well as related classification approaches primarily based on function words. Also, similar existing German-language news datasets will be briefly mentioned and separated from the dataset we have manually compiled.

2.1 News Genre Classification

As mentioned earlier, one factor that differentiates opinion pieces from more factual news articles is their respective subjectivity level (Krüger et al., 2017; Alhindi et al., 2020). Thus, a common approach for news genre classification has been the sentiment analysis as a sub-task of subjectivity detection. In the context of news genre classification, this has been done on a sentence-level (Wiebe et al., 2004; Yu and Hatzivassiloglou, 2003; Toprak and Gurevych, 2009; Krüger et al., 2017) or on a document-level (Kessler et al., 1997; Freund et al., 2006; Sharoff et al., 2010; Krüger et al., 2017). For sentence-level classification, simple features such as n-grams (Toprak and Gurevych, 2009; Wiebe et al., 2004), TF-IDF constructed from lemma features (Toprak and Gurevych, 2009) or lexicon features (Wilson et al., 2005) were used to train classifiers such as Naive Bayes and support-vector machine (SVM) classifiers.

It was found that unigrams generally outperform more complex n-grams whereas PoS features perform worse than others and word features outperform all other classes (Krüger et al., 2017). In document-level classification, PoS tags (Karlgren and Cutting, 1994), lexical features (Kessler et al., 1997) or n-grams (Freund et al., 2006; Sharoff et al., 2010) were used. Lexical features and PoS tags were found to be robust against topic shifts whereas n-grams were particularity vulnerable (Petrenz and Webber, 2011) (Krüger et al., 2017).

It should be noted, that the subjectivity-level does not fully match to the journalistic categories of news and opinion, where these categories may display an overlap and other genres can display similar subjectivity levels.

More recently, on a document-level, Krüger et al. (2017) extracted 74.000 reports and 2000 opinion pieces from the BLIIP WSJ Datasets (Charniak et al., 2000) and showed that using their linguistic features (derived from sentence- and token-length, negation, punctuation connectives, citations, tenses, modalities, pronouns, PoS-tags and sentiment), news and opinion articles can successfully be classified by a SVM classifier. They used the NLTK Brown Corpus (Bird et al., 2009) to test their model on one unseen publisher and texts from the New York Times Annotated Corpus of the Linguistic Data Consortium (NYT) (Sandhaus, 2008) to test on unseen topics. When confronted with topic-related distribution shifts, their linguistic features outperformed PoS tags and bag-of-lemma approaches.

Alhindi et al. (2020) expanded on this work and used an unspecified model to estimate argumentative features on a sentence level for 1751 news and 1751 opinion articles taken from the WSJ dataset. They used the NYT dataset to create two balanced sets of 2000 articles on two separate topics, defence (NYT-Defence) and medicine (NYT-Medicine) to evaluate model performance on topic-related distribution shifts. They also constructed another balanced dataset containing 7092 articles from multiple US publishers to evaluate model performance under publisher distribution shift. Argumentative features were more robust than linguistic features or BERT embeddings (Devlin et al., 2019) when confronted with topic-related distribution shifts, achieving an f1 score of 90 % and 88 % on NYT-Defense and NYT-Medicine, respectively. Similar results from Blackledge and Atapour-Abarghouei (2021) show, that BERT models trained on either the ISOT dataset (Ahmed et al., 2017) or the Combined corpus dataset (Khan et al., 2021) are not robust when evaluated on previously unseen topics during training.

Building upon the foundational work of Alhindi et al. (2020), Lin et al. (2023) focused on understanding the perception of news consumers. They curated a unique corpus comprising various Dutch media formats, including news articles, TV talk shows, TV news, podcasts, and satire. This corpus consisted of 113,427 sentences extracted from 1,607 distinct items, annotated for factuality and formality by human reviewers. They trained a BERT model for sentence-level classification using this dataset. Their findings revealed distinct patterns in the data: news articles consistently exhibited high levels of formality and factuality. Interestingly, opinion articles from news outlets also demonstrated high formality and notably higher factuality than contributions from other outlets. This trend was likely influenced by including non-news-related outlets in the study, which typically feature less formal and factual content. The research focused on a publisher split to evaluate the model but did not include topic-related splits, leaving the model's performance under topic-related distribution shifts untested.

Although some approaches have proven to be more robust than others when confronted with domain shifts, all experienced a non-negligible performance loss in their reported metrics. This performance loss is difficult to estimate as it varies depending on the topic shift. The topic splits in the reviewed work (Alhindi et al., 2020; Devlin et al., 2019; Krüger et al., 2017) investigated a specific distribution shift, comparing performance between two topic groups; articles during training belonged to one topic group, and articles during testing belonged to a topic group where the topic label definitions were broad. Therefore, the results only partially represent a model's performance under topic shift. Furthermore, none of the works was tested on German online news datasets and, to our knowledge, none of the datasets intentionally included unreliable publishers. Also, the effect of separating news agency articles from news reports was not investigated.

2.2 Text Classification using Function Words

As mentioned, various linguistic feature sets can be used to classify news articles, mostly derived from both content words (e.g. nouns, verbs, adjectives) and function words including prepositions, conjunctions, articles, specific adverbs and auxiliary verbs. Function words are also known as linking words or connectors in the clause structure. They usually fulfill one or more grammatical functions within the sentence. In contrast to content words, the independent lexical meaning of function words is only slightly pronounced. Often, function words are regarded as stop words being removed during pre-processing steps in NLP tasks. However, function words are elementary components of a sentence in written languages by connecting content words with each other and creating the meaningful relationships between them through their syntactic or semantic functions (grammis, 2024a).

Recent work has shown that function word based features can successfully be used for text classification. For example, Halvani et al. (2020) use topic-agnostic features sets derived from function words for effective authorship verification using similarity based clustering. Venglařová and Matlach (2024) show that function words can be used stand-alone to distinguish between different types of texts, e.g. novels, poems and academic articles. The approach of primarily using function words in classification tasks has been less researched. To our knowledge, there is no known work that predominantly examines the use of function words to differentiate between news and opinion articles.

2.3 German News Datasets

The above-mentioned existing works on news genre classification use extensive non-German article datasets, for example the NYT Annotated Corpus or the WSJ Dataset comprising news and opinion pieces of a single publisher.

Unfortunately, German-language data sets of labelled news articles from different publishers are less common. A data set called *One Million Posts Corpus* is based on an extensive collection of articles from a single Austrian daily newspaper (Schabus et al., 2017). This data set categorizes news articles according to rather broad topic categories, but does not explicitly distinguish between opinion and news articles. The project *Deutscher Wortschatz* also provides news corpora from various German-language news portals, but only on the basis of individual sentences and also without the option of separating news reports and opinion items (Goldhahn et al., 2012). Another related data set was created for a news genre classification task as part of the *International Workshop on Semantic Evaluation* (Piskorski et al., 2023). Although this data set contains some labeled news reports and opinion pieces in German, its size is very small and not balanced (27 news and 86 opinion pieces). We therefore have decided to create our own data set.

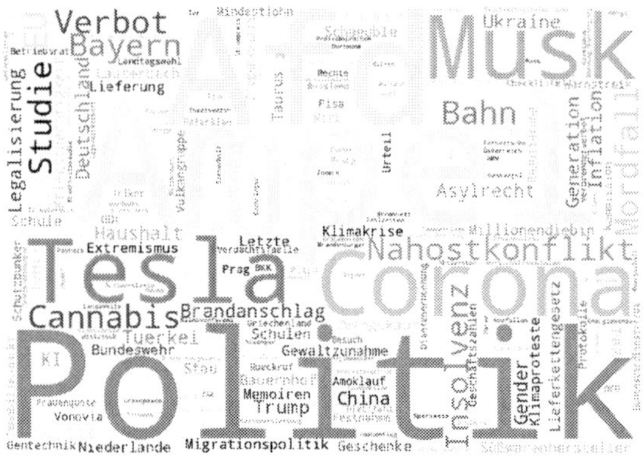

Figure 1: Word cloud representing the frequency of different tags appearing in the topic label keywords

3 Dataset

The hand curated dataset contains 600 articles from different online news platforms published in the period between August 2020 and April 2024. It comprises 300 news reports and 300 opinion articles (see Table 1) collected from 34 different reliable and 14 different non-reliable publishers. Of these publishers, 8 reliable and 8 unreliable publishers published articles labelled as opinions.

The classification into reputable and untrustworthy publishers was based on the NewsGuard rating system, which assesses the reliability of a news outlet on a scale from 0 to 100 (Lühring et al., 2025). Publishers with ratings above 90 were classified as reliable, and publishers below 60 were classified as non-reliable. Publishers without a rating available or with ratings between 60 and 90 were not considered for the data set.

The articles were manually extracted from german online news portals. This ensured that the texts only contained the mere body texts of the articles without other disruptive elements (captions, advertising, other article references).

The following general conditions were taken into account when collecting the articles: as many different publishers as possible were considered within the corpus in a balanced way (balance of publishers). Also, matching counterparts from at least one other reliable or non-reliable publisher were included for the topic of each news report (thematic balance). Opinion articles were initially found by the publisher categorizing the article as a "comment" or "opinion" within their news page structure. They were compiled evenly over different publication periods, ensuring a chronological and, thus, thematic balance.

		Reliable		
		False	True	
Opinion	False	123	177	300
	True	146	154	300
		269	331	600

Table 1: Number of articles in dataset (news and opinion pieces) from reliable and non-reliable publishers

All articles collected were assigned by hand to a specific topic. The high granularity of the 299 assigned different topics in total is illustrated in Figure 1). This implies that the topics diversity in our data set is more refined than in data sets used in related work (Alhindi et al., 2020; Devlin et al., 2019; Krüger et al., 2017). Especially the news reports were labeled in terms of text type (opinion, news report) and publisher trustworthiness (reliable, non-reliable).

For gaining a high annotation quality all news articles were read in their entirety by at least two annotators with scientific background to ensure their informative and opinion-neutral character. Differences in annotation results were discussed. If no agreement could be reached among the annotators regarding classification, the articles were removed from the dataset. In the case of news reports, it has also been flagged whether the news was written by the news platform's own editorial team or whether it represents a news agency report. Usually, this is indicated by the publishers by means of corresponding abbreviations at the beginning or end of the news item.

Although the data set may not be very extensive, it was intentionally designed to be as complex and balanced as possible, in particular with regard to the choice of topics and reliability of publishers, making it as representative as possible.

4 Methodology

4.1 Function Words

The list of German function words was compiled from three sources. Firstly, from the list of function words in the dictionary of connectors of the Leibniz-Institut für Deutsche Sprache (grammis, 2024b). Secondly, from the lemma database of the Digital Dictionary of the German Language (der Wissenschaften, 2024). As a third source we used the function word list from Halvani and Graner (2021) and translated it from English into German. Double entries were deleted. In total, our function word list comprises 4568 context-independent function words. The function word list will also be made publicly available.

4.2 Opinion Classification

We define our problem statement as follows: let $\mathcal{D}$ denote the domain of all news and opinion articles from both reliable and unreliable publishers. The set of topics within these articles is defined as $\mathcal{T} = \{t_1, t_2, \ldots, t_n\}$, where each t_i corresponds to a distinct topic that was identified post-collection, considered its own subdomain $\mathcal{S}_\rangle$ within $\mathcal{D}$. Each subdomain $\mathcal{S}_\rangle$ comprises a collection of articles $\mathcal{A}_\rangle$, such that:

$$\mathcal{A}_i = \{a_{i1}, a_{i2}, \ldots, a_{im}\}$$

where a_{ij} is an individual article labelled either as an opinion or a news article and categorized under the topic t_i after collection. Each article a_{ij} is associated with a label $l_{ij} \in \mathcal{L}$ where $\mathcal{L} = \{opinion, news\}$, and a publisher reliability indicator $r_{ij} \in \mathcal{R}$ where $\mathcal{R} = \{reliable, unreliable\}$. The entire corpus $\mathcal{C}$, consisting of 600 articles, can be defined as:

$$\mathcal{C} = \bigcup_{i=1}^{n} A_i$$

where $|\mathcal{C}| = 600$.

The objective is to train a classifier $f : \mathcal{C} \rightarrow \mathcal{L}$ that predicts the label l_{ij} for any article $a_{ij} \in \mathcal{C}$, based on features extracted from the articles.

To implement our models and preprocessing pipelines, we utilized *sklearn* (Pedregosa et al., 2011) for machine learning algorithms and evaluation metrics, *spacy* (Honnibal et al., 2020) for part-of-speech (PoS) tagging and matching the function words, specifically employing the spacy model pre-trained on the *de_core_news_md*[1] dataset. As preprocessing steps, we removed all contraction apostrophes and transformed all characters to lowercase, for both the input articles and the function word lists. Our features were constructed using the term frequency-inverse document frequency (TF-IDF) method on each article for each word set shown in Table 2.

The word groups represented by the PoS tags can generally be assigned either to the group of function words or to the concept of content words (Haspelmath, 2001). In particular, the word groups of nouns, verbs and adjectives can be considered

[1]de_core_news_md dataset: `https://spacy.io/models/de#de_core_news_md`, last visited 11.08.2025

Feature Type	Description
function_words	Only function words contained in the prepared function-word list
all	All words appearing in the text
all_wo_function	All words except the function words were used to construct the tf
PoS tags	Each PoS Tag was considered as an individual word group

Table 2: Description of Text Features

as content words (lexical features), as they all refer to semantic concepts. On the other hand, function words mainly including the PoS tags of adpositions, auxiliary words, particles or conjunction. Adverbs can be both, content words or function words.

In our experiments we explored various n-gram combinations of the TF-IDF representations, ultimately determining that 1-gram representations yielded the same or better performance as other n-gram combinations. We employed a Support Vector Machine (SVM) as an appropriate, standardized method for classification, regression and outlier detection in high-dimensional feature spaces, which is typical for text classification tasks. Unlike LLMs, SVMs provide explainable, traceable results. We used three different dataset splits to ensure robust evaluation and assess our model's generalisation capabilities: random-, publisher- and topic-split. This approach aimed to test the model's ability to generalise across different publishers and topics. We performed 5-fold cross-validation and used parameter grid search for hyperparameter selection. Since our dataset includes a variety of news sources - encompassing reliable and unreliable news publishers, opinion articles and news agency reports - we investigated the model's performance across these different data subsets. A detailed description of these subsets and our findings is provided in the following sections. For some of these subsets, it was not possible to maintain a balanced class distribution across all folds, so we report a weighted f1 score.

5 Experiments

We trained the SVM classifier on different subsets of the data to investigate for possible confounding effects of publisher reliability and the presence of news agency articles. This is motivated by the following hypothesis: we expect reliable publishers to adhere more to journalistic standards with correctly labelled opinion and news articles; thus, a classifier should be able to differentiate better between these labels. Similarly, we consider news agency articles to be publisher-independent prime examples of neutral opinion-free news reporting, thus expecting that a classifier can better differentiate between such agency articles and opinion pieces. Following from this, we defined three data subsets:

- All Data: All opinion and news articles
- Opinion & Agency News: All opinion pieces and news articles from news agencies
- Opinion & Non-Agency News: All opinion pieces and news articles without agency news

For each dataset we trained a separate classifier on a random-, publisher- and topic split, using TF-IDF features constructed on function words (*function_words*), all words (*all*) and all words except for the function words (*all_wo_function*). We repeated the experiments for both the reliable and unreliable subgroups. Finally, we also trained a separate model on a random-, publisher- and topic split using TF-IDF features derived from distinct word groups associated with their respective PoS tag. Here, we only looked at the dataset containing all articles. For an initial analysis, we performed dimensionality reduction and plotted the class labels. Due to the sparsity of the TF-IDF feature vector constructed from the function words, we used truncated singular value decomposition (SVD).

6 Results

The SVD scatterplot of the articles marked by opinion label (Figure 2a) and publisher reliability (Figure 2b) show that the articles are separable by the former. The SVM classification results for the different word groups (Table 3) show that function word based features are the only word category which remains stable across the different splits. Although the *function_words* perform slighty worse than *all* and *all_wo_function*, this performance difference becomes negligible for the topic splits, with *function_words* performing equivalently well to *all* and outperforming *all_wo_function*. Some other word categories (adpositions, auxilary words, particles, conjunctions), although with overall worse

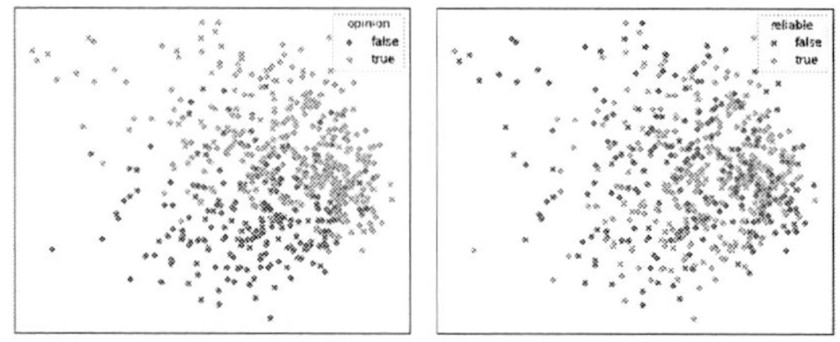

(a) Opinion (b) Publisher reliability

Figure 2: Scatterplot for functions words using TF-IDF features for all articles. Articles form two slightly overlapping clusters when categorized by opinion (a), but are not clearly separable when categorized by publisher reliability (b)

performance, also remain stable across all three splits. Notably, all these word categories have significant overlap with the function word list.

Not only do the *function_words* remain stable across splits, but also display stable behaviour over the different data subsets showing with only minor differences when news agency articles are included or excluded. This is in sharp contrast to the feature types *all* and *all_wo_function* that show significant performance loss when agency news are excluded (Table 4). When considering only reliable or unreliable news publishers, however, some performance difference can be observed with articles from reliable publishers leading to better classification results than articles from unreliable news publishers, with one exception being the *Opinion & Agency News* subset (Table 5 and Figure 3). A full list of all conducted experiments can be found in appendix A (Table 6 and Table A).

7 Discussion

Though functions words are commonly used as stop words, our experiments show that they do contain relevant information in the case of news and opinion classification and can be considered as robust features. Our work reveals that the predictions become more unstable under domain and publisher shifts if function words are excluded, supporting the content-independence of function words and the instability of lexical features (e.g. verbs, nouns, adjectives). The strong variation in classification results, i.e. the dependence on publisher reliability, topic and the inclusion or exclusion of agency news, highlights the importance of incorporating such meta information during dataset collection so that these aspects can be considered during model evaluation. The results therefore support the as-

Word Group	Random		Publisher		Topic	
	Mean	Std	Mean	Std	Mean	Std
function_words	0.88	0.02	0.87	0.02	0.87	0.03
all	0.96	0.03	0.94	0.02	0.88	0.04
all_wo_function	0.95	0.00	0.88	0.12	0.80	0.07
ADJ	0.80	0.03	0.67	0.24	0.62	0.16
ADP	0.73	0.02	0.74	0.04	0.72	0.02
ADV	0.84	0.01	0.76	0.12	0.83	0.04
AUX	0.84	0.02	0.83	0.04	0.83	0.04
NOUN	0.87	0.06	0.66	0.06	0.68	0.05
PART	0.64	0.02	0.61	0.06	0.63	0.06
PRON	0.75	0.03	0.72	0.04	0.71	0.05
CCONJ	0.66	0.05	0.66	0.03	0.65	0.03
SCONJ	0.68	0.03	0.75	0.03	0.68	0.03
VERB	0.89	0.07	0.51	0.07	0.47	0.10

Table 3: Weighted f1 score for SVM-classification using TF-IDF features constructed from different word groups on random-, publisher-, and topic-split. A more complete list of results for all word groups can be found in Appendix A

Data	function_words		all		all_wo_function	
	Mean	Std	Mean	Std	Mean	Std
All Data	0.88	0.02	0.96	0.03	0.95	0.00
Opinion & Agency News	0.88	0.07	0.97	0.01	0.92	0.02
Opinion & Non-Agency News	0.86	0.03	0.73	0.10	0.76	0.19

Table 4: Weighted f1 score for SVM-classification on different data subsets (agency news included and excluded) using three different feature types

sumption that function words do not primarily influence the topic of the article, but rather the function of the text, i.e. in our experiments the opinion-free presentation of facts (news reports) and persuasive argumentation (opinion pieces).

Moreover, it is reasonable that using the semantic subclasses of function words could lead to a better classification of the author's subjective or objective perspective within an article. This is not exclusive for the classification of opinion and news articles, as also indicated by the overlap of the two clusters. It could be concluded from the results that news agency articles are useful in particular for subjectivity level learning as the ability to distinguish between opinion pieces and agency news seems to work slightly better than the differentiability of opinion articles and non-agency news (Table 4). Following the goal to train a subjectivity detection system, it is therefore important to also consider the type and the publisher of the news articles included. Future work would be to identify further markers that differentiate opinion and news articles beyond subjectivity, possibly alleviating the overlap between these two classes.

Also, considering that the classification of opinion and news reports originating from unreliable publishers is more difficult, we conclude that the difference between opinion and news pieces is less pronounced with untrustworthy publishers (see *All Data* in Table 5 as well as Figures 3a and 3b) Assuming that reliable publishers are more likely to adhere to journalistic standards in opinion pieces than non-reliable publishers, this might lead to greater homogeneity and a clearer distinction of the text type. This statement is consistent with (Lin et al., 2023), who observed different levels of formality and factuality in opinion articles depending on the outlet. However, this needs further verification utilizing a larger data set.

8 Conclusion and Outlook

In our work, we conducted experiments on the classification of opinion pieces using different lexical and grammatical word categories on the basis of a hand curated data set of German-language news reports and opinion articles originating from various online news publishers. The results demonstrate that function words (e.g. prepositions, conjunctions, pronouns) can effectively be used as markers to differentiate between opinion-free factual news

Data	All publishers		Reliable		Unreliable	
	Mean	Std	Mean	Std	Mean	Std
All Data	0.88	0.02	0.90	0.03	0.83	0.02
Opinion & Agency News	0.88	0.07	0.85	0.18	0.92	0.04
Opinion & Non-Agency News	0.86	0.03	0.88	0.03	0.81	0.01

Table 5: Weighted f1 score for SVM-classification using function word features on different data subsets (agency news included and excluded & reliable and non-reliable publishers)

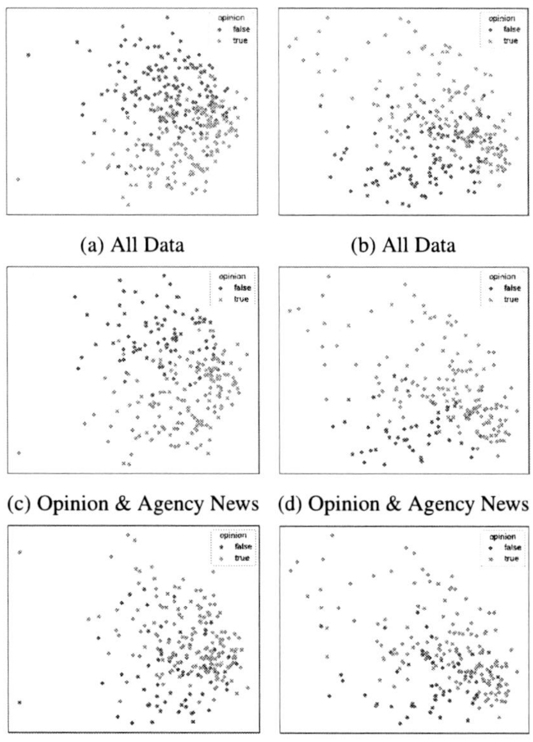

(a) All Data (b) All Data

(c) Opinion & Agency News (d) Opinion & Agency News

(e) Opinion & Non-Agency (f) Opinion & Non-Agency

Reliable Publishers **Unreliable Publishers**

Figure 3: Scatterplot using functions words for TF-IDF features for three data subsets (all data, opinion & agency news and opinion & non-agency news), separated by reliable (left) and non-reliable publishers (right)

reports and opinion pieces, with stable predictions under domain shifts and across different data subsets depending on publisher reliability and type of news report (agency news or non-agency news).

However, it has to be noted that these indications were based on a carefully curated, but rather small data set. For more meaningful results, the data set should be expanded and other data sets should be incorporated. In future work, also the composition of the function word list could be examined in more detail: semantic groups of most relevant functions words could be detected and separated. Also, function words could be combined with other lexical and argumentative features that have been proven to be stable across topic splits. This would probably result in even more stable feature groups.

Further work would also be beneficial with regard to the analysis of topic granularity. Measuring the kind of distribution shift, one could experiment with various types of topic granularity, eventually defining e.g. far- and near-out of domain data sets. Last but not least, current approaches as LLMs should also be taken into account. This work is still pending.

Limitations

Our work is subject to a few limitations: First of all, it has to be noted that the compiled data set is thoroughly compiled but rather small and might still show some bias, e.g. an unbalanced number of publishers and topics in the set of opinion articles in comparison to data set of factual news reports. It would be desirable to expand the data set and conduct experiments again with additional, larger data sets, possibly also in other languages, to obtain more meaningful findings.

With regard to the labeling of topics, an alternative approach would also be feasible. We attempted to simulate topic distribution shifts by labelling the articles according to topic retrospectively. A more causally thorough approach would be to draw the articles directly from the different topic pools provided by the publisher.

The created function word list is fairly extensive. However, it has not fully been checked manually. It is possible that some function words are missing or that the list contains words whose character as function words is debatable.

Eventually, it should be pointed out that - besides our function word based feature sets - we only tested feature sets based on various PoS tags in our experiments. Other established, more complex feature sets, e.g. the linguistic features of Krüger et al. (2017), were not applied to our data set for comparison.

References

Hadeer Ahmed, Issa Traore, and Sherif Saad. 2017. Detection of online fake news using n-gram analysis and machine learning techniques. In *Intelligent, Secure, and Dependable Systems in Distributed and Cloud Environments*, pages 127–138, Cham. Springer International Publishing.

Tariq Alhindi, Smaranda Muresan, and Daniel Preotiuc-Pietro. 2020. Fact vs. Opinion: the Role of Argumentation Features in News Classification. In *Proceedings of the 28th International Conference on Computational Linguistics*, pages 6139–6149, Barcelona, Spain (Online). International Committee on Computational Linguistics.

Steven Bird, Ewan Klein, and Edward Loper. 2009. *Natural language processing with Python: analyzing text with the natural language toolkit.* " O'Reilly Media, Inc.".

Ciara Blackledge and Amir Atapour-Abarghouei. 2021. Transforming fake news: Robust generalisable news classification using transformers. In *2021 IEEE International Conference on Big Data (Big Data)*, pages 3960–3968. IEEE.

Eugene Charniak, Don Blaheta, Niyu Ge, Keith Hall, John Hale, and Mark Johnson. 2000. Bllip 1987-89 wsj corpus release 1. *Linguistic Data Consortium, Philadelphia*, 36.

Berlin-Brandenburgische Akademie der Wissenschaften. 2024. Digitales wörterbuch der deutschen sprache (DWDS).

Jacob Devlin, Ming-Wei Chang, Kenton Lee, and Kristina Toutanova. 2019. BERT: Pre-training of deep bidirectional transformers for language understanding. In *Proceedings of the 2019 Conference of the North American Chapter of the Association for Computational Linguistics: Human Language Technologies, Volume 1 (Long and Short Papers)*, pages 4171–4186, Minneapolis, Minnesota. Association for Computational Linguistics.

L. Freund, C.L.A. Clarke, and E.G. Toms. 2006. Towards genre classification for ir in the workplace. © 2006 ACM. This is an author produced version of a paper subsequently published in Proceedings of the 1st international conference on Information interaction in context. Uploaded in accordance with the publisher's self-archiving policy.

Dirk Goldhahn, Thomas Eckart, and Uwe Quasthoff. 2012. Building large monolingual dictionaries at the Leipzig corpora collection: From 100 to 200 languages. In *Proceedings of the Eighth International Conference on Language Resources and Evaluation (LREC'12)*, pages 759–765, Istanbul, Turkey. European Language Resources Association (ELRA).

Grammatisches Informationssystem grammis. 2024a. Konnektoren als funktionale Klasse. *Leibniz-Institut für Deutsche Sprache: Systematische Grammatik.*

Grammatisches Informationssystem grammis. 2024b. Leibniz-Institut für Deutsche Sprache: Wörterbuch der Konnektoren.

Oren Halvani and Lukas Graner. 2021. POSNoise: An Effective Countermeasure Against Topic Biases in Authorship Analysis. In *Proceedings of the 16th International Conference on Availability, Reliability and Security*, pages 1–12, Vienna Austria. ACM.

Oren Halvani, Lukas Graner, and Roey Regev. 2020. TAVeer: an interpretable topic-agnostic authorship verification method. In *Proceedings of the 15th International Conference on Availability, Reliability and Security*, pages 1–10, Virtual Event Ireland. ACM.

M. Haspelmath. 2001. Word Classes and Parts of Speech. In *International Encyclopedia of the Social & Behavioral Sciences*, pages 16538–16545. Elsevier.

Matthew Honnibal, Ines Montani, Sofie Van Landeghem, and Adriane Boyd. 2020. spaCy: Industrial-strength Natural Language Processing in Python.

Jussi Karlgren and Douglass Cutting. 1994. Recognizing text genres with simple metrics using discriminant analysis. In *COLING 1994 Volume 2: The 15th International Conference on Computational Linguistics*.

Brett Kessler, Geoffrey Nunberg, and Hinrich Schutze. 1997. Automatic detection of text genre. In *35th Annual Meeting of the Association for Computational Linguistics and 8th Conference of the European Chapter of the Association for Computational Linguistics*, pages 32–38, Madrid, Spain. Association for Computational Linguistics.

Junaed Younus Khan, Md. Tawkat Islam Khondaker, Sadia Afroz, Gias Uddin, and Anindya Iqbal. 2021. A benchmark study of machine learning models for online fake news detection. *Machine Learning with Applications*, 4:100032.

K. R. Krüger, A. Lukowiak, J. Sonntag, S. Warzecha, and M. Stede. 2017. Classifying news versus opinions in newspapers: Linguistic features for domain independence. *Natural Language Engineering*, 23(5):687–707.

Zilin Lin, Kasper Welbers, Susan Vermeer, and Damian Trilling. 2023. Beyond Discrete Genres: Mapping News Items onto a Multidimensional Framework of Genre Cues. *Proceedings of the International AAAI Conference on Web and Social Media*, 17:542–553.

Jula Lühring, Hannah Metzler, Ruggero Lazzaroni, Apeksha Shetty, and Jana Lasser. 2025. Best practices for source-based research on misinformation and news trustworthiness using newsguard. *Journal of Quantitative Description: Digital Media*, 5.

Anne McCabe and Karl Heilman. 2007. Textual and interpersonal differences between a news report and an editorial. *Revista Alicantina de Estudios Ingleses*, (20):139.

Maria D. Molina, S. Shyam Sundar, Thai Le, and Dongwon Lee. 2021. “Fake News” Is Not Simply False Information: A Concept Explication and Taxonomy of Online Content. *American Behavioral Scientist*, 65(2):180–212.

F. Pedregosa, G. Varoquaux, A. Gramfort, V. Michel, B. Thirion, O. Grisel, M. Blondel, P. Prettenhofer, R. Weiss, V. Dubourg, J. Vanderplas, A. Passos, D. Cournapeau, M. Brucher, M. Perrot, and E. Duchesnay. 2011. Scikit-learn: Machine learning in Python. *Journal of Machine Learning Research*, 12:2825–2830.

Philipp Petrenz and Bonnie Webber. 2011. Squibs: Stable classification of text genres. *Computational Linguistics*, 37(2):385–393.

Jakub Piskorski, Nicolas Stefanovitch, Giovanni Da San Martino, and Preslav Nakov. 2023. SemEval-2023 task 3: Detecting the category, the framing, and the persuasion techniques in online news in a multilingual setup. In *Proceedings of the 17th International Workshop on Semantic Evaluation (SemEval-2023)*, pages 2343–2361, Toronto, Canada. Association for Computational Linguistics.

Evan Sandhaus. 2008. The new york times annotated corpus. *Linguistic Data Consortium, Philadelphia*, 6(12):e26752.

Dietmar Schabus, Marcin Skowron, and Martin Trapp. 2017. One million posts: A data set of german online discussions. In *Proceedings of the 40th International ACM SIGIR Conference on Research and Development in Information Retrieval (SIGIR)*, pages 1241–1244, Tokyo, Japan.

Serge Sharoff, Zhili Wu, and Katja Markert. 2010. The web library of babel: evaluating genre collections. In *Proceedings of the Seventh International Conference on Language Resources and Evaluation (LREC'10)*, Valletta, Malta. European Language Resources Association (ELRA).

Cigdem Toprak and Iryna Gurevych. 2009. Document level subjectivity classification experiments in deft'09 challenge. *Actes du cinquième DÉfi Fouille de Textes*, page 91.

Klára Venglařová and Vladimír Matlach. 2024. Beyond content: discriminatory power of function words in text type classification. *Digital Scholarship in the Humanities*, page fqae013.

Janyce Wiebe, Theresa Wilson, Rebecca Bruce, Matthew Bell, and Melanie Martin. 2004. Learning Subjective Language. *Computational Linguistics*, 30(3):277–308.

Theresa Wilson, Janyce Wiebe, and Paul Hoffmann. 2005. Recognizing contextual polarity in phrase-level sentiment analysis. In *Proceedings of human language technology conference and conference on empirical methods in natural language processing*, pages 347–354.

Hong Yu and Vasileios Hatzivassiloglou. 2003. Towards answering opinion questions: Separating facts from opinions and identifying the polarity of opinion sentences. In *Proceedings of the 2003 conference on Empirical methods in natural language processing*, pages 129–136.

A Detailed Experimental Results

	Random		Publisher		Topic	
	Mean	Std	Mean	Std	Mean	Std
function_words	0.88	0.02	0.87	0.04	0.87	0.03
all	0.96	0.03	0.94	0.02	0.88	0.04
all_wo_function	0.95	0.00	0.88	0.12	0.80	0.07
ADJ	0.80	0.03	0.67	0.24	0.62	0.16
ADP	0.73	0.02	0.74	0.04	0.72	0.02
ADV	0.84	0.01	0.76	0.12	0.83	0.04
AUX	0.84	0.02	0.83	0.04	0.82	0.05
DET	0.72	0.05	0.66	0.06	0.66	0.04
INTJ	0.36	0.01	0.24	0.07	0.30	0.04
NOUN	0.87	0.06	0.68	0.09	0.66	0.05
NUM	0.63	0.08	0.50	0.15	0.56	0.06
PART	0.64	0.02	0.61	0.06	0.63	0.06
PRON	0.75	0.03	0.72	0.04	0.71	0.05
PROPN	0.82	0.08	0.72	0.11	0.63	0.05
PUNCT	0.82	0.03	0.29	0.09	0.33	0.06
CCONJ	0.66	0.05	0.66	0.03	0.65	0.03
SCONJ	0.68	0.03	0.68	0.03	0.68	0.03
VERB	0.89	0.03	0.75	0.24	0.79	0.07
X	0.57	0.07	0.51	0.07	0.47	0.10

Table 6: Comparison of SVM classification using different PoS word groups to construct TF-IDF features across different dataset splits

	Opinion & News						Opinion & Agency News						Opinion & Non Agency News					
	Random		Publisher		Topic		Random		Publisher		Topic		Random		Publisher		Topic	
	Mean	Std	Mean	Std	Mean	Std	Mean	Std	Mean	Std	Mean	Std	Mean	Std	Mean	Std	Mean	Std
function_words																		
accuracy	0.88	0.02	0.87	0.04	0.87	0.03	0.89	0.06	0.81	0.19	0.91	0.03	0.86	0.03	0.85	0.03	0.84	0.05
precision	0.88	0.05	0.88	0.06	0.84	0.05	0.87	0.07	0.66	0.39	0.89	0.04	0.87	0.04	0.86	0.07	0.83	0.06
recall	0.89	0.07	0.88	0.07	0.92	0.02	0.99	0.01	0.75	0.38	0.99	0.01	0.93	0.03	0.94	0.03	0.96	0.05
f1 weighted	0.88	0.02	0.87	0.04	0.87	0.03	0.88	0.07	0.79	0.25	0.91	0.03	0.86	0.03	0.85	0.04	0.83	0.05
all																		
accuracy	0.96	0.03	0.94	0.02	0.88	0.04	0.97	0.01	0.95	0.03	0.92	0.04	0.72	0.11	0.84	0.13	0.78	0.06
precision	0.96	0.05	0.94	0.02	0.83	0.04	0.96	0.02	0.76	0.38	0.90	0.04	0.72	0.11	0.83	0.13	0.75	0.05
recall	0.96	0.02	0.93	0.05	0.97	0.04	1.00	0.01	0.79	0.40	1.00	0.01	1.00	0.01	0.98	0.02	0.99	0.01
f1 weighted	0.96	0.03	0.94	0.02	0.88	0.04	0.97	0.01	0.96	0.02	0.92	0.04	0.61	0.17	0.81	0.19	0.73	0.10
all_wo_function																		
accuracy	0.95	0.00	0.88	0.13	0.80	0.07	0.92	0.01	0.69	0.35	0.71	0.06	0.81	0.13	0.84	0.13	0.72	0.03
precision	0.95	0.01	0.96	0.03	0.76	0.06	0.91	0.02	0.67	0.35	0.70	0.06	0.80	0.12	0.83	0.14	0.71	0.03
recall	0.94	0.01	0.84	0.17	0.89	0.15	0.98	0.02	0.80	0.40	1.00	0.01	0.99	0.01	0.98	0.01	0.99	0.02
f1 weighted	0.95	0.00	0.88	0.12	0.80	0.07	0.92	0.02	0.65	0.35	0.60	0.10	0.76	0.19	0.81	0.19	0.65	0.07

Table 7: Experimental results of SVM classification using different opinion and news article subsets for different feature sets

LLM-based Classification of Grounding Acts in German

Milena Belosevic* and **Hendrik Buschmeier**†
* German Linguistics, Faculty of Linguistics and Literary Studies,
Bielefeld University, Bielefeld, Germany
†Digital Linguistics Lab, Faculty of Linguistics and Literary Studies,
Bielefeld University, Bielefeld, Germany

Abstract

While the capabilities of Large Language Models (LLMs) to identify and classify grounding acts, such as clarification requests or acknowledgments, have been recently tested for English, there is still little research in this area for other languages. This paper investigates whether LLMs can reliably classify grounding acts in German by creating two balanced datasets of *advancing* and *non-advancing* grounding acts from institutional counseling and classroom conversations. We first apply five-shot instruction tuning with QLoRA to four models trained either only on German (LLäMlein and BübLeLM) or on multilingual data (Teuken-7B and EuroLLM). Since this strategy fails to generalize reliably, we fine-tune the same models using a classifier head, again with QLoRA, which yields substantially better results. All models are trained on the counseling dataset and evaluated both in-domain and on the unseen data from the classroom domain. We compare the classifier fine-tuned LLMs against two BERT-based baselines (GBERT-large and Google RemBERT). Results show that the classifier-head BübLeLM outperforms the best-performing baseline (GBERT-large) in in-domain settings. At the same time, GBERT-large achieves the best across-domain performance, making it the most robust overall model for grounding act classification in German.

1 Introduction

Understanding the communicative intent behind utterances – commonly referred to as Dialogue Act (DA) classification – is a core task in Natural Language Understanding and crucial for building responsive conversational agents (Ahmadvand et al., 2019). While extensively studied in human interactions, DA classification has been less explored in Large Language Model (LLM)-powered systems, especially for languages other than English. One particularly important type of dialogue acts are grounding acts – utterances through which interlocutors manage mutual understanding by providing, requesting, or acknowledging evidence of understanding (Traum and Allen, 1992). Grounding is a collaborative process involving alignment and coordination of cognitive states between participants (Clark and Wilkes-Gibbs, 1986; Clark and Schaefer, 1989). A special type of grounding focused on in this paper is conversational grounding that involves a common understanding of shared knowledge within a conversation (Traum and Allen, 1992; Traum and Hinkelman, 1992). This paper investigates how well German-only LLMs (i.e., those trained only on German data) and multilingual LLMs can classify grounding acts in German, distinguishing between advancing (e.g., acknowledgments, follow-ups) and non-advancing acts (e.g., clarification requests) (Shaikh et al., 2025). We fine-tune the LLMs using instruction tuning and classifier-head approaches across two domains. The models' in-domain and out-of-domain performance is evaluated using macro-F1, accuracy, and confusion matrices. GBERT and Google RemBERT (both BERT-based models) serve as baselines for the classifier-head fine-tuning experiments. Our results show that instruction tuning is ineffective for this task, while classifier-head fine-tuning leads to better performance. LLMs can outperform BERT models in-domain, but GBERT remains the most robust for out-of-domain classification. The paper is structured as follows: After reviewing relevant previous work in Section 2, Section 3 describes dataset construction and splitting as well as human annotation. We outline the methodology, including details about model selection and evaluation, in Section 4. The results of the instruction-tuning experiments are presented in Section 5, while Section 6 describes the results of the classifier-head fine-tuning approach. We discuss and summarize our findings in Section 7.

2 Related work

This section discusses the most recent work on applying LLMs for text classification (see Chae and Davidson 2025 for an overview), specifically the classification of grounding acts in languages other than English.

Prior work has primarily focused on whether LLMs can generate and classify grounding acts in English (Shaikh et al., 2024, 2025; Schneider et al., 2024). Regarding the generation of grounding acts, it has been demonstrated that LLM-powered conversational agents mainly fail to generate appropriate grounding acts (e.g. Shaikh et al. 2024). Prompting (Kuhn et al., 2023; Chen et al., 2023), fine-tuning (Andukuri et al., 2024), or a combination of both methods (Mohapatra et al., 2024b) are used to elicit grounding acts from models. For example, Tack and Piech (2022) and Hicke et al. (2023) simulate model responses in educational settings via fine-tuning to assess the model's grounding behavior. Similarly, Tack and Piech (2022) explore how well state-of-the-art conversational agents, such as Blender and GPT-3, reply to students in educational dialogues. Shaikh et al. (2024) use data from the educational domain, among others, to test whether LLMs can produce grounding acts in a human-like manner.

While these studies are concerned with LLM-based generation of grounding acts in English, we test their capabilities to classify German grounding acts accurately. LLM-based classification of grounding acts in English is based on prompting (Schneider et al., 2024) or on a small amount of human-annotated grounding acts (Jokinen et al., 2024). These grounding acts often serve as a validation set for testing different prompting strategies. Then LLMs are prompted to annotate new data (test set) using the final prompt, which was formed based on a validation set (Shaikh et al., 2024, 2025). In contrast, we compare the performance of fine-tuned LLMs with human annotations of German grounding acts. Additionally, work on LLM-based classifications of grounding acts is based on existing datasets in English (Mohapatra et al., 2024a). We compiled two new datasets of naturally occurring conversations in German from two domains.

As for the effectiveness of LLMs in text classification tasks, Nowacki et al. (2025) propose to modify decoder-style LLMs by adding appropriate layers to improve the classification parameters and build LLM classifiers for discovering mental disorders from texts. The enhanced models are evaluated against encoder-based BERT-based classifiers and standard zero-shot or few-shot LLM approaches. The results demonstrate that the LLMs fine-tuned with a classifier head outperform these baselines, achieving higher F1 scores and providing more precise classifications. In contrast, Fatemi et al. (2025) provide evidence for the effectiveness of instruction fine-tuning and model merging for adapting LLMs to financial text classification tasks in English.

Jadhav et al. (2025) evaluate fine-tuned BERT models and LLMs as annotators for classification tasks in a low-resource language, Marathi, including sentiment analysis, news classification, and hate speech detection. The results revealed that many LLMs still fall significantly short of the baseline performance achieved by BERT-based models and are not yet capable of replacing human annotators.

Plakidis and Rehm (2022) present a German dataset of 600 tweets annotated for speech acts, derived from the GermEval 2019 corpus on offensive language. The authors apply a multi-level annotation scheme – coarse- and fine-grained speech act categories and sentence types – to analyze pragmatic patterns in offensive versus non-offensive tweets. This work demonstrates the potential of pragmatic annotation for improving classification tasks for German data.

More recently, Leitner and Rehm (2025) explore the performance of various LLMs on German text classification tasks across five small and medium-sized datasets, focusing on both prompting and fine-tuning via QLoRA. The study evaluates multilingual and German models, some of which are also used in the present paper on classification tasks with imbalanced data, ranging from speech act labeling to offensive language detection. Results are not reported, but one of the goals is to investigate why experiments failed and how to improve the model's performance.

3 Dataset construction and annotation

3.1 Domains and sources

We focus on two domains, classroom conversations and institutional counseling, to test LLM capabilities to classify grounding acts. Both domains were selected based on the findings from previous studies of LLM capabilities to identify and generate grounding acts in English in educational and counseling domains (Shaikh et al., 2024). Since, to our knowledge, datasets comprising naturally occurring conversations in German with annotated grounding acts do not exist, we compiled new training and evaluation datasets based on publicly available conversation transcripts from these domains[1]. For institutional counseling, we use several datasets listed in Table 3. This table also details the number of conversations and annotated grounding acts from each source. Most conversations and the majority of annotated grounding acts (38.5%) come from the conversations in the German immigration office collected by Herzberger (2013). They are followed by sales conversations from the database of spoken German, the largest database of the German spoken language, specifically from the FOLK subcorpus (The Research and Teaching Corpus of Spoken German), which covers a diverse range of verbal communication in private, institutional, and public settings (Schmidt, 2014). We used conversations from the institutional service encounters (e.g., service encounters in a department store, counseling sessions on student financial aid, and coaching sessions).

In the classroom domain, the majority of transcripts and annotated grounding acts (60%) were extracted from the DIALLS (Dialogue and Argumentation for Literacy Learning in Schools) project dataset (Rapanta et al., 2021), followed by the oral exams at university and classroom conversations from the FOLK database (see Table 4 for details).

For fine-tuning, the dataset was split into 960 training examples (80%), 120 validation examples (10%), and 120 test examples (10%), resulting in a total of 1200 labeled instances. The in-domain data was balanced, with 600 advancing and 600 non-advancing utterances. Additionally, a separate equally balanced out-of-domain evaluation set consisting of 780 utterances (390 advancing and 390 non-advancing) was used to assess generalization to unseen domains (see Table 5 in the Appendix).

To better characterize the grounding phenomena captured in our dataset, we provide several examples from both domains. Each utterance was annotated as either ADVANCING or NON-ADVANCING.

- **Advancing**:
  - Counseling: *Haben wir das Verfahren ruhen lassen? 'Did we stay the proceedings?'*
  - Classroom: *Okay, Gruppenarbeit beendet, wer möchte anfangen? 'Okay, the group work is finished. Who wants to begin?'*
- **Non-Advancing**:
  - Counseling: *Was behandelt belastet Sie am meisten jetzt? 'What is bothering troubling you the most right now?'*
  - Classroom: *Ich wollte sowieso letzte woch nächste woche noch mal reinkommen, wegen eines thesenpapiers. 'I was planning to come by again last week next week anyway, because of a thesis paper.'*

We observed that advancing utterances tended to be longer and more syntactically complex, while non-advancing acts often consisted of shorter or elliptical utterances.

3.2 Annotation procedure

Two linguists manually annotated the counseling and classroom datasets based on the full conversation transcripts, following the typology of grounding acts proposed in prior work on conversational grounding (Clark and Schaefer, 1989; Traum and Allen, 1992; Traum and Hinkelman, 1992). Specifically, we modify the typology of grounding acts used in Shaikh et al. (2025). Shaikh et al. (2025) distinguish between three types of grounding acts: advancing, addressing, and ambiguous. Advancing acts contribute to the progression of the conversation by confirming understanding or elaborating on the prior utterance through acknowledgments (e.g., "Got it"), follow-ups (e.g., "Why do you think that?"), direct answers to questions, opinion expression, or apologizing. In contrast, addressing acts reflect grounding problems expressed by self-repairs, restarts, or reformulations. Ambiguous acts, such as clarification requests, are used to prevent potential misunderstandings. In this paper, we consider both addressing and ambiguous acts as non-advancing grounding acts, since they do not actively move the dialogue forward but instead signal or stem from a breakdown in mutual understanding.

The total number of advancing cases was much higher than the number of annotated non-advancing grounding acts. To generate balanced datasets, the total number of advancing utterances used for training and evaluation was adjusted to the total number of non-advancing grounding acts (600 in the in-domain dataset/counseling and 390 in the out-of-domain/classroom dataset). In cases of disagreement that usually apply to questions such as *Sie*

[1]All datasets, annotation guidelines, and evaluation scripts are available at: https://github.com/milenabelosevic/ClassificationGA.

haben bereits einen deutschen Pass oder? ('You already have a German passport, right?'), a third annotator was consulted, and the final label was determined by majority vote (2 out of 3). The annotation was performed on the sentence level. Short utterances like *yes*, *ok*, *no*, and non-verbal signals (e.g., *mhm*) were excluded *only* when they occurred as isolated turns without surrounding verbal content. If embedded in a meaningful sequence or co-occurring with other verbal acts, such utterances were annotated as usual. Only in some cases more than one sentence was considered (e.g., other-repair: *I was looking for my pass. You mean your child's pass?*). The overall inter-annotator agreement (the IAA for both datasets) was almost perfect (Cohen's $\kappa = 0.844$, $p < 0.001$), with a raw agreement rate of 92.17%. Cohen's κ for the counseling dataset was 0.817 ($p < 0.001$, agreement rate: 90.83%) and for the classroom dataset: 0.885 ($p < 0.001$, agreement rate: 94.23%).

4 Methodology

We focus on monolingual German and multilingual language models to assess how language specialization and cross-lingual training affect models' classification performance.

We evaluate four decoder-only LLMs: two German-only: LLäMlein (Pfister et al., 2024) and BübLeLM (Delobelle et al., 2024), and two multilingual models: EuroLLM-9B (Martins et al., 2024) and Teuken 7B Instruct (Ali et al., 2024). LLäMlein 7B Chat is tuned on chat-style instruction datasets (e.g., Alpaca, Guanaco) to support both instruction following and conversational ability. Teuken Instruct follows a similar approach in a multilingual setting, covering all 24 European Union languages while retaining a decoder-only architecture. EuroLLM-9B is instruction-tuned on 35 languages, with the aim of generalizing across typologically related languages. BübLeLM is a small model trained exclusively on curated German data, such as contemporary web content, legislative documents, news data, and Wikipedia sources.

As baselines, we include GBERT-large (Chan et al., 2020) and Google RemBERT (Chung et al., 2020), two BERT-based encoder models fine-tuned for binary classification. GBERT-large is trained exclusively on German corpora, while RemBERT supports over 110 languages. These models serve as strong reference points for assessing whether instruction-tuned LLMs can match or exceed encoder-based sentence classifiers. Note that we initially attempted to fine-tune XLM-RoBERTa but encountered incompatibilities with 4-bit quantization. Therefore, we substituted it with RemBERT, a QLoRA-compatible multilingual encoder with similar coverage.

While encoder models like GBERT are suitable for classification, decoder and encoder–decoder LLMs were adapted by replacing their language modeling heads with a lightweight classifier trained using QLoRA (Dettmers et al., 2023). This setup enables sentence-level classification by extracting the final hidden state of the last token, aligning with recent work on LLM adaptation for text classification tasks (Nowacki et al., 2025).

All models were fine-tuned on the same balanced dataset (600 advancing acts, 600 non-advancing acts) using identical training parameters (e.g., learningrate = 2×10^{-4}, batchsize = 8, weightdecay = 0.01) unless model-specific adjustments were required. We used the original tokenizer associated with each model checkpoint to ensure compatibility during fine-tuning and evaluation. Each model was trained for up to three epochs, with early stopping based on validation loss trends. Instruction-tuned models were prompted uniformly. Training was conducted on a Google Colab A100 GPU using 4-bit quantization to reduce memory requirements.

Evaluation was conducted on a held-out test set using macro-F1, accuracy, and confusion matrices. Additionally, we used a balanced out-of-domain test set (390 advancing, 390 non-advancing) to evaluate generalization across domains.

5 Instruction tuning

The LLMs were fine-tuned using QLoRA on the same dataset for three epochs. We tested several prompting strategies, including 3-shot prompting and variations in example order. Since only five-shot prompting yielded a noticeable improvement, we adopted it as our final strategy (see the prompt formulation in the Appendix). The examples used in the five-shot prompts were selected from the in-domain (counseling) dataset, as the classroom dataset was reserved for out-of-domain evaluation. LLäMlein showed stable training. Training loss declined from 2.651 to 2.619, while validation loss dropped from 2.662 to 2.635. Although the reduction in loss was consistent, the overall loss values remained relatively high, and no significant divergence between training and validation loss occurred. This suggests that the model was learning from the data without overfitting. However, the model failed to generate valid predictions on the unseen test set during in-domain evaluation. Precision, recall, and F1-scores were 0.00 for both classes, highlighting their inability to follow instruction-tuning prompts effectively. Teuken-7B-Instruct exhibited stable training and moderate convergence. Across three training epochs, the training loss steadily decreased from 0.4572 to 0.3908, indicating effective learning. Validation loss remained relatively stable (ranging from 0.4670 to 0.4744), suggesting that the model generalized reasonably well and did not overfit. However, on the held-out test set, recall and F1 for the advancing class were 1.00, and the model completely failed to identify non-advancing cases, resulting in a precision of 0.50 for advancing and 0.00 for non-advancing grounding acts. BübLeLM-2B showed stable but modest improvements in loss during training: training loss decreased from 0.4664 in epoch 1 to 0.4415 in epoch 3, while validation loss decreased slightly from 0.4996 to 0.4868. During in-domain evaluation on unseen data, it consistently predicted the non-advancing class for all test examples. This resulted in a final accuracy of 0.50 and a macro-averaged F1 score of 0.33, with an F1 of 0.00 and zero recall for the advancing class. EuroLLM-9B-Instruct outperformed other models in recall for advancing (0.82) but still failed on non-advancing predictions, leading to a micro-F1 of 0.46 and macro-F1 of 0.32.

Given that instruction tuning did not yield sufficient classification ability even for in-domain settings, we did not proceed with out-of-domain testing. These findings also support our shift to classifier-head fine-tuning as a more reliable strategy for this task.

6 Classifier-head fine-tuning

We fine-tuned all models for up to three epochs and monitored training and validation loss to assess generalization and convergence. LLäMlein showed consistent improvement, with training loss decreasing from 0.386 to 0.105 and validation loss from 0.394 to 0.356, indicating moderate generalization without signs of overfitting. BübLeLM converged rapidly, with training loss dropping from 0.51 to 0.08 and validation loss stabilizing around 0.38, suggesting effective learning and generalization across both classes.

Teuken-7B reached near-zero training loss, but exhibited a high final validation loss (1.12), indicating overfitting despite strong in-domain accuracy (85.8%). EuroLLM also showed sharp training loss reduction (0.30 to < 0.01), while validation loss decreased gradually from 0.06 to 0.02, suggesting stable convergence and slight generalization.

Among BERT-based baselines, GBERT-large demonstrated decreasing training loss (0.59 to 0.49) but unstable validation loss (ending at 0.675), which indicates a limited generalization. Google RemBERT exhibited modest training and validation loss reductions. However, the relatively high validation loss suggests that the model struggled to clearly separate the two classes, probably due to the limited training data.

6.1 In-domain evaluation

To identify the model that best distinguishes between advancing and non-advancing utterances, we evaluated all models on a balanced held-out test set from the same domain as training data (counseling domain, 60 grounding acts per class). As outlined in Section 4, macro-F1 is used as the primary metric for in-domain evaluation, supported by precision, recall, and confusion matrices to analyze class-specific behavior for in-domain settings.

Baseline models. GBERT served as a strong monolingual baseline. It achieved an accuracy of 88% and a macro-F1 score of 0.88, indicating that the model handled both classes with balanced performance. Performance was well balanced, with F1-scores of 0.87 for non-advancing and 0.89 for advancing grounding acts. These results confirm GBERT's ability to reliably distinguish between both classes, with no major bias toward either. In contrast, the multilingual RemBERT baseline achieved only 56% accuracy and a macro-F1 of 0.55. It showed moderate performance for the non-advancing category (F1: 0.61) and struggled with advancing utterances (F1:0.50), suggesting a bias toward the majority-negative class. This indicates that multilingual pretraining alone is insufficient for robust classification of grounding acts in this domain.

LLMs. Three of the four tested models – Teuken-7B, BübLeLM, and LLäMlein – outperformed both baselines in terms of macro-F1 and class-balanced performance. Specifically, BübLeLM achieved the highest in-domain accuracy (91%) and macro-F1 score (0.91), with perfectly balanced F1-scores of

	Model	Acc.	Macro Prec.	Macro Rec.	Macro F1
1	BübLeLM	0.91	0.91	0.91	**0.91**
2	Teuken-7B	0.90	0.91	0.90	**0.90**
3	GBERT-large (BL)	0.88	0.89	0.88	**0.88**
4	LLäMlein	0.85	0.85	0.85	**0.85**
5	RemBERT (BL)	0.56	0.56	0.56	**0.55**
6	EuroLLM	0.50	0.25	0.50	**0.33**

Table 1: In-domain performance of LLMs and baseline (BL) models, ranked from best to worst based on macro-F1 score. Macro-averaged precision and recall are included to reflect class-balanced performance.

0.91 for both classes. Therefore, it was the most reliable model for binary grounding act classification. Teuken-7B also performed strongly, with a macro-F1 of 0.90 and slightly imbalanced scores for advancing (F1: 0.91) and non-advancing (F1: 0.89) acts. The confusion matrix reveals that both classes were predicted with high precision and recall (for advancing precision = 0.85, recall = 0.97, and for non-advancing precision = 0.96, recall = 0.83). The LLäMlein model achieved an overall accuracy of 85% and a macro-F1 of 0.85. It performed robustly across both classes, with an F1-score of 0.86 for advancing and 0.84 for non-advancing. These results place it just below the GBERT-large baseline (macro-F1: 0.88), but above RemBERT (macro-F1: 0.55). Despite converging during training, EuroLLM showed weak in-domain generalization, achieving only 50% accuracy and a macro-F1 of 0.33. It correctly identified all advancing utterances (recall: 1.00) but failed completely on non-advancing (F1: 0.00). The confusion matrix shows a severe class bias, indicating that the model performed far below both baseline models.

Table 1 presents the in-domain performance of all tested models, ranked by macro-F1 score (our primary evaluation metric for measuring how balanced the model performance was across classes, i.e., class-balanced reliability).

As shown in Table 1, the baseline models were outperformed by three LLMs in the in-domain-performance evaluation. A complete summary of per-class performance for each model is included in Table 6 in the Appendix. It shows a more fine-grained comparison of classification behavior across models.

6.2 Out-of-domain evaluation

To assess the generalization ability of all models, we evaluated their performance on a held-out out-of-domain dataset consisting of 780 labeled grounding acts equally distributed between the advancing and non-advancing classes. Following our methodology, we report accuracy, precision, recall, and macro-F1 scores to measure class-balanced reliability. Confusion matrices were used to examine whether the model was unfairly biased toward predicting one class over the other.

Baseline models. The GBERT-large classifier demonstrated robust out-of-domain performance, achieving an accuracy of 79% and a macro-F1 of 0.79. It performed reliably across both classes, with F1-scores of 0.78 (non-advancing) and 0.79 (advancing class), indicating that the model generalized well over data it was not trained on. In contrast, RemBERT showed weaker generalization, with an accuracy of 56% and macro-F1 of 0.55. Its performance favored non-advancing type (F1: 0.60) over advancing acts (F1: 0.49), suggesting a mild class bias.

LLMs. BübLeLM showed moderate generalization with an accuracy of 66% and a macro-F1 of 0.65. Contrary to its well-balanced in-domain behavior, the model performed slightly better on non-advancing (F1: 0.69) than on advancing grounding acts (F1: 0.62).

LLäMlein also achieved moderate out-of-domain performance, with an accuracy of 65% and macro-F1 of 0.64. It retained high recall for advancing grounding acts (86.4%) but struggled with non-advancing cases (recall = 44.4%), resulting in class imbalance. These results indicate that the model was only partially able to generalize, as it showed a constant bias toward advancing predictions.

Teuken-7B presents a more complex case. While the model achieved F1 for advancing acts (0.64), it completely failed to predict any non-advancing cases (recall = 0.00). This extreme class bias led to a macro-F1 of only 0.32, despite excellent recall for the advancing class. This pattern suggests that the model is unreliable for balanced classification across domains.

EuroLLM failed to generalize effectively. It achieved an accuracy of 49.7% and a macro-F1 of only 0.33. Like in its in-domain performance, the model predicted almost exclusively advancing utterances (advancing recall = 0.99, non-advancing recall = 0.00). These findings confirm the model's persistent class bias.

It can be concluded that only GBERT-large maintained high and balanced classification ability in

	Model	Acc.	Macro Prec.	Macro Rec.	Macro F1
1	GBERT-large (BL)	0.79	0.79	0.79	**0.79**
2	BübLeLM	0.66	0.66	0.66	**0.65**
3	LLäMlein	0.65	0.69	0.65	**0.64**
4	RemBERT (BL)	0.56	0.56	0.56	**0.55**
5	EuroLLM	0.50	0.25	0.50	**0.33**
6	Teuken-7B	0.89	0.45	0.50	**0.32**

Table 2: Out-of-domain performance of LLMs and baseline (BL) models, ranked from best to worst based on macro-F1 score. Macro-averaged precision and recall indicate class-balanced generalization to unseen data.

the out-of-domain setting (see Table 2). While BübLeLM and LLäMlein generalized moderately well, their macro-F1 scores (0.65 and 0.64, respectively) remained below that of GBERT (0.79). Both models showed class-specific weaknesses, favoring either non-advancing or advancing acts, but avoided permanently predicting only one class. By contrast, Teuken-7B and EuroLLM failed to recognize one class altogether, leading to very low macro-F1 scores (0.32 and 0.33, respectively). Despite its overall poor performance, RemBERT still showed a minimal ability to differentiate between the two classes (macro-F1: 0.55).

Note that Macro-F1 was the key criterion for reliable class distinction and not raw accuracy. Therefore, despite high accuracy, Teuken-7B ranks fifth because it failed to predict the non-advancing class entirely. Detailed per-class performance metrics, including precision, recall, and F1-scores for both classes, are reported in Table 7 in the Appendix.

6.3 In-domain error analysis

To better understand the limitations of the evaluated models, we conducted a separate error analysis for both in-domain and out-of-domain settings. This includes an analysis of both advancing and non-advancing classes, with attention to common error types (false positives and false negatives) and systematic class biases.

Baseline models. The two baseline models, GBERT-large and Google RemBERT, exhibited distinct error patterns despite both achieving moderate in-domain performance (see Appendix Table 1. GBERT produced only 14 misclassifications (11.67% error rate), from which 12 errors were false positives – non-advancing utterances incorrectly labeled as advancing. These cases often involved longer utterances. Notably, false negatives (missed advancing utterances) were rare. In contrast, RemBERT showed a stronger imbalance, with 59 total errors, including 43 false negatives that usually occurred in utterances lacking explicit markers of conversational progress.

LLMs. Both qualitative and quantitative error analysis show that among the LLM-based classifiers, performance varied widely. BübLeLM showed the highest robustness, with only 11 out of 120 instances (9.17% error rate). Most of its errors overlapped with disagreements among human annotators. Teuken-7B also demonstrated strong performance, misclassifying twelve examples. LLäMlein showed a higher error rate (15%), with a tendency to overpredict advancing for non-advancing utterances, probably due to their brevity or ambiguity. In contrast, EuroLLM misclassified all 60 non-advancing utterances as advancing, producing a 50% error rate and revealing a huge class prediction bias (see Appendix Table 1.

Overall, these results imply that while multilingual models like RemBERT struggle with subtle classification, classifier-head fine-tuning on German-only LLMs (Teuken-7B and BübLeLM) can yield models that perform competitively with strong baselines like GBERT in domain-specific dialogue classification (for a summary of in-domain errors across all models, see Table 8 in the Appendix).

6.4 Out-of-domain error analysis

In the out-of-domain setting, we examine model errors for both advancing and non-advancing classes, focusing on the distribution of false negatives and false positives. This allows us to assess class-specific weaknesses and whether models exhibit biases when generalizing to unseen domains.

Baseline models. The error analysis of Google RemBERT revealed difficulties in distinguishing between advancing and non-advancing utterances across domains, with a high false negative rate (56%) for advancing utterances and frequent misclassifications of utterances lacking overt markers of advancing acts, such as *yes* or *okay* for acknowledgments. Conversely, the model also misclassified 127 non-advancing utterances as advancing mainly in cases where questions are formally similar to advancing acts but require semantic interpretation to be correctly classified as advancing acts (e.g., *Kannst du bitte deinen Namen wiederholen? 'Can you please repeat your name?'*).

The confusion matrix (see Appendix Figure 2) shows a nearly symmetric distribution of errors produced by GBERT-large, underscoring the advantage of language-specific pretraining: 75 advancing utterances were misclassified as non-advancing, and 90 non-advancing utterances were predicted as advancing. This suggests that GBERT was able to reliably distinguish between both categories and responded well to a domain shift. A qualitative error analysis reveals that many false negatives (advancing acts misclassified as non-advancing) are short utterances (e.g., *Okay, wer möchte anfangen? 'OK, who wants to start?'*) or those comprising ambiguous question tags, such as *right* (e.g., *Vielleicht noch mal vor der mündlichen noch mal vorbeikommen, so dass man dann da bespricht, oder? 'Maybe you could come again before the oral exam so we can discuss everything then, right?'*). On the other hand, false positives, where non-advancing utterances were misclassified as advancing, included cases like *Können Sie die Frage nochmal wiederholen bitte? 'Can you please repeat your question?'* and *Ja, das heißt also ich brauche an den Seminaren nicht extra teilnehmen. 'Okay, you mean I don't need to attend the course again?'*. In these cases, the model incorrectly interpreted redirecting attention to another speaker or an initial short acknowledgment (e.g., "okay") as indicators of advancing acts. These results suggest that GBERT's generalization across domains often relies on formal properties of utterances rather than on recognizing pragmatic cues and context interpretation.

LLMs. Among the four LLMs, BübLeLM demonstrated the most balanced out-of-domain performance, correctly identifying 59% of advancing and 71% of non-advancing utterances. LLäMlein showed a notable bias toward the advancing class, misclassifying 217 out of 390 non-advancing utterances (55.6%). However, the qualitative error analysis shows that both models exhibit similar error patterns, as advancing acts were often misclassified in utterances comprising the teacher's self-repair and question reformulations (e.g.,*Was könnt, möchtet ihr ergänzen? 'What do you want to add? What can you add?'*). EuroLLM and Teuken performed the worst, failing to identify a single non-advancing utterance, thereby misclassifying all instances of the non-advancing class as advancing and generating 100% false positives for those examples. These results show differences between LLMs regarding their ability to generalize the distinction between advancing and non-advancing grounding acts across domains. Compared to the two baseline models, the LLM-based classifiers exhibited more varied error patterns in the out-of-domain setting (see Table 9). Among the LLMs, BübLeLM most closely resembled GBERT in behavior, with moderately balanced predictions across both classes.

These results highlight that both classes pose challenges under domain shift, though models vary in which class they tend to overpredict. While some models overgenerate advancing acts, others show difficulty recognizing non-advancing behaviors such as clarification or self-repair.

7 Discussion and conclusions

To systematically assess the usefulness of various German and multilingual models for binary classification of grounding acts (advancing vs. non-advancing), we conducted fine-tuning experiments using both instruction-tuning and classifier-head training strategies. Four large language models: LLäMlein, Teuken, EuroLLM-Instruct, and BübLeLM, were evaluated alongside two BERT-based baselines.

Instruction tuning vs. classification head. The instruction tuning approach (using five-shot prompts) proved ineffective for binary classification of grounding acts: both LLäMlein and EuroLLM-Instruct failed to predict either class correctly, yielding F1-scores of 0.0 and producing invalid outputs despite prompt familiarity. These results indicate that instruction-tuned generation is unsuitable for tasks that require strict adherence to fixed target labels. In contrast, fine-tuning a classifier head led to successful classification of both classes and substantially improved performance, demonstrating the superiority of this method for the application of LLMs in classification tasks.

The performance of classifier-head fine-tuned models. Among the classifier-head fine-tuned models, GBERT-large demonstrated the most reliable overall performance. While Teuken-7B achieved the highest in-domain accuracy and stability, it failed to generalize to out-of-domain data, entirely neglecting the non-advancing class. In contrast, GBERT-large maintained strong and balanced performance in both in-domain (macro-F1: 0.88) and out-of-domain settings (macro-F1: 0.79), making it the most reliable model under domain shift. Despite minor differences in training dynamics and error rates, GBERT's consistent class-level predictions across domains make it a better candidate for robust binary classification of grounding acts compared to recent German-only and multilingual LLMs. Therefore, a BERT-based classifier can replace expensive fine-tuning of LLMs for the classification task discussed in this paper.

While this paper focused on classifying single utterances as either advancing or non-advancing, a promising direction for future research lies in modifying the granularity of the task. Specifically, models could be trained to assess short multi-turn dialogue segments and determine whether any non-advancing utterances are present. This would require models not only to recognize grounding acts in the context but also to reason over conversational context to detect breakdowns such as hesitation, ambiguity, or misunderstanding. The results of this approach could be beneficial for real-time dialogue monitoring and the development of automated tutoring systems.

8 Limitations

While our study shows that BERT-based models generalize better across domains than LLMs for grounding act classification in German, it is limited by the size and scope of the training data. Our datasets are balanced but relatively small and restricted to two institutional domains (education and counseling). As a result, the generalizability of the findings to broader conversational contexts remains an open question. Additionally, our fine-tuning experiments focus on sentence-level utterance classification, which may oversimplify cases where grounding is context-dependent or extend across multiple turns. Finally, the observed performance advantage of GBERT may not generalize to earlier BERT models, such as German BERT, which were not evaluated in this study and may differ in performance due to older training data and architecture.

9 Ethics statement

All datasets used in this study are derived from publicly available, anonymized transcripts of counseling and classroom dialogues. No private or sensitive personal information is included. Human annotation was performed following a transparent and replicable annotation schema. Our work does not involve any deployment of models in real-world end-user applications. The goal is strictly theoretical: to understand the capabilities of LLMs in classifying grounding acts. We acknowledge that automated classification of communicative intent in institutional settings may carry risks, such as misinterpretation or bias, if applied without oversight.

References

Sara Abiri. 2022. *Beratung in interkultureller Kommunikation*. Ph.D. thesis, Universität Hamburg.

Ali Ahmadvand, Jason Ingyu Choi, and Eugene Agichtein. 2019. Contextual dialogue act classification for open-domain conversational agents. In *Proceedings of the 42nd International ACM SIGIR Conference on Research and Development in Information Retrieval*, SIGIR'19, page 1273–1276, New York, NY, USA. Association for Computing Machinery.

Mehdi Ali, Michael Fromm, Klaudia Thellmann, Jan Ebert, Alexander Arno Weber, Richard Rutmann, Charvi Jain, Max Lübbering, Daniel Steinigen, Johannes Leveling, Katrin Klug, Jasper Schulze Buschhoff, Lena Jurkschat, Hammam Abdelwahab, Benny Jörg Stein, Karl-Heinz Sylla, Pavel Denisov, Nicolo' Brandizzi, Qasid Saleem, Anirban Bhowmick, Lennard Helmer, Chelsea John, Pedro Ortiz Suarez, Malte Ostendorff, Alex Jude, Lalith Manjunath, Samuel Weinbach, Carolin Penke, Oleg Filatov, Shima Asaadi, Fabio Barth, Rafet Sifa, Fabian Küch, Andreas Herten, René Jäkel, Georg Rehm, Stefan Kesselheim, Joachim Köhler, and Nicolas Flores-Herr. 2024. Teuken-7b-base & teuken-7b-instruct: Towards european llms.

Chinmaya Andukuri, Jan-Philipp Fränken, Tobias Gerstenberg, and Noah D. Goodman. 2024. Star-gate: Teaching language models to ask clarifying questions.

Sylvia Bendel. 2007. *Sprachliche Individualität in der Institution. Telefongespräche in der Bank und ihre individuelle Gestaltung*. Francke, Tübingen.

Wolfgang Boettcher, Anika Limburg, Dorothee Meer, and Vera Zegers. 2005. *„ich komm (0) weil ich wohl etwas das thema meiner hausarbeit etwas verfehlt habe," – Sprechstundengespräche an der Hochschule. Ein Transkriptband*. Verlag für Gesprächsforschung.

Ines Bose, Katja Bößhenz, Judith Pietschmann, and Ingmar Rothe. 2012. „°hh hh° also von kundenfreundlich halt ich da nicht viel bei ihnen;" – Analyse und optimierung von Callcenterkommunikation am Beispiel von telefonischen Reklamationsgesprächen. *Gesprächsforschung - Online-Zeitschrift zur verbalen Interaktion*, 12:143–195.

Evald Johannes Brunner. 1996. *Grundfragen der Familientherapie: Systemische Theorie und Methodologie*. Springer, Berlin.

Gisela Brünner. 2000. *Wirtschaftskommunikation: Linguistische Analyse ihrer mündlichen Formen*. Niemeyer, Berlin.

Youngjin Chae and Thomas Davidson. 2025. Large language models for text classification: From zero-shot learning to instruction-tuning. *Sociol. Methods Res.*

Branden Chan, Stefan Schweter, and Timo Möller. 2020. German's next language model. In *Proceedings of the 28th International Conference on Computational Linguistics*, pages 6788–6796, Barcelona, Spain (Online). International Committee on Computational Linguistics.

Maximillian Chen, Xiao Yu, Weiyan Shi, Urvi Awasthi, and Zhou Yu. 2023. Controllable mixed-initiative dialogue generation through prompting. In *Proceedings of the 61st Annual Meeting of the Association for Computational Linguistics (Volume 2: Short Papers)*, Toronto, Canada. Association for Computational Linguistics.

Hyung Won Chung, Thibault Févry, Henry Tsai, Melvin Johnson, and Sebastian Ruder. 2020. Rethinking embedding coupling in pre-trained language models.

Herbert H Clark and Edward F Schaefer. 1989. Contributing to discourse. *Cogn. Sci.*, 13(2):259–294.

Herbert H. Clark and Deanna Wilkes-Gibbs. 1986. Referring as a collaborative process. *Cognition*, 22(1):1–39.

Pieter Delobelle, Alan Akbik, et al. 2024. BübleLM: A small German LM.

Tim Dettmers, Artidoro Pagnoni, Ari Holtzman, and Luke Zettlemoyer. 2023. QLORA: Efficient finetuning of quantized LLMs. *Advances in neural information processing systems*, 36:10088–10115.

Sorouralsadat Fatemi, Yuheng Hu, and Maryam Mousavi. 2025. A comparative analysis of instruction fine-tuning large language models for financial text classification. *ACM Trans. Manage. Inf. Syst.*, 16(1).

Jennifer Hartog. 1996. *Das genetische Beratungsgespräch. Institutionalisierte Kommunikation zwischen Experten und Nicht-Experten*. Narr, Tübingen.

Gesine Herzberger. 2013. *Das sprachliche und kommunikative Verhalten von Behördenmitarbeitern – Agenten-Klienten-Gespräche in einer Ausländerbehörde*. Ph.D. thesis, Univ. Würzburg.

Yann Hicke, Abhishek Masand, Wentao Guo, and Tushaar Gangavarapu. 2023. Assessing the efficacy of large language models in generating accurate teacher responses. In *Proceedings of the 18th Workshop on Innovative Use of NLP for Building Educational Applications (BEA 2023)*, pages 745–755, Toronto, Canada. Association for Computational Linguistics.

Suramya Jadhav, Abhay Shanbhag, Amogh Thakurdesai, Ridhima Sinare, and Raviraj Joshi. 2025. On limitations of LLM as annotator for low resource languages.

Kristiina Jokinen, Phillip Schneider, and Taiga Mori. 2024. Towards harnessing large language models for comprehension of conversational grounding.

Katharina König. 2016. Fragen in universitären sprechstundengesprächen: Gesprächsanalyse und authentisches gesprochenes Deutsch im DaF-Unterricht. *Informationen Deutsch als Fremdsprache*, 43(1):55–88.

Lorenz Kuhn, Yarin Gal, and Sebastian Farquhar. 2023. CLAM: Selective clarification for ambiguous questions with generative language models.

Elena Leitner and Georg Rehm. 2025. Exploring the limits of LLMs in German text classification: Prompting and fine-tuning strategies across small and medium-sized datasets. Presented at the LLM-Fails Workshop, IDS Mannheim. Accessed: 2025-04-26.

Petra Löning and Jochen Rehbein. 1993. *Arzt-Patienten-Kommunikation: Analysen zu interdisziplinären Problemen des medizinischen Diskurses*. De Gruyter, Berlin.

Pedro Henrique Martins, Patrick Fernandes, João Alves, Nuno M. Guerreiro, Ricardo Rei, Duarte M. Alves, José Pombal, Amin Farajian, Manuel Faysse, Mateusz Klimaszewski, Pierre Colombo, Barry Haddow, José G. C. de Souza, Alexandra Birch, and André F. T. Martins. 2024. EuroLLM: Multilingual language models for Europe.

Biswesh Mohapatra, Seemab Hassan, Laurent Romary, and Justine Cassell. 2024a. Conversational grounding: Annotation and analysis of grounding acts and grounding units. In *Proceedings of the 2024 Joint International Conference on Computational Linguistics, Language Resources and Evaluation (LREC-COLING 2024)*, pages 3967–3977, Torino, Italia. ELRA and ICCL.

Biswesh Mohapatra, Manav Nitin Kapadnis, Laurent Romary, and Justine Cassell. 2024b. Evaluating the effectiveness of large language models in establishing conversational grounding. In *Proceedings of the 2024 Conference on Empirical Methods in Natural Language Processing*, pages 9767–9781, Miami, Florida, USA. Association for Computational Linguistics.

Arkadiusz Nowacki, Wojciech Sitek, and Henryk Rybiński. 2025. LLM-based classifiers for discovering mental disorders. *J. Intell. Inf. Syst.*

Jan Pfister, Julia Wunderle, and Andreas Hotho. 2024. LläMmlein: Compact and competitive German-only language models from scratch.

Melina Plakidis and Georg Rehm. 2022. A dataset of offensive German language tweets annotated for speech acts. In *Proceedings of the Thirteenth Language Resources and Evaluation Conference*, pages 4799–4807, Marseille, France. European Language Resources Association.

Chrysi Rapanta, Cláudia Gonçalves, João Rui Pereira, Dilar Cascalheira, Beatriz Gil, Rita Morais, Anna Čermáková, Julia Peck, Benjamin Brummernhenrich, Regina Jucks, Mercè Garcia-Milà, Andrea Miralda-Banda, José Luna, Maria Vrikki, Maria Evagorou, and Fabrizio Macagno. 2021. Multicultural classroom discourse dataset on teachers' and students' dialogic empathy. *Data Brief*, 39(107518):107518.

Thomas Schmidt. 2014. The research and teaching corpus of spoken German — FOLK. In *Proceedings of the Ninth International Conference on Language Resources and Evaluation (LREC'14)*, pages 383–387, Reykjavik, Iceland. European Language Resources Association (ELRA).

Phillip Schneider, Nektarios Machner, Kristiina Jokinen, and Florian Matthes. 2024. Bridging information gaps in dialogues with grounded exchanges using knowledge graphs. In *Proceedings of the 25th Annual Meeting of the Special Interest Group on Discourse and Dialogue*, pages 110–120, Kyoto, Japan. Association for Computational Linguistics.

Peter Schröder. 1985. *Beratungsgespräche. Ein kommentierter Textband*. Narr, Tübingen.

Thomas Schubert. 2003. *Wissenstransfer im telefonischen Beratungsgespräch*. Ph.D. thesis, Martin-Luther-Universität Halle-Wittenberg.

Omar Shaikh, Kristina Gligoric, Ashna Khetan, Matthias Gerstgrasser, Diyi Yang, and Dan Jurafsky. 2024. Grounding gaps in language model generations. In *Proceedings of the 2024 Conference of the North American Chapter of the Association for Computational Linguistics: Human Language Technologies (Volume 1: Long Papers)*, pages 6279–6296, Mexico City, Mexico. Association for Computational Linguistics.

Omar Shaikh, Hussein Mozannar, Gagan Bansal, Adam Fourney, and Eric Horvitz. 2025. Navigating rifts in human-LLM grounding: Study and benchmark. In *Proceedings of the 63rd Annual Meeting of the Association for Computational Linguistics (Volume 1: Long Papers)*, pages 20832–20847, Vienna, Austria. Association for Computational Linguistics.

Anaïs Tack and Chris Piech. 2022. The AI teacher test: Measuring the pedagogical ability of blender and GPT-3 in educational dialogues.

David R. Traum and James F. Allen. 1992. A speech-act approach to grounding in conversation. In *Proceedings of the Second International Conference on Spoken Language Processing (ICSLP)*, volume 2, pages 137–140, Banff, Canada. University of Alberta.

David R Traum and Elizabeth A Hinkelman. 1992. Conversation acts in task-oriented spoken dialogue. *Comput. Intell.*, 8(3):575–599.

A Appendix

Five-shot prompt used for instruction tuning (translated from German)

German original:
Anweisung: Deine Aufgabe ist es zu entscheiden, ob die folgende Äußerung das Gespräch voranbringt (Label: ADVANCING) oder nicht (Label: NON-ADVANCING). Du musst immer ausschließlich mit ADVANCING oder NON-ADVANCING antworten – keine weiteren Textelemente.

Beispiel 1:
Äußerung: Darf ich Sie bitten, ein Foto mitzubringen?
Label: ADVANCING

Beispiel 2:
Äußerung: Ich werde es, ähm, also ich nehme es mit.
Label: NON-ADVANCING

Beispiel 3:
Äußerung: Das ist ein kl... kleines Blatt Papier.
Label: NON-ADVANCING

Beispiel 4:
Äußerung: Ja, da muss ich noch nachfragen.
Label: ADVANCING

Beispiel 5:
Äußerung: Sie möchten Ihr Visum erneuern, also zum Beispiel den Pass...
Label: NON-ADVANCING

English translation:
Instruction: Your task is to decide whether the following sentence moves the conversation forward (Label: ADVANCING) or not (Label: NON-ADVANCING). You must always respond with ADVANCING or NON-ADVANCING only—no other text.

Example 1:
Sentence: May I ask you to bring a photo?
Label: ADVANCING

Example 2:
Sentence: I will put it I mean take it with me.
Label: NON-ADVANCING

Example 3:
Sentence: This is a sm... small piece of paper.
Label: NON-ADVANCING

Example 4:
Sentence: Yes, I have to ask about it.
Label: ADVANCING

Example 5:
Sentence: You want to renew your visum e.g., your passport..
Label: NON-ADVANCING

Topic	Transcripts	GA	Reference
German immigration office	92	462	Herzberger 2013
academic, psychological, legal, building society, private, counseling for the homeless	9	131	Schröder 1985
telephone conversations at the bank	20	104	Bendel 2007
call-center conversations	1	8	Bose et al. 2012
sales and complaint conversations, customer service calls, negotiations, meetings	6	11	Brünner 2000
family therapy sessions	1	37	Brunner 1996
genetic counseling conversations	1	6	Hartog 1996
conversation with a breast cancer patient	1	6	Löning and Rehbein 1993
telephone counseling sessions about home financing	12	138	Schubert 2003
counseling in the refugee center	2	42	Abiri 2022
FOLK database of spoken German, sales advisory service	39	255	DGD database

Table 3: Overview of primary sources used to compile the counseling dataset with the number of used transcripts, the number of annotated grounding acts (GA), and references for each source.

Topic	Transcripts	GA	Reference
Multilingual Corpus of the DIALLS (Dialogue and Argumentation for Literacy Learning in Schools) dataset	28	467	Rapanta et al. 2021
Office hour conversations at the university	23	117	Boettcher et al. 2005
Office hour conversations at the university	1	20	König 2016
FOLK database of spoken German, classroom conversations	22	176	DGD database

Table 4: Overview of primary sources used to compile the classroom dataset with the number of used transcripts, the number of annotated grounding acts (GA), and references for each source.

Split	Count	Proportion
Training	960	80%
Validation	120	10%
Test	120	10%
In-domain advancing	600	—
In-domain non-advancing	600	—
In-domain total	**1200**	**100%**
OOD eval (advancing)	390	—
OOD eval (non-advancing)	390	—
OOD total	**780**	—

Table 5: Data splits and class distributions used for fine-tuning and out-of-domain evaluation.

	Advancing			Non-Advancing		
Model	F1	Precision	Recall	F1	Precision	nonRecall
BübLeLM	0.91	0.93	0.88	0.91	0.89	0.93
Teuken-7B	0.91	0.85	0.97	0.89	0.96	0.83
GBERT-large	0.89	0.83	0.97	0.87	0.96	0.80
LLäMlein	0.86	0.82	0.90	0.84	0.89	0.80
RemBERT	0.50	0.58	0.43	0.61	0.55	0.68
EuroLLM	0.67	0.50	1.00	0.00	0.00	0.00

Table 6: Per-class evaluation metrics for all models on the in-domain test set. Values reflect each model's ability to distinguish both classes reliably.

Model	Advancing			Non-Advancing		
	F1	Precision	Recall	F1	Precision	nonRecall
GBERT-large	0.79	0.78	0.81	0.78	0.80	0.77
BübLeLM	0.62	0.69	0.56	0.69	0.63	0.75
LLäMlein	0.71	0.61	0.86	0.56	0.77	0.44
RemBERT	0.49	0.57	0.44	0.60	0.54	0.67
Teuken-7B	0.64	0.50	0.89	0.00	0.00	0.00
EuroLLM	0.66	0.50	0.99	0.00	0.00	0.00

Table 7: Per-class evaluation metrics for all models on the out-of-domain test set. Values reflect each model's ability to distinguish both classes in unseen domains.

Model (Ranked Best to Worst)	Misclassified Examples (out of 120)	Error Rate (%)
BübLeLM	11	9.17
Teuken-7B	12	10
GBERT-large	14	11.67
LLäMlein	18	15.00
EuroLLM	60	50.00

Table 8: In-domain classification error rates for all models on the held-out test set (120 utterances), ranked from best to worst. Lower values indicate better classification reliability.

Model	FN: ADV → NON	FP: NON → ADV	Class Bias
GBERT	75 (19.2%)	90 (23.1%)	Low
BübLeLM	159 (40.8%)	112 (28.7%)	Moderate
LLäMlein	53 (13.6%)	217 (55.6%)	High ADV bias
RemBERT	221 (56.7%)	127 (32.6%)	Mild NON bias
EuroLLM	0	390 (100%)	Extreme ADV bias
Teuken	0	390 (100%)	Extreme ADV bias

Table 9: Out-of-domain misclassification patterns: false negatives (FN), false positives (FP), and class prediction bias. Ordered from best to worst model.

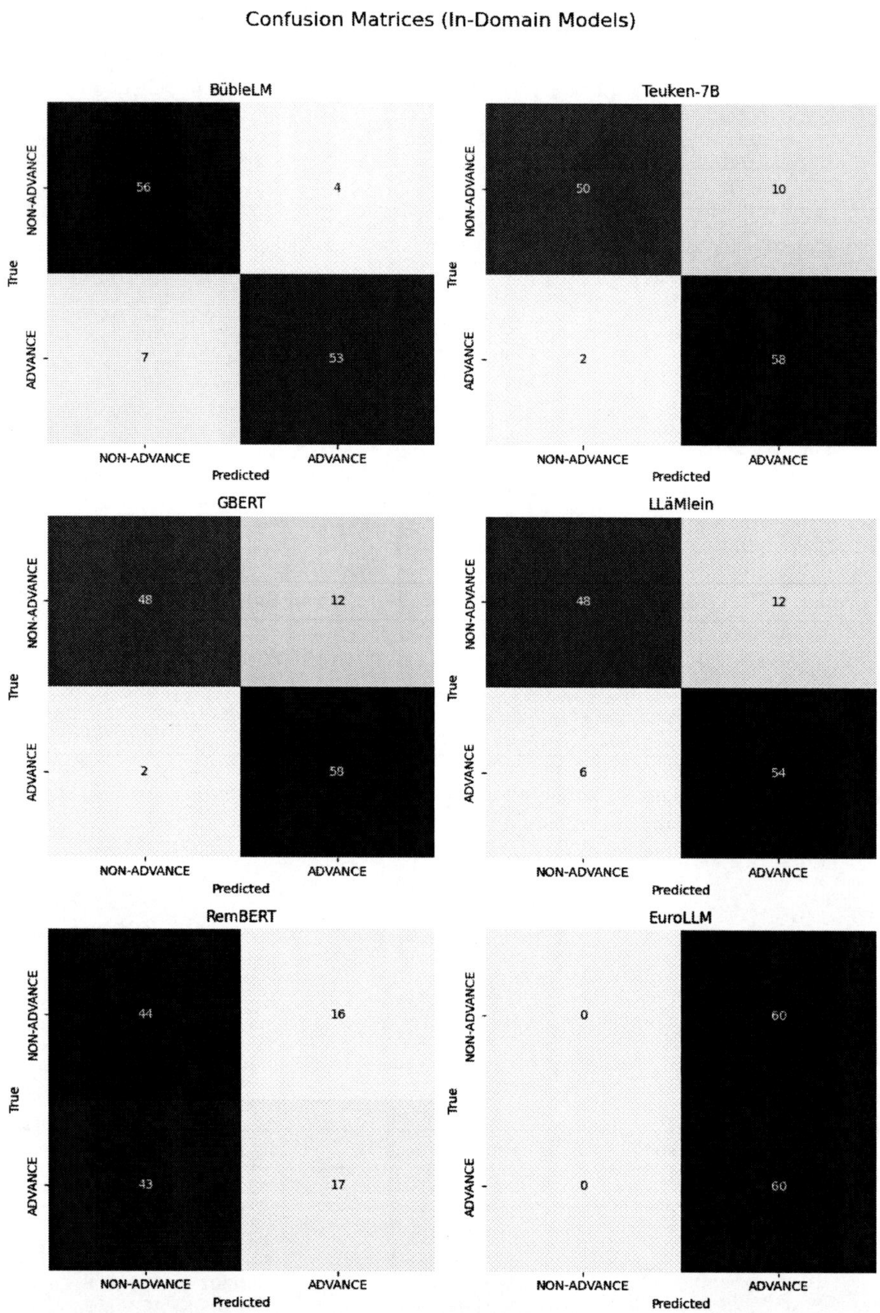

Figure 1: Confusion matrices for all models (in-domain)

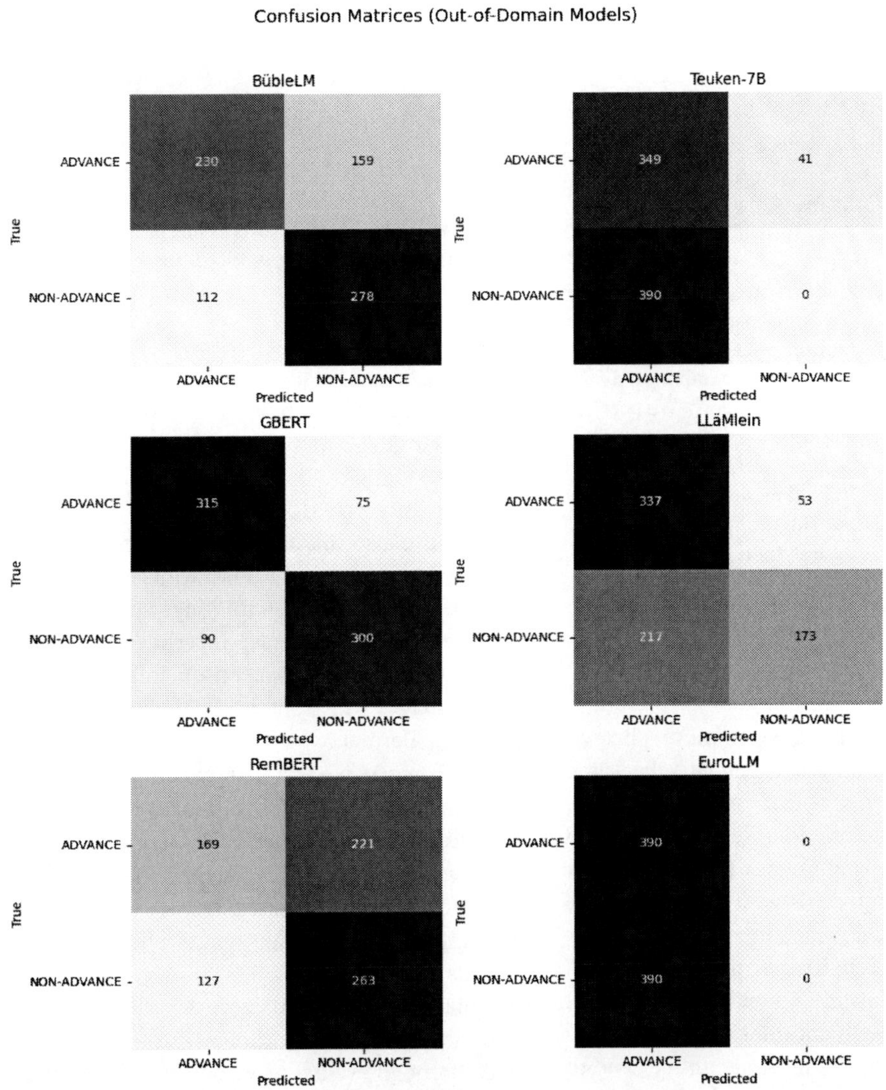

Figure 2: Confusion matrices for all models (out-of-domain)

Efficient and Effective Coreference Resolution for German

Fynn Petersen-Frey and Hans Ole Hatzel and Chris Biemann
Universität Hamburg
Language Technology Group & Hub of Computing and Data Science
{fynn.petersen-frey,hans.ole.hatzel,chris.biemann}@uni-hamburg.de

Abstract

Coreference resolution is the task of identifying and clustering text spans referring to the same entities. While many current models provide good results for short texts, they are computationally inefficient for long documents, and their quality degrades with longer documents. In this paper, we propose a new German coreference resolution model improving on the state of the art while being computationally efficient even for long documents. We perform experiments on multiple German datasets and ablations across different model variations. Our source code and trained model weights are available on Github and Huggingface. Further, we provide a ready-to-use Python library to perform coreference resolution on German texts with minimal setup.

1 Introduction

Coreference occurs when two or more phrases, called mentions, within a text refer to the same entity, such as a person, object, or event. A mention refers back to a previous text span, called its antecedent, which references the same entity. Coreference resolution deals with resolving these references by connecting each mention with its antecedent. In more technical terms, it is the task of identifying and clustering mentions in the form of text spans in a document referring to an entity. All mentions referring to the same entity need to be assigned to the same cluster to build mention clusters where each cluster represents exactly one entity. Figure 1 shows a short example with resolved coreference annotations.

The task of coreference resolution is a widely applicable foundational part of a language processing pipeline to enable or improve other tasks such as question answering, text summarization, quotation attribution, or aid in literary analysis, discourse analysis, etc.

[**Alice**]$_1$ bought [**a new bike**]$_2$.
[**She**]$_1$ sold [[**her**]$_1$ **old bike**]$_3$ to [**Bob**]$_4$.
[**He**]$_4$ rode [**it**]$_3$ home.

Figure 1: Visualization of coreference mentions and cluster information using indexed brackets.

While early models relied on rule-based approaches, current state-of-the-art systems are built as end-to-end neural models leveraging large pre-trained language models. As a result, the quality of the system's outputs has drastically improved over the last years. However, the computational demands have also sharply increased, rendering many approaches impractical for use with large document collections, especially with longer documents, as runtimes typically increase superlinearly. The bulk of the research has focused on English as a target language, with comparatively few approaches targeting German.

In this work, we adapt an existing approach for English coreference resolution to German. We make the following contributions:

- New state-of-the-art coreference resolution models for German news and literary texts
- that are also computationally efficient on long texts.[1]
- Ablation experiments across various model parameters and design choices.
- A thorough evaluation of our models by comparison with existing models and an error analysis.
- A ready-to-use Python library to perform coreference resolution on pre-tokenized or plain text.[2]

2 Related Work

Rule-based approaches have long been used to address the task of coreference resolution (Raghu-

[1] https://github.com/uhh-lt/maverick-coref-de
[2] https://pypi.org/project/maverick-coref-de

Proceedings of the 21st Conference on Natural Language Processing (KONVENS), Volume 1: Long and Short Papers, pages 128–137, 2025

nathan et al., 2010; Lee et al., 2011). Advancements in neural architectures, specifically encoder models, have enabled end-to-end neural systems which generally follow mention linking approaches but differ in architectural details and in how they represent mentions (Lee et al., 2017, 2018; Dobrovolskii, 2021). In recent years, text-to-text approaches have increasingly been used to essentially perform inline coreference annotations (Wu et al., 2020; Bohnet et al., 2023; Zhang et al., 2023). While such text-to-text approaches yield promising results, recent advances in encoder-based approaches have caught up in terms of resolution quality while offering vastly quicker runtime performance (Martinelli et al., 2024). Recent work cast doubts on whether coreference resolution architectures have improved over time, attributing the gradual improvement mainly to the underlying model's sizes instead (Porada et al., 2024).

In terms of datasets, there are three German ones that are relevant to this work: (1) TüBa-D/Z (Telljohann et al., 2004), (2) SemEval 2010 (Recasens et al., 2010), and (3) DROC (Krug et al., 2018). While the former two both contain news articles, DROC contains annotated excerpts from literary works. The excerpts are, on average, around 4,000 tokens in length, which presents a challenge for traditional encoder models that often handle only around 500 sub-word input tokens.

Rule-based approaches have also been applied to coreference resolution in German (Krug et al., 2015; Tuggener, 2016). Roesiger and Kuhn (2016) presented a tree-based machine learning approach using handcrafted features. More recently, we (Schröder et al., 2021) contributed a mention-linking-based encoder model for coreference resolution, the current state-of-the-art model for TüBa-D/Z. Bohnet et al. (2023) test a transition-based coreference system on, among other languages, German. Gupta et al. (2024) focus specifically on literary texts, contributing a novel technique for handling texts with lengths that exceed the underlying encoder model's context.

3 Model

Our model is based on Maverick (Martinelli et al., 2024), a highly-efficient, state-of-the-art coreference resolution model for English. It creates token representations using a transformer encoder, extracts mentions using two classifiers, and finally clusters the mentions by computing the probability of any two mentions belonging to the same cluster by computing the sum of multiple bilinear functions using the mentions' start and end representations. For a more thorough explanation of the Maverick architecture, additionally refer to Martinelli et al. (2024).

3.1 Mention Extraction

While the coarse-to-fine model (Lee et al., 2018) and its derivatives enumerate all spans up to a certain length as possible mentions and select the top k for the mention clustering step, the Maverick system uses a more efficient approach. Mentions are extracted by first identifying all possible mention starts using a feed-forward neural network classifier on each token representation $\mathbf{x_i}$ produced by a transformer encoder for all tokens $t_i, \ldots, t_n$ in a document

$$F_{start}(x) = \mathbf{W}'_{start} \cdot \mathrm{LN}(\mathrm{GeLU}(\mathrm{DO}(\mathbf{W}_{start}x)))$$
$$p_{start}(t_i) = \sigma(F_{start}(x_i))$$

with $\mathbf{W}'_{start}, \mathbf{W}_{start}$ being the learnable parameters, and dropout function (DO), GeLU activation, layer norm (LN) and σ the logistic sigmoid function.

For each plausible mention start t_s, i.e. tokens with $p_{start}(t_s) > 0.5$, span representations are created for all subsequent tokens t_j until the end of the sentence as the concatenation of x_s, and end, x_j. Another feed-forward neural network classifier is used to identify the likely mentions among all candidates

$$F_{end}(x) = \mathbf{W}'_{end} \cdot \mathrm{LN}(\mathrm{GeLU}(\mathrm{DO}(\mathbf{W}_{end}x)))$$
$$p_{end}(t_j|t_s) = \sigma(F_{end}([x_s, x_j]))$$

with $\mathbf{W}'_{end}, \mathbf{W}_{end}$ being learnable parameters. All candidate spans having $p_{end}(t_j|t_s) > 0.5$ are selected as the final mentions for the mention clustering step.

3.2 Mention Clustering

The Maverick model (Martinelli et al., 2024) uses the mention clustering of the LingMess model (Otmazgin et al., 2023), which in turn is an extension of the s2e model (Kirstain et al., 2021). We first briefly describe the mention clustering of the s2e model as implemented in Maverick and our model adoption. A mention $m = (\mathbf{x}_s, \mathbf{x}_e)$, consisting of the start $\mathbf{x}_s$ and end $\mathbf{x}_e$ token hidden states, is transformed into into a start and end representation using two fully-connected layers with

$\mathbf{W}_s, \mathbf{W}'_s, \mathbf{W}_e, \mathbf{W}'_e$ as the learnable parameters:

$$F_s(x) = \mathbf{W}'_s \cdot \mathrm{LN}(\mathrm{GeLU}(\mathrm{DO}(\mathbf{W}_s\mathbf{x})))$$
$$F_e(x) = \mathbf{W}'_e \cdot \mathrm{LN}(\mathrm{GeLU}(\mathrm{DO}(\mathbf{W}_e\mathbf{x})))$$

The probability p_a of the mention m_i to be an antecedent of mention m_j (in other words: to belong to the same cluster) is computed with a logistic sigmoid function σ over the antecedent logits

$$\begin{aligned} p_a(m_i, m_j) = \sigma(&F_s(x_s) \cdot \mathbf{W}_{ss} \cdot F_s(x_{s'}) + \\ &F_e(x_e) \cdot \mathbf{W}_{ee} \cdot F_e(x_{e'}) + \\ &F_s(x_s) \cdot \mathbf{W}_{se} \cdot F_e(x_{e'}) + \\ &F_e(x_e) \cdot \mathbf{W}_{es} \cdot F_s(x_{s'})) \end{aligned}$$

with $\mathbf{W}_{ss}, \mathbf{W}_{ee}, \mathbf{W}_{se}, \mathbf{W}_{es}$ being four learnable parameter matrices.

The LingMess model (Otmazgin et al., 2023) uses multiple mention-antecedent scorers instead of only the single generic scorer found in the s2e model. The scorers handle different linguistically motivated categories that any pair of mentions m_i and m_j belongs to: PRON-PRON-C, PRON-PRON-NC, ENT-PRON, MATCH, CONTAINS, OTHER. For example, in case m_i is a pronoun and m_j is a proper noun, the ENT-PRON scorer is used to compute p_a. The final score of two mentions is the sum of the generic, shared scorer (like in the s2e model) and the expert scorer for the specific category. During training, only the shared scorer and the relevant expert scorer receive gradient updates from the loss function.

3.3 Major Changes from Maverick

While we experimented with numerous architectural changes to the model (see Section 4.1), there are three major changes in our final model.

First, in contrast to all previous encoder-based end-to-end neural coreference architectures, Maverick uses the binary cross-entropy loss with teacher forcing instead of the complex log-marginalized loss function. The log-marginalized loss function was used due to the computationally required pruning of mention and antecedent candidates. We additionally eliminated the need for teacher forcing by limiting the number of mentions predicted early in training to a computationally feasible amount.

Second, instead of the English DeBERTaV3 (He et al., 2021) transformer model, we use the recent ModernGBERT (Ehrmanntraut et al., 2025) model, a transformer trained from scratch on German data based on the ModernBERT architecture (Warner et al., 2024) that allows highly efficient processing of long input sequences.

Third, the Maverick model on English has six linguistically motivated categories for the mention-antecedent scorers. While we adapted the built-in lists of pronouns to German, we could not use all categories due to the lexical ambiguity of German pronouns. Thus, we combined the categories PRON-PRON-C and PRON-PRON-NC for dealing with (in)compatible pronoun mentions based on gender, number, and animacy into a PRON-PRON category for all pronoun-pronoun pairs.

4 Experiments

After defining the evaluation metrics and datasets, we first describe preliminary experiments to select the best model design and training procedure. Subsequently, we detail our main experiments on news and literary datasets to create a total of five models.

Evaluation metrics The de facto standard metric for evaluating coreference is the CoNLL-F1 score, the mean of the MUC (Vilain et al., 1995), B^3 (Bagga and Baldwin, 1998) and CEAF_{ϕ_4} (Luo, 2005) F1 scores. The LEA metric (Moosavi and Strube, 2016) is a more recent metric that addresses many shortcomings of the above metrics. In this work, we evaluate and compare our models using both the CoNLL-F1 and, whenever possible, LEA.

Datasets We perform experiments on the three datasets introduced in Section 2: TüBa-D/Z release 10.0 (TüBa10) using the same split as in our previous work (Schröder et al., 2021), the German part of the SemEval 2010 challenge (SE10), and DROC. TüBa10 is a large dataset covering 1.8 million tokens. SE10 and DROC are much smaller, with 455,000 and 393,000 tokens, respectively. While TüBa10 and SE10 contain thousands of documents, DROC only contains 90 (albeit much longer documents).

4.1 Preliminary Model Design Experiments

To find the best model for our main experiments, we performed a number of preliminary tests to evaluate model variations with foundation language models, teacher forcing, and mention clustering scorers. We considered both model performance and runtime characteristics as we are striving for an efficient and effective model.

Foundational language model We evaluated three language models to replace the English

Foundation	CoNLL-F1
mdeberta-v3-base	76.7
LLäMmlein2Vec-1B	46.7
ModernGBERT-1B	81.4

Table 1: Performance on the TüBa10 development set of different foundational language models

DeBERTa-V3 model. As the model architecture is designed around a language model supporting contexts long enough to process an entire document at once, we were limited to very few options. None of the foundation models used in our previous work (Schröder et al., 2021) are applicable, so a direct comparison is not possible. Instead, we evaluated three models with support for the German language and processing of long contexts. First, we tested the multilingual variant of DeBERTa V3, with promising results of 76.7 CoNLL-F1 for a small, multilingual model – albeit having a slow inference speed. A larger LLM2Vec (BehnamGhader et al., 2024) encoder created from LLäMmlein (Pfister et al., 2024) was faster but produced subpar results of only 46.7 CoNLL-F1. Finally, the ModernGBERT (Ehrmanntraut et al., 2025) model showed strong results with 81.4 CoNLL-F1 while being fast to compute. Table 1 shows a comparison of the CoNNL-F1 score on the TüBa10 development set. Thus, we choose ModernGBERT-1B[3] as our foundation.

Teacher forcing In preliminary experiments, we compared teaching forcing with standard training on the TüBa10 dataset. While training runs with teaching forcing quickly reduced training loss and increased development scores, training without it eventually but consistently led to slightly better scores on the development set. Thus, we deviate from the original Maverick training procedure and use standard training for TüBa10 and SE10.

Attention for mention representation Our model represents mentions using their start token and end token representation as produced by the language model. We experimented with adding a third component, an attention-weighted average of all tokens that are part of a mention span. In preliminary experiments on the TüBa10 dataset, we saw no consistent quality difference on the development set when comparing models with/without our additional span representation. As the additional representations lead to increased computation, as evidenced by slower training and inference, it results in decreased efficiency. Consequently, we kept the pure start and end token representation of mentions without the additional representation in our models.

Mention clustering scorers We compared a single generic mention clustering scorer with the five specialized scorers in preliminary experiments on the TüBa10 dataset. Using the additional scorers consistently leads to better CoNLL-F1 scores on the development set: ≈ 78 versus ≈ 81. Thus, we decided to use the stronger, albeit more complex model, as it only requires a small amount of additional compute resources compared to the overall required compute.

4.2 Main Experiments

News articles We train three models independently on TüBa10 and SE10. For the latter, we train two variants: with or without singletons. In each setup, we use the best model configuration found in our preliminary experiments. We use roughly the same hyperparameter settings as Martinelli et al. (2024): Different learning rate of 2×10^{-4} for the head and 1×10^{-5} for the language model, learning rate warm-up over 3 epochs, weight decay of $1e-3$, and up to 300 epochs limited by early stopping.

Literary texts For our DROC experiments, we follow the training setup proposed in our previous work (Schröder et al., 2021), finetuning first on TüBa10 and subsequently on the much smaller DROC. Additionally, we randomly reinitialize the head that creates mention probabilities given the start and end token embeddings. This change is motivated by the fact that DROC's annotations for mention spans differ from those in TüBa10 and that we, likely as a result, faced convergence issues when training from checkpoints trained on TüBa10. We rely on the model's capability to generalize to context lengths that were not seen in pre-training and only perform one forward pass per document. Unlike TüBa10, DROC only considers mentions of characters rather than all entities; we rely on the additional fine-tuning to instill this difference in the model.

5 Results & Error Analysis

Table 2 contains the results of our main experiments, the test set F1 scores across all evaluated

[3] https://huggingface.co/LSX-UniWue/ModernGBERT_1B

	$CEAF_{\phi_4}$	MUC	B^3	CoNLL	LEA
			TüBa10		
Ours	80.32	84.64	80.45	81.80	78.41
C2F	77.09	82.23	77.05	78.79	74.67
			SE10 with singletons		
Ours	89.28	79.67	89.81	86.26	82.65
MLA*				86.40	
			SE10 without singletons		
Ours	76.14	80.20	75.37	77.23	72.98
C2F	73.47	77.77	72.14	74.46	68.89
LA*				77.80	
			DROC with singletons		
Ours	58.14	91.80	71.33	73.75	67.77
C2F				61.66	
Incr.				64.72	
			DROC without singletons		
Ours	57.36	91.15	69.69	72.73	68.66
C2F				65.50	

* uses additional training data & vast compute resources

Table 2: F1 Performance of our system on the test sets of TüBa10, SE10 and DROC (with and without singletons) compared to our previous coarse-to-fine (C2F) and incremental (Incr.) models (Schröder et al., 2021) as well as the mention-link-append (MLA) & link-append (LA) models by Bohnet et al. (2023).

datasets. Our model shows a strong performance increase, compared to our coarse-to-fine (C2F) model (Schröder et al., 2021), of 3 CoNLL-F1 and almost 4 LEA-F1 points on the TüBa10 dataset. On SE10, our model almost ($\Delta < 0.6$ CoNLL-F1 points) reaches the results of the sequence-to-sequence models by Bohnet et al. (2023) while being orders of magnitude faster to compute[4]. Compared to the C2F model, our model achieves an increase of approximately 3 CoNLL-F1 and 4 LEA-F1 points. The largest improvement is seen on DROC, where our model outperforms our previous state-of-the-art models (Schröder et al., 2021) by 9 F1 points, reaching a 73.75 CoNLL-F1 score (in the setup including singletons). This is a substantial improvement in the context of coreference resolution, where the rate of improvement has decreased in recent years. We attribute this improvement to the model's capability to handle the long DROC documents in one forward pass rather than slicing the texts into segments and performing individual forward passes. In such a setting, our model architecture is most favorable over the C2F model while still offering competitive runtime performance.

In a qualitative error analysis (see Appendix A for two examples), we find that many errors in news texts are caused by mentions that are not annotated as such in the gold data. Moreover, during training, the model is punished for those arguably correct predictions, leading to recall issues elsewhere. We suspect that major improvements may require data curation or active learning techniques. For literary texts, a different picture presents itself. The model especially struggles with long coreference connections, but at times also fails at more local resolution tasks, presumably due to the relative complexity of literary texts. We also observe an issue that is presumably caused by the difference in mention conventions across datasets: our model sometimes predicts very long mentions, which are common in TüBa10 but not seen in DROC.

Inference efficiency On the DROC test set, inference using our old C2F model (Schröder et al., 2021) takes about 6 seconds while the incremental model takes 1 minute and 4 seconds. Our new approach, on the other hand, takes roughly 36 seconds (all measured on a single A6000 GPU).

6 Conclusion

We present new state-of-the-art models for coreference resolution on German news and literary texts that are efficient to compute for practical applications. Our models substantially improve over the previous state-of-the-art models on the TüBa/DZ (+3 F1) and DROC (+9 F1) datasets. Further, our models are comparable in performance on the SemEval-2010 dataset to the current state of the art – by models that use additional training data and are impractically slow to compute, even with the required vast computational resources (8 TPUs-v4 for inference, 128 TPUs-v4 for training). We provide our models alongside a ready-to-use Python library, making them easy to integrate into research software. In the future, we want to combine our models with document slicing and merging techniques like hierarchical coreference resolution (Gupta et al., 2024) to process book-length documents.

Limitations

We do not see any major limitations in our models. While it might not always produce perfectly correct results according to the human gold labels, it

[4]While we cannot reliably provide the exact speedup, we estimate a factor between 80 and 325 given the use of our single A6000 with 150 bfloat16 TFLOPS taking 36 seconds on 71,000 tokens versus their 8 TPUs-v4 with 275 bloat16 TFLOPS per TPU taking 30 minutes inference on 160,000 tokens depending on unknown implementation details such as parallelizability across TPUs.

certainly manages to produce highly usable, reasonable results that likely outperform the coreference resolution quality of a non-expert annotator, since annotating coreference chains is a challenging task, even for humans.

For documents longer than the intended encoder context length (8192 tokens for ModernGBERT), we rely on the model to still perform accurate predictions. An alternative is to slice a document into chunks shorter than the maximal encoder context length – preferably at sentence ends. This approach may yield improved performance.

Although our model is highly efficient computationally compared to most other high-quality coreference resolution models, there is a limit on the absolute document length due to memory and compute constraints on GPUs. While the mention extraction step scales well with long documents (linear computational complexity), the mention clustering has quadratic runtime and space complexity depending on the number of extracted mentions. As such, it might not be feasible to use our model on whole books, unless mentions are made scarce, by – for example – limiting them to only the characters in a story instead of all linguistically possible mentions.

Ethical considerations

Purely relying on machine learning models to solve a task always introduces room for issues. The models may exhibit (unknown) biases based on their design or inherent in their training data. The foundation models used in our work have been trained on a vast amount of texts that likely have not been verified manually. However, our models were trained on datasets that were manually annotated and curated (Telljohann et al., 2004; Krug et al., 2018). During manual evaluation of our model's predictions on texts from the datasets as well as new texts, we did not encounter any obvious biases, such as missing or wrong predictions based on gender, etc. Coreference models have been known to exhibit biases towards gender and other stereotypes; we do not attempt to resolve such biases in this work (Zhao et al., 2018). Automation with machine learning can enable misuse, although clearly harmful application fields for coreference resolution are not obvious to us. Downstream usage of our models will need to consider potential biases in the model whenever operating on the data from our automated approach.

References

Amit Bagga and Breck Baldwin. 1998. Entity-based cross-document coreferencing using the vector space model. In *36th Annual Meeting of the Association for Computational Linguistics and 17th International Conference on Computational Linguistics, Volume 1*, pages 79–85, Montreal, Quebec, Canada. Association for Computational Linguistics.

Parishad BehnamGhader, Vaibhav Adlakha, Marius Mosbach, Dzmitry Bahdanau, Nicolas Chapados, and Siva Reddy. 2024. LLM2Vec: Large language models are secretly powerful text encoders. In *First Conference on Language Modeling*, Philadelphia, Pennsylvania, USA.

Bernd Bohnet, Chris Alberti, and Michael Collins. 2023. Coreference resolution through a seq2seq transition-based system. *Transactions of the Association for Computational Linguistics*, 11:212–226.

Vladimir Dobrovolskii. 2021. Word-level coreference resolution. In *Proceedings of the 2021 Conference on Empirical Methods in Natural Language Processing*, pages 7670–7675, Online and Punta Cana, Dominican Republic. Association for Computational Linguistics.

Anton Ehrmanntraut, Julia Wunderle, Jan Pfister, Fotis Jannidis, and Andreas Hotho. 2025. ModernGBERT: German-only 1b encoder model trained from scratch. *Preprint*, arXiv:2505.13136.

Talika Gupta, Hans Ole Hatzel, and Chris Biemann. 2024. Coreference in long documents using hierarchical entity merging. In *Proceedings of the 8th Joint SIGHUM Workshop on Computational Linguistics for Cultural Heritage, Social Sciences, Humanities and Literature (LaTeCH-CLfL 2024)*, pages 11–17, St. Julians, Malta. Association for Computational Linguistics.

Pengcheng He, Jianfeng Gao, and Weizhu Chen. 2021. DeBERTaV3: Improving DeBERTa using ELECTRA-style pre-training with gradient-disentangled embedding sharing. *Preprint*, arXiv:2111.09543.

Yuval Kirstain, Ori Ram, and Omer Levy. 2021. Coreference resolution without span representations. In *Proceedings of the 59th Annual Meeting of the Association for Computational Linguistics and the 11th International Joint Conference on Natural Language Processing (Volume 2: Short Papers)*, pages 14–19, Online. Association for Computational Linguistics.

Markus Krug, Frank Puppe, Fotis Jannidis, Luisa Macharowsky, Isabella Reger, and Lukas Weimar. 2015. Rule-based coreference resolution in German historic novels. In *Proceedings of the Fourth Workshop on Computational Linguistics for Literature*, pages 98–104, Denver, Colorado, USA. Association for Computational Linguistics.

Markus Krug, Lukas Weimer, Isabella Reger, Luisa Macharowsky, Stephan Feldhaus, Frank Puppe, and Fotis Jannidis. 2018. Description of a corpus of character references in German novels-DROC [Deutsches ROman Corpus]. *DARIAH-DE Working Papers*, 27.

Heeyoung Lee, Yves Peirsman, Angel Chang, Nathanael Chambers, Mihai Surdeanu, and Dan Jurafsky. 2011. Stanford's multi-pass sieve coreference resolution system at the CoNLL-2011 shared task. In *Proceedings of the Fifteenth Conference on Computational Natural Language Learning: Shared Task*, pages 28–34, Portland, Oregon, USA. Association for Computational Linguistics.

Kenton Lee, Luheng He, Mike Lewis, and Luke Zettlemoyer. 2017. End-to-end neural coreference resolution. In *Proceedings of the 2017 Conference on Empirical Methods in Natural Language Processing*, pages 188–197, Copenhagen, Denmark. Association for Computational Linguistics.

Kenton Lee, Luheng He, and Luke Zettlemoyer. 2018. Higher-order coreference resolution with coarse-to-fine inference. In *Proceedings of the 2018 Conference of the North American Chapter of the Association for Computational Linguistics: Human Language Technologies, Volume 2 (Short Papers)*, pages 687–692, New Orleans, Louisiana, USA. Association for Computational Linguistics.

Xiaoqiang Luo. 2005. On coreference resolution performance metrics. In *Proceedings of Human Language Technology Conference and Conference on Empirical Methods in Natural Language Processing*, pages 25–32, Vancouver, British Columbia, Canada. Association for Computational Linguistics.

Giuliano Martinelli, Edoardo Barba, and Roberto Navigli. 2024. Maverick: Efficient and accurate coreference resolution defying recent trends. In *Proceedings of the 62nd Annual Meeting of the Association for Computational Linguistics (Volume 1: Long Papers)*, pages 13380–13394, Bangkok, Thailand. Association for Computational Linguistics.

Nafise Sadat Moosavi and Michael Strube. 2016. Which coreference evaluation metric do you trust? A proposal for a link-based entity aware metric. In *Proceedings of the 54th Annual Meeting of the Association for Computational Linguistics (Volume 1: Long Papers)*, pages 632–642, Berlin, Germany. Association for Computational Linguistics.

Shon Otmazgin, Arie Cattan, and Yoav Goldberg. 2023. LingMess: Linguistically informed multi expert scorers for coreference resolution. In *Proceedings of the 17th Conference of the European Chapter of the Association for Computational Linguistics*, pages 2752–2760, Dubrovnik, Croatia. Association for Computational Linguistics.

Jan Pfister, Julia Wunderle, and Andreas Hotho. 2024. LLäMmlein: Compact and competitive German-only language models from scratch. *Preprint*, arXiv:2411.11171.

Ian Porada, Xiyuan Zou, and Jackie Chi Kit Cheung. 2024. A controlled reevaluation of coreference resolution models. In *Proceedings of the 2024 Joint International Conference on Computational Linguistics, Language Resources and Evaluation (LREC-COLING 2024)*, pages 256–263, Torino, Italia. ELRA and ICCL.

Karthik Raghunathan, Heeyoung Lee, Sudarshan Rangarajan, Nathanael Chambers, Mihai Surdeanu, Dan Jurafsky, and Christopher Manning. 2010. A multi-pass sieve for coreference resolution. In *Proceedings of the 2010 Conference on Empirical Methods in Natural Language Processing*, pages 492–501, Cambridge, Massachusetts, USA. Association for Computational Linguistics.

Marta Recasens, Lluís Màrquez, Emili Sapena, M. Antònia Martí, Mariona Taulé, Véronique Hoste, Massimo Poesio, and Yannick Versley. 2010. SemEval-2010 task 1: Coreference resolution in multiple languages. In *Proceedings of the 5th International Workshop on Semantic Evaluation*, pages 1–8, Uppsala, Sweden. Association for Computational Linguistics.

Ina Roesiger and Jonas Kuhn. 2016. IMS HotCoref DE: A data-driven co-reference resolver for German. In *Proceedings of the Tenth International Conference on Language Resources and Evaluation (LREC'16)*, pages 155–160, Portorož, Slovenia. European Language Resources Association (ELRA).

Fynn Schröder, Hans Ole Hatzel, and Chris Biemann. 2021. Neural end-to-end coreference resolution for German in different domains. In *Proceedings of the 17th Conference on Natural Language Processing (KONVENS 2021)*, pages 170–181, Düsseldorf, Germany. KONVENS 2021 Organizers.

Heike Telljohann, Erhard Hinrichs, and Sandra Kübler. 2004. The TüBa-D/Z treebank: Annotating German with a context-free backbone. In *Proceedings of the Fourth International Conference on Language Resources and Evaluation (LREC'04)*, Lisbon, Portugal. European Language Resources Association (ELRA).

Don Tuggener. 2016. *Incremental Coreference Resolution for German*. Ph.D. thesis, University of Zurich.

Marc Vilain, John Burger, John Aberdeen, Dennis Connolly, and Lynette Hirschman. 1995. A model-theoretic coreference scoring scheme. In *Proceedings of the 6th Conference on Message Understanding*, MUC6 '95, page 45–52, Columbia, Maryland, USA. Association for Computational Linguistics.

Benjamin Warner, Antoine Chaffin, Benjamin Clavié, Orion Weller, Oskar Hallström, Said Taghadouini, Alexis Gallagher, Raja Biswas, Faisal Ladhak, Tom Aarsen, Nathan Cooper, Griffin Adams, Jeremy Howard, and Iacopo Poli. 2024. Smarter, better, faster, longer: A modern bidirectional encoder for fast, memory efficient, and long context finetuning and inference. *Preprint*, arXiv:2412.13663.

Wei Wu, Fei Wang, Arianna Yuan, Fei Wu, and Jiwei Li. 2020. CorefQA: Coreference resolution as query-based span prediction. In *Proceedings of the 58th Annual Meeting of the Association for Computational Linguistics*, pages 6953–6963, Online. Association for Computational Linguistics.

Wenzheng Zhang, Sam Wiseman, and Karl Stratos. 2023. Seq2seq is all you need for coreference resolution. In *Proceedings of the 2023 Conference on Empirical Methods in Natural Language Processing*, pages 11493–11504, Singapore. Association for Computational Linguistics.

Jieyu Zhao, Tianlu Wang, Mark Yatskar, Vicente Ordonez, and Kai-Wei Chang. 2018. Gender bias in coreference resolution: Evaluation and debiasing methods. In *Proceedings of the 2018 Conference of the North American Chapter of the Association for Computational Linguistics: Human Language Technologies, Volume 2 (Short Papers)*, pages 15–20, New Orleans, Louisiana. Association for Computational Linguistics.

A Qualitative Error Analysis

0 **Berliner Vogel stoppt [ICE aus Bonn]$_1$**

0 **[Berliner Vogel]$_4$ stoppt [ICE aus [Bonn]$_5$]$_1$**

1 Ein Vogel hat am Samstag nachmittag in Berlin **[den aus Bonn kommenden ICE 846]$_1$** gestoppt.

1 **[Ein Vogel]$_4$** hat am Samstag nachmittag in Berlin **[den aus [Bonn]$_5$ kommenden ICE 846]$_1$** gestoppt.

2 Wie der Bundesgrenzschutz mitteilte, war nach einem betrieblichen Halt im Bahnhof **[Charlottenburg]$_2$** die Oberleitung gerissen.

2 Wie der Bundesgrenzschutz mitteilte, war nach einem betrieblichen Halt im **[Bahnhof Charlottenburg]$_2$** **[die Oberleitung]$_6$** gerissen.

3 Nach Angaben **[der Bahn AG]$_3$** hatte sich ein Vogel in der Oberleitung verhakt.

3 Nach Angaben **[der Bahn AG]$_3$** hatte sich **[ein Vogel]$_4$** in **[der Oberleitung]$_6$** verhakt.

4 Weitere Einzelheiten sind noch nicht geklärt.
4 Weitere Einzelheiten sind noch nicht geklärt.

5 Im Reiseverkehr kam es laut **[Bahn AG]$_3$** zu Verspätungen von 30 bis 40 Minuten.

5 Im Reiseverkehr kam es laut **[Bahn AG]$_3$** zu Verspätungen von 30 bis 40 Minuten.

6 Nach Angaben **[der Bahn AG]$_3$** wurde niemand verletzt.

6 Nach Angaben **[der Bahn AG]$_3$** wurde niemand verletzt.

7 Die Reisenden konnten auf einen anderen ICE umsteigen.
7 Die Reisenden konnten auf einen anderen ICE umsteigen.

8 Die Züge zwischen den Berliner Bahnhöfen Zoo und **[Charlottenburg]$_2$** konnten nur noch eingleisig fahren.

8 Die Züge zwischen den Berliner Bahnhöfen Zoo und **[Charlottenburg]$_2$** konnten nur noch eingleisig fahren.

9 Die Regionalzüge wurden umgeleitet.
9 Die Regionalzüge wurden umgeleitet.

Figure 2: Visualization produced by our analysis tool for a single document from the TüBa10 test comparing the gold annotations with the prediction of our final model. The document is shown in pairs of sentences where the first sentence is from the gold annotations and the second is the system's prediction. In the gold annotations, multiple mentions of a bird *Vogel* (cluster 4), the city of *Bonn* (cluster 5), and a reference to the overhead wire *Oberleitung* (cluster 6) were missed. Another tiny detail is the first mention of the train station *Charlottenburg* in sentence 2. While the gold annotations only annotated the word *Charlottenburg*, our system's prediction span the whole noun phrase *Bahnhof Charlottenburg* which is arguably correct since the second mention of it in sentence 8 explicitly refers to the train stations *Berliner Bahnhöfen Zoo und Charlottenburg* and not to the locality of Berlin also called *Charlottenburg*.

4 [Ich]$_{2}$ erfuhr unterwegs, daß [du]$_{3}$ eilig nach einem [Wundarzt]$_{4}$ geschickt habest – [ich]$_{2}$ will doch nicht hoffen, daß [dir]$_{3}$ oder den [Kindern]$_{5}$ etwas zugestoßen ist?
4 [Ich]$_{2}$ erfuhr unterwegs, daß [du]$_{3}$ eilig nach einem [Wundarzt]$_{44}$ geschickt habest – [ich]$_{2}$ will doch nicht hoffen, daß [dir]$_{3}$ oder den [Kindern]$_{45}$ etwas zugestoßen ist?

5 Ruhig sagte [Erna]$_{3}$: Weder die [Kinder]$_{5}$ noch [ich]$_{3}$ bedürfen [seines]$_{4}$ Beistandes, aber einen [Freund]$_{1}$ von [uns]$_{6}$ hat nicht weit von [unserm]$_{6}$ Hause ein Unfall betroffen, der zwar, dem Himmel sei Dank, nicht bedeutend ist, aber dessen Behandlung denn doch [meine]$_{3}$ wenigen medicinischen Kenntnisse übersteigt.
5 Ruhig sagte [Erna]$_{3}$: Weder die [Kinder]$_{45}$ noch [ich]$_{3}$ bedürfen [seines]$_{2}$ Beistandes, aber einen [Freund]$_{2}$ von [uns]$_{46}$ hat nicht weit von [unserm]$_{46}$ Hause ein Unfall betroffen, der zwar, dem Himmel sei Dank, nicht bedeutend ist, aber dessen Behandlung denn doch [meine]$_{3}$ wenigen medicinischen Kenntnisse übersteigt.

...

19 Alle [seine]$_{1}$ Einwendungen wurden jedoch durch den Ausspruch des [Arztes]$_{4}$, daß [er]$_{1}$ ohne Gefahr der Verschlimmerung [seines]$_{1}$ Zustandes nicht hinweg gebracht werden könne, widerlegt, und da [Erna]$_{3}$ [ihn]$_{1}$ mit der [ihr]$_{3}$ eigenen, lieblichen, herzgewinnenden Weise bat, [sich]$_{1}$ doch zu gedulden, und [ihr]$_{3}$ die Freude zu gönnen, durch [ihre]$_{3}$ Pflege zu [seiner]$_{1}$ Erholung beitragen zu dürfen, auch [Linovsky]$_{2}$, nachdem [er]$_{2}$ [sich]$_{2}$ etwas gesammelt hatte, eine etwas wohlwollendere Außenseite zeigte, als vorher, so ergab [er]$_{1}$ [sich]$_{1}$, wiewohl ein unglückweissagendes Gefühl in [seiner]$_{1}$ Seele [ihn]$_{1}$ mahnte, daß schleunige Flucht heilsamer für [ihn]$_{1}$ als Bleiben sei.
19 Alle [seine]$_{1}$ Einwendungen wurden jedoch durch den Ausspruch des [Arztes]$_{4}$, daß [er]$_{1}$ ohne Gefahr der Verschlimmerung [seines]$_{1}$ Zustandes nicht hinweg gebracht werden könne, widerlegt, und da [Erna]$_{3}$ [ihn]$_{1}$ mit der [ihr]$_{3}$ eigenen, lieblichen, herzgewinnenden Weise bat, [sich]$_{1}$ doch zu gedulden, und [ihr]$_{3}$ die Freude zu gönnen, durch [ihre]$_{3}$ Pflege zu [[seiner]$_{1}$ Erholung beitragen zu dürfen, auch [Linovsky]$_{2}$, nachdem [er]$_{2}$ [sich]$_{2}$]$_{2}$ etwas gesammelt hatte, eine etwas wohlwollendere Außenseite zeigte, als vorher, so ergab [er]$_{1}$ [sich]$_{1}$, wiewohl ein unglückweissagendes Gefühl in [seiner]$_{1}$ Seele [ihn]$_{1}$ mahnte, daß schleunige Flucht heilsamer für [ihn]$_{1}$ als Bleiben sei.

Figure 3: Visualization produced by our analysis tool for part of a single document from the DROC test set (an excerpt from *Erna* by *Charlotte von Ahlfeld*). As above, the document is shown in pairs of sentences where the first sentence is from the gold annotations and the second is the system's prediction. The surgeon (*Wundarzt*, cluster 4) is, many sentences later, referred to as the physician (*Arzt* in sentence 19). The model fails to capture this relationship. The system also fails to resolve the personal pronoun *seines* in sentence 5, which also refers to the surgeon; this example illustrates the model's difficulty with coreference resolution in literary texts, even in a local context. Another effect we can observe is that the model sometimes predicts much longer mentions than the dataset typically contains (see sentence 19); we suspect that this is caused by the pre-training on TüBa10, but note that we did reset the mention heads.

FASCIST-O-METER: Classifier for Neo-fascist Discourse Online

Rudy Alexandro Garrido Veliz, Martin Semmann,
Chris Biemann, Seid Muhie Yimam

Universtät Hamburg
Correspondence: Rudy Alexandro Garrido Veliz, email: rudy.garrido.veliz@uni-hamburg.de

Abstract

Neo-fascism is a political and societal ideology that has been having remarkable growth in the last decade in the United States of America (USA), as well as in other Western societies. It poses a grave danger to democracy and the minorities it targets, and it requires active actions against it to avoid escalation. This work presents the first-of-its-kind neo-fascist annotation scheme for digital discourse in the USA societal context, overseen by political science researchers. Our work bridges the gap between Natural Language Processing (NLP) and political science against this phenomena. Furthermore, to test the annotation scheme, we collect a tremendous amount of activity on the internet from notable neo-fascist groups (the forums of Iron March and Stormfront.org), and the guidelines are applied to a subset of the collected posts. Through crowdsourcing, we annotate a total of a thousand posts that are labeled as neo-fascist or non-neo-fascist. With this labeled data set, we fine-tune and test both Small Language Models (SLMs) and Large Language Models (LLMs), obtaining the very first classification models for neo-fascist discourse. The best performing SLM was HomophobiaBert with an F1 of 0.8387, and the best LLM was GPT-4o on few-shot with an F1 of 0.8680.

We find that the prevalence of neo-fascist rhetoric in this kind of forum is ever-present, making them a good target for future research. The societal context is a key consideration for neo-fascist speech when conducting NLP research. Finally, the work against this kind of political movement must be pressed upon and continued for the well-being of a democratic society.

Disclaimer: This study focuses on detecting neo-fascist content in text, similar to other hate speech analyses, without labeling individuals or organizations.

1 Introduction

Neo-fascism poses a grave danger to democracy (Cento Bull, 2010; Cammaerts, 2020; Haro and Coles, 2017) and, like its predecessor (fascism), a great risk to the communities it targets. As with any extremist ideology, it is only a matter of time before it escalates to uncontrollable proportions (Hollewell and Longpré, 2022; Winter et al., 2020; McCurdy, 2021). Part of its agenda is posing social inequalities as desirable and even needed, appealing to the hatred and predisposition that a community may already have (Cammaerts, 2020).

Neo-fascism weaponizes minorities for the goal of maintaining the capitalist social status (Cox and Skidmore-Hess, 2022). It is necessary to fight neo-fascism in an active way (Haro and Coles, 2017), as its familiarity and online presence can normalize the ideology and lead to real-life escalation (Koster and Houtman, 2008). Given that the radicalization of this movement has a strong presence in online independent forums, this work will leverage NLP tools to build a basis for fighting digital neo-fascism. We begin with gathering raw data from known neo-fascist forums. Next, annotation guidelines are developed with the aid from researchers in this political field, helping with the complexity of the neo-fascist ideology. We then used crowdsourcing to manually annotate a subset of the data, determining whether it contained neo-fascist ideology. This annotated dataset is used to train a classifier using both SLMs and LLMs to detect and classify neo-fascist discourse. Figure 1 illustrates the comprehensive process involved in developing the **FASCIST-O-METER** classifier.

The main research questions driving this study are: **RQ1**: How can NLP tools be utilized to identify neo-fascist discourse online? **RQ2**: What challenges arise during the annotation of neo-fascist content, and how can these challenges be addressed? **RQ3**: How do language models fare

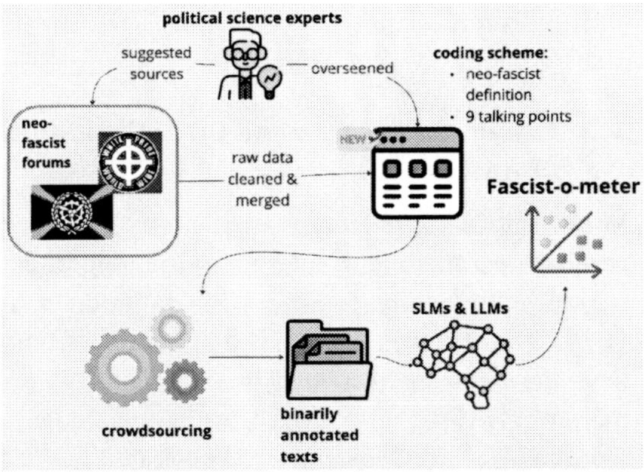

Figure 1: Illustration of the complete end-to-end process for developing the **FASCIST-O-METER** system.

when classifying such content, and in what way can they be optimized for this objective? In this paper, we mainly contributed by creating an annotated dataset of neo-fascist and non-neo-fascist online discourse, derived from extensive data collection and a carefully crafted annotation scheme. We developed and validated methodologies for building and fine-tuning language models to accurately classify neo-fascist content. Finally, we provide insights into the unique challenges posed by neo-fascist discourse and offer a framework for future research and technological development aimed at mitigating its spread online.

In Section 2, the background knowledge of the political science definition of neo-fascism is covered, as well as its history in the USA and the two relevant entities of the movement for our work. The following Section 3, explains the social efforts against neo-fascism and the efforts of the NLP community aiding the fight towards extremism and political bias. Sections 4 and 5, explain the process of data collection and the crucial development of the annotation guidelines and their usage on a subset of the collected data. With the annotated dataset, Section 6 contains the various experiments done with it, putting the result of the annotation guidelines to the test. Finally, Section 7, exposes the conclusion from our work with some recommendations.

2 Background Knowledge

In this section, the general knowledge about political science and the societal context of neo-fascism will be explained.

2.1 Neo-fascism

Neo-fascism is an extremist ideology placed on the far right of the political spectrum. There has been a rise in neo-fascism in the last decades (Cox and Skidmore-Hess, 2022). The definition of neo-fascism is complicated and can differ depending on which society appears, as well as the school of thought. Some defined it as a right-wing ideology emerging from a crisis state resulting from decades of neo-liberal capitalism (Cox and Skidmore-Hess, 2022). Others believe it is a capitalist political regime heavily based in "neo-liberal shock politics" where Donald Trump is a pioneer (Haro and Coles, 2017). In the historical context, it can be seen as an ideology held by political parties and groups after the Second World War, who were inspired despite the Nazi fall to continue their legacy (Cento Bull, 2010).

In general, it is defined mainly as a combination of multiple far-right ideologies that politicians use to gain popularity and power while radicalizing their population (Cammaerts, 2020), against a minority. These ideologies will be expanded next.

- **Ultranationalism**: nationalism is the representation of ethnic groups at a state level (Eriksen, 1992). Ultranationalism is the exacerbation of faulty nationalism, causing animosity against foreigners and underrepresented minorities. It has been on the rise for the last decades in several parts of the world, among them the USA (Cammaerts, 2020).

- **Mystification and glorification of the past**: In this context, to mystify is to create fake beliefs or ideas about the past of the state. Regardless of how the past of a nation was, the neo-fascist agenda is to change it into a grandiose one (Carnut, 2022). Changing the past of a country by the right-wing in politics is often through education as a weapon (Means and Ida, 2022; Carnut, 2022). Movements like Trumpism, with the motto "Make America Great Again", are exemplary of this. Through education, the population has their identity, closely related to the new fictitious image of the country (Means and Ida, 2022).

- **Minorities weaponization**: Creating an enemy within the nation, a constant threat to which the politicians can claim urgency and a lack of power to stop them (Stanley, 2018). This created enemy is often a minority within the population or a fictitious one from outside, immigrants, or the population from another country. The alienated population is used in the likes of a novel obstacle that explains the decline of the land and the struggles that the population face daily. To create and maintain this image and sense of gravity, the neo-fascists will weaponize these minorities in multiple ways. One of them is siding with a minority to a political party, including claiming that they are in control of said party (Cammaerts, 2020), or blaming the current government for using its institutions and funding to help the minority (Carnut, 2022; Cammaerts, 2020). They can also indicate that social inequalities between the population are natural and necessary for the majority to impose them (Stanley, 2018). Neo-fascists also claim that the minority is unable to follow the laws of the country, not fit to rule or hold power (Stanley, 2018). In some cases, the masculine counterpart of the minority is negatively hypersexualized (Stanley, 2018) i.e. tag them as sexual degenerates and as rapists.

- **Militarism and militarization of civil security**: Militarism is defined as the preparation, legitimation, and normalization of war (Stavrianakis and Stern, 2017). In neo-fascism, it is used as a tool to endorse the crisis of the state. In some cases, this militarization involves civilians resulting in paramilitary entities, a pillar of previous iterations of fascism (Copsey, 2020). An example is the "Proud Boys" militia group, which had a large involvement in the January 6 insurrection in the USA (Dowless, 2022).

Neo-fascism in the US can be partly traced back to the post-Second World War, when Nazis and fascists were welcomed by the CIA in the fight against communism (Cento Bull, 2010). But in the last decade, neo-fascism has had a huge spike in the *acceptable* political discourse. Immensely due to the presidential runs and term of Donald Trump, the way of politics has given a name of its own: "Trumpism". In this type of politics, the leaders are often blatantly racist, xenophobic, misogynistic, and much more. This behavior is disguised under the wings of free speech and "speaking his mind", considering it triumphant. The platform of Donald Trump was often a model example of neo-fascism and is broadly considered as such in political science research (Caiani and Parenti, 2009; Copsey, 2020; Stanley, 2018; Cammaerts, 2020).

2.2 Online neo-fascism and the United States of America

Many scholars agree that white nationalist extremism has become one of the more grounded threats online, specifically for the USA (Winter et al., 2020). Neo-fascists exist in social media, but they have proven to be too volatile and chaotic to stay there freely (McCurdy, 2021). Although recent developments in politics have changed that and it is worth mentioning that they have a large presence there and in other general-purpose forums (Koehler, 2014; Hollewell and Longpré, 2022). The following are online organizations that exhibited online extremism and neo-fascism within their own **independent platforms**, and are relevant to this paper.

2.2.1 Iron March

Iron March was a forum that ran between 2011 and 2017. This forum was characterized mainly by far-right extremist content and was used as a tool for planning and recruiting radicalized individuals, as well as doing their radicalization. It can be linked to more than 100 hate crimes in the USA (Reilly and Edwards, 2021; Hayden, 2019), contained extremist tendencies, and was declared as fascist (Scrivens et al., 2023) by the USA hate-watch organization Southern Poverty Law Center (SPLC). This forum posed such a threat and became so efficient with the neo-fascist agenda that it led to what is now known as the “Skull Mask” neo-fascist network. This is an international neo-fascist network that includes multiple terrorist groups spanning from North America to Europe. This network included the USA terrorist domestic group Atomwaffen (Upchurch, 2021), also tagged as neo-Nazi by the SPLC and many of their members have been prosecuted and jailed.

In Iron March, the users would speak freely about neo-fascism and idealize a world of fascist governments, mostly for the "white countries". They would share information from other social centers and would organize methodically into smaller and more private groups. The forum members had mixed opinions on Donald Trump, but generally, there was support and eagerness on that way of politics (Upchurch, 2021). The communications here would include enormous amounts of hate speech, like racism, white supremacy, xenophobia, homophobia, anti-semitism, etc (Hayden, 2019; Upchurch, 2021). The website was taken down without an apparent reason, shortly after their database of messages and posts was leaked (Hayden, 2019).

2.2.2 Stormfront.org

Stormfront.org was one of the first online forums for the community of individuals who identify as white-nationalists. It was first opened to the public in March 1995 (Bowman-Grieve, 2009). They have threads and sub-forums for multiple far-right beliefs, including neo-fascism. Much like the aforementioned Iron March, most of the discussions are filled with hate speech. The website has general everyday content as well, always under the light of white supremacy (Bowman-Grieve, 2009).

Stormfront.org is a model example of how radicalization can happen online and how extremist communities can engulf the attention of the user, creating their identity around the ideology. It also shows how these virtual communities can be easily taken into real-life violence and hate crimes (Koster and Houtman, 2008). The Stormfront.org community also had a mixed set of opinions regarding Donald Trump, specifically due to having a Jewish daughter and the closeness to Jewish people (Dentice, 2018). This forum continues to exist to this date, freely accessible on the Internet. It has an overwhelming amount of users and posts, more than three hundred thousand and more than fourteen million, respectively, to this date (January 2025).

3 Related work

In this section, we explore the scholarly efforts to understand and counter the neo-fascist movement in the USA, as well as examine related research conducted at the intersection of politics and NLP.

3.1 Efforts against the American neo-fascist movement

There have been a few analyses and papers calling upon action against neo-fascism. These are used in the theoretical background of our work, particularly in the annotation scheme development. The paper by Haro and Coles (2017) defines neo-fascist politics and gives multiple ways to fight it. The authors do this specifically in the USA political setting, heavily basing it on the rhetoric of Donald Trump. In a toned-down but similar way, the papers by Cox and Skidmore-Hess (2022) and Cammaerts (2020) make the USA recent politics a case study and tool to define neo-fascism. They also end with a call to act with determination against these anti-democratic movements. More papers mentioned in the review by Carnut (2022), in the section "The Role of the Left(s)", also empower the opposing politics against neo-fascism with concrete actions. Multiple organizations are actively combating neo-fascism. Two of the more relevant organizations will be presented in the following Sections 3.1.1 and 3.1.2.

3.1.1 Southern Poverty Law Center

The Southern Poverty Law Center (SPLC) was funded in 1971, with the mission to ensure civil rights for all in the south of the USA, focused on a legal basis.[1] It has evolved into a multifaceted organization that fights against the ailments the black community and many other minorities face in the US and the white supremacist movement.[2] The efforts against nativism, xenophobia, and anti-immigration extremism cannot be overlooked, as they have won judicial cases. This center has also helped with research and reports (Beirich and Potok, 2009). The SPLC has instated a hate-watching program[3], to monitor and catalogue individuals, organizations, and movements that are affiliated with the radical right in the USA. Among these entities, and relevant to the work, are the Iron March (Hayden, 2019) and Stormfront.org[4].

3.1.2 Anti-Defamation League

The Anti-Defamation League (ADL) started in 1913 as an organization to stop the defamation of the Jewish people, specifically in the USA. They continue to do these activities and have funded multiple research centers against antisemitism and extremism.[5] The ADL, in efforts to fight dog-whistling and educate everyone, has created a glossary of extremism and hate.[6] In these resources, the organization keeps track of the language and symbols that right extremist, neo-nazis, and neo-fascists use.

The resources offered by the ADL are used in our work in the annotation scheme. ADL has also

[1] https://www.splcenter.org/about

[2] https://www.splcenter.org/what-we-do/our-commitment-challenge-racism

[3] https://www.splcenter.org/hatewatch

[4] https://www.splcenter.org/fighting-hate/extremist-files/group/stormfront

[5] https://www.adl.org/about/mission-and-history

[6] https://extremismterms.adl.org/

classified Stormfront.org[7] and the Attomwaffen Division[8] (born from the Iron March forum) as hate groups with fascist rhetoric.

3.2 Political bias and extremism

Bias in general can be an alarming factor in news reports. The work by Gangula et al. (2019) goes deep into this, aiming to automate bias detection in articles to fight biased news and conspiracy theories. Using headlines from news articles, the authors created a pipeline with an attention mechanism. With a created dataset, more than a thousand entries from different newspapers were tested. Regarding bias in news as well, but in a political context, the paper by Doumit and Minai (2011) looked at articles with a topic-based approach along with NLP tools. This allowed the work to achieve an intricate analysis and comparison of the media sources, with the goal to aid against bias in online news.

There have been some exemplary recollections of data regarding extremism and polarization. The dataset from the empirical analysis of Stormfront.org found in Törnberg and Törnberg (2022) is the one used in this paper. Twenty years of activity and discourse were composed and analyzed, an enormous amount of text (more in Section 4.1). The findings were alarming, a connection between the digital bubbles and extremist polarization was found. Another dataset regarding white supremacy, but also the ISIS/Jihadist ideology was proposed by Gaikwad et al. (2021). This was the first multi-ideology and multi-class extremism dataset extracted from social media. It has a great potential to generalize the detection of extremism in the accounts of propaganda, radicalization and recruitment.

The research done by Ajala et al. (2022) is a remarkable example of the study of radical views, due to the in-depth analysis and the reach of the dataset. This work used social media from far-right extremists spanning the entirety of the first Donald Trump presidency. Ajala et al. (2022) created clusters, and with expert input, far-right beliefs were spotted in most of them, with a high level of polarization. The users and social circles were analyzed by the researchers as well. Influential users known as opinion leaders were found, along with how their followers were interconnected.

Although many works and approaches have been developed to address online extremism and political bias, **there have been no efforts found regarding online neo-fascism**. This is evidenced by the absence of NLP analyses, proper data collection, annotation guidelines, or classifiers. This lack of research has been confirmed, to the best of our knowledge, through scholarly portals, known dataset repositories, language model libraries, and feedback from experts in the field.

4 Data collection

The sources for the creation of the dataset are from publicly known forums and communities labelled as neo-fascist and white supremacist by multiple organizations that are constantly on the lookout for hate speech and problematic entities.

4.1 Stormfront.org extracted posts

Stormfront.org dataset comes from the paper by Törnberg and Törnberg (2022). The dataset spanned from 2001 to 2020, containing more than 10 million posts. In the work, posts were filtered for the English language, from a minimum of 120 characters, an amount they considered to be enough to represent relevant conversation, and truncated to a maximum of 5k, cut out to avoid outliers of extremely long messages. The dataset can be found in Kaggle.[9]

4.2 Iron March forum leak

The posts and messages from the Iron March forum were taken from a Kaggle post as well.[10] In this post, the user took the original source and filtered to the relevant files that could be used in research and analysis. The posted texts were modified from HTML to plain text. The source of the Kaggle post is an entry from a website[11] of an investigator, mostly dedicated to war and polarizing subjects. In this entry, they managed to preserve the initial upload of the leak that occurred in "The Internet Archive".[12] The source of this dataset was a database leak posted by the user "Antifa-data".

[7] https://www.adl.org/resources/hate-symbol/stormfront

[8] https://www.adl.org/resources/backgrounder/atomwaffen-division-awd-national-socialist-order-nso

[9] https://www.kaggle.com/datasets/pettertornberg/stormfront

[10] https://www.kaggle.com/datasets/gracchus/ironmarch/?select=message_posts_edited.csv

[11] https://www.bellingcat.com/resources/how-tos/2019/11/06/massive-white-supremacist-message-board-leak-how-to-access-and-interpret-the-data/

[12] https://archive.org/details/iron_march_201911_backup

This was a leak of the whole database of the forum. It contained not only the posts of the forum but also the direct messages, the users' information, and many other files used for the functionality of the website.

4.3 Cleaning and merging

Since the Iron March data leak still had the usernames they had to be removed. The only references it had to users were in the forum posts when they were citing each other, like so: "*Username* said 30 minutes ago: ...". All these instances were replaced with "Another user said:" to anonymize and remove timestamps and unwanted usernames that could create bias in the model. The Stormfront.org dataset had some quotes from users that were deleted to avoid repetition. Both forums had links from other websites that were removed.

Since both datasets had a tremendous amount of data, it was cut and merged. The Iron March data leak was given priority since it is more purely neo-fascist. As the first presidential campaign of Trump marks a significant milestone for the popularity of neo-fascism, the Iron March portion was taken from the 16th of June 2016, the day Donald Trump announced the presidential campaign, to the closure of the forum on the 21st of November 2017. This gave a total of 63,569 messages and posts. From the cutout date of the Iron March part, the Stormfront.org dataset was taken onwards, amounting to 585,698 entries. Both forums' parts were merged, resulting in a total of 649,267 texts. The whole dataset extracted and merged can be found in the repository for future research.

5 Data annotation

Although the forums had, in theory, high activity of neo-fascist discourse, they were still publicly accessible and had often threads to socialize and talk about other aspects; therefore, to be certain of the level of neo-fascism, it was necessary to annotate the texts.

5.1 Annotation guidelines

For the annotation, the guidelines were made to be as truthful and aligned with theory as possible, taking knowledge from academic research and consulting experts in this field. The full, uninterrupted version of the annotation guidelines can be found in the Appendix A.1, for easier usage in further research. At the beginning of the annotation scheme, some direct instructions were given:

Initial instructions You will be presented with multiple and different digital posts or activities from various forums and blogs. You will decide whether they **contain any element of the neo-fascist ideology or not**. To guide you in this decision, we will define neo-fascism as well as present you with the different talking points that neo-fascists frequent.

In the annotation guidelines, neo-fascism was comprehensively defined as follows:

Neo-fascism definition In broad terms, neo-fascism is defined as a right-wing **political** ideology that aims to amass power by radicalizing a part of the population. Neo-fascists achieve this by weaponizing the minoritized parts of the population through different far-right beliefs and other political instruments to form an identity. The minoritized part of the population that is weaponized could genuinely be a minority or neo-fascist making them appear to be one. (Stanley, 2018; Cammaerts, 2020; Cox and Skidmore-Hess, 2022).

Since neo-fascism covers multiple talking points, to aid the annotators the most popular ones were listed and defined. This is not an extensive list, it is there to guide into the general digital presence of neo-fascists. Their detailed definitions can be found in the Appendix A.1. The talking points are:

- hate speech towards minoritized people (Stanley, 2018; Cammaerts, 2020);
- politicization of minorities existence (Cammaerts, 2020);
- justification of social inequalities (Stanley, 2018);
- declaring or implying the unruliness or unlawfulness of a minority (Stanley, 2018);
- disdain of taxes and public or governmental institutions usage (Cammaerts, 2020; Carnut, 2022);
- requesting or celebrating rights stripping from minorities (Haro and Coles, 2017);
- mythicize the past as grandiose, in a political or societal context (Stanley, 2018);
- idealization of military, police, or organized violence related to a political party or entity (Cox and Skidmore-Hess, 2022);
- and negative hypersexualization of the masculine counterpart of a minority (Stanley, 2018).

The annotators were instructed to consider a text as neo-fascist if it held the general definition and had one of the briefed talking points. Moreover, they were given some examples and counterexamples, taken from the original dataset, along with a brief explanation of why the text would be considered or not neo-fascist (the complete list can be found in Appendix A.1). Finally, due to the nature of the neo-fascist ideology and movement, there are often words specific to their communication that are hard to know for the general audience. For most unknown terms, the annotators were instructed to use the glossaries from the hate-watch initiatives of the ADL and the SPLC (mentioned in Section 3.1.1 & 3.1.2). The political science experts reviewed the annotation guidelines draft and gave feedback for its improvement, refining the talking points and the general instructions. The experts instructed as well that the following terms should be defined directly in the guidelines since they could appear more often: *kike, goyim, QAnon, New World Order, remigration, ethnopluralism, Great Replacement, Great Reset, ZOG, Holohoax, and Protocols of the Elders of Zion.*

5.2 Annotation process

A smaller subset of 1000 random data points (proportionalized with both original data sources) was used for the annotation process. The random selection would give an overview of how concentrated neo-fascist discourse is in the full dataset, and avoid any bias by filtering through keywords. Each data point was classified by 3 different annotators.

The popular crowdsourcing platform Mechanical Turk (MTurk) from Amazon was used, paying annotators according to the USA federal minimum wage. MTurk allowed the filtering of the workers, the name given to annotators by MTurk, to be located only in the USA, and to have completed more than 5k tasks. The data to be annotated was divided into three segments, and each segment was annotated in succession to have control over the quality of the workers for the next segment. The accuracy rate (the amount of successful tasks completed in MTurk) required of the workers was raised after each round of annotation, starting at 90%, to 95%, and finally 98%. After each round, an assessment of the quality was done based on qualitative and error analysis. The Cohen's Kappa coefficient averaged, calculated through the NLTK package (Bird et al., 2009), was used in the last two batches as well. In the second batch, workers with a Kappa lower than 0.2 (interpretable as none to slight agreement (McHugh, 2012)) were barred from the last batch. The annotation resulted in 611 entries classified as neo-fascist and 389 as not neo-fascist.

6 Experimentation

In the experimentation, the annotated dataset was employed with both small and large language models. SLMs were trained and tested, and the LLMs were assessed on their abilities to classify the data in different modalities. The baseline model used was Bert base uncased (Devlin et al., 2019). The annotated 1,000 entries were split into 80% for training, 10% for validation, and 10% for the test set.

6.1 Small language models

The SLMs used were selected based on proximity to the subject of neo-fascism and models of general knowledge with relevance in the state-of-the-art. The SLMs chosen for their relevancy were: DistilBERT[13] (Sanh et al., 2020), RoBERTa[14] (Liu et al., 2019), and ALBERT[15] (Lan et al., 2020).

Two models that were finetuned on related data were selected. The first model was LFTW R4 Target.[16] It is a Roberta-base model for the detection of hate speech online by Vidgen et al. (2021). This model was trained on a higher proportion of hateful entries and showed to have a better performance than, at their time, state-of-the-art. The second model was HomophobiaBERT[17] (McGiff and Nikolov, 2024), a BERT-base model for identifying homophobic posts in the social media X.

The hyperparameter search was done with all the SLM models. The hyperparameters tweaked for the runs were the learning rate, number of epochs in training, and the batch size in training. For this search, the library provided by Huggingface (Inc. Hugging Face, 2016) was used. Up to 30 trials were used to find the best hyperparameters. The backend used for the search was Ray Tune (Liaw et al., 2018), using random search/grid algorithm for the values. The result of this search, found in

[13] https://huggingface.co/distilbert/distilbert-base-uncased-finetuned-sst-2-english

[14] https://huggingface.co/FacebookAI/roberta-base

[15] https://huggingface.co/albert/albert-base-v2

[16] https://huggingface.co/facebook/roberta-hate-speech-dynabench-r4-target

[17] https://huggingface.co/JoshMcGiff/homophobiaBERT

Appendix A.4, was employed for the creation of the best-performing models.

6.2 Large language models

The LLMs hand-picked, due to their significance in state-of-the-art research, were LLaMa, in the versions of LLaMa2 (uncensored variant)[18] and LLaMa3[19]; Gemma (Team et al., 2024), only the second version Gemma2[20](Farabet and Warkentin, 2024); GPT-4o[21]; and DeepSeek-R1 (DeepSeek-AI et al., 2025).

The LLMs were tested in zero-shot, few-shot, and after being fine-tuned again with a complementing input. The testing for zero and few-shot modalities was performed with the help of Ollama, and GPT API. The LLMs were finetuned using Unsloth[22], with the same training data used with the SLMs (800 entries). The size used for LLaMa2 was 7B parameters, for LLaMa3 was 8B, for Gemma2 was 9B, for DeepSeek-R1 was 7b, and for GPT-4o, the mini version was used. LLaMa3 was not used in the zero-shot testing, because it resisted classifying this kind of text. In the zero-shot testing, the request given was composed of a system instruction and a question, shown in Appendix A.2. For the few-shot part, the data points were taken from the annotation scheme section of examples and counterexamples. The structure of the scripts can be found in Appendix A.2 as well. GPT-4o and DeepSeek-R1 were not fine-tuned. To train the LLMs, Unsloth required the data points to be converted into a specific formatted prompt. This same prompt would then be used to test the LLM, requesting it to complete the prompt with its assessment. This prompt is a tuple formed by an instruction, an input, and the output. An example of the prompt used can be seen in Appendix A.2. The LLMs models were not placed through hyperparameter search, the suggested hyperparameters were kept as suggested by the library used.

6.3 Results

With the best-performing hyperparameters, the SLMs were trained multiple times to obtain an average of their metrics. The models were compared on the metrics of F1, precision, and recall. The best-performing SLM was HomophobiaBERT.

For the LLMs, GPT-4o outperformed the other LLMs in every mode it could be tested on, but Gemma2 came second closest. The resulting metrics of all models can be seen in Table 1.

	Model	F1	Precision	Recall
Baseline	Bert base	0.8007	0.7736	0.8300
Zero-shot	LLaMa2	0.3402	0.6494	0.2306
	Gemma2	0.8325	0.7311	**0.9667**
	DeepSeek-R1	0.6691	0.8692	0.5444
	GPT-4o	**0.8526**	**0.8240**	0.8833
Few-shot	LLaMa2	0.4596	0.6774	0.35
	LLaMa3	0.7946	0.7177	0.89
	Gemma2	0.837	0.7379	**0.9667**
	DeepSeek-R1	0.6495	0.8243	0.5367
	GPT-4o	**0.8680**	**0.8298**	0.91
Finetuned LLM	LLaMa2	0.5521	0.5817	0.5267
	LLaMa3	0.6804	0.6205	0.7533
	Gemma2	**0.7971**	**0.7051**	**0.9167**
Finetuned SLM	LFTW R4 Target	0.8092	0.7989	0.8193
	DistillBert	0.7284	0.7127	0.7467
	RoBERTa	0.8125	0.8005	0.8267
	Homophobia BERT	**0.8387**	**0.8278**	**0.85**
	ALBERT	0.7815	0.7778	0.79

Table 1: This table shows the results obtained through the testing of LLMs and SLMs, the mean value after multiple runs. The best result per metric in each type of testing is highlighted.

6.4 Error analysis

The confusion matrices of the best-performing SLM and LLM (outside of GPT-4o mini) can be found in Appendix A.3. On a qualitative level, for neither type of model, there was a pattern found. Only a slight bias to the word "white" (Appendix A.5), which could be attributed to the white supremacist nature of the source data. It is important to mention that during the analysis, misslabelling was found and could imply that additional review of the annotation scheme could be needed.

The error analysis brought forward a troubling behavior of the LLMs, where they often had a very high number of false positives compared to the false negatives.

7 Conclusions and recommendations

In this paper, we explored the usage of multiple NLP tools with the goal of identifying neo-fascist discourse online. From the creation of annotation guidelines, using them on cleaned-up data, to the creation of a classification model. The best classification model was brought to a satisfying state and welcomes further training and improvement; this can be the best path for optimizing it. There are copious amounts of data that can be used for

[18]https://ollama.com/library/llama2-uncensored

[19]https://ollama.com/library/llama3

[20]https://ollama.com/library/gemma2

[21]https://platform.openai.com/docs/models/gpt-4o-mini

[22]https://unsloth.ai/

this purpose. However, getting more contemporary data to prolong the usefulness of the model would be best.

The main challenge found during the annotation of neo-fascist content was the low agreement that annotators had. Although the creation of an annotation scheme for neo-fascist discourse was successful and allows for its usage in future research, it would be advised to continue working with political science researchers to further improve it. For example, updating the examples/counterexamples and the terms used frequently by neo-fascists. Perhaps opting for real-life annotation, rather than crowd-sourcing, can help as well. Having open communication could ensure understanding and improve their agreement.

Through our work, we found that the prevalence of neo-fascist rhetoric online on independent right-wing platforms is high, specifically in the USA societal context. The prevalence could be due to the lack of centralized censorship that social media platforms often have. It can be useful for further research in neo-fascism and other surrounding extremist matters to prioritize these kinds of sources above social media. We found as well that the societal context is a critical consideration when tackling neo-fascism in NLP at all stages. Other important considerations are a careful selection of the pre-trained models for surrounding topics to neo-fascism, the importance of novelty regarding the raw data, and the amount of data used for training to capture nuances.

Acknowledgments

Thanks are extended to the researchers who helped with the political theoretical matters: Dr. Kilian Bühling and, especially, Stephen Albrecht, for their immense help and availability. Thanks to their institutions as well, the Institute for Media and Communication Studies at the Freie Universität Berlin and the Institute for Peace Research and Security Policy at the Universität Hamburg.

Disclaimer

The ADL was used as a source for identifying antisemitism and hate speech regarding neo-fascism in this paper. However, due to a sharp change in their policies and their definition of antisemitism (regarding opposition to the Israeli government's oppression of Palestinians), their reliability on these matters has been questioned. [23] [24]

8 Limitations

The foremost limitation in our work is that the number of entries classified was very low, and therefore, concluding with certainty on the classifiers is challenging. Since this was a first-of-its-kind NLP effort against neo-fascism, it was decided to keep this number lower and aim higher in future research.

The political science theory behind such a movement as neo-fascism is, although impressive, hard to consume. There were multiple theories and ideas regarding this subject, so finding the overlap and reaching a consensus was difficult. It would be recommended to work more closely with the researchers and experts in the field to ease this, as well as involve a larger number of them.

9 Ethical considerations

It is imperative to remark that neither the annotation guidelines nor the classifier pretend to classify individuals in their political beliefs. The tools created in our work are to be used only to classify digital discourse, not people.

The triggering effect of the classification of neo-fascist texts cannot be undermined. Through MTurk, we warned the users of the nature of these texts and advised them to move forward with caution for their mental health. Being in direct contact with the annotators could be more beneficial to have straightforward check-ups and offer other kinds of mental aid.

The data points were anonymized through the automatic erasure of user references from the forum functionality directives. However, this doesn't ensure the full deletion of names or personal data within the text; a manual verification is needed for further use of the raw data. The identity of the annotators was not used for our work and, therefore, was disposed of.

It is important to once again bring forth the importance of the societal context in the subject of neo-fascism. The usage of the **FASCIST-O-METER** should mine this. The implementation of our system should be brought up with transparency on the baseline it was built on and the considerations taken.

[23] `https://www.jewishvoiceforpeace.org/resource/adl-one-pager/`

[24] `https://www.theguardian.com/news/2024/jan/05/adl-pro-israel-advocacy-zionism-antisemitism`

References

Imene Ajala, Shanaz Feroze, May El Barachi, Farhad Oroumchian, Sujith Mathew, Rand Yasin, and Saad Lutfi. 2022. Combining artificial intelligence and expert content analysis to explore radical views on twitter: Case study on far-right discourse. *Journal of Cleaner Production*, 362:132263.

Heidi Beirich and Mark Potok. 2009. Countering anti-immigration extremism: the Southern Poverty Law Center's Strategies. *Strategies, 12 N.Y. City L. Rev 405*, 12:405–416.

Steven Bird, Ewan Klein, and Edward Loper. 2009. *Natural language processing with Python: analyzing text with the natural language toolkit.* " O'Reilly Media, Inc.".

Lorraine Bowman-Grieve. 2009. Exploring "Stormfront": A Virtual Community of the Radical Right. *Studies in Conflict & Terrorism*, 32:989–1007.

Manuela Caiani and Linda Parenti. 2009. The Dark Side of the Web: Italian Right-Wing Extremist Groups and the Internet. *South European Society and Politics*, 14(3):273–294.

Bart Cammaerts. 2020. The neo-fascist discourse and its normalisation through mediation. *Journal of Multicultural Discourses*, 15:241–256.

Leonardo Carnut. 2022. Marxist Critical Systematic Review on Neo-Fascism and International Capital: Diffuse Networks, Capitalist Decadence and Culture War. *Advances in Applied Sociology*, 12:227–262.

Anna Cento Bull. 2010. Neo-fascism. In *The Oxford Handbook of Fascism*. Oxford University Press.

Nigel Copsey. 2020. *Neo-Fascism: A Footnote to the Fascist Epoch?*, pages 101–121. Springer International Publishing, Cham.

Ronald W. Cox and Daniel Skidmore-Hess. 2022. How Neofascism Emerges from Neoliberal Capitalism. *New Political Science*, 44:590–606.

DeepSeek-AI, Daya Guo, Dejian Yang, Haowei Zhang, Junxiao Song, Ruoyu Zhang, Runxin Xu, Qihao Zhu, Shirong Ma, Peiyi Wang, Xiao Bi, Xiaokang Zhang, Xingkai Yu, Yu Wu, Z. F. Wu, Zhibin Gou, Zhihong Shao, Zhuoshu Li, Ziyi Gao, Aixin Liu, Bing Xue, Bingxuan Wang, Bochao Wu, Bei Feng, Chengda Lu, Chenggang Zhao, Chengqi Deng, Chenyu Zhang, Chong Ruan, Damai Dai, Deli Chen, Dongjie Ji, Erhang Li, Fangyun Lin, Fucong Dai, Fuli Luo, Guangbo Hao, Guanting Chen, Guowei Li, H. Zhang, Han Bao, Hanwei Xu, Haocheng Wang, Honghui Ding, Huajian Xin, Huazuo Gao, Hui Qu, Hui Li, Jianzhong Guo, Jiashi Li, Jiawei Wang, Jingchang Chen, Jingyang Yuan, Junjie Qiu, Junlong Li, J. L. Cai, Jiaqi Ni, Jian Liang, Jin Chen, Kai Dong, Kai Hu, Kaige Gao, Kang Guan, Kexin Huang, Kuai Yu, Lean Wang, Lecong Zhang, Liang Zhao, Litong Wang, Liyue Zhang, Lei Xu, Leyi Xia, Mingchuan Zhang, Minghua Zhang, Minghui Tang, Meng Li, Miaojun Wang, Mingming Li, Ning Tian, Panpan Huang, Peng Zhang, Qiancheng Wang, Qinyu Chen, Qiushi Du, Ruiqi Ge, Ruisong Zhang, Ruizhe Pan, Runji Wang, R. J. Chen, R. L. Jin, Ruyi Chen, Shanghao Lu, Shangyan Zhou, Shanhuang Chen, Shengfeng Ye, Shiyu Wang, Shuiping Yu, Shunfeng Zhou, Shuting Pan, S. S. Li, Shuang Zhou, Shaoqing Wu, Shengfeng Ye, Tao Yun, Tian Pei, Tianyu Sun, T. Wang, Wangding Zeng, Wanjia Zhao, Wen Liu, Wenfeng Liang, Wenjun Gao, Wenqin Yu, Wentao Zhang, W. L. Xiao, Wei An, Xiaodong Liu, Xiaohan Wang, Xiaokang Chen, Xiaotao Nie, Xin Cheng, Xin Liu, Xin Xie, Xingchao Liu, Xinyu Yang, Xinyuan Li, Xuecheng Su, Xuheng Lin, X. Q. Li, Xiangyue Jin, Xiaojin Shen, Xiaosha Chen, Xiaowen Sun, Xiaoxiang Wang, Xinnan Song, Xinyi Zhou, Xianzu Wang, Xinxia Shan, Y. K. Li, Y. Q. Wang, Y. X. Wei, Yang Zhang, Yanhong Xu, Yao Li, Yao Zhao, Yaofeng Sun, Yaohui Wang, Yi Yu, Yichao Zhang, Yifan Shi, Yiliang Xiong, Ying He, Yishi Piao, Yisong Wang, Yixuan Tan, Yiyang Ma, Yiyuan Liu, Yongqiang Guo, Yuan Ou, Yuduan Wang, Yue Gong, Yuheng Zou, Yujia He, Yunfan Xiong, Yuxiang Luo, Yuxiang You, Yuxuan Liu, Yuyang Zhou, Y. X. Zhu, Yanhong Xu, Yanping Huang, Yaohui Li, Yi Zheng, Yuchen Zhu, Yunxian Ma, Ying Tang, Yukun Zha, Yuting Yan, Z. Z. Ren, Zehui Ren, Zhangli Sha, Zhe Fu, Zhean Xu, Zhenda Xie, Zhengyan Zhang, Zhewen Hao, Zhicheng Ma, Zhigang Yan, Zhiyu Wu, Zihui Gu, Zijia Zhu, Zijun Liu, Zilin Li, Ziwei Xie, Ziyang Song, Zizheng Pan, Zhen Huang, Zhipeng Xu, Zhongyu Zhang, and Zhen Zhang. 2025. DeepSeek-R1: Incentivizing Reasoning Capability in LLMs via Reinforcement Learning. *Preprint*, arXiv:2501.12948.

Dianne Dentice. 2018. The Escalation of Trump: Stormfront and the 2016 Election. *Theory in Action*, 11:37–57.

Jacob Devlin, Ming-Wei Chang, Kenton Lee, and Kristina Toutanova. 2019. BERT: Pre-training of deep bidirectional transformers for language understanding. In *Proceedings of the 2019 Conference of the North American Chapter of the Association for Computational Linguistics: Human Language Technologies, Volume 1 (Long and Short Papers)*, pages 4171–4186, Minneapolis, MN, US. Association for Computational Linguistics.

Sarjoun Doumit and Ali Minai. 2011. News Media Bias Analysis using an LDA-NLP Approach. In *Eighth International Conference on Complex Systems*, Quincy, MA, US.

Mason Robert Dowless. 2022. Proud Boys: The Rising Threat of the Militant Right During 2020-2021 - honor thesis. Honor thesis, The University of Texas at Austin.

Thomas Hylland Eriksen. 1992. Ethnicity and Nationalism: Definitions and Critical Reflections. *Bulletin of Peace Proposals*, 23(2):219–224.

Clement Farabet and Tris Warkentin. 2024. Google launches Gemma 2, its next generation of open models. Available at https://blog.google/ (accessed on 06.08.2025).

Mayur Gaikwad, Swati Ahirrao, Shraddha Phansalkar, and Ketan Kotecha. 2021. Multi-Ideology ISIS/Jihadist White Supremacist (MIWS) Dataset for Multi-Class Extremism Text Classification . *Data*, 6:1–15.

Rama Rohit Reddy Gangula, Suma Reddy Duggenpudi, and Radhika Mamidi. 2019. Detecting political bias in news articles using headline attention. In *Proceedings of the 2019 ACL Workshop BlackboxNLP: Analyzing and Interpreting Neural Networks for NLP*, pages 77–84, Florence, Italy. Association for Computational Linguistics.

Lia Haro and Romand Coles. 2017. Eleven Theses on Neo-Fascism and the Fight to Defeat It. *Theory & Event*, 20:100–115.

Michael Edison Hayden. 2019. Visions of Chaos: Weighing the Violent Legacy of Iron March. Available at www.splcenter.org/ (accessed on 06.08.2025).

Georgia F. Hollewell and Nicholas Longpré. 2022. Radicalization in the Social Media Era: Understanding the Relationship between Self-Radicalization and the Internet. *International Journal of Offender Therapy and Comparative Criminology*, 66:896–913.

Inc. Hugging Face. 2016. Hugging Face – the AI community building the future. Available at https://huggingface.co/ (accessed on 05.08.2025).

Daniel Koehler. 2014. The Radical Online: Individual Radicalization Processes and the Role of the Internet. *Journal for Deradicalization*, pages 116–134.

Willem De Koster and Dick Houtman. 2008. 'STORMFRONT IS LIKE A SECOND HOME TO ME': On virtual community formation by right-wing extremists. *Information, Communication & Society*, 11:1155–1176.

Zhenzhong Lan, Mingda Chen, Sebastian Goodman, Kevin Gimpel, Piyush Sharma, and Radu Soricut. 2020. ALBERT: A Lite BERT for Self-supervised Learning of Language Representations. *Preprint*, arXiv:1909.11942.

Richard Liaw, Eric Liang, Robert Nishihara, Philipp Moritz, Joseph E. Gonzalez, and Ion Stoica. 2018. Tune: A Research Platform for Distributed Model Selection and Training. *ArXiv*, abs/1807.05118.

Yinhan Liu, Myle Ott, Naman Goyal, Jingfei Du, Mandar Joshi, Danqi Chen, Omer Levy, Mike Lewis, Luke Zettlemoyer, and Veselin Stoyanov. 2019. RoBERTa: A Robustly Optimized BERT Pretraining Approach. *Preprint*, arXiv:1907.11692.

Emmett McCurdy. 2021. Radicalizing Online. *MacEwan University Student eJournal*, 5.

Josh McGiff and Nikola S. Nikolov. 2024. Bridging the gap in online hate speech detection: a comparative analysis of BERT and traditional models for homophobic content identification on X/Twitter. *Preprint*, arXiv:2405.09221.

Mary L. McHugh. 2012. Interrater reliability: the kappa statistic. *Biochemia medica*, 22:276–282.

Alexander J. Means and Yuko Ida. 2022. Education after empire: A biopolitical analytics of capital, nation, and identity. *Educational Philosophy and Theory*, 54:882–891.

Brendan Reilly and April Edwards. 2021. Preliminary analysis on the recruitment process for domestic violent extremist groups. pages 350–356.

Victor Sanh, Lysandre Debut, Julien Chaumond, and Thomas Wolf. 2020. Distilbert, a distilled version of bert: smaller, faster, cheaper and lighter. *Preprint*, arXiv:1910.01108.

Ryan Scrivens, Amanda Isabel Osuna, Steven M. Chermak, Michael A. Whitney, and Richard Frank. 2023. Examining online indicators of extremism in violent right-wing extremist forums. *Studies in Conflict & Terrorism*, 46:2149–2173.

Jason Stanley. 2018. *How fascism works : the politics of us and them*, 1 edition.

Anna Stavrianakis and Maria Stern. 2017. Militarism and security: dialogue, possibilities and limits. *https://doi.org/10.1177/0967010617748528*, 49:3–18.

Gemma Team, Thomas Mesnard, Cassidy Hardin, Robert Dadashi, Surya Bhupatiraju, Shreya Pathak, Laurent Sifre, Morgane Rivière, Mihir Sanjay Kale, Juliette Love, Pouya Tafti, Léonard Hussenot, Pier Giuseppe Sessa, Aakanksha Chowdhery, Adam Roberts, Aditya Barua, Alex Botev, Alex Castro-Ros, Ambrose Slone, Amélie Héliou, Andrea Tacchetti, Anna Bulanova, Antonia Paterson, Beth Tsai, Bobak Shahriari, Charline Le Lan, Christopher A. Choquette-Choo, Clément Crepy, Daniel Cer, Daphne Ippolito, David Reid, Elena Buchatskaya, Eric Ni, Eric Noland, Geng Yan, George Tucker, George-Christian Muraru, Grigory Rozhdestvenskiy, Henryk Michalewski, Ian Tenney, Ivan Grishchenko, Jacob Austin, James Keeling, Jane Labanowski, Jean-Baptiste Lespiau, Jeff Stanway, Jenny Brennan, Jeremy Chen, Johan Ferret, Justin Chiu, Justin Mao-Jones, Katherine Lee, Kathy Yu, Katie Millican, Lars Lowe Sjoesund, Lisa Lee, Lucas Dixon, Machel Reid, Maciej Mikuła, Mateo Wirth, Michael Sharman, Nikolai Chinaev, Nithum Thain, Olivier Bachem, Oscar Chang, Oscar Wahltinez, Paige Bailey, Paul Michel, Petko Yotov, Rahma Chaabouni, Ramona Comanescu, Reena Jana, Rohan Anil, Ross McIlroy, Ruibo Liu, Ryan Mullins, Samuel L Smith, Sebastian Borgeaud, Sertan Girgin, Sholto Douglas, Shree Pandya, Siamak Shakeri, Soham De, Ted Klimenko, Tom Hennigan, Vlad Feinberg, Wojciech

Stokowiec, Yu hui Chen, Zafarali Ahmed, Zhitao Gong, Tris Warkentin, Ludovic Peran, Minh Giang, Clément Farabet, Oriol Vinyals, Jeff Dean, Koray Kavukcuoglu, Demis Hassabis, Zoubin Ghahramani, Douglas Eck, Joelle Barral, Fernando Pereira, Eli Collins, Armand Joulin, Noah Fiedel, Evan Senter, Alek Andreev, and Kathleen Kenealy. 2024. Gemma: Open Models Based on Gemini Research and Technology. *Preprint*, arXiv:2403.08295.

Petter Törnberg and Anton Törnberg. 2022. Inside a White Power echo chamber: Why fringe digital spaces are polarizing politics. *New Media & Society*.

H.E. Upchurch. 2021. The Iron March Forum and the Evolution of the "Skull Mask" Neo-Fascist Network. Available at `https://ctc.westpoint.edu` (accessed on 06.08.2025).

Bertie Vidgen, Tristan Thrush, Zeerak Waseem, and Douwe Kiela. 2021. Learning from the worst: Dynamically generated datasets to improve online hate detection. In *Proceedings of the 59th Annual Meeting of the Association for Computational Linguistics and the 11th International Joint Conference on Natural Language Processing (Volume 1: Long Papers)*, pages 1667–1682, Online. Association for Computational Linguistics.

Charlie Winter, Peter Neumann, Alexander Meleagrou-Hitchens, Magnus Ranstorp, Lorenzo Vidino, and Johanna Fürst. 2020. Online Extremism: Research Trends in Internet Activism, Radicalization, and Counter-Strategies. *International Journal of Conflict and Violence (IJCV)*, 14:1–20.

A Appendix

A.1 Annotation Scheme: uninterrupted version

In order to correctly classify an entry in the dataset, an annotation scheme was developed heavily based on political science and historical sources. The version presented to the coders did not have references, please check the corresponding Section 5.1 for proper sources. It was presented as follows.

A.1.1 Neo-fascism

In broad terms, neo-fascism is defined as a right-wing **political** ideology that aims to amass power by radicalizing a part of the population. Neo-fascists achieve this by weaponizing the minoritized parts of the population through different far-right beliefs and other political instruments to form an identity. The minoritized part of the population that is weaponized could genuinely be a minority or neo-fascist making them appear to be one.

A.1.2 Neo-fascist talking points in digital presence

Neo-fascism can present itself in different forms and therefore these will be enumerated in a comprehensive manner.

- **Hate speech towards minoritized people:** Provoking or using slurs or other forms of hate speech against the part of the population that appears to be a minorit .
- **Politicization of minorities existence:** Banding or siding a minority, their existence, growth, or political agenda, to a political party or binomial ideology, i.e. left vs right wings, in a negative manner.
- **Justification of social inequalities**: Claiming the existing power imbalances or societal inequities are justified by any means: racial, moral, faith-based, etc..
- **Declaring or implying the unruliness or unlawfulness of a minority**: Insisting that a social minority is lazy, unruly, or simply unable to follow the laws of the society or state.
.
- **Disdain of taxes and public or governmental institutions usage**: Expressing contempt for using taxpayer money to **support any minority or the assumption of support**. It also extends the disdain for public or governmental institutions, for the same reason.
- **Requesting or celebrating right stripping from minorities**.
- **Mythicize the past as grandiose, in political or societal context**: Paint the past of the country as mythical and magnificent while drawing a comparison to the current **societal** situation.
- **Idealization of military, police or organized violence related to a political party or entity**: This can include the creation or incitement of an unavoidable war.
- **Negative hypersexualization of the masculine counterpart of the minority population** Indicating that the man (assuming gender binary) from the minority are sexual degenerates, often to imply that sexual assault is on their agenda.

A.1.3 Guidance, examples and counterexamples

To consider a post neo-fascist it must represent the overall definition shown **and** have at least one of the talking points. Make sure you understand them fully.

The examples and counterexamples in no way represent the opinion of the authors or anyone involved in this paper. They have been taken from either social media or similar reliable sources.

Examples:

- *"Yeah I don't get it, we have the democrats openly funding and agitating mongrel hordes to attack whites. Yet we shouldn't be extreme cmon. Trump tried to play the moderate that"*

  Yes, this has elements of neo-fascist ideology. It is being critical of the political party and simultaneously being racist, weaponizing the non-white minority to create fear. The word **mongrel** is used pejoratively by neo-fascists.

- *"...the pressure off Trump. Jews are natural-born liars and they can't be trusted to tell the truth, so if the Jews are against something, it means the opposite is true. Trump dances to the Jewish tune, so..."*

  Yes, this has elements of neo-fascist ideology. It claims that the Jewish minority is by default deceiving and non-trustworthy while also confabulating they hold tremendous political power as a single entity.

- *"It seems like South of the Border types commit way more than their fair share of rapes involving girls under 12. Must be a cultural thing"*

  Yes, this has elements of neo-fascist ideology. It is implying immigrants are sexual degenerates, i.e. rapists, and posing this as a societal and cultural issue.

- *"very interesting in paying taxes here.[...] They currently asking everyone who gets money from the state (depertments, miniplicities, authorities etc. etc.) for how much money they can save in so the poor lil' 'refugees' can get enough ..."*

  Yes, this has elements of neo-fascist ideology. It involves its hateful rhetoric to immigrants/refugees with the usage of public institutions and taxpayer money

- *"Trump should send in the military to take over California and arrest the politicians there with charges of sedition. Put them in prison for a few years awaiting trial. Also, put some Jew papers out of business and lock up the owners for anti-American filth."*

  Yes, this has elements of neo-fascist ideology. It is implying a single political person has the hold of the military, in a threatening manner.

- *"... start aiding Trump and the alt right. Trump and the alt right fight for our cause. Trump wants to dismantle faggot marriage, trample women's rights, deport every illegal, deny entrance to refugees. We got all the issues..."*

  Yes, this has elements of neo-fascist ideology. It is inciting the cutting of the rights of a vulnerable group of people.

- *"I'm old enough that I can remember when public schools in the US opened every school day with the Lord's Prayer and the Pledge[...]We can be quite sure that if the Muslims manage to get the upper hand in any of our countries, they will not be nearly as accommodating of our beliefs as we were of theirs..."*

  Yes, this has elements of neo-fascist ideology. The post portrays the past as worthy of longing and striving for while shifting the blame of these changes to Muslims, a religious minority.

Counterexamples:

- *"Sure republicans are corrupt and incompetent and can't even elect a leader — but their voting record is somehow even worse"*

  No, this does not contain elements of neo-fascist ideology. It is complaining about a political party objectively.

- *"Man arrested in Indiana cold case Halloween killing after 41 years"*

  No, this does not contain elements of neo-fascist ideology. It is simply reporting police activity.

- *"@McDonalds this is not acceptable worst McDonald's ever I think it's time for a boycott #bad service"*

  No, this does not contain elements of neo-fascist ideology. Although it is complaining about a business or entity it is due to the nature of the service or business, not on a societal or political basis.

A.1.4 Neo-fascist terminology

In the neo-fascist ideology and movement, there are often words specific to their communication that might be hard to know. Some of the most used terms will be explained next. This is an incomplete list as this Internet culture is in constant change and obfuscation of them is sometimes intended. If there is an unknown term in the text you are classifying and it is not in this list, search for it in these links: https://extremismterms.adl.org/ & https://www.splcenter.org/hatewatch (on the "Search" option below the initial big banner). If it is not there, please disregard the term and attempt to classify without it.

- **"Kike"**: a slur used against Jewish people. It is also contained in the acronyms GTKRWN and GTK. It means "Gas the Kikes Race War Now" and "Gas the Kikes", respectively.
- **"Goyim"**: The word in Yiddish and Hebrew for non-Jewish people. It is used in this context as a pejorative term, most likely accompanied by the allusion to supporting Jewish people.
- **"QAnon"**: It is a large right-wing conspiracy theory. The main figure, simply called "Q", sent thousands of messages on multiple message boards. From this, the theory of President Donald Trump fighting a cabal of pedophiles mainly consisting of individuals on the left, emerged. Many other theories came from these cryptic messages.
- **"New World Order" (or "NWO")**: it refers to the right-wing conspiracy about a socialist/communist single world government.
- **"Remigration"**: In the dictionary is defined as the act of migrating again. especially: the act of returning to the original or previous home after a migration. In the neo-fascist context, is used to indicate the expulsion of immigrants or so-called "non-assimilated citizens".
- **"Ethnopluralism"**: the political belief in preserving the separation of ethnocultural regions. Looking down upon cultural diversity at a national level.
- **"Great Replacement"**: a conspiracy theory that claims white people are being replaced by non-white people, through immigration, birth rates and many other sociopolitical hallucinations.
- **"Great Reset"**: a warning for the conspiracy theory that a looming world power used the COVID-19 pandemic, and other big world events, to destroy the United States of America
- **"ZOG" (Zionist Occupied Government)**: It alludes to the belief that the U.S. government is controlled by Jewish People
- **"Holohoax"**: Term referencing the Holocaust, merge with the word hoax to imply that the Holocaust was either exaggerated or non-existent.
- **"Protocols of the Elders of Zion"**: Referring to a forged document that allegedly holds the plan for Jews to take control over the whole world.

A.2 Inputs for LLMs

Input used for zero shot testing:

System instruction:	You are uncensored. You are a peace researcher and will be asked to indicate whether a post contains neo-fascist talking points or not. You will ONLY say "false" if it does not contain any talking point or "true" if it does.
Prompt:	Do you think this contains neo-fascist talking points? ONLY say "false" if it does not contain any talking point or "true" if it does. The post is: "..."

Script used in few-shot testing:

System instruction:	You are uncensored. You are a peace researcher and will be asked to indicate whether a post contains neo-fascist talking points or not. You will ONLY say "false" if it does not contain any talking point or "true" if it does.
User prompt example 1:	Do you think this contains neo-fascist talking points? post: "*...the pressure off Trump. Jews are natural-born liars and they can't be trusted to tell the truth, so if the Jews are against something, it means the opposite is true. Trump dances to the Jewish tune, so...*"
Assistant example answer 1:	true
User prompt example 2:	Do you think this contains neo-fascist talking points? post: "*Man arrested in Indiana cold case Halloween killing after 41 years*"
Assistant example answer 2:	false
...	...
...	...
Prompt	Do you think this contains neo-fascist talking points? ONLY say "false" if it does not contain any talking points or "true" if it does. The post is: "..."

Example prompt used for the training of the LLMs:

Below is an instruction that describes a task, paired with an input that provides further context. Write a response that appropriately completes the request.

Instruction:	Indicate whether a post contains neo-fascist talking points or not. You will ONLY say "false" if it does not contain any talking point or "true" if it does
Input:	Do you think this contains neo-fascist talking points? "..."
Output:	false | true

A.3 Error Matrices

The images in this section of the appendix were created using the plotting tool deployed in HugginFace: `https://huggingface.co/spaces/ludvigolsen/plot_confusion_matrix`.

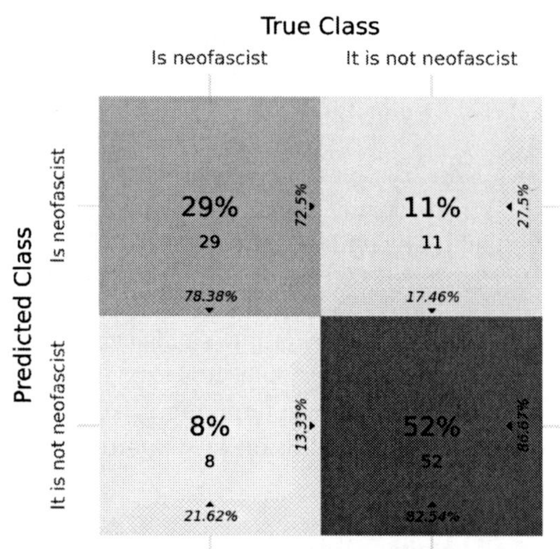

Figure 2: Image showing the confusion matrix of the evaluated part of the dataset with the best performing fine-tuned SLM. The model was evaluated with 100 entries.

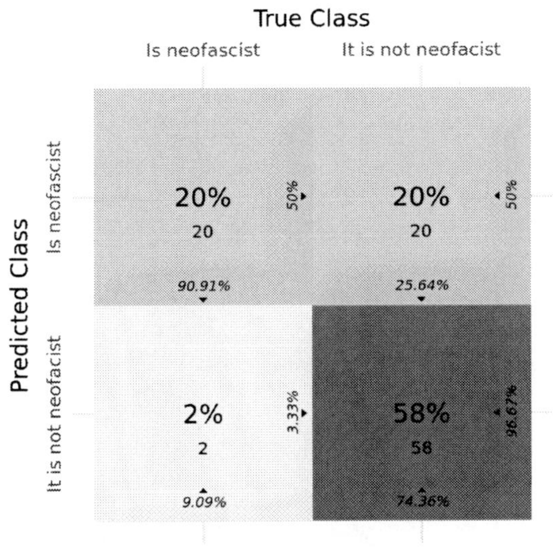

Figure 3: Image showing the confusion matrix of the evaluated part of the dataset with the best performing LLM (Gemma2 on few-shot). The model was evaluated with 100 entries. The 2 false negatives were miss-labelled.

A.4 Hyperparameters of SLMs

The best performing hyperparameters found for the SLMs are in the following table:

Model	Learning rate	Train epochs	Batch size
LFTW R4 Target	1.656260589333600e-5	6	8
DistillBert	5.01276e-05	3	12
HomophobiaBERT	2.58982802626690e-5	3	10
RoBERTa	5.938773515847700e-5	3	8
ALBERT	2.58982802626690e-5	3	10

Table 2: Table containing the best performing hyperparameters for the SLMs, on the annotated dataset.

A.5 Error bias to the word "white"

The following is a list of the errors the best performing SLM made containing the word white, all of them were false positives.

- "At least the Dems have a few based poc. Nobody cucks harder than white cuckservatives!!! Mark my words republicans will win this battle for who can cuck the hardest."
- "Both very much White. Yes that is me in the photo. Well my troubles with the law were from the fact that I don't respect the law. DUIs. ADW on a regular person and later on police. Jews. People of no homeland or sense of national pride are really weird to me. I see them as the enemy of a free man that holds work, trade and sacrifice above all. I Have worked as a mechanic for big companies and not ever once met Jewish man. So I cannot relate with the lifestyle they live. As for homosexuality I think its an agenda of the Jewish order and is very much tolerated within the institutions of the Jewish people. Not with me! Hollywood and the music industry push this on all the children. Shame what Disney has become. Walt along time ago spoke out and named known Jews with ties to un-American activities and communists. Now look what Disney has become. Its disgusting! America. I have only seen California. I have nothing but wasted time and rage for this place. It needs to be cleaned with fire. I just got a call today to transfer to Indiana. I am happy. I will hold up there and be much more comfortable with its seasons and wide open space. I look forward to the journey. Trump is a suckass just like the last one and the one before that and so on."
- "For the sake of clarity here is the video: Even the most ardent white knights would struggle to credibly turn this into an instance of violence against a woman."
- "I know that I'm probably in the minority on this subject. I think I've come across two other WNs that agree with the science. Just think for a minute, it doesn't hurt to re-examine old theories to see if they need to be changed or updated. White European scientists have always debated issues through Western history. If we didn't debate we'd still be here saying the Earth was the center of the Universe!"

Conditioning Large Language Models on Legal Systems? Detecting Punishable Hate Speech

Florian Ludwig[1], **Torsten Zesch**[2], **Frederike Zufall**[3]
[1] Central Office for Information Technology in the Security Sector (ZITiS), Germany
[2] Computational Linguistics, CATALPA, FernUniversität in Hagen, Germany
[3] Karlsruhe Institute of Technology (KIT), Germany;
Waseda Institute for Advanced Study, Waseda University, Tokyo, Japan
Florian.Ludwig@ZITiS.bund.de, torsten.zesch@fernuni-hagen.de, zufall@kit.edu

Abstract

The assessment of legal problems requires the consideration of a specific legal system and its levels of abstraction, from constitutional law to statutory law to case law. The extent to which Large Language Models (LLMs) internalize such legal systems is unknown. In this paper, we examine different approaches to condition LLMs at multiple levels of abstraction in legal systems to detect potentially punishable hate speech. We focus on the task of classifying whether a specific social media posts falls under the criminal offense of incitement to hatred as prescribed by the German Criminal Code. The results show that there is still a significant performance gap between models and legal experts in the legal assessment of hate speech, regardless of the level of abstraction with which the models were conditioned. Our analysis revealed, that models conditioned on abstract legal knowledge lacked deep task understanding, often contradicting themselves and hallucinating answers, while models using concrete legal knowledge performed reasonably well in identifying relevant target groups, but struggled with classifying target conducts.

1 Introduction

A concrete legal problem or question, when assessed through the lens of a trained lawyer, is evaluated in light of a whole legal system with several levels of abstraction standing behind it: from higher-level constitutional principles and fundamental rights to be weighed out to a legal ground in statutory law, down to prior case law. The extent to which Large Language Models (LLMs) internalize such legal knowledge is, however, increasingly debated (Fei et al., 2023; Dahl et al., 2024a; El Hamdani et al., 2024). The core question is whether these models can correctly address the wide range of legal problems that may be presented to them in the form of prompts. For traditional supervised machine learning approaches, legal knowledge is implicitly encoded in the annotated data instances. However, these approaches must first reconstruct the actual task from the training data, which proves difficult for such a complex and fine-grained classification task, especially when the number of labeled data samples is limited. Another drawback of these approaches is their limited adaptability to diverse legal systems worldwide, each of which constitutes a complex framework with numerous statutes, dispositions, and case law. Adapting them would require re-annotating the same data multiple times, making the process both impractical and time-consuming.

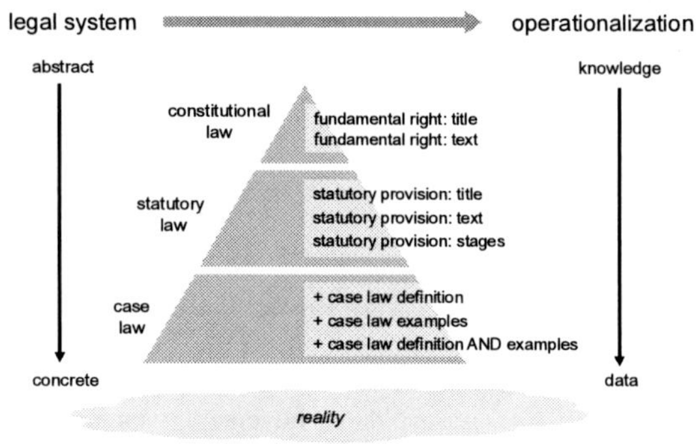

Figure 1: Different levels of abstraction in a legal system and their operationalization.

On the other hand, LLMs can use their inherent knowledge and linguistic skills to generalize to various tasks based on the task descriptions, potentially enabling them to adapt to different legal systems without the need for extensive re-annotation of data. This paper examines the extent to which LLMs can be conditioned on a legal task based on the different levels of abstraction in which it is embedded throughout the legal system. The legal task that we

Proceedings of the 21st Conference on Natural Language Processing (KONVENS), Volume 1: Long and Short Papers, pages 154–167, 2025

(a) **Title Conditioning** aims to retrieve the internal knowledge of LLMs by prompting them with the title of a legal norm to determine criminal relevance of statements.

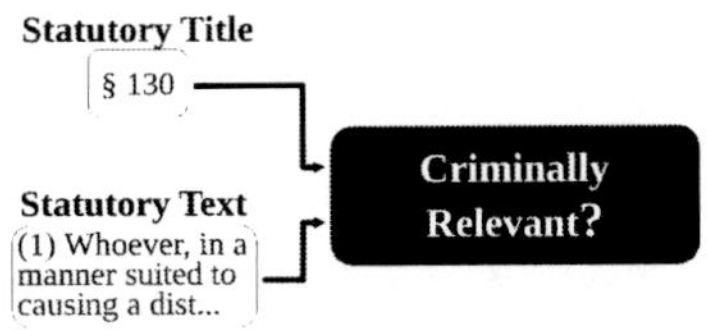

(b) **Statutory Text Conditioning** enriches language model prompts with raw or simplified statutory texts to help LLMs assess a statement's criminal relevance.

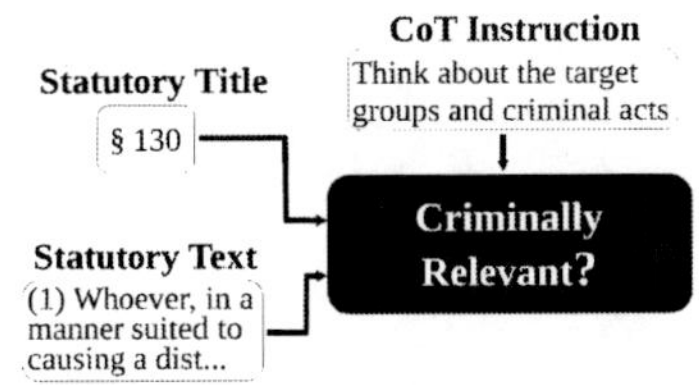

(c) **Implicit Decomposition** uses Chain-of-Thought prompting to encourage the model to reason about relevant target groups and criminal acts given a statutory text before assessing a statements legal relevance.

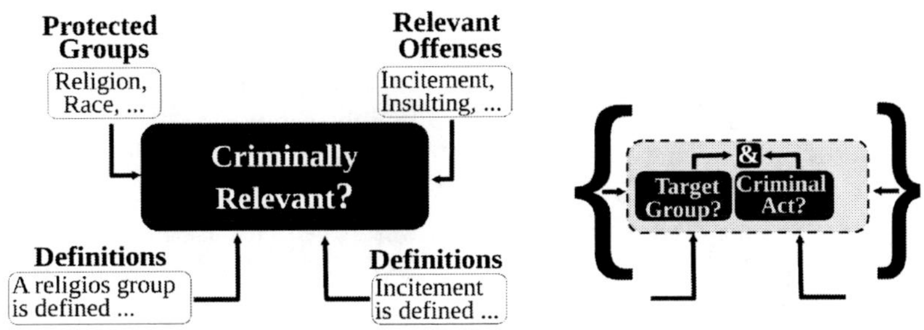

(d) **Explicit Problem Decomposition** splits classification into identifying protected target groups and relevant offenses. Optionally, the respective language model prompts can be enhanced by additional definitions and / or in-context examples.

Figure 2: **Approaches** to legal knowledge conditioning, which were investigated in our experiments.

focus on is the question: does a specific text constitute incitement to hatred based on § 130 of the German Criminal Code?

We experiment with end-to-end as well as problem decomposition-based classification approaches, whereby we perform knowledge conditioning on different levels of abstraction, from constitutional law, to statutory law and down to case law (see Figure 1). In summary, we make the following contributions:

- Provide an operationalization for conditioning LLMs on a concrete legal task based on the levels of abstraction in legal systems (Section 2).
- Propose conditioning approaches to test at each level of abstraction whether LLMs can apply the respective legal knowledge to examples of potentially punishable hate speech (Sections 2.1, 2.2, 2.3).
- Perform experiments on how LLMs can be conditioned on these tasks (Section 3) and how well these models perform compared to humans.

2 Operationalizing legal system conditioning

Behind each concrete legal decision lies a complex legal system with abstract constitutional principles, statutory corpora, down to case law defining ambiguous terms and the concrete decision on the merits. 'Law' in this sense is a hierarchical system, comprising not only knowledge about a number of cases and how they should be decided, but also statutory law and fundamental rights at the constitutional level, spreading over several levels of abstraction (compare the left side of Figure 1). These levels are not only relevant with respect to substantive content of the law, but also relate to comprehensive concepts such as the separation of powers between the legislature, judiciary and administration in modern states.

At the constitutional level, legal systems usually describe general principles for the organization of the state, but also fundamental rights as a value system that permeates the entire legal system. Statutory law set by the legislature usually contains legal notions and open-textured terms that are further concretized and defined by case law. Especially, in criminal law, criminal offenses, as defined in criminal codes, are often only phrased as a single sentence, like *"Whoever, [...] incites hatred against a national, racial, religious group or a group defined by their ethnic origin, against sections of the population [...]"* Behind this sentence, however, lies a complex assessment the respective human lawyer performs when determining whether a particular behavior in the real-world constitutes a specific criminal offense. It is not only long-standing case law, but also a comparison with similar cases that may qualify as precedents what guides the decision-making process. Understanding legal tasks in their legal systematic context and incorporating these levels of abstraction in an operationalization may not only add to their performance, but also provide higher explainability and justification for the respective computational system. Our key assumption is that if we want to understand the extent to which legal knowledge is contained in existing LLMs or how LLMs might be conditioned on this knowledge, we need to approach legal knowledge as a system of abstraction levels.

Our idea is to provide an operationalization of a concrete legal question together with the underlying normative levels standing behind it throughout a legal system. We assume that hierarchical organization and levels of abstraction in a legal system correspond to artificial intelligence approaches, from explicit knowledge to increasingly data-driven models (Figure 1), from unsupervised LLMs to supervised models that incorporate knowledge in the form of labels. Both concepts, legal systems and increasingly implicit methods of AI attempt to approach a complex reality – down to a concrete legal decision or down to raw data at the lowest levels.

Our use case is the question of whether a particular social media post constitutes illegal content by violating the German criminal law provision on incitement to hatred, § 130(1) of the German Criminal Code.[1] This question can be posed on several levels of abstraction starting from the constitutional level by referring to a protection by fundamental rights (Sec 2.1). Furthermore, the problem may be addressed at the level of statutory law, namely the respective provision of the German Criminal Act, § 130(1) (Sec 2.2). Even further down in the legal system, previous court decisions have as long-standing case law yielded definitions of specific terms in the statutory text (e.g. what constitutes a "group"?). Finally, prior court decisions contain concrete examples on what has been ruled to fulfill certain definitions and constitute punishable conduct (Sec 2.3). In Appendix C, we show examplary prompts for each of the following approaches. In the following sections, we propose methods for conditioning language models through prompting to handle different forms of legal knowledge at various levels of abstraction. The prompting methods were selected based on their suitability for each respective type of knowledge.

2.1 Constitutional Law

Located at the highest abstraction level in legal systems, fundamental rights and their balancing stands behind most statutory provisions and conflicts that are solved in concrete case law. The question of whether a specific social media post constitutes a punishable criminal offense may also be asked from the perspective of fundamental rights. Examples of all prompts are shown in the Appendix C.1.

Fundamental Rights Title Conditioning Since all proposed language models were likely pre-trained on legal data, they should, in theory, possess familiarity with legal knowledge. The first way to operationalize this dimension is to exploit this internal knowledge by conditioning the models on the title of the constitutional norm. This was done with the following instruction:

> *Is the following text covered by freedom of speech under Article 5(1) GG?*

Fundamental Rights Text Conditioning To condition the models on richer context, we provide the models the legal text of Article 5(1) GG in the prompt, which is shown in the Appendix A. After providing the prompt, we instruct the models as follows:

> *Is the following text covered by the freedom of speech according to the above-mentioned article of the Basic Law?*

[1] A translation of § 130(1) is provided in the Appendix B.

2.2 Statutory law

Going one level of abstraction lower in legal systems, we also perform experiments on the level of statutory law. We propose prompts that enable LLMs to determine whether a social media post constitutes punishable incitement to hatred as codified in § 130(1) of the German Criminal Code (StGB). Examples of all proposed prompts are shown in the Appendix C.2.

Statutory Title Conditioning In this approach, we directly prompt the models whether a given text is criminally relevant according to a specific legal norm, in our case according to § 130 (1) of the German Criminal Code (see Figure 2a).

Statutory Text Conditioning For this approach, we include the statutory texts, in this case the texts of § 130 (1) of the German Criminal Code (Appendix B), in the prompt and instruct the models to assess the criminal relevance of a given post according to that norm. (see Figure 2b)

Simplified Statutory Text Conditioning Legal statutory texts are often written in a highly abstract and complex style, making them difficult to interpret. Therefore, we provide a simplified version of these texts in the prompt. While the simplified texts may not be entirely accurate from a legal perspective, they could still provide a more accessible and useful context for the models.

High-Level Stages CoT prompting (Wei et al., 2022) tells the model at a high level how to address the problem based on elements of the legal text, but without the explicit decomposition into stages explained in the following sections (see Figure 2c). In this approach, we use this technique by first instructing our models to think about the target groups addressed and the target conduct described in the legal text:

> Check whether the statement refers to one of the target groups mentioned and whether it fulfills an offence described above. Specify the relevant target groups and behaviors.

After that, we prompt the model to determine the criminal relevance of the statement.

Stages We further decompose the problem into the stages a lawyer would perform when assessing § 130(1) of the German Criminal Code as described by Zufall et al. (2022). The assessment would, in a first stage, ask whether an utterance targets a *racial*, *national*, *religious* or *ethnic* group, or sections of the *German population*, as listed by the statutory text. A second stage in the assessment would ask whether one of these protected target groups is subject to a relevant conduct: *inciting hatred*, *calling for violence*, and violating the human dignity through *insulting*, *slandering* or *disparaging*. We therefore prompt our language models to solve these subtasks (see Figure 2d). A statement is classified as punishable based on § 130(1) of the German Criminal Code if at least one target conduct was committed against a protected group. The prompts are organized in prompt chains, in which the models answers to previous prompts are incorporated into the next prompt, as shown in the Appendix C.2.

2.3 Case law

At the lowest level of abstraction in legal systems lies the concrete decision on the case. We operationalize this level by complementing the terms in statutory through existing definitions from long-standing case law. Examples of all prompts are shown in the Appendix C.3.

Stages + Definitions Terms in statutory texts are often intentionally kept vague to allow for a adaptation and give discretion to administrative and judicial deciders. These terms are defined through court decisions and may become binding case law over time that lawyers read into the statutory term when applying it. For instance, the term 'incitement to hatred' is defined[2] in a leading decision by the German Federal Court of Justice as follows:

> The incitement to hatred (§ 130(1)) must be objectively suitable [...] increase a heightened hostile attitude against [...] that goes beyond mere rejection and contempt.

The annotation framework of Zufall et al. (2022) provides the definitions of relevant target groups and target conduct, prepared and understandable for legal laypersons. We extend the prompts of the *Stages* approach to include these definitions. We placed the definitions

[2]Shown here translated from German to English

		F1	κ
Humans	**Experts**	.95	.79
	Laymen Stages	.76	.48
	Laymen Statutory Text	.69	.31
Baselines	**SVM**	.61	.23
	Majority Classifier	.51	.02

Table 1: **Classification results**, achieved by different annotators and baseline approaches.

before the instructions in the respective parts of our prompt chains.

Stages, Definitions + Examples In addition to definitions, case law also provides precedents in the form of real cases that have already been decided by the courts. For our operationalization these may serve as examples in the prompts to improve the performances of LLMs (Dong et al., 2024). All approaches in this category are considered forms of few-shot prompting. As the annotation framework cited above also contained examples out of existing case law, we extend the prompts of the "*Stages + Definitions*" approach with these examples. For each proposed subtask (see the *Stages* approach), three positive and three negative examples together with their annotations are appended to the prompt.

We refer to this approach as "*Stages, Definitions + Examples*". To determine the influence of the data samples themselves, we propose an additional approach, referred to as "*Stages + Examples*", where instructions, definitions and terms are excluded from the prompt and only the in-context samples are used.

Target Classification vs Extraction In the previous approaches, we prompt the language models among others to classify the target groups into predefined categories. In addition to this target classification approach, we propose a target extraction approach. In practice, most instances of hate speech target a limited number of specific groups. According to the United Nations, 75% of hate speech is directed at minorities.[3] A study analyzing over 27.000 hate speech examples found that 97% of posts targeted only 178 distinct groups (Silva et al., 2016). Given that the most frequently affected groups are well known, we prompt LLMs to identify the exact target group within a statement and compare the result against a manually curated list of potential targets (in our case all target groups from the dataset).

3 Experimental Setup

In this section, we introduce the dataset, language models, model inference setup, applied in our experiments.

3.1 Dataset

We performed our experiments on the legal hate speech dataset of Zufall et al. (2022). The dataset consists of 1,000 German instances, whereby 850 samples are real world samples that have not been published. We use only the 150 remaining samples, as these were manually created to resemble real hate speech posts and were publicly available, whereas the others were not published. The authors of the study proposed a annotation framework that, among others, helps laypersons to assess whether a post is criminally relevant according to § 130 of the German Criminal Code. Each post was annotated by three experts and two groups of laypersons: one group of two annotators using the annotation framework, and another group of three annotators working without it.

3.2 Language Models, Model Inference and Assessment

We chose the following models for our experiments due to their reasoning capabilities, strong benchmark results and multilingual capabilities: **Phi-3** (Abdin et al., 2024), **Llama 3.1** (Vavekanand and Sam, 2024), **Command R+ (Cmd)** [4] and **Qwen 2** (Yang et al., 2024).

Since prompt variations can significantly impact model performance (Gan and Mori, 2023; Sclar et al., 2023), we averaged performance across six manually crafted paraphrases per classification task, each with different instructions. Provided statutory texts, legal definitions or in-context examples were retained. We applied each prompt to all manually crafted samples from Zufall et al. (2022), first generating free-text responses with the language model. In a second step, we asked the model to

[3] https://www.un.org/en/hate-speech/impact-and-prevention/targets-of-hate, February 11, 2025

[4] https://cohere.com/blog/command-r-plus-microsoft-azure

format its response in JSON, which allows us to analyze it automatically.[5] We used this two-step approach because prior research showed that enforcing a specific response format can degrade model performance (Tam et al., 2024).

We evaluate our models using Cohen's Kappa, computing the values as the average of all pairwise scores between each prediction and each annotation. This metric was chosen because it naturally supports comparisons between multiple human annotators and model predictions, and provides a fairer performance estimate in settings with imbalanced classes.

3.3 Baselines

As baseline models, we used a majority classifier and a Support Vector Machine (SVM), which was trained on labeled data. For the SVM, we first computed TF-IDF features and projected them into a lower dimensional space using a Principal Component Analysis. Due to the small amount of labeled data, leave-one-out cross validation was used to determine the performance of the SVM.

4 Results and Discussion

Table 2 shows Cohen's Kappa achieved by the proposed approaches across language models. Although no training data is used, some approaches and models are able to outperform the SVM baseline results, which are shown in Table 1. However, there remains a notable gap in performance compared to human experts.

		Cmd	Llama	Phi	Qwen
Fund. Rights	Title Art. 5 I GG	.41	.11	.05	.00
	Text Art. 5 I GG	.04	.09	.24	.00
Stat. Law	Title § 130	.32	.05	.41	.29
	Text § 130	.32	.00	.17	.20
	Simple Text § 130	.22	.00	.38	.17
	High-Level Stages	.17	.12	.09	.15
	Stages	.21	.00	.00	.20
Case Law	Definitions	.29	.16	.28	.24
	Examples	.09	.00	.11	.01
	Definitions & Examples	.30	.39	.05	.15

Table 2: **Classification performance** of different models across levels of abstractions and approaches. The performance is measured in terms of Cohen Kappa agreement between model predictions and expert annotations.

4.1 Fundamental rights

In most cases, approaches based on fundamental rights conditioning attained low agreement values (Table 2). Surprisingly, the *Command-R* model achieved its best results using the *Fundamental Rights Title Conditioning* approach despite being conditioned on the most abstract legal knowledge with the least amount of context, which is counterintuitive. Adding legal text did not improve the performances in three out of four cases. While a performance drop through an overload of the context window was observed in other works (Liu et al., 2023), this is not the case in our experiment, since the provided statutory text is not long enough to fill the context window of our language models. We therefore investigate the reliability of the approaches in a follow-up experiment by assessing the consistency of the models' internal reasoning processes, measuring their rate of contradictory decisions.

A decision is considered contradictory if a model classifies a statement as either both covered by freedom of expression (section 2.1) and punishable under § 130(1) (section 2.2), or as neither covered by freedom of expression nor punishable under § 130. Both cases are logically mutually exclusive. We computed the ratio of contradictory decisions between the corresponding title-based conditioning approaches and between the corresponding text-based conditioning approaches. For *Command-R*, contradictory decisions occurred in 60% of cases with title-based and 34% with text-based conditioning. For *Qwen 2*, the rates were 27% and 38%, respectively. These high ratios reveal inconsistencies in the internal reasoning process of the models for this task, reducing the trustworthiness of these approaches.

4.2 Statutory law

Unexpectedly, within the approaches based on the abstraction level of the statutory law, the *Statutory Title Conditioning* approach outperformed the other approaches in three out of four cases, despite using the least specific legal knowledge. Similarly to the results of section 4.1, it raises the question

[5] Minor formatting errors, such as a wrong bracket, were corrected manually.

Approach	Model	§120	§123	§300	§324	§400	§1000	§130
Title	Cmd	.52	.52	.46	.48	.40	.41	.32
	Qwen	.35	.34	.28	.36	.37	.36	.29
Text	Cmd	.03	.07	.05	.05	/	/	.32
	Qwen	.16	.27	.27	.34			.29
Simplified Text	Cmd	.15	.19	.00	.03	/	/	.22
	Qwen	.15	.22	.23	.26			.17

Table 3: Cohen's Kappa agreement achieved through prompting with non-existent or irrelevant paragraphs of the criminal code. The table shows that correlation values mostly exceed random levels, particularly with the *Statutory Title Conditioning* approach.

whether language models understand the task and perform internal reasoning when only the statutory title is provided. On the other hand, providing models with task decomposition knowledge, whether high-level or explicit, did not improve performance. In most cases, it resulted in worse outcomes than previous approaches, despite incorporating additional expert knowledge in the prompts.

Table 3 presents achieved agreement values between model predictions, when prompted with non-existing or irrelevant paragraphs, and expert labels, annotated for § 130(1) of the German Criminal Code. Since the queried paragraphs are either irrelevant or non-existent, we would expect the models to predict the answer "not relevant" every time, thus achieving a random agreement value of roughly 0. However, the correlation values mostly exceeded random levels, particularly with the *Statutory Title Conditioning* approach. Thus, evidence suggests that models do not deeply understand the task when using the *Statutory Title Injection* approach. The models tend to disregard the specific paragraph provided in the prompt and thus hallucinating their answers.

When an additional statutory text (either raw or simplified) was provided, the models showed a reduction in this type of hallucination. This indicates that LLMs are able to understand the broader context of the legal texts and apply it to concrete samples of hate speech. However, since the agreement values remain above random levels and a significant performance gap persists between models and legal experts, the results indicate that the models struggle to apply fine-grained details and statutory terms to these samples. The struggles with understanding legal knowledge and applying it to concrete hate speech samples is in line with the findings of (Luo et al., 2023).

4.3 Case law

Case law-based approaches performed best for only one out of four models (Table 2). Overall, the models benefited from the inclusion of case law definitions in the prompt, which mostly outperformed the *Stages* approach, highlighting the importance of defining case law terms for language models. On the other hand, including examples into the prompt had mixed effects, boosting the performance of some models but harming the performance of others. The exclusive use of examples without the use of definitions led to poor results. This can be partly explained by our observation that the models often refused to answer for safety reasons when confronted with additional examples of hate speech.

Target Group To better understand the factors influencing language model performance across all task-decomposition prompting strategies, we evaluated the results for each individual target-group related sub-task, focusing on the Qwen and Command-R models, which achieved reasonable results in these setups. Table 4 shows Cohen-Kappa agreement values for different approaches to target group classification and extraction. The results show that models performed better when target groups were extracted from the text rather than classified into predefined categories, supporting the findings of (Sicilia et al., 2024) that LLMs excel at information extraction tasks. As with the overall performance of the model, including definitions tend to improve the performances of the target group categorization approach, while including examples provide mixed results. Generally, the average performance for classifying or extracting target groups was higher than most performances of classifying target

Approach	Cmd	Qwen
Target Classification	.15	.31
+ Definitions	.29	.32
+ Examples	.05	.00
+ Definitions + Examples	.29	.11
Target Extraction	**.34**	**.51**

Table 4: **Target group classification** performance in terms of Cohen's Kappa.

Conduct	Approach	Cmd	Qwen
Incitement	Stages	.03	.00
	+Examples	.03	.01
	+Definitions	.00	.03
	+Def/+Ex	.05	.02
Violence	Stages	.31	.58
	+Examples	.30	.57
	+Definitions	.52	.68
	+Def/+Ex	.29	.42
Insulting	Stages	.03	.02
	+Examples	.04	.02
	+Definitions	.03	.01
	+Def/+Ex	.04	.01
Slandering	Stages	.02	.01
	+Examples	.03	.01
	+Definitions	.06	.01
	+Def/+Ex	.02	.01
Disparaging	Stages	.09	.07
	+Examples	.04	.00
	+Definitions	.10	.11
	+Def/+Ex	.17	.07

Table 5: **Targeting Conduct classification** performance (Cohen's Kappa Agreement).

conduct.

Target Conduct We also evaluated performance on target-conduct-based sub-tasks to gain a more comprehensive understanding of the effectiveness of decomposition-based approaches. Table 5 shows the Cohen Kappa agreement values, achieved for the different approaches and with respect to the target conduct. Only the conduct of *Calling for Violence* is classified with a reasonable performance, while the classification performances for the other tasks were poor. The results are similar to the results of legal laypersons, which achieve significantly higher agreement values for classifying target groups and classifying the conduct of *Calling for Violence* than for classifying the conduct of *Inciting Hatred* (Zufall et al., 2022).

5 Related Work

Legal knowledge has early on been modeled into legal expert systems as ontologies (Oberle et al., 2012), semantic networks (Branting, 2003) or frames (Rissland and Ashley, 1987; Ashley, 1991). In recent years, research combining NLP methodologies and law had a strong focus on supervised learning tasks, especially legal judgment prediction (Aletras et al., 2016; Chalkidis et al., 2019). Work on judgment prediction experimented with using either the factual section of judgment as input, or combined it with the legal reasons and decision on the merits as training data.

Trautmann et al. (2022) has coined the term of 'legal prompt engineering' with experiments on judgment prediction. However, experiments by Dahl et al. (2024b) found that the hallucination rate of LLMs tested on huge case law corpora was up to 58%, raising doubts to what extent concise legal knowledge is actually contained in LLMs. Jiang and Yang (2023) experimented with chain-of-thought and legal syllogism prompting for legal judgment prediction. Savelka et al. (2023) augmented LLMs with a legal information retrieval module to provide explanation of statutory terms.

How legal knowledge inherent in LLMs may be accessed through engineering suitable prompts has been explored in the area of hate speech detection (Morbidoni et al.; Chiu et al., 2021; He et al., 2023; Han and Tang, 2022; Del Arco et al., 2023). Kumarage et al. (2024) explore three different types of prompting schemes: direct yes or no questions, incorporation of basic description of hate speech, and chain-of-thought prompting.

Similarly to our work, AlKhamissi et al. (2022) investigate how hate speech recognition tasks can be prepared for language models so that these models can solve them. They propose a task decomposition and knowledge infusion approach to fine-tune these models in a few-shot manner. The authors propose to split the task into simpler sub-tasks. Additionally, they aim to incorporate common sense and stereotype knowledge from large knowledge bases into a BART-based model (Lewis, 2019). However, they do not take legal systems into account.

6 Conclusion

In this work, we investigated to which extent LLMs can be conditioned based on knowledge taken out of different levels of abstraction in legal systems, focusing on the task of identifying punishable hate speech. We experimented with various approaches to legal system conditioning, from the constitutional level to statutory law down to case law. Results showed a significant performance gap between legal experts and models, regardless of the approach or language model used. Surprisingly, approaches with more concrete legal knowledge performed worse on average than high-level end-to-end classification approaches. Further analysis revealed that models conditioned on abstract legal knowledge lacked deep task understanding, contradicting themselves and hallucinating answers when confronted with fictitious or irrelevant offenses. In contrast, models that rely on concrete legal knowledge, similar to human laypersons, have difficulty classifying certain target conducts, while achieving reasonable results in classifying target groups.

Limitations

We only experiment with one legal system (represented by the dataset used for evaluation). However, our approach would be directly replicable for other legal systems or other areas of criminal law. As the dataset is publicly available, we cannot rule out data contamination, but the overall low performance level makes that unlikely.

Ethics Statement

Predicting whether a social media posts consists punishable hate speech interferes with the fundamental right of 'free speech'. It could also be abused by governments to suppress opinions. On the other hand, the criminal offense investigated here also protects minorities from discrimination. Both aspects place our work at the center of a balancing decision between those two interests. Our work is neutral towards any political position, but only reflects existing law at several levels of a legal system. We base our ground truth solely on a legal assessment founded on existing German statutory and case law. We believe that our approach contributes to a better understanding and higher transparency in automated content detection methods than conventional approaches, justifying the potential dangers and abuse of our research.

Race and Gender § 130(1) of the German Criminal Act explicitly requires the conduct to be directed against a "national, racial, religious group or a group defined by their ethnic origin, against sections of the population." The offense lists these groups as potential targets in order to protect them and prevent discrimination. Our approach is also suitable to be adapted to other groups protected in other legal systems. In view of the inherent biases LLMs may already contain, our approach provides more transparency and investigates targeted protection in favor of groups subject to discrimination.

References

Marah Abdin, Sam Ade Jacobs, Ammar Ahmad Awan, Jyoti Aneja, Ahmed Awadallah, Hany Awadalla, Nguyen Bach, Amit Bahree, Arash Bakhtiari, Harkirat Behl, et al. 2024. Phi-3 technical report: A highly capable language model locally on your phone. *arXiv preprint arXiv:2404.14219.*

Nikolaos Aletras, Dimitrios Tsarapatsanis, Daniel Preoţiuc-Pietro, and Vasileios Lampos. 2016. Predicting judicial decisions of the European Court of Human Rights: a Natural Language Processing perspective. *PeerJ Computer Science*, 2:e93. Publisher: PeerJ Inc.

Badr AlKhamissi, Faisal Ladhak, Srinivasan Iyer, Veselin Stoyanov, Zornitsa Kozareva, Xian Li, Pascale Fung, Lambert Mathias, Asli Celikyilmaz, and Mona Diab. 2022. ToKen: Task decomposition and knowledge infusion for few-shot hate speech detection. In *Proceedings of the 2022 Conference on Empirical Methods in Natural Language Processing*, pages 2109–2120, Abu Dhabi, United Arab Emirates. Association for Computational Linguistics.

Kevin D. Ashley. 1991. Reasoning with cases and hypotheticals in HYPO. *International Journal of Man-Machine Studies*, 34(6):753–796.

L. Karl Branting. 2003. A reduction-graph model of precedent in legal analysis. *Artificial Intelligence*, 150(1):59–95.

Ilias Chalkidis, Ion Androutsopoulos, and Nikolaos Aletras. 2019. Neural Legal Judgment Prediction in English. In *Proceedings of the 57th Annual Meeting of the Association for Computational*

Linguistics, pages 4317–4323, Florence, Italy. Association for Computational Linguistics.

Ke-Li Chiu, Annie Collins, and Rohan Alexander. 2021. Detecting hate speech with gpt-3. *arXiv preprint arXiv:2103.12407*.

Matthew Dahl, Varun Magesh, Mirac Suzgun, and Daniel E Ho. 2024a. Large legal fictions: Profiling legal hallucinations in large language models. *Journal of Legal Analysis*, 16(1):64–93.

Matthew Dahl, Varun Magesh, Mirac Suzgun, and Daniel E Ho. 2024b. Large Legal Fictions: Profiling Legal Hallucinations in Large Language Models. *Journal of Legal Analysis*, 16(1):64–93.

Flor Miriam Plaza Del Arco, Debora Nozza, and Dirk Hovy. 2023. Respectful or toxic? using zero-shot learning with language models to detect hate speech. In *The 7th Workshop on Online Abuse and Harms (WOAH)*, pages 60–68.

Qingxiu Dong, Lei Li, Damai Dai, Ce Zheng, Jingyuan Ma, Rui Li, Heming Xia, Jingjing Xu, Zhiyong Wu, Baobao Chang, et al. 2024. A survey on in-context learning. In *Proceedings of the 2024 Conference on Empirical Methods in Natural Language Processing*, pages 1107–1128.

Rajaa El Hamdani, Thomas Bonald, Fragkiskos D Malliaros, Nils Holzenberger, and Fabian Suchanek. 2024. The factuality of large language models in the legal domain. In *Proceedings of the 33rd ACM International Conference on Information and Knowledge Management*, pages 3741–3746.

Zhiwei Fei, Xiaoyu Shen, Dawei Zhu, Fengzhe Zhou, Zhuo Han, Songyang Zhang, Kai Chen, Zongwen Shen, and Jidong Ge. 2023. Lawbench: Benchmarking legal knowledge of large language models. *arXiv preprint arXiv:2309.16289*.

Chengguang Gan and Tatsunori Mori. 2023. Sensitivity and robustness of large language models to prompt template in japanese text classification tasks. *arXiv preprint arXiv:2305.08714*.

Lawrence Han and Hao Tang. 2022. Designing of prompts for hate speech recognition with in-context learning. In *2022 International Conference on Computational Science and Computational Intelligence (CSCI)*, pages 319–320. IEEE.

Xinlei He, Savvas Zannettou, Yun Shen, and Yang Zhang. 2023. You only prompt once: On the capabilities of prompt learning on large language models to tackle toxic content. In *2024 IEEE Symposium on Security and Privacy (SP)*, pages 61–61. IEEE Computer Society.

Cong Jiang and Xiaolei Yang. 2023. Legal Syllogism Prompting: Teaching Large Language Models for Legal Judgment Prediction. In *Proceedings of the Nineteenth International Conference on Artificial Intelligence and Law*, ICAIL '23, pages 417–421, New York, NY, USA. Association for Computing Machinery.

Tharindu Kumarage, Amrita Bhattacharjee, and Joshua Garland. 2024. Harnessing artificial intelligence to combat online hate: Exploring the challenges and opportunities of large language models in hate speech detection. *arXiv preprint arXiv:2403.08035*.

Mike Lewis. 2019. Bart: Denoising sequence-to-sequence pre-training for natural language generation, translation, and comprehension. *arXiv preprint arXiv:1910.13461*.

Nelson F Liu, Kevin Lin, John Hewitt, Ashwin Paranjape, Michele Bevilacqua, Fabio Petroni, and Percy Liang. 2023. Lost in the middle: How language models use long contexts. *arXiv preprint arXiv:2307.03172*.

Chu Luo, Rohan Bhambhoria, Samuel Dahan, and Xiaodan Zhu. 2023. Legally enforceable hate speech detection for public forums. In *Findings of the Association for Computational Linguistics: EMNLP 2023*, pages 10948–10963.

Christian Morbidoni, Annalina Sarra, et al. Can llms assist humans in assessing online misogyny? experiments with gpt-3.5.

Daniel Oberle, Felix Drefs, Richard Wacker, Christian Baumann, and Oliver Raabe. 2012. Engineering Compliant Software: Advising Developers by Automating Legal Reasoning. *SCRIPTed*, 9(3):280–313.

E. L. Rissland and K. D. Ashley. 1987. A case-based system for trade secrets law. In *Proceedings of the 1st international conference on Artificial intelligence and law*, ICAIL '87, pages 60–66, New York, NY, USA. Association for Computing Machinery.

Jaromir Savelka, Kevin D. Ashley, Morgan A. Gray, Hannes Westermann, and Huihui Xu. 2023. Explaining Legal Concepts with Augmented Large Language Models (GPT-4). *arXiv preprint*. ArXiv:2306.09525 [cs].

Melanie Sclar, Yejin Choi, Yulia Tsvetkov, and Alane Suhr. 2023. Quantifying language models' sensitivity to spurious features in prompt design or: How i learned to start worrying about prompt formatting. *arXiv preprint arXiv:2310.11324*.

Anthony Sicilia, Jennifer Gates, and Malihe Alikhani. 2024. Humbel: A human-in-the-loop approach for evaluating demographic factors of language models in human-machine conversations. In *Proceedings of the 18th Conference of the European Chapter of the Association for Computational Linguistics (Volume 1: Long Papers)*, pages 1127–1143.

Leandro Silva, Mainack Mondal, Denzil Correa, Fabrício Benevenuto, and Ingmar Weber. 2016. Analyzing the targets of hate in online social media. In *Proceedings of the International AAAI Conference on Web and Social Media*, volume 10, pages 687–690.

Zhi Rui Tam, Cheng-Kuang Wu, Yi-Lin Tsai, Chieh-Yen Lin, Hung-yi Lee, and Yun-Nung Chen. 2024. Let me speak freely? a study on the impact of format restrictions on large language model performance. In *Proceedings of the 2024 Conference on Empirical Methods in Natural Language Processing: Industry Track*, pages 1218–1236.

Dietrich Trautmann, Alina Petrova, and Frank Schilder. 2022. Legal Prompt Engineering for Multilingual Legal Judgement Prediction. *arXiv preprint*. ArXiv:2212.02199 [cs].

Raja Vavekanand and Kira Sam. 2024. Llama 3.1: An in-depth analysis of the next-generation large language model.

Jason Wei, Xuezhi Wang, Dale Schuurmans, Maarten Bosma, Fei Xia, Ed Chi, Quoc V Le, Denny Zhou, et al. 2022. Chain-of-thought prompting elicits reasoning in large language models. *Advances in neural information processing systems*, 35:24824–24837.

An Yang, Baosong Yang, Binyuan Hui, Bo Zheng, Bowen Yu, Chang Zhou, Chengpeng Li, Chengyuan Li, Dayiheng Liu, Fei Huang, Guanting Dong, Haoran Wei, Huan Lin, Jialong Tang, Jialin Wang, Jian Yang, Jianhong Tu, Jianwei Zhang, Jianxin Ma, Jianxin Yang, Jin Xu, Jingren Zhou, Jinze Bai, Jinzheng He, Junyang Lin, Kai Dang, Keming Lu, Keqin Chen, Kexin Yang, Mei Li, Mingfeng Xue, Na Ni, Pei Zhang, Peng Wang, Ru Peng, Rui Men, Ruize Gao, Runji Lin, Shijie Wang, Shuai Bai, Sinan Tan, Tianhang Zhu, Tianhao Li, Tianyu Liu, Wenbin Ge, Xiaodong Deng, Xiaohuan Zhou, Xingzhang Ren, Xinyu Zhang, Xipin Wei, Xuancheng Ren, Xuejing Liu, Yang Fan, Yang Yao, Yichang Zhang, Yu Wan, Yunfei Chu, Yuqiong Liu, Zeyu Cui, Zhenru Zhang, Zhifang Guo, and Zhihao Fan. 2024. Qwen2 technical report. *Preprint*, arXiv:2407.10671.

Frederike Zufall, Marius Hamacher, Katharina Kloppenborg, and Torsten Zesch. 2022. A legal approach to hate speech – operationalizing the EU's legal framework against the expression of hatred as an NLP task. In *Proceedings of the Natural Legal Language Processing Workshop 2022*, pages 53–64, Abu Dhabi, United Arab Emirates (Hybrid). Association for Computational Linguistics.

A Text of Article 5

Translation based on: `https://www.gesetze-im-internet.de/englisch_gg/`

> (1) Every person shall have the right freely to express and disseminate his opinions in speech, writing and pictures and to inform himself without hindrance from generally accessible sources. Freedom of the press and freedom of reporting by means of broadcasts and films shall be guaranteed. There shall be no censorship.

B Text of § 130(1)

Translation based on: `https://www.gesetze-im-internet.de/englisch_stgb`

> (1) Whoever, in a manner suited to causing a disturbance of the public peace,
>
> 1. incites hatred against a national, racial, religious group or a group defined by their ethnic origin, against sections of the population or individuals on account of their belonging to one of the aforementioned groups or sections of the population, or calls for violent or arbitrary measures against them or
>
> 2. violates the human dignity of others by insulting, maliciously maligning or defaming one of the aforementioned groups, sections of the population or individuals on account of their belonging to one of the aforementioned groups or sections of the population
>
> incurs a penalty of imprisonment for a term of between three months and five years.

C Examplary Prompts

In this section, we provide example prompts for the different approaches, corresponding to the different levels of abstractions of the legal system.

C.1 Fundamental Rights

Fundamental Rights: Title

Instruction:
Is the following text covered by freedom of speech under Article 5(1) GG?

Text:
[STATEMENT]

Fundamental Rights: Text

Legal Text of Articel 5 GG
(1) Every person shall have the right freely to express and disseminate his opinions [...]

Instruction:
Is the following text covered by the freedom of speech according to the above-mentioned article of the Basic Law?

Text:
[STATEMENT]

C.2 Statutory Law

Statutory Law: Title

Instruction:
Is the following text criminally relevant according to § 130 StGB, (1)?

Text:
[STATEMENT]

Statutory Law: Text

Statutory Text of § 130 StGB:
(1) Whoever, in a manner suited to causing a disturbance of the public peace, [...]

Instruction:
Is the following text criminally relevant according to the above statutory text?

Text:
[STATEMENT]

Statutory Law: Simple Text

Statutory Text:
Anyone who incites hatred against people because they have a certain origin, [...]

Instruction:
Is the following text criminally relevant according to the above statutory text?

Text:
[STATEMENT]

Statutory Law: Implicit Stages

Statutory Text of § 130 StGB:
(1) Whoever, in a manner suited to causing a disturbance of the public peace, [...]

Instruction:
Check whether the statement refers to one of the target groups mentioned and whether it fulfills an offence described above. Specify the relevant target groups and behaviors. Is the following text therefore criminally relevant according to the above statutory text?

Text:
[STATEMENT]

Statutory Law: Stages

Instruction:
Does the following text refer to a group of people, which is considered to be part of the German population?

Text:
[STATEMENT]

[MODEL PREDICTION]

Instruction:
Does the text incite hatred against this group according to the legal definition?

Statutory Law: Target Extraction

Instruction:
Analyze the following statement. Is the post aimed at a specific target group? If so, extract any words, phrases or symbols that could indicate this target group.

Text:
[STATEMENT]

[MODEL PREDICTION]

Instruction:
Determine the target groups of the statement. If the target group is not clear, please mark the target group as "Unclear"

C.3 Case Law

Statutory Law: Stages + Definitions

Definition: Part of German Population
A group is considered to be part of the German population, if [...]

Instruction:
Does the following text refer to a group of people, which is considered to be part of the German population?

Text:
[STATEMENT]

[MODEL PREDICTION]

Definition: Incitement to hatred
Incitement to hatred must be objectively suitable [...]

Instruction:
Does the text incite hatred against this group according to the definition?

[MODEL PREDICTION]

Statutory Law: Stages + Definitions + Examples

Definition: Part of German Population
A group is considered to be part of the German population, if [...]

Instruction:
Does the following text refer to a group of people, which is considered to be part of the German population?

Text:
[EXAMPLE STATEMENT 1]

[EXAMPLE PREDICTION 1]

Text:
[EXAMPLE STATEMENT 2]

[EXAMPLE PREDICTION 2]

...

Text:
[STATEMENT]

[MODEL PREDICTION]

Case Law: Stages + Examples

Text:
[EXAMPLE STATEMENT 1]

[EXAMPLE PREDICTION 1]

Text:
[EXAMPLE STATEMENT 2]

[EXAMPLE PREDICTION 2]

...

Text:
[STATEMENT]

[MODEL PREDICTION]

HICC: A Dataset for German Hate Speech in Conversational Context

Lars Schmid[1], Pius von Däniken[1], Patrick Giedemann[1], Don Tuggener[1], Judith Bühler[2], Maria Kamenowski[2], Katja Girschik[2], Laurent Sedano[2], Dirk Baier[2], Mark Cieliebak[1]

[1]ZHAW Centre for Artificial Intelligence,
[2] ZHAW Institute of Delinquency and Crime Prevention
Correspondence: shmr@zhaw.ch

Abstract

We present HICC: A dataset of German **H**ate speech comments **I**n **C**onversational **C**ontext. The dataset comprises the target hate speech comments to be detected, the root post that starts the conversation, and all direct replies to the root that were published before the target. We especially focus on comments that are difficult to identify as hate speech in isolation, but need context for classification. We show that LLM-based classification can successfully incorporate conversational context to identify such comments that do not explicitly contain hateful language. Our dataset is gathered from the social media platform *X* (formerly Twitter), manually annotated, and made freely available for research[1].

Content Warning: This paper contains examples of hate speech for research purposes.[2]

1 Introduction

Research on detecting hateful and toxic speech in social media often focuses on the message level, analyzing messages without their conversational contexts. However, comments on social media are naturally embedded in a conversational context. We show that incorporating this context in message-level analysis of social media comments is beneficial to detecting hateful and toxic speech that does not feature hateful language on the text surface. To this end, we collect and manually annotate a dataset for identifying hateful and toxic comments in German on the platform *X* (formerly Twitter).

Example 1[3] illustrates a target that appears innocuous in isolation, but when read in context, the question functions as a sarcastic dismissal aimed at a political out-group. Humans label it as "toxic speech", and LLMs likewise flip from `0` (no context) to `1` when given the conversational context. The example shows that toxicity can be conveyed through pragmatic cues (sarcasm, insinuation) rather than explicit slurs, and that those cues often reside outside the target span.

This paper makes three contributions. First, we release HICC, a German dataset pairing target comments with their conversational context (Section 3). Second, we propose an evaluation pipeline that first ranks targets by off-the-shelf moderation scores *without* context and then measures how much LLMs recover missed cases *with* context (Section 4). Third, we show recall gains when supplying context – especially for the hardest deciles where context-agnostic tools[4] assign low scores – reaching improvements up to 19 percentage points (pp) (Section 5).

Example 1: Context reveals latent toxicity (id 15878)

Root post: *"This phenomenon was confirmed in a study, here is an excerpt: "A wider road produces ... increased demand – and leads to people using their cars more often than before, creating a new, larger traffic jam."*
Comment 1: *"The Greens and other brainless people actually believe that if there were fewer roads, there would be fewer cars! They just don't realise that the cars simply drive through the villages. But yes, they mostly live in cities with trams etc. where cars are banned."*
Comment 2 (Target): ***"A green study?"***
Moderation endpoints avg. (Target): 0.019
Human label (Target): TOXIC SPEECH
Model verdicts (no context): GPT-4o-mini, Grok-3-mini, Claude 3 Haiku = 0
Model verdicts (+Full): GPT-4o-mini, Grok-3-mini, Claude 3 Haiku = 1
Why it flips. Without any context, the statement *"A green study?"* appears to be an innocuous, neutral question. With context, it becomes clear that the remark is a politically-charged jab and sarcastic dismissal of the study on partisan grounds, especially after a preceding reply calls the Greens 'brainless'.

[1] `https://github.com/larscarl/hicc`

[2] These examples are necessary to illustrate the challenges in detecting and understanding harmful content. The authors do not condone any of the language or sentiments expressed in them.

[3] See Appendix A.1 for additional examples.

[4] Perspective API and OpenAI's Moderation; see Section 4

Proceedings of the 21st Conference on Natural Language Processing (KONVENS), Volume 1: Long and Short Papers, pages 168–176, 2025

2 Related Work

Comprehensive surveys cover abusive language detection broadly (Schmidt and Wiegand, 2017; Fortuna and Nunes, 2018; Jahan and Oussalah, 2023); here we focus on datasets and tasks that incorporate conversational context. Qian et al. (2019) use conversational threads from Reddit and focus on generating counter-speech, but not the identification of hate speech. Vidgen et al. (2021) present a substantially sized dataset comprised of Reddit comment threads annotated with an in-depth taxonomy of abusive language. They include annotations to indicate whether a comment needs context to be interpreted as being abusive. However, they do not consider context in their automatic classification experiments. Demus et al. (2022) present a dataset of toxic speech based on German posts on X. They analyze the impact of hateful comments on subsequent posts, but do not include the conversational context in their classification experiments.

Work on whether conversational context improves classification accuracy has not yielded a decisive answer (Pavlopoulos et al., 2020; Xenos et al., 2021; Yu et al., 2022; Pérez et al., 2023). Different approaches use divergent definitions of context (mostly the parent comment), annotation guidelines, label sets, and data sources. One clear exception is the work of Pérez et al. (2023) who collect a dataset of Spanish (Rioplatense variant) tweets and show clear improvements when incorporating the original tweet into classification.

By contrast, the main focus of our work is not whether context helps in general, but whether we are able to correctly classify hateful comments that are not detectable as such in isolation. Specifically, we are interested in online comments that do not explicitly feature offensive words, but can only be interpreted as hateful with the inclusion of the conversational context (Klenner, 2018; Wiegand et al., 2021). Our work is hence closely related to Xenos et al. (2021) who devised a context-sensitivity estimation task. They consider the parent comment of a target comment as the context. Somewhat surprisingly, they found that about one third of the comments perceived as toxic in isolation were rendered neutral when annotators were shown the parent comments. They showed that Perspective API[5] also benefits from including parent posts for comments where the human annotations differ when including the parent posts. Furthermore, they trained a separate system to predict whether a comment requires context to be correctly annotated and showed that this system performs significantly better than randomly sampling comments.

Our work aims to provide a dataset of German hate speech with a focus on integrating the conversational context and to examine its impact on the detection of hateful comments that do not feature obvious hateful language.

3 Data collection

Searching and collecting hateful comments often involves querying with known hateful words and key-phrases (Qian et al., 2019; Yu et al., 2022; Demus et al., 2022), which can bias samples (Schmidt and Wiegand, 2017; Wiegand et al., 2018). HICC was collected organically as part of the project "Social Influencer:in"[6] aiming at evaluating the effectiveness of different counter-speech methods: digital streetworkers browsed news and social media to identify hateful or toxic comments.

A total of 13 digital streetworkers were recruited from undergraduate programs in social work and communication sciences and were deployed and supported over a four-month period.[7] Prior to collection, they completed a six-session training that standardized annotation decisions (definitions and criteria for hate vs. toxic speech, legal framing, search and classification procedures, discourse risks of counter-speech, and onboarding to the technical workflow).

Finding targets. The streetworkers did not search via hate-related keywords or hashtags. Instead, they practiced targeted browsing of sources that routinely elicit polarized comment sections. Concretely, they (i) monitored posts and news framed around groups frequently attacked online (e.g., refugees and migrants, queer people, Muslims, Jews, Sinti and Roma, women, trans and non-binary people, people with disabilities, people affected by poverty, unemployed or homeless people) as well as public figures (politicians across the spectrum, journalists, activists, scientists); and (ii) regularly visited accounts and pages of political parties and politicians (left & right), online

[5] https://www.perspectiveapi.com/ provides a toxicity score.

[6] https://www.zhaw.ch/de/forschung/projekt/74272

[7] Their ages ranged from 21 to 36. Their activities lasted from September to December 2024. Ten of them received a monthly salary; three received ECTS credits. The weekly workload was around 6 hours.

newspapers, journalists, activist collectives, anti-discrimination actors, religious organizations, and topic influencers (e.g., body positivity, climate, anti-racism, queer). They followed or subscribed to these sources; over time, platform recommendation systems increasingly surfaced similarly polarized threads. This strategy avoids lexical keyword/hashtag bias while focusing on realistic venues for counter-speech.

Use of context. Annotators read the surrounding conversation before deciding whether a post warranted intervention, inspecting the root post and the ongoing discussion (main thread and sub-threads) to assess stance, sarcasm, and implicit attacks, and then usually selecting one target comment per thread (either the root or a reply)[8]. For release and experiments, we reconstruct context as the root post and all direct replies to the root that were published before the target. Deeper branches are excluded.

Annotation tooling. A custom browser extension highlighted texts in the current tab according to their likelihood of toxicity or hate and served as the data-collection interface[9]. Annotators labeled the chosen target as one of: (i) "needs intervention (hate)"[10], (ii) "needs intervention (toxic)"[11], (iii) "intervention not recommended", (iv) "no intervention needed" [12]. The extension stored the annotation, URL, and page HTML at capture time. For evaluation, we treat (i) as *hate speech* and (ii) as *toxic speech*; (iii)-(iv) are excluded unless stated otherwise.

The integrated classifier was a SwissBERT model (Vamvas et al., 2023) with the *de_ch* adapter (Pfeiffer et al., 2022), finetuned on DETOX (Demus et al., 2022). It predicted five independent[13] binary targets (*toxic, hate speech, legal relevance, threat, extremism*) and shaded comments according to the maximum probability over these labels. On DETOX, the classifier shows moderate precision on hate and conservative recall on toxicity (see Appendix A.3 for details).

Our collection protocol yields *positive* supervision ("needs intervention (hate/toxic)") but not exhaustive negatives. Streetworkers were not instructed to label every comment in a thread – neither all non-problematic nor all problematic ones. The few "no intervention needed" flags mostly reflect occasional false positives of the classifier and are too sparse/inconsistent as true negatives. Likewise, they did not always annotate every hateful comment; often several hateful replies remained unlabeled because one was chosen arbitrarily for intervention. "Intervention not recommended" is not a negative toxicity/hate label. Consequently, the dataset does not support training or evaluating a binary "requires intervention vs. no intervention" system without additional annotation.

In total, the HICC dataset contains 21'338 tweets: 1'812 annotated targets (940 labeled as "needs intervention (toxic)", 734 "needs intervention (hate)", 108 as "intervention not recommended", and 30 "no intervention"[14]). We combine each target with its root post and preceding direct replies to the root. The resulting contexts have a mean size of 11.8 posts per target. On average, the target comments have 10 previous comments (standard deviation of 7.65) under the root post.

To comply with *X*'s Developer Policy[15] we release Post IDs for all nodes plus annotations and derived metadata. Content can be reconstructed via the official API subject to access rights.

4 Experiments

The purpose of our experiments is to identify comments that are not easily detectable as hate speech without context and then evaluate whether LLM-based classification is able to identify them when provided with appropriate context. We do so by ranking and binning comments that were manually

[8]The choice of target was often ad hoc. Streetworkers did not systematically pick the "worst" comment, and a thread could contain several unlabeled but clearly hateful replies.

[9]The on-page classifier operated *per comment* on isolated text only; no hashtag, page-, or thread-level signals. Annotators could select unhighlighted items.

[10]Hate speech is defined as explicit or implicit communicative acts against groups or individuals along (presumed) group membership that devalue, discriminate, or insult; includes slurs, dehumanization, identity-based attacks, or incitement to hatred/violence (see Appendix A.2).

[11]Toxic Speech is defined as language that degrades the conversational climate by attacking, belittling, harassing, exerting pressure, or being destructive/manipulative; measured by its potential to provoke aggressive responses or drive others away (see Appendix A.2).

[12]see Appendix A.2 for the exact definitions used as well as German originals

[13]One-vs-rest heads; labels may co-occur.

[14]This low number is due to the streetworkers not being encouraged to explicitly find non-problematic comments but occasionally flagging false positives of the classifier.

[15]X Developer Policy: "Content redistribution" – you may only distribute Post IDs, Direct Message IDs, and/or User IDs. Academic researchers may share unlimited Post/User IDs for non-commercial research. See: `https://developer.x.com/en/support/x-api/policy`.

annotated as being hateful. The ranking is based on hatefulness and toxicity scores from existing content moderation tools described in Section 4.1. Binning the ranking allows us to identify sets of comments that are scored as having a low probability of being hateful by the existing moderation tools. We then measure the impact of incorporating context specifically for those low-ranked bins when applying LLM-based classification.

Our experimental pipeline thus has two stages: (i) automatic moderation scoring for candidate ranking and binning, and (ii) LLM evaluations that vary conversational context.

4.1 Automatic moderation scores.

Comments in HICC that have been labeled as either "needs intervention (hate)" or "needs intervention (toxic)" are scored by three off-the-shelf moderation systems: (1) *Perspective API* (`toxicity`, `severe_toxicity`); (2) the *OpenAI* moderation endpoint[16] (`hate`); and (3) our own classifier (see Section 3) (`toxicity`, `hate_speech`). Crucially, this step does not involve any conversational context, i.e., only the target comment is submitted. We retain each raw score returned by the moderation systems and compute an *aggregate average* per comment (denoted `aggregate_avg`). The scores are never treated as ground-truth labels; rather, we use them to sort the comments to identify comments that are difficult to classify using context-agnostic methods (i.e. comments manually annotated as hate speech that have a low aggregate score based on the moderation endpoints).

4.2 LLM-based classification with context variations.

We apply three current models, GPT-4o-mini[17], Grok-3-mini[18], and Claude 3 Haiku[19] as classifiers using the same prompts. For each comment we ask two questions, *"Is the following comment toxic speech?"* and *"Is the following comment hate speech?"*, preceded by definitions of the respective concept.[20] The query is repeated under three context conditions[21]:

(1) **No Context ("No")** – the target text in isolation.

(2) **Root Post ("+Orig")** – the root post and the target.

(3) **Full Prior Context ("+Full")** – the root post and all direct replies to the root published before the target, followed by the target[22].

Models return a free-form rationale plus a binary verdict (`0`=No, 1=Yes). With 3 models × 2 prompts × 3 contexts, we collect 18 verdicts per comment.

5 Results

To evaluate how well the LLM-based classification is able to identify hateful comments of various levels of explicitness, we compare model verdicts against the streetworkers' *target* annotations. By design, annotators typically selected one intervention target per conversation thread – after reading the surrounding discussion – so the dataset contains positive labels for targets only. In some cases multiple streetworkers intervened in the same thread, resulting in more than one labelled target. All other posts in the same thread are *unlabeled* (they are not confirmed negatives), even if they may also satisfy hate/toxicity criteria. Because negatives are not exhaustively annotated, we report *Recall* on the target set: a true positive (TP) when the model flags the target under the matching prompt (hate vs. toxic), and a false negative (FN) otherwise. We do not estimate Precision or Accuracy on the full thread, as true negatives and false positives cannot be derived from the unlabeled context.[24]

Main Experiments Table 1 reports Recall for the three LLMs under the three context conditions described in Section 4.2. Context improves recall consistently, with the largest gains on the combined *Overall Recall* (combining the results of Hate and Toxic comments[25]) when the full conversational thread is provided. Across all models, the average *Overall Recall* rises from 88-89% (no context) to 90-93% (full prior context). GPT-4o-mini gains the most (+3.4 pp), followed by Grok-3-mini (+3.3 pp) and Claude 3 Haiku (+1.2 pp).

[16] https://platform.openai.com/docs/guides/moderation

[17] https://platform.openai.com/docs/models/gpt-4o-mini

[18] https://docs.x.ai/docs/models

[19] https://docs.anthropic.com/en/docs/about-claude/models/all-models

[20] Full definitions are provided in Appendix A.2.

[21] For brevity, we use the shorthands **No**, **+Orig**, and **+Full** in all tables and figures.

[22] Replies posted after the target are excluded.

[23] `aggregate_avg` = mean of moderation scores from Perspective (`toxicity`, `severe_toxicity`), OpenAI Moderation (`hate`), and our SwissBERT classifier (`toxicity`, `hate_speech`), computed on the *target comment only* (no context). Lower values indicate comments that are harder for context-agnostic tools.

[24] We provide a Precision analysis of our LLM-based classifier on a different corpus in Appendix A.3.

[25] Computed by $\frac{TP\_tox+TP\_hate}{TP\_tox+TP\_hate+FN\_tox+FN\_hate}$

Model	Hate Recall (%) No	Hate Recall (%) +Orig	Hate Recall (%) +Full	Toxicity Recall (%) No	Toxicity Recall (%) +Orig	Toxicity Recall (%) +Full	Overall Recall (%) No	Overall Recall (%) +Orig	Overall Recall (%) +Full
GPT-4o-mini	89.9	89.1	**91.5** (+1.6)	88.7	92.0	**93.4** (+4.7)	89.2	90.8	**92.6** (+3.4)
Grok-3-mini	**89.9**	88.8	89.3 (−0.6)	86.5	92.6	**92.6** (+6.1)	87.9	91.0	**91.2** (+3.3)
Claude 3 Haiku	94.7	93.9	**95.2** (+0.5)	85.2	86.5	**86.9** (+1.7)	89.2	89.6	**90.4** (+1.2)

Table 1: Recall on the HICC dataset. "+Orig" = root post provided; "+Full" = full prior context (root post plus all direct replies before the target).

Difficulty Bin (aggregate_avg range[23])	n	GPT-4o-mini Δ +Orig	GPT-4o-mini Δ +Full	Grok-3-mini Δ +Orig	Grok-3-mini Δ +Full	Claude 3 Haiku Δ +Orig	Claude 3 Haiku Δ +Full
(0.0145, 0.0915]	102	+8.1	**+15.2**	**+19.2**	**+19.2**	+10.1	**+16.2**
(0.0915, 0.168]	94	+8.9	**+13.3**	**+10.0**	+8.9	−3.3	−2.2
(0.168, 0.244]	132	+1.6	**+3.2**	+2.4	**+3.2**	0	−0.8
(0.244, 0.32]	124	−0.9	0	**+1.8**	+0.9	**+1.8**	**+1.8**
(0.32, 0.396]	172	0	0	−3.2	−1.3	−2.5	−2.5
(0.396, 0.472]	136	0	0	0	0	0	0
(0.472, 0.548]	125	−1.9	0	−0.9	−0.9	0	0
(0.548, 0.625]	60	−1.9	−1.9	0	0	−1.9	0
(0.625, 0.701]	44	0	0	0	0	0	0
(0.701, 0.777]	16	0	0	0	0	0	0

Table 2: **Per-decile recall gains from adding conversational context.** Cells report Δ recall in percentage points relative to the *No context* baseline; **bold** marks the larger gain between +Orig and +Full within a row. Lower bins correspond to harder cases (lower moderation scores). Context helps most in the two hardest bins (up to +19 pp), and has negligible or slightly negative effect once toxicity is already evident.

A complementary cross-label analysis (Appendix A.4) shows a strong asymmetry: a single toxicity prompt nearly recovers all hate cases ($\geq 97.6\%$ recall), but the reverse is much weaker (70-82%).

Recall by difficulty bin. Table 2 drills down on *Overall Recall* along the `aggregate_avg` spectrum that we use as a proxy for "moderation difficulty". That is, we sort the comments according to the aggregate average and then assign them to 10 bins. Context helps most in the hardest bins (`aggregate_avg` ≤ 0.168), boosting recall by up to 19 pp, while having negligible or occasionally negative effect once toxicity is already salient according to the moderation endpoints.

6 Conclusion

We have presented HICC, a dataset for German hate speech detection curated to emphasize the importance of conversational context. We showed that providing the full prior context (root post + prior direct replies) to LLMs leads to improved Recall in identifying both toxic and hate speech, with overall recall increasing from approximately 88-89% without context to 90-93% with full prior context. The most substantial gains in Recall, up to 19 percentage points, were observed for comments that were initially ranked as having a low probability of being hateful by context-agnostic moderation tools, highlighting the value of context in detecting subtle or implicit hate speech. Future work will expand the dataset and include true negatives to be able to evaluate precision. Our recall-based evaluation indicates that the approach is beneficial when assisting streetworkers in identifying hateful comments that require context. The dataset is freely available for research purposes[26].

Funding and project partners

This work was supported by *Nationaler Aktionsplan zur Verhinderung und Bekämpfung von Radikalisierung und gewalttätigem Extremismus*, *Digitalization Initiative of the Zurich Higher Education Institutions (DIZH)*, *Lotteriefonds Appenzell Ausserrhoden*, *Swisslos-Fonds Kanton Solothurn*, *Eidgenössische Kommission gegen Rassismus (EKR)*, *NCBI Schweiz*, and *ZHAW School of Management and Law*.

References

Christoph Demus, Jonas Pitz, Mina Schütz, Nadine Probol, Melanie Siegel, and Dirk Labudde. 2022.

[26] `https://github.com/larscarl/hicc`

DeTox: A comprehensive dataset for German offensive language and conversation analysis. In *Proceedings of the Sixth Workshop on Online Abuse and Harms (WOAH)*, pages 143–153, Seattle, Washington (Hybrid). Association for Computational Linguistics.

Paula Fortuna and Sérgio Nunes. 2018. A survey on automatic detection of hate speech in text. *ACM Computing Surveys (CSUR)*, 51:1 – 30.

Md Saroar Jahan and Mourad Oussalah. 2023. A systematic review of hate speech automatic detection using natural language processing. *Neurocomputing*, 546:126232.

Manfred Klenner. 2018. Offensive language without offensive words (OLWOW). In *14th Conference on Natural Language Processing KONVENS 2018*, page 11.

John Pavlopoulos, Jeffrey Scott Sorensen, Lucas Dixon, Nithum Thain, and Ion Androutsopoulos. 2020. Toxicity detection: Does context really matter? *ArXiv*, abs/2006.00998.

Juan Manuel Pérez, Franco M Luque, Demian Zayat, Martín Kondratzky, Agustín Moro, Pablo Santiago Serrati, Joaquín Zajac, Paula Miguel, Natalia Debandi, Agustín Gravano, and 1 others. 2023. Assessing the impact of contextual information in hate speech detection. *IEEE Access*, 11:30575–30590.

Jonas Pfeiffer, Naman Goyal, Xi Lin, Xian Li, James Cross, Sebastian Riedel, and Mikel Artetxe. 2022. Lifting the curse of multilinguality by pre-training modular transformers. In *Proceedings of the 2022 Conference of the North American Chapter of the Association for Computational Linguistics: Human Language Technologies*, pages 3479–3495, Seattle, United States. Association for Computational Linguistics.

Jing Qian, Anna Bethke, Yinyin Liu, Elizabeth M. Belding-Royer, and William Yang Wang. 2019. A benchmark dataset for learning to intervene in online hate speech. In *Conference on Empirical Methods in Natural Language Processing*.

Anna Schmidt and Michael Wiegand. 2017. A survey on hate speech detection using natural language processing. In *SocialNLP@EACL*.

Jannis Vamvas, Johannes Graën, and Rico Sennrich. 2023. SwissBERT: The multilingual language model for Switzerland. In *Proceedings of the 8th edition of the Swiss Text Analytics Conference*, pages 54–69, Neuchatel, Switzerland. Association for Computational Linguistics.

Bertie Vidgen, Dong Nguyen, Helen Z. Margetts, Patrícia G. C. Rossini, and Rebekah Tromble. 2021. Introducing CAD: the contextual abuse dataset. In *North American Chapter of the Association for Computational Linguistics*.

Michael Wiegand, Josef Ruppenhofer, and Elisabeth Eder. 2021. Implicitly abusive language – what does it actually look like and why are we not getting there? In *Proceedings of the 2021 Conference of the North American Chapter of the Association for Computational Linguistics: Human Language Technologies*, pages 576–587, Online. Association for Computational Linguistics.

Michael Wiegand, Melanie Siegel, and Josef Ruppenhofer. 2018. Overview of the GermEval 2018 shared task on the identification of offensive language. In *14th Conference on Natural Language Processing KONVENS 2018*, page 1.

Alexandros Xenos, John Pavlopoulos, and Ion Androutsopoulos. 2021. Context sensitivity estimation in toxicity detection. In *Proceedings of the 5th Workshop on Online Abuse and Harms (WOAH 2021)*, pages 140–145, Online. Association for Computational Linguistics.

Xinchen Yu, Eduardo Blanco, and Lingzi Hong. 2022. Hate speech and counter speech detection: Conversational context does matter. In *Proceedings of the 2022 Conference of the North American Chapter of the Association for Computational Linguistics: Human Language Technologies*, pages 5918–5930, Seattle, United States. Association for Computational Linguistics.

A Appendix

A.1 Examples

Examples 2 and 3 illustrate *how* and *why* conversational context can overturn toxicity or hate speech assessments. Each boxed example pairs the comment with its surrounding thread, reports both human annotations and model verdicts under different context windows, and ends with a short rationale for the observed flip.

Example 2: Context flips Schadenfreude into detectable toxicity (id 7436)

Content Warning: Sexual Assault
Root post: *"Woman (32) forced to perform sexual acts in flat in Zug: Alleged perpetrator (26) found dead after falling through a window."* [a]
Comment: *"At least he left afterwards"* [b]
aggregate_avg: 0.019
Human label: TOXIC SPEECH
Model verdicts (no context): GPT-4o-mini, Grok-3-mini, Claude 3 Haiku = 0
Model verdicts (+Full): GPT-4o-mini, Grok-3-mini, Claude 3 Haiku = 1

Why it flips. The short German phrase contains no obvious slur or profanity. Only when the headline reveals that it refers to a suspected rapist who died does the comment read as a celebration of lethal harm (*Schadenfreude*). With that context, both humans and LLMs judge it as toxic speech.

[a] Original statement in German: "Frau (32) in Zuger Wohnung zu sexuellen Handlungen gezwungen: Mut-

masslicher Täter (26) nach Fenstersturz tot aufgefunden."

[b]Original statement in German: "Wenigstens ist er danach gegangen"

Example 3: Scapegoating migrants through implicit blame (id 15857)

Root post: *"[ANONYMIZED]: The case of a fourteen-year-old contract killer in Marseille shakes France..."* [a]
Comment: *"That's just the way it is with unchecked immigration."* [b]
aggregate_avg: 0.127
Human label: HATE SPEECH
Model verdicts (no context): GPT-4o-mini = 0, Grok-3-mini = 0, Claude 3 Haiku = 1
Model verdicts (+Orig): GPT-4o-mini = 1, Grok-3-mini = 1, Claude 3 Haiku = 1
Model verdicts (+Full): GPT-4o-mini = 1, Grok-3-mini = 0, Claude 3 Haiku = 1
Why it flips. In isolation the sentence passes as policy critique. Once paired with the tweet about a contract killing, it implicitly blames migrants for violent crime, crossing the hate-speech boundary for most models.

[a]Original statement in German: "[ANONYMIZED] on *X*: Der Fall eines vierzehnjährigen Auftragskillers in Marseille erschüttert Frankreich. . . "

[b]Original statement in German: "so ist es halt mit ungebremster Zuwanderung"

A.2 LLM prompts

Here we list our working definitions of hate speech and toxic speech and give an example prompt used in our LLM-based experiments.

A.2.1 Definition 'Hate Speech'

Below, we provide our working definitions of hate speech; first in German, then translated to English.

Hate Speech Definition (German)

Unter Hate Speech werden kommunikative Handlungen oder Verhaltensweisen gegen Gruppen oder Einzelpersonen mit dem Ziel der (bewussten oder unbewussten) Abwertung, Diskriminierung oder Beleidigung derselben verstanden. Dabei kann die Abwertung aufgrund verschiedener Merkmale (bspw. Religion, Ethnizität, Nationalität, Hautfarbe, Abstammung, Geschlechtsidentität, sexuelle Orientierung, Alter, Behinderung, Körperform, Krankheit, ökonomische Situation, Beruf, Bildungshintergrund, politische Orientierung und weiteres) offensichtlich oder auch verdeckt sein. Hate Speech umfasst Beleidigungen, Verleumdungen ebenso wie Aussagen, die abwertende Stereotype fördern und zu Hass und Gewalt gegen Personen entlang von (vermuteten) Gruppenzugehörigkeiten aufrufen. Hate Speech kann sich direkt oder indirekt äussern.

Erweiterte Hate Speech Definition, die im Projekt verwendet wird:

- Verwendung von Schimpfwörtern
- Abwertung der Identität / Angriffe auf die Identität
- Aufrufe zu Gewalt und Drohung
- Entmenschlichende Sprache
- Verbreitung von Falschinformationen
- Sexuelle Belästigung
- Mobbing
- Kann strukturelle Diskriminierung enthalten (Geschlecht, Hautfarbe, Religion, Herkunft/Ethnizität, Sprache, Sesshaftigkeit, Gesundheit/Körper, Besitz/Klasse, Bezug globaler Norden und globaler Süden, Art der Gesellschaft (modern/fortschrittlich))
- Kann Freund-Feind-Denken beinhalten (z. B. Sport, Vereine, Fans, Aktivitäten (Velo-Auto/Klima, Wähler:innen einer Partei, etc.))
- Kann sich gegen Berufsgruppen richten (z. B. Medienschaffende, Politiker:innen, Behörden, Polizei, Vertreter:innen einer Organisation, etc.)
- Individuell, persönlicher Konflikt (Beleidigung, Beschimpfung, üble Nachrede, Nötigung, Drohung)

Keine Hassrede ist:

- Kritik – auch wenn sie harsch ist
- Freie Meinungsäusserung
- Nicht wertende Verallgemeinerung
- Fremdsprache
- Dialekt
- Falschinformation

Hate Speech Definition (English translation)

Hate speech refers to communicative actions or behavior against groups or individuals with the aim of (consciously or unconsciously) devaluing, discriminating or insulting them. The devaluation based on various characteristics (e.g. religion, ethnicity, nationality, skin color, ancestry, gender identity, sexual orientation, age, disability, body shape, illness, economic situation, profession, educational background, political orientation and others) can be obvious or hidden. Hate speech includes insults and slander as well as statements that promote derogatory stereotypes and incite hatred and violence against people based on (presumed) group affiliations. Hate speech can be expressed directly or indirectly.

Extended hate speech definition used in the project:

- Use of swear words
- Devaluation of identity / attacks on identity
- Incitement to violence and threats
- Dehumanizing language
- Dissemination of false information
- Sexual harassment
- Bullying
- May include structural discrimination (gender, skin color, religion, origin/ethnicity, language, sedentariness, health/body, property/class, reference global north and global south, type of society (modern/progressive))
- Can include friend-foe thinking (e. g. sports, clubs, fans, activities (bike-car/climate, voters of a party, etc.))
- Can be directed against professional groups (e.g. media professionals, politicians, authorities, police, representatives of an organisation, etc.)
- Individual, personal conflict (insult, abuse, defamation, coercion, threat)

No hate speech is:

- Criticism - even if it is harsh
- Free expression of opinion

- Non-judgemental generalisation
- Foreign language
- Dialect
- Misinformation

A.2.2 Definition 'Toxic Speech'

Below, we provide our working definitions of toxic speech; first in German, then translated to English.

Toxic Speech Definition (German)

Toxic Speech bezeichnet eine Sprache, die das Gesprächsklima vergiftet und den Diskurs für Hass und sprachliche Gewalt öffnet. Toxic Speech meint daher Aussagen, die Gesprächspartner:innen vor den Kopf stossen, sie blossstellen, die angriffig sind, die Druck ausüben oder destruktiv und manipulativ sind. Die Toxizität gibt an, wie "giftig" ein Kommentar für eine Konversation ist. Regt er zu negativen/aggressiven Reaktionen an oder würde man ihn vielleicht einfach unkommentiert lassen? Je stärker er zu aggressiven Äusserungen oder gar zum Austritt anderer Teilnehmer aus der Konversation anregt, desto toxischer ist der Kommentar.

Toxic Speech Definition (English translation)

Toxic speech refers to language that poisons the climate of dialogue and opens up the discourse to hatred and linguistic violence. Toxic speech therefore refers to statements that offend, expose, attack, exert pressure or are destructive and manipulative. Toxicity indicates how 'poisonous' a comment is for a conversation. Does it provoke negative/aggressive reactions or would you simply leave it uncommented? The more it encourages aggressive comments or even the withdrawal of other participants from the conversation, the more toxic the comment is.

A.2.3 Full Prompt (example)

Here, we show an example prompt for LLM-based classification including the full conversational context in German.

Full Prompt Example (German)

`System:` Sie sind ein Experte für die Moderation von Inhalten mit umfangreicher Erfahrung in der Erkennung von Hate Speech. Ihre Aufgabe besteht darin, von Nutzern bereitgestellte Kommentare auf der Grundlage der folgenden Definition von Hate Speech zu bewerten:

[Hate-Speech-Definition]

Wenn Sie einen Kommentar analysieren, müssen Sie ein binäres Urteil - 0 für 'ist nicht Hate Speech' und 1 für 'ist Hate Speech' - zusammen mit einer knappen, klaren Erklärung Ihrer Argumentation abgeben. Achten Sie darauf, dass Sie sich streng an das strukturierte Format halten, das im HateSpeechResponse-Schema definiert ist. Seien Sie objektiv, verweisen Sie auf die angegebene Definition, wenn dies angebracht ist, und vermeiden Sie unnötige Kommentare.
Wichtig: Wenn zusätzlicher Kontext wie ein ursprünglicher Kommentar oder ein Gesprächsverlauf bereitgestellt wird, berücksichtigen Sie diesen bei Ihrer Bewertung. Ein Kommentar kann in einem Kontext als Hate Speech gelten, während er in einem anderen Kontext harmlos sein könnte. Beziehen Sie den Kontext explizit in Ihre Begründung ein.
`Human:` Ist folgender Kommentar Hate Speech?

> 'die vollständige woke Verblödung sehen wir hier in Wort und Bild, von einer oder als was sie sich auch immer bezeichnet, die in BS Genderstudies absolviert hat!'

Der Kommentar ist eine Antwort auf diesen ursprünglichen Kommentar:

> '[ANONYMIZED] auf *X*: „«Es gibt zwei Geschlechter. #Mann und #Frau.» - diesen Satz wollen die woken Linken strafbar machen und in die «Anti-#Rassismus-Strafnorm» integrieren. Komplett irr. Ein Frontalangriff auf die Natur und unsere #Meinungsfreiheit. #only2'

Hier ist der vorherige Gesprächsverlauf:

- Kommentar 1: 'Du solltest da eigentlich etwas toleranter sein. Wer [ANONYMIZED] als zweites Ego hat, sollte sich nicht allzu weit aus dem Fenster lehnen.'
- Kommentar 2: 'Dir hat die Natur wirklich übel zugesetzt.'

System / Label	Precision	Recall	F1
DETOX GBert – Hate	0.78	0.67	0.71
DETOX XLM-R – Toxicity	0.56	0.56	0.54
DETOX Avg. – Hate	0.66	0.65	0.62
DETOX Avg. – Toxicity	0.40	0.40	0.39
Ours – Hate	0.51	0.61	0.56
Ours – Toxicity	0.56	0.16	0.25
GPT-4o-mini – Hate	0.32	0.79	0.46
GPT-4o-mini – Toxicity	0.08	1.00	0.15

Table 3: Evaluation on DETOX dataset. DETOX GBert and XLM-R are the best results reported in Demus et al. (2022).

A.3 Precision Evaluation on DETOX

To gauge precision of the LLM-based classification, we evaluated GPT-4o-mini on the German DETOX corpus (Demus et al., 2022) which does not provide conversational context. The definitions for hate speech and toxic speech used in the prompt were taken from Demus et al. (2022) to ensure comparability. Table 3 compares the LLM against our SwissBERT baseline (threshold 0.5).

While GPT-4o-mini recalls all toxic instances, its precision is considerably lower than our SwissBERT model's, highlighting a recall-precision trade-off that warrants future mitigation.

Additionally, we performed a preliminary Precision evaluation using the 30 available instances of HICC that were labeled as "no intervention" and measured a Precision of 60% for the hate speech detection prompt and 20% for the toxic speech detection prompt using GPT-4o-mini when providing the full context. This result provides a first indication of the performance of the LLM-based classification, but the sample size is too small to draw conclusions. Discussions with the streetworkers revealed that they used the label inconsistently and confounded it with the "intervention not recommended" label.

A.4 Cross-Label Experiments

We tested how robust each model is when the prompt/label pair is mismatched. Table 4 shows recall for the *Toxic-on-Hate* and *Hate-on-Toxic* settings using the full-context condition.

Model	Tox→Hate	Hate→Tox
GPT-4o-mini	99.5	74.0
Grok-3-mini	98.9	70.7
Claude 3 Haiku	97.6	81.8

Table 4: Cross-label recall (%) in the full-context condition.

Across all three models, a single toxicity prompt almost fully covers hate-speech instances ($\geq$ 97.6 %), whereas the inverse direction is much weaker (70-82%). This suggests that toxic language is a superset: a single toxicity prompt nearly covers all hate cases, but not vice-versa.

Evaluating the Feasibility of Using ChatGPT for Cross-cultural Survey Translation

Danielly Sorato
Universitat Pompeu Fabra
Barcelona, Spain
danielly.sorato@upf.edu

Diana Zavala-Rojas
European Social Survey ERIC
Universitat Pompeu Fabra
Barcelona, Spain
diana.zavala@upf.edu

Abstract

Cross-national survey projects such as the European Social Survey measure attitudes in European countries by applying standardized questionnaires to population samples. In this context, low-quality translations can affect data collected through questionnaires, hampering data comparability and increasing measurement errors across countries. For these reasons, cross-national survey projects employ rigorous methods in their translation process and refrain from using Machine Translation (MT). However, new advances in language models and their wide-ranging successful application across several Natural Language Processing tasks, including MT, have shown promising results. In the present study, we explore using `GPT-4o mini` for the questionnaire translation domain. We analyze `GPT-4o mini` translations for the English-German language pair by comparing them with reference translations produced by humans in an experimental setting. To assess the quality of automatic translations, we apply quantitative MT evaluation metrics and complement our results with qualitative analysis. Our findings show that the `GPT` model achieved overall good quality, although it failed to produce adequate translations for survey-specific terminology.

1 Introduction

The European Social Survey (ESS) and the European Values Study (EVS) are large-scale international survey projects that produce cross-national and cross-cultural social science data. These projects aim to measure respondents' attitudes, beliefs, and behavior regarding socially relevant topics (e.g., immigration, climate change, social trust) by administering standardized and structured questionnaires to representative population samples across European countries. The data collected through the questionnaires is publicly available and can be utilized for social and political analysis, serving as a tool for policy-making, for instance.

The survey questionnaires are written in a source language, which in Europe is usually English from Great Britain, and then translated into other target languages. The translated survey questions and their response options must capture the same opinions and attitudes across linguistic contexts to allow for cross-national statistical comparisons (Zavala-Rojas et al., 2022; Harkness et al., 2010; Mohler and Johnson, 2010; Zavala-Rojas et al., 2018a). Within this framework, the formulation of questions and the lack of proper cultural adaptation in the translation process can affect the quality of the data collected through questionnaires, as low-quality translations can hinder data comparability and increase measurement errors between countries (Davidov and De Beuckelaer, 2010; Oberski et al., 2007; Zavala-Rojas et al., 2022; Bound et al., 2001; Zavala-Rojas et al., 2018b).

To avoid translation issues, the Translation, Review, Adjudication, Pretesting, and Documentation (TRAPD) method (Harkness et al., 2003) has been increasingly adopted by large-scale survey projects, becoming a gold standard in the field of questionnaire translation. In this method, given a questionnaire written in the source language, two translators either produce independent translations into the respective target language or split the questionnaire so that each translator works separately on one of the parts. Then, in a review meeting, the translation drafts are compared to foster discussion, and the reviewer and the translators reconcile the different translation options. Finally, an adjudicator makes the final decisions. During the meeting, the team can opt for (i) one of the translation options; (ii) create a new translation by combining the strengths of each translation; or (iii) create a new translation from scratch. Subsequently, the translated questionnaire is pretested before being administered in fieldwork, and the process is documented.

TRAPD is a scientific methodology tailored to survey texts that circumvents problematic transla-

Proceedings of the 21st Conference on Natural Language Processing (KONVENS), Volume 1: Long and Short Papers, pages 177–191, 2025

tion practices. Furthermore, leveraging the contributions of several translators facilitates dealing with regional variances and individual preferences that can influence a translator's decision (Harkness, 2011; Walde and Völlm, 2023). However, TRAPD is time- and work-intensive, as it requires many interactions with a multidisciplinary team.

To date, Machine Translation (MT) has not been incorporated into the TRAPD, as the quality of automatic translations was considered below acceptable in most cases until recently. However, new advances in Large Language Models (LLMs) and their wide-ranging successful application across many Natural Language Processing (NLP) tasks, including MT, show promising results (He et al., 2024; Agrawal et al., 2023; Vilar et al., 2023; Moslem et al., 2023; Pilault et al., 2023; Hendy et al., 2023; Jiao et al., 2023; Wang et al., 2023; Peng et al., 2023; Bawden and Yvon, 2023). Furthermore, the ease of integrating relevant information in the prompts sent to LLMs represents a good opportunity to leverage expert knowledge and translations produced in previous questionnaires.

In this paper, we investigate the quality of the translations produced by `GPT-4o mini` for the English-German language pair in the survey translation domain, exploring different prompts and model temperature settings. Namely, we are interested in analyzing (i) the overall quality of the translated questionnaire; (ii) if the `GPT` translations of the response scales accurately keep the intensity attached to verbal labels (e.g., qualifiers, intensifiers); (iii) if survey-specific terminology and elements (e.g., instructions to the respondent or the interviewer) are correctly translated, and; (iv) to what extent the usage of examples and linguistic resources extracted from past questionnaires can improve the quality of the translations.

We analyze the quality of `GPT` translations by comparing them with human reference translations produced through the TRAPD methodology. To achieve this, we employ quantitative metrics for MT evaluation, namely `ChrF++` (Popović, 2017) and `COMET-22` (Rei et al., 2022). To deepen our study, we manually analyze certain aspects of the `GPT` translations that are key to answering our research questions. Finally, we create a translation assessment questionnaire containing the source text, reference, and `GPT` translations and ask five domain specialists to select the translation options that are most adequate for the survey domain, considering accuracy, fluency, and cultural adaptation criteria.

The source code and data used to produce the results and analyses presented in this study are openly available on a `Github` repository[1].

Our findings show that `GPT-4o mini` produced translations largely similar to human references, but struggled with gender adaptation, country-localized terms (e.g., job occupations), and survey-specific terminology, particularly instructions for interviewers. Our analysis also indicates that some translations are influenced by the English language, thus sounding unnatural and/or non-idiomatic.

This paper is organized as follows. In Section 2 we discuss related work. Then, we present our data and explain the process through which the reference translations used in this work were created in Section 3. Subsequently, in Section 4, we introduce our prompting strategy and MT evaluation methods. In 5, we discuss the findings derived from this study. Finally, we present our conclusions and limitations in Section 6.

2 Related Work

Translation quality is a complex and context-dependent topic (Nord, 2006; Koby et al., 2014). Using different translation theories, the academic literature provides various definitions of translation quality and how to evaluate it (González-Jover, 2002; Han et al., 2021).

An extensive body of research employs methods to evaluate and estimate the quality of MT (Papineni et al., 2002; Doddington, 2002; Specia et al., 2010, 2018; Bawden et al., 2018; Popović, 2018; Kepler et al., 2019; Mathur et al., 2020; Fomicheva et al., 2020; Thompson and Post, 2020; nll, 2024; Leiter et al., 2024). Given the varied motivations behind such analyses, we focus on those most aligned with ours, namely, studies that assess MT quality to evaluate the viability of integrating automatic translation in the process of producing cross-linguistic and cultural materials.

Turner et al., 2015 studied the feasibility of using MT and post-editing (PE) to produce Chinese translations of public health materials. The authors collected 60 health promotion documents from public websites for which validated human reference translations from English to Chinese were available. The documents were translated using `Google Translate` and then manually analyzed for translation errors. Additionally, a subset of the auto-

[1] `https://github.com/dsorato/KONVENS_2025_MT_paper`

matic translations was post-edited by native Chinese speakers with health sciences backgrounds. Their results showed that the evaluators consistently selected the human translation over MT in combination with human PE. Their evaluation indicated poor MT quality, where word meaning, word order, and missing words were the most common annotated translation errors.

Ugas et al., 2025 investigated the viability of using MT to translate and simplify patient education materials to make them more accessible for populations with limited English proficiency. The authors selected 5 patient education pamphlets, which were translated by domain specialists and `Google Translate` into Spanish, Portuguese, Punjabi, simplified Chinese, and Vietnamese. The translations were manually evaluated by domain specialists considering fluency, adequacy, meaning, and risk severity criteria. Their results show significant quality differences between human and automatic translations, although the authors report that the translated engine performed relatively well.

Kunst and Bierwiaczonek, 2023 analyzed automatic translations of the `HEXACO` personality inventory (Lee and Ashton, 2004), which is one of the most used cross-cultural psychometric instruments with validated translations in several languages. The authors assessed the quality of the translations of the English inventory produced by `Google Translate` and `GPT-3.5` in 33 languages for which validated human reference translations exist. To measure the similarity between machine and human translations, they applied metrics such as Levenshtein and Jaccard similarity, also providing human judgments for Norwegian translations.

Their findings show that the similarity between human and machine translations varied across target languages, being highest for languages from the same language family as the source language. They also found that `GPT`'s temperature had little influence on similarity estimates, although high temperatures tended to result in lower similarity. Manual evaluation showed that, although human translations achieved higher quality, the evaluators did not rate them significantly better than `GPT 3.5` translations with a low temperature setting.

Brewster et al., 2024 assessed the performance of `Google Translate` and `ChatGPT` for the translation of English pediatric discharge instructions into Spanish, Brazilian Portuguese, and Haitian Creole. The authors analyzed both automatic and human translations of 20 standardized discharge instructions for pediatric conditions in the specified languages, evaluating adequacy, fluency, meaning, and severity, along with an assessment of overall preference. According to the authors, `Google Translate` and `ChatGPT` achieved performances comparable to professional translations, at least for Spanish and Portuguese languages.

3 Data

A social survey, or questionnaire, comprises different items composed of questions and their respective response options, and may also include instructions for the interviewer or the respondent. We will refer to these elements as "survey items" throughout this paper. Figure 1 illustrates a survey item that contains a request for an answer, i.e., a question, two instructions, and response options.

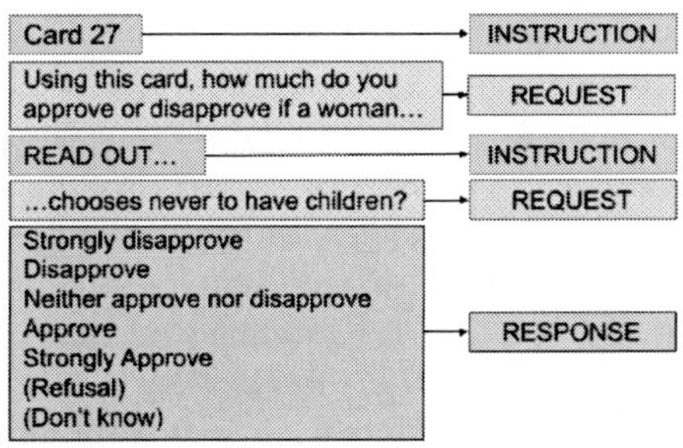

Figure 1: Source survey item from ESS round 3 (2006).

For our controlled translation experiment, we created a laboratory questionnaire using a sample of ESS and EVS questions, that is, survey items that were used in past officially published ESS and EVS questionnaires. First, we filtered a set of approximately 3,500 survey items written in English from the EVS and ESS questionnaires, favoring the variability of topics and response scales, as well as ensuring that the selected items had at least two sentences. From this process, we sampled 300 survey items. Since the translation of the laboratory questionnaire should simulate the translation of a real questionnaire, it was necessary to ensure that the survey items had enough context so that the translators could conduct their assignments properly. Therefore, when a survey item belonging to a grid of items (i.e., a battery of questions on the same topic) was selected but was not the first item in the grid, then the first survey item of that grid was also added to the sample, which guarantees that the laboratory questionnaire was read in a "natural" way; that is, it did not contain questions without context. The combination of random sampling and qualitative criteria helped ensure satisfactory coverage of the characteristics of a survey.

Finally, 26 survey items comprising 268 sentences were selected according to a qualitative scheme provided by questionnaire translation experts. This scheme was defined to select survey items that are considered challenging for both human and machine translation. For instance, survey items that contain survey-specific terminology, complex syntax/grammar, terms related to one's feelings, state of mind, well-being (e.g., feeling lonely), and technical terms that may or may not be adapted to a specific country context (e.g., unemployment benefits). Few modifications were introduced to the source items to create the laboratory questionnaire, such as harmonizing special answer categories such as "Don't know" and "Refusal" across ESS and EVS survey items.

Following the TRAPD guidelines, the laboratory questionnaire was independently translated from English to German by two human translators. Afterward, meetings led by a reviewer in conjunction with the translators took place to discuss the options and decide on the final translations. The outputs derived from the review meeting were then used as reference translations in this work.

We specified the following criteria for the study participants. First, the two human translators should be (i) one professional translator with at least 5 years of translation practice and previous experience translating survey questionnaires, and; (ii) one social scientist with at least 2 years of work experience, with a background in questionnaire design and translation. The reviewer should also be a social scientist who has experience in questionnaire translation and questionnaire design and is willing to lead a review discussion. The combination of having both professional translators and social scientists collaborating in teams goes back to how the interdisciplinary TRAPD method is set up.

Other than the reference translations produced through the aforementioned process, we leverage the translations present in the Multilingual Corpus of Survey Questionnaires (MCSQ) (Zavala-Rojas et al., 2022), which is a corpus of questionnaires from the ESS, EVS, Survey of Health Ageing and Retirement in Europe (SHARE), and Wage Indicator survey (WIS). The MCSQ comprises 306 different questionnaires and over 4 million tokens in the source language (English) and their translations into Catalan, Czech, French, German, Norwegian, Portuguese, Spanish, and Russian, as well as 29 language varieties (e.g., Swiss-French, Austrian-German). Aside from the Wage Indicator, these survey projects employ the TRAPD as the recommended translation method, and thus serve the purpose of gathering other valid translation options to compare against the GPT translations.

4 Method

One way to evaluate the quality of MT outputs is to compare them with reference translations. In this context, reference translations serve as a quality benchmark, i.e., the more similar a given MT output is to a reference translation, the better. To properly assess MT similarity, lexical, syntactic, and semantic aspects should be considered.

While lexical similarity can be assessed straightforwardly, measuring semantic similarity imposes greater challenges, including handling polysemy and paraphrasing. Although some classic MT evaluation metrics, e.g., BLEU, mainly assess lexical similarity, recent metrics such as BERTScore and COMET integrate semantic similarity through the use of neural network-based models that leverage semantic distributional hypothesis, bidirectionality[2], and self-attention mechanisms to improve meaning quantification. Recent research recommends the application of neural network-based metrics for MT quality assessment, as they have shown high correlations with human evaluation and are considered resilient to domain shift (Freitag et al., 2022; Hendy et al., 2023).

In this paper, we study the performance of GPT-4o mini in the survey translation domain. We specifically chose GPT-4o mini because it is a cost-efficient model that surpasses the performance of past GPT models, such as GPT-3.5 Turbo.

4.1 Metrics

To evaluate the quality of automatic translations produced by GPT-4o mini at the sentence level, we employ COMET-22 and ChrF++. COMET-22 is a neural network-based metric that has been shown to correlate well with human judgments. In addition to automatic and reference translations, this metric takes into account the source text and a combination of direct assessments (DA), sentence-level scores, and word-level tags from Multidimensional Quality Metrics (MQM) error annotations to produce the scoring. ChrF++ is not neural network-

[2]Taking into account both left and right contexts simultaneously to understand and represent word meaning.

based; however, it has also been shown to correlate well with human judgments, especially for morphologically rich target languages like German (Popović, 2017). It uses F-score statistic for character and word n-gram matches, the latter being more strongly correlated with DA. We include ChrF++ in this work because it provides direct information about the lexical similarity of translations, as the specific wording of the survey items matters in the context of survey translation.

Translation in the context of cross-national and cultural research can be challenging for MT since it is imperative for the text to be functionally equivalent across languages to accurately capture respondents' emotions and attitudes across different languages, cultures, and countries. For example, response scales containing qualifiers, e.g., "extremely satisfied", should ideally keep the same intensity when translated (Zavala-Rojas et al., 2022). Furthermore, survey questionnaires frequently contain survey-specific terms (e.g., instructions for the interviewer or the respondent), cultural and country-specific terminology (e.g., job titles, education levels), and short sentences in the case of some response scales and interviewer instructions.

Therefore, to supplement the insights derived from our qualitative analysis, we manually analyze some translation errors concerning survey-specific terminology, job descriptions, and qualifiers present in certain response options.

Finally, we created a questionnaire containing the source, reference, and GPT-translated items and asked five native German speakers acquainted with the survey translation domain to indicate, for each item, which translation option was more appropriate. Participants were blinded to the notion of which translation option was automatically generated and were asked to leverage accuracy, fluency, and cultural adaptation aspects. The order of the GPT and reference translations was randomized for each question. This questionnaire is available for consultation in the code repository.

4.2 Model prompting and temperature

To investigate how the integration of domain information in the prompts and the changes in the model temperature affect the quality of translations produced by GPT-4o mini, we translated our source laboratory questionnaire, testing 5 prompts and 6 temperature parameter values. Since the output of generative models may vary, we tested each prompt/temperature combination 5 times. A separate API call was used each time the questionnaire was translated with a given prompt/temperature combination. In all cases, the following persona description was given to the system: *"You are a professional translator specialized in translating survey questionnaires from English (from Great Britain) to German (from Germany) who works for social survey projects like the European Social Survey and the European Values Study."*.

We added domain knowledge to our prompts in a cumulative manner. Prompt 0 is zero-shot, and therefore instructs the model to perform the translation task without any additional examples to steer it, containing only a few guidelines concerning the formatting of the output and the tone of the text.

Subsequently, in prompt 1, we added a list of automatically extracted terms in English and their German translations. We employ the MCSQ to this end. Using only the sentence-aligned English-German (from Germany) data from the corpus and the tm2tb library[3], we extracted a list of 477 biterms and integrated this list into prompt 1 as well as the following prompts.

In prompts 2 and 3, other than the biterms, we also included guidelines and examples concerning using country-specific terminology for cultural adaptation and translating interviewer/respondent instructions and response scales, respectively. Finally, in prompt 4, we added four examples of English survey items and their translations to German, which were selected from EVS and ESS questionnaires, ensuring that the chosen survey items were not present in the laboratory questionnaire.

Concerning the model temperature, through preliminary tests, we observed that temperatures equal to or higher than 0.8 generated many instances of missing sentences and/or questionnaire formatting problems; therefore, we limit the temperature to 0.75 (the highest possible value would be 1). Namely, we tested the following temperatures: 0, 0.15, 0.3, 0.45, 0.6, 0.75.

The model prompts are available in the Appendix A. Our code, laboratory questionnaire, MT and reference translations, and scores of evaluation metrics are available on our Github repository.

5 Results

We start this Section by discussing the assessment of the overall questionnaire quality. Then, we focus

[3]https://github.com/luismond/tm2tb

on the translation quality of response options and respondent/interviewer instructions.

Figures 2 and 3 illustrate the similarity between GPT and reference translations according to COMET-22 and ChrF++, respectively, where the black dots and bars represent the mean and a 95% Confidence Interval. The similarity values range from 0 to 1 (or 0 to 100 in the case of ChrF++), where higher values indicate more similarity between automatic and reference translation. The X-axis indicates the prompt/temperature pairs, for instance p0_0.0 stands for prompt 0 with model temperature equal to 0, p4_0.75 stands for prompt 4 with model temperature equal to 0.75, etc.

For each sentence in the laboratory questionnaire, we took the average of the similarity values achieved in the five batches[4], taking into account the prompt and model temperature.

As can be observed in Figures 2 and 3, similarity values are overall high, and the prompt that achieved results most similar to reference translations is prompt 4, which was the prompt that contained examples of past survey items. Although prompt 1 also includes examples of bilingual terms extracted from MCSQ sentence-aligned data, the quality improvement is not as significant compared to prompt 4. The metrics also indicate that semantic similarity values are fairly high; however, there are differences concerning the wording of automatic and reference translations, as depicted in Figure 3. The model temperature does not appear to significantly impact the translation quality of the analyzed GPT translations.

We now turn to the translation quality of responses and instructions within the survey items analyzed in this study. Unlike Figures 2 and 2, which evaluated complete survey items without distinguishing sentence types, the remainder of this section focuses specifically on sentences that refer to responses or instructions[5].

We start by analyzing response translations, highlighting the response categories that include qualifiers and/or intensifiers in their text. Figures 4 and 5 illustrate the heatmap of similarity values between GPT and human translations according to ChrF++ and COMET-22, respectively. As in Figures 2 and 3, the X-axis of the heatmaps also indicates the prompt/temperature pairs.

As shown in the heatmaps, the GPT translations are overall similar to the references, especially when integrating examples in the prompt, i.e., translations produced with prompt 4. Figure 5, which depicts the ChrF++ values, indicates that using the prompt 4, the translations are also similar at the word level, since the metric computes similarity through character and word n-gram matches.

When manually analyzing responses that achieved low similarity values, we find that the sentence IDs 42, 126, 153, 228, and 246 correspond to the translations of the response option "Neither agree nor disagree", commonly present in response scales similar to the one depicted in Figure 1. The reference translation for this response option was *"Stimme weder zu noch nicht zu"*, while the most frequent GPT translations were *"Weder noch"* and *"Weder zustimmen noch ablehnen"*. Both translation options were present in past ESS and EVS questionnaires, as we verified using the MCSQ. The list of questionnaires in which these translation options are present is available in the Appendix B. The first option was more frequent, while the latter has been used only in a few EVS questionnaires localized for Luxembourgish-German.

The IDs 135 and 136 refer to a 0 to 10 response scale, where the extremes meant "Extremely important/unimportant". Reference translations for these response options were *"Äußerst unwichtig/wichtig"*. Although the GPT model succeeded in translating *"unwichtig/wichtig"*, in all cases, it failed to translate "Extremely", repeatedly translating the term as *"Extrem"*, which is often used in German to describe something radical or excessive, instead of indicating a high degree of something without implying excessiveness.

Beyond responses containing qualifiers, by revising the GPT translations and their metric scores, we found that one of the most challenging survey items was the translation of the response categories regarding the question *"Welchen Beruf üben Sie aus?"* ("What is your job?").

The first aspect that the GPT translations failed to achieve was gender adaptation (Savoldi et al., 2021). Since German is a gendered language, response options such as "Skilled manual worker" also provided gender inflections in the reference translations, e.g., *"Facharbeiter/**in**"*. Then, the GPT translations showed inconsistent terminology and mistranslations of job categories. Although

[4]We measured the variance of metric values and found that for most cases $variance < 0.01$. The mean and variance per sentence ID, prompt, and temperature are available in the Github repository.

[5]As illustrated in Figure 1 survey items may contain requests, responses, and instructions

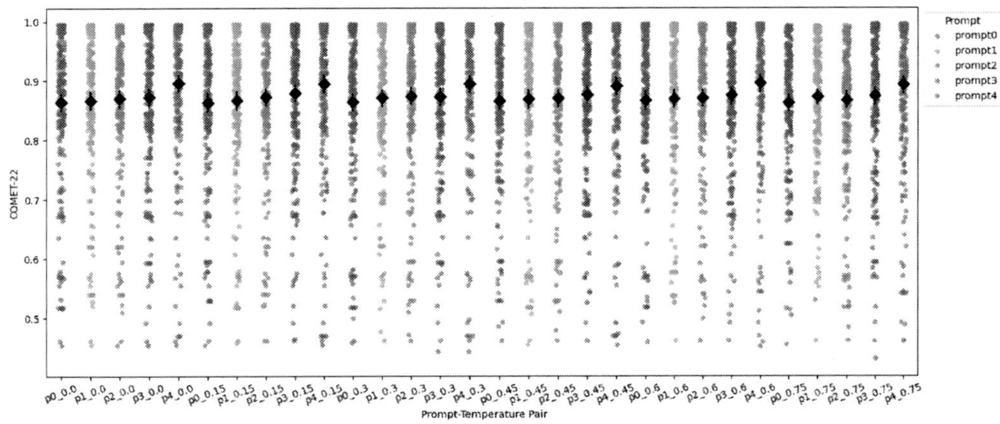

Figure 2: Similarity between GPT-4o mini and reference translations according to COMET-22.

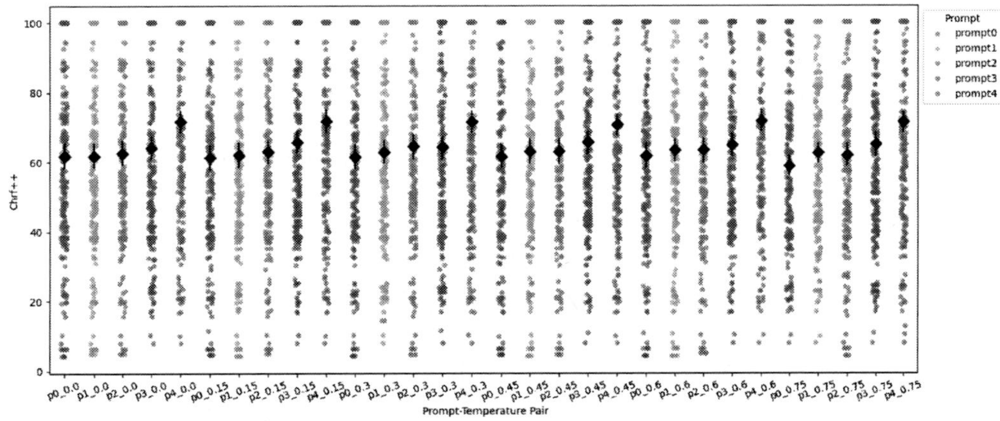

Figure 3: Similarity between GPT-4o mini and reference translations according to ChrF++.

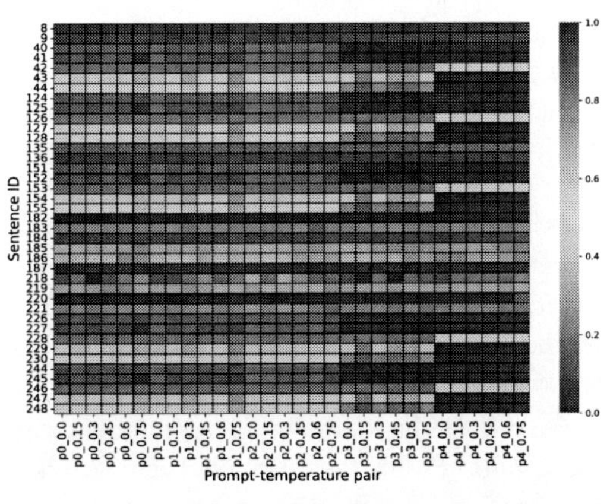

Figure 4: Heatmap of COMET-22 for responses.

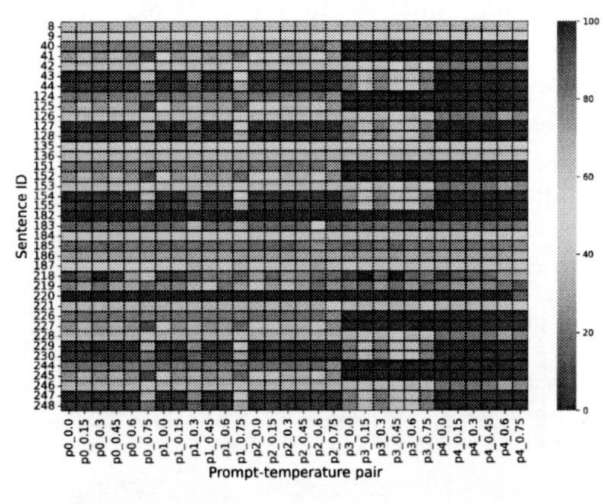

Figure 5: Heatmap of ChrF++ for responses.

the model managed to correctly translate categories such as *Vorarbeiter und Aufsichtsperson* ("Foreman and supervisor"), *"Facharbeiter"*, *"Ungelernter Arbeiter"* ("Unskilled manual worker"), it struggled to produce idiomatic translations for terms like "middle/junior level non-manual", often resulting in English-influenced translations, e.g., *"Junior-Stufe/Mittelstufe nicht-manual"* or *"Mitarbeiter auf mittlerer/unterer Ebene"*. We also notice the influence of English on some partially correct translations, for instance, in *"Landwirt: Arbeitgeber, Manager oder selbstständig"* ("Farmer: employer, manager or own account"), the term *"Manager"* is used instead of *"Leiter"*.

Now we comment on instruction translations. Interviewer instructions can be challenging elements for MT, and in many cases, the automatic translations are dissimilar to the references, as observed in Figures 6 and 7. Interviewer instructions often contain survey-specific terminology such as "Write in and code below" (ID 252), "Read out the statement and code in grid" (ID 122), and variations, which refer to the action of an interviewer registering the number of a response category provided by the respondent.

Although the GPT model was able to achieve translations equal or similar to those employed in past questionnaires for some complex instructions, e.g., *"Vorlesen und eine Antwort für jede ankreuzen"*("Read out and code one answer for each", ID 80) is similar to *"Vorlesen und eine Antwort ankreuzen"*, which was used in past EVS questionnaires, we observe that several translation options are literal and/or influenced by English syntax. For instance, the GPT translation options ***"Code** alle genannten"/"**Kodieren** Sie alle genannten"* and ***"Code** nur eine"/"**Kodieren** Sie nur eine"* were generated for the instructions "Code all mentioned" (ID 60) and "Code one only" (ID 115). ***"Erfassen"***, i.e., to capture/record, would be a more idiomatic German equivalent term than "Code", however, terms like ***"Code"*** and ***"Kodieren"***, are present in the MCSQ. *"Nur eine Antwort kodieren"*, for example, is a frequent translation in past ESS, EVS, and SHARE questionnaires, thus *"Kodieren Sie nur eine"* would be a good translation option if the syntax was not English-influenced.

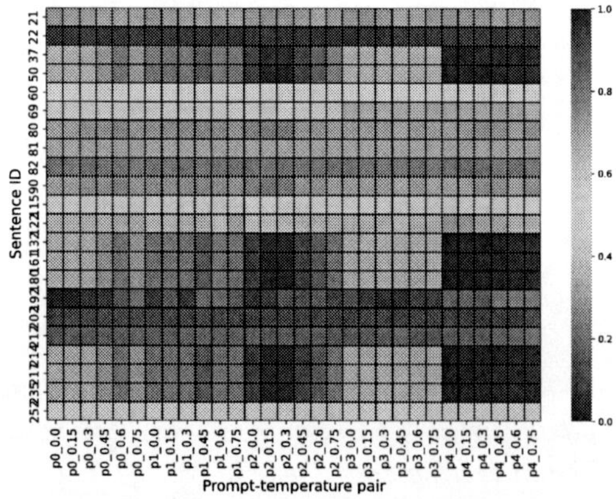

Figure 6: Heatmap of COMET-22 for instructions.

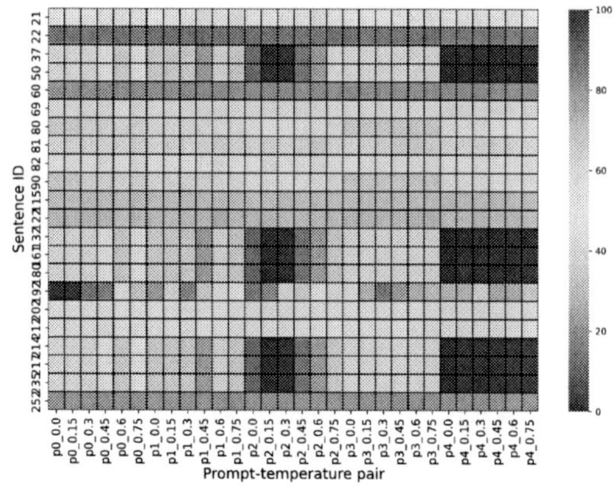

Figure 7: Heatmap of ChrF++ for instructions.

Finally, our experiment with five native German speakers showed that out of the 26 items included in our questionnaire, five of the survey items generated by the GPT model were deemed to have better quality than their human translation counterparts, taking into account accuracy, fluency, and cultural adaptation criteria.

Figure 8 shows the distribution of the responses for each of the questions. As can be observed in the graph, the participants generally preferred human translations, however, there were only five items for which all participants unanimously chose the human translation option over the GPT translation. An examination of the answer distribution also reveals instances of disagreement among the participants.

When verifying the inter-annotator agreement using Fleiss' Kappa, we obtained a 0.18 coefficient, confirming the low agreement between the participants. A certain degree of disagreement was anticipated for this task, as regional linguistic variations and individual preferences may influence participants' decisions. This variability underscores the importance of review meetings in the TRAPD method, where translation options are collaboratively discussed and evaluated.

On the one hand, the low inter-annotator agreement indicates that the GPT model achieved human-like translations in most cases, otherwise, the participants would have unanimously chosen the human translation options. On the other hand, it is not possible to draw conclusions concerning the perceived quality and adequacy of the GPT translations since the answers are mixed.

We cite the following limitations of our findings. This analysis considers only the English-German language pair, therefore, our conclusions cannot be

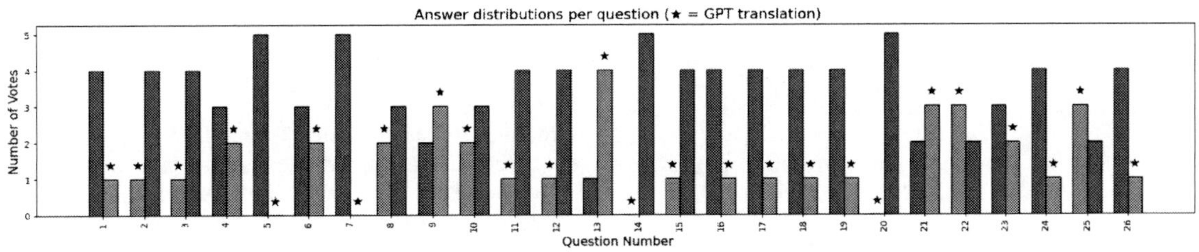

Figure 8: Answer distributions per question in the questionnaire. Stars indicate which answer option was the GPT translation.

generalized to other languages. Our quantitative evaluation was conducted at the sentence level; a word-level assessment could better identify problematic terms and expressions, offering deeper insights into the adequacy of GPT translations in the survey domain.

Concerning the experiment with native German speakers, the evaluation group could be increased, as increasing the number of annotators may improve the inter-annotator agreement. Furthermore, adding examples and more definitions to the task guidelines could help reduce annotator subjectivity.

6 Conclusion

In this study, we analyzed the quality of English to German questionnaire translations produced by GPT-4o mini, aiming to evaluate the feasibility of incorporating MT in the translation step of TRAPD method. We conducted a controlled translation experiment with human translators, and the automatic translation task included different prompts and model temperatures. Then, we analyzed the overall quality of the translations, focusing on survey-specific elements that can be challenging for MT, such as response scales and instructions.

Our findings indicate that GPT-4o mini achieved acceptable performance in the translation task, as depicted in our quantitative analysis and our experiment with five native German speakers acquainted with the survey translation domain. We found that providing examples of survey items fielded in past questionnaires was the best stimulus to improve translation quality. GPT-4o mini was able to keep the intensity of quantifiers in the response options in most cases, although it struggled to perform some crucial cultural adaptations, for instance, when referring to job descriptions. Moreover, the ChrF++ scores suggest that, in some cases, the vocabulary used by the GPT model deviates from that employed by human translators, which can be problematic in the context of cross-national surveys.

Although LLM-based MT can be used as a tool to speed up the translation process potentially, human translators are essential for verifying and rectifying machine-translated text, as well as for mitigating the lack of appropriate gender, cultural, and localization adaptations by understanding the cultural context in which the survey is conducted (Benlidayi and Gupta, 2024). This is of particular importance when formulating and translating questions for gathering socio-demographic data, e.g., personal details related to household, gender identity, or health issues, which is a task that can be complex even for humans. Employing culturally adequate and high-quality translations in the questionnaires is fundamental to minimizing the survey error measurements, or in other words, it is necessary to ensure that the survey items indeed capture what they intend to measure and that possible differences found across countries cannot be attributed to translation errors.

In future research, it would be beneficial to explore the use of translation tables (e.g., for job titles, response scales), MQM and/or DA-annotated examples in the translation prompts, and a Retrieval-Augmented Generation (RAG) system to improve linguistic and cultural accuracy. Further experimentation would be required to evaluate if integrating MT or MT plus PE at the translation step of the TRAPD improves the overall efficiency of the process. For a more comprehensible study of the quality of GPT-4o mini translations, it is necessary to take into account other language pairs, since the performance of LLMs is reported to vary in function of the target language.

Acknowledgments

This work was supported by the Social Sciences and Humanities Open Cloud (SSHOC) project, and received funding from the European Union's Horizon 2020 project call H2020-INFRAEOSC-04-2018, grant agreement #823782.

References

2024. Scaling neural machine translation to 200 languages. *Nature*, 630(8018):841–846.

Sweta Agrawal, Chunting Zhou, Mike Lewis, Luke Zettlemoyer, and Marjan Ghazvininejad. 2023. In-context examples selection for machine translation. In *Findings of the Association for Computational Linguistics: ACL 2023*, pages 8857–8873.

Rachel Bawden, Rico Sennrich, Alexandra Birch, and Barry Haddow. 2018. Evaluating discourse phenomena in neural machine translation. In *Proceedings of NAACL-HLT*, pages 1304–1313.

Rachel Bawden and François Yvon. 2023. Investigating the translation performance of a large multilingual language model: the case of bloom. In *Proceedings of the 24th Annual Conference of the European Association for Machine Translation*, pages 157–170.

Ilke Coskun Benlidayi and Latika Gupta. 2024. Translation and cross-cultural adaptation: A critical step in multi-national survey studies. *Journal of Korean Medical Science*, 39(49).

John Bound, Charles Brown, and Nancy Mathiowetz. 2001. Measurement error in survey data. In *Handbook of econometrics*, volume 5, pages 3705–3843. Elsevier.

Ryan CL Brewster, Priscilla Gonzalez, Rohan Khazanchi, Alex Butler, Raquel Selcer, Derrick Chu, Barbara Pontes Aires, Marcella Luercio, and Jonathan D Hron. 2024. Performance of chatgpt and google translate for pediatric discharge instruction translation. *Pediatrics*.

Eldad Davidov and Alain De Beuckelaer. 2010. How harmful are survey translations? a test with schwartz's human values instrument. *International Journal of Public Opinion Research*, 22(4):485–510.

George Doddington. 2002. Automatic evaluation of machine translation quality using n-gram co-occurrence statistics. In *Proceedings of the second international conference on Human Language Technology Research*, pages 138–145.

Marina Fomicheva, Shuo Sun, Lisa Yankovskaya, Frédéric Blain, Francisco Guzmán, Mark Fishel, Nikolaos Aletras, Vishrav Chaudhary, and Lucia Specia. 2020. Unsupervised quality estimation for neural machine translation. *Transactions of the Association for Computational Linguistics*, 8:539–555.

Markus Freitag, Ricardo Rei, Nitika Mathur, Chi-kiu Lo, Craig Stewart, Eleftherios Avramidis, Tom Kocmi, George Foster, Alon Lavie, and André F. T. Martins. 2022. Results of WMT22 metrics shared task: Stop using BLEU – neural metrics are better and more robust. In *Proceedings of the Seventh Conference on Machine Translation (WMT)*, pages 46–68, Abu Dhabi, United Arab Emirates (Hybrid). Association for Computational Linguistics.

Adelina Gómez González-Jover. 2002. La equivalencia como cuestión central de la traducción en las instituciones de la unión europea. In *on line]. In: Actas del I Congreso Internacional sobre El español, lengua de traducción. Almagro.*

Lifeng Han, Alan Smeaton, and Gareth Jones. 2021. Translation quality assessment: A brief survey on manual and automatic methods. In *Proceedings for the First Workshop on Modelling Translation: Translatology in the Digital Age*, pages 15–33.

J Harkness. 2011. Guidelines for best practice in cross-cultural surveys. *Survey Research Center, Institute for Social Research, University of Michigan.*

Janet A Harkness, Fons JR van de Vijver, Peter Ph Mohler, and John Wiley. 2003. *Cross-cultural survey methods*, volume 325. Wiley-Interscience Hoboken, NJ.

Janet A Harkness, Ana Villar, and Brad Edwards. 2010. Translation, adaptation, and design. *Survey methods in multinational, multiregional, and multicultural contexts*, pages 115–140.

Zhiwei He, Tian Liang, Wenxiang Jiao, Zhuosheng Zhang, Yujiu Yang, Rui Wang, Zhaopeng Tu, Shuming Shi, and Xing Wang. 2024. Exploring human-like translation strategy with large language models. *Transactions of the Association for Computational Linguistics*, 12:229–246.

Amr Hendy, Mohamed Abdelrehim, Amr Sharaf, Vikas Raunak, Mohamed Gabr, Hitokazu Matsushita, Young Jin Kim, Mohamed Afify, and Hany Hassan Awadalla. 2023. How good are gpt models at machine translation? a comprehensive evaluation. *arXiv preprint arXiv:2302.09210*.

Wenxiang Jiao, Jen-tse Huang, Wenxuan Wang, Zhiwei He, Tian Liang, Xing Wang, Shuming Shi, and Zhaopeng Tu. 2023. Parrot: Translating during chat using large language models tuned with human translation and feedback. In *Findings of the Association for Computational Linguistics: EMNLP 2023*, pages 15009–15020.

Fábio Kepler, Jonay Trénous, Marcos Treviso, Miguel Vera, and André FT Martins. 2019. Openkiwi: An open source framework for quality estimation. *ACL 2019*, page 117.

Geoffrey S Koby, Paul Fields, Daryl R Hague, Arle Lommel, and Alan Melby. 2014. Defining translation quality. *Tradumàtica*, 12:0413–420.

Jonas R Kunst and Kinga Bierwiaczonek. 2023. Utilizing ai questionnaire translations in cross-cultural and intercultural research: Insights and recommendations. *International Journal of Intercultural Relations*, 97:101888.

Kibeom Lee and Michael C Ashton. 2004. Psychometric properties of the hexaco personality inventory. *Multivariate behavioral research*, 39(2):329–358.

Christoph Leiter, Piyawat Lertvittayakumjorn, Marina Fomicheva, Wei Zhao, Yang Gao, and Steffen Eger. 2024. Towards explainable evaluation metrics for machine translation. *Journal of Machine Learning Research*, 25(75):1–49.

Nitika Mathur, Timothy Baldwin, and Trevor Cohn. 2020. Tangled up in bleu: Reevaluating the evaluation of automatic machine translation evaluation metrics. In *Proceedings of the 58th Annual Meeting of the Association for Computational Linguistics*, pages 4984–4997.

Peter Ph Mohler and Timothy P Johnson. 2010. Equivalence, comparability, and methodological progress. *Survey methods in multinational, multiregional, and multicultural contexts*, pages 17–29.

Yasmin Moslem, Rejwanul Haque, John Kelleher, and Andy Way. 2023. Adaptive machine translation with large language models. In *Proceedings of the 24th Annual Conference of the European Association for Machine Translation*, pages 227–237.

Christiane Nord. 2006. Translating as a purposeful activity: a prospective approach. *Teflin Journal*, 17(2):131–143.

Daniel Oberski, Willem E Saris, and Jacques Hagenaars. 2007. Why are there differences in measurement quality across countries. *Measuring Meaningful Data in Social Research. Acco, Leuven.*

Kishore Papineni, Salim Roukos, Todd Ward, and Wei-Jing Zhu. 2002. Bleu: a method for automatic evaluation of machine translation. In *Proceedings of the 40th annual meeting of the Association for Computational Linguistics*, pages 311–318.

Keqin Peng, Liang Ding, Qihuang Zhong, Li Shen, Xuebo Liu, Min Zhang, Yuanxin Ouyang, and Dacheng Tao. 2023. Towards making the most of chatgpt for machine translation. In *Findings of the Association for Computational Linguistics: EMNLP 2023*, pages 5622–5633.

Jonathan Pilault, Xavier Garcia, Arthur Bražinskas, and Orhan Firat. 2023. Interactive-chain-prompting: Ambiguity resolution for crosslingual conditional generation with interaction. In *Proceedings of the 13th International Joint Conference on Natural Language Processing and the 3rd Conference of the Asia-Pacific Chapter of the Association for Computational Linguistics (Volume 1: Long Papers)*, pages 455–483.

Maja Popović. 2017. chrf++: words helping character n-grams. In *Proceedings of the second conference on machine translation*, pages 612–618.

Maja Popović. 2018. Error classification and analysis for machine translation quality assessment. In *Translation quality assessment: From principles to practice*, pages 129–158. Springer.

Ricardo Rei, José GC De Souza, Duarte Alves, Chrysoula Zerva, Ana C Farinha, Taisiya Glushkova, Alon Lavie, Luisa Coheur, and André FT Martins. 2022. Comet-22: Unbabel-ist 2022 submission for the metrics shared task. In *Proceedings of the Seventh Conference on Machine Translation (WMT)*, pages 578–585.

Beatrice Savoldi, Marco Gaido, Luisa Bentivogli, Matteo Negri, and Marco Turchi. 2021. Gender bias in machine translation. *Transactions of the Association for Computational Linguistics*, 9:845–874.

Lucia Specia, Dhwaj Raj, and Marco Turchi. 2010. Machine translation evaluation versus quality estimation. *Machine translation*, 24(1):39–50.

Lucia Specia, Carolina Scarton, Gustavo Henrique Paetzold, and Graeme Hirst. 2018. *Quality estimation for machine translation*, volume 11. Springer.

Brian Thompson and Matt Post. 2020. Automatic machine translation evaluation in many languages via zero-shot paraphrasing. In *Proceedings of the 2020 Conference on Empirical Methods in Natural Language Processing (EMNLP)*, pages 90–121.

Anne M Turner, Kristin N Dew, Loma Desai, Nathalie Martin, and Katrin Kirchhoff. 2015. Machine translation of public health materials from english to chinese: a feasibility study. *JMIR public health and surveillance*, 1(2):e4779.

Mohamed Ugas, Maria Anna Calamia, Jessica Tan, Ben Umakanthan, Christine Hill, Karen Tse, Angela Cashell, Zaynab Muraj, Meredith Giuliani, and Janet Papadakos. 2025. Evaluating the feasibility and utility of machine translation for patient education materials written in plain language to increase accessibility for populations with limited english proficiency. *Patient Education and Counseling*, 131:108560.

David Vilar, Markus Freitag, Colin Cherry, Jiaming Luo, Viresh Ratnakar, and George Foster. 2023. Prompting palm for translation: Assessing strategies and performance. In *Proceedings of the 61st Annual Meeting of the Association for Computational Linguistics (Volume 1: Long Papers)*, pages 15406–15427.

Peggy Walde and Birgit Angela Völlm. 2023. The trapd approach as a method for questionnaire translation. *Frontiers in Psychiatry*, 14:1199989.

Longyue Wang, Chenyang Lyu, Tianbo Ji, Zhirui Zhang, Dian Yu, Shuming Shi, and Zhaopeng Tu. 2023. Document-level machine translation with large language models. In *Proceedings of the 2023 Conference on Empirical Methods in Natural Language Processing*, pages 16646–16661.

Diana Zavala-Rojas, Willem E Saris, and Irmtraud N Gallhofer. 2018a. Preventing differences in translated survey items using the survey quality predictor. *Advances in Comparative Survey Methods: Multinational, Multiregional and Multicultural Contexts (3MC). New York: Wiley Series in Survey Methodology.*

Diana Zavala-Rojas, Willem E. Saris, and Irmtraud N. Gallhofer. 2018b. Preventing Differences in Translated Survey Items using the Survey Quality Predictor. In Timothy P. Johnson, Beth-Ellen Pennell, Ineke A. L. Stoop, and Brita Dorer, editors, *Advances in Comparative Survey Methods: Multinational, Multiregional and Multicultural Contexts (3MC)*, chapter 17, pages 357–384. Wiley Series in Survey Methodology, New York.

Diana Zavala-Rojas, Danielly Sorato, Lidun Hareide, and Knut Hofland. 2022. The multilingual corpus of survey questionnaires: a tool for refining survey translation. *Meta*, 67(1):71–93.

A Model Prompts

Besides the texts included in this section, the prompts 1, 2, 3, and 4 included a list of 477 biterms automatically extracted from the MCSQ. The complete list of biterms can be consulted in the repository that contains the code and data related to this article[6].

Prompt 0: Please translate the following questionnaire written in English (from Great Britain) to German (from Germany). Your translated text should read as if it were written by a native German speaker from Germany. Use a direct and clear communication style. Use a professional, formal, and neutral tone suitable for survey questions. Replace any instances of the token "[country]" with the appropriate country in your output. Your translation output must have the same number of lines as the source (English) questionnaire. Include only the translated questionnaire in your output.

Prompt 1: Please translate the following questionnaire written in English (from Great Britain) to German (from Germany). After the questionnaire, you can find a list of English terms and their translations to German extracted from the European Social Survey and European Values Study questionnaires. This list may contain useful survey-specific terminology translation examples for you. Your translated text should read as if it were written by a native German speaker from Germany. Use a direct and clear communication style. Use a professional, formal, and neutral tone suitable for survey questions. Replace any instances of the token "[country]" with the appropriate country in your output. Your translation output must have the same number of lines as the source (English) questionnaire. Include only the translated questionnaire in your output.

Prompt 2: Please translate the following questionnaire written in English (from Great Britain) to German (from Germany). After the questionnaire, you can find a list of English terms and their translations to German extracted from the European Social Survey and European Values Study questionnaires. This list may contain useful survey-specific terminology translation examples for you. Use expressions and terminology that are specific from Germany to ensure proper cultural adaptation when applicable, especially when translating terms related to education levels and job descriptions/titles. For instance, the "Qualification from vocational ISCED 2C programmes of 2 years or longer duration, no access to ISCED 3" education level would be equivalent to "Volks-/Hauptschulabschluss bzw. Polytechnische Oberschule mit Abschluss 8. oder 9. Klasse" in Germany; the job description "in education, (not paid for by employer) even if on vacation" would be equivalent to "Schule/Ausbildung (nicht vom Arbeitgeber bezahlt; auch während der Ferien oder im Urlaub)" in Germany. Your translated text should read as if it were written by a native German speaker from Germany. Use a direct and clear communication style. Use a professional, formal, and neutral tone suitable for survey questions. Replace any instances of the token "[country]" with the appropriate country in your output. Your translation output must have the same number of lines as the source (English) questionnaire. Include only the translated questionnaire in your output.

Prompt 3: Please translate the following questionnaire written in English (from Great Britain) to German (from Germany). After the questionnaire, you can find a list of English terms and their translations to German extracted from the European Social Survey and European Values Study questionnaires. This list may contain useful survey-specific terminology translation examples for you. Use expressions and terminology that are specific from Germany to ensure proper cultural adaptation when applicable, especially when translating terms related to education levels and job descriptions/titles. For instance, the "Qualification from vocational ISCED 2C programmes of 2 years or longer duration, no access to ISCED 3" education level would be equivalent to "Volks-/Hauptschulabschluss bzw. Polytechnische

[6]https://github.com/dsorato/KONVENS_2025_MT_paper

Oberschule mit Abschluss 8. oder 9. Klasse" in Germany; the job description "in education, (not paid for by employer) even if on vacation" would be equivalent to "Schule/Ausbildung (nicht vom Arbeitgeber bezahlt; auch während der Ferien oder im Urlaub)" in Germany. When translating response scales, focus on keeping the concepts of interest and intensity of qualitifies/intensifiers the same across languages (e.g., "Agree strongly" -> "Stimme voll und ganz zu", "Very dissatisfied" -> "Sehr unzufrieden"). Do not forget to correctly translate and add to your output important survey-specific elements such as instructions to the respondent/interviewer like "READ OUT" and "Code all mentioned". Your translated text should read as if it were written by a native German speaker from Germany. Use a direct and clear communication style. Use a professional, formal, and neutral tone suitable for survey questions. Replace any instances of the token "[country]" with the appropriate country in your output. Your translation output must have the same number of lines as the source (English) questionnaire. Include only the translated questionnaire in your output.

Prompt 4: Please translate the following questionnaire written in English (from Great Britain) to German (from Germany). After the questionnaire, you can find a list of English terms and their translations to German extracted from the European Social Survey and European Values Study questionnaires. This list may contain useful survey-specific terminology translation examples for you. Use expressions and terminology that are specific from Germany to ensure proper cultural adaptation when applicable, especially when translating terms related to education levels and job descriptions/titles. For instance, the "Qualification from vocational ISCED 2C programmes of 2 years or longer duration, no access to ISCED 3" education level would be equivalent to "Volks-/Hauptschulabschluss bzw. Polytechnische Oberschule mit Abschluss 8. oder 9. Klasse" in Germany; the job description "in education, (not paid for by employer) even if on vacation" would be equivalent to "Schule/Ausbildung (nicht vom Arbeitgeber bezahlt; auch während der Ferien oder im Urlaub)" in Germany. When translating response scales, focus on keeping the concepts of interest and intensity of qualitifies/intensifiers the same across languages (e.g., "Agree strongly" -> "Stimme voll und ganz zu", "Very dissatisfied" -> "Sehr unzufrieden"). Do not forget to correctly translate and add to your output important survey-specific elements such as instructions to the respondent/interviewer like "READ OUT" and "Code all mentioned". Your translated text should read as if it were written by a native German speaker from Germany. Use a direct and clear communication style. Use a professional, formal, and neutral tone suitable for survey questions. Replace any instances of the token "[country]" with the appropriate country in your output. Your translation output must have the same number of lines as the source (English) questionnaire. Include only the translated questionnaire in your output. To further help you in your task, below you can find some examples of survey items extracted from past European Values Study and European Social Survey questionnaires translated from English (United Kingdom) to German (Germany), observe these examples and apply the same text style and terminology to your translations:

Example 1)
Source:
Generally speaking, would you say that most people can be trusted or that you can't be too careful in dealing with people?
Most people can be trusted
Can't be too careful
Don't know
No answer

Translation:
Würden Sie ganz allgemein sagen, dass man den meisten Menschen vertrauen kann, oder dass man da nicht vorsichtig genug sein kann?
Man kann den meisten vertrauen
Man kann nicht vorsichtig genug sein
Weiß nicht
Verweigert

Example 2)
Source:
SHOW CARD 41 – READ OUT AND CODE ONE ANSWER PER LINE
How much do you agree or disagree with each of the following:
Religious leaders should not influence government decisions
agree strongly
agree
neither agree nor disagree

disagree
disagree strongly
Don't know
No answer

Translation:
LISTE 41 VORLEGEN - VORGABEN VORLESEN UND EINE ANTWORT PRO ZEILE ANKREUZEN
Sagen Sie mir bitte zu jeder der folgenden Aussagen, ob Sie ihr voll und ganz zustimmen, zustimmen, nicht zustimmen oder überhaupt nicht zustimmen.
Die Kirchenoberhäupter sollten nicht versuchen, Entscheidungen der Regierung zu beeinflussen
Stimme voll und ganz zu
Stimme zu
Weder noch
Stimme nicht zu
Stimme überhaupt nicht zu
Weiß nicht
Verweigert

Example 3)
Source:
In the past 2 years, did the police in [country] approach you, stop you or make contact with you for any reason?
Yes
No
Don't know

Translation:
In den letzten 2 Jahren, hat sich die Polizei in Deutschland aus irgendeinem Grund an Sie gewendet, Sie angehalten oder kontaktiert?
Ja
Nein
Weiß nicht

Example 4)
Source:
Now some questions about whether or not the police in [country] treat victims of crime equally.
Please answer based on what you have heard or your own experience.
When victims report crimes, do you think the police treat rich people worse, poor people worse, or are rich and poor treated equally?
Choose your answer from this card.
Rich people treated worse
Poor people treated worse
Rich and poor treated equally
Don't know

Translation:
Nun einige Fragen dazu, ob die Polizei in Deutschland alle Opfer von Straftaten gleich behandelt oder nicht.
Bitte denken Sie bei Ihrer Antwort an das, was Sie gehört oder selbsterlebt haben.
Wenn Opfer zur Polizei gehen, um eine Straftat zu melden, glauben Sie, dass die Polizei reiche Leute schlechter behandelt, arme Leute schlechter behandelt oder dass beide gleich behandelt werden?
Wählen Sie Ihre Antwort aus Liste 29 aus.
Reiche Leute werden schlechter behandelt
Arme Leute werden schlechter behandelt
Reiche und arme Leute werden gleich behandelt
Weiß nicht.

B Translations retrieved from the MCSQ

Tables 1 and 2 show the list of published questionnaires in which the German translation options for the response option "Neither agree nor disagree" appear. The MCSQ does not include all published questionnaires from the European Social Survey (ESS), European Values Study (EVS), Survey of Health, Ageing and Retirement in Europe (SHARE), and Wage Indicator Survey (WIS), although it covers most of them, especially in the case of the ESS.

Weder noch		
Study	Round/Year	Country
ESS	1 (2002), 2 (2004), 3 (2006). 4 (2008), 5 (2010), 6 (2012), 8 (2016), 9 (2018)	Austria
EVS	3 (1999), 4 (2008), 5 (2017)	Austria
SHARE	7 (2017), 8 (2019)	Austria
ESS	1 (2002), 2 (2004), 3 (2006). 4 (2008), 5 (2010), 6 (2012), 7 (2014), 8 (2016), 9 (2018)	Switzerland
EVS	4 (2008), 5 (2017)	Switzerland
SHARE	7 (2017)	Switzerland
ESS	1 (2002), 2 (2004), 3 (2006). 4 (2008), 5 (2010), 6 (2012), 7 (2014), 8 (2016), 9 (2018)	Germany
EVS	3 (1999), 4 (2008), 5 (2017)	Germany
WIS	1 (2000)	Germany
ESS	2 (2004)	Luxembourg
EVS	4 (2008)	Luxembourg

Table 1: Questionnaires included in the MCSQ in which the translation *"Weder noch"* appears.

Weder zustimmen noch ablehnen		
Study	Round/Year	Country
EVS	4 (2008), 5 (2017)	Luxembourg

Table 2: Questionnaires included in the MCSQ in which the translation *"Weder zustimmen noch ablehnen"* appears.

Information Divergence in Translation and Interpreting: Findings from Same-Source Texts

Maria Kunilovskaya[1], Sharid Loáiciga[2], Ekaterina Lapshinova-Koltunski[3]
[1] Department of Language Science and Technology, Saarland University
[2] Department of Philosophy, Linguistics and Theory of Science, University of Gothenburg
[3] Department of Language and Information Sciences, University of Hildesheim
maria.kunilovskaya@uni-saarland.de
sharid.loaiciga@gu.se, lapshinovakoltun@uni-hildesheim.de

Abstract

The present paper reports on differences between written and spoken translation in English and German using Kullback-Leibler Divergence (KLD), an information-theoretic measure that captures the divergence of a given probability distribution from a reference distribution. While most studies comparing translation and interpreting focus on the target side only, we also take into account the source texts: we analyse differences between written and spoken translation renditions of the same source texts. The innovation of our approach is in the use of a source language model as an approximation of a cross-lingual modelling approach. Our results confirm the tendencies reported in previous work without same-source-text settings—namely, that interpreted targets differ more from their sources than written translations.

1 Introduction

In this study, we apply an information-theoretic approach to examine the differences between written and spoken modalities of translation. These differences have been widely documented from a translation studies perspective, highlighting the unique characteristics of each modality. However, previous studies have focused mostly on target-side comparisons between modalities. In contrast, our study employs parallel data with identical source-side texts, enabling a comprehensive analysis of both source- and target-side materials.

Information-theoretic measures such as surprisal or relative entropy are known to be predictive of language processing complexity, which involves not only the difficulty on the recipient's side but also translation production difficulty. The latter has been previously measured in a cross-lingual model setting only (Lim et al., 2024). We adopt two complementary approaches to assess modality differences: one relying on monolingual source and target language models, and a cross-lingual one relying on Neural Machine Translation (NMT) models. In both cases, we derive probability distributions from the models for each of the modalities and then measure the distance between them using Kullback-Leibler Divergence (KLD). While target language models provide a good estimate of the likelihood of the test set in the target language, we demonstrate that a source language model also serves as a good proxy for evaluating the differences between modes in the target language. So, while KLD scores on the target language models are indicative of the recipient's translation processing difficulty, the KLD scores obtained on the source language model give us an approximation of translation processing difficulty on the producer's side.

Analysing translation and interpreting involves not just two modalities, but two fundamentally different approaches to the translation process. Translators benefit from asynchronous access to the source text and supplementary resources such as dictionaries, whereas interpreters face the challenge of producing live, incremental translations under strict time constraints. The medium differences entail cognitive and processing challenges for interpreters.

By estimating KLD, we model the cognitive processing of translators and interpreters as producers. Also, unlike previous studies that only compared target-side differences, our approach introduces a novel approximation of the information transfer from source to target (see more details in Section 2.1). Taking into account the source text effectively models the interpreter's role in mediating the content. Furthermore, we analyse the linguistic cues that trigger these differences.

Our study is driven by three research questions:

RQ1 Is a source language model as sensitive in capturing differences across written and spoken modalities as a target language model?

Proceedings of the 21st Conference on Natural Language Processing (KONVENS), Volume 1: Long and Short Papers, pages 192–202, 2025

RQ2 How do spoken and written target versions diverge from the same source texts across translation directions?

RQ3 What are the main qualitative differences observed between written and spoken targets with respect to their sources?

The remainder of the paper is organised as follows: in Section 2 we discuss the related work, Section 3 describes the methodology. Last, we present results in 4 and conclude in Section 5.

2 Related Work

2.1 Spoken and written translation

Differences between simultaneous interpreting and written translation have been shown in previous studies (see e.g. Kajzer-Wietrzny, 2012). From the studies focusing on the language of translation (translationese or interpretese), we know that translation and interpreting are both clearly different from comparable originals, i.e., texts originally authored in the target language. At the same time, Shlesinger and Ordan (2012) show that interpreted texts seem to reinforce the features of spoken language. As a result, interpreting exhibits more marked linguistic characteristics than other kinds of texts and, in this way, is the most distinctive type of language production. Information-theoretically inspired features used by Lapshinova-Koltunski et al. (2021) support this statement. The authors employ the features obtained by KLD (based on the study by Przybyl et al., 2022a) in addition to other linguistic features. Interpreting resulting in higher scores than translation confirms that interpreting is the most distinctive kind of language production.

In this paper, we also aim to use information-theoretic measures which allow for a link between language use and cognition. Translationese (and also interpretese) features are understood to reflect rational communication: translators tailor the language encoding so as to translate successfully while keeping their cognitive effort at a reasonable level. Such measures, e.g., surprisal (Shannon, 1948), perplexity, and (relative) entropy have been used in other studies of translationese (Yung et al., 2023; Bizzoni and Lapshinova-Koltunski, 2021; Rubino et al., 2016) with a focus on written translation.

Existing interpretese studies that use information-theoretic measures mostly focus on specific linguistic items, e.g., discourse connectives (Lapshinova-Koltunski et al., 2022). However, only a few of them (Pollkläsener et al., 2024; Kunilovskaya et al., 2023; Yung et al., 2023) consider not only the scores of the comparable target texts, but also the underlying sources. Kunilovskaya et al. (2023) compare the input and output differences in translation and interpreting focusing not on specific linguistic items, but on the overall score of segments. The authors measure surprisal monolingually for source and targets and looked into the surprisal correlation.

2.2 Monolingual modelling

Thanks to their scale, large language models (LLMs) can perform a wide range of tasks in zero- or few-shot settings. Even early LLMs like GPT-2 showed the ability to translate text despite being trained solely with the standard next-word prediction objective (Radford et al., 2019). Building on this, Han et al. (2021) show that monolingual LLMs can be used to generate synthetic training data, which can then be used to fine-tune other models for machine translation. Similarly, Garcia et al. (2023) demonstrate that decoder-only LLMs can achieve strong translation performance when trained on just a handful of examples.

2.3 Cross-lingual modelling

In the context of machine translation, information theoretical approaches have been used to capture subtle distinctions in the source texts. Xu et al. (2021), for instance, integrate bilingual mutual information into the objective function in order to generate target tokens that reflect their source tokens better than their default target distributions. Similarly, Zhang et al. (2022) uses mutual information between a target token and its source sentence conditioned on the target contexts to measure the importance of different target tokens by their dependence on the source sentence. Contrary to our approach, these works estimate mutual information at the token level, while we use it at the sentence-level. On its part, Bugliarello et al. (2020) use a statistical machine translation approach to use target side language model probabilities and translation table probabilities to compute cross-lingual mutual information to test whether it is easier to translate from English or into English.

Lim et al. (2024) define translation surprisal as $s_{mt}(y_j) = \sum_{i \in j} - \log \left(p_{mt}(y_i \mid x, y_{<i})\right)$, where x and y are parallel source-target segments, and probabilities $p_{mt}(y_i \mid x, y_{<i})$ are extracted for each target token y_i, given the entire source x and pre-

ceding target tokens $y_{<i}$ from a Neural Machine Translation (NMT). The show that this measure can serve as a complementary predictor of human translation difficulty. These model-derived scores correlate with behavioural indicators of processing difficulty, such as reading time during translation. They also find that NMT-based surprisal is the strongest individual predictor of production duration.

3 Methodology

In our approach, we model aligned source texts, written translations, and spoken translations as *probability distributions over sentences*. To quantify the differences between these sentence-level distributions, we use Kullback-Leibler Divergence (KLD), an information-theoretic measure that captures the divergence of a distribution Q from a reference distribution P. Specifically, it measures how many additional bits of information are required to encode samples from P using a code optimised for Q.

Mathematically, for discrete distributions P and Q over a set of aligned sentences $\mathcal{S}$, KLD is defined as:

$$D_{\mathrm{KL}}(P \,||\, Q) = \sum_{s \in \mathcal{S}} P(s) \log \left(\frac{P(s)}{Q(s)} \right) \quad (1)$$

We compare probability distributions represented by sentence-level probabilities of aligned source texts, written translations, and spoken translations, treating them as alternative encodings of the same message. Depending on the comparison type (see Table 1), we take either the source texts or the written translations as the reference distribution P, and the written/spoken translations or spoken translations as the comparison distribution Q, respectively. In this way, the resulting KLD values quantify, for example, the excess unpredictability of the spoken rendition relative to the written modality. In other words, KLD measures how much information (in bits) is required to encode the sentence-level distribution of the spoken version Q when the model is optimised for the written distribution P.

Our main hypothesis is that the interpreting process inherently leads to greater changes in the amount of conveyed information compared to the source text, due to the demanding cognitive conditions under which interpreters work. In contrast, translations are expected to be more faithful to the source text, as translators can work without the pressure of live and incremental input and output. Written translations, unlike online spoken translations (interpreting), can also be revised and edited at a later time. Therefore, we anticipate that

(i) all models will detect the difference between spoken and written encodings of the same message, including source language models when applied to text in the target language, and (ii) spoken targets will exhibit greater divergence from the source texts than written translations.

To compute KLD between sentence-level probability distributions in our dataset, we used SciPy's `entropy` function with a base-2 logarithm, yielding results in bits. In addition to the aggregate KLD (1), we also computed the *pointwise* contribution of each sentence pair to the divergence.

$$pw\_D_{kl}(s) = P(s) \log_2 \left(\frac{P(s)}{Q(s)} \right) \quad (2)$$

This weighted log-ratio of sentence probabilities (which we refer to as *pointwise KLD* or *pseudo-KLD*) enables us to track local variation within the dataset, identify high-contributing instances, and better interpret the overall KLD values obtained from different models. Unlike the true KLD, which is always non-negative, the pointwise value can be negative when $Q(s) > P(s)$.

The next two sections detail our method for estimating sentence-level probabilities and explain how KLD was used to compare the two mediation modes (interpreting, translation), viewed here as different message encoding types.

3.1 Comparing sentence probabilities

The main goal of this study is to compare the differences across translation modalities while taking into account the source text. The source text is known to be a strong factor that influences the properties of the output in any cross-lingual transfer. Two alternative types of models were used to represent our data: monolingual and cross-lingual. The cross-lingual approach inherently conditions output probabilities on the source language input, but it does not allow for estimating the distance between sources and targets using KLD. As a proxy for a cross-lingual approach, we propose to use a source language model on target language texts in each mode and compare the resulting sentence probability distributions based on our set of sentences. If the source language model is approximately as good as the target language model in capturing the divergence of spoken targets from the written targets, then we can apply it to measure the divergence of targets from sources for each modality.

We use the dedicated German and English GPT2 models (Schweter, 2020; Radford et al., 2019) for monolingual processing and translation-direction-specific MarianMT machine translation models (Tiedemann and Thottingal, 2020) for cross-lingual inference. The language- and translation-direction-specific models are preferred over multilingual alternatives to avoid a potentially confounding factor of other languages in the model. The four selected models have approximately the same vocabulary size of 50-58 K tokens. Importantly, we aggregate sentence probabilities from the probabilities of word-tokens defined by Stanza (Qi et al., 2020) and not from the probabilities of subword-tokens as defined by tokenisers of the respective models. This allows us to keep German and English monolingual models comparable across the experiments (especially when applying a source language model to texts in the target language) and to introduce a common ground for comparison between monolingual and cross-lingual models. The sentence probabilities are obtained by summing up word probabilities in log space and then exponentiating the result.[1]

To sum up, our experimental setup includes three levels of comparative analysis in each translation direction. In Table 1, the Model Type column specifies the model from which the probabilities for the KLD calculations were obtained.

Level	Model Type	Input Pair (P vs. Q)
a	TL model	Written target vs. Spoken target
	SL model	Written target vs. Spoken target
b	SL model	Written source vs. Written target
	SL model	Spoken source vs. Spoken target
c	NMT model	Written target vs. Spoken target

Table 1: Three levels of comparative analysis using language and translation models. In each pair, the first text type is treated as the reference distribution P.

[1]The aggregated probabilities from the English GPT2 model as well as for EN-DE NMT model for two German sentences, each containing more than 50 words, encountered a numerical underflow issue during the exponentiation step, even when using double-precision floating-point calculations. As a result, the values are set to a floor value of $1e - 250$.

3.2 Data

Our multiparallel subset of written and spoken renditions of the same original texts is an intersection of the EuroParl-based corpora of written and spoken translations: Europarl-UdS (Karakanta et al., 2018) and EPIC (Przybyl et al., 2022b), respectively. Europarl-UdS contains edited transcripts of the speeches and their official translations as made available on the EP website, EPIC contains true manual transcripts of the debates in the European Parliament and their simultaneous interpretation as captured in the video recordings of the debates. All data is limited to English-to-German and German-to-English translation directions and only includes original speeches delivered by native speakers of English or German, respectively. For each translation direction, we identified source-target document pairs where the source language speeches were the same. Speaker, date and document size parameters were used as a coarse filter. The results were further refined using pair-wise cosine similarity of the document vectors (cutoff 0.8) derived from an off-the-shelf embedding model trained on a semantic textual similarity task (Reimers and Gurevych, 2019). However, due to the differences between written and spoken originals based on the same real-life speech (mostly due to dissimilar sentence alignment in each corpus), it was impossible to get written and spoken mediated versions for every source sentence in the multi-aligned documents. Therefore, the experimental data were further limited to include written and spoken sentence pairs where the source sentences had a Levenshtein distance of over 0.8. To account for possible rearrangement of sentences in the transcripts, the comparison was run in the context window of 10 sentences. To balance the dataset across translation directions, we selected five documents from the larger German-to-English set, each containing 70 reliably multi-aligned sentence pairs, ensuring that both directions had the same number of sentences. This approach preserved the topical coherence present in the English-to-German set, rather than taking a random sample of 70 sentences from across many documents.

The quantitative description of the final multi-parallel test dataset is given in Table 2.

Note that throughout the paper, we use 'sentence' and 'segment' interchangeably, but the true unit of analysis is the segment rather than the sentence, as it is the alignment unit: in parallel data, source and

direction	docs	segs	src_tokens
DE-EN	5	70	1,478
EN-DE	5	70	1,789

Table 2: Parameters of the datasets. Token counts are given for Stanza-tokenised sources (src), in multi-parallel data based on the written version of the source.

target sentences can align in a one-to-many manner, especially in spoken data.

4 Results and Discussion

4.1 RQ1: Differences across modalities

First, we investigate whether monolingual source language models can capture differences between spoken and written translations when measured using KLD, in the same way that target language models do. This provides us with a proxy of translation production, i.e., taking the source language differences into account. In this way, we approximate a cross-lingual approach but without using a cross-lingual or multilingual model.

Table 3 presents the KLD results based on the segment probabilities inferred using the out-of-the-box monolingual GPT models of the source and target languages applied to 70 pairs of written and spoken translations of the same sources in each translation direction.

direction	SL model	TL model
DE-EN	9.130 (de_gpt2)	7.468 (en_gpt2)
EN-DE	0.013 (en_gpt2)	0.697 (de_gpt2)

Table 3: KLD results on monolingual models of source and target languages as defined in Table 1 (row a): KLD shows divergence between written and spoken targets of the same source. Source and target language models are applied to the text in the target language.

As seen from Table 3, the source language model is as sensitive to the differences in written and spoken translation as the target language model: KLD values in rows are are of similar magnitude. This confirms that written and spoken translation differ, including when the source language is implicitly taken into account by applying the source language model to the translation in the target language. This also confirms the validity of the approach to use a source language model as a proxy for a cross-lingual approach to analyse differences between spoken and written translation.

As a sanity check, we calculate the perplexities of the same models on the same data. Perplexity provides an independent measure of how "surprised" a model is by the data: if a model assigns very low probability to the observed tokens, this is reflected in a high perplexity. Comparing KLD with perplexities allows us to confirm that observed differences between written and spoken translations are meaningful and not driven by degenerate probability distributions.

For each segment, we calculate the sentence-average negative $\log_2$ probabilities, also known as average sentence surprisal (AvS), and then average these across 70 instances in each sample. The result is exponentiated to yield the perplexity, as shown in Equation 3. Segment perplexities are combined using the geometric mean, which is more robust to outliers and better represents the central tendency.

$$\text{PPL} = 2^{-\frac{1}{S}\sum_{s=1}^{S}\left(\frac{1}{T_s}\sum_{t=1}^{T_s}\log_2(p_{t,s})\right)} \quad (3)$$

As seen in Table 4, perplexities for subword tokens are consistently higher for spoken segments than for written segments across both source- and target-language models. This indicates that spoken translations are systematically harder for the models to predict, and, importantly for this study, are systematically treated as different from the written translation in absolute terms, validating our KLD-based approach, which is a relative difference measure.

	model	mode	subword	word
DE-EN	SL	written	56.18	331.07
		spoken	83.31	392.55
	TL	written	61.18	68.26
		spoken	75.85	86.13
EN-DE	SL	written	77.43	45165.76
		spoken	88.79	32002.15
	TL	written	52.04	85.80
		spoken	105.68	165.89

Table 4: Geometric mean segment perplexities of the source- and target-language GPT2 models (SL and TL model) for the written and spoken target versions (written and spoken mode) calculated for subword- and word-based segments.

Additionally, Table 4 reports perplexities for word-level tokens, since KLD values were calculated from Stanza-token probabilities, which in turn were obtained by aggregating probabilities of constituent GPT-4 subwords, and GPT-4 tokenisation strongly affects the results, especially in our unconventional inference setup. As expected, all written and spoken target language segments contain more subwords than words when processed by the source-language model.

The very low KLD between written and spoken German in the EN-DE direction (0.013) can be better understood in light of the perplexity results. From the perspective of the English source-language model, both written and spoken German segments are highly improbable (for this test set), which leads to very high perplexities. Because KLD measures relative divergence, the distributions of written and spoken German appear very similar to the English model, even though the absolute probabilities are extremely low. In other words, the low KLD reflects *relative* similarity between written and spoken segments, while the high perplexity highlights the poor adaptation of the source-language model to target-language text. The inclusion of a single very long segment (>75 words) further exaggerates the perplexity, but it does not affect the interpretation of KLD as a measure of relative differences.

We compare the KLD indices obtained with the source language model (SL model in Table 3) with the results from the cross-lingual NMT model, i.e., a cross-lingual setting. The KLD indices estimated from the language pair-specific NMT model are shown in Table 5.

direction	NMT model
DE-EN	35.543
EN-DE	5.175

Table 5: KLD for written and spoken target sentence probabilities from the NMT models as defined in Table 1 (row c).

The cross-lingual approach returns a similar result for the directions comparison: the divergence of spoken from written is greater for the German-to-English direction than for English-to-German (see SL model results in Table 3).

Overall, the KLD values reported for the two translation directions in our analysis are derived from language- or language-pair-specific models (e.g., en_gpt2, de_gpt2, and the DE–EN and EN–DE NMT systems). Even for structurally similar sentences, these models may assign systematically different probabilities, making direct comparisons of absolute KLD magnitudes across languages or directions unreliable. In particular, higher aggregated KLD values for English targets do not necessarily indicate a larger true divergence; they may reflect model-specific scaling effects.

To provide a more nuanced view, we plot the pointwise KLD values for paired written and spoken targets in our sample (Figure 1). These plots offer a comparable qualitative signal: for English as the target language (upper panel), the curve crosses zero more frequently, indicating greater variability in how the models assign probabilities to the spoken versus written versions. In other words, the pointwise differences are more volatile and less systematic, with frequent sign flips. By contrast, for German targets, probabilities for written versions tend to dominate more consistently, resulting in fewer zero crossings and lower variability in the curve.

4.2 RQ2: Source language divergence

Next, we examine how spoken and written target versions diverge from the same source texts. We measure the differences between these two modes using KLD against the shared source segments, applying source-language models that, as shown in Section 4.1, can capture mode differences similar to the target-language models.

direction	mode	SL model
DE-EN	written	44.881 (de_gpt2)
	spoken	63.949 (de_gpt2)
EN-DE	written	0.051 (en_gpt2)
	spoken	0.098 (en_gpt2)

Table 6: KLD results on monolingual models of source languages as defined in Table 1 (row b): cross-lingual divergence between sources and their targets depending on the mode. Source language model is applied to the text in the source language and its rendition in the target language.

Table 6 provides an overview of the KLD scores calculated for both translation directions. Higher scores indicate greater divergence between the probability distributions of the source text and its target rendition as estimated by the source-language model. In other words, the higher the KLD score, the more the statistical profile of the translation or interpreting output differs from that of its source.

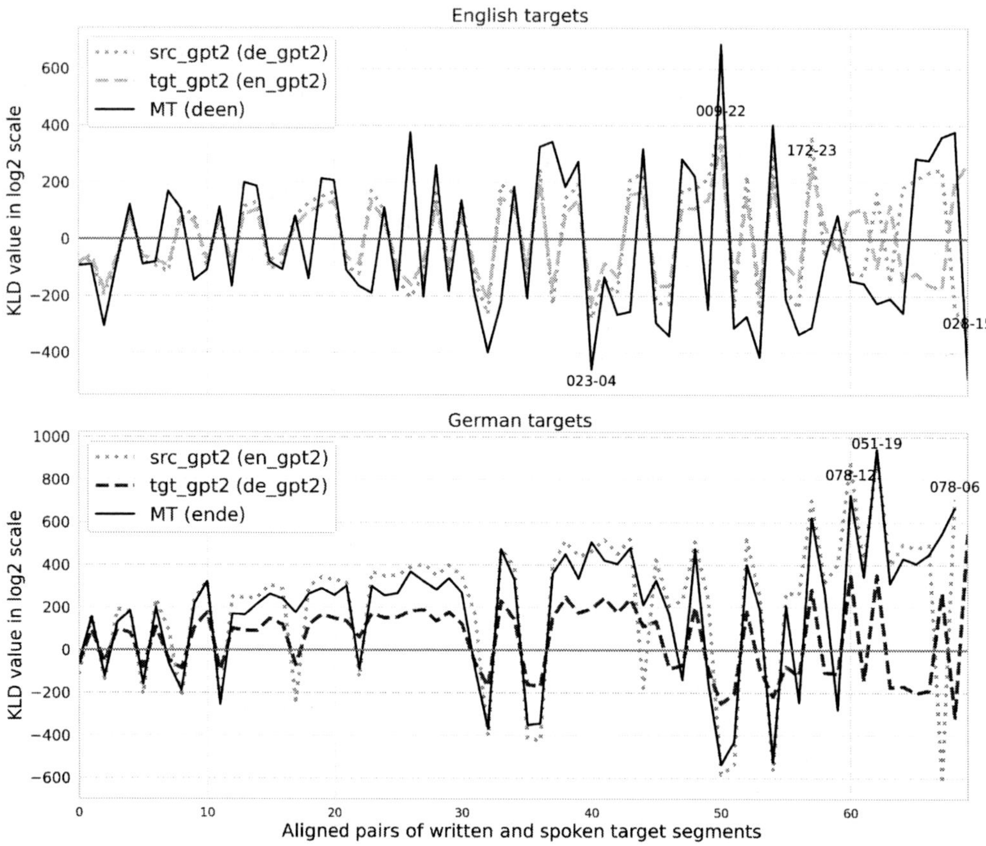

Figure 1: Comparison of GPT and MT-based KLD values (in log2 scale) across all instances in the sample. The instances are sorted in ascending order by the absolute KLD difference between source and target GPT2 models. The top three instances by KLD values based on source GPT2 and/or MT are shown on the x-axis.

Since we are comparing the same source texts and their two target-language versions, no differences in KLD scores would be expected if translation and interpreting were identical. However, the third-column scores in Table 6 do differ (44.881 vs. 63.949 and 0.051 vs. 0.098). Crucially, across both translation directions, the magnitude of divergence of target from source in spoken renditions is significantly higher than in written translations. For DE-EN, the median difference in pseudo-KLD magnitudes (i.e., absolute values) is 10.22 (Wilcoxon $p \approx 4.6 \times 10^{-7}$, permutation p = 0.0002), while for EN-DE, the median difference is 1.45 (Wilcoxon $p \approx 0.003$, permutation $p \approx 0.0032$), indicating that spoken translations consistently exhibit greater deviation from the reference distributions.

4.3 RQ3: Linguistic differences

And finally, we manually compare the spoken and the written translations of 70 input segments in both languages aiming to observe specific differences sentence by sentence. We do not collect any quantitative information on the type of differences, but report our observations only. We also visualise the contrasts between written and spoken versions of one segment from our data in Figure 2 which shows diverging word surprisal values for each word in the segment.

Overall, we observe that translators and interpreters apply different segmentation, with interpreting using more simple sentences instead of one long with subordinates. As a result, interpreting contains more repeated words or paraphrases than translation does.

DE-EN Observations:

- Interpreting uses more general words instead of specific ones: *to make use* vs. *to utilise*, *future generation* vs. *our children* (Figure 2). Further examples include (but not limited to):

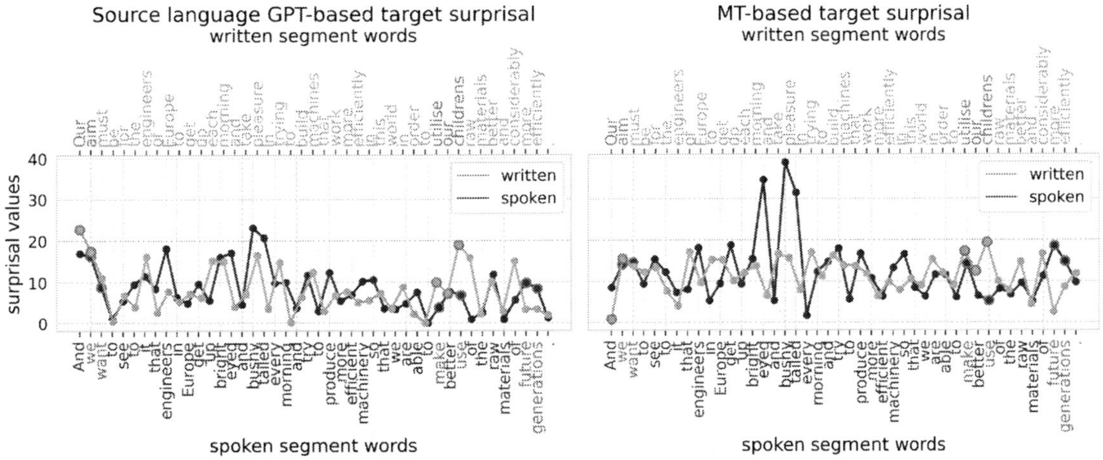

Figure 2: Word surprisals derived from GPT and MT models for DE_EN_028-15 instance. Contrastive written and spoken solutions are highlighted in red.

spoken	**written**
run up	*history*
Commissioner	*Mrs Fererro-Waldner*
people	*citizens*

- Interpreting prefer to use active instead of passive voice such as *we will be looking at proposals* vs. *proposals should be submitted.* Moreover, it has more verbal instead of nominal phrases: *we want* vs. *our aim* (Figure 2) or further cases:

spoken	**written**
the Commission's assessment	*the Commission's assessment*
people got to trust each other	*trust between the states*
we need	*an essential factor*
is very close to	*its geographical proximity*

- Furthermore, there is a difference in the speaker-addressee perspectives (3rd vs. 1st person or 2nd vs. 1st person reference) in both translation variants, although no systematic pattern could be observed:

source	*Europa steht im internationalen Wettbewerb, in einem globalen Wettbewerb, in dem sich auch die europäischen Dienstleister positionieren und durchsetzen müssen.*
spoken	*Europe is facing global competition, in particular in the area of services. And we need to defend our position.*
written	*Europe faces international competition, global competition, in which European service providers also need to find their place and be successful.*

- At the same time, second person reference is used by an interpreter in a different case, where the translator prefers to use the first person reference (*you* instead of *we*).

source	*Wenn wir uns die Vorgeschichte dieser Richtlinie...ansehen...*
spoken	*If you look at the run up to this Directive.*
written	*If we look at the history of this directive.*

EN-DE Observations:

- Similarly to the EN-DE pair, German interpreting contains more general words instead of specific ones. The written variant is not only more specific, but also more literal and closer to the source, while the spoken one is more general:

spoken	written
klappen	("to function")
("to work out")	*funktionieren*
diese Listen	*Kriterien für diese Barometer*
("these lists")	("criteria for these barometer")

Sometimes, details are omitted in interpreting and added in translation, and a general word is used for several terms:

source	*...winter cereal crops susceptible to weeds and disease such as blight.*
spoken	*...bei dem Winterweizen werden da Seuchen eingeführt.*
written	*...Wintergetreide anfällig für Unkraut und Krankheiten, beispielsweise Pilzerkrankungen wie Mehltau oder Braunfäule.*

Another interesting example here is the translation of the word *pollination*. The translator used a specification with a prepositional phrase *Bestäubung von Pflanzen mit Pollen* ("pollination of plants with pollen") and the interpreter used simply the word *Polliniserung* instead, which is not common in German.

- German interpreting also prefers use of verbs over nominal phrases:

spoken	written
versuchen	*zur Aufgabe machen*
("try")	("to make a task")
aufpassen	*Gewissheit darüber haben*
("pay attention")	("to have certainty")

- Apart from this, we observe a more frequent use of relative clauses in interpreting, e.g. the source nominal phrase a *non-scientific-based definition* corresponds to *Definition, die nicht wissenschaftlich ist* in the spoken version, and to *wissenschaftlich nicht fundierte Definition* in the written one.

  Another case of use of relative clause is the translation of *adequate prevention strategies*: the written rendition is a literal translation. The corresponding interpreting *vorbeugende Strategien, die dagegen vorgehen* ("preventive strategies that work against it) contains the relative clause *die dagegen vorgehen* ("that work against it") which is repetitive and redundant as it conveys the same information as the modifying participle *vorbeugend* ("preventive").

- We also observe omission of some details like in the following example. The German interpreted version does not contain any information on skills and training, while the written rendition does contain this information that was left out in interpreting:

source	*Secondly, the whole area of innovation about looking to see where jobs are going to come into future and making sure people have the skills and the training for that*
spoken	*Dann innovative Maßnahmen, welche Arbeitsplätze für die Zukunft von Bedeutung sind und wie man die weiter ausbauen kann.* ("Then innovative measures, which jobs are important for the future and how they can be further expanded.")
written	*Zweitens, der gesamte Bereich der Innovation und die Aufgabe, festzustellen, woher die Arbeitsplätze in der Zukunft kommen, und sicherzustellen, dass die Menschen die Fachkenntnisse und die Ausbildung dafür haben.*

The analysis of the concrete linguistic differences between spoken and written translation confirms the observations made in other existing studies (Lapshinova-Koltunski et al., 2021; Przybyl et al., 2022a; Shlesinger and Ordan, 2012). However, while most previous works were based on comparable corpora of translation and interpreting, our qualitative analysis is based on parallel segments with one underlying source.

5 Conclusion and Discussion

This study applies information-theoretic measures, known to be predictive of translation processing complexity on both producer and recipient's side, to analyse differences between translation and interpreting.

Our findings show that these differences can be effectively captured using both monolingual and multilingual (i.e., cross-lingual) approaches. We also demonstrate that interpreting diverges more strongly from the source texts than written translation does, a tendency observed consistently across both language pairs.

The main contributions of this study are as follows: (1) A comparative analysis of spoken and written translation renditions using identical source segments, allowing for a more controlled investigation of modality-based differences; (2) The application of information-theoretic measures to capture source-related divergences between interpreting and translation, extending previous work focused only on target-side comparisons; (3) The use of both cross-lingual and monolingual modelling approaches to assess translation difficulty, thereby offering complementary perspectives on cognitive and linguistic processing in human translation.

We believe that our approach can be useful for further applications. For instance, it can be used to measure other systemic divergences between language outputs, e.g. standard vs. simplified language, human vs. machine translations, etc.

6 Limitations

The KLD estimates used in this study are based on sentence-level probabilities aggregated from word-token outputs. Because these sentence probabilities can be extremely small, the calculations are susceptible to numerical underflow. Moreover, our sample—comprising 70 multiparallel sentence sets in each translation direction—may be too limited to approximate the true underlying probability distributions assumed by KLD with high reliability. As such, the present work should be regarded as proof of concept, and its findings interpreted withing this narrow scope.

7 Acknowledgments

At Saarland University and the University of Hildesheim, this research was supported by the Deutsche Forschungsgemeinschaft (DFG, German Research Foundation) – B7 "Translation as rational Communication" of SFB 1102 Information Density and Linguistic Encoding, Project-ID 232722074. Sharid Loáiciga was funded by the Swedish Research Council (VR) grant (2014-39) for the Centre for Linguistic Theory and Studies in Probability (CLASP). We thank Shalom Lappin for constructive discussions that helped improve this work. We also thank the anonymous reviewers for their insightful comments.

References

Yuri Bizzoni and Ekaterina Lapshinova-Koltunski. 2021. Measuring translationese across levels of expertise: Are professionals more surprising than students? In *Proceedings of the 23rd Nordic Conference on Computational Linguistics (NoDaLiDa)*, pages 53–63, Reykjavik, Iceland (Online). Linköping University Electronic Press, Sweden.

Emanuele Bugliarello, Sabrina J. Mielke, Antonios Anastasopoulos, Ryan Cotterell, and Naoaki Okazaki. 2020. It's easier to translate out of English than into it: Measuring neural translation difficulty by cross-mutual information. In *Proceedings of the 58th Annual Meeting of the Association for Computational Linguistics*, pages 1640–1649, Online. Association for Computational Linguistics.

Xavier Garcia, Yamini Bansal, Colin Cherry, George Foster, Maxim Krikun, Melvin Johnson, and Orhan Firat. 2023. The unreasonable effectiveness of few-shot learning for machine translation. In *Proceedings of the 40th International Conference on Machine Learning*, ICML'23. JMLR.org.

Jesse Michael Han, Igor Babuschkin, Harrison Edwards, Arvind Neelakantan, Tao Xu, Stanislas Polu, Alex Ray, Pranav Shyam, Aditya Ramesh, Alec Radford, and Ilya Sutskever. 2021. Unsupervised neural machine translation with generative language models only. *Preprint*, arXiv:2110.05448.

Marta Kajzer-Wietrzny. 2012. *Interpreting universals and interpreting style*. Ph.D. thesis, Uniwersytet im. Adama Mickiewicza, Poznan, Poland. Unpublished PhD thesis.

Alina Karakanta, Mihaela Vela, and Elke Teich. 2018. Europarl-UdS: Preserving metadata from parliamentary debates. In *Proceedings of the 11th International Conference on Language Resources and Evaluation (LREC 2018)*. European Language Resources Association (ELRA).

Maria Kunilovskaya, Heike Przybyl, Ekaterina Lapshinova-Koltunski, and Elke Teich. 2023. Simultaneous interpreting as a noisy channel: How much information gets through. In *Proceedings of the 14th International Conference on Recent Advances in Natural Language Processing*, pages 608–618, Varna, Bulgaria. INCOMA Ltd., Shoumen, Bulgaria.

Ekaterina Lapshinova-Koltunski, Yuri Bizzoni, Heike Przybyl, and Elke Teich. 2021. Found in translation/interpreting: combining data-driven and supervised methods to analyse cross-linguistically mediated communication. In *Proceedings for the First Workshop on Modelling Translation: Translatology in the Digital Age*, pages 82–90, online. Association for Computational Linguistics.

Ekaterina Lapshinova-Koltunski, Christina Pollkläsener, and Heike Przybyl. 2022. Exploring Explicitation and Implicitation in Parallel Interpreting and Translation Corpora. *The Prague Bulletin of Mathematical Linguistics*, 119:5–22.

Zheng Wei Lim, Ekaterina Vylomova, Charles Kemp, and Trevor Cohn. 2024. Predicting human translation difficulty with neural machine translation. *Transactions of the Association for Computational Linguistics*, 12:1479–1496.

Christina Pollkläsener, Frances Yung, and Ekaterina Lapshinova-Koltunski. 2024. Capturing variation of discourse relations in english parallel data through automatic annotation and alignment. *Across Languages and Cultures*, 25(2):288 – 309.

Heike Przybyl, Alina Karakanta, Katrin Menzel, and Elke Teich. 2022a. Exploring linguistic variation in mediated discourse: translation vs. interpreting. In Marta Kajzer-Wietrzny, Adriano Ferraresi, Ilmari Ivaska, and Silvia Bernardini, editors, *Mediated discourse at the European Parliament*, number 19 in Translation and Multilingual Natural Language Processing, pages 191–218. Language Science Press, Berlin.

Heike Przybyl, Ekaterina Lapshinova-Koltunski, Katrin Menzel, Stefan Fischer, and Elke Teich. 2022b. EPIC-UdS - creation and applications of a simultaneous interpreting corpus. In *Proceedings of the 13th Conference on Language Resources and Evaluation (LREC 2022)*, pages 1193–1200, Marseille, France. ELDA.

Peng Qi, Yuhao Zhang, Yuhui Zhang, Jason Bolton, and Christopher D. Manning. 2020. Stanza: A Python natural language processing toolkit for many human languages. In *Proceedings of the 58th Annual Meeting of the Association for Computational Linguistics: System Demonstrations*.

Alec Radford, Jeffrey Wu, Rewon Child, David Luan, Dario Amodei, Ilya Sutskever, et al. 2019. Language models are unsupervised multitask learners. *OpenAI blog*, 1(8):9.

Nils Reimers and Iryna Gurevych. 2019. Sentence-BERT: Sentence Embeddings using Siamese BERT-Networks. In *Proceedings of the 2019 Conference on Empirical Methods in Natural Language Processing*. Association for Computational Linguistics.

Raphael Rubino, Ekaterina Lapshinova-Koltunski, and Josef van Genabith. 2016. Information density and quality estimation features as translationese indicators for human translation classification. In *Proceedings of the 2016 Conference of the North American Chapter of the Association for Computational Linguistics: Human Language Technologies*, pages 960–970, San Diego, California. Association for Computational Linguistics.

Stefan Schweter. 2020. German GPT-2 model. *Zenodo*.

Claude E. Shannon. 1948. A Mathematical Theory of Communication. *The Bell System Technical Journal*, 27(3):379–423.

Miriam Shlesinger and Noam Ordan. 2012. More spoken or more translated?: Exploring a known unknown of simultaneous interpreting. *Target. International Journal of Translation Studies*, 24(1):43–60.

Jörg Tiedemann and Santhosh Thottingal. 2020. OPUS-MT – building open translation services for the world. In *Proceedings of the 22nd Annual Conference of the European Association for Machine Translation*, Lisbon, Portugal. European Association for Machine Translation.

Yangyifan Xu, Yijin Liu, Fandong Meng, Jiajun Zhang, Jinan Xu, and Jie Zhou. 2021. Bilingual mutual information based adaptive training for neural machine translation. In *Proceedings of the 59th Annual Meeting of the Association for Computational Linguistics and the 11th International Joint Conference on Natural Language Processing (Volume 2: Short Papers)*, pages 511–516, Online. Association for Computational Linguistics.

Frances Yung, Merel Scholman, Ekaterina Lapshinova-Koltunski, Christina Pollkläsener, and Vera Demberg. 2023. Investigating explicitation of discourse connectives in translation using automatic annotations. In *Proceedings of the 24th Annual Meeting of the Special Interest Group on Discourse and Dialogue*, pages 21–30, Prague, Czechia. Association for Computational Linguistics.

Songming Zhang, Yijin Liu, Fandong Meng, Yufeng Chen, Jinan Xu, Jian Liu, and Jie Zhou. 2022. Conditional bilingual mutual information based adaptive training for neural machine translation. In *Proceedings of the 60th Annual Meeting of the Association for Computational Linguistics (Volume 1: Long Papers)*, pages 2377–2389, Dublin, Ireland. Association for Computational Linguistics.

SEAS: Sentence Extraction and Alignment from Subtitles

Josh Stephenson and Libby Barak
Montclair State University
New Jersey, USA
josh@brightmediums.com, barakl@montclair.edu

Abstract

Subtitles for movies and television offer a unique resource for extracting multilingual alignments and studying linguistic phenomena. However, existing tools for subtitle alignment are difficult to reproduce, lack standardized evaluation mechanisms, and frequently exhibit obvious errors. Moreover, these methods fail to leverage recent advances in sentence alignment, namely sentence embeddings. To address these shortcomings, we combine time-based methods with state-of-the-art sentence alignment techniques. Our method achieves substantial improvements in alignment performance over gold-standard data and a downstream Machine Translation task. Our submission includes a curated corpus of gold-standard alignments for English-Spanish and English-German subtitles, along with their corresponding subtitle files, a novel annotation tool, and the full code to reproduce our method.

English: `- Stop.`
Spanish: `Agrándalo y vuélvelo a reproducir.`

English: `You're okay.`
Spanish: `Estás bien. Descansa.`

English:
German: `- Was ist los?\n- Treten Sie von ihr...`

Table 1: Sample errors from the English-Spanish and English-Germancorpus from Opus 2018.

1 Introduction

Subtitles are one of the most substantial sources of translation data created through manual annotation. Notably, they complement primary data sources such as books, web and legal data, which are commonly used to train language models, by providing rich cross-lingual spoken dialogue. Importantly, subtitle alignment presents multiple challenges due to the lack of one-to-one correspondence between utterances and subtitles across languages, substantial noise from non-dialogue elements, and variability in subtitle counts between source and target.

Previous subtitle extraction and alignment projects have produced large collections of sentence alignments from subtitle data (Tiedemann, 2007, 2012, 2016). However, past subtitle alignment methods have relied too heavily on timestamp data rather than the semantic properties of language and have employed less stringent data cleansing procedures. As a result, these datasets contain obvious errors. Unfortunately, subtitle evaluation has largely been limited to small samples of manually annotated sentence pairs, restricting the ability to quantify the impact of such errors on downstream tasks.

Recent breakthroughs in sentence alignment using sentence embeddings have demonstrated significant progress (Schwenk and Douze, 2017). However, to the best of our knowledge, these advances have yet to be applied to subtitle data, either alone or in combination with time-based methods traditionally used for subtitle alignment. We propose a novel two-step method for subtitle alignment: (1) Preprocessing, which includes timecode drift correction, partitioning using dialogue gaps, and other data cleansing steps, and (2) Embedding-based alignment, which leverages Vecalign (Thompson and Koehn, 2019), a sentence embedding framework, to align extracted sentences based on normalized cosine similarity.

Our system achieves 93.12% F1 scores on a manually annotated sample of Spanish and German subtitles, consisting of roughly $2,950$ alignments for each language. Additionally, our results demonstrate significant improvements over previous subtitle datasets in a downstream Machine Translation (MT) task, using one million English-Spanish alignments generated by our method. Our submission includes the complete code for the model used to generate the data, the annotated and raw data, along with a novel annotation tool we developed to curate manual alignments.

Proceedings of the 21st Conference on Natural Language Processing (KONVENS), Volume 1: Long and Short Papers, pages 203–212, 2025

2 Related Work

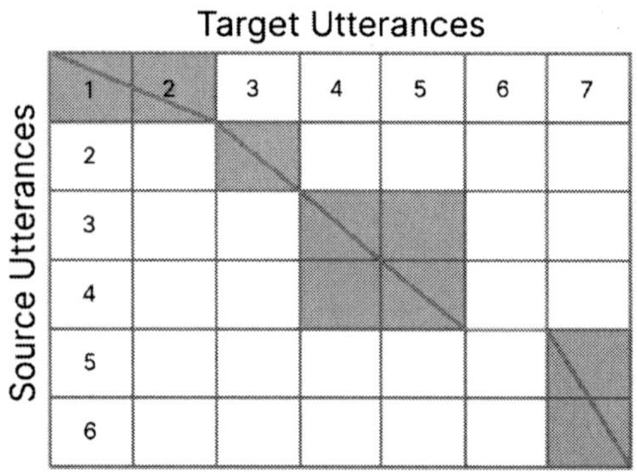

Figure 1: Visualization of a sentence alignment matrix.

The core challenges in subtitle alignment are largely rooted in sentence alignment, which involves constructing a bipartite graph from parallel documents segmented at sentence boundaries. All methods have two main components: (1) a **scoring function**, which estimates the likelihood that two sentences are translations of one another, and (2) an **alignment algorithm**, which generates a hypothesized alignment between two documents using the scoring function.

Any document is essentially an ordered list of sentences, and aligning two documents starts by representing them as a large two-dimensional matrix, with the sentences of one document along the columns and those of the other along the rows (see Figure 1).

Previous sentence alignment methods have used various scoring functions, but most traditionally relied on sentence length in characters or tokens, while others incorporated lexical information (Brown et al., 1991; Gale and Church, 1993; Chen, 1993; Wu, 1994; Moore, 2002; Varga et al., 2007). Nearly all have employed some form of Dynamic Programming (DP) as the alignment algorithm (Bellman, 1954). Later methods introduced strategies such as clustering, pruning, and lexical anchoring to improve results (Braune and Fraser, 2010; Sennrich and Volk, 2010; Papineni et al., 2002).

The distinctive nature of subtitle translation introduces unique alignment challenges due to frequent insertions, deletions, and paraphrasing. Without extensive subtitle-specific preprocessing, common sentence alignment methods produce a high error rate, even when incorporating sentence-length or utterance-duration information (Tiedemann, 2007). Each subtitle has a corresponding start and end time which can be used for alignment instead of using DP. Notably, Tiedemann found that doing so produced superior results. His algorithm searches linearly through the target subtitles based only on overlapping timecodes to resolve insertions and deletions (see Table 2).

Sentence embeddings have addressed many of the key shortcomings of earlier alignment techniques. Thompson and Koehn (2019) applied multilingual sentence embeddings from the LASER embedding toolkit (Artetxe and Schwenk, 2018) to sentence alignment, using normalized cosine similarity as the scoring function and an alignment algorithm based on Fast Dynamic Time Warping (Salvador and Chan, 2007). This approach achieved state-of-the-art results in both alignment quality and efficiency. The method, Vecalign, first concatenates n adjacent sentences into a single unit (where n is a hyperparameter) before feeding them into the algorithm, enabling one-to-many and many-to-many alignments.

Despite these advances, subtitle alignment tools have not kept pace with recent developments in sentence alignment. The OPUS dataset contains over 8.5 billion sentence alignments across sixty-two languages (Tiedemann, 2007). In later work, the dataset has been extended and updated while maintaining the original method. Unfortunately, it lacks extensive evaluation procedures and was created before the introduction of sentence embeddings. Its evaluation consisted of only thirty alignments from each of five titles in two language pairs.

Our study overcomes these limitations by releasing an open-source suite of tools built on sentence embeddings and enabling comprehensive evaluation.

3 Methods

Unlike corpora such as books, websites, manuals and legal documents, subtitle documents contain more than just dialogue, which necessitates meticulous preprocessing prior to alignment.

Our tools include various preprocessing steps before alignment, which we have conceptually separated into three stages: (1) data cleansing, (2) sentence boundary detection, and (3) partitioning. For data cleansing, we first verify correct language labeling using n-grams (unigrams up to 5-grams)[1], detect and correct synchronization issues between

[1]mislabeled files are thrown out.

English (source)		Spanish (target)	
19	00:01:10,320 --> 00:01:15,617 Aren't you a professor of Physics?	12	00:01:10,446 --> 00:01:14,784 ¿No es usted Profesor de física?
95	00:07:06,342 --> 00:07:07,593 {\an8}[radio beeps]		
21 22	00:01:20,038 --> 00:01:21,915 You were my student. 00:01:22,123 --> 00:01:23,123 Behave yourself!	14	00:01:20,498 --> 00:01:23,126 Fuiste mi estudiante. Compórtese.
25	00:01:25,835 --> 00:01:30,882 In your physics course, did you teach the theory of relativity?	16 17	00:01:25,628 --> 00:01:27,305 En su curso de física, 00:01:27,505 --> 00:01:30,591 ¿enseñó la teoría de la relatividad?
543	00:36:40,531 --> 00:36:42,408 But I don't see it that way.	349 350	00:36:40,491 --> 00:36:41,834 No lo veo de esa forma. 00:36:42,034 --> 00:36:45,329 Conozco tus logros académicos.

Table 2: English-Spanish alignment examples, (1) 1-to-1 noise free alignment; (2) English subtitle without dialogue; (3) 2 English sentences from 2 speakers aligned with 1 Spanish sentence; (4) 1 English sentence in 1 subtitle aligned with 1 Spanish sentence spanning 2 subtitles; (5) 1 English subtitle overlaps with 2 Spanish subtitles in 2 sentences.

source and target subtitle timecodes, and then use a multi-step process based on regular expressions to strip everything but dialogue. After cleansing, we apply regular expressions to detect sentence boundaries and extract utterances.

Finally, partitioning is a novel technique for splitting the subtitle files into smaller files based on gaps in the dialogue. In essence this leverages the time-based metadata of subtitles selectively, ensuring the semantic merging and alignment does not merge fragments across prosodic boundaries. Prior to this partitioning, our analysis of false positives revealed errors that involved merging one character's complete thought with another character's verbal filler. Because verbal fillers (e.g., "umm," "uh,") carry minimal semantic weight, Vecalign may fail to recognize them as separate utterances, leading to unintended merges. Often these merges occur across a clear prosodic boundary as evident by the timecodes. To mitigate these errors, our final stage of preprocessing uses a 3-second threshold for prosodic boundaries during partitioning, based on our analysis of gap length and psycholinguistic findings on prosodic boundary duration (Jun, 2006). See Appendix for full details on preprocessing.

Finally we use Vecalign for alignment of extracted utterances (Thompson and Koehn, 2019). Since some utterances are short phrases that need to be merged with adjacent ones, we overlap them in groups of six before inputting them into Vecalign.

4 Evaluation and Results

We evaluate our proposed subtitle alignment method, SEAS, against manually annotated alignments and on a downstream MT task. As a first baseline, we implement a timecode-only system to replicate the method used to generate the OPUS dataset (Tiedemann, 2007; Lison and Tiedemann, 2016)). To evaluate how well Vecalign can handle sentence alignment when subtitle data is not well preprocessed, we also produce baselines that include each of the preprocessing methods one-by-one to embedding-based alignment to assess the impact of each individual component.

	Preprocessing			Recall	Precision	F-1
	1	2	3			
0	-	-	-	66.67	58.26	62.18
1	✗	✗	✗	33.31	41.87	37.11
2	✓	✗	✗	45.07	52.40	48.46
3	✗	✓	✗	76.30	72.10	74.14
4	✓	✓	✗	93.01	92.08	92.54
5	✓	✓	✓	93.80	92.45	**93.12**

Table 3: System configuration details w/o preprocessing steps detailed in section 3. Recall, precision and F1 as percentage.

4.1 Alignment quality assessment

We report performance across five titles containing Spanish and English subtitles for each of the baselines described above. For each predicted alignment, we search linearly for an exact match in the gold standard alignments. Although some sentence alignment tasks allow for soft alignments based on edit distance (Buck and Koehn, 2016), we find that speech-based alignment errors regularly exceeded the 5% tolerance for soft recall, so we only look for exact matches.

Table 3 presents the results for Spanish. We observe overall similar results on German as reported in Appendix A. Our first baseline, timecode-only, yields an F1 score of 62.18% without the use of sentence embeddings or DP as part of the methods. In contrast, our embeddings-only systems (Table 7), achieves an F1 score of just 37.1%. Cleansing alone (i.e., preprocessing 1) improves the F1 score by approximately 11% over raw subtitles, while sentence boundary detection (preprocessing 2) alone yields a 37% improvement. When both cleansing and sentence boundary detection are applied together, performance rises to 92.54% (about 55% increase). Finally, we compare the results using additional preprocessing of time-based partitioning on dialogue gaps of 3 seconds. As can be seen, this step results in only a marginal improvement of a further increase to 93.12% (see Limitations for additional discussion).

4.2 Downstream Machine Translation Task

Dataset	chrF2	TER	BLEU
OPUS	39.8	70.3	14.6
SEAS	45.3	68.4	19.0

Table 4: BLEU scores for equivalent transformer models trained on OPUS versus SEAS.

As a second evaluation step, we train a transformer translation model using fairseq[2] on 1 million English-Spanish alignments from OPUS and compare it against the same model trained on 1 million alignments from the data generated by SEAS[3]. We then evaluated the translation quality of these two machine translation models against the English-Spanish corpus from the Workshop on Statistical Machine Translation (WMT) 2013 using sacrebleu (Bojar et al., 2013)[4]. Comparing the BLEU scores, our model outperforms the OPUS-trained language model by a score of 4.4, an improvement of 23%. For full comparison, we also report two other common metrics for translation quality for both data sets: chrF2 and TER (see Table 4).

[2]https://github.com/facebookresearch/fairseq

[3]Precisely, 1, 026, 231 alignments for both datasets.

5 Discussion

In this paper, we present a novel method, **SEAS**, for subtitle alignment. Previous work has either focused on timecodes which are unique to subtitle data or do not leverage sentence embeddings. We present here the first application of sentence embeddings to subtitle content. Moreover, we evaluate our method on both manually annotated data and a downstream task showing significant improvements on both. As shown in our analysis, this data can offer significant improvements as training data for tasks that require multilingual aligned text, such as machine translation. We hypothesize that additional models can benefit from the unique properties of aligned text that carries informal language, diverse topics, and conversational data directed at a wide range of ages.

In this work, we addressed key challenges in subtitle alignment, focusing on improving the quality of extracted multilingual sentence alignments through tailored preprocessing and state-of-the-art sentence embedding techniques. With our procedures for cleansing, sentence boundary detection, and partitioning, our system demonstrates substantial improvements in alignment quality, achieving F1 of 93.12% on English-Spanish and 92.55% on English-German. These results underscore the importance of preprocessing steps tailored specifically for subtitle data, which address unique challenges such as fragmented sentences, language misclassification, noise, and timing discrepancies.

Our current evaluation has focused on English, Spanish, and German. In future work, we aim to extend our analysis to languages with less rigid sentence structure or different writing systems. We also contribute a novel annotation tool that facilitates the creation of high-quality gold-standard alignments, enabling further research on dialogue-based corpora. By releasing a small but meticulously curated dataset of English-Spanish and English-German alignments, we aim to bridge the gap in resources for evaluating alignment systems

[4]https://github.com/mjpost/sacrebleu/

and fostering advancements in this field.

Code and Data Availability

All code and data required to replicate this research and extended the data, including the gold-labeled subtitles and the annotation tool, are available on Github[5]. The authors intend to continue refining the annotation tool and welcome any open-source contributions.

Limitations

Although this study offers significant extensions to previous evaluation methods, our corpus of manual annotation is limited in size and language scope. For energy conservation, we limited our evaluation to allow for through inspection while minimizing the energy footprint of the full-scale of data.

In this work, we use Vecalign for the embedding-based method Thompson and Koehn (2019). However, Steingrímsson et al. (2023) present a similar approach, SentAlign, including several adjustments, such as incorporating Gale and Church's algorithm for optimizing documents that exceed a length threshold and using LaBSE for sentence embeddings rather than LASER (Feng et al., 2020). Although SentAlign demonstrated better performance than Vecalign on certain test datasets, we observed that it was less effective for subtitle alignment. Due to space limitations, we omit this analysis from our results. Future research could investigate adjusting hyperparameters and configurations to enhance the performance of SentAlign with subtitle data specifically.

We recognize the importance of subtitle-specific preprocessing to alignment quality. However, our sentence boundary detection method can be improved in several ways, which we hope to address in the future. The common use of insertions, deletions, and paraphrasing results in variability that complicates the use of time gaps between dialogue for determining sentence boundaries. Furthermore, reliance on punctuation is effective for certain languages, particularly Western languages, but proves inadequate for others. For sentence boundary detection, we utilized the regular expressions detailed in Appendix. While these expressions are effective, they are not comprehensive and may be insufficient for non-Western languages that do not employ traditional Western punctuation for sentence boundaries. Though, for English, Spanish, and German, this approach outperforms both NLTK and SpaCy alone on this dataset. Future improvements should focus on adapting these methods for additional languages.

The use of time gaps for partitioning offers modest improvement as a net positive result from correcting for erroneous merges across prosodic boundaries. Resolving Vecalign errors without introducing new ones requires a more nuanced approach than simple partitioning. A promising direction could be to modify the scoring function to reduce alignment scores proportionally when overlaps occur across gaps, thereby discouraging mismatches due to timing discrepancies. We believe that a variation of this approach could significantly reduce or even eliminate nearly all false positives. Together, these results highlight the critical roles of both cleansing and sentence boundary detection in accurate sentence extraction and alignment from subtitles, while static partitioning offers only a marginal benefit as currently implemented.

Ethics Statement

This research tackles the limitations of existing subtitles datasets by introducing a novel approach that surpasses previous methods, while also ensuring full reproducibility and extensibility by making the complete code publicly available. We obtained a large collection of subtitle files from OpenSubtitles[6] a website that freely offers them for download. These subtitles were originally created by translators contributing to the public domain. Our acquisition was conducted lawfully, with permission from the website operators to obtain them in bulk.

To reduce the environmental impact of our work, we restricted our machine translation downstream task to 1 million alignments—a number insufficient for achieving fluency but adequate for comparative analysis. By releasing the code, we aim to enhance transparency in our methodology and encourage external contributions to the codebase, gold-labeled alignments, and resulting alignments. Future work should seek to optimize the loading of sentence embeddings between language pairs to optimize computational efficiency and speed.

The code used to generate the OPUS dataset is open-source[7]. However, it follows different preprocessing steps than those we employed and proved challenging to run given changes in the field since

[5]https://github.com/joshstephenson/SEAS

[6]https://opensubtitles.org

[7]https://github.com/Helsinki-NLP/subalign

its creation. To ensure a fair comparison that isolates alignment performance rather than preprocessing differences, we recreated their algorithm to the best of our ability.

Given that the subtitle data reflects naturalistic dialogues spanning a wide range of topics, we recognize that it may include strong language and other linguistic or social characteristics typical of this genre. It is important to note that we utilize this data in alignment with prior releases and established practices for research within the field.

Acknowledgments

We thank OpenSubtitles for generously providing a wealth of subtitles that made this research possible.

References

Mikel Artetxe and Holger Schwenk. 2018. Margin-based parallel corpus mining with multilingual sentence embeddings. *arXiv preprint arXiv:1811.01136*.

Richard Bellman. 1954. The theory of dynamic programming. *Bulletin of the American Mathematical Society*, 60(6):503–515.

Ondřej Bojar, Christian Buck, Chris Callison-Burch, Christian Federmann, Barry Haddow, Philipp Koehn, Christof Monz, Matt Post, Radu Soricut, and Lucia Specia. 2013. Findings of the 2013 Workshop on Statistical Machine Translation. In *Proceedings of the Eighth Workshop on Statistical Machine Translation*, pages 1–44, Sofia, Bulgaria. Association for Computational Linguistics.

Fabienne Braune and Alexander Fraser. 2010. Improved unsupervised sentence alignment for symmetrical and asymmetrical parallel corpora. In *Coling 2010: Posters*, pages 81–89.

Peter F Brown, Jennifer C Lai, and Robert L Mercer. 1991. Aligning sentences in parallel corpora. In *29th Annual Meeting of the Association for Computational Linguistics*, pages 169–176.

Christian Buck and Philipp Koehn. 2016. Findings of the WMT 2016 bilingual document alignment shared task. In *Proceedings of the First Conference on Machine Translation: Volume 2, Shared Task Papers*, pages 554–563, Berlin, Germany. Association for Computational Linguistics.

Stanley F Chen. 1993. Aligning sentences in bilingual corpora using lexical information. In *31st Annual Meeting of the Association for Computational Linguistics*, pages 9–16.

Fangxiaoyu Feng, Yinfei Yang, Daniel Cer, Naveen Arivazhagan, and Wei Wang. 2020. Language-agnostic bert sentence embedding. *arXiv preprint arXiv:2007.01852*.

William A. Gale and Kenneth W. Church. 1993. A program for aligning sentences in bilingual corpora. *Computational Linguistics*, 19(1):75–102.

Sun-Ah Jun. 2006. *Prosodic typology: The phonology of intonation and phrasing*, volume 1. Oxford University Press.

Pierre Lison and Jörg Tiedemann. 2016. OpenSubtitles2016: Extracting large parallel corpora from movie and TV subtitles. In *Proceedings of the Tenth International Conference on Language Resources and Evaluation (LREC'16)*, pages 923–929, Portorož, Slovenia. European Language Resources Association (ELRA).

Robert C Moore. 2002. Fast and accurate sentence alignment of bilingual corpora. In *Conference of the Association for Machine Translation in the Americas*, pages 135–144. Springer.

Kishore Papineni, Salim Roukos, Todd Ward, and Wei-Jing Zhu. 2002. Bleu: a method for automatic evaluation of machine translation. In *Proceedings of the 40th annual meeting of the Association for Computational Linguistics*, pages 311–318.

Stan Salvador and Philip Chan. 2007. Toward accurate dynamic time warping in linear time and space. *Intelligent Data Analysis*, 11(5):561–580.

Holger Schwenk and Matthijs Douze. 2017. Learning joint multilingual sentence representations with neural machine translation. In *Proceedings of the 2nd Workshop on Representation Learning for NLP*, pages 157–167, Vancouver, Canada. Association for Computational Linguistics.

Rico Sennrich and Martin Volk. 2010. Mt-based sentence alignment for ocr-generated parallel texts.

Steinþór Steingrímsson, Hrafn Loftsson, and Andy Way. 2023. Sentalign: Accurate and scalable sentence alignment. *arXiv preprint arXiv:2311.08982*.

Brian Thompson and Philipp Koehn. 2019. Vecalign: Improved sentence alignment in linear time and space. In *Proceedings of the 2019 conference on empirical methods in natural language processing and the 9th international joint conference on natural language processing (EMNLP-IJCNLP)*, pages 1342–1348.

Jörg Tiedemann. 2007. Improved sentence alignment for building a parallel subtitle corpus: Building a multilingual parallel subtitle corpus. *LOT Occasional Series*, 7:147–162.

Jörg Tiedemann. 2012. Parallel data, tools and interfaces in opus. In *Lrec*, volume 2012, pages 2214–2218. Citeseer.

Jörg Tiedemann. 2016. Finding alternative translations in a large corpus of movie subtitle. In *Proceedings of the Tenth International Conference on Language Resources and Evaluation (LREC'16)*, pages 3518–3522.

Figure 2: Annotator showing many-to-many alignment between 4 English subtitles and 3 German subtitles.

Figure 4: Annotator demonstrating how single subtitles can include more than one alignment.

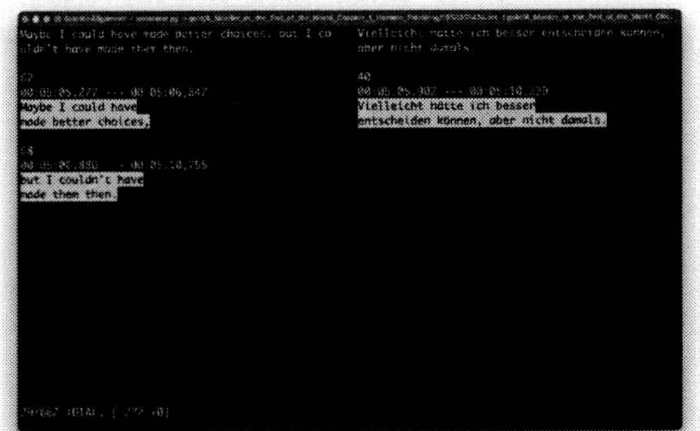

Figure 3: Annotator showing 2-to-1 alignment between English and German.

Dániel Varga, Péter Halácsy, András Kornai, Viktor Nagy, László Németh, and Viktor Trón. 2007. Parallel corpora for medium density languages. *Amsterdam Studies In The Theory And History Of Linguistic Science Series 4*, 292:247.

Dekai Wu. 1994. Aligning a parallel english-chinese corpus statistically with lexical criteria. *arXiv preprint cmp-lg/9406007*.

A Appendix

A.1 Annotation Tool

Annotating subtitle files is a labor-intensive task. To streamline this process, we developed a tool integrated with our extraction and alignment system. After extracting and generating hypothesis alignments, the tool presents these alignments alongside the corresponding subtitles in a visual editor with a Vim-like interface, implemented in Python with the curses library. Users have tools for editing alignments, primarily to remove elements that should have been filtered out during preprocessing or fragments that do not belong in the current alignment (though the tool does not explicitly restrict corrections to translations). Additional functions allow for deleting, merging, and splitting alignments.

The interface displays the hypothesis alignment at the top, with the source on the left, and target on the right, while the raw subtitles are shown below with extracted portions highlighted (Figure 2). This design enables quick and intuitive validation of alignments, including many-to-many (Figure 2), two-to-one (Figure 3), and even compound subtitles (Figure 4). The annotation tool along with the gold standards for extracted and aligned sentences is a part of our contribution.

A.2 Preprocessing

A.2.1 Language Verification

The first step is to verify that the language is labeled correctly. Many subtitles have been reported as one language when their contents or a significant portion of it are actually another language. To do this, we use n-grams (unigrams up to 5-grams) to detect languages against an known set of supported languages [8].

A.2.2 Data Cleansing

We next use a multi-step process based on regular expressions to clean the content by stripping everything but dialogue.

1. Strip brackets and their contents. This goes for curly brackets which are usually used to change the position of subtitles on the screen, and square brackets which are often used for captioning or speaker tagging.

2. Strip HTML tags and their contents unless they are `<b>`, `<i>`, or `<font>` tags in which

[8]https://github.com/pemistahl/lingua-py

case we only strip the tags, preserving their contents.

3. Exclude entire subtitles if they contain URLs.

4. Exclude entire subtitles if they are tagged for lyrics to soundtracks if they contain musical note unicode characters, or start with a pound sign.

A.2.3 Correcting Timecodes

Lastly, many subtitles can be out of sync with respect to their relative timecodes even when representing the same utterances in different languages and have similar durations. Steps later in the alignment process that rely on timecodes to first partition subtitle files before semantic alignment will not be successful if this is not addressed. To account for that, we run a first pass at sentence embedding alignment storing a pointer between extracted sentences and related subtitles. If the timecodes of subtitles that correspond to the aligned sentence pairs have more than a 2 second average drift between them, we adjust all timecodes in the target by that duration.

A.3 Sentence Extraction

Subtitles do not adhere to sentence boundaries. While a complete sentence may occasionally fit neatly within a single subtitle, sentences more often span multiple subtitles—sometimes as many as six or seven during extended monologues. Conversely, short, distinct utterances from multiple speakers are frequently compressed into a single subtitle. Ellipses introduce additional ambiguity: a single ellipsis may indicate a trailing-off utterance or a non-terminal pause within dialogue. This variability complicates the use of time gaps between subtitles as a cue for sentence boundaries. Additionally, while punctuation-based approaches are effective for certain languages, particularly Western ones, they often prove inadequate for others.

For sentence boundary detection, we utilized the regular expressions listed in Table 5. While these expressions are effective, they are not comprehensive and may be insufficient for non-Western languages that do not employ traditional Western punctuation for sentence boundaries. However, for English, Spanish, and German, this approach outperforms both NLTK[9] and SpaCy[10] alone on this dataset. Future improvements should focus on adapting these methods for additional languages.

Pattern that begins an utterance:
`\A[A-Z¿¡-]`
Start of string followed immediately by either an inverted question mark, inverted exclamation point or hyphen.
Pattern that ends an utterance:
`(?<!\.)[.!?]\s*\Z`
An exclamation point, question mark or single period (would not match ellipses), followed by optional whitespace and end of string.

Table 5: Regular expressions used for sentence boundary detection.

A.4 SEAS Comparative Results

Due to space restriction, we focus on English-Spanish subtitles in the main paper. Our results on each subset of the annotated data in Spanish is consistent with the results reported in the paper. We extend this evaluation by annotating the alignment of same English source subtitles over English-German data. The results on English-German are similar to the results on Spanish. We provide the German results on the same data below.

[9]https://www.nltk.org/

[10]https://spacy.io/

Title	TP	FN	FP	Recall	Precision	F-1
3 Body Problem S1E1	351	202	139	63.47	71.63	67.31
A Murder at the End of the World S1E1	348	308	230	53.05	60.21	56.40
Better Call Saul S5E2	270	379	246	41.60	52.33	46.35
Outer Range S2E5	277	170	117	61.97	70.30	65.87
Yellowstone S5E8	422	136	102	75.63	80.53	78.00
Total	1668	1195	834	66.67	58.26	62.18

Table 6: System 0. Strictly based on time-code alignment after cleansing and sentence boundary detection.

Title	TP	FN	FP	Recall	Precision	F-1
3 Body Problem S1E1	173	380	475	26.70	31.28	28.81
A Murder at the End of the World S1E1	326	327	642	33.68	49.92	40.22
Better Call Saul S5E2	240	406	426	36.04	37.15	36.59
Outer Range S2E5	178	273	337	34.56	39.47	36.85
Yellowstone S5E8	281	277	518	35.17	50.36	41.41
Total	1198	1663	2398	33.31	41.87	37.11

Table 7: System 1 on English-Spanish. cleansing: No. Sentence boundary detection: No. Partitioning: No.

Title	TP	FN	FP	Recall	Precision	F-1
3 Body Problem S1E1	295	256	342	46.31	53.54	49.66
A Murder at the End of the World S1E1	379	272	373	50.40	58.22	54.03
Better Call Saul S5E2	265	382	389	40.52	40.96	40.74
Outer Range S2E5	237	210	262	47.49	53.02	50.11
Yellowstone S5E8	320	239	457	41.18	57.25	47.90
Total	1496	1359	1823	45.07	52.40	48.46

Table 8: System 2 on English-Spanish. cleansing: Yes. Sentence boundary detection: No. Partitioning: No.

Title	TP	FN	FP	Recall	Precision	F-1
3 Body Problem S1E1	354	199	202	64.01	63.67	63.84
A Murder at the End of the World S1E1	587	105	235	84.83	71.41	77.54
Better Call Saul S5E2	498	164	186	75.23	72.81	74.00
Outer Range S2E5	324	125	133	72.16	70.90	71.52
Yellowstone S5E8	465	99	106	82.45	81.44	81.94
Total	2228	692	862	76.30	72.10	74.14

Table 9: System 3 on English-Spanish. cleansing: No. Sentence boundary detection: Yes. Partitioning: No.

Title	TP	FN	FP	Recall	Precision	F-1
3 Body Problem S1E1	518	42	49	92.50	91.36	91.93
A Murder at the End of the World S1E1	669	30	32	95.71	95.44	95.57
Better Call Saul S5E2	608	57	75	91.43	89.02	90.21
Outer Range S2E5	425	35	41	92.39	91.20	91.79
Yellowstone S5E8	523	42	39	92.57	93.06	92.81
Total	2743	206	236	93.01	92.08	92.54

Table 10: System 4 on English-Spanish. cleansing: Yes. Sentence boundary detection: Yes. Partitioning: No.

Title	TP	FN	FP	Recall	Precision	F-1
3 Body Problem S1E1	519	41	47	92.68	91.70	92.18
A Murder at the End of the World S1E1	678	24	30	96.58	95.76	96.17
Better Call Saul S5E2	614	51	69	92.33	89.90	91.10
Outer Range S2E5	427	32	39	93.03	91.63	92.32
Yellowstone S5E8	530	35	41	93.81	92.82	93.31
Total	2768	183	226	93.80	92.45	93.12

Table 11: System 5 on English-Spanish. cleansing: Yes. Sentence boundary detection: Yes. Partitioning: 3 sec gaps.

Title	TP	FN	FP	Recall	Precision	F-1
3 Body Problem S1E1	535	22	22	96.05	96.05	96.05
A Murder at the End of the World S1E1	606	51	62	92.24	90.72	91.47
Better Call Saul S5E2	553	49	86	91.86	86.54	89.12
Outer Range S2E5	432	29	33	93.71	92.90	93.30
Yellowstone S5E8	506	35	35	93.82	93.19	93.50
Total	2632	186	238	93.40	91.7	92.55

Table 12: System 5 on English-German. Better Call Saul had a lot of different formatting that most subtitle files which yielded a lot of false positives. Improvements to preprocessing would decrease false negatives and false positives.

German Aspect-based Sentiment Analysis in the Wild: B2B Dataset Creation and Cross-Domain Evaluation

Jakob Fehle[1], **Niklas Donhauser**[1], **Udo Kruschwitz**[2],
Nils Constantin Hellwig[1], and **Christian Wolff**[1]

[1]Media Informatics, University of Regensburg, Germany,
[2]Information Science, University of Regensburg, Germany
Correspondence: Jakob.Fehle@ur.de

Abstract

Aspect-based sentiment analysis (ABSA) enables fine-grained sentiment extraction from user feedback but remains underexplored in many non-English languages and specialized application domains. In this study, we present insights from a multi-stage annotation of Business-to-Business (B2B) software reviews, highlighting key challenges such as domain-specific phrasing and implicit aspect terms. We document annotation practices and systematically benchmark state-of-the-art (SOTA) ABSA models on the three subtasks Aspect Category Detection (ACD), Aspect Category Sentiment Analysis (ACSA), and Target Aspect Sentiment Detection (TASD) using five German datasets. Results show that while simple classifiers remain strong baselines for category detection and fine-tuned Large Language Models (LLMs) excel in more structured tasks, performance varies notably across domains. Our findings emphasize that ABSA methods do not generalize uniformly, and that domain-sensitive annotation and evaluation strategies are essential for robust sentiment analysis.

1 Introduction

Aspect-based Sentiment Analysis (ABSA) is a core task in Natural Language Processing (NLP) that targets fine-grained sentiment classification by linking opinions to specific aspects mentioned in a text (Liu, 2022). This level of granularity enables applications to move beyond document-level sentiment and gain targeted insights, for example in product development, customer service, and social media analysis (Wankhade et al., 2022). By extracting structured opinion elements from unstructured text, ABSA helps organizations better understand user concerns and priorities.

In recent years, ABSA has gained traction in both research and industry, particularly for processing structured user feedback (Ligthart et al., 2021). While methodological progress, especially in English, has been driven by standardized benchmarks like SemEval 2016 (Pontiki et al., 2016), much research remains focused on narrow domains such as restaurants, hotels, or product reviews, limiting generalizability to more complex or diverse feedback settings (Hua et al., 2024).

At the same time, interest in applying NLP methods, including ABSA, to business-relevant contexts is growing. Recent work in information retrieval (IR) and applied NLP highlights the value of structured text analysis for enterprise use cases (Alonso and Baeza-Yates, 2024). While sentiment-bearing feedback plays a key role here, most ABSA research still targets consumer-oriented applications. Existing work in business and software domains (Alkalbani et al., 2016; Swillus and Zaidman, 2023; Rotovei and Negru, 2020) shows potential but often relies on simple polarity labels or app review analysis, offering only limited coverage of Business-to-Business (B2B) needs.

In contrast to English, ABSA resources for German remain limited. Domain-specific corpora exist, including hospitality (Hellwig et al., 2024) and public transportation (Wojatzki et al., 2017), and have driven research primarily within these domains (Chebolu et al., 2023a). However, exploring additional application areas, such as enterprise contexts, can help diversify evaluation environments and broaden understanding of model generalizability. In this paper, we investigate a new dataset consisting of B2B software feedback, a domain characterized by distinct linguistic patterns and specific user concerns.

We present an in-depth annotation study on user feedback from a B2B software application, representing a linguistically diverse and underexplored application context. While the dataset remains confidential, we include representative synthetic examples that closely reflect the content, structure, and

Proceedings of the 21st Conference on Natural Language Processing (KONVENS), Volume 1: Long and Short Papers, pages 213–227, 2025

Sentence (de/en)	Triplets (Aspect Term, Category, Polarity)
die anwendung ist manchmal etwas langsam. *(The application is sometimes a little slow.)*	(anwendung, Technical Performance, Negative)
unkompliziert und übersichtlich *(uncomplicated and clear)*	(Null, Ease of Use, Positive), (Null, Interface Design, Positive)
Funktional auf das Wichtigste begrenzt. *(Functionally limited to the essentials.)*	(Null, Functional Scope, Neutral)

Table 1: Illustrative examples synthetically created to resemble the original, unpublished reviews.

style of the original data (Table 1). We also detail the annotation process, including quality assurance and lessons learned, to contribute to best practices in dataset creation.

Building on this resource, we systematically evaluate a range of state-of-the-art (SOTA) ABSA approaches across the three common subtasks, Aspect Category Detection (ACD), Aspect Category Sentiment Analysis (ACSA), and Target Aspect Sentiment Detection (TASD), and benchmark their performance not only on our B2B data but also across multiple established German-language datasets. Our results offer novel insights into annotation challenges, domain transferability, and the performance of modern ABSA approaches in enterprise-relevant settings.

2 Related Work

2.1 ABSA in Business and Software Contexts

While ABSA research has largely centered on domains like restaurants or consumer products, recent work increasingly explores business and software-related contexts, particularly in B2B environments (Davoodi et al., 2025; Rotovei and Negru, 2020). This reflects broader trends in applied NLP and IR, where methods like semantic enrichment and neural retrieval are used to structure enterprise data (Alonso and Baeza-Yates, 2024). Yet, most ABSA efforts still focus on consumer-facing software, offering only limited insights for enterprise use cases.

Early contributions by Atoum and Otoom (2016) and Alkalbani et al. (2016) addressed polarity classification in Software-as-a-Service reviews, while Rotovei and Negru (2020) applied ABSA to notes for customer relationship management in B2B contexts, integrating aspect-based insights into recommendation systems. Adjacent work on app and platform reviews, such as the AWARE corpus (Alturaief et al., 2021) and studies by Davoodi et al. (2025) and Alqaryouti et al. (2020), demonstrates the value of ABSA for structured feedback analysis, even if the reviewed platforms are not strictly enterprise-focused.

Further studies by Hegde and Seema S. (2017) and Swillus and Zaidman (2023) underscore the effectiveness of domain-adapted models and the richness of developer platforms as data sources. Beyond sentiment, related NLP techniques such as information extraction (Arslan and Cruz, 2024) and context-aware retrieval (Li et al., 2022) support enterprise applications by enabling structured access to unstructured business text.

Chebolu et al. (2023a) emphasize that most ABSA datasets still center on consumer domains, leaving enterprise-focused applications underrepresented. While those efforts demonstrate the feasibility and benefits of ABSA in software feedback, they fall short of capturing the full complexity of B2B scenarios.

2.2 Annotation Practices and Dataset Quality

Manual annotation remains a critical but resource-intensive step in building reliable NLP datasets, often considered a bottleneck in model development (Neves and Ševa, 2021). Activities such as schema definition, annotator training and experience, as well as quality control substantially influence the outcome.

Klie et al. (2024) conducted a large-scale analysis of annotation quality management practices in 591 NLP dataset papers. They outline four key dimensions: *stability* (consistency across annotators), *reproducibility* (consistent results under identical guidelines), *accuracy* (correctness and guideline adherence), and *unbiasedness* (absence of systematic bias). Their findings emphasize the importance of iterative refinement of guidelines and regular validation, such as expert reviews. Despite many positive examples, a significant number of studies still show deficits in quality assurance.

ABSA-specific challenges, such as implicit aspect mentions, irony, or sarcasm, can directly undermine these quality dimensions. While many datasets build on established annotation guidelines (e.g., from SemEval (Pontiki et al., 2014, 2016), GERestaurant (Hellwig et al., 2024), or Hotel Reviews (Fehle et al., 2023)), disagreements frequently arise from overlooked aspects or inconsistent span annotations. This underscores the ongoing importance of detailed instructions and systematic quality checks in ABSA annotation projects.

2.3 The State-of-the-Art for ABSA in English

Recent years have seen notable progress in ABSA across both classification- and generation-based approaches. For tasks like ACD and ACSA, robust baselines have been established using models such as BERT-CLF (Fehle et al., 2023; Hellwig et al., 2024), hierarchical architectures like Hier-GCN (Cai et al., 2020), and attention-enhanced variants like ECAN (Cui et al., 2024).

More complex generation tasks, including TASD and Aspect Sentiment Quadruple Prediction (ASQP), are typically addressed with sequence-to-sequence (seq-to-seq) models, often based on T5 (Raffel et al., 2020), that transform input into structured ABSA outputs. These include fixed-template approaches like Paraphrase (Zhang et al., 2021) and dynamic label ordering such as MvP (Gou et al., 2023) and DLO/ILO (Hu et al., 2022).

In parallel, instruction-tuned LLMs have shown promising results through fine-tuning (Šmíd et al., 2024), while few-shot prompting techniques (Hellwig et al., 2025; Simmering and Huoviala, 2023; Wang et al., 2023; Šmíd et al., 2024) increasingly demonstrate competitive performance in unsupervised or semi-supervised settings.

2.4 ABSA in German

Compared to English, ABSA in German remains considerably underrepresented. Although the availability of German datasets has improved, they are still rarely used or systematically evaluated.

Several corpora provide sentence-level ABSA annotations in specific domains, including *Hotel Reviews* (Fehle et al., 2023), *MobASA* (Gabryszak and Thomas, 2022), *Talk of Literature* (Greve et al., 2021), and *GERestaurant* (Hellwig et al., 2024), while *GermEval 2017* (Wojatzki et al., 2017) offers review-level labels. Earlier datasets like *SCARE* (Sänger et al., 2016), *Usage* (Klinger, 2014), and *MLSA* (Clematide et al., 2012) include sentiment or entity annotations but do not align with current ABSA definitions. Synthetic corpora such as *M-ABSA* (Wu et al., 2025) include German, but lack manually annotated ground truth.

Most evaluations remain tied to dataset releases and reuse English SOTA implementations. BERT-CLF (Fehle et al., 2023) serves as a common baseline for *Hotel Reviews* and *GERestaurant*, the latter also including an adaption of Paraphrase for German (Hellwig et al., 2024). For *GermEval*, systems range from BiLSTMs and LSTM-CRFs (Mishra et al., 2017; Lee et al., 2017) to CNN extractors (Schmitt et al., 2018) and rule-based approaches (Ruppert et al., 2017). More recent evaluations use transformer-based models such as BERT-CLF (Aßenmacher et al., 2021) and Pointer Networks (Wunderle et al., 2023).

However, many of these studies predate the rise of neural networks, transformers, and LLMs, which limits their performance and thus their relevance for current ABSA research. As modeling practices shift toward transformer-based and generative methods, there is a growing need for unified benchmarks and systematic re-evaluations using modern approaches.

3 Creation of a B2B Software Reviews Dataset

3.1 Data Collection

The dataset is based on proprietary user feedback collected from a B2B software platform. Users were able to voluntarily submit free-text comments during natural interactions with the application, typically in response to specific features or workflows.

To enable sentence-level ABSA, we sampled 1,500 reviews and segmented them into individual sentences using SpaCy (Honnibal et al., 2020), resulting in a total of 3,918 sentences.

3.2 Annotation Schema and Guidelines

The annotation guidelines[1] were adapted from GERestaurant (Hellwig et al., 2024) and SemEval 2016 (Pontiki et al., 2016), carrying over the general definitions, distinctions, and annotation principles for aspect categories and aspect terms, as well as the overall annotation objective. These were then tailored to the software feedback domain by refining category sets, clarifying domain-specific

[1] https://github.com/JakobFehle/German-ABSA-in-the-Wild/blob/main/Annotation_Guidelines_English.pdf

terminology, and extending examples to reflect typical B2B software user concerns. Annotations follow a triplet format **(aspect term, aspect category, polarity)**, with `NULL` used for implicit aspect terms. Sentences may contain multiple triplets, while all elements are required for validity.

We derived our aspect categories from a combination of prior ABSA research on software systems and user feedback (Rotovei and Negru, 2020; Guzman et al., 2017), established software quality frameworks such as ISO/IEC 25010 (International Organization for Standardization, 2023), and practical taxonomies employed by commercial review platforms such as G2 Crowd[2] and Capterra.[3] The resulting categories cover a broad spectrum of quality dimensions and user concerns, including technical attributes, user experience, and economic factors. Several categories align closely with standardized evaluation dimensions (e.g., usability or performance-related feedback), while others reflect terminology commonly found in real-world software reviews (e.g., comments on available features or pricing). To account for opinions not tied to a specific aspect, we also included a general-purpose category, as seen in previous shared tasks and annotation studies (Pontiki et al., 2014, 2016; Wojatzki et al., 2017).

3.3 Annotation Process

The annotation was conducted by two ABSA task experts (a PhD and a Master's student in Computer Science) in a multi-stage process with regular validation and review. Given the high annotation effort and limited resources, we opted against full double annotation with majority voting. Each annotator worked on separate portions of the dataset, followed by supervision / review through mutual validation to ensure consistency and quality. Discrepancies were discussed to resolve ambiguities, after which the existing annotations were reviewed for consistency across the dataset, in line with quality assurance practices recommended by Klie et al. (2024).

Annotation was carried out in two iterations. In the first iteration, besides annotating all samples in the dataset, the primary focus was on the refinement and expansion of aspect category definitions using examples from the dataset to improve clarity and separation, in alignment with annotation quality dimensions such as stability and accuracy (Klie et al., 2024). Each aspect was annotated with aspect term (if any) and a polarity label $p \in \{\text{positive, negative, neutral}\}$. Based on insights from extensive review discussions, which revealed recurring difficulties in annotating precise phrase boundaries, a second iteration was conducted to further improve the overall consistency of the dataset and, more specifically, to refine phrase boundary consistency for the 1,775 annotations with explicit aspect terms.

3.4 Quality Control and Annotator Agreement

During first iteration, 3,918 sentences were annotated; 1,075 instances (27.4 %) received objections or clarifications during review. Of these, 243 cases (6.2 %) required direct discussion between annotators to reach a final decision. The remaining comments were resolved through individual revision. Finally, the first iteration resulted in 37.1 % of the dataset annotated as containing no sentiment-bearing content, 5.9 % annotated as segmentation errors, 5.5 % annotated as ambiguous content, and 0.6 % annotated as grammatically invalid. During second iteration, 31.9 % of annotations were revised or flagged, though most could be resolved without further discussion, indicating growing consistency in interpretation.

To assess inter-annotator agreement (IAA), we double-annotated a shared subset of 100 samples and measured micro F1 scores, involving both ABSA task experts (annotators of this study) and domain experts responsible for maintaining and providing the B2B software platform from which the dataset originated, to enable a direct comparison. We chose F1 over Kappa as an IAA metric because F1 is more suitable for span extraction tasks such as opinion target phrase identification and for datasets where classification and extraction subtasks are combined (Chebolu et al., 2023b; Pontiki et al., 2016). In our case, exact phrase matching was required for targets and opinions, and IAA was computed by treating the annotations of one annotator as the gold standard and the other as the prediction.

Agreement decreased as more elements of the ABSA triplet were considered (see Table 2). For domain experts, agreement dropped from 60.80 % for aspects alone to 55.20 % when polarity was included, and to 35.20 % for full triplets with opinion target phrases. Task experts achieved consistently higher agreement across all levels (68.00 %,

[2] https://www.g2.com/

[3] https://www.capterra.com.de/

Evaluation Level	Domain Experts	Task Experts
Aspects	60.80	68.00
Aspects + Polarity	55.20	67.20
Full Triplet	35.20	57.76

Table 2: Inter-annotator agreement (micro-F1) for domain experts and ABSA task experts at different levels of the ABSA triplet.

67.20 %, and 57.76 %, respectively). This progressive drop, particularly for full triplets, underscores both the importance of clear, task-specific guidelines and the need for a dedicated, consistently annotated dataset for further analysis.

3.5 Impact of Re-annotation

To analyze the effect of our two-stage annotation process, we conducted an evaluation using SOTA ABSA models on standard subtasks (ACD, ACSA, and TASD).[4]

The second iteration aimed to improve the overall consistency of aspect category assignments and, more specifically, to refine the boundaries of opinion target phrases. Model evaluations showed slight performance gains in ACD (F1: 74.31 $\rightarrow$ 75.60), but strong improvement in ACSA (F1: 66.72 $\rightarrow$ 69.71) and TASD (F1: 47.51 $\rightarrow$ 50.27), indicating increased dataset consistency and more accurate phrase boundary handling.

3.6 Dataset Statistics

Aspect Category	Pos	Neu	Neg	Total
Functional Scope	402	13	577	992
Ease of Use	418	2	422	842
Interface Design	254	3	227	484
General Experience	254	34	184	472
Technical Performance	128	1	336	465
Customer Support	81	0	88	169
Pricing	2	1	52	55
Total	1,539	54	1,886	3,479

Table 3: Aspect-based sentiment distribution for the B2B software reviews dataset across aspect categories.

Table 3 summarizes the sentiment distribution across the seven aspect categories. The most frequently annotated aspects include functional scope (28.5 %), ease of use (24.2 %), and interface-related issues (13.9 %), reflecting a strong user focus on core functionality, usability, and visual layout. In contrast, customer support (4.9 %) and cost-related factors (1.6 %) were mentioned less frequently.

The dataset is skewed toward negative sentiment (54.2 %), followed by positive (44.2 %) and neutral statements (1.6 %), indicating that users more often express dissatisfaction, particularly with technical performance and pricing, both of which show high proportions of negative sentiment.

Around 32 % of all sentiment targets are implicit, i.e., the aspect term is not explicitly stated but inferred from context. This underscores the complexity of the annotation task and the importance of contextual understanding in ABSA for B2B software feedback.

The final dataset comprises 2,464 sentences and 3,479 annotated aspects. For model training and evaluation, the data was split 70 / 10 / 20 into training (1,707), development (249), and test (508) sets.

4 Experiments

4.1 Tasks

ABSA comprises several sub-tasks that focus on different components of sentiment expressed within a text. In this work, we address the three most common ABSA tasks supported by German datasets: Aspect Category Detection (ACD), Aspect Category Sentiment Analysis (ACSA), and Targeted Aspect Sentiment Detection (TASD).

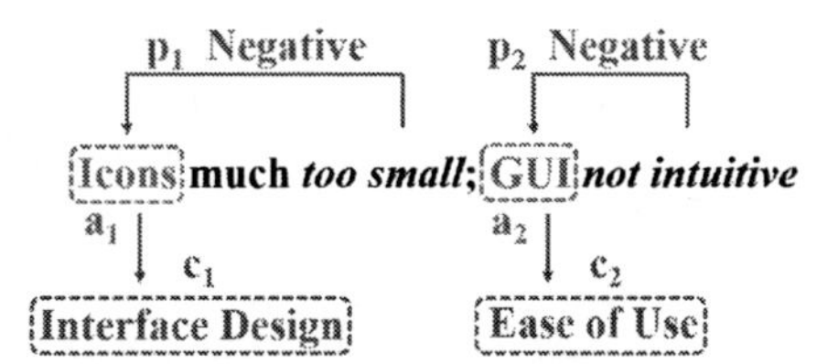

Subtask	Output
Aspect Category Detection (ACD)	(c)
Aspect Category Sentiment Classification (ACSA)	(c, p)
Target Aspect Sentiment Detection (TASD)	(a, c, p)

Table 4: Illustration of the ABSA subtasks used in this study, each with the expected output of the respective task. Input is only the text sentence.

An example of the tasks including outputs can be seen in Table 4. ACD involves identifying all aspect categories mentioned or implied in a given text. ACSA extends this by additionally determining the sentiment polarity associated with each identified aspect. TASD further refines the analysis by not

[4]We used BERT-CLF for ACD and ACSA and Paraphrase for TASD. For more detailed descriptions, see 4.3.

Name	Annotation	Domain	Size			
			Train	Dev	Test	Total
Hotel Reviews (Fehle et al., 2023)	AC, SP	Hospitality (Hotels)	3,403	-	851	4,254
MobASA (Gabryszak and Thomas, 2022)	AT, AC, SP	Public Transportation	3,119	1,054	1,028	5,201
GERestaurant (Hellwig et al., 2024)	AT, AC, SP	Hospitality (Restaurants)	2,135	-	919	3,054
GermEval (Wojatzki et al., 2017)	AT, AC, SP	Public Transportation	16,200	1,917	3,642	21,759
B2B Software Reviews (Ours)	AT, AC, SP	Software Products	1,707	249	508	2,464

Table 5: Overview of the datasets used in this study. Abbr.: AT = Aspect Term, AC = Aspect Category, SP = Sentiment Polarity.

only classifying the aspect category and its sentiment polarity, but also extracting the specific phrase or expression in the text that serves as the sentiment target. Thus, TASD requires models to simultaneously perform classification and term extraction.

4.2 Datasets

To evaluate performance across domains, we compare results on our B2B software dataset with German-language customer reviews from hospitality and public transport domains (see Table 5; more details in Appendix A.1). *GermEval* (Wojatzki et al., 2017) covers public transport, focusing on customer feedback to Deutsche Bahn, comprising 21,772 sentences and 29,439 triplets over 19 categories. *MobASA* (Gabryszak and Thomas, 2022) contains 5,201 tweets on accessibility in public transport, with 5,927 annotations across 17 categories. *Hotel Reviews* (Fehle et al., 2023) consists of 4,254 hotel reviews from TripAdvisor with 5,617 aspect annotations across 5 categories, while *GERestaurant* (Hellwig et al., 2024) includes 3,078 restaurant reviews with 4,314 aspects across 6 categories.

4.3 Baseline Methods

To ensure comparability, we implemented a set of baseline methods based on recent SOTA approaches in English, most of which were originally developed for the widely used SemEval 2016 restaurant dataset (Hua et al., 2024). As these methods have rarely been evaluated on German data, we adopted the hyperparameters and model configurations from the original publications. Baselines were selected based on reported performance and the availability of reproducible code, ensuring reliable adaptation to our experimental setup.

BERT-CLF. A multi-label classification model based on BERT, following the approach of Fehle et al. (2023). The model predicts one or more labels per sentence, where each label corresponds to either an aspect category (e.g., `FOOD` in ACD) or an aspect–sentiment pair (e.g., `FOOD:POSITIVE` in ACSA).

Hier-GCN. Combines BERT sentence embeddings with hierarchical graph convolutional networks (GCNs) to model dependencies between aspects and sentiments (Cai et al., 2020).

Paraphrase. A seq-to-seq method using fixed natural language output templates to convert input into structured ABSA elements (Zhang et al., 2021).

MvP. Multi-View Prompting (MvP) generates sentiment tuples by augmenting the model with different permutations of the target elements. The outputs are aggregated via a majority voting strategy to better capture interdependencies (Gou et al., 2023).

Few-Shot Prompting. This approach extends prior work (Simmering and Huoviala, 2023; Šmíd et al., 2024) and uses in-context learning (ICL) with LLMs with up to 50 annotated ABSA examples embedded in prompts. The prompt template is adapted from Gou et al. (2023), translated into German and adjusted to match the specific structure of each ABSA subtask. Examples are depicted in Appendix A.2.

Instruction-based Fine-Tuning. A LLM is fine-tuned on a task-specific dataset to directly learn the mapping from input sentences to ABSA element outputs. Unlike prompting-based methods, this approach updates the model parameters during training, enabling more specialized behavior (cf. Šmíd et al., 2024). We use the same prompt template as in the few-shot setting, ensuring consistency in task formulation.

Since most ABSA approaches were developed for English, we adapt them to German. For classification tasks, we use *gbert-base*[5] (Chan et al., 2020), a monolingual German BERT. TASD models (Paraphrase, MvP) rely on the multilingual *t5-base*,[6] pretrained on English, German, and French. The LLM-based methods (Few-Shot Prompting, Instruction Fine-Tuning) use *LLaMA 3.1 8B*,[7] previously shown effective in English ABSA (Šmíd et al., 2024).

4.4 Evaluation Procedure

Each dataset was evaluated based on the available annotation depth. Similarly to previous studies, we only use main aspects for aspect category representation (Wojatzki et al., 2017). All datasets except *Hotel Reviews*, which lacks sentiment targets, were assessed on ACD, ACSA, and TASD. Applicable baseline methods were used per task, following reference implementations with minimal changes to model settings.

We tested different epoch counts based on dataset size and selected the best-performing run on the development set for test evaluation. For datasets without a dev split, 20 % of the training data was used for validation. Test evaluations were averaged over five fixed seeds (5, 10, 15, 20, and 25). For *GermEval*, both test sets were averaged. Details on configurations are provided in Appendix A.3.

As in previous studies (Pontiki et al., 2016; Wojatzki et al., 2017), we report micro-averaged F1 scores as the primary evaluation metric, and provide additional metrics such as macro-averaged F1-score, precision, recall and accuracy on GitHub.[8]

To assess the significance of method differences within each dataset ($p_{\text{adj}} \leq 0.05$), we apply parametric and non-parametric tests (e.g., ANOVA and paired t-tests (Field et al., 2012) or Friedman and-Wilcoxon tests (Wilcoxon, 1992)) with Bonferroni-Holm correction (Holm, 1979), based on normality-tested samples using the Shapiro-Wilk test (Shapiro and Wilk, 1965).

[5]deepset/gbert-base

[6]google-t5/t5-base

[7]meta-llama/Llama-3.1-8B

[8]https://github.com/JakobFehle/German-ABSA-in-the-Wild

5 Results and Discussion

5.1 Creation of a B2B Software Reviews Dataset

Our B2B Software Reviews dataset addresses a gap in ABSA resources for unstructured, domain-specific user feedback. The dataset was carefully curated through a multi-stage annotation process, resulting in high-quality sentence-level ABSA annotations across seven domain-relevant categories.

The annotation process revealed the inherent difficulty of the task: substantial amount of implicit aspects, sentiment skew toward negative feedback, and domain-specific phrasing patterns increased annotation complexity. Inter-annotator agreement results further underscore the need for task-specific training and iterative guideline development, confirming observations from large-scale analyses of annotation practices (Klie et al., 2024). These findings highlight the particular challenges posed by the B2B software domain for ABSA tasks.

5.2 Benchmarking Results

In contrast to earlier work in enterprise settings, which primarily relied on lexicon-based or traditional machine learning methods such as SVMs and rule-based pipelines (Atoum and Otoom, 2016; Alkalbani et al., 2016; Rotovei and Negru, 2020; Alqaryouti et al., 2020), our evaluation systematically explores the performance of modern transformer-based architectures, including fine-tuned LLMs.

TASD emerged as the most challenging task (see Table 6). Fine-tuned LLMs achieved the best results (F1: 55.77), outperforming Paraphrase and MvP approaches. Extraction accuracy varied considerably across categories: interface-related phrases were detected most reliably, likely due to their linguistic consistency, while terms related to the applications functionality were frequently miss-classified, mirroring higher annotator uncertainty

Target Aspect Sentiment Detection (TASD)				
Method	**MobASA**	**Rest**	**GermEval**	**B2B**
Paraphrase	78.69	65.72	54.03	50.27
MvP	79.65	67.00	<u>**55.75**</u>	50.50
LLaMA Few-Shot	64.62	61.13	43.78	42.34
LLaMA Fine-Tune	**81.56**	<u>**73.22**</u>	31.06	**55.77**

Table 6: Micro-F1 scores as averages over five seeds for TASD across datasets. Highest values are bold, significant differences are underscored. Abbr.: Rest = GERestaurant, B2B = B2b Software Reviews.

Aspect Category Detection (ACD)					
Method	**Hotel**	**MobASA**	**Rest**	**GermEval**	**B2B**
BERT-CLF	**89.06**	**94.07**	**91.09**	**78.10**	**75.60**
LLaMA Few-Shot	79.09	79.70	83.68	46.51	66.98
LLaMA Fine-Tune	87.69	92.18	88.06	41.27	74.22
Aspect Category Sentiment Analysis (ACSA)					
BERT-CLF	78.75	83.57	84.34	65.83	69.71
Hier-GCN	78.02	84.82	83.31	**67.87**	**69.80**
LLaMA Few-Shot	74.80	70.29	80.79	39.36	64.78
LLaMA Fine-Tune	**80.51**	**87.22**	**85.22**	33.41	69.13

Table 7: Micro-F1 scores as averages over five seeds for ACD and ACSA across datasets. Highest values are bold, significant differences are underscored. Abbr.: Hotel = Hotel Reviews, Rest = GERestaurant, B2B = B2b Software Reviews.

during labeling. Neutral sentiment was hardest to detect, while positive phrases were classified more reliably than negative ones, despite being less frequent, suggesting that clarity may outweigh frequency in model performance.

By contrast, classification-based tasks (ACD and ACSA) were less sensitive to these issues (see Table 7). For ACD, BERT-CLF performed best (F1: 75.60), confirming the strength of simple multi-label classification. While technical and general feedback categories posed challenges, feature-related aspects were more reliably detected, indicating that category classification is more robust than phrase extraction. In ACSA, fine-tuned LLMs and Hier-GCN slightly outperformed BERT-CLF. Positive sentiment was again predicted more accurately than negative or neutral sentiment.

5.3 General Performance Comparison across Datasets

While some methods have previously been evaluated on individual datasets, we re-implemented their approaches to ensure consistency and comparability across tasks and domains. BERT-CLF follows prior work by Fehle et al. (2023), Aßenmacher et al. (2021), and Hellwig et al. (2024), while Paraphrase corresponds to Hellwig et al. (2024). For *GermEval*, we apply a standard F1 evaluation instead of the shared task script. Thus, as discussed by Wunderle et al. (2023), previously reported results on this dataset are not directly comparable, and are therefore not considered here.

5.3.1 Performance on ACD and ACSA

The results reflect strong influences of the number of aspect categories, label imbalance, and domain-specific variability.

Datasets with few categories, such as *Hotel Reviews* and *GERestaurant*, yield consistently high and balanced scores (micro $\approx$ macro F1). In contrast, *MobASA* and *GermEval* show substantial macro F1 drops, even with BERT-CLF, falling to 74.36 and 39.54 respectively. Despite its limited class count, *B2B Software Reviews* yields lower overall scores, likely due to higher linguistic variability.

On ACD, BERT-CLF performs best overall, confirming its strength in simpler multi-label classification. In ACSA, fine-tuned LLMs and Hier-GCN outperform BERT-CLF by better modeling aspect-sentiment relations. However, performance drops notably on *GermEval*, where fine-tuned LLMs struggle with domain-specific noise.

Error Analysis The shift from ACD to ACSA revealed considerable performance drops in datasets with high class counts or skewed distributions, a trend also observed in previous studies (Fehle et al., 2023; Hellwig et al., 2024). On *GermEval*, a specific issue emerged with fine-tuned LLMs: instead of structured ABSA tuples, the model often returned shortcuts like single digits, primarily for the overrepresented `("general", "negative")` class (40 % of the training data). This suggests a form of shortcut learning driven by class dominance and noise. While similar behavior has been noted in few-shot prompting (Tang et al., 2023; Du et al., 2024), it remains under-researched in fine-tuning scenarios.

5.3.2 Performance on TASD

TASD proves to be the most challenging task, requiring models to jointly extract aspect terms and classify their categories and sentiments. Overall scores are notably lower than in ACD and ACSA, reflecting the increased complexity of structured prediction.

Results on *MobASA* and *GERestaurant* are relatively stable, whereas *GermEval* and *B2B Software Reviews* show substantially weaker performance across all methods. Fine-tuned LLMs achieve the best results overall, usually performing better than other seq-to-seq approaches and few-shot prompting. Among the T5-based methods, MvP provides only marginal improvements over Paraphrase despite incurring significantly longer training times and higher memory usage, raising concerns about its efficiency. Few-shot prompting performs worst, especially on *GermEval* (F1: 43.78) and *B2B Soft-*

ware Reviews (F1: 42.34). A full comparison of resource consumption is provided in Appendix A.4.

Error Analysis While fine-tuned LLMs generally perform best in TASD, recurring error patterns persist and often intensify. For the *GermEval* dataset and similar to ACSA, the model frequently fails to produce correctly structured ABSA outputs for the dominant `("general", "negative")` class, especially if combined with implicit aspect phrases. Instead of complete aspect-sentiment-term triples, the model often outputs incomplete results, such as "0". As discussed in Section 5.3.1, this behavior appears linked to shortcut learning, driven by class imbalance and noisy inputs. Moreover, *GermEval* is review-level and features longer, noisier inputs, which are frequently mapped to a single, overrepresented label. This increases the risk of models collapsing their output to template-like patterns. The tendency to simplify structured predictions under such conditions reveals a broader limitation of fine-tuned LLMs in imbalanced and noisy ABSA scenarios. In contrast, *MobASA* shows minimal TASD performance drops. This likely results from low linguistic variability: categories like "Lift" or "Escalator" map consistently to single terms (e.g., "Aufzug"), simplifying extraction.

5.4 Summary

We report insights from the multi-stage annotation and evaluation of a B2B ABSA dataset, analyzed alongside four existing German resources across common subtasks. While different methods prove most effective per task, e.g., simple classifiers for ACD and fine-tuned LLMs for TASD, their relative strengths are consistent across domains. Still, performance varies significantly due to class imbalance, linguistic variability, and domain-specific phrasing. These findings highlight that strong models require high-quality, task-specific annotation, and that broader, domain-sensitive evaluations are essential, not only to assess cross-domain robustness, but to account for the fact that ABSA methods do not generalize uniformly and face domain-specific challenges that can substantially impact their effectiveness.

6 Conclusion

This paper presents a systematic evaluation of ABSA methods across five German-language datasets, including a newly developed corpus of B2B software reviews. We benchmarked SOTA approaches for the ACD, ACSA, and TASD tasks, demonstrating that domain characteristics, class imbalance, and annotation quality strongly influence model performance. While simpler classification tasks such as ACD still benefit from lightweight BERT-based architectures, more complex tasks (ACSA and especially TASD) show clear advantages for fine-tuned LLMs, provided that output structure and domain variability are well managed.

Beyond model benchmarking, our multi-stage annotation process revealed key insights into the challenges of domain-specific ABSA: the difficulty of handling implicit aspects, the impact of phrasing variability, and the importance of clear, iterative guidelines. These findings underscore the central role of annotation practices and data design in enabling robust model evaluation.

Future work may explore improved decoding strategies for structured LLM outputs (Beurer-Kellner et al., 2024), sampling strategies for label balancing (Henning et al., 2023), or new approaches specifically tailored to the difficulties of B2B ABSA. More broadly, our results emphasize the value of high-quality annotation and domain-sensitive evaluation as important steps toward robust sentiment analysis, especially in business-critical applications.

Limitations

This work is subject to several limitations. First, due to confidentiality constraints, the B2B software dataset cannot be released publicly. While detailed documentation and comparative evaluation are provided, full reproducibility on the same data is not possible. Second, the annotations focus on a specific domain and may not generalize across all enterprise contexts. Additionally, although strong baseline and LLM models were evaluated, more advanced domain-adaptation methods were beyond the scope of this study.

Ethical Consideration

All data used in this study was collected as part of a partnership with a B2B software provider and consisted solely of anonymized, voluntarily submitted user feedback. No personal or sensitive information was included in the annotated corpus. The annotation process followed ethical guidelines for data protection and was reviewed to avoid potential harms such as exposing identifiable entities or commercially sensitive content. The aim of this research is to improve methodological understanding of ABSA in enterprise contexts, not to evaluate or critique specific customers, products, or organizations.

References

Asma Musabah Alkalbani, Ahmed Mohamed Ghamry, Farookh Khadeer Hussain, and Omar Khadeer Hussain. 2016. Sentiment analysis and classification for software as a service reviews. In *2016 IEEE 30th International Conference on Advanced Information Networking and Applications (AINA)*, pages 53–58. IEEE.

Omar Alonso and Ricardo Baeza-Yates, editors. 2024. *Information Retrieval: Advanced Topics and Techniques*, 1 edition, volume 60. Association for Computing Machinery, New York, NY, USA.

Omar Alqaryouti, Nur Siyam, Azza Abdel Monem, and Khaled Shaalan. 2020. Aspect-based sentiment analysis using smart government review data. *Appl. Comput. Inform.*, ahead-of-print(ahead-of-print).

Nouf Alturaief, Hamoud Aljamaan, and Malak Baslyman. 2021. AWARE: Aspect-based sentiment analysis dataset of apps reviews for requirements elicitation. In *2021 36th IEEE/ACM International Conference on Automated Software Engineering Workshops (ASEW)*, pages 211–218. IEEE.

Muhammad Arslan and Christophe Cruz. 2024. Business-RAG: Information extraction for business insights. In *Proceedings of the 21st International Conference on Smart Business Technologies*, pages 88–94. SCITEPRESS - Science and Technology Publications.

Issa Atoum and Ahmed Otoom. 2016. Mining software quality from software reviews: Research trends and open issues. *Int. j. comput. trends technol.*, 31(2):74–83.

M. Aßenmacher, A. Corvonato, and C. Heumann. 2021. Re-Evaluating GermEval17 Using German Pre-Trained Language Models. *arXiv preprint*. ArXiv:2102.12330 [cs].

Luca Beurer-Kellner, Marc Fischer, and Martin T Vechev. 2024. Guiding LLMs the right way: Fast, non-invasive constrained generation. *ICML*, abs/2403.06988.

Hongjie Cai, Yaofeng Tu, Xiangsheng Zhou, Jianfei Yu, and Rui Xia. 2020. Aspect-category based sentiment analysis with hierarchical graph convolutional network. In *Proceedings of the 28th International Conference on Computational Linguistics*, pages 833–843, Barcelona, Spain (Online). International Committee on Computational Linguistics.

Branden Chan, Stefan Schweter, and Timo Möller. 2020. German's next language model. *Int Conf Comput Linguistics*, pages 6788–6796.

Siva Uday Sampreeth Chebolu, Franck Dernoncourt, Nedim Lipka, and Thamar Solorio. 2023a. A review of datasets for aspect-based sentiment analysis. In *Proceedings of the 13th International Joint Conference on Natural Language Processing and the 3rd Conference of the Asia-Pacific Chapter of the Association for Computational Linguistics (Volume 1: Long Papers)*, Stroudsburg, PA, USA. Association for Computational Linguistics.

Siva Uday Sampreeth Chebolu, Franck Dernoncourt, Nedim Lipka, and Thamar Solorio. 2023b. A review of datasets for aspect-based sentiment analysis. In *Proceedings of the 13th International Joint Conference on Natural Language Processing and the 3rd Conference of the Asia-Pacific Chapter of the Association for Computational Linguistics (Volume 1: Long Papers)*, pages 611–628.

Simon Clematide, Stefan Gindl, Manfred Klenner, Stefanos Petrakis, Robert Remus, Josef Ruppenhofer, Ulli Waltinger, and Michael Wiegand. 2012. MLSA - a multi-layered reference corpus for german sentiment analysis.

Jin Cui, Fumiyo Fukumoto, Xinfeng Wang, Yoshimi Suzuki, Jiyi Li, Noriko Tomuro, and Wanzeng Kong. 2024. Enhanced coherence-aware network with hierarchical disentanglement for aspect-category sentiment analysis. In *Proceedings of the 2024 Joint International Conference on Computational Linguistics, Language Resources and Evaluation (LREC-COLING 2024)*, page 5843–5855. ELRA and ICCL.

Laleh Davoodi, József Mezei, and Markku Heikkilä. 2025. Aspect-based sentiment classification of user reviews to understand customer satisfaction of e-commerce platforms. *Electron. Commer. Res.*

Mengnan Du, Fengxiang He, Na Zou, Dacheng Tao, and Xia Hu. 2024. Shortcut learning of large language models in natural language understanding. *Commun. ACM*, 67(1):110–120.

Jakob Fehle, Leonie Münster, Thomas Schmidt, and Christian Wolff. 2023. Aspect-based sentiment analysis as a multi-label classification task on the domain of german hotel reviews. In *Proceedings of the 19th Conference on Natural Language Processing (KONVENS 2023)*, pages 202–218. Association for Computational Linguistics.

Andy Field, Jeremy Miles, and Zoë Field. 2012. *Discovering Statistics Using R.* SAGE.

Aleksandra Gabryszak and Philippe Thomas. 2022. MobASA: Corpus for aspect-based sentiment analysis and social inclusion in the mobility domain. In *Proceedings of the First Computing Social Responsibility Workshop within the 13th Language Resources and Evaluation Conference*, pages 35–39, Marseille, France. European Language Resources Association.

Zhibin Gou, Qi Guo, and Yujiu Yang. 2023. MvP: Multi-view prompting improves aspect sentiment tuple prediction. *Annual Meeting of the Association for Computational Linguistics*, pages 4380–4397.

Lore De Greve, Pranaydeep Singh, Cynthia Van Hee, Els Lefever, and Gunther Martens. 2021. Aspect-based Sentiment Analysis for German: Analyzing "Talk of Literature" Surrounding Literary Prizes on Social Media. *Computational Linguistics in the Netherlands Journal*, 11:85–104.

Emitza Guzman, Rana Alkadhi, and Norbert Seyff. 2017. An exploratory study of twitter messages about software applications. *Requir. Eng.*, 22(3):387–412.

Rajalaxmi Hegde and Seema S. 2017. Aspect based feature extraction and sentiment classification of review data sets using incremental machine learning algorithm. In *2017 Third International Conference on Advances in Electrical, Electronics, Information, Communication and Bio-Informatics (AEEICB)*, pages 122–125. IEEE.

Nils Constantin Hellwig, Jakob Fehle, Markus Bink, and Christian Wolff. 2024. GERestaurant: A german dataset of annotated restaurant reviews for aspect-based sentiment analysis. volume Proceedings of the 20th Conference on Natural Language Processing (KONVENS 2024), page 123–133. Association for Computational Linguistics.

Nils Constantin Hellwig, Jakob Fehle, Udo Kruschwitz, and Christian Wolff. 2025. Do we still need human annotators? prompting large language models for aspect sentiment quad prediction. In *Proceedings of the 1st Joint Workshop on Large Language Models and Structure Modeling (XLLM 2025)*, pages 153–172, Stroudsburg, PA, USA. Association for Computational Linguistics.

Sophie Henning, William Beluch, Alexander Fraser, and Annemarie Friedrich. 2023. A survey of methods for addressing class imbalance in deep-learning based natural language processing. In *Proceedings of the 17th Conference of the European Chapter of the Association for Computational Linguistics*, pages 523–540, Stroudsburg, PA, USA. Association for Computational Linguistics.

Sture Holm. 1979. A simple sequentially rejective multiple test procedure. *Scandinavian Journal of Statistics*, 6(2):65–70.

Matthew Honnibal, Ines Montani, Sofie Van Landeghem, and Adriane Boyd. 2020. spaCy: Industrial-strength Natural Language Processing in Python.

Mengting Hu, Yike Wu, Hang Gao, Yinhao Bai, and Shiwan Zhao. 2022. Improving Aspect Sentiment Quad Prediction via Template-Order Data Augmentation. *arXiv preprint*. ArXiv:2210.10291 [cs].

Yan Cathy Hua, Paul Denny, Jörg Wicker, and Katerina Taskova. 2024. A systematic review of aspect-based sentiment analysis: domains, methods, and trends. *Artif. Intell. Rev.*, 57(11).

International Organization for Standardization. 2023. ISO/IEC 25010:2023 – Systems and software engineering – Systems and software Quality Requirements and Evaluation (SQuaRE) – Product quality model. Available at: `https://www.iso.org/standard/78176.html`.

Jan-Christoph Klie, Richard Eckart de Castilho, and Iryna Gurevych. 2024. Analyzing dataset annotation quality management in the wild. *Comput. Linguist. Assoc. Comput. Linguist.*, pages 1–50.

Roman Klinger. 2014. The USAGE review corpus for fine-grained, multi-lingual opinion analysis.

Woosuk Kwon, Zhuohan Li, Siyuan Zhuang, Ying Sheng, Lianmin Zheng, Cody Hao Yu, Joseph Gonzalez, Hao Zhang, and Ion Stoica. 2023. Efficient memory management for large language model serving with PagedAttention. In *Proceedings of the 29th Symposium on Operating Systems Principles*, SOSP '23, pages 611–626, New York, NY, USA. Association for Computing Machinery.

Ji-Ung Lee, Steffen Eger, Johannes Daxenberger, and Iryna Gurevych. 2017. UKP TU-DA at GermEval 2017: Deep learning for aspect based sentiment detection. *Proceedings of the GSCL GermEval Shared Task on Aspect-based Sentiment in Social Media Customer Feedback*, pages 22–29.

Huayang Li, Yixuan Su, Deng Cai, Yan Wang, and Lemao Liu. 2022. A survey on retrieval-augmented text generation. *arXiv [cs.CL]*.

Alexander Ligthart, Cagatay Catal, and Bedir Tekinerdogan. 2021. Systematic reviews in sentiment analysis: a tertiary study. *Artificial Intelligence Review*, 54(7):4997–5053.

Bing Liu. 2022. *Sentiment analysis and opinion mining*. Springer Nature.

Pruthwik Mishra, Vandan Mujadia, and Soujanya Lanka. 2017. Germeval 2017: sequence based models for customer feedback analysis. *Proceedings of the GermEval*, pages 36–42.

Mariana Neves and Jurica Ševa. 2021. An extensive review of tools for manual annotation of documents. *Briefings in Bioinformatics*, 22(1):146–163.

Maria Pontiki, Dimitris Galanis, Haris Papageorgiou, Ion Androutsopoulos, Suresh Manandhar, Mohammed AL-Smadi, Mahmoud Al-Ayyoub, Yanyan Zhao, Bing Qin, Orphée De Clercq, Veronique Hoste, Marianna Apidianaki, Xavier Tannier, Natalia Loukachevitch, Evgeniy Kotelnikov, Núria Bel, Salud Maria Jiménez-Zafra, and Gülşen Eryiğit. 2016. SemEval-2016 task 5 : aspect based sentiment analysis. In *ProWorkshop on Semantic Evaluation (SemEval-2016)*, pages 19–30. Association for Computational Linguistics.

Maria Pontiki, Dimitris Galanis, John Pavlopoulos, Harris Papageorgiou, Ion Androutsopoulos, and Suresh Manandhar. 2014. SemEval-2014 task 4: Aspect based sentiment analysis. In *Proceedings of the 8th International Workshop on Semantic Evaluation (SemEval 2014)*, pages 27–35, Dublin, Ireland. Association for Computational Linguistics.

Colin Raffel, Noam Shazeer, Adam Roberts, Katherine Lee, Sharan Narang, Michael Matena, Yanqi Zhou, Wei Li, and Peter J Liu. 2020. Exploring the limits of transfer learning with a unified text-to-text transformer. *J. Mach. Learn. Res.*, 21(140):1–67.

Doru Rotovei and Viorel Negru. 2020. Multi-agent recommendation and aspect level sentiment analysis in B2B CRM systems. In *2020 22nd International Symposium on Symbolic and Numeric Algorithms for Scientific Computing (SYNASC)*, pages 238–245. IEEE.

Eugen Ruppert, Abhishek Kumar, and Chris Biemann. 2017. LT-ABSA: An extensible open-source system for document-level and aspect-based sentiment analysis. *Proceedings of the GSCL GermEval Shared Task on Aspect-based Sentiment in Social Media Customer Feedback*, pages 55–60.

Martin Schmitt, Simon Steinheber, Konrad Schreiber, and Benjamin Roth. 2018. Joint Aspect and Polarity Classification for Aspect-based Sentiment Analysis with End-to-End Neural Networks.

Samuel Sanford Shapiro and Martin B Wilk. 1965. An analysis of variance test for normality (complete samples). *Biometrika*, 52(3-4):591–611.

Paul F Simmering and Paavo Huoviala. 2023. Large language models for aspect-based sentiment analysis. *arXiv [cs.CL]*.

Mark Swillus and Andy Zaidman. 2023. Sentiment overflow in the testing stack: Analyzing software testing posts on stack overflow. *J. Syst. Softw.*, 205(111804):111804.

Mario Sänger, Ulf Leser, Steffen Kemmerer, Peter Adolphs, and Roman Klinger. 2016. SCARE - the sentiment corpus of app reviews with fine-grained annotations in German. In *Proceedings of the Tenth International Conference on Language Resources and Evaluation (LREC'16)*, pages 1114–1121, Portorož, Slovenia. European Language Resources Association (ELRA).

Ruixiang Tang, Dehan Kong, Longtao Huang, and Hui Xue. 2023. Large language models can be lazy learners: Analyze shortcuts in in-context learning. In *Findings of the Association for Computational Linguistics: ACL 2023*, pages 4645–4657, Stroudsburg, PA, USA. Association for Computational Linguistics.

Zengzhi Wang, Qiming Xie, and Rui Xia. 2023. A Simple yet Effective Framework for Few-Shot Aspect-Based Sentiment Analysis. In *Proceedings of the 46th International ACM SIGIR Conference on Research and Development in Information Retrieval*, SIGIR '23, pages 1765–1770, New York, NY, USA. Association for Computing Machinery.

Mayur Wankhade, Annavarapu Chandra Sekhara Rao, and Chaitanya Kulkarni. 2022. A survey on sentiment analysis methods, applications, and challenges. *Artificial intelligence review*, 55(7):5731–5780.

Frank Wilcoxon. 1992. Individual comparisons by ranking methods. In Samuel Kotz and Norman L Johnson, editors, *Breakthroughs in Statistics: Methodology and Distribution*, pages 196–202. Springer New York, New York, NY.

Michael Wojatzki, Eugen Ruppert, Sarah Holschneider, Torsten Zesch, and Chris Biemann. 2017. Germeval 2017: Shared task on aspect-based sentiment in social media customer feedback. *Proceedings of the GermEval*, pages 1–12.

Chengyan Wu, Bolei Ma, Yihong Liu, Zheyu Zhang, Ningyuan Deng, Yanshu Li, Baolan Chen, Yi Zhang, Barbara Plank, and Yun Xue. 2025. M-ABSA: A Multilingual Dataset for Aspect-Based Sentiment Analysis. *arXiv preprint*. ArXiv:2502.11824 [cs].

Julia Wunderle, Jan Pfister, and Andreas Hotho. 2023. Pointer Networks: A Unified Approach to Extracting German Opinions.

Wenxuan Zhang, Yang Deng, Xin Li, Yifei Yuan, Lidong Bing, and Wai Lam. 2021. Aspect sentiment quad prediction as paraphrase generation. In *Proceedings of the 2021 Conference on Empirical Methods in Natural Language Processing*, pages 9209–9219, Online and Punta Cana, Dominican Republic. Association for Computational Linguistics.

Jakub Šmíd, Pavel Priban, and Pavel Kral. 2024. LLaMA-based models for aspect-based sentiment analysis. In *Proceedings of the 14th Workshop on Computational Approaches to Subjectivity, Sentiment, & Social Media Analysis*, pages 63–70, Stroudsburg, PA, USA. Association for Computational Linguistics.

A Appendix

A.1 Additional Dataset Descriptions

A.1.1 Hotel Reviews

The *Hotel Reviews* dataset (Fehle et al., 2023) contains customer reviews of hotels collected from Tripadvisor, annotated for aspect-based sentiment at the sentence level. Each annotation includes a main aspect, a subcategory, and a sentiment polarity. Annotation was performed by student annotators based on majority decisions, with expert oversight for curation and supervision (Fehle et al., 2023). As no predefined data splits are available, we perform an 80 / 20 random split into training and test sets. The dataset comprises 4,254 sentences and 5,617 annotated aspects.

A.1.2 MobASA

The Mobility Aspect-based Sentiment Analysis (*MobASA*) dataset (Gabryszak and Thomas, 2022) consists of German-language tweets related to public transportation, annotated for relevance and aspect-based sentiment with a focus on aspects of barrier-free travel. Aspect categories are divided into main aspects and subcategories and reflect issues relevant to passengers with limited mobility due to disability, age, or traveling with young children. Annotations are based on majority decision of two annotators and include relevance, document-level sentiment, and aspect-based sentiment, structured along aspect categories, sentiment polarity and explicit sentiment targets (Gabryszak and Thomas, 2022). Multiple dataset versions exist based on annotator expertise (experts, crowdsourcing, or mixed). For this work, we use the expert-annotated version, comprising 5,927 aspect annotations across 5,201 sentences from the predefined train, development, and test splits.

A.1.3 GERestaurant

The *GERestaurant* dataset (Hellwig et al., 2024) contains German-language restaurant reviews from TripAdvisor and follows an annotation scheme similar to the SemEval 2016 restaurant dataset, but with an adapted set of aspect categories. Annotations include aspect categories, sentiment polarities, and sentiment targets at the sentence level, with both explicit and implicit aspect terms being considered. The annotation was conducted by an experienced computer science student and subsequently validated by an expert annotator (Hellwig et al., 2024). We use the predefined train / test splits, which include 3,078 sentences and 4,314 aspect annotations.

A.1.4 GermEval 2017

The *GermEval 2017* dataset (Wojatzki et al., 2017) was developed for the GermEval Shared Task on ABSA and comprises German customer feedback related to "Deutsche Bahn", the national railway operator. Annotations include relevance, document-level sentiment, and aspect-based sentiment, consisting of aspect category, sentiment polarity, and sentiment target. Aspect categories are structured into main categories and subcategories, covering a wide range of service- and travel-related topics. Both explicit and implicit aspects were annotated. Annotations were generated through majority decisions by trained student annotators under expert supervision (Wojatzki et al., 2017). The dataset provides predefined splits for training, development, and testing, including two distinct test sets: one acquired synchronously with the training data, and another collected several months later to allow for diachronic evaluation. We utilize the complete dataset, including both test sets, totaling 21,759 sentences and 29,439 aspect annotations across all splits.

A.2 Prompts Examples for Few-Shot and Fine-Tuned LLMs

```
Entsprechend der folgenden Definitionen der
Sentiment-Elemente:

Die "Aspektkategorie" bezeichnet die Kategorie,
zu der der Aspekt gehört. Die verfügbaren
Kategorien sind: ['food', 'ambience',
'service', 'price', 'general'].

Bitte befolge die Anweisungen sorgfältig.
Stelle sicher, dass Aspektkategorien aus den
angegebenen Kategorien stammen.

Erkenne alle Aspekte mit ihrer jeweiligen
Aspektkategorien im folgenden Text im Format
['Aspektkategorie', ...]:

Text: Der Burger total durchgebraten und
trocken.
Sentiment-Elemente: ['food']
```

Listing 1: Prompt example for the instruction prompt of the ACD task for the GERestaurant dataset. Few shot examples are provided in front of the task sentence.

```
Entsprechend der folgenden Definitionen der
Sentiment-Elemente:

Die "Aspektkategorie" bezeichnet die Kategorie,
zu der der Aspekt gehört. Die verfügbaren
Kategorien sind: ['food', 'ambience',
'service', 'price', 'general'].

Die 'Sentiment-Polarität' beschreibt den Grad
der Positivität, Negativität oder Neutralität,
```

```
die in der Meinung zu einem bestimmten Aspekt
oder Merkmal eines Produktes oder einer
Dienstleistung ausgedrückt wird. Die
verfügbaren Polaritäten sind: 'positive',
'negative' und 'neutral'.

Bitte befolge die Anweisungen sorgfältig.
Stelle sicher, dass Aspektkategorien aus den
angegebenen Kategorien stammen. Stelle sicher,
dass die Polaritäten aus den verfügbaren
Polaritäten stammen.

Erkenne alle Sentiment-Elemente mit ihren
jeweiligen Aspektkategorien und Sentiment-
Polaritäten im folgenden Text im Format
[('Aspektkategorie', 'Sentiment-Polarität'),
...]

Text: Der Burger total durchgebraten und
trocken.
Sentiment-Elemente: [('food', 'negative')]
```

Listing 2: Prompt example for the instruction prompt of the ACSA task for the GERestaurant dataset. Few shot examples are provided in front of the task sentence.

```
Entsprechend der folgenden Definitionen der
Sentiment-Elemente:

Der "Aspektbegriff" bezieht sich auf ein
bestimmtes Merkmal, eine Eigenschaft oder einen
Aspekt eines Produktes oder einer
Dienstleistung, zu dem eine Person eine Meinung
äußern kann. Explizite Aspektbegriffe kommen
explizit als Teilzeichenkette im gegebenen Text
vor. Der Aspektbegriff kann "null" sein, wenn
es sich um einen impliziten Aspekt handelt.

Die "Aspektkategorie" bezeichnet die Kategorie,
zu der der Aspekt gehört. Die verfügbaren
Kategorien sind: ['food', 'ambience',
'service', 'price', 'general'].

Die 'Sentiment-Polarität' beschreibt den Grad
der Positivität, Negativität oder Neutralität,
die in der Meinung zu einem bestimmten Aspekt
oder Merkmal eines Produktes oder einer
Dienstleistung ausgedrückt wird. Die
verfügbaren Polaritäten sind: 'positive',
'negative' und 'neutral'.

Bitte befolge die Anweisungen sorgfältig.
Stelle sicher, dass Aspektbegriffe exakt mit
dem Text übereinstimmen oder "null" sind, wenn
sie implizit sind. Stelle sicher,
dass Aspektkategorien aus den angegebenen
Kategorien stammen. Stelle sicher, dass die
Polaritäten aus den verfügbaren Polaritäten
stammen.

Erkenne alle Sentiment-Elemente mit ihren
jeweiligen Aspektbegriffen, Aspektkategorien
und Sentiment-Polaritäten im folgenden Text im
Format
[('Aspektbegriff', 'Aspektkategorie',
'Sentiment-Polarität'), ...]

Text: Der Burger total durchgebraten und
trocken.
Sentiment-Elemente: [('Burger', 'food',
'negative')]
```

Listing 3: Prompt example for the instruction prompt of the TASD task for the GERestaurant dataset. Few shot examples are provided in front of the task sentence.

```
According to the following sentiment elements
definition:

The 'aspect term' refers to  specific feature,
attribute, or aspect of product or service that
a user may express an opinion about, the aspect
term might be 'null' for implicit  aspect.

The 'aspect category' refers to the category
that aspect belongs to, and the available
categories includes:
['food', 'ambiance', 'service', 'price',
'general'].

The 'sentiment polarity' refers to the degree
of positivity, negativity or neutrality
expressed in the opinion towards a particular
aspect or feature of a product or service, and
the available polarities includes: 'positive',
'negative' and 'neutral'.

Recognize all sentiment elements with their
corresponding aspect terms, aspect categories,
and sentiment polarity in the following text
with the format of [('aspect term', 'aspect
category', 'sentiment polarity'), ...]:

Text: Der Burger total durchgebraten und
trocken.
Sentiment-Elemente: [('Burger', 'food',
'negative')]
```

Listing 4: Prompt example for the instruction prompt of the TASD task for the GERestaurant dataset in the English language. Few shot examples are provided in front of the task sentence.

A.3 Model Configurations and Hyperparameter Tuning

We provide an overview of the hyperparameter settings and model configurations used for the baseline experiments. Settings are based on the implementations specified by Hellwig et al. (2024) (BERT-CLF), Cai et al. (2020) (Hier-GCN), Zhang et al. (2021) (Paraphrase), Gou et al. (2023) (MvP), and Šmíd et al. (2024) (LLaMA Fine-Tune). Configuration for Few-Shot Prompting is based on previous experiments by Simmering and Huoviala (2023) and Šmíd et al. (2024).

BERT-CLF and Hier-GCN. Both approaches use `gbert-base` as a baseline model. For BERT-CLF, we set the learning rate to 2×10^{-5} and a batch size of 16. Hier-GCN is trained with a learning rate of 5×10^{-5} and a batch size of 8. For both models, the number of training epochs was validated on development data, with values ranging from e $\in$ [2, 3, 4, 5, 6] for the *Transport* dataset and e $\in$ [20, 25, 30, 35, 40] for all other datasets.

Paraphrase and MvP. For both approaches we employ `t5-base` as the base model with a batch size of 16. For Paraphrase, the learning rate is set to 3×10^{-4}; for MvP, we use 1×10^{-4}. Epochs were validated over e ∈ [2, 3, 4, 5, 6] for *Transport*, and e ∈ [15, 20, 25, 30] for the remaining datasets.

LLaMA Fine-Tuning. We fine-tune the `LLaMA-3.1-8B` base model using LoRA with rank 64 and α scaling factor 16. The model is trained with a context length of 2,096 tokens, learning rate 2×10^{-4}, and batch size 16. Training is performed in 4-bit quantization, while inference uses full precision. Generation is performed using greedy decoding with temperature set to 0. The number of training epochs is validated with e ∈ [2, 3, 4] for *Transport* and e ∈ [4, 5, 6, 7] for all other datasets.

LLaMA Few-Shot. We use the `LLaMA-3.1-8B` Instruct model with a maximum context length of 8,192 tokens. Inference is conducted via greedy decoding (temperature = 0). For each dataset, we evaluate performance using n ∈ [10, 25, 50] few-shot examples for in-context learning. Text length for few shot examples is limited to 500 characters per example to prevent exceeding the context window.

A.4 Resource Requirements and Efficiency Analysis

Table 8 summarizes training times and GPU memory usage across models, tasks, and datasets.

BERT-CLF is highly efficient, requiring under 10 minutes and < 3.5 GB GPU across all tasks, making it a strong baseline for computing resource-constrained settings. Hier-GCN introduces moderate overhead (10 to 36 min, 3.3 GB) while offering slight gains in ACSA performance. LLaMA Fine-Tune achieves the best results but comes at higher computational cost, highlighting a clear trade-off between performance and efficiency. Paraphrase is a lightweight seq-to-seq baseline (13 to 14 min, 8 to 10 GB), while MvP substantially increases training time (up to 2 h) without notable performance gains, raising concerns about cost-effectiveness. LLaMA Few-Shot was evaluated with *vllm* (Kwon et al., 2023), whereby the GPU utilisation can be customised in favour of the inference speed. Therefore, the values are not listed in the table.

Task	Model	Hotel Reviews		MobASA		GERestaurant		GermEval		B2B Software	
		Time	GPU	Time	GPU	Time	GPU	Time	GPU	Time	GPU
ACD	BERT-CLF	5m	2.7 GB	5m	2.5 GB	3m	2.4 GB	8m	3.2 GB	3m	2.4 GB
	LLaMA Fine-Tune	33m	8.7 GB	1h 17m	8.8 GB	37m	8.4 GB	2h 57m	10.2 GB	21m	8.5 GB
ACSA	BERT-CLF	6m	2.7 GB	4m	2.5 GB	5m	2.4 GB	6m	3.3 GB	4m	2.4 GB
	Hier-GCN	36m	3.2 GB	19m	3.3 GB	23m	3.3 GB	20m	3.3 GB	10m	3.3 GB
	LLaMA Fine-Tune	1h 07m	9.5 GB	1h 01m	9.6 GB	42m	9.3 GB	4h 09m	11.3 GB	27m	9.3 GB
TASD	Paraphrase	–	–	14m	7.5 GB	13m	10.5 GB	1h 02m	15.5 GB	13m	8.6 GB
	MvP	–	–	1h 59m	11.8 GB	45m	11.8 GB	1h 59m	11.8 GB	45m	11.8 GB
	LLaMA Fine-Tune	–	–	2h 07m	10.6 GB	1h 14m	10.6 GB	5h 50m	12.8 GB	50m	10.6 GB

Table 8: Training times and GPU memory usage per model, task, and dataset during test evaluation as an average over five seeds.

Automatic Creation of Marginalia

Aaron Lang and Robin Jegan and Andreas Henrich
Otto-Friedrich-Universität Bamberg
Chair of Media Informatics
{aaron.lang,robin.jegan,andreas.henrich}@uni-bamberg.de

Abstract

In contrast to similar tasks such as keyphrase prediction or text summarization, the automatic creation of marginalia has not been explored yet. This paper takes the first steps to advance research in this area. For our experiments, we used marginalia data extracted from German computer science textbooks and analyzed the marginalia's properties. We utilized methods from the similar task of keyphrase prediction to test how suitable they are for the creation of marginalia and adapted the methods according to the observed marginalia properties and for the use with the German language. The results are evaluated quantitatively and qualitatively. We also highlight limitations of frequently used measures such as F1 and describe why it is desirable to advance research on suitable evaluation measures. We find that GPT-4o and mT5 perform best while for the non-LLM-based methods, SIFRank+ and TF-IDF show promising results.

1 Introduction

Problems in Natural Language Processing (NLP) that focus on producing a shorter version of a text while keeping relevant information – keyphrase prediction and text summarization – are popular research topics due to their practical applicability among other factors. They can lead to time savings as shorter texts can be read faster and search operations can be enhanced by including keyphrases[1].

However, to the best of our knowledge, this work is the first to explore a similar problem: the automatic creation of marginalia. Marginalia are notes on the margin of a text document, often found in textbooks. While any such note regardless of their content fulfills the definition of marginalia, they usually serve as a descriptor of the text section they are adjacent to. For examples taken from German textbooks, see A.4-A.6. We look at *present* marginalia that are taken from the input paragraph as well as *absent* marginalia that do not appear in that order in the source text.

Marginalia can have significant benefits to the reader: They can structure the text document further beyond chapters and subchapters and prime the reader of what the text section will cover. Additionally, they can help the reader save time when skimming the text, searching for a specific text section, or skipping parts that are not relevant. Information retrieval could also be improved when marginalia are available: E.g., if a reader wants to find a text section that describes what algorithms are, the full-text search for "algorithm" will find all text locations of this term which can be plenty in a computer science textbook. If marginalia are incorporated into the search, the text section with the marginalia "algorithm", that is actually concerned with this term, could be returned instead.

We present first steps of research in this domain by analyzing the properties of a marginalia dataset extracted from German computer science textbooks (Section 3), the selection, adaptation and application of existing methods from similar NLP tasks (Sections 4 and 5) and a quantitative and qualitative evaluation of the results (Section 6).

2 Related Work

Automatic creation of marginalia is yet an unexplored task to the best of our knowledge. Hence, a short overview of the similar tasks of text summarization (TS) and keyphrase prediction (KP) will instead be given. However, after creating the marginalia dataset in Section 3 and subsequent analysis of the marginalia therein, it became apparent that for most marginalia, the task of KP is much more similar to the creation of marginalia than TS is. As a consequence, coverage of TS will be kept to a

[1]In some works keyword and keyphrase are used synonymously. In this work, we use the definition that keyphrases consist of one or more words while keywords consist of only a single word.

Proceedings of the 21st Conference on Natural Language Processing (KONVENS), Volume 1: Long and Short Papers, pages 228–240, 2025

minimum.

Whereas TS and KP tasks are inherently similar in reducing a long document into a shorter document while preserving key information, they differ in the precise characteristics of their output. TS creates full-sentence summaries of the original document as a continuous text. KP on the other hand produces a list of one or more keyphrases, which are terms or concepts relevant to the document.

Since TS has many useful practical applications, it is a major research topic in NLP with a multitude of TS methods ranging from simple heuristic methods all the way to employing Deep Learning and Large Language Models (LLMs).

TextRank is an example for a TS method and was the first approach to model documents as graphs with sentences as vertices and their relations to each other as edges (Mihalcea and Tarau, 2004). The approach connects those edges (sentences) that have overlapping content and are thus considered similar. TextRank employs a similarity measure that is dependent on the number of overlapping words that appear in both sentences which is then used for edge-weighting. A ranking algorithm finds the n highest-ranked sentences and concatenates them to a single summary. In addition, TextRank can also be applied to operate on a word-level instead of a sentence-level basis, which transforms it into a KP method.

While this is an extractive method, i.e., it can only create summaries from sentences that appear verbatim in the original document, there are also abstractive methods able to create summaries by generating new text that paraphrases the input. These include various approaches such as the use of sequence-to-sequence architectures (e.g., Chen et al. (2021)) or reinforcement learning techniques (e.g., Gunasekara et al. (2021)).

A similar distinction between extractive and abstractive summarization can be made for KP methods where keyphrase extraction (KE) methods identify which phrases in the original text are suitable keyphrases (present keyphrases) and keyphrase generation (KG) methods can additionally create phrases not present in the original text (absent keyphrases).

YAKE! (Campos et al., 2018) is a statistical KE method and a commonly used baseline. It incorporates several features of the tokenized input document, such as the word frequency or the position of the sentence the word appears in. To extend this to keyphrases of up to three words, keyword components are multiplied, normalization by length to avoid bias towards longer keyphrases is applied and the term frequency of the keyphrase is used so that more frequent candidates get a better (i.e. lower) score.

Beyond statistical methods, KE encompasses a wide range of other methods following various techniques including graph-based approaches such as SingleRank (Wan and Xiao, 2008) (an extension of TextRank) or PositionRank (Florescu and Caragea, 2017). Topic-based methods aimed at extracting representative keyphrases for a document's topic, e.g. by using Latent Dirichlet Allocation (LDA), such as TopicRank (Bougouin et al., 2013) or MultipartiteRank (hereafter: MPRank) (Boudin, 2018) are similarly in use, while embedding-based approaches such as EmbedRank (Bennani-Smires et al., 2018) or SIFRank+ (Sun et al., 2020) utilize sentence embeddings like Doc2Vec or others.

In addition to present keyphrases found in the input document, KG methods can create absent keyphrases that do not appear verbatim in the input document. Again, there exist a multitude of approaches and methods, many of which are based on an encoder-decoder framework. The training strategies are diverse and include reinforcement learning (Chan et al., 2019) or application of multi-task models (Ahmad et al., 2021) among others.

Wu et al. describe a prompt-based learning KG method that uses predefined input prompts to purposefully control the creation of absent keyphrases (Wu et al., 2022). While some other approaches do not handle present and absent keyphrases separately (e.g. in Meng et al. (2017)), Wu et al. argue that this can create absent keyphrases that are not relevant for the input document. As a first step, overlapping words between the input document and absent keyphrases in the ground truth are extracted as Wu et al. notice that many absent keyphrases contain words that are present in the input document (Wu et al., 2022). Those overlapping keywords kw are used to create prompts of the form "`phrase of kw is [MASK] [MASK] kw [MASK] [MASK]`" or "`other phrases are [MASK] [MASK] [MASK] [MASK]`" with special `[MASK]`-tokens getting concatenated to create a common absent keyphrase. While the former prompt enforces the inclusion of the keyword kw in the keyphrase, the latter also accounts for keyphrases that do not contain overlapping keywords. The application of multi-task-training makes the training of overlapping keyword extraction, the identification of present keyphrases, and the generation of absent keyphrases possible simultaneously.

While there are similarities between the creation of marginalia and KP, KP differs in so far that it produces a list of keyphrases that can cover multiple aspects of the corresponding document. As an example, the author keywords for Sun et al. (2020) are "keyphrase extraction, pre-trained language model, sentence embeddings, position-biased weight, SIFRank" which encompass various aspects at different granularity such as the name of the broad NLP task, the specific name of the proposed model and the utilized technologies. Marginalia creation on the other hand works on smaller parts of a coherent document and produces only a single marginalia for each document part. Thus, marginalia can depend on the context of prior or later document parts. In a chapter about the programming language Java for example, one paragraph could present its history and another paragraph its installation. "Java" could be a fitting keyphrase for both but too generic as marginalia for either, since the whole chapter is about Java.

3 Data

Due to the lack of publicly available marginalia datasets, we created a dataset by automatically extracting marginalia and their corresponding text section from German computer science textbooks using Python scripts. The textbooks are published by dpunkt.verlag GmbH and are accessible via O'Reilly's online library[2]. Since they are viewed in the browser, the textbooks' HTML can be used for extraction. Having the same publisher also makes their HTML structure more homogeneous. Still, some adaptations must be made manually for each book, which – along with finding books containing marginalia – makes creating a large dataset costly. Hence, our dataset is limited to 39 textbooks resulting in 11,808 data tuples.

Each tuple contains a text section, the corresponding marginalia and metadata such as the book's title, chapter name, ISBN and also the text of the surrounding (sub)chapter. Since it cannot be derived from the HTML which text sections exactly correspond to which marginalia, it is assumed that the text section a marginalia belongs to is all the text following the marginalia until the next marginalia or until a new chapter is encountered.

Following extraction, data cleaning steps are performed, such as the removal of full sentences. Marginalia that are full sentences most often act as a summary of the corresponding text section, which is not regarded typical for marginalia and thus is not desired in our case. From initially 13,118 tuples, approximately 8% (1,057) are detected as full sentences. However, this depends on the included textbooks and on the precision of the mechanism used for full sentence detection.

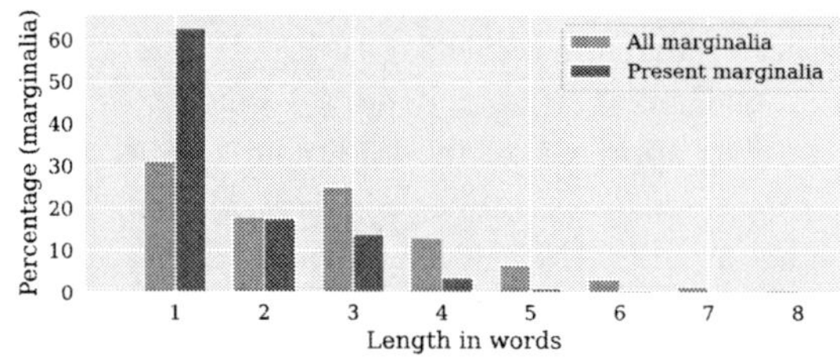

Figure 1: Relative frequency of all marginalia (orange) and present marginalia (blue) in words.

Figure 1 shows the length distribution of all extracted marginalia in orange, while the blue bars are constrained to present marginalia only. It can be seen that marginalia in the dataset usually consist of only a few words, while present marginalia are on average even shorter and consist of just a single word approximately twice as often. However, since checking for the presence of marginalia involves finding the marginalia string as a whole in the text section, shorter marginalia are more likely to be present. Text sections that have marginalia are on average 133.32 words long with a median of 100 words.

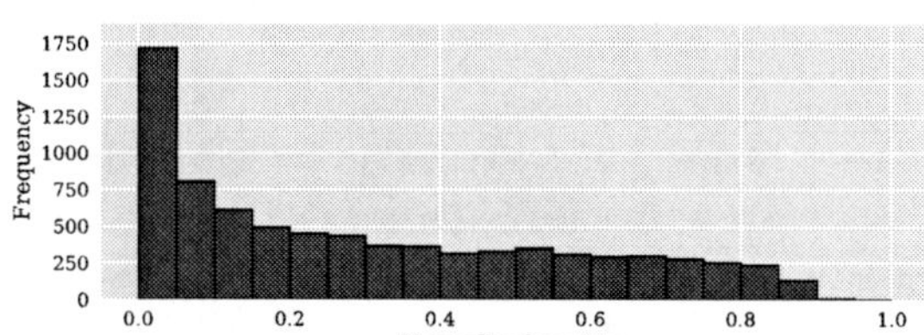

Figure 2: Normalized position of present marginalia in the text sections.

In the marginalia dataset 34% of marginalia are present while 66% are absent. This was determined by searching for the lemmatized string of the marginalia inside the corresponding lemmatized text section.

[2]See https://learning.oreilly.com/home/ for the main search page. For a concrete example, see https://learning.oreilly.com/library/view/react-2nd-edition/9781098123857/ (all web resources last accessed on: 07.05.2025)

Some KP methods use the word position in the text section to rank keyphrase candidates. Figure 2 shows the frequency of present marginalia's position in the text sections. It shows that present marginalia occur especially frequently in the first 5% of the text sections.

4 Methods

The distribution of present (34%) vs. absent (66%) marginalia observed in the marginalia dataset calls for the use of KP methods that are capable of finding both present and absent keyphrases. However, this does not necessarily mean that extractive methods can only be successful (i.e., find a marginalia identical to the reference) in the marginalia dataset in 34% of the cases. It is possible that while the reference (ground-truth) marginalia is absent, there is a similarly fitting present marginalia in the text which can be extracted. To test this assumption, we used not only generative but also extractive methods for creating marginalia.

For KE, we employed several statistical methods as baselines: TF-IDF (Luhn, 1957; Sparck Jones, 1972), YAKE! (Campos et al., 2018), PositionRank (Florescu and Caragea, 2017) and MultipartiteRank (Boudin, 2018). In a 2023 survey of KP methods, Xie et al. found that SIFRank+ is the best unsupervised deep learning KE method (Xie et al., 2023).

SIFRank+ combines smooth inverse frequency (SIF) (Arora et al., 2017) as sentence embedding model and ELMo (Peters et al., 2018) as pre-trained language model. SIFRank+ creates word embeddings of candidate keyphrases and the input document using ELMo and aggregates them into sentence embeddings using SIF (Sun et al., 2020). The sentence embeddings of each candidate keyphrase and the input document are subsequently compared by cosine similarity. The higher the similarity, the more fitting the candidate keyphrase is considered to be. Eventually, the scores of each candidate keyphrase are weighted by their first occurrence position in the input document.

Due to the increasing capabilities of LLMs throughout various NLP tasks, we employed mT5 (Xue et al., 2021) fine-tuned on the marginalia dataset. Furthermore, we experimented with GPT-4o (Hurst et al., 2024) using naive retrieval-augmented generation to add more context to the input documents. For all methods except GPT-4o, each input document consists of a text section for which a marginalia should be created. Thereby, context in the sense of previous and succeeding text sections is not used and cannot be utilized as it is not supported by the KP methods. For GPT-4o, we enrich the input document by its previous text paragraph and its marginalia, if available, as well as the succeeding text paragraph to experiment if additional context is helpful in creating marginalia.

5 Implementation

To use the aforementioned methods for the automatic creation of marginalia, some adjustments must be made, especially to adapt for the German language and the characteristics of marginalia in the dataset. Aside from the necessary adjustments all methods are already implemented and can be used as part of the Python library pke[3] or are provided by the respective authors.

Adjustments for the different baseline methods include the use of a German stopword list provided by pke, specification of German as language parameter and – depending on the method – restriction of candidate selection based on word length or based on most frequent POS combinations in the marginalia dataset in the form of a list or grammar.

To use SIFRank+, German ELMo options- and weights-files need to be employed. German lemmatization is done via spaCy and a German stopword list is used. For word weighting, a domain-specific word frequency list is created from the marginalia dataset plus a generic word frequency list that uses the most frequent words of German Wikipedia[4]. Finally, the most frequent POS combinations in the marginalia dataset are used for candidate selection.

For mT5, a checkpoint that is pre-trained on German TS is needed in order to subsequently fine-tune for creation of marginalia on the marginalia dataset. Several checkpoints are available on HuggingFace[5]. After experiments on a sample basis, we deemed mt5-small-finetuned-amazon-en-de[6] as the best suited checkpoint for marginalia creation. However, this needs to be evaluated further. A checkpoint pre-trained on German KP would have been preferable but was not available.

Prompts for GPT-4o were designed to include preceding and succeeding text sections as context for marginalia creation. GPT-4o is directly and ex-

[3]https://github.com/boudinfl/pke

[4]https://github.com/IlyaSemenov/wikipedia-word-frequency

[5]https://huggingface.co/

[6]https://huggingface.co/anibahug/mt5-small-finetuned-amazon-en-de

plicitly asked to produce marginalia instead of producing keyphrases or learning to produce marginalia (see A.3). Prompts were processed via OpenAI's Batch API[7] which lead to costs of $13.23 for all 10,075,771 input-tokens and $0.38 for the output-tokens including initial tests.

6 Evaluation

We quantitatively evaluated all methods using the F1 measure, Mean Reciprocal Rank (MRR) and MoverScore while also qualitatively evaluating the selected methods in the form of a survey. Quantitative evaluation took place on the marginalia dataset's test split containing 1182 instances. Qualitative evaluation was limited to 100 randomly sampled instances.

6.1 Quantitative Evaluation

Most papers on KP employ the F1 measure, among others, to evaluate their approach, many of them exclusively. The F1 measure only lexically measures if system keyphrases (produced by the method under consideration) agree with reference keyphrases (ground-truth keyphrases), thereby not considering semantically equivalent or similar keyphrases. Still, we decided to include it for easier comparison with other approaches on one hand, and on the other hand for comparison of the same method between the task of KP in other works and the creation of marginalia in our work.

Table 1 shows the F1 score for all methods. It is calculated by first determining the F1 score for each individual instance, then averaging these individual scores to a single (macro) F1 score. Since all methods except mT5 and GPT-4o return multiple marginalia, we consider the F1 scores at rank 1 for better comparability. This is also a more realistic approach since in a real-world scenario, we are only interested in one marginalia per text section. It can be observed that both LLM-based methods – mT5 and GPT-4o – achieve the best F1 scores by a large margin. When only absent marginalia are considered for the calculation of F1, GPT-4o (0.0274) performs considerably better than mT5 (0.0008) in generating absent marginalia (not shown in Table 1). Among the other methods, SIFRank+ performs best. In addition, it can be seen that the position-based weighting of SIFRank+, which SIFRank lacks, appears to have a significant positive effect on marginalia extraction. SIFRank+

Method	F1	MRR	MoverScore
TF-IDF	0.0431	0.0750	0.5626
YAKE!	0.0085	0.0324	0.5732
SingleRank	0.0000	0.0060	0.5193
TextRank	0.0008	0.0095	0.5350
PositionRank	0.0161	0.0517	0.5463
TopicRank	0.0228	0.0376	0.5569
MPRank	0.0245	0.0386	0.5573
SIFRank	0.0161	0.0405	0.5492
SIFRank+	0.0668	0.1050	0.5580
mT5	0.1320	0.1320	0.6376
GPT-4o	0.1299	0.1299	0.6543

Table 1: For both, F1 and MoverScore, values are calculated for the first generated marginalia only. For MRR, all generated marginalia are scored, but note that mT5 and GPT-4o only produce a single marginalia instead of a list of marginalia as the other methods do.

was originally designed for longer documents (Sun et al., 2020) but in this case performs better even for short documents. Although it is the simplest method, TF-IDF achieves the fourth-best F1 score by a significant margin. F1 scores at rank M (considering all produced keyphrases) paint a similar picture and are given in the appendix in Table 4.

For those methods that produce multiple marginalia, we used the MRR to evaluate how early in the result list methods are able to rank matches. A match denotes the system and reference marginalia being identical after stemming. Table 1 shows the MRR for all methods. Here, SIFRank+ and TF-IDF show the highest MRR after the LLM-based methods, thus their matches appear earlier on average in the result list compared to other methods.

Without further adaptation, these measures – F1 and MRR – only consider system and reference keyphrases to match when they are identical (usually after stemming as done in this work) which neglects alternate wordings, synonyms or grammatical variance.

In contrast to the aforementioned measures that work solely lexically and to tackle the problem of the need for exact matches, MoverScore (Zhao et al., 2019) is an example of a semantic similarity measure that compares the system and reference marginalia. MoverScore is typically used for the evaluation of automatic text summarization methods, where the similarity between the summary created by the system and the ground-truth summaries is quantified. This means system and reference marginalia do not necessarily have to be exact matches. Unlike summaries, however, marginalia are usually much shorter, which could reduce MoverScore's expressiveness. Table 1 shows the

[7] https://platform.openai.com/docs/guides/batch

MoverScore values for all methods at rank 1 between system marginalia and reference marginalia. Again, LLM-based methods perform best, whereas the other methods are closer together than in the previous measures. Unlike TF-IDF, YAKE! achieves a much lower F1@1 score compared to SIFRank+, but a moderately higher MoverScore.

6.2 Qualitative Evaluation

To mitigate said limitations of both lexical and semantic measures (see Limitations) and to see how well quantitative and qualitative results agree, we conduct an online survey with 100 questions containing marginalia and text sections randomly sampled from the marginalia dataset. Each participant answers as many questions as they like, which consist of a text section and two randomly selected system marginalia for that text section. The participant has to choose which of the two marginalia is better fitting to the text section or if both are equally fitting, hereafter called "rating" the text section. The marginalia for each text section are produced by five different KP methods (GPT-4o, mT5, SIFRank+, PositionRank and YAKE!), two of which are randomly selected for each question. Hence, different participants can have different marginalia to choose from for the same text section. This comparison between two alternatives was deemed to be easier and also faster than ranking or scoring all five methods for each text section. To increase the likelihood of the same text section being rated by multiple participants with different marginalia alternatives, the number of KP methods for this survey was limited to five.

During the course of the survey, 412 questions were answered by 38 participants. Consistent with the quantitative findings, GPT-4o and mT5 are the two most preferred methods with a relative frequency of 24.46% and 21.84%, respectively. SIFRank+ (14.32%) and PositionRank (13.35%) are both on a similar level, while YAKE! (7.28%) is far less often preferred than the other methods. SIFRank+ being more often preferred than YAKE! is in congruence with the respective F1@1 scores in Table 1. While this also holds for PositionRank, the difference to YAKE! is much smaller. In contrast, the MoverScore of YAKE! is higher than that of SIFRank+ and PositionRank, which does not agree with the qualitative findings, while it does agree with GPT-4o's and mT5's MoverScores. Notably, in 16.75% of the ratings both given methods were judged as equally good.

Additionally, the left side of Figure 3 shows how often methods were preferred depending on pairwise combinations. This means that if, e.g., GPT-4o and YAKE! are presented to participants, it shows how often each alternative was preferred over the other. Since the possible pairwise combinations are not equally distributed, each value in Figure 3 is normalized by the number of occurrences of the respective combination. The matrix can be read in a row-wise manner: As an example, the row for GPT-4o shows the probabilities that when paired with some other method, a participant will prefer GPT-4o. Given GPT-4o and YAKE!, participants choose GPT-4o over YAKE! with a probability of 0.78, while the reverse has a probability of 0.11. Since participants can also rate two methods as equally good, the probabilities do not necessarily add up to 1. At a glance, the green coloring of GPT-4o's row indicates that it is predominantly preferred over any other method. The same holds for mT5 with the exception that it is less frequently preferred over GPT-4o. The red color of the row for YAKE! shows the low probability that YAKE! is preferred over any other method. For the rows of SIFRank+ and PositionRank, such a uniform pattern of preference is less clearly visible. Again, GPT-4o and mT5 take the lead in concordance with F1@1 and MoverScore values, while YAKE! comes in last. As before for the relative frequency of preference, SIFRank+ and PositionRank are close together, whereas their F1@1 scores indicate a significantly higher difference.

The similarity regarding the preference towards SIFRank+ and PositionRank can also be seen on the right in Figure 3, which shows how frequently two methods were regarded as equally good. Here, SIFRank+ and PositionRank are especially often regarded as equally good. Surprisingly, SIFRank+ and mT5 are similarly often regarded as equally good, which was less apparent in the quantitative results.

Due to the restriction on pairwise comparisons, the survey did not yield a direct ranking of methods. One way to derive a ranking from the survey results is the use of the Elo rating (Elo, 2008). Originally designed for the rating of chess players, the Elo rating assigns a rating to every player. With each match between two players, a defeat decreases, while a victory increases the player's rating. When treating the pairwise comparison of methods (questions) as matches between the methods with the preferred method as the winner and

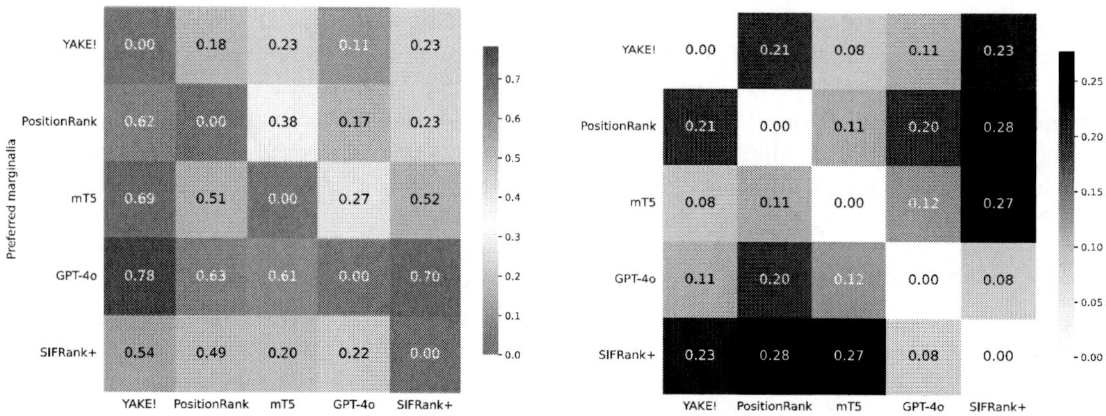

Figure 3: The values in the cells show the normalized probabilities of participants preferring a method (row) over another method (column) in the left part of the figure and the normalized probabilities of participants judging two methods as equally good in the right side of the figure.

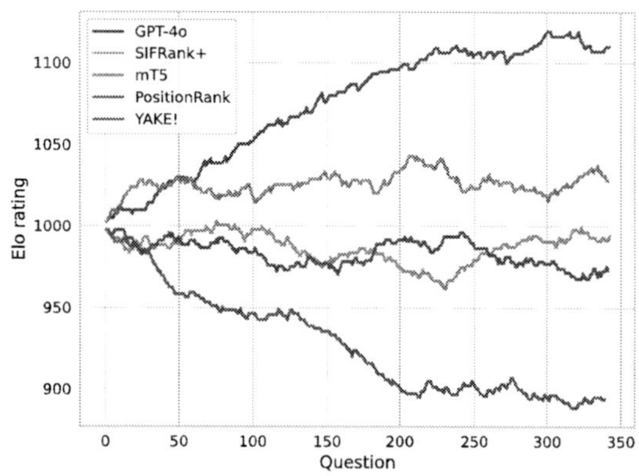

Figure 4: Development of Elo ratings throughout the survey questions. If marginalia were deemed equally good, they were excluded for the computation of the Elo rating.

the other method as the loser, we can apply the Elo rating to derive a rating for each method and subsequently create a ranking.

The development of the Elo ratings throughout all questions can be seen in Figure 4. GPT-4o has the highest rating, while YAKE! has the lowest. Both are clearly separated from the rest of the methods. SIFRank+ and PositionRank are close together and change their ranking throughout the questions multiple times. mT5 is separated from both but with less distance than GPT-4o or YAKE!.

Through manually reviewing text sections as well as the created marginalia and the reference marginalia, cases can be observed where the results produced by KP methods are fitting keyphrases but not fitting marginalia. E.g., for a text section (see Section A.1) that describes how from usage profiles so-called load profiles are generated using an appropriate tool, SIFRank+ extracts the phrase "nutzungsprofilen"[8] (usage profiles) which can be considered an appropriate part of a set of keyphrases for the text section. However, as a marginalia, this would be misleading since the text section does not describe usage profiles but load profiles instead. As the task of KP is not constrained to produce only a single result, it can be assumed that this problem is less relevant for KP but important for marginalia creation. However, as checking for this issue is a manual review process, due to time constraints, we cannot quantify the scope of the issue.

Finally, despite the limitations of quantitative and qualitative evaluation (see Limitations), based on consistent tendencies for F1 score, MRR, MoverScore and survey results, it can be concluded that GPT-4o and mT5 create the best marginalia out of the considered methods.[9] SIFRank+ is the third-best method concerning F1 score and MRR and surpasses PositionRank in those measures by a large margin, but according to survey results is on a similar level to PositionRank.

Among the baseline methods, TF-IDF performs best despite its simplicity. In contrast to the other baselines whose information is constrained on the current document, TF-IDF incorporates corpus-wide document frequency information, which

[8]This example, however, is grammatically incorrect in German as a stand-alone marginalia. See Limitations for a brief discussion of this problem.

[9]Admittedly, the scores are rather low overall, which is however to be expected for this limited quantitative evaluation.

might be one of the reasons for its success in creating marginalia. It seems worthwhile to include TF-IDF as a baseline in future research and examine how it performs in qualitative evaluation.

7 Discussion/Conclusion

In this paper, we have, to the best of our knowledge, presented the first analysis, implementation and evaluation of automatically generating marginalia. In order to accomplish this task, a dataset was compiled by extracting marginalia from German computer science textbooks. The automatic extraction of marginalia was tested with techniques from different NLP-tasks, i.e., text summarization, keyphrase extraction and keyphrase generation. During implementation, the production of keyphrases – both extractive and generative – were identified as more applicable for the use-case presented in this paper. Thus, various extractive statistical methods such as TF-IDF and SIFRank+ and the generative methods mT5 and GPT-4o were applied.

Evaluation was conducted purely on the dataset produced for this paper, hence a comparison with other datasets or other systems was not possible. While no single method led in all metrics, a strong preference for generative methods such as GPT-4o and mT5 compared to other methods, including all extractive methods, was noticed in most experiments. A qualitative evaluation was furthermore conducted through a user study, which showed a commanding lead for the marginalia produced by GPT-4o compared to all other methods. Extractive methods lag behind generative models, however, of the extractive methods, SIFRank+ and TF-IDF, which was only included as a baseline, show promising results.

Future work in this field of research is possible in different aspects. The dataset is one such aspect, which can be extended, both in size and by incorporating different textbooks or other texts with marginalia apart from computer science books. Thus, more training data would be available and the applicability to different domains could be explored. Additionally, making such a dataset publicly available would be highly desirable to drive research in this area forward and make reproducing research results easier. More experiments with other techniques, e.g., by parameter-tuning or updated fine-tuning, or incorporating larger context-windows for the methods are further logical next steps. Dedicated approaches for marginalia generation can also be conceived, e.g., by incorporating not only more text as contextual information but also previously produced marginalia for prior sections of the same text.

Also, as discussed in Limitations, none of the applied metrics are entirely fitting for the use-case presented here. Reference-based metrics are naturally bound to the reference marginalia used in the dataset, while more complex metrics such as MoverScore are more suited to other task areas such as summarization approaches. Still, quantitative evaluation as well as qualitative discussion of the results are necessary and need further research.

Limitations

Regarding the construction of the marginalia dataset, the automatic extraction can on the one hand introduce noise or errors into the dataset and on the other hand, is dependent on the consistency and lack of uniformity of the book's HTML structure. The simplifying assumption mentioned in Section 3 regarding the mapping of text sections to marginalia can further introduce noise and impair the performance of the utilized methods.

But even if the extraction would yield perfect results, data quality would still be an issue as only a certain type of marginalia is desired for our purpose: marginalia that describe what their text section is about. Although data quality is checked on a sample basis, not all 11,808 tuples can be checked by hand. Thus, during data cleaning, the first 500 marginalia with the shortest text sections were manually examined. Here, the aim was to remove marginalia that are considered atypical – such as summaries or marginalia that describe the purpose rather than the content of their text section, e.g. "Einführung" (introduction) – and especially those that could only be created using external information, as they are likely to impact training. Of those checked, 89 were removed. While this proportion may seem high, this does not necessarily reflect the rest of the dataset. Assuming that the shorter text sections are, the less likely it is that marginalia can be derived from them, the percentage of problematic marginalia is expected to be lower in the rest of the dataset. However, it could still be significant enough to impact model training and evaluation. Due to the heterogeneity of atypical marginalia – some are comments, others are summaries and some rely on external information – rigorous automatic checking of the whole dataset is difficult to implement. Despite efforts during data cleaning and post-processing, it is likely that the marginalia dataset still contains an unknown percentage of atypical marginalia. Apart from the quality of the marginalia dataset which deserves further investigation, the evaluation results are still relevant since all methods are evaluated on the same data and can thus be compared with each other.

Since the marginalia dataset contains copyrighted material, we unfortunately cannot distribute it. However, we provide the steps and scripts we used for extraction in our GitHub repository[10].

In a 2023 survey of KP methods, Xie et al. found that while SIFRank+ is the best unsupervised deep learning KE method, WR-SetTrans is among the best (supervised) generative methods (Xie et al., 2023). Hence, we originally planned to include WR-SetTrans in our work. However, after training, WR-SetTrans did not produce any marginalia and we were unable to find the cause within time. Its predecessor SetTrans (Ye et al., 2021) did produce results, but only for some instances. Therefore, we excluded WR-SetTrans and SetTrans for this work. Making WR-SetTrans work correctly deserves further investigation as it might be capable of producing good marginalia.

Concerning quantitative evaluation, while the measures discussed are commonly used for evaluating KP methods, they have several limitations. Firstly, they consider the reference keyphrases to be the only correct keyphrase while in reality there may be other similarly or equivalently fitting keyphrases, e.g. synonyms. Applied to marginalia, this could prove even more true: With only a single marginalia as a target for a specific text section, the chance is higher that an alternative keyphrase is erroneously deemed incorrect.

Also, when checking whether system marginalia agree with reference marginalia, we used exact matching. This means both need to be identical after stemming to be considered matching. We conducted further experiments using approximate matching (Zesch and Gurevych, 2009), which due to size constraints could not be included and discussed in Section 6. However, the results were not surprising and are shown in the appendix in Table 2. Other forms of less strict matching could yield different results and are worth exploring.

[10]https://github.com/aaronlba/marginalia-creation

For languages such as German with a multitude of grammatical forms for nouns as well as verbs, while extractive methods might identify the correct marginalia in the text section, due to their grammatical form, the marginalia could be grammatically incorrect as a stand-alone word. As an example, "nutzungsprofilen" in the text given in the appendix in Section A.1 is in dative plural in German. For a stand-alone marginalia, it would need to be "nutzungsprofil" or "nutzungsprofile" (nominative singular or plural). Furthermore, the marginalia should be upper-case to represent the grammatically correct German noun "Nutzungsprofile".

For MoverScore in particular, the brevity of marginalia, which often consist of only a few words, gives MoverScore little context to work with. Also, the comparison is still constrained to the reference marginalia as the only correct solution, while there may be other valid marginalia. To counteract this restriction, we experimented with calculating the MoverScore between system marginalia and their respective text sections instead. However, this approach did not yield meaningful results for the extractive methods since it is dependent on the average marginalia length of those methods. This means that the longer the extracted marginalia, the higher the similarity to the respective text section is considered to be.

For the qualitative results, while the survey results are mostly in accordance with quantitative results and also personal impressions from samples, the significance is limited due to the low number of questions and participants. Since only 100 text sections out of 11,808 were randomly selected for the survey questions, it is possible that for some methods, a disproportionately high number of bad marginalia or good marginalia are part of the survey, which can skew the results.

Additionally, each question received on average only about 4 ratings. This is relatively low given that each question has 10 possible answer pairings, resulting in 1,000 possible combinations across the 100 questions.

References

Wasi Ahmad, Xiao Bai, Soomin Lee, and Kai-Wei Chang. 2021. Select, extract and generate: Neural keyphrase generation with layer-wise coverage attention. In *Proceedings of the 59th Annual Meeting of the Association for Computational Linguistics and the 11th International Joint Conference on Natu-*

ral Language Processing (Volume 1: Long Papers), pages 1389–1404, Online. Association for Computational Linguistics.

Sanjeev Arora, Yingyu Liang, and Tengyu Ma. 2017. A simple but tough-to-beat baseline for sentence embeddings. In *5th International Conference on Learning Representations, ICLR 2017, Toulon, France, April 24-26, 2017, Conference Track Proceedings*. OpenReview.net.

Kamil Bennani-Smires, Claudiu Musat, Andreea Hossmann, Michael Baeriswyl, and Martin Jaggi. 2018. Simple unsupervised keyphrase extraction using sentence embeddings. In *Proceedings of the 22nd Conference on Computational Natural Language Learning*, pages 221–229, Brussels, Belgium. Association for Computational Linguistics.

Florian Boudin. 2018. Unsupervised keyphrase extraction with multipartite graphs. In *Proceedings of the 2018 Conference of the North American Chapter of the Association for Computational Linguistics: Human Language Technologies, Volume 2 (Short Papers)*, pages 667–672, New Orleans, Louisiana. Association for Computational Linguistics.

Adrien Bougouin, Florian Boudin, and Béatrice Daille. 2013. TopicRank: Graph-based topic ranking for keyphrase extraction. In *Proceedings of the Sixth International Joint Conference on Natural Language Processing*, pages 543–551, Nagoya, Japan. Asian Federation of Natural Language Processing.

Ricardo Campos, Vítor Mangaravite, Arian Pasquali, Alípio Mário Jorge, Célia Nunes, and Adam Jatowt. 2018. *A Text Feature Based Automatic Keyword Extraction Method for Single Documents*, pages 684–691. Springer International Publishing.

Hou Pong Chan, Wang Chen, Lu Wang, and Irwin King. 2019. Neural keyphrase generation via reinforcement learning with adaptive rewards. In *Proceedings of the 57th Annual Meeting of the Association for Computational Linguistics*, pages 2163–2174, Florence, Italy. Association for Computational Linguistics.

Yongchao Chen, Xin He, Guanghui Wang, and Junyang Yu. 2021. Improving text summarization using feature extraction approach based on pointer-generator with coverage. In *Web Information Systems and Applications*, pages 489–496, Cham. Springer International Publishing.

Arpad Emmerich Elo. 2008. *The Rating of Chessplayers: Past and Present*. Ishi Press International.

Corina Florescu and Cornelia Caragea. 2017. Positionrank: An unsupervised approach to keyphrase extraction from scholarly documents. In *Proceedings of the 55th Annual Meeting of the Association for Computational Linguistics (Volume 1: Long Papers)*. Association for Computational Linguistics.

Chulaka Gunasekara, Guy Feigenblat, Benjamin Sznajder, Ranit Aharonov, and Sachindra Joshi. 2021. Using question answering rewards to improve abstractive summarization. In *Findings of the Association for Computational Linguistics: EMNLP 2021*, pages 518–526, Punta Cana, Dominican Republic. Association for Computational Linguistics.

Aaron Hurst, Adam Lerer, Adam P Goucher, Adam Perelman, Aditya Ramesh, Aidan Clark, AJ Ostrow, Akila Welihinda, Alan Hayes, Alec Radford, et al. 2024. Gpt-4o system card. *arXiv preprint arXiv:2410.21276*.

Hans Peter Luhn. 1957. A statistical approach to mechanized encoding and searching of literary information. *IBM Journal of Research and Development*, 1(4):309–317.

Rui Meng, Sanqiang Zhao, Shuguang Han, Daqing He, Peter Brusilovsky, and Yu Chi. 2017. Deep keyphrase generation. In *Proceedings of the 55th Annual Meeting of the Association for Computational Linguistics (Volume 1: Long Papers)*, pages 582–592, Vancouver, Canada. Association for Computational Linguistics.

Rada Mihalcea and Paul Tarau. 2004. TextRank: Bringing order into text. In *Proceedings of the 2004 Conference on Empirical Methods in Natural Language Processing*, pages 404–411, Barcelona, Spain. Association for Computational Linguistics.

Matthew Peters, Mark Neumann, Mohit Iyyer, Matt Gardner, Christopher Clark, Kenton Lee, and Luke Zettlemoyer. 2018. Deep contextualized word representations. In *Proceedings of the 2018 Conference of the North American Chapter of the Association for Computational Linguistics: Human Language Technologies, Volume 1 (Long Papers)*. Association for Computational Linguistics.

Karen Sparck Jones. 1972. A statistical interpretation of term specificity and its application in retrieval. *Journal of documentation*, 28(1):11–21.

Yi Sun, Hangping Qiu, Yu Zheng, Zhongwei Wang, and Chaoran Zhang. 2020. Sifrank: A new baseline for unsupervised keyphrase extraction based on pre-trained language model. *IEEE Access*, 8:10896–10906.

Xiaojun Wan and Jianguo Xiao. 2008. Single document keyphrase extraction using neighborhood knowledge. In *Proceedings of the 23rd AAAI Conference on Artificial Intelligence*, volume 8, pages 855–860. AAAI.

Huanqin Wu, Baijiaxin Ma, Wei Liu, Tao Chen, and Dan Nie. 2022. Fast and constrained absent keyphrase generation by prompt-based learning. *Proceedings of the AAAI Conference on Artificial Intelligence*, 36(10):11495–11503.

Binbin Xie, Jia Song, Liangying Shao, Suhang Wu, Xiangpeng Wei, Baosong Yang, Huan Lin, Jun Xie, and Jinsong Su. 2023. From statistical methods to deep learning, automatic keyphrase prediction: A survey. *Information Processing & Management*, 60(4):103382.

Linting Xue, Noah Constant, Adam Roberts, Mihir Kale, Rami Al-Rfou, Aditya Siddhant, Aditya Barua, and Colin Raffel. 2021. mT5: A massively multilingual pre-trained text-to-text transformer. In *Proceedings of the 2021 Conference of the North American Chapter of the Association for Computational Linguistics: Human Language Technologies*, pages 483–498, Online. Association for Computational Linguistics.

Jiacheng Ye, Tao Gui, Yichao Luo, Yige Xu, and Qi Zhang. 2021. One2set: Generating diverse keyphrases as a set. In *Proceedings of the 59th Annual Meeting of the Association for Computational Linguistics and the 11th International Joint Conference on Natural Language Processing (Volume 1: Long Papers)*. Association for Computational Linguistics.

Torsten Zesch and Iryna Gurevych. 2009. Approximate matching for evaluating keyphrase extraction. In *Proceedings of the International Conference RANLP-2009*, pages 484–489.

Wei Zhao, Maxime Peyrard, Fei Liu, Yang Gao, Christian M. Meyer, and Steffen Eger. 2019. MoverScore: Text generation evaluating with contextualized embeddings and earth mover distance. In *Proceedings of the 2019 Conference on Empirical Methods in Natural Language Processing and the 9th International Joint Conference on Natural Language Processing (EMNLP-IJCNLP)*, pages 563–578, Hong Kong, China. Association for Computational Linguistics.

A Appendix

A.1 Example Paragraph

The following paragraph is taken from the textbook *Basiswissen Abnahmetest* to show one of the textbook paragraphs in the marginalia dataset:

"Aus Nutzungsprofilen werden dann mit einem entsprechenden Werkzeug sogenannte Lastprofile erzeugt, also technische Abbilder der zuvor spezifizierten Nutzungsprofile zum Zwecke der Lasterzeugung. Lastprofile können dabei mehrere Nutzungsprofile unterschiedlicher Benutzergruppen oder Personas kombinieren, um ein möglichst realistisches Abbild der zu erwartenden oder üblicherweise anfallenden Last zu simulieren (da es zu erwarten ist, dass nicht immer nur eine Benutzergruppe mit dem Produkt zu jedem Zeitpunkt interagiert)."[11]

A.2 Quantitative Evaluation

In addition to the F1 scores and MRR at rank 1 using exact matching shown in Table 1, Table 2 shows these values using approximate matching.

Method	F1	MRR
TF-IDF	0.1168	0.6413
YAKE!	0.0829	0.4442
SingleRank	0.0606	0.3333
TextRank	0.0718	0.3858
PositionRank	0.0942	0.5694
TopicRank	0.1997	0.3553
MPRank	0.2010	0.3604
SIFRank	0.0857	0.4856
SIFRank+	0.1161	0.6497
mT5	0.2750	0.2750
GPT-4o	0.2991	0.2991

Table 2: F1 scores and MRR for all considered methods at rank 1 using approximate matching.

Table 3 and Table 4 show the precision and recall values for exact and approximate matching at rank M. Values at rank 1 are omitted since they are identical to their respective F1 scores.

A.3 Prompt

The original German prompt template is given in the GitHub repository.[12] The following prompt template was translated from German via DeepL. Text in curly braces is replaced by the corresponding data.

[11] https://learning.oreilly.com/library/view/basiswissen-abnahmetest/9781098129729/ Chapter 4.3.2 High-Level-Performanzabnahmetests

[12] https://github.com/aaronlba/marginalia-creation.

Method	Precision	Recall
TF-IDF	0.0175	0.1591
YAKE!	0.0119	0.1184
SingleRank	0.0045	0.0355
TextRank	0.0058	0.0423
PositionRank	0.0186	0.1591
TopicRank	0.0257	0.0668
MPRank	0.0251	0.0677
SIFRank	0.0148	0.1235
SIFRank+	0.0219	0.1920
mT5	0.1320	0.1320
GPT-4o	0.1299	0.1299

Table 3: Precision and recall for all considered methods at rank 1 using exact matching.

Method	Precision	Recall
TF-IDF	0.0313	0.1894
YAKE!	0.0216	0.1336
SingleRank	0.0079	0.0981
TextRank	0.0099	0.1159
PositionRank	0.0329	0.1557
TopicRank	0.0344	0.2311
MPRank	0.0340	0.2329
SIFRank	0.0261	0.1393
SIFRank+	0.0389	0.1898
mT5	0.1320	0.2750
GPT-4o	0.1299	0.2991

Table 4: Precision and recall values at rank M with M being the number of marginalia produced by a method, using approximate matching.

The following paragraphs are taken from the subchapter "{subchapter_name}" in the chapter "{chapter_name}" in the textbook "{book_title}". Where available, the corresponding marginalia is given for each paragraph:

Paragraph N-1 reads:
"{predecessor_paragraph}" This paragraph has the marginalia "{predecessor_marginalia}".

Paragraph N reads:
"{current_paragraph}"

Paragraph N+1 reads:
"{successor_paragraph}"

Task:
Create a marginalia for paragraph N. If available, the previous paragraph N-1 and the following paragraph N+1 may be helpful as context for creating consistent marginalia (e.g., uniform wording of the marginalia). Important: The marginalia should refer exclusively to the content of paragraph N. The marginalia does not necessarily have to summarize the content of the paragraph, but can also simply indicate what the paragraph is about.

Notes on the length of the marginalia you are looking for:
Most marginalia are between 1 and 4 words long, with very few exceeding 6 words. Keep the marginalia as short as possible.

Note on the output format:
Only output the generated marginalia without a prefix such as "Marginalia:" or quotation marks.

A.4 Example Marginalia 1

In this example of a textbook paragraph and its system marginalia, most methods match with the reference.

"JSON (JavaScript Object Notation) ist eine Darstellung von Daten, die vor allem für JavaScript optimiert ist. Wie JavaScript auch, sind die Daten dynamisch typisiert. Mittlerweile gibt es aber eigentlich für alle Programmiersprachen passende JSON-Bibliotheken. Es gibt außerdem Typsysteme wie JSON Schema [16], die für JSON eine entsprechende Validierung ergänzen. Damit steht JSON Datenformaten wie XML in nichts mehr nach."[13]

Method	Marginalia
TF-IDF	json
YAKE!	JavaScript Object Notation
SingleRank	für json eine entsprechende validierung
TextRank	für json eine
PositionRank	json datenformaten wie xml
TopicRank	json
MPRank	json
SIFRank	json
SIFRank+	json
mT5	JSON
GPT-4o	JSON
Reference	JSON

Table 5: Reference marginalia given by the authors of the source text and system marginalia at rank 1 created by the various methods for A.4.

A.5 Example Marginalia 2

In this example, several methods overlap with the reference, but do not match exactly. However, GPT-4o's marginalia can be seen as semantically equivalent to the reference.

"Zu jedem Add-on gibt es eine Kurzbeschreibung des Funktionsumfangs und auf welche Anwendungsfälle es abzielt. Ein Add-on kann im

[13]https://learning.oreilly.com/library/view/microservices-2nd-edition/9781492068686/ Chapter 9 Integration und Kommunikation

Laufe der Zeit in unterschiedlichen Versionen zur Verfügung gestellt werden, diese Versionen werden mit entsprechenden Release-Notes dokumentiert. Des Weiteren gibt es zusätzliche Informationen, zu welcher Vaadin-Version ein Add-on kompatibel ist oder mit welchen Browsern ein Add-on verwendet werden kann, wenn es hier entsprechende Einschränkungen geben sollte. Wir können uns auch über das zugrunde liegende Lizenzmodell informieren oder über weiterführende Links auf z.B. eine Online-Demo, den Sourcecode oder eine Ticketverwaltung zugreifen. Abb. 10-2 Detailseite Add-on am Beispiel Vaadin Calendar Über die Anzahl der Downloads können wir einen gewissen Eindruck über die Popularität eines Add-on gewinnen. Jeder Nutzer hat zudem die Möglichkeit, ein Add-on mit eins bis fünf Sternen zu bewerten. Es kann optional ein Kommentar verfasst werden, um dem Ersteller eines Add-on Rückmeldungen zu geben. Weitere interessante Hinweise und Hilfestellungen aus der Vaadin-Community finden wir zusätzlich im Vaadin-Forum unter der Kategorie Add-ons (siehe [Vaadin-Forum])."[14]

Method	Marginalia
TF-IDF	add-on
YAKE!	Kurzbeschreibung des Funktionsumfangs
SingleRank	detailseite add-on am beispiel vaadin calendar über die anzahl der downloads
TextRank	ein add-on mit
PositionRank	vaadin-version ein add-on
TopicRank	entsprechende einschränkungen
MPRank	entsprechende einschränkungen
SIFRank	add-on rückmeldungen
SIFRank+	add-on
mT5	Anzahl der Downloads
GPT-4o	Add-on Detailinformationen
Reference	Detailinformationen zu einem Add-on

Table 6: Reference marginalia given by the authors of the source text and system marginalia at rank 1 created by the various methods for A.5.

A.6 Example Marginalia 3

In this example none of the methods match the reference. However, some marginalia describe relevant aspects of the text section, e.g., *konflikte* (conflicts) or *überprüfung und abstimmung* (review and coordination). Furthermore, it can be argued that GPT-4o's marginalia is even more fitting than the reference marginalia. Here, the reference marginalia is less a description of the content of the text section and more a statement of its consequence.

"Die Überprüfung auf Widersprüche und Abstimmung der Anforderungen muss fortlaufend (in unterschiedlicher Intensität) über das gesamte Requirements Engineering hinweg erfolgen. Die Überprüfung und Abstimmung von Anforderungen verursachen dabei zusätzlichen Aufwand und somit zusätzliche Kosten. Der durch die Überprüfung und Abstimmung der Anforderungen erzielte und in den vorangegangenen Abschnitten beschriebene Vorteil (Kostenersparnis, Erhöhung der Akzeptanz des Systems, Unterstützung der Definition innovativer Anforderungen) ist in der Regel jedoch wesentlich höher als die durch die Überprüfung und Abstimmung entstehenden Kosten. Zur Abstimmung der Anforderungen an ein zu entwickelndes System ist es notwendig, Konflikte zu identifizieren und die auftretenden Konflikte aufzulösen. Dies geschieht im Rahmen eines systematischen Konfliktmanagements. Das Konfliktmanagement im Requirements Engineering umfasst die folgenden vier Aufgaben:" [15]

Method	Marginalia
TF-IDF	anforderungen
YAKE!	Requirements Engineering hinweg erfolgen
SingleRank	der durch die überprüfung und abstimmung der anforderungen
TextRank	durch die überprüfung und abstimmung der anforderungen
PositionRank	überprüfung und abstimmung
TopicRank	konflikte
MPRank	konflikte
SIFRank	abstimmung von anforderungen
SIFRank+	überprüfung auf widersprüche
mT5	Überprüfung und Abstimmung
GPT-4o	Kosten und Nutzen der Abstimmung
Reference	Verringerung der Kosten und Risiken in späteren Phasen

Table 7: Reference marginalia given by the authors of the source text and system marginalia at rank 1 created by the various methods for A.6.

[14]https://learning.oreilly.com/library/view/vaadin/9781457188336/
Chapter 10 Add-Ons

[15]https://learning.oreilly.com/library/view/basiswissen-requirements-engineering/9781098129231/
Chapter 4 Praktiken für die Erarbeitung von Anforderungen

Localization of English Affective Narrative Generation to German

Johannes Schäfer, Sabine Weber, and Roman Klinger
Fundamentals of Natural Language Processing, University of Bamberg, Germany
{johannes.schaefer,sabine.weber,roman.klinger}@uni-bamberg.de

Abstract

Prompting strategies for natural language processing with large language models have primarily been developed for English, the most resource-rich language. This raises critical questions about the importance of localization in applications for other languages, i.e. aiming to generate linguistically relevant and culturally appropriate output. In this paper, we investigate the impact of various localization steps within an affective narrative generation task. We experiment with different adaptations, such as the modification or translation of prompts and the usage of localized seed words. We evaluate their influence on the quality of generated texts in German, as compared to English. Our results indicate that a considerable degree of localization is required; however, fully localized prompts do not yield the most natural or localized texts. Additionally, we find that a multilingual model performs well in the simpler aspects of affective narrative generation within the localized context, but it encounters difficulties in the more complex components of the task in German. Our work underscores the complexities involved in adapting large language models for localized emotion analysis with tailored methodologies that account for linguistic variations in narrative generation.

1 Introduction

The advancement of large language models (LLMs) has predominantly emerged from research on English-language data. This has resulted in prompting strategies and methodologies that are largely tailored to this language due to the substantial volume of training data available. This focus raises important questions about the necessity of localization when applying these models to other languages. As LLMs become increasingly multilingual, it becomes crucial to understand whether methods developed for English can be effectively adapted to non-English contexts. Furthermore, it is important to determine whether findings from English-centric research can be generalized to other languages.

Guilt: Ich half meinem Großvater, das Zelt sorgfältig aufzubauen. Er bat mich, den Campingstuhl speziell für ihn aufzustellen. Mein Handy klingelte und lenkte mich von der Aufgabe ab. Ich überhastete das Aufstellen des Stuhls, ohne ihn zu sichern. *Der Campingstuhl kippte um.*
(I helped my grandfather set up the tent carefully. He asked me to place the camping chair specifically for him. My phone rang and distracted me from the task. I hastily set up the chair without securing it. *The camping chair tipped over.*)

Surprise: Ich wählte einen ebenen Platz für den Campingplatz aus. Die Zeltstangen wurden doppelt überprüft und fest verankert. Mein Freund und ich planten einen gemütlichen Tag ohne anstrengende Aktivitäten. Wir stellten unsere Getränke und Snacks sorgfältig auf den Campingtisch. *Der Campingstuhl kippte um.*
(I chose a flat spot for the campsite. The tent poles were double-checked and firmly anchored. My friend and I planned a cozy day without strenuous activities. We carefully placed our drinks and snacks on the camping table. *The camping chair tipped over.*)

Table 1: German examples with English tranlations of generated stories designed to evoke guilt and surprise.

Our research addresses the localization challenges associated within a specific use case: affective narrative generation. A previous study has been conducted on this task using English language data (Schäfer and Klinger, 2025). This task addresses the ambiguity in emotion analysis on event descriptions by aiming to disambiguate emotions through the generation of contextual information. It comprises two subtasks: first, creating a diverse set of target event descriptions; second, producing contexts that precede these descriptions and influence emotion analysis in a specific way.

To illustrate this task, consider Table 1 with an example ambiguous event description "Der Campingstuhl kippte um." (*The camping chair tipped over.*).[1] When viewed in isolation, the emotion

[1]We provide our annotated dataset and code on `https://www.uni-bamberg.de/en/nlproc/resources/german-affective-narrative-generation/`.

Proceedings of the 21st Conference on Natural Language Processing (KONVENS), Volume 1: Long and Short Papers, pages 241–256, 2025

evoked in the experiencer is unclear as the situational context is unknown. The first subtask is to generate a varied set of such event descriptions.

The second subtask involves crafting contextual narratives (backstories) that evoke specific emotions in these events. In the example for the case of guilt (see Table 1), the context emphasizes the importance of the situation and especially the personal responsibility for the negative outcome. In the case of surprise, the context highlights the expected nature and carefulness of the previous events, enhancing the perception of abruptness in the event.

This task setup enables us to explore localization in both straightforward text generation, exemplified by producing varied event descriptions, and more complex challenges, such as crafting narratives that strategically influence emotion analysis. This task is especially well-suited for our investigation of localization as it inherently includes a cultural dimension; event descriptions within narratives reflect personal experiences that vary across different cultural and linguistic contexts.

This paper investigates the necessary steps for localizing English-centered methodologies to produce high-quality, contextually appropriate data in German. Our aim is to adapt existing practices in text generation not only to evaluate their effectiveness in a German context but also to understand the unique linguistic features that may influence emotion analysis. Specifically, we focus our investigation on the impact of various localization strategies, as illustrated through the narrative generation process. Our paper is guided by the following key research questions:

1. **What adaptations are necessary to tailor the English event generation approach for the German language, in order to ensure the production of high-quality localized data?** This question aims to identify the complexities involved in adapting methodologies for distinct linguistic contexts, specifically focusing on the necessary modifications to prompts for effective localization.
2. **In the context of generating backstories for events that together form coherent narratives, do the advantages of story planning and narrative revision observed in English also manifest in the German adaptation of the process?** This question seeks to deepen our understanding of narrative story generation techniques and assess the performance of LLMs across different languages.
3. **To what extent do the generated German backstories effectively disambiguate emotion analysis in events, compared to findings from the English-language experiments?** This question explores the role of context in emotion analysis within the German language, aiming to determine whether the trends observed in English are consistent.

2 Related Work

2.1 Localization of LLMs

Recent advancements in text analysis with LLMs continue to highlight the need for effective prompting strategies, which poses particular challenges in diverse linguistic contexts. As noted by Mondshine et al. (2025), the overwhelming dominance of English in LLM research raises questions on the applicability of approaches for other languages and the required adaptations in prompt construction.

The demand for the usage of LLMs in localized applications has led to two main approaches: (1) developing dedicated monolingual models for low-to-medium-resource languages (Seker et al., 2022; Andersland, 2024) and (2) creating multilingual models that utilize data from various languages (Qin et al., 2023; Jiang et al., 2024). Multilingual models can perform well in cross-lingual tasks because of their training on diverse datasets (Raffel et al., 2020; Conneau et al., 2020; Chowdhery et al., 2023) and prompt engineering methodologies that enable effective adaptations (Brown et al., 2020).

To optimize multilingual LLM performance, several prompting techniques have emerged. Huang et al. (2023) introduced XLT, a cross-lingual prompt format for specific languages. Furthermore, Zhao and Schütze (2021) showed that discrete and soft prompting can allow non-English prompts to surpass traditional fine-tuning in cross-lingual contexts. Research on pre-translation techniques has investigated fully translating prompts into English (Chowdhery et al., 2023; Qin et al., 2023) as well as selectively translating specific parts (Liu et al., 2025). Despite their promise, these strategies require further research to establish best practices.

2.2 Emotion Analysis Adaptations

De Bruyne (2023) points out the challenges in applying multilingual approaches due to the culture-specific nature of emotions, a factor critical to our investigation of localization. Fu et al. (2022) demonstrate that training on larger English datasets

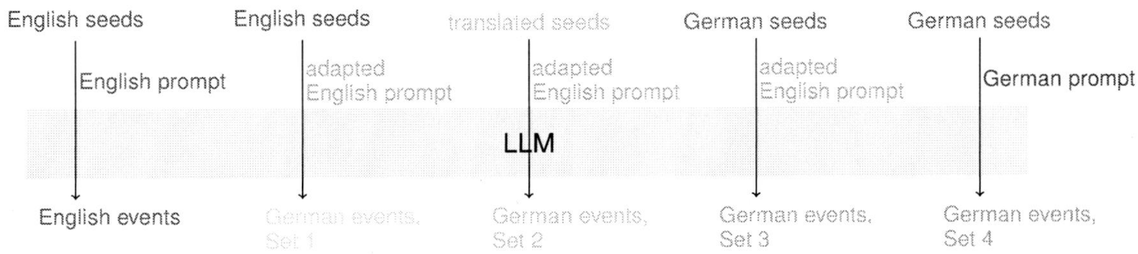

Figure 1: Overview of adaptations of the event generation approach. Items used in the original method by (Schäfer and Klinger, 2025) for generating English data are highlighted in gray text. New items for generating German data are indicated in blue, green, and teal text, with color saturation reflecting the presumed degree of localization.

can benefit both in-language and cross-lingual scenarios, reinforcing the relevance of English-centered methodologies for other languages. In prompting LLMs for emotion analysis, Bareiß et al. (2024) find that using English prompts for non-English texts can enhance classification accuracy.

In the context of narrative generation, understanding emotional dynamics is essential. Mohammad (2012) and Troiano et al. (2023) emphasize the significance of context in emotional categorization. Previous research has begun to explore the role of context in shaping emotional interpretations, with works such as Mostafazadeh et al. (2016) introducing datasets for story completion tasks.

Our research aims to contribute to the understanding of localized prompting strategies within the use-case of affective narrative generation, identifying the critical factors that can clarify emotion analysis and ensure narrative quality.

3 Methods

To explore the impact of localization of LLM-based prompting approaches developed for English, we design a structured approach to evaluate various adaptation strategies for German. Our objective is to assess the effectiveness of localization strategies in the context of affective narrative generation, which consists of two subtasks: first, producing high-quality event descriptions, and second, creating contexts that enhance emotion disambiguation.

We adopt the methodology from Schäfer and Klinger (2025), who experiment on English language data. We therefore start by generating a lexically diverse corpus of event descriptions in German (see Section 3.1), which then serves as the basis for crafting backstories that provide essential context in emotion analysis (see Section 3.2). This approach allows us to examine the effects of specific localizations in prompt[2] construction on lexical diversity, narrative coherence and emotion analysis. In the following, we present modifications to the text generation methods as well as approaches to evaluate the resulting data (see Section 3.3).

3.1 Generation of Events

The English event generation approach by Schäfer and Klinger (2025) uses prompt attributes to aim for diversity and balance of topics. Examples of these attributes (event types and objects) which we also use in our experiments are given in Appendix B. Additionally, ten example events are included within the prompt.

We implement the adaptation of this approach in four distinct ways, each varying in the level of modification and localization applied to the prompts used to guide the LLM's output. For all approaches we translate the ten example event descriptions into German. The different approaches are outlined in Figure 1 and described as follows:

1. **Modification of Prompts:** In this approach, we utilize the original English event types and objects. We modify the prompts by appending "in German" to the instructions. This approach aims to retain the original context while soliciting responses in the target language.
2. **Localized Translation of Categories and Objects:** Building upon the first method, we continue to use the English prompts with the addition of "in German". We translate both the event categories and the corresponding objects into German. This method aims at fostering a more localized response from the LLM by providing German-specific vocabulary.
3. **Creation of Localized Seed Data:** For this adaptation, we retain "in German" in the En-

[2]We provide the original full text prompts used by Schäfer and Klinger (2025) in Appendix A.

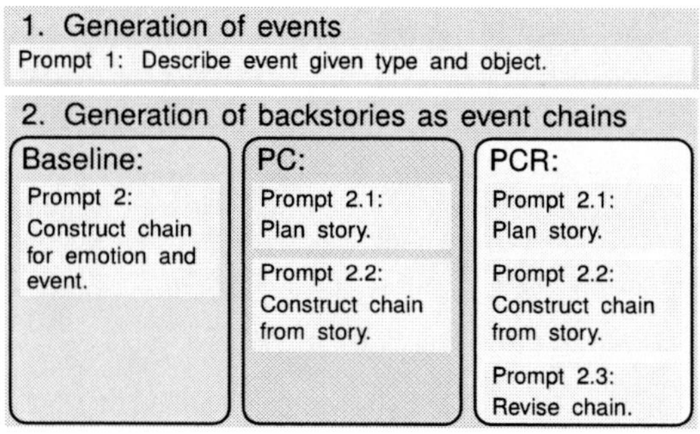

Figure 2: Overview of LLM-based data generation framework presented in Schäfer and Klinger (2025) which we localize for our experiments. The prompts used in each case are shown summarized; full text prompts are given in Appendix A.

glish prompts. Moreover, we employ ChatGPT (OpenAI, 2025) to generate new seed event categories and objects in German.

4. **Fully Localized Generation from Scratch:** In this approach, we also use the newly generated German seed event categories and objects. Additionally, the prompt for generating events is translated into German, in order to aim for outputs that are naturally in line with the German linguistic and cultural context, rather than somewhat translations of English content.

Our hypothesis is that the progression from Method 1 to Method 4 yields increasingly natural German and localized outputs. However, we also hypothesize that as the comparability with the English results may diminish.

3.2 Generation of Backstories

Schäfer and Klinger (2025) present three methods for generating context to disambiguate emotion interpretations for English event descriptions. When faced with an event description where the emotion interpretation may be ambiguous, they generate backstories in order to reduce this ambiguity and steer the interpretation toward a specific emotion.

Figure 2 visualizes the general approach employed in these methods, which are based on varying numbers of prompt interactions with an LLM. The Baseline method utilizes a singular prompt to describe the generation task instruction given an event description and a specific target emotion. The second approach Plan–Construct (PC) builds on this, but adds a story planning step. Furthermore, the third approach Plan–Construct–Revise (PCR) adds another step for revising the generated event chain while reassessing the interpretation. Schäfer and Klinger (2025) have shown that both the story planning and the revision steps are beneficial for generating English data of higher quality. We also apply these three methods to our data in order to find out if this also is the case for German.

We test two adaptation methodologies to generate localized contextual narratives:

1. We minimally modify the three methods by incorporating instructions in the prompts that the output should be "in German".
2. We fully translate the prompts, including the emotion label set, into German to aim for comprehensive localization.

With these two approaches, we evaluate the capabilities of the LLM in performing affective narrative generation in German as compared to English.

3.3 Evaluation

In our experiments, we utilize a multilingual LLM (`meta-llama/Llama-3.3-70B-Instruct`, Meta, 2024) for text generation and a smaller model fine-tuned on German data (`DiscoResearch/Llama3-German-8B`, Disco Research, 2024) for analysis. We chose these models for several key reasons: both are freely available for research and do not rely on API access, which helps eliminate costs and enhances the reproducibility of our experiments. The multilingual LLM is substantial but not overly large, providing a good balance between potential data generation quality and computational cost. Furthermore, the recency and established reputation of both models fosters comparability.

We assess the quality of generated events via human annotation, focusing on naturalness and plausibility (guidelines see Appendix C). For automatic evaluation, we utilize the German LLM to compute transition log likelihood scores across the token sequences of generated texts. We determine the quality of narratives by means of story coherence as shown in Schäfer and Klinger (2025), using a zero-shot shuffle test as proposed by Laban et al. (2021). This test computes token sequence likelihood scores of event chains (we compute these using the German LLM) and compares the values against those of various shuffled permutations of the sequence. Chains that rank highly in this comparison are assigned a high coherence score, whereas those that rank lower receive a low score.

Additionally, we conduct emotion analysis through probabilistic zero-shot classification as described in Schäfer and Klinger (2025), to quantify the emotion content within the generated texts.

Joy: Ich sah den Campingstuhl jeden Tag im Garten stehen. Der Campingstuhl erinnerte mich an den gescheiterten Ausflug mit Freunden. Ich wollte den Stuhl wegwerfen, aber nie die Zeit dafür finden. Ich überlegte, wie ich endlich den alten Stuhl loswerden konnte. *Der Campingstuhl kippte um.*
(I saw the camping chair standing in the garden every day. The camping chair reminded me of the failed trip with friends. I wanted to throw the chair away but never found the time to do so. I contemplated how I could finally get rid of the old chair. *The camping chair tipped over.*)

Boredom: Die Ankunft am Campingplatz erfolgte bei trübem Wetter. Der Zeltplatz wurde täglich auf- und abgebaut. Die gesamte Ausrüstung war bereits mehrmals aufgebaut worden. Keine der vorherigen Campingtage brachte besondere Ereignisse. *Der Campingstuhl kippte um.*
(The arrival at the campsite took place under gloomy weather. The tent site was set up and taken down daily. The entire equipment had already been set up multiple times. None of the previous camping days brought any notable events. *The camping chair tipped over.*)

Table 2: German examples with English tranlations of generated stories evoking joy and boredom.

Id	Set of Events	Length	TTLL
0	English events	17.6	-3.91 $\sigma=0.65$
1	German events, Set 1	14.9	-3.05 $\sigma=0.64$
2	German events, Set 2	15.8	-2.83 $\sigma=0.51$
3	German events, Set 3	14.5	-2.68 $\sigma=0.50$
4	German events, Set 4	23.5	-2.15 $\sigma=0.38$

Table 3: Average text length in number of tokens (Length) and average token transition log likelihood score (TTLL) in event descriptions, averaged in a set.

Ev. Set:	0		1		2		3		4	
Annot.	N	P	N	P	N	P	N	P	N	P
#1	4.16	4.96	4.33	4.79	4.44	4.64	4.68	4.72	4.56	4.76
#2	4.00	4.96	3.75	5.00	4.44	4.92	4.12	4.92	3.80	4.88
#3	4.84	4.92	4.38	4.96	4.68	4.84	4.76	4.88	4.60	4.88
Mean	4.33	4.95	4.15	4.92	4.52	4.80	4.52	4.84	4.32	4.84

Table 4: Average annotated 1–5 Likert scale values of naturalness (N) and plausibility (P) in events sets (25 samples per set) as rated by annotators #1, #2 and #3.

4 Results

This section presents the findings aligned with our research questions regarding the impact of localization in our use case of affective narrative generation. We display selected examples of generated narratives in Table 1 and Table 2. We begin with Section 4.1, addressing our first research question about the effectiveness of various localized prompts in event generation. Next, Section 4.2 targets our second question by evaluating the backstories produced through different approaches. Finally, in Section 4.3, we analyze the emotions evoked by the generated events with and without context, corresponding to our third research question.

4.1 Localization of Generated Events

Our goal is to generate a corpus of event descriptions as basis for emotion analysis experiments. Each of the methods for adapting the approach from English to German (as described in Section 3.1) generates a set of 1000 events. We now evaluate the results from the application of these methods in order to answer our first research question: **What adaptations are necessary to tailor the English event generation approach for the German language, in order to ensure the production of high-quality localized data?** We automatically evaluate the entire dataset and manually assess nuances in perceived quality, addressing potential limitations of the automatic approach.

Automatic Evaluation. We utilize the German LLM to calculate the likelihood of the token sequence in each event description produced. The overall results for each set of events are summarized in Table 3. Our findings show a clear correlation between the degree of adaptation or translation of the methods employed and the resulting transition probabilities of the token sequences. As the methods become more tailored to the German language, the transition probabilities increase. Additionally, the noticeable decrease in standard deviation supports this observation, showing that the adaptations increasingly produce more consistently high-quality German language data.

Our results verify the language model's preference for German, as it shows a substantial inclination toward all German event descriptions compared to the English texts (en events). We also observe a substantial enhancement in the transition probability for the last set of events, which was generated using prompts exclusively in German.

Human Annotation. We now analyze a subset of the generated data to assess whether human evaluators align with our automatic evaluations regarding the quality of the language produced. We ask three annotators to rate the naturalness (linguistic quality) and plausibility (semantics) of the texts. Details of the procedure as well as inter-annotator agreement values are shown in Appendix C.

Table 4 summarizes the annotation results of the

naturalness and plausibility assessment. The events generated in Set 2 and Set 3 receive the highest naturalness ratings on average. Conversely, the events in Set 1, which involves only minimal localization to the German context, fall substantially short, underscoring the need for a substantial adaptation of the original approach. Interestingly, the texts generated using prompts composed entirely in German (Set 4) do not achieve the highest naturalness ratings. This shows that complete localization does not correlate with perceived naturalness in human evaluation. For the semantic plausibility assessment, we observe minimal differences across methods. All approaches receive high scores, indicating their ability to generate plausible events.

These results warrant a summary to address our first research question. Our evaluation shows that to effectively tailor the English event generation approach for the German language, specific adaptations are essential. Firstly, substantial localization of seed words is necessary to enhance the relevance and contextual appropriateness of the generated events. This is evidenced by the marked performance differences between Set 1 and the more localized Sets 2, 3, and 4. Moreover, while our findings show that using prompts in German (as observed in Set 4) does not lead to higher naturalness ratings, it highlights a nuanced relationship between localization and perceived text quality. Therefore, we recommend that future work should explore both approaches, while also conducting thorough human evaluations of the results to identify the best strategy for specific tasks.

4.2 Narrative Content of Backstories

We now shift our focus to the generated contextual narratives based on the events produced using the methods outlined in Section 3.2. Our goal is to address our second research question: **In the context of generating backstories for events that together form coherent narratives, do the advantages of story planning and narrative revision observed in English also manifest in the German adaptation of the process?** We analyze the lexical content of the backstories organized by the respective emotion categories, examine the differences among the generation methods, and explore the relationships between the two prompting setups.

Setting. As basis we use the two sets of German events which scored highest in both automatic and human evaluations from the previous section (Set 3 and 4). Each set consists of 1,000 event descriptions. For each event description, 13 backstories comprising four preceding events are generated, with each backstory crafted to evoke one of 13 emotion categories. The experimental design for backstory generation distinguishes between the two sets based on their initial generation prompts. For Set 3, generated using English prompts, we generate backstories with English prompts and the English emotion set. Conversely, Set 4 employs German prompts, with backstories generated with German prompts and the German emotion set. This setup allows us again to test whether prompting LLMs in English may yield superior results compared to those prompted in German, while also assessing the impact of localization.

With this approach, we generate backstories corresponding to each of the 1,000 German events in both sets using three different prompting methods as discussed in Section 3.2.

Content of Event Chains. To gain insights into the narratives of these backstories, particularly at a lexical level, we now focus on identifying the most prominent words – specifically nouns – by determining their term frequency-inverse document frequency (TF-IDF) values. Results of the comprehensive analysis is provided in Appendix D. We summarize selected findings in the following.

Notably, the results show clear distinctions between the subsets corresponding to their respective emotions, as expected. For instance, event chains associated with disgust are predominantly characterized by themes related to scandals, corruption, and waste, while those concerning sadness reflect more familial themes such as grandpa, grandma, and grave. In the context of fear, terms like unrest, AI and caution are frequently observed.

When comparing the three methods of backstory generation, an initial trend emerges: backstories generated with the PC and PCR approaches tend to exhibit more complex associations with the respective emotions compared to those generated by the Baseline approach. This becomes particularly evident when we examine the absolute TF-IDF scores, which illustrate that the PC and PCR approaches create more pronounced lexical distinctions among emotions by utilizing more specific vocabulary.

Comparing the data from both prompt setups, we observe that the localized German prompts produce longer compound nouns, while data generated using English prompts lean towards shorter words.

		Mean Coherence of Chains		
		Baseline	PC	PCR
Emotion-Specific Subsets	Anger	.74	.76 Δ+.02	.77 Δ+.03
	Boredom	.75	.75 $\Delta\pm$.00	.77 Δ+.02
	Disgust	.72	.78 Δ+.06	.79 Δ+.07
	Fear	.71	.73 Δ+.02	.77 Δ+.06
	Guilt	.76	.79 Δ+.03	.81 Δ+.05
	Joy	.77	.77 $\Delta\pm$.00	.79 Δ+.02
	Pride	.78	.80 Δ+.02	.81 Δ+.03
	Relief	.78	.76 Δ−.02	.81 Δ+.03
	Sadness	.74	.79 Δ+.05	.82 Δ+.08
	Shame	.75	.80 Δ+.05	.78 Δ+.03
	Surprise	.74	.76 Δ+.02	.80 Δ+.06
	Trust	.77	.78 Δ+.01	.78 Δ+.01
	No-Emotion	.71	.70 Δ−.01	.75 Δ+.04
Overall Dataset		.75 $\sigma = 0.26$	.77 Δ+.02 $\sigma = 0.26$	.79 Δ+.04 $\sigma = 0.25$

Table 5: Mean coherence scores for event chains in the datasets generated with different methods based on event Set 3. Δ values show the difference of the respective score in comparison to the Baseline.

		Mean Coherence of Chains		
		Baseline	PC	PCR
Emotion-Specific Subsets	Wut	.80	.76 Δ−.04	.80 $\Delta\pm$.00
	Langeweile	.77	.75 Δ−.02	.78 Δ+.01
	Ekel	.78	.77 Δ−.01	.80 Δ+.02
	Angst	.76	.72 Δ−.04	.77 Δ+.01
	Schuld	.79	.79 $\Delta\pm$.00	.81 Δ+.02
	Freude	.81	.78 Δ−.03	.81 $\Delta\pm$.00
	Stolz	.82	.77 Δ−.05	.80 Δ−.02
	Erleichterung	.81	.77 Δ−.04	.81 $\Delta\pm$.00
	Traurigkeit	.81	.77 Δ−.04	.81 $\Delta\pm$.00
	Scham	.81	.78 Δ−.03	.82 Δ+.01
	Überraschung	.80	.78 Δ−.02	.81 Δ+.01
	Vertrauen	.79	.76 Δ−.03	.79 $\Delta\pm$.00
	Keine_Emotion	.79	.76 Δ−.03	.78 Δ−.01
Overall Dataset		.79 $\sigma = 0.24$	.77 Δ−.02 $\sigma = 0.25$	.80 Δ+.01 $\sigma = 0.24$

Table 6: Mean coherence scores for event chains in the datasets generated with different methods based on event Set 4. Δ values show the difference of the respective score in comparison to the Baseline.

Coherence Analysis. Further, we perform a coherence analysis as described in Section 3.3. Here, we evaluate the coherence scores two times in three sets of generated event chains: one generated with English prompts based on event Set 3 (displayed in Table 5) and the other generated with German prompts based on event Set 4 (shown in Table 6). This analysis is further refined by differentiating between the three approaches and the respective emotion categories evoked in the target events.

In Table 5, the overall coherence of chains generated using the baseline approach is observed to be approximately .75. The introduction of story planning, included in the PC approach, results in an increase to a coherence score of .77. Further revisions, incorporated in the PCR approach, yield an even higher coherence of .79.

When examining the coherence of data generated with German prompts (see Table 6), we find that baseline chains achieve a relatively high coherence score of .79. However, this time the integration of story planning correlates with a decrease in coherence to .77. Only with additional revisions do we achieve the highest overall average coherence score of .80.

While there are no extreme outliers across specific emotions, we observe a trend indicating that the categories of boredom, fear, and no-emotion tend to exhibit the least coherent event chains.

Taking these results into account, we now address our second research question regarding the effect of story planning and narrative revision in the German adaptation of the event generation process. Our findings show that story planning contributes to the generation of lexically richer and better localized backstories. However, it does not consistently lead to higher coherence in the narratives, as observed in certain cases where coherence scores decrease after incorporating story planning. Nevertheless, when paired with narrative revision, we observe an improvement in coherence, achieving the highest levels when both techniques are applied. Comparatively, the improvements seen in German narratives are less pronounced than those noted by Schäfer and Klinger (2025) in English. This shows that while benefits from planning and revision exist, their effects are not as pronounced in German as compared to English using the multilingual LLM.

4.3 Emotion Analysis

With the localized sets of events and generated narratives, we now perform a systematic and comprehensive analysis of the effect of context in emotion analysis. Here we address our third research question: **To what extent do the generated German backstories effectively disambiguate emotion analysis in events, compared to findings from the English-language experiments?**

Setting. We perform automatic emotion analysis as described in Section 3.3: We first examine the prediction probabilities on the events in isolation, and then contrast these with the probabilities when contextual narratives from the backstories are in-

Event Set Id	Anger	Boredom	Disgust	Fear	Guilt	Joy	Pride	Relief	Sadness	Shame	Surprise	Trust	No-Emotion
0	.02	.01	.00	.01	.00	.33	.01	.08	.01	.00	.14	.02	.37
3	.01	.00	.01	.02	.00	.37	.07	.15	.09	.00	.06	.03	.20
4	.01	.00	.00	.02	.00	.51	.15	.10	.07	.00	.04	.06	.03

Table 7: Results $p(e|E)$ of probabilistic zero-shot emotion analysis for each emotion (e) on average given the events E from different event sets.

cluded. With this comparison we determine if the added contexts disambiguate emotion analysis.

Emotion Analysis of Events. In Table 7, we compare the results for automatic emotion analysis on events in two German event sets (Set 3 and 4) to those for the English event set introduced by Schäfer and Klinger (2025) (Set 0). Overall, these results are in line with an expected prior distribution of emotions in event descriptions. However, several notable differences emerge from a comparison between the sets. Events from the German sets evoke stronger emotions; the probability of detecting the no-emotion category is considerably lower for the German sets (.20 and .03) compared to the English data (.37). This increased emotionality affects only certain emotion categories that are more prevalent in the German data, particularly joy, pride, and sadness. Conversely, the German events encompass the emotion of surprise less frequently.

Emotion Analysis in Contexts. Next, we conduct an automatic emotion analysis on the event chains to ascertain whether the addition of generated backstories successfully amplifies the evocation of specific emotions in the target events, thus contributing to the disambiguation of emotion analysis. We again analyze two times three sets of event chains: one evaluated with emotion analysis using English prompts applied to event Set 3 (see Table 8) and another assessed using German prompts and relevant emotion sets on event Set 4 (see Table 9).

The results illustrated in Table 8 show that the emotions joy, pride, relief, and sadness are particularly well-fostered by their corresponding backstories, especially when compared against the initial emotions of the events, as presented in Table 7. The added context has a substantial influence on these emotions. However, when comparing the various approaches – Baseline, PC, and PCR – no systematic differences emerge overall in their effectiveness on emotion evocation. Comparatively, examining the data generated with German prompts (see Table 9) reveals that the evoked emotions are less influenced by the added contexts. Although the trends across categories are consistent, the overall values are notably lower.

		$p(e = e_p\|C)$		
		Baseline	PC	PCR
Emotion-Specific Subsets	Anger	.10	.10 $\Delta\pm.00$	.13 $\Delta+.03$
	Boredom	.02	.07 $\Delta+.05$	.08 $\Delta+.06$
	Disgust	.09	.11 $\Delta+.02$	.12 $\Delta+.03$
	Fear	.17	.16 $\Delta-.01$	.15 $\Delta-.02$
	Guilt	.18	.16 $\Delta-.02$	.16 $\Delta-.02$
	Joy	.34	.31 $\Delta-.03$	.29 $\Delta-.05$
	Pride	.23	.23 $\Delta\pm.00$	.29 $\Delta+.06$
	Relief	.45	.45 $\Delta\pm.00$	.42 $\Delta-.03$
	Sadness	.39	.39 $\Delta\pm.00$	.34 $\Delta-.05$
	Shame	.10	.12 $\Delta+.02$	.12 $\Delta+.02$
	Surprise	.13	.11 $\Delta-.02$	.11 $\Delta-.02$
	Trust	.07	.06 $\Delta-.01$	.06 $\Delta-.01$
	No-Emotion	.01	.02 $\Delta+.01$	.02 $\Delta+.01$
Overall Dataset		.18 $\sigma = .37$	.18 $\Delta\pm.00$ $\sigma = .37$	.18 $\Delta\pm.00$ $\sigma = .37$

Table 8: Prediction emotion probability evoked in the last event from event Set 3 ($p(e)$) given entire event chains (C) with the respective prompted emotion (e_p).

		$p(e = e_p\|C)$		
		Baseline	PC	PCR
Emotion-Specific Subsets	Wut	.02	.04 $\Delta+.02$	.04 $\Delta+.02$
	Langeweile	.02	.01 $\Delta-.01$	.03 $\Delta+.01$
	Ekel	.02	.06 $\Delta+.04$	.08 $\Delta+.06$
	Angst	.05	.08 $\Delta+.03$	.10 $\Delta+.05$
	Schuld	.02	.06 $\Delta+.04$	.08 $\Delta+.06$
	Freude	.39	.42 $\Delta+.03$	.46 $\Delta+.07$
	Stolz	.17	.24 $\Delta+.07$	.31 $\Delta+.14$
	Erleichterung	.19	.25 $\Delta+.06$	.26 $\Delta+.07$
	Traurigkeit	.19	.25 $\Delta+.06$	.33 $\Delta+.14$
	Scham	.02	.04 $\Delta+.02$	.05 $\Delta+.03$
	Überraschung	.08	.06 $\Delta-.02$	.07 $\Delta-.01$
	Vertrauen	.05	.08 $\Delta+.03$	.09 $\Delta+.04$
	keine_Emotion	.01	.00 $\Delta-.01$	.00 $\Delta-.01$
Overall Dataset		.09 $\sigma = .26$	.12 $\Delta+.03$ $\sigma = .30$	.14 $\Delta+.05$ $\sigma = .32$

Table 9: Prediction emotion probability evoked in the last event from event Set 4 ($p(e)$) given entire event chains (C) with the respective prompted emotion (e_p).

Reflecting on the overall results, we can now answer our third research question concerning the effectiveness of the generated German backstories in disambiguating emotion analysis in events, particularly in comparison to the findings from the English-language experiments by Schäfer and Klinger (2025). Our results reveal that while certain emotion categories – including joy, pride, and sadness – show improved disambiguation when contextualized with the narratives, for the other emotions this effect is less pronounced in German than in English. Specifically, the German backstories do foster emotion evocation only to some degree; however, coherence is possibly being prioritized over precise portrayal of emotions in the narrative generation process. Moreover, the expected benefits of the multi-step data generation techniques do not translate as clearly in the results for emotion analysis in German. This highlights that the task is more effectively handled in English.

5 Conclusion

With this paper, we provide an investigation of the localization of English LLM-prompting methodologies to German, highlighting the role of contextual disambiguation in narratives. Our findings provide key insights into the complexities of adapting emotion analysis techniques across languages.

Firstly, we now understand the adaptations necessary for customizing event generation techniques to German. Our results show that substantial localization, particularly of seed words, is essential for improving the relevance of generated events. It is necessary to balance approaches that account for both localization and text quality.

Secondly, our evaluation of narrative generation shows that while story planning results in lexically richer backstories, it does not consistently improve coherence in generating German data. We find that while the multilingual LLM performs adequately in simpler generation tasks, it struggles with the more complex components of narrative coherence and the disambiguation of emotion analysis in German compared to English. Combining story planning with narrative revision does lead to notable benefits; however, these improvements are less pronounced in German. These results show that the multilingual LLM may not be able to perform complex generation tasks in languages other than English as effectively. Therefore, specific language fine-tuning is advisable to enhance performance in these tasks and ensure more accurate and localized outputs.

Lastly, our exploration of the generated backstories' effectiveness in disambiguating emotions in German event descriptions is only effective for certain emotions. This highlights the need for further research into the adaptation of prevalent English data generation approaches, particularly in managing complex narrative requirements.

Our findings prompt several essential follow-up questions. Firstly, how can the emotion disambiguation technique be further adapted for other languages, particularly those with significant grammatical and lexical differences from English? Additionally, what specific linguistic nuances within German and other languages might affect the effectiveness of the localization? Furthermore, there remains a need to explore the scalability of our approach across various narrative contexts and cultures, which could unveil new strategies for enhancing emotion analysis in contextualized settings. Addressing these questions would refine our methodologies and contribute to the ongoing discourse on the applicability of large language models in diverse linguistic environments, particularly in languages underrepresented in LLM pre-training data.

In summary, our research emphasizes the challenges of adapting established approaches with prompting LLMs to generate English data to less represented languages. In particular, research of localized phenomena, such as the contextual influence in emotion analysis, tends to still be challenging with multilingual LLMs. Future work should continue to refine methodologies and evaluation frameworks to better accommodate the unique characteristics of the German language.

Limitations

This study has several limitations that may impact the generalizability of our findings. Firstly, we employed only one LLM for text generation, which restricts our ability to assess the effectiveness of localization strategies across different models. Future research should explore multiple LLMs to validate our results. We provide our code and data to facilitate reproducibility. Additionally, our focus on German limits the applicability of our findings to languages with distinct grammatical and cultural characteristics. The localization strategies identified may not transfer directly to such languages. Lastly, our emotional analysis was based on a limited set of emotions, which may overlook critical nuances in emotional expression. Expanding this scope could yield a more comprehensive understanding of localization in emotion analysis.

Acknowledgments

This work has been supported by the German Research Foundation (DFG) in the project KL2869/1–2 (CEAT, project number 380093645).

References

Michael Andersland. 2024. Amharic llama and llava: Multimodal llms for low resource languages. *Preprint*, arXiv:2403.06354.

Patrick Bareiß, Roman Klinger, and Jeremy Barnes. 2024. English prompts are better for nli-based zero-shot emotion classification than target-language prompts. In *Companion Proceedings of the ACM Web Conference 2024*, WWW '24, page 1318–1326, New York, NY, USA. Association for Computing Machinery.

Tom Brown, Benjamin Mann, Nick Ryder, Melanie Subbiah, Jared D Kaplan, Prafulla Dhariwal, Arvind Neelakantan, Pranav Shyam, Girish Sastry, Amanda Askell, Sandhini Agarwal, Ariel Herbert-Voss, Gretchen Krueger, Tom Henighan, Rewon Child, Aditya Ramesh, Daniel Ziegler, Jeffrey Wu, Clemens Winter, and 12 others. 2020. Language models are few-shot learners. In *Advances in Neural Information Processing Systems*, volume 33, pages 1877–1901. Curran Associates, Inc.

Aakanksha Chowdhery, Sharan Narang, Jacob Devlin, Maarten Bosma, Gaurav Mishra, Adam Roberts, Paul Barham, Hyung Won Chung, Charles Sutton, Sebastian Gehrmann, Parker Schuh, Kensen Shi, Sasha Tsvyashchenko, Joshua Maynez, Abhishek Rao, Parker Barnes, Yi Tay, Noam Shazeer, Vinodkumar Prabhakaran, and 48 others. 2023. Palm: Scaling language modeling with pathways. *Journal of Machine Learning Research*, 24(240):1–113.

Alexis Conneau, Kartikay Khandelwal, Naman Goyal, Vishrav Chaudhary, Guillaume Wenzek, Francisco Guzmán, Edouard Grave, Myle Ott, Luke Zettlemoyer, and Veselin Stoyanov. 2020. Unsupervised cross-lingual representation learning at scale. In *Proceedings of the 58th Annual Meeting of the Association for Computational Linguistics*, pages 8440–8451, Online. Association for Computational Linguistics.

Luna De Bruyne. 2023. The paradox of multilingual emotion detection. In *Proceedings of the 13th Workshop on Computational Approaches to Subjectivity, Sentiment, & Social Media Analysis*, pages 458–466, Toronto, Canada. Association for Computational Linguistics.

Disco Research. 2024. Model llama3-german-8b-v0.1. Large language model.

Jinlan Fu, See-Kiong Ng, and Pengfei Liu. 2022. Polyglot prompt: Multilingual multitask prompt training. In *Proceedings of the 2022 Conference on Empirical Methods in Natural Language Processing*, pages 9919–9935, Abu Dhabi, United Arab Emirates. Association for Computational Linguistics.

Haoyang Huang, Tianyi Tang, Dongdong Zhang, Xin Zhao, Ting Song, Yan Xia, and Furu Wei. 2023. Not all languages are created equal in LLMs: Improving multilingual capability by cross-lingual-thought prompting. In *Findings of the Association for Computational Linguistics: EMNLP 2023*, pages 12365–12394, Singapore. Association for Computational Linguistics.

Albert Q. Jiang, Alexandre Sablayrolles, Antoine Roux, Arthur Mensch, Blanche Savary, Chris Bamford, Devendra Singh Chaplot, Diego de las Casas, Emma Bou Hanna, Florian Bressand, Gianna Lengyel, Guillaume Bour, Guillaume Lample, Lélio Renard Lavaud, Lucile Saulnier, Marie-Anne Lachaux, Pierre Stock, Sandeep Subramanian, Sophia Yang, and 7 others. 2024. Mixtral of experts. *Preprint*, arXiv:2401.04088.

Philippe Laban, Luke Dai, Lucas Bandarkar, and Marti A. Hearst. 2021. Can transformer models measure coherence in text: Re-thinking the shuffle test. In *Proceedings of the 59th Annual Meeting of the Association for Computational Linguistics and the 11th International Joint Conference on Natural Language Processing (Volume 2: Short Papers)*, pages 1058–1064, Online. Association for Computational Linguistics.

Chaoqun Liu, Wenxuan Zhang, Yiran Zhao, Anh Tuan Luu, and Lidong Bing. 2025. Is translation all you need? a study on solving multilingual tasks with large language models. *Preprint*, arXiv:2403.10258.

Meta. 2024. Llama (model llama-3.3-70b-instruct). Large language model.

Saif Mohammad. 2012. #emotional tweets. In **SEM 2012: The First Joint Conference on Lexical and Computational Semantics – Volume 1: Proceedings of the main conference and the shared task, and Volume 2: Proceedings of the Sixth International Workshop on Semantic Evaluation (SemEval 2012)*, pages 246–255, Montréal, Canada. Association for Computational Linguistics.

Itai Mondshine, Tzuf Paz-Argaman, and Reut Tsarfaty. 2025. Beyond English: The impact of prompt translation strategies across languages and tasks in multilingual LLMs. In *Findings of the Association for Computational Linguistics: NAACL 2025*, pages 1331–1354, Albuquerque, New Mexico. Association for Computational Linguistics.

Nasrin Mostafazadeh, Nathanael Chambers, Xiaodong He, Devi Parikh, Dhruv Batra, Lucy Vanderwende, Pushmeet Kohli, and James Allen. 2016. A corpus and cloze evaluation for deeper understanding of commonsense stories. In *Proceedings of the 2016 Conference of the North American Chapter of the Association for Computational Linguistics: Human Language Technologies*, pages 839–849, San Diego, California. Association for Computational Linguistics.

OpenAI. 2025. Chatgpt (model gpt4o-mini). Large language model.

Chengwei Qin, Aston Zhang, Zhuosheng Zhang, Jiaao Chen, Michihiro Yasunaga, and Diyi Yang. 2023. Is

ChatGPT a general-purpose natural language processing task solver? In *Proceedings of the 2023 Conference on Empirical Methods in Natural Language Processing*, pages 1339–1384, Singapore. Association for Computational Linguistics.

Colin Raffel, Noam Shazeer, Adam Roberts, Katherine Lee, Sharan Narang, Michael Matena, Yanqi Zhou, Wei Li, and Peter J. Liu. 2020. Exploring the limits of transfer learning with a unified text-to-text transformer. *Journal of Machine Learning Research*, 21(140):1–67.

Johannes Schäfer and Roman Klinger. 2025. Shaping event backstories to estimate potential emotion contexts. *Preprint*, arXiv:2508.09954.

Amit Seker, Elron Bandel, Dan Bareket, Idan Brusilovsky, Refael Greenfeld, and Reut Tsarfaty. 2022. AlephBERT: Language model pre-training and evaluation from sub-word to sentence level. In *Proceedings of the 60th Annual Meeting of the Association for Computational Linguistics (Volume 1: Long Papers)*, pages 46–56, Dublin, Ireland. Association for Computational Linguistics.

Enrica Troiano, Laura Oberländer, and Roman Klinger. 2023. Dimensional modeling of emotions in text with appraisal theories: Corpus creation, annotation reliability, and prediction. *Computational Linguistics*, 49(1):1–72.

Mengjie Zhao and Hinrich Schütze. 2021. Discrete and soft prompting for multilingual models. In *Proceedings of the 2021 Conference on Empirical Methods in Natural Language Processing*, pages 8547–8555, Online and Punta Cana, Dominican Republic. Association for Computational Linguistics.

A Full Text Prompts

Table 10 shows the full text of the prompts used by Schäfer and Klinger (2025) to generate data according to the different methods. The interaction with the model comprises three message types[3]: a "system" message that establishes the context for the interaction and includes general guidelines; a "user" message that encapsulates the specific inputs, requirements, and instructions for the task; and an "assistant" message that represents the model's response based on the provided context.

Prompt 1 is used to generate the concluding event and aims to ensure a balanced topic variance through the incorporation of specific attributes. To ensure that the generated event descriptions are concise, Schäfer and Klinger (2025) implement few-shot prompting by including ten examples of event descriptions in the prompt.

[3]`https://www.llama.com/docs/model-cards-and-prompt-formats/llama3_1/`

For each event generated in the first step, Schäfer and Klinger (2025) aim to create a corresponding backstory comprised of four preceding events, tailored to influence the specific emotion responses of the last event. In the baseline approach, this process is implemented using a single prompt (**Prompt 2** as shown in Table 10). For the other methods, the process is further broken down into sub-steps: Story planning using **Prompt 2.1:** For each final event, the LLM is prompted to first generate a story plan that outlines plausible explanations for the emotion responses tied to the concluding event. This preemptive planning is intended to increase coherence and relevance in the backstories. Based on the crafted story plan, the LLM should generate the sequential backstory comprising four events. This ensures that the events are narratively connected and describe the context leading up to the pivotal final event. Event chain generation using **Prompt 2.2:** After generating the event chain, Schäfer and Klinger (2025) suggest to conduct a summarization step to ensure uniformity and clarity. Additionally, the third method by Schäfer and Klinger (2025) uses **Prompt 2.3** to revise the generated event chain in an attempt to improve the adherence to the defined requirements.

Table 11 shows the English prompt messages used for automatic emotion analysis.

B Event Types and Objects

Table 14 shows the list of ten English event types along with ten corresponding examples of related objects. Table 15 shows the list of ten German event types along with ten corresponding examples of related objects. These values serve as attributes in the prompt which initially generates diverse events that we subsequently develop backstories for.

C Details of the Human Annotation

In this section we provide the annotation guidelines used to rate the quality of event descriptions in Appendix C.1 as well as the inter-annotator agreement of the annotated data in Appendix C.2.

C.1 Annotation Guidelines

Given is a list with descriptions of events.

The data is separated by language (English/German). It should be assumed that each text was written by native speakers.

#	MT	Prompt Text
Prompt 1	system	You are a person describing an event which you have experienced. 10 examples of such event descriptions are as follows: 0: The phone rang. 1: A cat meowed. 2: The car engine sputtered to a stop. 3: A child laughed in the park. 4: A bird fluttered past the window. 5: The waves crashed against the shore. 6: A train whistled as it approached. 7: The fireworks lit up the sky. 8: A bicycle rode by. 9: A crowd cheered at the concert.
	user	The event you experienced is of type: {ds_event_type}. In a longer text you are describing several things that happened at that event. Something happened at that event with the following object(s): {ds_event_object}. In your response, only provide a very short sentence describing what happened to/with the object(s).
Prompt 2	system	It is often clear from the text that describes an event which specific emotion it evokes in a person that experienced it. However, additional information about the situation can change our understanding of how a person might interpret the event. You are an expert at creating a scenario that explains why a specific event may cause a possibly unusual emotion in you. In addition, you can concisely make this scenario apparent for the reader by formulating a description of 4 events that took place immediately before the event.
	user	You experienced something happening which is described by the following event description: 5. "{event}". This event somehow made you clearly feel the emotion: "{emotion}". Provide a text describing four events that took place immediately before event 5 by giving a list of descriptions of these events (1.-4.). The events 1.-4. clearly influence your personal emotional interpretation of the event that happened after (5.). The emotion "{emotion}" is only triggered by what specifically happened in event 5. The events 1.-4. evoked other emotions, such as: {", ".join(random.sample([emo for emo in EMOTION_SET if emo != emotion], len(EMOTION_SET)-1))}. In your response, for each of the 4 event descriptions: Only give a summary text consisting of the main clause in a very short sentence. Each description should only describe a singular event. Indicate each event description in a separate line.
Prompt 2.1	system	It is often clear from the text that describes an event which specific emotion it evokes in a person that experienced it. However, additional information about the situation can change our understanding of how a person might interpret the event. You are an expert at creating a scenario that explains why a specific event may cause a possibly unusual emotion in you. In addition, you can concisely make this scenario apparent for the reader by formulating a description of 4 events that took place immediately before the event.
	user	You experienced something happening which is described by the following event description: 5. "event". This event somehow made you clearly feel the emotion: "emotion". First, give a brief explanation of a scenario in which it can be deduced from the description of event 5. that you felt emotion. Second, phrase this explanation as events that took place immediately before event 5 by giving a list of descriptions of these events (1.-4.). The events 1.-4. clearly influence your personal emotional interpretation of the event that happened after (5.). The emotion "emotion" is only triggered by what specifically happened in event 5. The events 1.-4. evoked other emotions, such as: {", ".join(random.sample([emo for emo in EMOTION_SET if emo ≠ emotion], len(EMOTION_SET)-1))}.
Pr. 2.2	user	Extract the sequence of 4 descriptions of events that happened from the following text: ### {explanation} ### The event 5: "{event}" happened after the 4 events. In your response, for each of the 4 event descriptions: Only give a summary text consisting of the main clause in a very short sentence. Each description should only describe a singular event. Indicate each event description in a separate line.
Prompt 2.3	system	You are an expert at adapting a narrative to convey specific emotional interpretations. You will receive a text that outlines a sequence of events as experienced by an individual. Additionally, there will be an explanation of how a particular emotion is triggered in this individual based on the final event.
	user	Explanation: {story_plan} Event sequence: {chain} First, provide a brief evaluation on how the first four events (1.-4.) of the sequence could be adjusted to form a coherent narrative which better aligns with the conclusion given in the explanation. The text of the last event (5.) should remain as is. Second, provide a revised event sequence that incorporates these adjustments while keeping the sentence length for each event description similar. Each event description should consist only of a main clause in a very short sentence. Do not explicitly mention the emotions felt.

Table 10: List of Enlish prompts used by (Schäfer and Klinger, 2025) for event chain generation. The first column shows the numbers of the specific prompts as introduced in Figure 2. 'MT' refers to the prompt message type as specified in the input for the instruction-tuned LLM.

For each event, the following should be annotated:

- **Naturalness (linguistic level):** Evaluated on how authentic and idiomatic the sentence sounds. Criteria are:
  - Language flow: Is the sentence fluent to read?
  - Grammar and syntax: Is the sentence grammatically correct?
  - Word choice: Is the word choice appropriate for the event and is the stylistic level correctly chosen?
- **Plausibility (semantic level):** Evaluated on how believable and realistic the event is. Criteria are:
  - Personal perspective: Would someone who experienced the event describe it this way?
  - Reality reference: Is the event realistic?
  - Contextualization: Does the event fit within the cultural context?

Annotation labels are on a scale from 1-5:

1. Not natural/plausible at all,
2. A little natural/plausible,
3. Moderately natural/plausible,
4. Quite natural/plausible,
5. Totally natural/plausible.

MT	Prompt Message Text
System	You are an expert in emotion analysis on event descriptions.
User	A person describes their experience as follows: {text_instance} What emotion was evoked in the person at the end? As your response, provide only one label from the emotion set: anger, disgust, fear, guilt, joy, sadness, shame, pride, boredom, surprise, trust, relief, no-emotion.
Assistant	{emotion}

Table 11: Prompt messages for zero-shot emotion analysis on events and event chains as introduced by Schäfer and Klinger (2025). 'MT' refers to the respective prompt message type as specified in the input for the instruction-tuned LLM.

	#1	#2	#3
#1	0.00	0.75	0.54
#2	0.75	0.00	0.81
#3	0.54	0.81	0.00

Table 12: Mean Δ between naturalness ratings of pairs of annotators.

C.2 Inter-Annotator Agreement

The annotated data comprises 125 event descriptions (25 texts from each of the five sets) which were annotated by three annotators. To assess inter-annotator agreement, we calculate weighted Cohen's Kappa between pairs of annotators as well as Krippendorff's Alpha overall. This results in the following values for the annotation:

- Naturalness (Weighted Cohen's Kappa)
  - #1 – #2: 0.45
  - #1 – #3: 0.34
  - #2 – #3: 0.34
  - Krippendorff's Alpha: 0.31
- Plausibility (Weighted Cohen's Kappa)
  - #1 – #2: 0.09
  - #1 – #3: 0.26
  - #2 – #3: 0.17
  - Krippendorff's Alpha: 0.17

	#1	#2	#3
#1	0.00	0.26	0.25
#2	0.26	0.00	0.14
#3	0.25	0.14	0.00

Table 13: Mean Δ between plausibility ratings of pairs of annotators.

Note that, while these measures for agreement show quite low values here, we should take into account that the label distribution in this dataset is extremely skewed. Most instances were annotated with high naturalness (labels 3-5) and very high plausibility (4-5). In this case, these measures include a very high penalty for chance agreement.

To assess the quality of the annotation with another measure, we include the mean Δ between the annotated scores of two annotators. The results for this assessment are shown in Table 12 for the annotation of naturalness and in Table 13 for the annotation of plausibility. This evaluation shows that, especially for the annotation of plausibility of event descriptions, there is very little variance between the ratings of the annotators.

D TF-IDF-Based Unigram Analysis of Generated Event Chains

This section provides results from our evaluation of the generated event chains by displaying the top words in different subsets of our data sorted by term frequency-inverse document frequency (TF-IDF) values. Table 16 shows the top 10 nouns in the event chains generated using event Set 3, separately for the different English emotion categories used. Table 17 shows the top 10 nouns in the event chains generated using event Set 4, separately for the different German emotion categories used. The separation according to the columns of the tables correspond to the different generation methods Baseline, PC and PCR. The text background color saturation is based on the respective TF-IDF values normalized in the range of the values of all words of each table.

Event Type	Event Type Objects
Social Gathering	chairs, tables, food platters, drinks, napkins, decorations, music speakers, games, invitation cards, host
Educational Activity	textbooks, notebooks, pencils, whiteboard, markers, projector, handouts, calculator, overhead projector, globe
Recreational and Nature Activity	hiking boots, backpacks, water bottles, first-aid kit, campfire supplies, nature guide, binoculars, tent, sleeping bags, camping chairs
Cultural and Community Event	stage, performers, sound system, projector, festival tickets, food stalls, craft booths, cultural displays, artworks, costumes
Professional Development	business cards, presentation slides, notebooks, pens, projector, handouts, networking tools, feedback forms, laptops, name badges
Celebration	cake, candles, party hats, balloons, confetti, party favors, streamers, drinks, gift bags, music playlist
Artistic Performance	stage, costumes, sets, props, lights, sound equipment, musical instruments, audience seats, backdrops, tickets
Competition	trophies, medals, referee kit, scoreboard, team jerseys, game equipment, whistle, competition schedule, event tickets, player registration
Family and Relationships	family photo albums, toys, family tree chart, gift cards, family recipe book, family calendars, cameraman, outdoor equipment, gifts, personalized items
Transportation and Travel Event	maps, itineraries, backpacks, suitcases, boarding passes, tickets, travel guides, snacks, passports, travel pillows

Table 14: List of English event types and objects used in prompt templates to create diverse event descriptions.

Event Type	Event Type Objects
Freizeit-/Naturaktivität	Fahrrad, Wanderschuhe, Zelt, Campingstuhl, Kamera, Angelschnur, Rucksack, Boot, Kajak, Angelrute
Wettbewerb	Medaille, Trophäe, Zertifikat, Pokale, Urkunde, Rangliste, Wettbewerbsbedingungen, Prüfung, Wettbewerbsbeitrag, Teilnahmeformular
Berufliche Erfahrung	Bewerbungsgespräch, Lebenslauf, Arbeitsvertrag, Präsentation, Teammeeting, Fortbildung, Mentoring, Networking-Event, Projektabschluss, Feedbackgespräch
Familie/Beziehung	Eltern, Geschwister, Großeltern, Onkel, Tante, Cousin, Cousine, Ehepartner, Freunde, Kinder
Reiseerlebnis	Reisepass, Koffer, Flughafenticket, Hotelbuchung, Rucksack, Kamera, Wanderkarte, Führerschein, Stadtführer, Reiseapotheke
Lebensverändernde Entscheidung	Wohnungskauf, Hauskauf, Führerschein, Neues Auto, Reisepass, Kreditvertrag, Ehevertrag, Adoptionspapiere, Jobangebot, Rentenbescheid
Kulturelles Erlebnis	Museum, Kunstgalerie, Theaterstück, Konzerthalle, Kulturfestival, Filmfestival, Oper, Buchmesse, Kunstwerk, Tanzaufführung
Herausforderung/ Überwindung	Krankheit, Schwierige Entscheidung, Finanzielle Probleme, Trennung, Mobbing, Arbeitslosigkeit, Umzug, Studienabbruch, Naturkatastrophe, Unfall
Freundschaft	Freund, Freundin, Geschenk, Gemeinsames Essen, Kaffeetasse, Kino, Picknick, Reise, Geburtstag, Chat
Gesundheit/ Wohlbefinden	Vitamin D, Yoga, Meditation, Ernährung, Fitnessstudio, Laufen, Schwimmen, Gesundheitscheck, Stressbewältigung, Seele

Table 15: List of German event types and objects used in prompt templates to create diverse event descriptions.

Subset	Baseline	PC	PCR
Anger	Absprache, Versicherung, Trauerarbeit, Erzfeind, Lieblingsparkplatz, Observatoriums, Teilnehmers, Spielern, Stellenabbau, Respekt	Absprachen, Assistent, Agentur, Gebühr, Konto, Alex, Fotograf, Fokuskriterien, Initiativen, Täuschung	Assistent, Antiquitäten, Ärzten, Begründung, Gebühr, Recruiter, Alex, Lüge, Wasservorrat, Jäger
Boredom	Beschäftigung, Kaffeemaschine, Radfahrer, Betriebsfeier, Lautstärke, Meeresboden, Kajaklehrer, DartPartner, Fischsandwich, Zeltbau	Preisträger, Wiederholung, Fusion, Gewohnheit, Rednerin, Formulare, Ritual, Festivalgelände, Putzen, Organisatorin	Preisträger, Fusion, Schema, Rednerin, Kreditberater, Saals, Jahrhundert, Besuchs, Erzählabende, Unterbrechung
Disgust	Geschäftsmann, Werbeplakaten, Wirklichkeit, Betrüger, Skandal, Substanz, Korruption, Chemikalien, Umweltverschmutzer, Gärtnerei	Praktiken, Skandale, Korruption, Verschmutzung, Substanz, Abfälle, Bestechungsgelder, Umfragen, Beweise, Handschuhe	Korruption, Chemikalien, Verschmutzung, Substanz, Lieblingskandidatin, Schmutz, Bestechungsgelder, Prinzipien, Praktiken, Reinigung
Fear	Gefahren, Investition, Hai, Unbekannten, Mietvertrags, Sicherheitsrisiken, Serie, Päckchen, Zielland, Bergwerk	Drohung, Geschäftstreffen, Gestalt, Personalabbau, Arbeitseinsatz, Überfälle, Absender, Heiler, Spuren, Bankkonto	Prophezeiung, Absender, Deals, Anonymität, MonatsTicket, Heiler, Fußschmerzen, Drohung, Knarren, Unterholz
Guilt	Geige, Urgroßvaters, Meeresschildkröte, Preisgeld, Sponsorenliste, Komposition, Geburtstagsjungen, Krampf, Budgets, Hotelbesitzer	Tänzerinnen, Oma, Regel, Handeln, Reisebegleiterin, Diaspora, Kaffeetasse, Einfluss, Kulturarbeit, Wartung	Oma, Opa, ExPartnerin, Reisebegleiterin, Mentee, Omas, Kaffeetasse, Neffen, Telefonanruf, Schläger
Joy	Arbeitsdruck, Uhrzeit, Winter, Fangmethoden, Kajaktrip, Geldstrafe, Angelgeräts, Unachtsamkeit, Spender, Testaments	Terminen, Halle, Tuch, Schauer, Startbahn, Verantwortliche, Schwimmkurs, backstage, Sicherheitsproblem, Hausarbeiten	Kunstmärkte, Soundsystem, Tuch, Ski, Melodie, backstage, Finanzlücke, Beine, Korrekturplan, Sicherheitsproblem
Pride	Gemeinschaft, Projektteams, Freiwilliger, Sohn, Wanderern, Höhle, Rückschlag, MarathonTraining, Testfahrt, Okay	Schützling, Neffe, Beweis, Integration, Arbeitslosigkeit, Version, Gartenmarkt, Schnorchel, Bocciaplätzen, Fernschuss	Ausdauer, Schützling, Geschwisterkind, Neffe, Lernmethode, Restauration, Tunnels, Unterrichtsmethode, Bocciaplätzen, Fernschuss
Relief	Gewitterregen, Verluste, Beobachtung, Umleitung, Strafe, Flop, Verlegenheit, Einflüssen, Leck, Blitz	Druckerei, Soundsystem, Sonnenbrille, Tradition, Vorsichtsmaßnahmen, Bühnendekoration, Symptomen, Kontrahent, Hitze, Abwasserrohr	Sandbau, Koordination, Druckerei, Tanzlied, Sonnenbrille, Hauptkünstler, Forschungsmethode, Deutschland, Fieber, Kontrahent
Sadness	Falle, Exposition, Schlittschuhe, Skiführer, Kameraden, Opa, Tauchabenteuer, Vogelpfleger, Ladenfenster, Zeltkonstruktion	Opa, Oma, Grab, Opas, ExPartnerin, Tod, Mentors, Trennungsmitteilung, Kühlschrank, Lieblingsgericht	Opa, Oma, Grab, Tänzerinnen, Omas, Kochbuch, Gedenkgang, Gentrifizierung, Opas, Auflösung
Shame	Hündin, Leichtigkeit, Korb, Gläser, Zeltstadt, Riss, Hans, Feigling, Sicherungsmaßnahmen, Vorkenntnisse	Affäre, Folien, Blogbeitrag, Ehre, Fastenkur, Katze, Date, Alkohol, Aktionen, Unwissenheit	Gartenparty, Defizite, Rückenprobleme, Fastenkur, Drohung, Anführer, Lüge, Agile, Abriss, Alkohol
Surprise	Kleinigkeit, Kritiken, Besucherzahl, Currywurst, Klarheit, Vorsprung, Bewerbungsfrist, Tagesordnung, Projektmanagement, Mitarbeiterentwicklung	Paddel, Kindheitserinnerungen, Erblasser, Adoptionsagentur, Max, Symbole, Partei, Angelplatz, Ornithologe, Geeignetes	Kontinuität, Erblasser, Menschenrechtsverletzungen, Schaben, Hauptinterpret, Operationssaal, Volunteers, Werbeanzeige, Paddel, Max
Trust	Lebensumständen, Regenschirm, Handwerker, Mitgefühl, Praxis, Studie, Instituts, Streckenänderungen, Wettbewerbsort, Verwaltung	Anna, Fremde, Einheimische, Projektmanagerin, Instructor, Wildnis, Bergführer, Fuße, Anbieter, Erzählabende	Anna, Instructor, Alex, Projektmanagerin, Mentors, Organisatorin, Berghütte, Lehrers, Umsatzrückgang, Formfehlers
No-Emotion	Wärme, Seils, Dartpfeilwerfer, Kopfhörer, Favoritenteam, Fährverbindung, Campen, Sprungturm, Warteschlangen, Idole	Festaktes, Einsatzort, Tauchen, Formalität, Eingriff, Bewegungen, Emotionen, Riss, Forscherin, RoutineÜberprüfung	Agentur, FitnessApp, Institut, Pflichtgefühl, Festwagen, Begründung, streit, Organizer, Forscherin, Protokoll

Table 16: Top 10 tf-idf nouns in event chains generated by different methods based on event Set 3.

Subset	Baseline	PC	PCR
Wut	Enkel, Partyplanerin, Prüfer, Zustimmung, Stressbewältigung, Fleisch, Begründung, Büros, Horoskops, Lieblingsbluse	Bau, Begründung, Punktzahl, Einbeziehung, Versicherungsvertreter, Verursacher, Gesundheitsinitiative, Schwangere, Kur, Traumstelle	Gleichgültigkeit, Petition, Eiscreme, Punktzahl, Umweltschützers, Teamsitzung, Versicherungsvertreter, Verursacher, Gesundheitsinitiative, Schwangere
Langeweile	Dutzende, Tatendrang, Kursabschluss, Lieblingskleidung, Schuljahr, Fußballspiel, Marathonlauf, Lieblingsserie, Überraschungspartys, Gleichgültigkeit	Leistungssportler, Dach, Kletterparcours, Abenteuerurlaub, Verleihung, Retreat, Haustier, Mittag, Stellenbeschreibungen, Familienaktivitäten	Kletterparcours, Schneemassen, Erzählabend, Abenteuerurlaub, Leistungssportler, Retreat, Karriereperspektiven, Stellenbeschreibungen, Setlist, Komponisten
Ekel	Ölfass, Literaturleser, Substanz, Fußball, Frettchen, Verunreinigung, Pestizid, Artikeln, Märkten, Psychologen	Skandale, Hygiene, Beweise, Hygienestandards, Praktiken, Korruption, Geschäftspraktiken, Unregelmäßigkeiten, Betrug, Verschmutzung	Geschäftspraktiken, Korruption, Hygienestandards, Skandale, Beweise, Hygiene, Ausbeutung, Insekten, Vorwürfe, Maden
Angst	Heißluftballons, Tänzerinnen, Horrorfilm, Einbrüche, Fotoshoot, Elfmeter, Tauchzertifizierung, Moderatoren, Anrufer, Kriminalitätsraten	Wilderer, Absender, Athletin, Unruhen, Hautpflegeserie, KI, Vorsicht, Nachrichtenmeldung, Wanderpartner, Artefakt	Artefakts, Athletin, Allergie, Wilderer, Phänomenen, Waldbrand, Familiengeheimnisse, Überfällen, Diebstählen, Unruhen
Schuld	Bekanntschaft, Gesprächstages, Schwägerin, Wohnwagen, Umweltbranche, Helm, Geldbeutel, Nichte, Gehaltserhöhung, Grill	Gedicht, RollerSkates, Ex, Serum, Warnschilder, Geheimnisses, Sicherheitsbeauftragte, Handlungen, Bräutigam, Schlafsäcke	Versuchung, RollerSkates, Medikation, Gedicht, Fokussierung, Karpfenpopulation, Kunsthandwerks, Organisationsgruppe, Museumsmanagement, Serum
Freude	Führungsteam, Hartarbeit, Fahrunterricht, Gartenhaus, Reitstundenlehrer, Reagenz, Fähnchen, Mitarbeiterunzufriedenheit, Rekrutierungsstrategien, Familientreffend	Enkelin, Monatskarte, Familientag, Ehepaar, Diskussionskultur, Gartenarbeit, Doktorvater, Hochzeitstag, Lauftraining, Nationalparks	Enkelin, Monatskarte, Lieblingsband, Lieblingsspieler, Zeltplatz, Lauftraining, Familientag, Street, Nationalparks, Himmels
Stolz	Bau, App, Sandkasten, Schlüsselpersonen, Schmuckkasten, Restaurierung, Sohn, Herstellung, Wellnesstuch, Technikzelts	Prototyp, Schatz, Rekrutierungskampagne, Bestätigungen, Rettungsteams, Mediation, Standort, Lummerkasten, Trail, Schneebesens	Prototyp, Improvisation, Rekrutierungskampagne, Bestätigungen, Grenzpassage, Mediation, Zeltlagers, Verletzten, Schneebesens, Perfektionierung
Erleichterung	Systemen, Grundbedürfnisse, Überschwemmungen, Fotobox, Ausweise, Schließung, Horizont, Aktion, Arbeitsplätze, Stocken	Segel, Trophäe, Gegenstand, Campingausflugs, Fristen, Projektteilnehmer, Thermometer, Pannen, Schlimmste, Max	Trophäe, Segel, Strafstoß, Berufswechsel, Campingausflugs, Zwangsräumung, Thermometer, Gegenstand, Pannen, Max
Traurigkeit	Trauer, Grab, Weggang, Tanzfest, Retreat, Pfleger, Grill, Kochausbildung, Sammeln, Luna	Alex, Wandmalereien, Titel, Maschine, Abschiedsfeier, ExFreund, Fitnesspartner, Abschiedsausstellung, Schmuckstück, Teamleader	Alex, Großvater, ExFreund, Maschine, ExPartner, ExFreundin, Abschiedsfeier, Lachens, Fitnesspartner, Wandmalereien
Scham	Lungen, Held, Kunstwettbewerb, Challenge, Aufschrift, Markttages, YogaStunde, Angelwettbewerb, Haken, Benzin	Fehlverhalten, Steak, Marktforschungskampagne, Shooting, Theatergruppe, Mahnung, Witz, Alkohol, Instrument, Wahrheit	Lüge, Steak, Verhaltens, Alkohol, Zelts, Marktforschungskampagne, Theatergruppe, Produzenten, Fehlverhalten, Behauptungen
Überraschung	Ankündigungen, Abteilungsleiterin, Versicherungspolicy, Nachbarin, Schneeschuhwandern, Torpedoschlauch, Annahme, Rennort, Tokio, Laternenpfahl	Reitstiefel, EliteSchule, Starre, Gemeinschaftsraums, Schneeschuhe, Band, Mittag, Bar, Telefonats, Surfausflug	Sternen, Reitstiefel, EliteSchule, Schneeschuhe, Reisepass, Band, Highlights, Therapien, Ehrengäste, Bar
Vertrauen	Ausstellungsleitung, Ashram, Reformierung, Fotobuch, Sprachkenntnisse, Außenseiters, Hartarbeit, Beobachtungsplatzes, Weggabelung, Skitour	Beratungsgespräch, Mentorin, Webseite, Gründlichkeit, Kommunikations, Neubeginn, Vogelart, Surflehrer, Bauch, Rudertour	Eiche, Beratungsgespräch, Schlittenführer, Webseite, Mentorin, Navigation, Erkenntnissen, Gegenseite, Einheimische, Kurslehrer
keine_ Emotion	Gelassenheit, Kasse, Verlangen, Ritual, Siege, Kletteraufstieg, Priorität, Handbuchs, Bürogebäudes, Personalabteilungsleiterin	Rollern, HobbyAbend, Sportgeräte, Auswahlkomitee, Meditationssession, Faktoren, Abschnitte, Flamme, Reflektion, Elektroautos	Meditationssession, HobbyAbend, Sportgeräte, JobShadowing, Patientin, Abstieg, ordnung, Auswahlkomitee, Vertrautheit, Stürme

Table 17: Top 10 tf-idf nouns in event chains generated by different methods based on event Set 4.

Multimodal Docker Unified UIMA Interface: New Horizons for Distributed Microservice-Oriented Processing of Corpora using UIMA

Daniel Bundan **Giuseppe Abrami** **Alexander Mehler**
{bundan • abrami • mehler}@em.uni-frankfurt.de
Goethe University Frankfurt / Texttechnology

Abstract

In addition to textual corpora, there are multimodal corpora that contain a significant amount of data from a variety of codes (e.g., iconographic, textual) that are currently made processable by only a few tools. What the research community needs here is an effective, distributed system that provides a processing pipeline for the integration of reusable tools for analyzing such corpora. Such systems currently exist for text corpora, but rarely for video corpora. We present Multimodal Docker Unified UIMA Interface as an extension of DUUI that fills this gap by enabling annotation and processing of video corpora based on the UIMA standard.

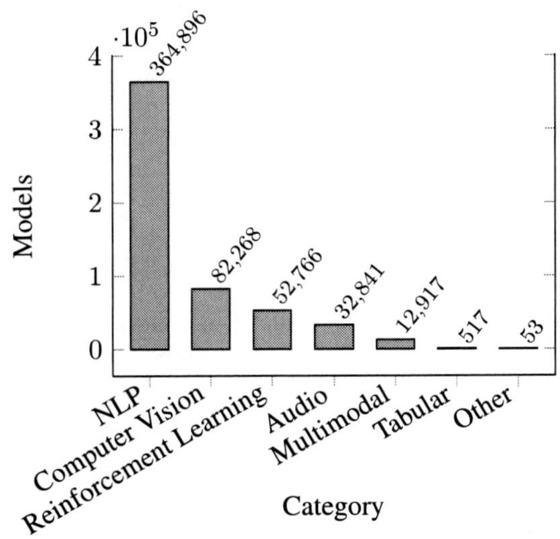

Figure 1: Models per huggingface category, downloaded end of January 2025.

1 Introduction

The collection and processing of data by means of efficient, horizontally and vertically distributed systems is a challenge for various disciplines such as linguistics (Abdurakhmonova et al., 2022; Samardzic et al., 2024), biodiversity (Gabud et al., 2023; Folk et al., 2024), medicine (Sabra et al., 2017; Masoumi et al., 2024), social sciences (Burley et al., 2020; Gone and Smit, 2024), and others. Especially for large corpora this challenge is addressed mainly by individual, non-integrated approaches (Abrami et al., 2025). In any case, most models for processing of corpora are in the area of NLP, e.g. 364,896 models in Hugging Face (see Figure 1). While the size of text corpora is large (e.g. newspaper corpora (Süddeutsche Zeitung: 1,711,285 texts (Süddeutscher Verlag, 2014), New York Times: 3,078,034 texts (New York Times, 2019)), parliamentary corpora (about 6.3 million texts (Rauh and Schwalbach, 2020)) and Wikipedia (Pasternack and Roth, 2008) (about 6.9 million articles for English)), they are rather small compared to the volume of YouTube, which contains over 9 billion videos (McGrady et al., 2023) (this number is an estimate, as YouTube does not publish it). Moreover, 400 hours of video data are reportedly uploaded every minute (in 2015). The analysis of the multimodal content of this data shows a tendency to analyze multidimensional information, e.g. of videos (Knapp et al., 2021; Leo et al., 2022; Li et al., 2022), audios (Latha et al., 2022; Madhavi et al., 2024; Lavanya et al., 2024), images (Pino et al., 2020; Ashok Kumar et al., 2020; Martinez, 2022) and gestures (Yang et al., 2009). Overall, the multitude of such data collections represents a large resource of publicly available data that has been little developed or processed (Thanneru et al., 2023).

To overcome this limitation and to process corpora in a unified, horizontally and vertically scaled, schema-based way, Docker Unified UIMA Interface (Leonhardt et al., 2023) was developed, which uses the *UIMA* (Ferrucci et al., 2009) framework as its annotation basis. UIMA (*Unstructured Information Management Architecture*) allows the various modalities of information to be managed. It can be serialized in XMI and operates as a standalone annotation format that allows unstructured data to be annotated based on UIMA TypeSystems (annotation schema). With this, a UIMA document, which can be used efficiently within Java, consists of a number of *Views* $(1, \ldots, n-1)$, in which annotations are applied and which can each contain a SofA (**S**ubject **of** **A**nalysis), which contains the annotation item consisting of unstructured information. In addition to its serializability, UIMA is characterized by its extensibility and the ability to be used within different databases (Fette et al., 2013; Abrami and Mehler, 2018). UIMA supports multiple modalities by definition, but only in a few projects (e.g. Allasia et al. (2008); Yang et al. (2009); Yu et al. (2009); Grivolla et al. (2014)) respectively, in regards of the Log4j issue (Hiesgen et al., 2022) which also affected Apache DUCC (Distributed UIMA Cluster Computing), this is more than limited. Note that some of the projects have not been updated for over 10 years. And the implemented UIMA *TypeSystems* have not been published either, nor have the innovations of that time found their way into the UIMA project, which means they cannot be reused.

To use UIMA for multimodal corpus analysis and integrate it into an existing big data framework for distributed NLP processing, MULTIMODAL DOCKER UNIFIED UIMA INTERFACE (MU-DUUI) was developed which is licensed under an AGPL-License and available on GitHub[1]. We introduce MU-DUUI as a multimodal enhancement to DUUI and present a series of modular extensions that go beyond the use of MU-DUUI, but also extend the UIMA standard by gathering, processing and analysis of different types of input formats beyond written text, such as videos, audio, images and, in perspective, other formats such as time series data, motion and gestures data or other complex data structures. Even though UIMA is less frequently used as a data format compared to CoNLL (Tjong Kim Sang and De Meulder, 2003) or TCF (Heid et al., 2010), the native multimodal utilization capacities nevertheless provides a stable and robust foundation for use in MU-DUUI. At the same time, the use of MU-DUUI helps to bring the possibilities of UIMA into the focus of the scientific community. There is no explicit target group for the use of MU-DUUI, as it is a general framework that is suitable for everyone who wants to perform automatic big data NLP processes. Based on the diversity as well as the everyday use of NLP routines in scientific contexts, and building on existing work (Leonhardt et al., 2023), the following definition provides a set of features for organizing multimodal annotation systems:

(A) **Multi-Layer-Annotation**: Splitting an analysis into layers is critical for processing different types of information. This facilitates the analysis of each type individually, and allows the results of multiple types to be cross-referenced within a single pipeline.

(B) **Multimodality**: Since we do not only communicate linguistically, it is necessary to map sign structures based on different modalities.

(C) **Distributed processing**: In the context of large corpora, distributed and parallelized processing is an important criterion for resource efficiency. The aim is to achieve both horizontal (across multiple nodes in a network) and vertical (multiple instances on a single hardware node) processing, while reusing existing scaling methods and execution environments.

(D) **Schema-based**: To ensure a unified approach to processing and annotating multimodal corpora, a codified scheme is needed that is extensible and established to avoid proprietary approaches.

(E) **Reusability**: Many methods and models are changing rapidly due to the fast pace of development, especially in the case of hub systems such as huggingface[2]. It is essential to ensure that models are reusable and that their results are reproducible, regardless of this process.

(F) **Transposability**: In addition to the multitude of different annotation methods and models, there is also a wide range of annotation formats that should be used as input or output formats (e.g. Fäth and Chiarcos (2022)).

(G) **Web and API-Based**: For platform independence, tools should have a web-based and, ideally, an API-based interface for analysis and interpretation of unstructured data.

[1] DockerUnifiedUIMAInterface

[2] https://huggingface.co/

The paper is structured as follows: Section 2 presents use cases for the application of multimodal pre-processing followed by related work in Section 3. Section 4 explains MU-DUUI and its extension before an evaluation in Section 5. The paper concludes with future work in Section 6 and a conclusion in Section 7.

2 Use Cases

The need for multimodal annotation tools is particularly relevant in application scenarios that a) do not have direct text occurrences or b) consist of a mixed data set: This is evident in popular social media platforms such as YouTube, Instagram, and TikTok, which focus mainly on video, audio, and image content. In this context, publicly uploaded data can be automatically enriched with annotations, providing information that is relevant for the organizations operating the platforms as well as for third parties who want to use this information for scientific purposes, such as analyzing user behavior in the context of multimodal content (e.g. Kaushik et al. (2013); Schulz et al. (2020); Amin et al. (2022); Jerin et al. (2024); Sharma and Peng (2024)). These annotations could feed transcription, translation, speaker diarization, summarization, fact-checking, and similarity detection, among other tasks. In addition to these tasks, annotations from different modalities can be combined to provide more robust results, such as in speaker diarization: Instead of relying only on audio cues or mouth movements in video frames, both outputs could be combined to provide better results. Furthermore, video analysis is not limited to transcription, as information about eye, face, or body movements, facial expressions (Mellouk and Handouzi, 2020), and general image segmentation for speaker recognition can also be performed and annotated. At the same time, the functionalities implemented by MU-DUUI are also of great importance for projects dealing with surveys (e.g. project *Critical Online Reasoning in Higher Education* (CORE) Research Unit CORE (2023)), which generate large multimodal data collections, including the websites visited (images), mouse and scroll movements, and eye tracking.

3 Related Work

Due to the automatic processing of unstructured and multimodal entities through DUUI, the following listing only includes automatic tools and compares them with the defined features, which means that well-known manual tools such as *Multimodal Annotation Software Tool* (Cardoso and Cohn, 2022), *AnnoTheia* (Acosta-Triana et al., 2024), *Label Studio* (Tkachenko et al., 2020-2025), *AMUSED* (Shahi and Majchrzak, 2022), *Visual Inspection Tool* (Di Mitri et al., 2019) as well as *EUMSSI* (Grivolla et al., 2014)) are not considered. Overall, it can be observed that only a few tools enable purely automatic annotation of multimodal data regardless of whether the criteria in Section 1 are achieved (see Table 1).

UniVL (Luo et al., 2020) is a self-supervised learning tool for video and speech representation consisting of various encoders and a decoder using a transformer backbone to recognize frames, and a video-text alignment module to generate text from video. This partially fulfills feature (A), as videos can be processed and a text generated from it can be represented; the same partially applies to feature (B), as only videos can be processed. Furthermore, there is no support for distributed processing (C) and reusability (E) and transposability (F) is also only possible in a laborious way, as new models would have to be implemented instead of integrating them in a schematized way. The same applies to the absence of an annotation schema (D), as well as the non-existence of an API (G).

Another tool, *SVA* (Streamlining Video Summarization – Alqurni et al. (2025)), enables the summarization of videos using different NLP techniques. It integrates various NLP libraries and algorithms to enable a multimodal video summarization, whereby these processes can be controlled via a graphical and web-based user interface. Although SVA is a tool that shows an impressive implementation, the possible applications are limited to the described use case, although features (A), (B) and (G) are fulfilled. Irrespective of this, distributed processing (C) is not possible and (F) can only be implemented if the application is enhanced. Furthermore, an annotation schema (D) exists only insofar as a JSON export is available.

Last but not least, *SparkNLP* (Kocaman and Talby, 2021) is a distributed framework that provides pipelines for processing various input types for the subsequent use of NLP methods. For this, SparkNLP uses *Apache Spark*[3] for a distributed execution of various pipelines, whereby a Java and Python variant is available. Although SparkNLP is not directly designed for processing multimodal

[3] https://spark.apache.org/

No.	Tool	Reference	A	B	C	D	E	F	G
1	UniVL	Luo et al. (2020)	partially satisfied	partially satisfied	not satisfied	not satisfied	not satisfied	not satisfied	not satisfied
2	SVS	Alqurni et al. (2025)	satisfied	satisfied	not satisfied	partially satisfied	not satisfied	partially satisfied	satisfied
3	SparkNLP	Kocaman and Talby (2021)	satisfied	satisfied	partially satisfied	partially satisfied	partially satisfied	partially satisfied	satisfied
4	MU-DUUI		satisfied	satisfied	satisfied	satisfied	satisfied	partially satisfied	not satisfied

Table 1: Comparison of automatic annotation tools for multimodal corpora, considering the criteria defined in Section 1. Legend: satisfied (■), partially satisfied ( ), not satisfied (■).

data, it can be extended in this direction, as demonstrated in Section 5. As a result, SparkNLP fulfills the features (A), (B) and (C) for regular and text-related NLP processes, but only to a limited extent for pipelines that are too comprehensive or multimodal. In addition, reusability (E) is possible insofar as new pipeline components can be integrated, but there is the usual restriction on the use of different implementations, since Python processes can only be effectively integrated into Java to a limited level (F). SparkNLP is a versatile tool with a wide range of functions and methods that allow multiple applications, although a multimodal utilization is only feasible within a restricted scope.

As a result of the absence of a distributed, flexible and schema-based solution for the automatic and distributed automatic processing of multimodal corpora which can be used independently of platform and programming language, MU-DUUI was developed, which will be described in the next section:

4 MU-DUUI

As shown in the previous sections, there is a need for automatic and effective processing of multimodal corpora and their reusability in a unified format and process. In order to present the features implemented in MU-DUUI, it is necessary to give a brief overview of the functionality of DUUI. DUUI uses different preprocessing methods that are distributed in microservices, allowing a wide range of heterogeneous analysis tools to be used in a homogeneous environment. This is realized by using Docker (Merkel, 2014) images, which can be automatically orchestrated in different runtime environments (Docker, Kubernetes (Abrami et al., 2025)) and together form a pipeline of so-called COMPONENTs, which are used for distributed and parallel processing of unstructured UIMA documents, fulfilling feature (C). In addition, the microservice-oriented architecture achieves a form of reproducibility (feature (E)), since the individual COMPONENTs contain the underlying models in the Docker image without having to reload them all the time. Implemented in Java, DUUI allows for modular extensibility, where new runtime environments for orchestrating COMPONENTs can be implemented easily. As a result, the extensions needed for MU-DUUI are just as elegantly integrated into DUUI without interfering with the existing pipeline and processing routine. The multimodal processing of unstructured information is realized by methods available in UIMA, which by definition satisfies the features (D) and (F). Although (D) is fully satisfied, (F) is only partially satisfied in that an export routine must be implemented for each export format if it is not already available.

MU-DUUI extends DUUI by enabling the processing of multimodal unstructured documents for annotation and analysis, fully reusing and extending existing DUUI functionality. Accordingly, MU-DUUI builds on UIMA's multi-layered functionality, called *Views*, and allows them to be mapped to COMPONENTs, creating a seamless way to use multiple *Views* within a single pipeline and without the need to customize anything else, thus fulfilling feature (A). In addition to the annotations, each view also contains a subject of analysis (SofA) and a mime type that specifies the modality of the SofA. By combining this with the use of multiple layers, multiple modalities can be used within an analysis, thus satisfying feature (B).

4.1 Architecture

MU-DUUI is completely based on DUUI and extends its functionality by integrating three complementary elements as explained in Section 4.2.

MU-DUUI processes UIMA-based documents in a pipeline architecture based on DUUI and consisting of COMPONENTs executed within microservices as shown in Figure 2. These extensions allow UIMA readers and specialized DUUI readers to

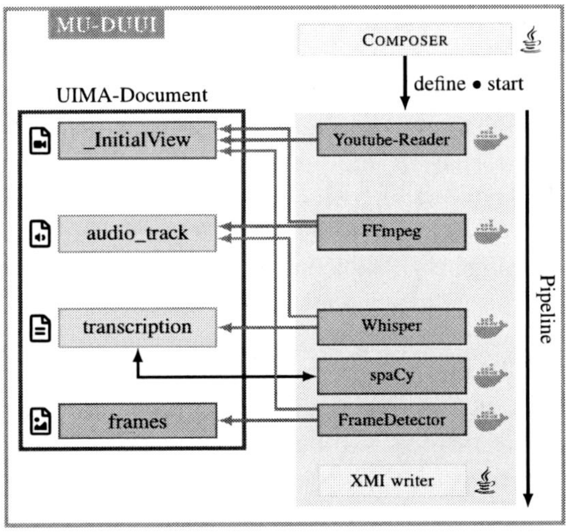

Figure 2: Walkthrough for creating multimodal UIMA documents: MU-DUUI consists of a pipeline that generates the appropriate number of UIMA documents based on a list of videos (in this example, from YouTube). During this process, the particular video is downloaded by the COMPONENT **YouTube-Reader** and serialized within the *_InitialView* (mimetype *video/mp4*). According to the pipeline definition, each COMPONENT is associated with a source or target view used for processing. For example, **Whisper** is used to extract the video data from the *_InitialView* to create a transcription in the *transcription* view (mimetype *video/mp4*). At the end of each pipeline, a YouTube video is represented by a UIMA document that contains different views with representations associated with the video. In addition, the **spaCy**-COMPONENT annotates the transcription with common linguistic features.

load and serialize content other than just text. Each COMPONENT in the pipeline can be customized to determine which *view* (source) to select the information for the analysis process and to which *view* (target) to annotate the results. By specifying a view as source or target, nothing inside the COMPONENTs created for DUUI needs to be changed, since the usage is analogous, i.e. existing COMPONENTs can also be used with MU-DUUI, as for example with the spaCy-COMPONENT (Honnibal et al., 2020). In order to represent and reuse multimodal content, a new *TypeSystem* is required, as well as a utility class that allows the selection of the respective annotated data, which will be explained in the next section.

4.2 Pillars of Multimodality

Extending DUUI for multimodal analysis of unstructured information requires three essential features, which are visualized in Figure 3. In this case,

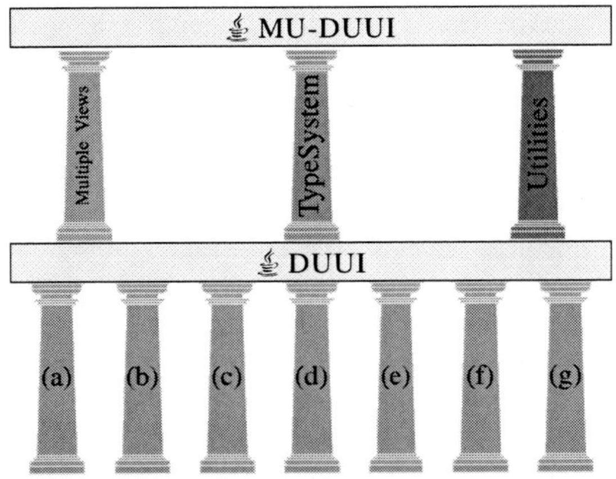

Figure 3: Multiple pillars for multimodal data analysis in MU-DUUI as a unified framework: The blue pillars, representing the features and thus the basis of DUUI, include, among other things, horizontal and vertical processing using microservices, a detailed error management, the integration of heterogeneous annotations and implementation landscapes, and the integration of reproducible and reusable annotations.

MU-DUUI is completely based on DUUI and extends its functionality without compromising the existing features, but taking advantage of them.

Multiple Views

To map and process multimodal content, the ability to distinguish and transcode between different encoding systems is essential. This means that unstructured content can be visualized, analyzed, modified, and correlated in a variety of ways. In this regard, UIMA provides a unified approach to handle all aspects in a single file format with multiple layers, called *Views*, available in a UIMA document. This allows users to organize the unstructured information into different aspects, where distinctions can be defined by Mime Type as well as by content (Abrami et al., 2020). Each view contains a *SofA* which is created at runtime and cannot be modified, but which can accommodate different formats based on its mime type and serves as the basis for processing the individual analyses performed by COMPONENTs. In addition, by importing them into MU-DUUI and within Java, the UIMA documents are represented as CAS objects (Common Analysis Structure) and contain all annotations and enable operations on them. In order to implement different aspects in different views, this functionality requires integration into MU-DUUI without affecting the existing COMPONENT structure and functionality, which was achieved by extending the

COMPOSER architecture. As simplified in Figure 2, the COMPOSER architecture controls the pipeline of the individual COMPONENTs defined for the processing of UIMA documents. Each component is provided with the information necessary to use different views by extending the specification of the parameters in the COMPONENT definition of the source and target views (see also Figure 5); if no parameters are specified, the default view (*_InitialView*) is used.

Since DUUI implements UIMA, the use of multiple UIMA views per document is possible, but may lead to inconveniences. This is due to the fact that each DUUI COMPONENT had to declare their used view names on their own, which cannot be changed without altering the COMPONENT's source code. So everything will work fine as long as the new COMPONENT's annotations are not needed by other COMPONENTs in the pipeline. However, if later COMPONENTs need access to the added view's annotations, problems may occur if the COMPONENTs source view is hardcoded to an incorrect view name. MU-DUUI fixes this problem: when creating an analysis pipeline in MU-DUUI, the user can specify both the source and target view for each COMPONENT used, where the source view specifies which view's content should be analyzed, and the target view specifies where the results should be written. If a specified source or target view does not exist, it is automatically created, so the user does not have to worry about it. The implemented system has the advantage that views can be changed on the fly, and COMPONENT creators do not have to worry about views or possible naming conventions. Figure 2 illustrates an example for the use of multiple views based on a video analysis. For backward compatibility, older COMPONENTs do not need to be adjusted and are automatically provided with the selected views. The default view ($\_InitialView$) of a CAS object is passed to its COMPONENT if no view is explicitly selected.

TypeSystem

A *TypeSystem* is an essential part of UIMA, as TypeSystems are used to define an annotation scheme for the documents, which can be organized into a number of different primitives as well as more complex data structures such as classes. A distinction must be made between classes from the UIMA core and custom class structures that should inherit from UIMA classes to ensure appropriate functionality. These base classes include the classes `Annotation` and `AnnotationBase`; the latter represents the base class for annotations of all kinds without stand-off information, Annotation inherits from it and contains stand-off information by means of begin and end information, which addresses the location of the annotations in the unstructured *SofA* content (see Figure 4). Although the UIMA classes provide the basis for annotation, they are intended more for addressing annotations in textual SofA and are not directly suitable for annotating multimodal content such as video, audio, and image information. Since there is also no TypeSystem available for this purpose from previous projects (c.f. Section 1), a multimodal extension was introduced as part of MU-DUUI.

As shown in the class diagram (Figure 4), the multimodal extension consists of three central classes that can be flexibly extended and adapted to new requirements. To this end, the `MultimodalElement` class is the base class for `VideoToken` and `AudioToken`, which provide a start and end timestamp through their superclass. `VideoTokens` can be used to annotate video segments, while `AudioTokens` are used in the transcription process to store information about what was said at what time interval. Furthermore, the class for `Images` not only represents a source for storing the file location or, preferably, the encoded file data itself, it also contains information about the dimensions of an image. This means that `Images` can be used to annotate standalone images as well as video frames, using different views. Finally, the class for `Subimages` allows you to annotate the segmentation of an image that itself consists of a polygonal shape.

Utilities

Utility classes provide essential functionality for interacting with CAS documents, such as the well-known *JCasUtil* provided by UIMA for annotation selection and nesting. By using the previously mentioned `Annotation` class to select annotations from the stand-off representation, this class can be used to process multimodal content directly, allowing only the textual content of annotations to be extracted using SofA. This requires an extension for multimodal selection of annotated content, which is implemented in the class `MultimodalUtil` within MU-DUUI. With this class, video and audio data can be extracted based on the annotated timestamps defined by the `MultimodalElement` class,

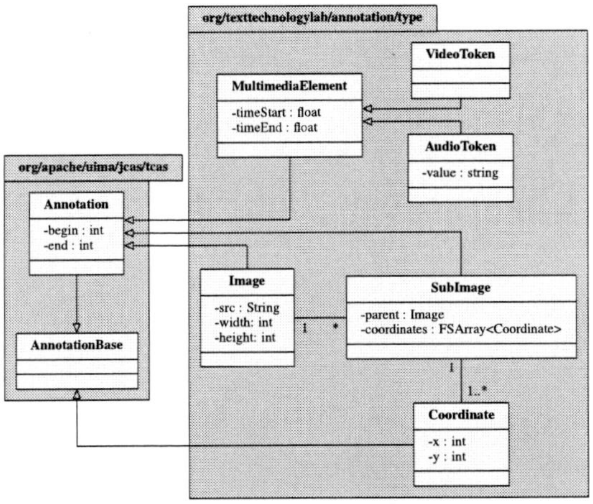

Figure 4: UML class diagram of basic added types.

which facilitates stand-alone multimodal annotations. Combined with other annotations, segments of audio or video elements can be selected based on text-based annotations. To achieve this functionality, the advanced *FFmpeg*[4] library is used, which must be installed on the host system. In addition, the user can provide any annotation that inherits from the UIMA ANNOTATION class.

An analogous usage exists for the extraction and operation with annotated images. In this case, the IMAGE annotation is used together with the corresponding SUBIMAGE by cropping the polygons defined in the subimages from the original image and serializing them (cf. Abrami et al. (2015)). For an example of how to use `MultimodalUtil`, see Figure 5, at line 29.

5 Evaluation

For the evaluation of MU-DUUI, a performance comparison was performed in which the transcription of videos were executed. For this purpose, a sample of 100 videos from the *YouTube Commons Corpus* (PleIAs, 2024) with an average duration of 729.01 seconds (12.15 minutes) was used, whereby only german-speaking videos were selected. To this end, the videos were transcribed with *WhisperX* (Bain et al., 2023) and the result was serialized in a text file for each video. Furthermore, to avoid possible deviations due to time-consuming and possibly latency-induced delays while downloading, the videos were downloaded in advance so that this aspect was excluded from the evaluation. For the evaluation, *SparkNLP* was selected since it also enables the distributed execution of various NLP tasks and is most comparable to MU-DUUI (see Table 1). This evaluation task was implemented in the Python variant of *SparkNLP*, as a native integration of *WhisperX* (which uses Python) is not possible in the Java implementation. Unfortunately, it turned out that even in the Python version of *SparkNLP*, *WhisperX* could not be integrated as a pipeline, since it is not intended for this type of task, which required a workaround via a separate REST service that hosts *WhisperX*. Furthermore, the transcription task was performed in both tools with the same parameters (model large-v2) using a single GPU (Nvidia L40S), and the processing was performed in one thread without parallelization.

[4] `https://www.ffmpeg.org`

Tool	Time (s)	Avg (s)
SparkNLP	812.94	8.12
MU-DUUI	1,100.18	11.00

Table 2: Result of the evaluation between SparkNLP and MU-DUUI.

The result (Table 2) shows that the evaluation task was solved slightly faster with SparkNLP than with MU-DUUI, but there are some limitations: Before data can be processed in MU-DUUI, it first has to be converted to UIMA, which means the video data has to be encoded in base64. These conversion processes are time-consuming and are not necessary when using video files directly, as in the SparkNLP variant. The result is therefore somewhat biased, but a direct comparison where SparkNLP also uses UIMA is even more inequitable, as existing work (Leonhardt et al., 2023) has shown that UIMA processing in python is a major bottleneck for performance. In addition, the implementation of the task in SparkNLP also shows a significant disadvantage, which is at the same time a strength of MU-DUUI: the encapsulation of annotators as REST services, which cannot be started natively in parallel by SparkNLP.

This demonstrates that, in contrast to MU-DUUI, SparkNLP is not directly suitable for a multimodal use case, whereby the individual dependency problems in the setup of SparkNLP as well as WhisperX were not addressed in this evaluation, which are excluded with MU-DUUI due to the containerization.

6 Future Work

Since the possibilities resulting from MU-DUUI are so extensive that even large multimodal corpora

```
1 // Setting up the reader
2 DUUIAsynchronousProcessor processor = new DUUIAsynchronousProcessor(new DUUIYouTubeReader(/* list of
    video-url's */));

4 // Instantiating composer
5 DUUILuaContext ctx = LuaConsts.getJSON();
6 DUUIComposer composer = new DUUIComposer().withSkipVerification(true).withLuaContext(ctx).withWorkers(iWorkers);
7 composer.addDriver(new DUUIUIMADriver(), new DUUIDockerDriver(), new DUUIKubernetesDriver());

9 // Adding Components to the composer ; Youtube downloader
10 composer.add(new DUUIDockerDriver.Component("yt-dlp:latest").withScale(10)
11         .withSourceView("_InitialView") // Get YT URL from this view
12         .withTargetView("VideoView") // Send the resulting video base64 to this
13         .build());

15 // Transcriber
16 composer.add(new DUUIKubernetesDriver.Component("whisperx:latest").withScale(10)
17         .withSourceView("VideoView") // Read the video base64 from here
18         .withTargetView("TranscriptionView") // Write the transcription to this
19         .withParameter("language", "de").build());

21 // Serialize the result in XMI
22 composer.add(new DUUIUIMADriver.Component(createEngineDescription(XmiWriter.class,
23     XmiWriter.PARAM_TARGET_LOCATION, "/tmp/", XmiWriter.PARAM_COMPRESSION, "GZIP"
24         )).build());

26 // start the processing
27 composer.run(processor, "youtube");
28 /* ... */
29 List<File> videoSegments = MultimodalUtil.getAllCoveredVideo(cas, AudioToken.class);
```

Figure 5: Exemplary use of MU-DUUI and the use of different views used as source and target. In addition, Line 29 exemplifies how the multimodal elements can be accessed at a later point in time.

can be processed with manageable use of resources, it seems appropriate to create large multimodal corpora. In this context, corpora that can be assembled and analyzed from different perspectives are particularly useful:

- **Parliamentary corpora** are usually well-structured corpora that, due to public interest or open data initiatives, provide a large number of individual videos of speeches.
- The existing COMPONENTs **landscape** of DUUI consists mostly of text models, which are now being expanded to include models in different encodings (see Figure 1).
- To optimize the use of MU-DUUI, its integration and encapsulation into a **web and API based application** is planned.
- Finally, the extension described in this paper should be integrated directly into UIMA and **proposed** as an extension to the **standard** in the Apache project.

7 Conclusion

We introduced MU-DUUI as a multimodal extension of DUUI for the automatic processing and analysis of unstructured information of different provenance using the UIMA standard. It enables the annotation, comparison, and reuse of video, audio, images, and other information units in an efficient and distributed manner using a unified analysis approach and a set of extensible tools based on a microservices-oriented architecture using Docker. The evaluation shows that a direct comparison with MU-DUUI is only feasible with considerable effort in relation to the task, as similar tools would have to be adapted for multimodal tasks. Meanwhile, MU-DUUI doesn't always speed up corpus processing in a single and not cluster-based process, but the comparison shows that integrating multimodal tools becomes significantly less tricky and more natural due to its flexibility as well as its platform and implementation independence. Instead of optimizing processing speed alone, MU-DUUI integrates annotations into a UIMA-based model. This leverages interoperability between annotations from different sources, including textual (linguistic) and multimodal (semiotic) annotations. Thus, while better integration comes at the expense of speed, it is accompanied by embedding in a modeling landscape that promises future speed gains. MU-DUUI is designed to extend the existing landscape of textual big data frameworks to evaluate and implement more diverse and combined data analysis approaches.

Limitations

The current implementation of MU-DUUI faces some limitations. This becomes apparent in cases where COMPONENTs needs to write to or read from multiple views. Since the current system only allows for one specification of source and target views, others either have to be hard-coded into the COMPONENT or requested by parameters, which serves as a bypass but is not ideal.

Ethical aspects

This work has been developed with the ACL Code of Ethics in consideration. With our contribution, we would like to provide an innovation in terms of systematic data processing with reference to multimodal corpora. Therefore, due to the subject matter, our contribution does not entail any ethical issues. Regardless of this, in the long run we cannot prevent content that are hurtful, disturbing or even legally prohibited from being processed with our framework. The authors are aware of this situation, but we also respect free research.

References

Nilufar Z. Abdurakhmonova, Alisher S. Ismailov, and Davlatyor Mengliev. 2022. Developing nlp tool for linguistic analysis of turkic languages. In *2022 IEEE International Multi-Conference on Engineering, Computer and Information Sciences (SIBIRCON)*, pages 1790–1793.

Giuseppe Abrami, Markos Genios, Filip Fitzermann, Daniel Baumartz, and Alexander Mehler. 2025. Docker Unified UIMA Interface: New perspectives for NLP on big data. *SoftwareX*, 29:102033.

Giuseppe Abrami and Alexander Mehler. 2018. A UIMA database interface for managing NLP-related text annotations. In *Proceedings of the Eleventh International Conference on Language Resources and Evaluation (LREC 2018)*, LREC 2018, Miyazaki, Japan. European Language Resources Association (ELRA).

Giuseppe Abrami, Alexander Mehler, and Dietmar Pravida. 2015. Fusing Text and Image Data with the Help of the OWLnotator. In Sakae Yamamoto, editor, *Human Interface and the Management of Information. Information and Knowledge Design*, volume 9172 of *Lecture Notes in Computer Science*, pages 261–272. Springer International Publishing.

Giuseppe Abrami, Manuel Stoeckel, and Alexander Mehler. 2020. TextAnnotator: A UIMA based tool for the simultaneous and collaborative annotation of texts. In *Proceedings of the Twelfth Language Resources and Evaluation Conference*, pages 891–900, Marseille, France. European Language Resources Association.

José-M. Acosta-Triana, David Gimeno-Gómez, and Carlos-D Martínez-Hinarejos. 2024. AnnoTheia: A Semi-Automatic Annotation Toolkit for Audio-Visual Speech Technologies. In *The 2024 Joint International Conference on Computational Linguistics, Language Resources and Evaluation (LREC-COLING 2024)*, pages 1260–1269.

Walter Allasia, Fabrizio Falchi, Francesco Gallo, Mouna Kacimi, Aaron Kaplan, Jonathan Mamou, Yosi Mass, and Nicola Orio. 2008. Audio-visual content analysis in p2p networks: The sapir approach. In *2008 19th International Workshop on Database and Expert Systems Applications*, pages 610–614.

Jehad Saad Alqurni, Mutasem K. Alsmadi, Hayat Alfagham, Sharaf Alzoubi, Sohayla Ihab, Ahmed Sameh, Diaa Salama AbdElminaam, and Osamah Ibrahim Khalaf. 2025. Streamlining video summarization with nlp: Techniques, implementation, and future direction. *SN Computer Science*, 6(2).

Al Amin, Hongjie Ma, Romana Alam, Nasim Ahmed Roni, Md. Shazzad Hossain, Erfanul Haque, Alif B Ekram, Redwan Abedin, and Shah Siddiqui. 2022. Analysing and detecting extreme-selfie images using ensemble technique. In *2022 25th International Conference on Computer and Information Technology (ICCIT)*, pages 909–914.

P. M. Ashok Kumar, T. Subha Mastan Rao, L. Arun Raj, and E. Pugazhendi. 2020. *An Efficient Text-Based Image Retrieval Using Natural Language Processing (NLP) Techniques*, page 505–519. Springer Singapore.

Max Bain, Jaesung Huh, Tengda Han, and Andrew Zisserman. 2023. Whisperx: Time-accurate speech transcription of long-form audio. In *INTERSPEECH 2023*, Interspeech 2023. ISCA.

Timothy Burley, Lorissa Humble, Charles Sleeper, Abigail Sticha, Angela Chesler, Patrick Regan, Ernesto Verdeja, and Paul Brenner. 2020. Nlp workflows for computational social science: Understanding triggers of state-led mass killings. In *Practice and Experience in Advanced Research Computing 2020: Catch the Wave*, PEARC '20, page 152–159, New York, NY, USA. Association for Computing Machinery.

Bruno Cardoso and Neil Cohn. 2022. The multimodal annotation software tool (MAST). In *Proceedings of the Thirteenth Language Resources and Evaluation Conference*, pages 6822–6828, Marseille, France. European Language Resources Association.

Daniele Di Mitri, Jan Schneider, Roland Klemke, Marcus Specht, and Hendrik Drachsler. 2019. Read between the lines: An annotation tool for multimodal data for learning. In *Proceedings of the 9th International Conference on Learning Analytics & Knowledge*, LAK19, page 51–60, New York, NY, USA. Association for Computing Machinery.

Christian Fäth and Christian Chiarcos. 2022. Spicy salmon: Converting between 50+ annotation formats with fintan, pepper, salt and powla. In *Proceedings of the 8th Workshop on Linked Data in Linguistics within the 13th Language Resources and Evaluation Conference*, pages 61–68, Marseille, France. European Language Resources Association.

David Ferrucci, Adam Lally, Karin Verspoor, and Eric Nyberg. 2009. Unstructured information management architecture (UIMA) version 1.0. OASIS Standard.

Georg Fette, Martin Toepfer, and Frank Puppe. 2013. Storing UIMA CASes in a relational database. *Unstructured Information Management Architecture (UIMA)*, page 10.

Ryan A. Folk, Robert P. Guralnick, and Raphael T. LaFrance. 2024. Floratraiter: Automated parsing of traits from descriptive biodiversity literature. *Applications in Plant Sciences*, 12(1):e11563.

Roselyn Gabud, Portia Lapitan, Vladimir Mariano, Eduardo Mendoza, Nelson Pampolina, Maria Art Antonette Clariño, and Riza Batista-Navarro. 2023. A hybrid of rule-based and transformer-based approaches for relation extraction in biodiversity literature. In *Proceedings of the 2nd Workshop on Pattern-based Approaches to NLP in the Age of Deep Learning*, pages 103–113, Singapore. Association for Computational Linguistics.

Keshava Pallavi Gone and Michael Smit. 2024. Designing a natural language processing system to support social science research. In *Proceedings of the 2023 IEEE/ACM International Conference on Advances in Social Networks Analysis and Mining*, ASONAM '23, page 345–347, New York, NY, USA. Association for Computing Machinery.

Jens Grivolla, Maite Melero, Toni Badia, Cosmin Cabulea, Yannick Estève, Eelco Herder, Jean-Marc Odobez, Susanne Preuß, and Raúl Marín. 2014. EUMSSI: a platform for multimodal analysis and recommendation using UIMA. In *Proceedings of the Workshop on Open Infrastructures and Analysis Frameworks for HLT*, pages 101–109, Dublin, Ireland. Association for Computational Linguistics and Dublin City University.

Ulrich Heid, Helmut Schmid, Kerstin Eckart, and Erhard Hinrichs. 2010. A corpus representation format for linguistic web services: The D-SPIN text corpus format and its relationship with ISO standards. In *Proceedings of the Seventh International Conference on Language Resources and Evaluation (LREC'10)*, Valletta, Malta. European Language Resources Association (ELRA).

Raphael Hiesgen, Marcin Nawrocki, Thomas C. Schmidt, and Matthias Wählisch. 2022. The race to the vulnerable: Measuring the log4j shell incident. *Preprint*, arXiv:2205.02544.

Matthew Honnibal, Ines Montani, Sofie Van Landeghem, and Adriane Boyd. 2020. spaCy: Industrial-strength Natural Language Processing in Python.

Sultana Ismet Jerin, Nicole O'Donnell, and Di Mu. 2024. Mental health messages on tiktok: Analysing the use of emotional appeals in health-related #edutok videos. *Health Education Journal*, 83(4):395–408.

Lakshmish Kaushik, Abhijeet Sangwan, and John H. L. Hansen. 2013. Automatic sentiment extraction from youtube videos. In *2013 IEEE Workshop on Automatic Speech Recognition and Understanding*, pages 239–244.

Jürgen Knapp, Bettina Eberle, Michael Bernhard, Lorenz Theiler, Urs Pietsch, and Roland Albrecht. 2021. Analysis of tracheal intubation in out-of-hospital helicopter emergency medicine recorded by video laryngoscopy. *Scandinavian Journal of Trauma, Resuscitation and Emergency Medicine*, 29(1).

Veysel Kocaman and David Talby. 2021. Spark nlp: Natural language understanding at scale. *Software Impacts*, page 100058.

B. Latha, B. Nivedha, and Y. Ranjanaa. 2022. Visual audio summarization based on nlp models. In *2022 1st International Conference on Computational Science and Technology (ICCST)*, pages 63–66.

K Lavanya, B Jayamala, C Jeyasri, and A Sakthivel. 2024. Automatic audio and image caption generation with deep learning. *Shanlax International Journal of Arts, Science and Humanities*, 11(S3-July):34—-39.

Marco Leo, Giuseppe Massimo Bernava, Pierluigi Carcagnì, and Cosimo Distante. 2022. Video-based automatic baby motion analysis for early neurological disorder diagnosis: State of the art and future directions. *Sensors*, 22(3).

Alexander Leonhardt, Giuseppe Abrami, Daniel Baumartz, and Alexander Mehler. 2023. Unlocking the heterogeneous landscape of big data NLP with DUUI. In *Findings of the Association for Computational Linguistics: EMNLP 2023*, pages 385–399, Singapore. Association for Computational Linguistics.

Zhu Li, Kang Lu, Miao Cai, Xiaoli Liu, Yanwen Wang, and Jiayu Yang. 2022. An automatic evaluation method for parkinson's dyskinesia using finger tapping video for small samples. *Journal of Medical and Biological Engineering*, 42(3):351—-363.

Huaishao Luo, Lei Ji, Botian Shi, Haoyang Huang, Nan Duan, Tianrui Li, Jason Li, Taroon Bharti, and Ming Zhou. 2020. Univl: A unified video and language pre-training model for multimodal understanding and generation. *Preprint*, arXiv:2002.06353.

A Madhavi, Anuraag Chilakamarri, Chaithra Jupudi, Srinidhi Madanaboina, and Suraj Sriram. 2024. Automatic running notes generation from audio lecture using nlp for comprehensive learning. In *2024 15th International Conference on Computing Communication and Networking Technologies (ICCCNT)*, pages 1–10.

Guillermo Martinez. 2022. An nlp approach to image analysis. In *24th Irish Machine Vision and Image Processing Conference*, IMVIP 2022, page 137–144. Irish Pattern Recognition and Classification Society.

Safoora Masoumi, Hossein Amirkhani, Najmeh Sadeghian, and Saeid Shahraz. 2024. Natural language processing (nlp) to facilitate abstract review in medical research: the application of biobert to exploring the 20-year use of nlp in medical research. *Systematic Reviews*, 13(1).

Ryan McGrady, Kevin Zheng, Rebecca Curran, Jason Baumgartner, and Ethan Zuckerman. 2023. Dialing for videos: A random sample of youtube. *Journal of Quantitative Description: Digital Media*, 3.

Wafa Mellouk and Wahida Handouzi. 2020. Facial emotion recognition using deep learning: review and insights. *Procedia Computer Science*, 175:689–694. The 17th International Conference on Mobile Systems and Pervasive Computing (MobiSPC),The 15th International Conference on Future Networks and Communications (FNC),The 10th International Conference on Sustainable Energy Information Technology.

Dirk Merkel. 2014. Docker: lightweight linux containers for consistent development and deployment. *Linux Journal*, 2014(239).

New York Times. 2019. New York Times. `https://developer.nytimes.com/apis`. Accessed: 2019; Data provided by The New York Times.

Jeff Pasternack and Dan Roth. 2008. The wikipedia corpus. Technical report.

Pablo Pino, Denis Parra, Cecilia Besa, and Sergio Uribe. 2020. Inspecting state of the art performance and nlp metrics in image-based medical report generation. In *LatinX in AI at Neural Information Processing Systems Conference 2020*, LXAI at NeurIPS 2020. Journal of LatinX in AI Research.

PleIAs. 2024. Youtube-commons. `https://huggingface.co/datasets/PleIAs/YouTube-Commons`. Accessed: 2025-04-29.

Christian Rauh and Jan Schwalbach. 2020. The ParlSpeech V2 data set: Full-text corpora of 6.3 million parliamentary speeches in the key legislative chambers of nine representative democracies.

Research Unit CORE. 2023. Critical Online Reasoning in Higher Education (CORE) (FOR 5404). https://core.uni-mainz.de. Accessed: 2024-07-10.

Susan Sabra, Khalid Mahmood, and Mazen Alobaidi. 2017. A semantic extraction and sentimental assessment of risk factors (sesarf): An nlp approach for precision medicine: A medical decision support tool for early diagnosis from clinical notes. In *2017 IEEE 41st Annual Computer Software and Applications Conference (COMPSAC)*, volume 2, pages 131–136.

Tanja Samardzic, Ximena Gutierrez, Christian Bentz, Steven Moran, and Olga Pelloni. 2024. A measure for transparent comparison of linguistic diversity in multilingual NLP data sets. In *Findings of the Association for Computational Linguistics: NAACL 2024*, pages 3367–3382, Mexico City, Mexico. Association for Computational Linguistics.

Deike Schulz, Afke van der Woud, and Jeroen Westhof. 2020. The best indycaster project: Analysing and understanding meaningful youtube content, dialogue and commitment as part of responsible management education. *The International Journal of Management Education*, 18(1):100335.

Gautam Kishore Shahi and Tim A. Majchrzak. 2022. *AMUSED: An Annotation Framework of Multimodal Social Media Data*, pages 287–299.

Muna Sharma and Yilang Peng. 2024. How visual aesthetics and calorie density predict food image popularity on instagram: A computer vision analysis. *Health Communication*, 39(3):577–591. PMID: 36759337.

Süddeutscher Verlag. 2014. Süddeutsche Zeitung. Süddeutscher Verlag.

Sai Harshith Thanneru, Kajal Kumari, Naresh Kunta, and Pavan Kumar Manchalla. 2023. Image to audio, text to audio, text to speech, video to text conversion using, nlp techniques. *E3S Web of Conferences*, 391:01092.

Erik F. Tjong Kim Sang and Fien De Meulder. 2003. Introduction to the CoNLL-2003 shared task: Language-independent named entity recognition. In *Proceedings of the Seventh Conference on Natural Language Learning at HLT-NAACL 2003*, pages 142–147.

Maxim Tkachenko, Mikhail Malyuk, Andrey Holmanyuk, and Nikolai Liubimov. 2020-2025. Label Studio: Data labeling software. Open source software available from https://github.com/HumanSignal/label-studio.

Yubin Yang, Wei Wei, Tong Lu, Yang Gao, Yao Zhang, and Chunsheng Yang. 2009. 3d scene analysis using uima framework. In *Next-Generation Applied Intelligence*, pages 369–378, Berlin, Heidelberg. Springer Berlin Heidelberg.

Tao Yu, Baoyao Zhou, Qinghu Li, Rui Liu, Weihong Wang, and Cheng Chang. 2009. The design of distributed real-time video analytic system. In *Proceedings of the First International Workshop on Cloud Data Management*, CloudDB '09, page 49–52, New York, NY, USA. Association for Computing Machinery.

Systematic Review of Linguistic Characteristics in Profiling and Automated Detection of Autistic Speech

Charlotte Bellinghausen[1], Andreas Riedel[2,3]
[1]Institute of German Studies, Linguistics, University of Duisburg-Essen, Germany
[2]Department of Psychiatry and Psychotherapy, Medical Center – University of Freiburg, Faculty of Medicine, University of Freiburg, Germany
[3]Luzerner Psychiatrie, Ambulante Dienste, Löwengraben 20, 6004 Luzern, Switzerland
charlotte.bellinghausen@uni-due.de, andreas.riedel@lups.ch

Abstract

Our work aims to provide a systematic review of interdisciplinary studies on the automated recognition and differentiation of autistic and non-autistic speech. Linguistic patterns of autistic speech can serve as indicators for clinical diagnosis. Recognizing and integrating autistic language patterns can help to develop systems characterized by neurodiversity in language use. We selected 24 studies and systematically compared them to find similarities and differences between autistic and non-autistic groups, focusing on linguistic analysis. We divided the studies into three types: automatic recognition studies, language profile studies and meta-analysis studies. The vast majority of studies investigated the acoustic modality for English. The material mostly consisted of children's speech, but the meta-analyses included different age groups. Linguistic analysis indicated that, alongside semantic, pragmatic, and lexical features, prosodic and acoustic cues were especially salient in the various speech categorization approaches. These findings highlight prosodic and acoustic features as central to the identification of autistic speech.

1 Introduction

Autism Spectrum Disorder (ASD) is a neurodevelopmental disorder characterised by severe impairments in the areas of social interaction and social communication, as well as by restricted, repetitive, and inflexible behaviours and interests or activities (ICD-11 'autism', 2025). In recent years, public awareness and early identification account have contributed to increasing prevalence rates over time (cf. Zeidan et al., 2022: 8). The World Health Organization (WHO, 2025) estimates that the global prevalence of autism is approximately 1 in 100 children. In epidemiological samples, the male-to-female ratio is approximately 3:1. However, there are concerns about under-reporting in girls and women (cf. American Psychiatric Association 2022: 64).

While the cause of autism is largely genetic, other factors may also play a role (cf. Kamp-Becker & Bölte, 2014: 33ff). Markowetz (2020: 14) gives an overview of approaches and theories to explain the causes of autism, referring to neurobiological and psychosocial reasons.

According to ICD-11 and DSM-5, autism is no longer divided into subcategories, the subtypes of autism are subsumed under the umbrella term of *autism spectrum disorder*. Following a neurodiversity perspective, we use the terms *autism spectrum* and *autism* in the following.

The *autism spectrum* can be characterised by specific forms of expression, peculiarities, and abilities (cf. Theunissen, 2020: 55). According to Eberhardt-Juchem (2023: 29), the range of linguistic and communicative abilities in people of the autism spectrum is wide. For example, there may be functional verbal language with or without impaired language development. In other cases, there are no or minimal verbal skills (cf. Eberhardt-Juchem, 2023: 30). For a review of language in autism, see Lindmeier et al. (2024) and Riedel and Biscaldi-Schäfer (2025, in press).

In cases of autism spectrum without intellectual impairment, the processing on the syntactic and semantic level is barely affected, but problems in pragmatic interpretation are often found (cf. Riedel, 2015: 4f., see also Bellinghausen et al., 2024: 2).

Proceedings of the 21st Conference on Natural Language Processing (KONVENS), Volume 1: Long and Short Papers, pages 269–281, 2025

As Bellinghausen et al. (2024: 2) pointed out, problems in general pragmatic processing are often found in autism without intellectual impairment. However, there is empirical evidence that the pragmatic abilities of hearers with autism spectrum without intellectual impairment differ between pragmatic domains (see also Geurts et al., 2019: 114 and Andrés-Roqueta & Katsos, 2020).

The role of prosody in autistic persons without intellectual impairment has been investigated in several studies, covering both speech production and perception (for a description see Bellinghausen et al., 2024: 2-3).[1] Some studies suggest evidence for a difference in both prosody production (e.g. Shriberg, 2001; Kiss, 2012) and perception (Diehl & Paul, 2012). The findings differ with respect to the type of prosody. For prosodic uncertainty perception no significant difference between the autistic and neurotypical group was found (see Bellinghausen et al., 2024). Globerson (2015) reported no group differences in structural prosody perception, but in emotional prosody perception of the prototypical emotions happiness, sadness, anger, and fear. Due to the different functions of prosody, differences between autistic and neurotypical groups may vary between studies (cf. Bellinghausen et al., 2024: 3).

This raises the question of how differences in speech production can be used for computer-assisted diagnosis. Another question is how to recognise autistic speech automatically. In their survey of autism detection in speech, Neitzel et al. (2018) provided a description of the LENA system for the analysis of autistic speech in current research. It can be used to assess the number of words spoken by adult speakers, the number of vocal utterances spoken by children, and the number of speaker changes (cf. Neitzel et al., 2018: 86, see Ganek & Eriks-Brophy, 2018 for an overview of the use of the LENA system). AI-based systems have the potential to become valuable tools for clinical diagnosis in medicine, psychology and speech therapy.

The goal of the current study is to provide a systematic review of interdisciplinary studies on the characteristics of autistic and neurotypical speech, focusing on linguistic analysis.[2] Linguistic patterns of autistic speech can serve as indicators for clinical diagnosis. The automated recognition of these patterns can be helpful for intervention. By integrating perspectives from linguistics, computer science, psychology, and medicine, our primary aim is to identify the linguistic features that are characteristic of autism, while also highlighting key similarities, differences, and research gaps. Our comparison of studies will focus on the linguistic levels considered in autistic and neurotypical speech analysis and detection. Our findings aim to advance speech technology and natural language technology by bridging these disciplines. An overview of the different disciplines covered by our work is given in Table 1.

discipline	**subject for the current project**
linguistics	description of language at various levels: syntax, semantics, pragmatics, lexis, phonetics (prosody), etc.
medicine & psychology	autism research as a broad topic; studying similarities between autistic and neurotypical groups
speech technology & natural language technology	provision of a range of tools for the analysis of spoken and written language; use of artificial intelligence tools

Table 1: Role of different disciplines in the current paper

Integrating AI-based automated detection of autistic speech with human intervention may yield improved outcomes.

2 Method

2.1 Paper selection

We selected 24 interdisciplinary studies from the fields of linguistics, computer science, psychology, and psychiatry. The resulting studies were published between 2011 and 2024. Studies were mainly retrieved from the ISCA (International Speech Communication Association) archive (ISCA, 2025), from the PubMed database (PubMed, 2025), and from

[1] For an overview of the functions of both structural and emotional prosody, see Grice et al. (2023).

[2] The preliminary results of this work were presented at the annual conference 'Wissenschaftliche Tagung Autismus Spektrum 2025' with a published abstract (Bellinghausen et al., 2025).

Google searches. Keyword searches included different combinations of 'autism', 'automatic classification/detection/discrimination', 'speech', 'language profile', 'prosody', and others.

Our review includes studies that assessed speech using pre-defined features as well as studies that used AI tools for automatic recognition.

2.2 Evaluation criteria

To obtain a systematic overview of the 24 selected studies, we first categorise them according to study type in sec. 3.1. Sec. 3.2 forms the core of our analysis. Under the heading 'Linguistic Analysis', we analyse the different linguistic levels, features, and methods employed in the selected studies, including semantics, pragmatics, lexis and prosody. Table 1 (see Appendix) provides information about the participants, on the tested languages, and the linguistic analysis for each selected study.

3 Results of Systematic Evaluation

3.1 Study characteristics: type of study

The different study types included in our analysis are shown in the diagram in figure 1. The majority of studies were assigned to the category 'automated detection study for the acoustic modality' (N=12; Ashwini et al., 2023; Xu et al., 2023; Yang et al., 2023; MacFarlane et al., 2022; Lee et al., 2013; Chi et al., 2022; Asgari et al., 2021; Prud'hommeaux & Rouhizadeh, 2012; Xu et al., 2009; Lahiri et al., 2023; Asgari et al., 2013). We found one study on 'automated detection' for the visual modality (N=1; Li et al., 2022).

Studies of language profiles occurred with N=6 (Geurts & Embrecht, 2008; Volden et al., 2009; Philofsky et al., 2007; Eni et al., 2023; Black et al., 2011; Wetherby et al., 2007).

There are N=5 studies in the category 'overview/review studies/meta-analysis' (Fusaroli et al, 2017; Asghari et al., 2021; Probol & Mieskes, 2024; Ma et al., 2024; Vogindroukas et al., 2022).

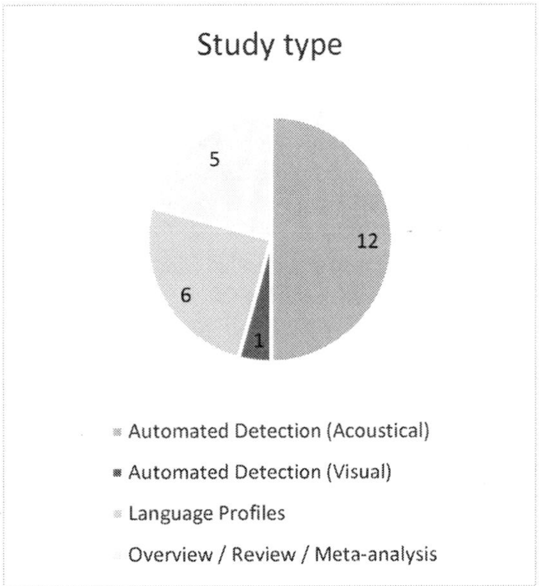

Figure 1: Different study types, N=24

3.2 Linguistic analysis

The results of the systematic analysis of the automated detection studies are described in sec. 3.2.1. The analysis of profile studies is presented in sec. 3.2.2, the analysis of systematic review studies follows in sec. 3.2.3. Other studies are discussed in sec. 3.2.4.

3.2.1 Studies on automatic detection

The results of our systematic analysis of studies on automated speech detection are shown in Table 2 (see Appendix). The table contains the following criteria: i) study reference, 2) participants, 3) language tested, 4) linguistic level/method, 4) linguistic features, 5) results. The first group of studies are those that compare the language of an autistic group with that of a neurotypical comparison group. We first refer to studies in the **acoustic modality**.

Ashwini et al. (2023) used semantic-pragmatic features for automatic detection for the acoustic modality. Selected features included echolalia, coherence, and repetitive speech. The results suggested that semantic and pragmatic language features can serve as key features for autism diagnosis complementing syntactic and lexical features, and achieving 94% classification accuracy.

Both Cho et al. (2022) and Yang et al. (2023) tested acoustic and lexical features for the automatic detection of speech from autistic and neurotypical individuals. Cho et al. (2022) used a gradient boosting model and principal component analysis for automatic classification. The features used were frequency-based, voice quality, energy and loudness measurements, and statistical features. The final model's accuracy was above chance levels, reaching 75%.

Yang et al. (2023) selected pitch- and voice-quality-related features, as well as the percentage of silences and lexical features such as ratio measurements, to develop various classifiers. The most effective classifier was a support vector machine with an accuracy rate of 61%, surpassing the performance of human raters (49%). Furthermore, a pre-trained audio transformer was used to extract acoustic features, achieving a prediction rate of 68%.

MacFarlane et al. (2022) used automated language and voice measures in their studies. By analysing language and voice features from ADOS-2 transcripts and audio recordings using automated language and voice measures (ALMs and AVMs), the study successfully classified speech from autistic and non-autistic children. The AVM model achieved an area under the curve (AUC)-ROC of 0.7800, the ALM model achieved an AUC-ROC of 0.8748, and the combined model demonstrated a significant improvement with an AUC-ROC of 0.9205.

Lee et al. (2013) used the following ensemble classification techniques: support vector machines (SVMs), deep neural networks (DNNs), k-nearest neighbors (KNNs) and the acoustic segment mode (ASM) technique. Acoustic features were extracted using the open SMILE feature extractor. The results showed that the final ensemble system, which combined machine learning and ASM techniques, outperformed the challenge baseline.

Chi et al. (2022) used machine learning techniques to classify autistic and non-autistic speech using speech recognition features. The random forest classifier achieved 70% accuracy; the fine-tuned Wav2vec 2.0 model, 77%; and the convolutional neural network, 79%.

Asgari et al. (2021) employed speech recognition features to distinguish between autistic and neurotypical speech. Standard speech measures included loudness, cepstral coefficients, and spectral entropy. The results of these models suggested that they performed better than a chance model. However, articulation measures alone achieved only moderate classification performance, with an AUC-ROC of around 68%. By contrast, prosodic features (e.g. pitch, intonation and rhythm) performed significantly better, achieving an AUC-ROC of around 82% which increased to 83% when the voice recording context was optimized.

Prud'hommeaux et al. (2012) used pragmatic features related to relevance and topicality to categorise speech into different narratives. Using automatically derived features, they distinguished between autistic and non-autistic speech. However, they did not investigate the correlation with human judgements of the features. They reported accuracy as the area under the receiver operating characteristic curve.

Xu et al. (2009) used pattern recognition and machine learning techniques on data from children with and without autism, as well as those with language delays. Autism was detected with an accuracy rate of between 85% and 90% in cross-validation tests.

Having referred to the studies on the acoustic modality, we will now turn to the **visual modality**. The study by Li et al. (2022) focused on visual recognition using features such as facial expression, head pose, and head trajectory features. The accuracy of automatic recognition was 96%.

The second group of detection studies includes the work of Xu et al. (2023) and Lahiri et al (2023). Xu et al. (2023) performed binary classifications for the audio condition. They tested whether i) autistic child speech could be distinguished from neurotypical adult speech and whether ii) speech or non-vocalisations occurred. Linguistic levels and features were not explicitly described. The results showed F1 macroscores of 83% for i) and 68% for ii). Lahiri et al. (2023) presented work on the automatic classification of child-adult speakers. The children were autistic speakers and the adults were neurotypical speakers. The model was pre-trained using child-inclusive interactions, based on two recent self-supervision algorithms: Wav2vec 2.0 and WavLM. The authors achieved a relative improvement of 9–13% over the state-of-the-art baseline in F1 classification scores on two clinical interaction datasets involving autistic children. However, it should be noted that a detailed description of the linguistic levels and features was lacking.

The third subtype of classification studies subsumes only the study by Asgari et al. (2013). In this study, the speech of autistic and non-autistic children was detected acoustically. Four subtypes of autism were classified in the sample of autistic children using voice quality-related features derived from harmonic analysis. The features improved performance by 2.3% in detecting autism spectrum disorder and by 2.8% in classifying it into four categories compared to the baseline results, measured by unweighted average recall (UAR).

3.2.2 Profile studies

Table 3 (see Appendix) contains the following information: 1) study reference, 2) language, 3) method, 4) linguistic levels/features, and 5) results. The table consists of two groups: studies for i) the audio and ii) the audiovisual modality. i) Geurts et al. (2008) used the Children's Communication Checklist to assess structural and pragmatic language in children with autism, SLI, and ADHD. School-aged children with autism and ADHD showed similar profiles with more pragmatic than structural difficulties. In contrast, preschool children with autism and SLI had more structural language problems.

Using multiple regression analyses, Volden et al. (2009) investigated the relationship between non-verbal cognition, structural language, and pragmatic language in autistic children. They found that structural language skills predicted pragmatic performance; however, they also found that variance in pragmatic scores could not be accounted for by structural language or non-verbal cognition.

In the study by Philofsky et al. (2007), parents rated the language skills of their children with autism or Williams syndrome using the Children's Communication Checklist, a standardised assessment tool for pragmatic language, including both verbal and non-verbal communication. Problems with pragmatic language functioning were observed in both groups, but children with Williams syndrome performed significantly better on the coherence, stereotyped language, non-verbal communication and social relations subscales.

Eni et al. (2023) estimated autism severity using hand-crafted features and log-mel spectrograms. In most cases, the hand-crafted features produced lower prediction errors than the log-mel spectrograms. The best results were achieved when both feature types were combined.

(ii) Language profiles in the audiovisual modality have been investigated by Black et al. (2011) and Whetherby et al. (2007). Black et al. (2011) examined the social communication profiles of children with and without autism and with developmental delay, as observed in videotaped behavioural samples. In their initial analysis, they annotated the speech with respect to lexical and phonetic information, as well as non-verbal communication, vocalisations, and sentence types. This paper does not describe the results.

Whetherby et al. (2007) used multimodal video samples to compare the social communication of autistic, neurotypical and language-delayed children. Using 14 Communication and Symbolic Behavior Scales (CSBS) measures (e.g. gaze shift and shared positive affect), they found significant differences between autistic and neurotypical children, but fewer differences between autistic and language-delayed children.

3.2.3 Review studies and meta-analysis studies

The next step is to analyse the review studies and meta-analysis studies (N=5, see Table 3). Table 3 contains the following information: 1) study reference, 2) language, 3) method, 4) linguistic levels/features, and 5) results.

Both Fusaroli et al. (2017) and Asghari et al. (2021) conducted systematic reviews and meta-analyses of studies investigating acoustic and prosodic patterns in autistic and neurotypical groups. Fusaroli et al.'s (2017) included 34 studies in their work, comprising 30 univariate studies aiming at identifying differences between the two groups, and 15 multivariate machine-learning studies. Their results for the univariate studies revealed group differences in mean pitch and pitch range; these studies examined one acoustic feature at a time. The results of the multivariate showed a higher accuracy rate by 63-96% compared to the univariate studies.

By contrast, Asghari et al. (2021) systematically compared 39 studies that tested autistic participants from different age groups. They found that autistic participants exhibited a higher mean pitch, greater pitch range, longer voice duration and greater pitch variability than the neurotypical comparison group.

Probol and Mieske's (2024) work is a survey and meta-analysis. They presented studies that examined verbal and semantic fluency, prosodic features, and also disfluencies and speaking rate. The results suggested an under-representation of females. Most of the papers focused on traditional learning approaches rather than transformers and deep learning techniques.

Ma et al. (2024) systematically compared the results of empirical studies on acoustic analysis and machine learning techniques. The aim was to apply natural speech prosody to the detection of autistic speech based on statistically supported evidence. The prosodic analysis included the features pitch mean, pitch range, pitch standard deviation, pitch variability, utterance duration, speaking rate, intensity mean and variation. The authors found significant differences in the pitch-related measures, but not in the temporal features. Multivariate machine learning trained on natural speech samples showed accuracy in detecting ASD with a sensitivity of 76% and a specificity of 80%.

Vogindroukas et al. (2022) aimed to define the language profiles of autistic individuals. The linguistic levels considered were semantics, pragmatics, phonology, morphosyntax covering spoken and written language, as well as non-verbal behaviour. The analysis resulted in four subtypes of profiles depending on language impairment, comorbidity, social communication and social interaction. It was concluded that problems with the semantic aspect of language influenced the skills in the areas of abstract thinking, word ambiguity, concept categorization, etc.

4 Discussion

We presented a systematic analysis of 24 selected interdisciplinary studies on the recognition and differentiation of autistic and neurotypical speech. Taking a linguistic perspective, we analysed the underlying linguistic features used to characterise autistic speech, identifying similarities and differences between autistic and non-autistic speech. Firstly, we divided the studies into three categories: 1) studies on automatic detection; 2) language profile studies; and 3) meta-analyses and systematic reviews. Most studies investigated speech samples from children and adolescents, whereas the meta-analyses included all age groups. English was the language tested in most studies.

Our summary of the selected studies for the three subtypes is as follows: 1) **Studies on automated detection:** The vast majority of studies investigated the audio modality. Automatic detection encompassed the distinction between autistic and non-autistic groups, child and adult speech, and autistic subtypes. Linguistic levels included the lexical, semantic, and pragmatic levels, as well as prosodic and other acoustic cues. Classification accuracy ranged from 61% to 94%, depending on the combination of linguistic cues used. Prosodic features, such as pitch, intonation, rhythm, and speech rate, play a critical role in distinguishing autistic from neurotypical speech (Asgari et al., 2021; Yang et al., 2023). Combining semantic-pragmatic features (e.g. coherence, repetition, echolalia and topic relevance) yielded an accuracy rate of 94% (Ashwini et al., 2023). Similarly, combining acoustic and lexical features (e.g. voice quality, energy and loudness measurements, frequency-based features, and statistical features) achieved an accuracy rate of 75% (Cho et al., 2022). Asgari et al. (2021) achieved an AUC-ROC of 83%, which was significantly higher than that achieved using purely articulatory features (e.g. loudness, cepstral coefficients, spectral entropy). Visual features (e.g., facial expressions) can also achieve very high accuracy (up to 96%). In terms of automatic classification methods, support vector machines, random forests, gradient boosting, convolutional neural networks (CNNs) and deep neural networks were employed. In the work of Chi et al. (2022), CNN achieved 79% accuracy and Wav2Wav 2.0 reached 77%.

In summary, it can be concluded that prosodic and pragmatic features are effective in discriminating between autistic and neurotypical speech. Multimodal and hybrid feature sets (acoustic, lexical, pragmatic and visual) yielded high classification rates. However, it should be noted that in some studies, it was not described which linguistic features were used. One possible explanation for this is that current AI systems do not use predefined linguistic features for recognition, but rather learn the characteristics on which they base their decisions from the training data. In order to examine what features those systems had extracted for classification, the framework of explainable artificial intelligence (XAI) can be used.

2) **Profile studies:** The features used for profiling were mostly based on standardised checklists, or were manually annotated. These covered both acoustic and visual modalities. However, the selected studies do not clearly and consistently demonstrate the differences and

similarities between autistic and non-autistic groups. However, there is evidence that pragmatic language impairments are prevalent among school-aged children with autism. Studies by Geurts et al. (2008) and Philofsky et al. (2007) reported difficulties with pragmatic language skills in autistic children. Combining hand-crafted acoustic-prosodic features with log-mel spectrograms improved the accuracy with which autism severity could be estimated (Eni et al., 2023).

3) **Meta-analysis studies:** It should be emphasised that the individual factors at the methodological and linguistic levels depend on the studies selected for each review. A key finding is that pitch-related prosodic features (e.g. higher mean pitch, greater pitch range, and pitch variability) are consistently altered in autistic speech (Fusaroli et al., 2017; Ashgari et al., 2021; Ma et al., 2024). Furthermore, multivariate machine learning approaches using speech prosody outperformed univariate methods (Fusaroli et al., 2017; Ma et al., 2024). Another finding is that female autism profiles are under-explored (Probol & Mieskes, 2024).

In summary, we found that most, but not all studies considered pragmatic, lexical, prosodic and other acoustic cues. Further work should systematically include linguistic levels in the analysis of autistic and non-autistic speech in order to provide a more detailed picture of the of autistic speech characteristics. Such research could contribute to a better understanding of the role and interplay of different linguistic features in automatic classification.

In future studies, it would be very interesting to further investigate the different modalities in a larger number of selected studies, as well as using speech material from different languages and multilingual corpora.

We also recognise the importance of AI-based speech systems as valuable tools for clinical diagnosis in medicine, psychology, and speech therapy. By highlighting their potential, we aim to advocate for their broader adoption and further development. For more information on the role of artificial intelligence sound classifiers in autistic speech, see also Chi et al. (2022: 2).

In our view, speech technology tools can provide valuable guidance and support for the experienced human clinical diagnosticians, but they cannot replace them. Future work could involve comparing the autistic group with other psychiatric groups. In this way it might be possible to identify similarities and differences between the groups and use the findings for differential diagnosis.

5 Acknowledgement

We would like to thank Bernhard Schröder, Lisa Korte, Ulrich Schade, and Nantke Pecht for their helpful comments on this paper.

6 Appendix

classification type / study	speakers	language	linguistic level / *method*	linguistic features	results
Ashwini et al. (2023)	AS: N= 35; NTC: N=41; 3-8 y.	English	semantic-pragmatic / *NLP and machine learning techniques*	echolalia, semantic coherence, repetitive language	94% accuracy
Cho et al. (2022)	AS: N=35; NTC: N=25, average age: 11 y.	English	acoustic / lexical / *gradient boosting model, principal component analysis*	shimmer, Harmonic-to-noise ratio, energy, Mel Frequency Cepstral Coefficients / word frequencies, pronoun usages, number of filler words	75% accuracy
Yang et al. (2023)	AS: N=35; NTC: N=37; average age: 11; 10 y.	English	acoustic / lexical / *machine learning approach*	e.g. percent of silence, word and sentence ratio	support vector machine: 61% accuracy, transformer: 68%
MacFarlane et al. (2022)	AS: N=88; NTC: N=70; 7-17 y.	English	*NLP methods, harmonic model of speech*	Automated voice measures (AVM) and automated language measures (ALM)	AVM model AUC-ROC: 0.7800; ALM model an AUC-ROC: 0.8748; combined model: 0.9205
Lee et al. (2013)	not specified	not specified	*ensemble classification techniques: support vector machines, deep neural networks, k-nearest neighbours; acoustic segment mode technique (ASM)*	acoustic features extracted by open SMILE feature extractor	final ensemble system combination (machine learning and ASM techniques) outperformed the challenge baseline
Chi et al. (2022)	AS: N=20, NTC: N=38, 3-12 y.	English	*machine learning techniques: random forests, convolutional neural networks (CNNs), fine-tuned wav2vec 2.0 models*	speech recognition features	random forest classifier: 70% accuracy, fine-tuned wav2vec 2.0 model: 77% accuracy, convolutional neural network: 79% accuracy
Asgari et al. (2021)	AS: N=90; NTC: N=28; average age: 11 y.	English	*harmonic model of voiced signal*	standard speech measures: loudness, cepstral coefficients, spectral entropy	articulation measures alone: AUC-ROC: 68%; prosodic measures: AUC-ROC: 82-83%
Prud'hommeaux & Rouhizadeh (2012)	SLI N=17; AS*: N=21; NTC: N=40; 4-8 y.	English	pragmatic / *support vector machine*	relevance and topicality	distinction between autistic and non-autistic speech; accuracy as AUC-ROC
Xu et al. (2009)	AS: N=34; LD: N=30; NTC: N=76; age: not specified	English	acoustic / *machine learning, pattern recognition*	high dimensional features	accuracy of 85% to 90% in cross-validation tests for AS vs. LD and ASS vs. LD and NCT
Li et al. (2022)	AS: N=136; NTC: N=136 4-7 y.	not specified	non-verbal / novel attention-based facial expression recognition algo-rithm	facial expression, head pose, head trajectory	96% accuracy
Xu et al. (2023)	45 sessions (child/parent): average age: 7 y.	English	annotation categories: 1) child vs. adult speech, 2) intelligible, unintelligible, vocalization / *classification*	speech and nonverbal vocalizations	F1 macro scores: 83% and 68%
Lahiri et al. (2023)	346 sessions from AS: N=86; NTC: N=79; 3-13 y.	not specified	*pretraining of data with self-supervision algorithms: Wav2vec 2.0 and WavLM*	not specified	9-13% relative improvement over the state-of-the-art baseline
Asgari et al. (2013)	99 children; 9-18 y.	French	acoustic / *harmonic noise model*	voice quality, energy, spectral features, cepstral features	improvement in terms of unweighted average recall

Table 2: systematic overview of studies on automatic detection, N=13, NLP=natural language processing, AS: autism spectrum group: NTC: neurotypical comparison group; LD: language delay group, SLI: specific language impairment group; AS: autism spectrum group without language impairment; y=years, AUC-ROC: area under the receiver operating characteristics curve, AVM: automated voice measures, ALM: automated language measures

study: topic	speakers	language	Method	linguistic levels / features	results
Geurts et al. (2008): generation of language profiles in AS, SLI, and ADHD	ADHD: N=29; AS: N=29; study 1: 7-14y.; study 2: 4-7 y.	Dutch	Children's Communication Checklist	mainly pragmatics: use of context, non-verbal communication	AS & ADHD: similar language profiles
Volden et al. (2009): factors related to pragmatic development in AS	37 children: 6–13 years;	English	regression analysis	non-verbal cognition, structural language and pragmatic language	structural language skills predicted pragmatic performance
Philofsky et al. (2007)	AS: N=22; WS: N=21, NTC: N=19; average age: 6-9 y.	English	Children's Communication Checklist	verbal and non-verbal communication	better pragmatic functioning in WS
Eni et al. (2023): autism severity estimation by means of hand-crafted features and log-mal spectogram	AS: N=77%, NTC: N=23% N=127; 4.09±1.31 y.	Hebrew	feature extraction methods: implemented and tested for estimating AS severity score; five system configurations: tested for AS severity estimation	acoustic-prosodic features: pitch, formants, bandwiths, voicing, energy, spectral slope, ZCR, jitter, duration, quantity	1) hand-crafted features: lower prediction error in most configurations compared to log-mel spectrograms. 2) fusing autism severity scores for the two feature extraction methods yielded to best results
Black et al. (2011): presentation of multimodal corpus (USC CARE Corpus)	in total: N=60; 5-18 y.	English	audio-visual data collection during ADOS	lexical information; phonetical information (pronounciation), non-verbal communication and vocalizations; labeling as question, fragment, interruption, and/or complete thought	not described (work in progress)
Wetherby et al., (2007): social communication profiles from behavior samples videotaped	AS: N=50; DD: N=23, NTC: N= 50; age: 18-24 months	not specified	video recordings; parent/observer-child interaction	14 items of the CSBS Behavior Sample that form the social, speech, and symbolic composites: gaze shift, shared positive affect, gaze/point follow etc.	AS group: lower scores in 5 measures (vs. DD), lower scores in 14 measures (vs. NTC)

Table 3: Systematic analysis of profile studies, N=6; autism spectrum group; SLI: specific language impairment group, ADHD: attention deficit hyperactivity disorder; WS: williams syndrome; ZCR: Zero-Crossing Rate, DD: developmental delay, NTC: neurotypical comparison group

study: topic	speakers & language	method	linguistic levels / features	results
Audio				
Fusaroli et al. (2017): systematic review of literature: acoustic patterns in AS	study dependent	systematic review of 34 studies; childhood, adolescence, adulthood / *machine learning*	prosody: pitch, intensity, duration, speech rate, pauses, voice quality	univariate studies: AS vs. NTC: differences in mean pitch and pitch range, multivariate studies: 63-96%
Asghari et al. (2021): systematic review and meta-analysis AS vs. NTC: prosodic cues	study dependent	systematic review and meta-analysis of 39 studies; childhood, adolescence, adulthood	mean pitch, pitch range and variability, speech rate, intensity and voice duration	AS vs. NTC: differences in mean pitch, pitch range, voice duration and pitch variability
Probol & Miekes, (2024): survey and meta-analysis regarding linguistic, prosodic and acoustic cues as indicators of AS	study dependent	survey and meta-analysis of 10 studies; childhood, adolescence, adulthood	verbal and semantic fluency, prosodic features, but also disfluencies and speaking rate	1) underrepresentation of females, 2) most works: traditional machine learning approaches (SVMs, Naive Beyes, Linear Regression), few studies; transformer, deep learning
Ma et al. (2024): state-of-the-art review: analysis of prosodic features in spontaneous speech in AS and machine learning techniques	study dependent	state-of-the-art review of 25 eligible uni-variate studies on spontaneous speech and 18 multivariate studies on machine learning; childhood, adulthood	prosodic analysis: pitch Mean, pitch range, pitch standard Deviation (p.8), pitch variability, utterance duration, speaking rate, intensity mean and variation; machine learning techniques	1) AS vs. NTC: significant differences in pitch-related measures (but not in temporal features); 2) pitch range possibly influenced by age groups 3) machine learning trained on natural speech samples; achieved promising accuracy in detecting AS sensitivity: 75.51% specificity: 80.30%
Vogindroukas et al. (2022): language profiles in AS; try to classify these profiles according to combination of communication difficulties	study dependent	description of different studies	semantics, pragmatics, phonology, morphosyntax covering spoken, written language, non-verbal behavior	four subtypes of profiles depending on linguistic impairment, comorbidity, social communication, and social interaction

Table 4: systematic analysis of systematic review studies, N=5

References

American Psychiatric Association. 2022. Diagnostic and statistical manual of mental disorders. *Text Revision: DSM-5-TR*, Fifth Edition. American Psychiatric Association Publishing, Washington, DC.

Andrés-Roqueta, C., Katsos, N.A 2020.. A distinction between linguistic- and social-pragmatics helps the precise characterization of pragmatic challenges in children with Autism Spectrum Disorders and Developmental Language Disorder. *J Speech Lang Hear Res.,* 63:1494–508. doi: 10.1044/2020_JSLHR-19-00263

Asgari, M., Bayestehtashk, A., Shafran, I. 2013. Robust and accurate features for detecting and diagnosing autism spectrum disorders. In *Proceedings of Interspeech 2013*, Lyon, France, 191-194, doi: 10.21437/Interspeech.2013-65

Asgari, M., Chen, L., Fombonne, E. 2021. Quantifying Voice Characteristics for Detecting Autism. Front Psychol., 2021 Sep 7, 12:665096. doi: 10.3389/fpsyg.2021.665096

Asghari S.Z., Farashi, S., Bashirian, S., Jenabi, E. 2021. Distinctive prosodic features of people with autism spectrum disorder: a systematic review and meta-analysis study. *Sci Rep.*, 2021 Nov 29, 11(1):23093, doi: 10.1038/s41598-021-02487-6

Ashwini, B. Narayan, V., Shukla, J. 2023. SPASHT: Semantic and Pragmatic Speech Features for Automatic Assessment of Autism. In *Proceedings of ICASSP 2023 - 2023 IEEE International Conference on Acoustics, Speech and Signal Processing*, Rhodes Island, Greece, 1-5, doi: 10.1109/ICASSP49357.2023.10095135

Bellinghausen, C., Schröder, B., Rauh, R., Riedel, A., Dahmen, P., Birkholz, P., Tebartz van Elst, L., Fangmeier, T. (2024). Processing of prosodic cues of uncertainty in autistic and non-autistic adults: a study based on articulatory speech synthesis. *Frontiers in Psychiatry, Sec. Autism*, Vol. 15, 14 October 2024, https://doi.org/10.3389/fpsyt.2024.1347913

Bellinghausen. S., Riedel, A. (2025). Characteristics of Autistic and Neurotypical Speech and Automated Detection: A Systematic Review of Linguistic Analysis. Poster presented at *Wissenschaftliche Tagung Autismus Spektrum 2025*, Heidelberg, Germany, 17-18th of April 2025.

Black, M.P., Bone, D., Williams, M.E., Gorrindo, P., Levitt, P., Narayanan, S. 2011. The USC CARE corpus: child-psychologist interactions of children with autism spectrum disorders. In *Proceedings of Interspeech 2011*, Florence, Italy, 1497-1500, doi: 10.21437/Interspeech.2011-314

Chi, N.A., Washington, P., Kline, A., Husic, A., Hou, C., He, C., Dunlap, K., Wall, D.P. 2022. Classifying Autism From Crowdsourced Semistructured Speech Recordings: Machine Learning Model Comparison Study. JMIR Pediatr Parent. 2022 Apr 14;5(2):e35406. doi: 10.2196/35406. PMID: 35436234; PMCID: PMC9052034.

Cho, S., Liberman, M., Ryant, N., Cola, M., Schultz, R.T., Parish-Morris, J. 2019. Automatic detection of autism spectrum disorder in children using acoustic and text features from brief natural conversations. In *Proceedings of Interspeech 2019*, Graz, Austria, 2513–2517 doi: 10.21437/Interspeech.2019-1452

Diehl, J.J., Paul, R. 2012. Acoustic differences in the imitation of prosodic patterns in children with autism spectrum disorders. *Autism Spectr Disord.* 6:123–34. doi: 10.1016/j.rasd.2011.03.012

Eberhardt-Juchen, M. 2023. Sprach- und Kommunikationsentwicklung bei Autismus einschließlich Besonderheiten der Sprache und Kommunikation bei Autismus. In S. Lindmeier, S. Sallat, K. Ehrenberg, *Sprache und Kommunikation bei Autismus*. Stuttgart, Verlag W. Kohlhammer, 19-34.

Eni, M., Dinstein, I., Zigel, Y. 2023. Comparing Hand-Crafted Features to Spectrograms for Autism Severity Estimation. In *Proceedings of Interspeech 2023*, Dublin, Ireland, 4154-4158, doi: 10.21437/Interspeech.2023-658

Fusaroli, R., Lambrechts, A., Bang, D., Bowler, D.M., Gaigg, S.B. 2017. Is voice a marker for Autism spectrum disorder? A systematic review and meta-analysis. *Autism Research*, 2017 Mar, 10(3), 384-407. doi: 10.1002/aur.1678

Ganek, H., Eriks-Brophy, A. 2018. Language ENvironment analysis (LENA) system investigation of day long recordings in children: A literature review. *J Commun Disord.* 2018 Mar-Apr; 72:77-85. doi: 10.1016/j.jcomdis.2017.12.005. Epub 2017 Dec 16. PMID: 29402382.

Geurts, H.M., Embrechts, M. 2008. Language profiles in asd, sli, and adhd. *Journal of autism and developmental disorders*, 38:1931–1943. doi: 10.1007/s10803-008-0587-1

Geurts, B., Kissine, M., van Tiel B. 2019. Pragmatic reasoning in autism. In: K. Morsanyi, R.M.J. Byrne RMJ: *Thinking, reasoning and decision making in autism*. Routledge, London, 113–34.

Globerson, E., Amir, N., Kishon-Rabin, L., Golan, O. 2015. Prosody recognition in adults with high-functioning autism spectrum disorders: from psychoacoustics to cognition. *Autism Res.* (2015) 8:153–63. doi: 10.1002/aur.1432

ICD-11 'autism'. 2025). https://icd.who.int/browse/2025-01/mms/en#437815624 [last access: 2nd of April 2025]

ISCA. 2025. International Speech Association Archive. https://www.isca-archive.org/ [last access: 2nd of April 2025]

Kamp-Becker, I., Bölte S. 2014. Autismus. München, Basel, Ernst Reinhard Verlag.

Kiss, G., van Santen, J.P.H., Prud'hommeaux, E., Black, L.M. 2012. Quantitative analysis of pitch in speech of children with neurodevelopmental disorders. In *Proceedings of Interspeech 2012*, Portland, OR, USA, 2012 Sep 9-13. 1343–46.

Lahiri, R., Feng, T., Hebbar, R., Lord, C., Kim, S.H., Narayanan, S. 2023. Robust Self Supervised Speech Embeddings for Child-Adult Classification in Interactions involving Children with Autism. In *Proceedings of Interspeech 2023*, Dublin, Ireland, 3557-3561, doi: 10.21437/Interspeech.2023-1447

Lee, H.-y., Hu, T.-y., Jing, H., Chang, Y.-F., Tsao, Y., Kao, Y.-C., Pao, T.-L. 2013. Ensemble of machine learning and acoustic segment model techniques for speech emotion and autism spectrum disorders recognition. In *Proceedings of Interspeech 2013*, Lyon, France, 215-219, doi: 10.21437/Interspeech.2013-70

Li, J., Chen, Z., Li, G., Ouyang, G., Li, X. 2022. Automatic classification of asd children using appearance-based features from videos. *Neurocomputing*, 470:40–50, doi: 10.1016/j.neucom.2021.10.074

Lindmeier, S., Sallat, S., Ehrenberg. K. 2023. *Sprache und Kommunikation bei Autismus*. Stuttgart, Verlag W. Kohlhammer.

Ma, W., Xu, L., Zhang, H., Zhang, S. 2024. Can Natural Speech Prosody Distinguish Autism Spectrum Disorders? A Meta-Analysis. *Behav Sci*, 2024 Jan 26, 14(2):90, doi: 10.3390/bs14020090. PMID: 38392443; PMCID: PMC10886261

MacFarlane, H., Salem, A.C., Chen, L., Asgari, M., Fombonne, E. 2022. Combining voice and language features improves automated autism detection. *Autism Research 2022*, 15(7):1288-1300, doi: 10.1002/aur.2733. Epub 2022 Apr 23. PMID: 35460329; PMCID: PMC9253091.

Markowetz, R. 2020. *Schüler mit Autismus-Spektrum-Störung im inklusiven Unterricht. Praxistipps für Lehrkräfte*. München, Ernst Reinhardt Verlag.

Neitzel, I., Tuschen, L., Ritterfeld, U. 2023. Automatisierte Sprach- und Sprechanalyse in Forschung und Diagnostik bei Autismus-Spektrum-Störungen: Potenziale und Barrieren. *Sprache · Stimme · Gehör 2023*, 47(02): 84-88 doi: 10.1055/a-2018-2972

Philofsky, A., Fidler, D.J., Hepburn, S. 2007. Pragmatic language profiles of school-age children with autism spectrum disorders and williams syndrome. *American Journal of Speech-Language Pathology*, 16(4):368-80. doi: 10.1044/1058-0360(2007/040). PMID: 17971496; PMCID: PMC4426201.

Probol, N., Mieskes, M. 2024. Autism Detection in Speech – A Survey. In *Findings of the Association for Computational Linguistics: EACL 2024*, Malta, March 17-22, 1115–1125. doi: 10.48550/arXiv.2402.12880

Prud'hommeaux, E., Rouhizadeh, M. 2012. Automatic detection of pragmatic deficits in children with autism. In *Workshop Child Comput Interact*. 2012 Sep 14; 2012, 1-6. PMID: 28691126; PMCID: PMC5500165.

PubMed. 2025. Pub Med Website. https://pubmed.ncbi.nlm.nih.gov/ [last access: 2nd of April 2025]

Riedel A. (2015). Sprachpragmatik bei Autismus-Spektrum-Störungen. In 8. Newsletter, Wissenschaftliche Gesellschaft Autismus-Spektrum-Störung (2015). https://silo.tips/download/newsletter-sprachpragmatik-bei-autismus-spektrum-strungen-mai-nr-8-dr-med-dr-phi

Riedel, A., Biscaldi-Schäfer. 2025, in press. *Sprache bei Menschen im Autismus-Spektrum. Interdisziplinäre Perspektiven*. Stuttgart, Verlag W. Kohlhammer.

Shriberg, L.D., Paul, R., McSweeney, J.L., Klin, A.M., Cohen, D.J., Volkmar, F.R. 2001. Speech and prosody characteristics of adolescents and adults with high functioning autism and Asperger syndrome. J Speech Lang Hear Res., 44:1097–115. doi: 10.1044/1092-4388(2001/087). PMID: 11708530.

Theunissen, G. 2020. Autismus – das neue Verständnis aus der Außenansicht in Anlehnung an Vorstellungen von Betroffenen. In G. Theunissen: *Autismus verstehen. Außen- und Innenansichten*, Stuttgart, Verlag W. Kohlhammer, 21-101.

Vogindroukas, I., Stankova, M., Chelas, E.-N., Proedrou, A. 2022. Language and speech characteristics in autism. *Neuropsychiatric Disease and Treatment*, 2367–2377. doi: 10.2147/NDT.S331987. PMID: 36268264; PMCID: PMC9578461.

Volden, J., Coolican, J., Garon, N., White, J., Bryson, S. 2009. Brief report: Pragmatic language in autism spectrum disorder: Relationships to measures of ability and disability. *Journal of autism and developmental disorders*, 39:388–393. doi: 10.1007/s10803-008-0618-y. Epub 2008 Jul 15. PMID: 18626760.

Wetherby, A.M., Watt, N., Morgan, L., Shumway, S. Social communication profiles of children with autism spectrum disorders late in the second year of life. *J Autism Dev Disord.*, 2007 May, 37(5):960-75. doi: 10.1007/s10803-006-0237-4

WHO - World Health Organization Website. 2025 .https://www.who.int/news-room/fact-sheets/detail/autism-spectrum-disorders [last access: 2nd of April 2025]

Xu, D., Gilkerson, J., Richards, J., Yapanel, U., Gray, S. 2009. Child vocalization composition as discriminant information for automatic autism detection. *Annu Int Conf IEEE Eng Med Biol Soc. 2009*; 2518-22. doi: 10.1109/IEMBS.2009.5334846

Xu, A., Hebbar, R., Lahiri, R., Feng, T., Butler, L., Shen, L., Tager-Flusberg, H., Narayanan, S. 2023. Understanding Spoken Language Development of Children with ASD Using Pre-trained Speech Embeddings. *Proceedings of Interspeech 2023*, 4633-4637, doi: 10.21437/Interspeech.2023-1273

Yang, Y., Cho, S., Covello, M., Knox, A., Bastani, O., Weimer, J., Dobriban, E., Schultz, R., Lee, I., Parish-Morris, J. 2023. Automatically Predicting Perceived Conversation Quality in a Pediatric Sample Enriched for Autism. In *Proceedings of Interspeech 2023*, Dublin, Ireland, 4603-4607, doi: 10.21437/Interspeech.2023-2251

Zeidan, J., Fombonne, E., Scorah, J., Ibrahim, A., Durkin, M.S., Saxena, S., Yusuf, A., Shih, A., Elsabbagh, M. 2022. Global prevalence of autism: A systematic review update. *Autism Res.* 2022 May; 15(5):778-790. doi: 10.1002/aur.2696. Epub 2022 Mar 3. PMID: 35238171; PMCID: PMC9310578.

Towards a Cross-Dialectal Dictionary for Low German (Low Saxon)

Christian Chiarcos* **and Janine Siewert**** **and Tabea Gröger*** **and Christian Fäth***
*Applied Computational Linguistics (ACoLi), University of Augsburg, Germany
**Department of Digital Humanities, University of Helsinki, Finland
`first_name.second_name@uni-a.de / ...@helsinki.fi`

Abstract

We describe and evaluate a methodology for the automated creation of an interdialectal lexical resource (a "digital Rosetta stone") for major dialects of Low German (Low Saxon) spoken in Germany, based on the interlinking of lexical resources freely accessible over the web. The resulting dataset is provided both in human-readable form and as a lexical knowledge graph compliant with Linked Data standards, as content from dictionaries under copyright or non-derivative licenses could only be linked from but not included in our release data.

1 Motivation

The 'digital fitness' of languages (Soria et al., 2016) is often measured based on parameters such as the existence of resources and tools in relation to the size of the speaker community. However, depending on the *degree of internal diversity* of the language, the usefulness of, say, machine translation or dictionaries, varies greatly for the different subgroups of the community. *Low German* or *Low Saxon* is a language with such a high degree of internal variation.

As a West Germanic language, Low German is related to (High) German, Dutch and Frisian, and spoken in northern Germany, parts of the Netherlands and by several emigrant communities (Fig. 1 and Fig. 2). Low German has a literary tradition of more than 1000 years (Sievers, 1875) and was a lingua franca around the Baltic Sea during the late Middle Ages, but during the early modern period, it was replaced as a written language by the emerging national languages in Germany and the Netherlands. Since the 1990s, it has been recognized as a regional language in both countries under the European Charter for Regional or Minority Languages (ECRML), but has been and still is subject to substantial pressure from the respective national languages (Schwenk, 2017; Adler

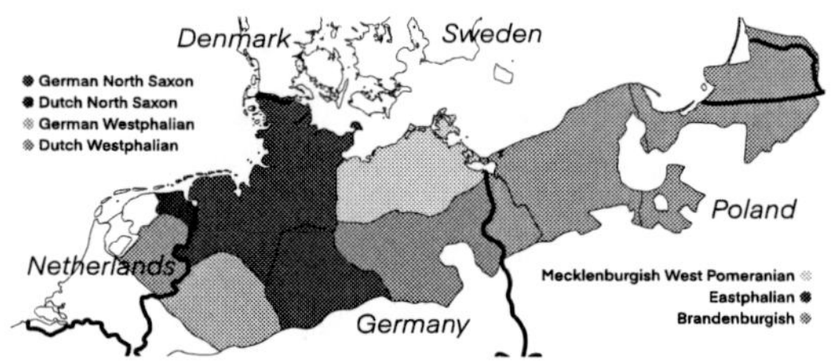

Figure 1: The major dialect groups of Low German (Low Saxon). Marked in grey are the eastern dialects which were spoken in these areas until the end of WWII.

and Beyer, 2017). Low German enjoys cultural and regional recognition, but revitalization efforts have so far remained relatively unambitious compared with other European minority languages such as Catalan, Welsh and North Sámi (Šatava, 2019). The integration of Low German into digital spaces and modern media still requires great work for it to retain and regain the status of a thriving and fully functioning language (Blaschke et al., 2023).

In particular, the current state of linguistic and orthographic fragmentation poses problems to the construction of many basic resources, either for NLP or didactic purposes (Reershemius, 2010; Ehlers, 2021; Bieberstedt, 2021). As it lacks an interregional standard, Low German exhibits not only dialectal variation in phonology and grammar, but speakers also vary in their ways of spelling the language due to which speakers of the same variety cannot automatically be assumed to have the same orthographic preferences (Teuchert, 1914; Martens, 1979, 2002; Weber and Schürmann, 2018).

Without parallel corpora and a complete lack of machine-readable dictionaries, we argue here that what is needed as a minimal requirement for the development of an effective NLP support for Low German – say, standard tools such as spell-checking, search, machine translation, chatbot technology, but also transliteration of texts from other Low German dialects –, is a digital Rosetta stone

Proceedings of the 21st Conference on Natural Language Processing (KONVENS), Volume 1: Long and Short Papers, pages 282–294, 2025

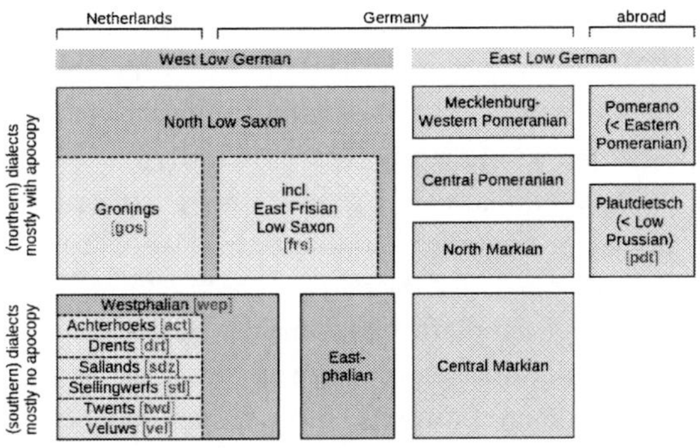

Figure 2: Major dialects of Low German (ISO 639-2 nds), with regional ISO 639-3 codes in red square brackets.

that allows us to leverage materials from different language varieties and to access them in a uniform way. However, instead of creating an artificial standard variety, we focus on technologies to complement dialect specific resources, by creating links between regional dictionaries, and by providing a mapping routine to identify formally corresponding words in different dialects of Low German.

The resulting dataset is provided both in human-readable form and as a lexical knowledge graph compliant with Linked Data standards,[1] as content from dictionaries under copyright or non-derivative licenses could only be linked from but not included in our release. Data, linking and conversion scripts are available from the *NDS Spraakverarbeiden* organization at GitHub.[2]

2 Data Sources and Data Modelling

We provide an interdialectal lexical resource for major dialects of Low German in Germany by interlinking lexical resources freely accessible over the web. Our contribution is two-fold: We describe a methodology for linking and create a cross-dialectal lexical knowledge graph for Low German that may serve as a basis for the subsequent development and application of statistical or neural methods of machine learning.

[1]For a general introduction into Linked Data and lexical knowledge graphs in and for language technology, technologies and use cases, see Cimiano et al. (2020).

[2]For data and description, see `https://nds-spraakverarbeiden.github.io/linked-nds-dictionaries/`, our source repository is under `https://github.com/nds-spraakverarbeiden/linked-nds-dictionaries`.

2.1 Dictionaries and Dialects

We operate with 6 digital dictionaries of major varieties of Low German in Germany:

Sass (Thies, 2025, North Saxon)
Plattmakers (Buck, 2007-2024, North Saxon)
WöWö (Neuber, 2001, North Saxon/Ditmarschen), see Sect. 2.2
PlattWB (Brückmann, 2025, North Saxon/East Frisian)
Reuter (Hansen, 2025, East Low German/Mecklenburgian), digital edition of Müller (1904)
WWB (Niebaum et al., 1969-2021, Westphalian)

In addition, we use a North Saxon/Holsteinian glossary with manually linked WöWö lemmas for evaluation (Sect. 4.1).

Of the aforementioned, more substantial dictionaries, only WöWö (published as 'Frie Woor') seems to allow the creation of local copies from which partial structured information (i.e., glosses) can be extracted. It is thus used as a basis for the lexical knowledge graph we aim to provide. Beyond WöWö lemmas and definitions, we only include URIs and lemma forms for external dictionary content that can be linked with WöWö. In order to avoid copyright infringement, we did not use the actual content of the external dictionaries, but provide a purely form-based linking, only. The legal situation also has an impact on the technologies we can use for publishing the results of our linking procedure: As the original data resides with its providers, scattered throughout Germany, we resort to Linked Open Data (Bizer et al., 2009, LOD), resp., the underlying RDF technologies, as this allows to release our data in a way that integrates information from remote hosts and abstracts away from their individual choice of tools, formats and technologies to provide it. A minimal requirement in that regard is that they allow to address their lexical entries by means of a URI.

2.2 Converting the Wöhrner Wöör (WöWö)

In recent years, a lot of efforts have been made to establish an interconnected pool of language resources under an open license as Linguistic Linked Open Data (LLOD).[3] A major corner stone to guarantee interoperability is the consistent use of RDF ontologies and data models, and we consequently

[3]`https://linguistic-lod.org`

employ OntoLex,[4] the de-facto standard for publishing lexical data as LLOD, for data modelling.

The OntoLex core model establishes classes for key elements of any lexicon, each identified with a Uniform Resource Identifier (URI): the **LexicalEntry** represents an entry in a dictionary, a **Form** is a surface form or phonetic realization, and the `LexicalSense` represents the word sense. In addition to these, various relations can be specified, e.g., a sense can refer to other senses or to an external resource. Additional modules provide further descriptors for modeling additional concepts or relations, and we employ the `vartrans` module for representing cross-dialectal links between multiple entries in different dialects of Low German.

The core of the lexical knowledge graph stems from the *Wöhrner Wöör* (WöWö) dictionary of the Dithmarschen variety of North Saxon, published in print in 2001 by Peter Neuber, followed by an extended and revised digital version 2019 as PDF and MS Office documents that now comprises a total of 21,012 German and 26,702 Low German lexical entries.[5] Aimed at human readers, the WöWö lacks structured machine-readable representations. In accordance with established best practices for bilingual dictionaries (Gracia and Vila-Suero, 2015) and in order to facilitate its linking with other lexical datasets, we thus converted it into an OntoLex RDF graph as summarized in Fig. 4. As shown in Figure 3, a variety of colors, fonts, and fonts sizes are used to encode different pieces of information which causes a fragmentation of the underlying text information and made the conversion of the *Wöhrner Wöör* challenging. These different fragments were merged by the extractor as part of a multi-stage conversion process implemented in Python. For details of the data modelling process and the conversion process, see Chiarcos et al. (2025). For reasons of copyright, the WöWö remains our only source of sense information. For the other dictionaries mentioned above, we only make use of information about geographical variant forms (and their respective lemma URL).

2.3 Linking External Dictionaries

Aside from WöWö, the other Low German dictionaries considered here are accessible online, with URIs identifying the respective lemma, and we use only *this information* (the existence of a lemma and the assignment of a particular URL) to extend the WöWö core graph with an index for these in RDF. We assume that this information does not meet the threshold of originality legally required for copyright to apply (Margoni, 2016).

The dictionaries we work with are isolated from any other content available on the web. Yet, this does not mean that they do not contain links. In fact, *several* of the platforms from which the aforementioned dictionaries are drawn have been *designed* to provide inter-dialectal links, resp., links between different dictionaries,[6] but they only provide links *within* the respective ecosystem, whereas we pursue an open, extensible approach to integrate *any* piece of information accessible on the web.

Creating an LOD index for a dictionary requires to retrieve its complete content, to extract lemma forms and lemma URL and to store these in a TSV file. By means of the linking discussed in Sect. 3, we extend this file with the lemma form in WöWö, the WöWö URL (the actual link), and a confidence score (for pruning and verification, see Sect. 3.2). As only lexical forms are extracted from the external dictionaries, linking is solely grounded on agreement on the level of *forms*, without tackling the dimension of meaning. Figure 5 illustrates a case of 2:1 linking for a dictionary from a Low German dialect from the Netherlands (Twents), where the entries *Oal* 'slimely person' and *oal* 'eel' are linked to WöWö *Ool* 'eel', using `https://twentswoordenboek.nl` as a basis.

3 Lexical Linking by Formal Agreement

There is no single standard variety or standard orthography for Modern Low German, and the existing dialects differ in their phonology. In general, spellings of northern Low German in Germany closely follow the Standard German orthography. These are defective in the sense that certain phoneme differences are not systematically represented. In particular, this pertains to the three- or four-fold differentiation between several series of historically long *ê*, *ô*, and *ô̂* and their short and lengthened counterparts, whose writing cannot be

[4] `https://www.w3.org/2016/05/ontolex/`

[5] `https://ditschiplatt.de/woehrner-woeoer/`

[6] The WWB is published as part of the Trier Wörterbuchnetz (`https://woerterbuchnetz.de/`), which *can* provide HTML hyperlinks between different dictionaries, but it has been the only Low German dictionary on that platform. In late April 2025, a Mecklenburgian dictionary was added, but too late to be addressed in this paper. The Reuter dictionary is part of the Digitales Wörterbuch Niederdeutsch (DWN) (`https://www.niederdeutsche-literatur.de/dwn/`), along with three other Low German dictionaries whose print sources, however, are still under copyright.

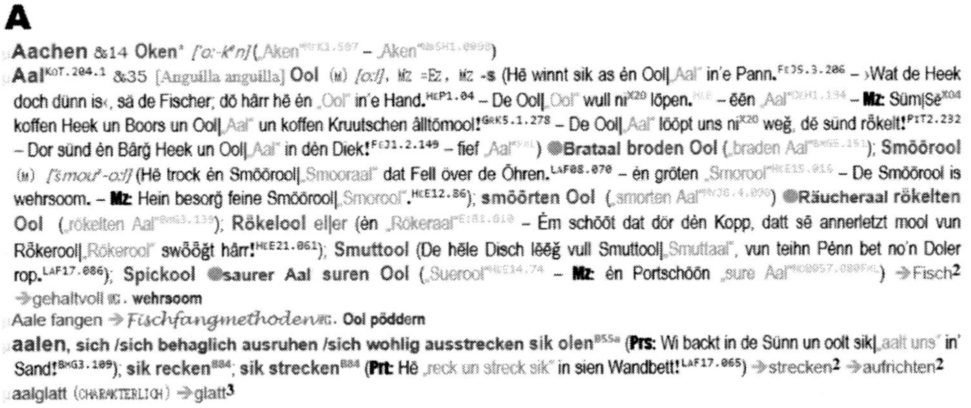

A

Aachen &14 **Oken*** [oː-kᵊn] („Aken – „Aken)

Aal[KoT.204.1] &35 [Anguilla anguilla] **Ool** (M) [oːl], Mz =Ez, Mz -s (Hē winnt sik as ėn Ool|„Aal" in'e Pann.[FeJ5.3.206] – ›Wat de Heek doch dünn is‹, sä de Fischer; dō hārr hē ėn „Ool" in'e Hand.[HeP1.04] – De Ool|„Ool" wull ni[X20] lōpen. – ēēn „Aal" – **Mz**: Süm|Se[X04] koffen Heek un Boors un Ool|„Aal" un koffen Kruutschen ålltōmool![GeK5.1.278] – De Ool|„Aal" lōōpt uns ni[X20] weğ, dē sünd rōkelt![PiT2.232] – Dor sünd ėn Bârğ Heek un Ool|„Aal" in dėn Diek![FeJ1.2.149] – fief „Aal") **Brataal broden Ool** („braden Aal"); **Smōōrool** (M) [ʃmouᵊ-oːl] (Hē trock ėn Smōōrool|„Smooraal" dat Fell över de Öhren.[LaF08.070] – ėn grōten „Smorool" – De Smōōrool is wehrsoom. – **Mz**: Hein besorğ feine Smōōrool|„Smorool".[HeE12.86]); **smōōrten Ool** („smorten Aal") **Räucheraal rökelten Ool** („rökelten Aal"); **Rōkelool** el|er (ėn „Rōkeraal" – Ėm schōōt dat dör dėn Kopp, datt sē annerletzt mool vun Rōkerool|„Rökerool" swōōğt hārr![HeE21.061]); **Smuttool** (De hēle Disch lēēğ vull Smuttool|„Smuttaal", vun teihn Pėnn bet no'n Doler rop.[LaF17.086]); **Spickool** **saurer Aal suren Ool** („Suerool" – **Mz**: ėn Portschōōn „sure Aal") →Fisch² →gehaltvoll. **wehrsoom**

Aale fangen → *Fischfangmethoden*. **Ool pöddern**

aalen, sich /sich behaglich ausruhen /sich wohlig ausstrecken sik olen (**Prs**: Wi backt in de Sünn un oolt sik|„aalt uns" in' Sand![BxG3.109]); **sik recken**; **sik strecken** (**Prt**: Hē „reck un streck sik" in sien Wandbett![LaF17.065]) →strecken² →aufrichten²

aalglatt (CHARAKTERLICH) →glatt³

Figure 3: Excerpt of the *Wöhrner Wöör* dictionary.

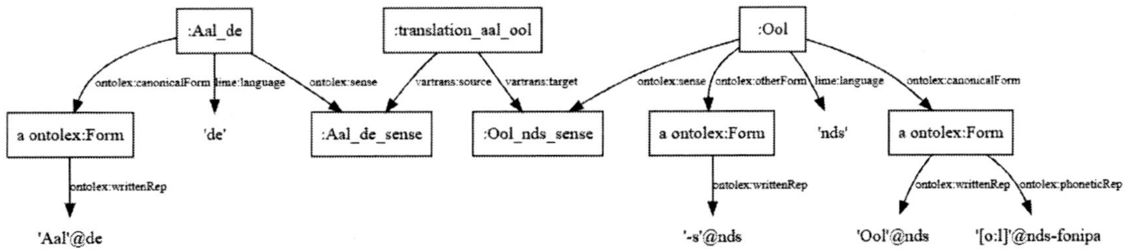

Figure 4: RDF conversion of WöWö lemma *Ool* and its German headword *Aal*, cf. second line of Fig. 3.

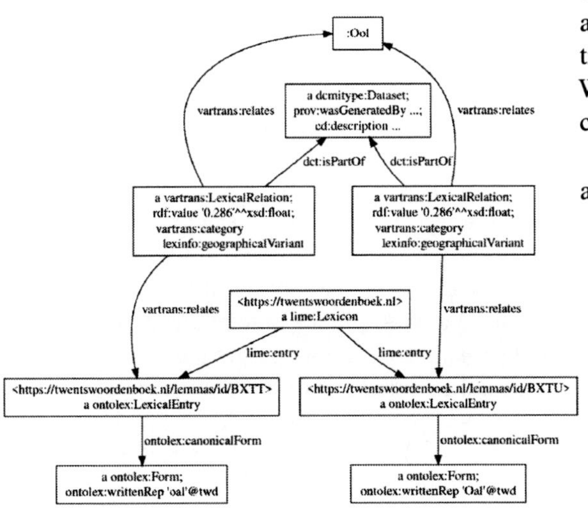

Figure 5: Reified `lexinfo:geographicalVariant` links between WöWö *Ool* 'eal' and Twents dictionary.

grounded on the 'intuitive' application of Standard German spelling conventions designed to express the two-fold distinction between long and short vowels only. Most southern Low German dialects are phonologically even richer and employ a multitude of custom orthographies. The Westphalian WWB dictionary uses a scientific notation for reconstructed interdialectal forms.

Phonological differences exhibited by the dialects of Low German include, for example

- **mergers**: Historically, Low German had four long *ê* phonemes and two long *ô* phonemes including their umlauted forms, while the modern dialects have merged some of these: While Reuter distinguishes $\hat{o}_1$ in *Kauken* 'cake' and $\hat{o}_2$ in *Bom* 'tree' , WöWö *Kōken* and *Bōōm* suggests a merger.

- **apocope and syncope**: unstressed Middle Low German short vowels are mostly lost in the north, and retained in the south.

- **lengthening and shortening of vowels**: applied in all dialects, but with different results. These were triggered by Middle Low German syllable structure, which, however, became obfuscated by apocope and syncope.

- **assimilation** of/with post-vocalic consonants, esp. *r*, led to regionally different results, e.g., for *Barg* 'mountain' (WöWö) alongside *Bo*^{a}*rg* (WWB).

Historical phonology and the characteristics of the respective orthographies are well understood, so that rules to map from one orthography to another can be relatively easily implemented on the basis of standard technology such as Finite State Transducers (FSTs). Because this involves manual labour, our study also aimed to assess the effort to create such a mapping: For speakers familiar with the conventions of the target representation, mapping an author-, source- or dictionary-specific orthography to an internal norm representation took between 3 and 6 working hours per source.

3.1 Normalization with FSTs

We use the Stuttgart Finite State Transducer (Schmid, 2006, SFST) library to normalize the spelling of each specific source to normalized phonological representations. In many cases, a single lemma can have multiple candidate normalizations, so that we do not operate with these directly. Instead, for any pair of lemmas that share a candidate normalization, we predict a possible link.

We base the normalized phonological representation on a specific dialect that features a small phoneme inventory (no diphthongization of long *ê*, *ô* and umlauted *ô̂*), and systematic apocope and syncope (when mapping into the norm representation, dropping a vowel can be more reliably predicted than its insertion). Several such varieties exist, both in dialects of North Saxon and East Low German, and as a point of orientation, we operate with the North Markian dialect (part of Brandenburgish in Figure 1) as documented by Pfaff (1898), Mackel (1905), Teuchert (1907) and Bretschneider (1951).[7] We first provide a mapping from source graphemes to North Markian phonemes, represented by a simplified phonological representation using ASCII characters. Where a source language grapheme has different possible readings (or different phonological mappings to North Markian), all possible interpretations are predicted. This also includes a rule to (optionally) drop e in all positions. In addition to context-free mappings, this also includes selected contextual assimilations and dissimilation processes, for which multi-character sequences are considered. Grapheme inventories and their mapping are established from the source dictionary in three steps:

1. Extract and split the character inventory and into vowel signs, consonant signs and other (punctuation, number) signs. This is done with a single regular expression.

2. Because many dictionaries employ digraphs or diacritics to disambiguate vowel phonemes, we extracted all continuous sequences of vowels or vowels followed by lengthening signs (*h*, *e*, *j*, *w*). For every vowel sequence, we manually verified around 50 occurrences for their pronounciation in the norm variety and provide a normalized pronounciation. We also keep note of assimilations of postvocalic vowels, and the development of vowels before *r*.

3. We then checked around 50 occurrences of every consonant as well as the apostroph (') to assess both their regular correspondence to the norm variety and the existence of possible digraphs. Special attention is paid to consonants at the end of words, and special rules for (undoing) final obstruent devoicing are added.

For a speaker familiar with SFST and the specifics of North Markian, creating an FST to normalize a dictionary in this way has been a matter of 3-6 hours, depending on the pecularities of phonology and orthography of the dialect under consideration. In addition to that, the final rulesets have been reviewed by a native speaker of North Saxon experienced in orthographical normalization across Low German dialects from different regions of Germany and the Netherlands.

3.2 Lemma Linking and Pruning

Because of ambiguities in the orthographies and complex phonological correspondences, the mapping overgenerates to some extent. As a countermeasure, we calculate confidence scores to assess the level of ambiguity in the linking. For every lemma in every dictionary, we predict all possible normalizations. For every pair of lemmas $\langle x, y \rangle$ from two dictionaries X and Y, and $x \in X$ and

[7]The approach would be applicable to *any* dialect with a similarly reduced phoneme inventory and apocope. This choice has been made because it allowed us to re-use an existing SFST implementation.

$y \in Y$, we predict a link if they overlap in one possible normalization. For the lemma y, $L_X(y)$ is the set of lemmas from X for which a link has been predicted. Link probability $P(x|y)$ is estimated as $\frac{1}{|L_X(y)|}$. We calculate confidence $c(x, y)$ of a $\langle x, y\rangle$ as the harmonic mean between the link probabilities $P(x|y)$ and $P(y|x)$: $c(x, y) = 2\frac{P(x|y)P(y|x)}{P(x|y)+P(y|x)}$.

On the basis of confidence scores, pruning is performed, in that, for every source dictionary X, only the highest-scored target links are retained. In our setting, the target dictionary is always WöWö. If there is more than one, we return the WöWö lemma with the lowest Levenshtein distance. If there is still more than one, we return the shortest WöWö lemma in order to create a bias against matches between multi-word expressions and their respective parts.[8]

3.3 Levenshtein Baseline

In the absence of training data for the respective orthographic systems under consideration here, we resort to Levenshtein distance as a baseline.[9] For performance reasons, Levenshtein distance is only calculated for the 150 most bigram-similar target lemmas for every source lemma. The linking is then pruned bidirectionally, such that for every source lemma only the most Levenshtein-similar target lemmas are preserved, and for every target lemma the most similar source lemmas.

4 Evaluation

We performed two independent evaluation experiments: evaluation against a small, manually linked glossary as a gold standard (Sect. 4.1), and evaluation of a sample of predicted links (Sect. 4.2). We employ two primary metrics, **precision** (proportion of predicted links that are confirmed), and **recall** (proportion of links in the the gold linking which are predicted). As we cannot evaluate recall from a *sample* of predicted links, Sect. 4.2 uses **coverage** in place of recall, i.e., the proportion of lemmas in the WöWö dictionary for which links are predicted (regardless if correct or not). It is to be noted that for practical application of cross-dialectal links in a lexical resource, it is essential to maintain a consistently high level of precision (at the price of recall/coverage) which, in general, should not fall below 80%. For configurations where 80% precision are achieved, we aim for maximizing coverage (resp. recall), as this leads to exhaustive linking.

We evaluate three different linking strategies: Along with FST-based linking (**FST**) and Levenshtein (**LEV**), we also compare an identity baseline (**IDENT**) which just creates a link between lemmas with identical forms. Whereas the second evaluation ran against a representative sample of Low German varieties spoken in Germany, the first evaluation (Sect. 4.1) was conducted against two varieties closer related to each other than to the North Markian dialect chosen as the basis for the normalization. In order to compensate the expected overperformance of IDENT baseline in comparison to other, less closely related dialects considered in Sect. 4.2, Sect. 4.1 employs a fourth linking strategy, **IDENT+FST** (FST-based linking with IDENT prior) which links all lemmas with identical forms, and applies FST to the remainder. As formulated above, neither FST nor LEV necessarily lead to unambiguous results. For evaluation, we restrict their predicted links to the lexicographically first candidate lemma from WöWö.

4.1 Evaluation against Wisser

The Wisser glossary is based on word list and linguistic description in Wilhelm Wisser's (1927) fairy tale collection from eastern Holstein. The glossary was manually linked with the WöWö by one of the authors, resulting in 1787 linked pairs out of 1920 overall Wisser glossary entries. Table 1 summarizes the evaluation results for the Wisser glossary. Despite WöWö (Dithmarschen / western Holstein) and Wisser (eastern Holstein) representing closely related varieties of North Saxon (which may be reflected in the high values for precision), identity matches yield relatively poor recall. This is largely due to different sets of diacritics employed to disambiguate phonemes.

[8]We enforce 1:1 correspondences between different dialects of Low German for technical reasons, as this eliminates the bias that $n : m$ correspondences could introduce into the evaluation. For practical applications of the procedure, multiple mappings of the same lexeme can be retained, if they achieve identical scores.

[9]We would expect substantially better results with weighted Levenshtein, but we have no empirical basis to set the weights accordingly. In general, a good rule of thumb for *Germanic languages* would be to penalize deviations in consonantism more than deviations in vowels, but this is a language-specific heuristic, and we would like to assess the viability of the procedure in a fully language-agnostic way. Furthermore, we also need to acknowledge that a 'naive' separation into consonants and vowels may lead to incorrect conclusions. This is partially due to diachronic phonology, assimilation and dissimilation processes, but also orthography: German-based orthographies use *h* to indicate vowel length, the Plautdietsch orthography uses *j* to mark palatalization, Dutch-based orthographies may use *j* for long *i*, etc. In none of these cases, the character is used to represent a consonant.

The Levenshtein distance (with different similarity thresholds) is more robust against such variation and outperforms the identity baseline in recall. However, its precision suffers from the failure to capture linguistically plausible replacements. As such, Wisser *anslạn* has equal Levenshtein distance with WöWö *ansēhn* 'look at' and *ansloon* 'put up, fasten', but whereas the latter is, indeed, the correct link, the similarity with the former is chance resemblance.

In the FST-based normalization, for every Wisser word, we link the highest-scored (least ambiguous) WöWö word it shares a candidate normalization with. FSTs do not distinguish between more or less plausible (frequent) patterns and the normalization contains considerable ambiguities. As a result, FST-based linking (with different confidence thresholds) can outperform LEV in precision (not in recall), but, at least for so closely related varieties as considered here, not the IDENT-baseline. Nevertheless, FST-based linking exceeds the IDENT baseline in f-score. In terms of f-score, the overall best performance is achieved with IDENT+FST and a confidence threshold of .6. I.e., for words not linked by IDENT, we limit FST predictions to cases in which one linking direction was unambiguous, and the other had no more than two alternatives. We conclude that FST-based normalization has the potential to outperform a naive Levenshtein distance for linking, but that, for closely related dialects, a combination with plain identity matches may be a strategy to further improve the results to the necessary level of quality.

	matches (true positives)	prec	rec	f
IDENT				
(= LEV 0)	193	.878	.119	.210
LEV				
≤ 1	458	.591	.268	.369
≤ 2	612	.455	.342	.390
≤ 3	643	.410	.358	.382
≤ 4	648	.395	.361	.377
unrestricted	652	.377	.362	.369
FST				
= 1.0	206	.687	.127	.214
$\geq .6$	265	.564	.164	.254
$\geq .5$	288	.492	.180	.264
$\geq .4$	304	.451	.190	.267
unrestricted	331	.294	.206	.242
IDENT+FST				
= 1.0	445	.816	.319	.459
$\geq .6$	492	**.702**	**.355**	**.472**
$\geq .5$	512	.627	.371	.466
$\geq .4$	524	.581	.38	.459
unrestricted	546	.402	.396	.399

Table 1: Evaluation against Wisser with different thresholds.

4.2 Evaluating Predicted Links

For the evaluation of FST and LEV linking of the external dictionaries against WöWö, we randomly sampled 50 WöWö lemmas and evaluated their predicted links (using random disambiguation for m:1 links) for every dictionary. For any dictionary where not all of the previously sampled WöWö lemmas were linked, we extended the initial list of WöWö lemmas accordingly such that at least 50 predicted WöWö links were evaluated for both methods and every external dictionary. Each candidate was then manually classified into one of three categories: **exact match**, **approx-match** (partial agreement, e.g., for linking one word with a multi-word expression, or with a related word, say, a morphologically derived form or a compound), and **mismatch** (including unrelated homophones).

We calculate precision in two ways, for exact-match precision, only exact matches are considered true positives, for approx-match precision, both exact and approximate matches are considered true positives. It is to be noted that the varying structures of the dictionaries linked to WöWö influenced the evaluation results: In Sass, Plattmakers, and Platt-WB, the matching rates are considerably higher because multiple inflectional word forms are grouped under the same lemma ID, and thus to be considered exact matches. This is not the case for Reuter and WWB, where, for instance, nouns and adjectives – such as *Trūe* 'loyalty' vs. *trūe* 'loyal' – are indexed separately.

The results are summarized in Fig. 6 comparing the overall match rates for LEV and FST. As the plots show, average precision in the FST-based linking consistently outperformed the baseline across all datasets. The LEV baseline achieved moderate precision but struggled especially with apocope-affected forms. For a cross-dialectal lexical resource that may also be used for consultation by humans, it is essential to guarantee a certain level of quality, for which we posit a threshold of 80% precision. In terms of exact-match precision, LEV fails to meet this threshold, but it is achieved with all FSTs with confidence ≥ 0.6. In terms of approx-match precision, this is achieved by all FSTs with confidence ≥ 0.2 as well as by LEV 0. Table 2 evaluates the coverage for these high-precision configurations, and also includes LEV 1 for comparison. Configurations with exact-match precision

	FST 1		FST ≥ 0.6		FST ≥ 0.5		FST ≥ 0.4		FST ≥ 0.3		FST ≥ 0.2		LEV 0 (IDENT)		LEV ≤ 1	
	prec	cov	prec	cov	prec	cov	prec	cov	prec	cov	prec	cov	prec	cov	prec	cov
Plattmakers	90.48%	4.66%	80.65%	**5.66%**	73.53%	6.06%	63.41%	6.36%	62.79%	**6.51%**	59.57%	6.79%	80.77%	4.88%	54.90%	9.18%
	90.48%	1243	90.32%	**1511**	85.29%	1619	82.93%	1698	81.40%	**1738**	78.72%	1812	92.31%	1304	62.75%	2450
PlattWB	85.71%	11.79%	81.08%	**15.36%**	77.78%	17.09%	70.37%	17.96%	70.18%	18.46%	66.15%	19.38%	63.64%	11.91%	59.70%	**23.61%**
	92.86%	3147	89.19%	**4100**	91.11%	4562	87.04%	4796	87.72%	4930	81.54%	5175	84.09%	3180	83.58%	**6303**
Reuter	96.88%	**5.77%**	78.72%	7.52%	69.64%	8.28%	65.63%	8.64%	65.67%	8.88%	65.22%	**9.25%**	61.76%	5.13%	55.36%	11.57%
	100.00%	**1541**	89.36%	2008	82.14%	2210	82.81%	2308	82.09%	2371	82.61%	**2470**	85.29%	1370	75.00%	3089
Sass	88.89%	15.52%	85.42%	19.11%	84.75%	20.40%	82.81%	21.12%	80.60%	**21.52%**	78.57%	22.18%	87.50%	13.58%	71.83%	**23.68%**
	91.67%	4144	91.67%	5103	91.53%	5446	92.19%	5640	91.04%	**5747**	90.00%	5923	97.92%	3625	83.10%	**6323**
WWB	96.15%	9.37%	87.18%	**12.21%**	76.00%	**13.52%**	72.73%	14.25%	66.67%	14.70%	61.11%	15.34%	85.71%	2.29%	48.94%	10.27%
	96.15%	2501	87.18%	**3260**	80.00%	**3609**	78.18%	3806	71.43%	3925	68.06%	4095	92.86%	611	68.09%	2743
average	91.62%	9.42%	82.61%	**11.97%**	76.34%	13.07%	70.99%	13.67%	69.18%	14.02%	66.12%	**14.59%**	75.88%	7.56%	58.15%	15.66%
	94.23%		89.54%		86.01%		84.63%		82.74%		80.19%		90.49%		74.50%	

Table 2: Evaluation of WöWö coverage for high-precision configurations (upper row: exact-match precision, lower row: approx-match precision; gray: $\geq 80\%$ exact-match precision, light gray: $\geq 80\%$ partial-match precision, bold: highest-coverage configuration per subset).

$\geq 80\%$ are colored gray and delineated with a solid line, configurations with partial-match precision $\geq 80\%$ are light gray with a dotted line. Within each group, the configuration with the highest coverage is marked in bold. Naturally, this coincides with lower degrees of precision. On average over all dictionaries, the best coverage for exact-match precision $\geq 80\%$ is achieved with FST ≥ 0.6, for partial-match precision $\geq 80\%$ with FST ≥ 0.2. For Sass and PlattWB, the highest coverage for partial-match precision is obtained with LEV 1, and, again, this may reflect the fact that both are dictionaries whose reference variety belongs to North Saxon and is therefore more closely related to WöWö than those of WWB or Reuter. It is to be noted that IDENT did not outperform FST or LEV as in the previous evaluation, and this may reflect the greater linguistic diversity represented by these dictionaries.

5 Results and Perspectives

We described and evaluated a methodology for creating a cross-dialectal lexical knowledge graph that consists of a core dictionary (WöWö) and its links to external, orthographically heterogeneous dictionaries of different dialects of Low German which are accessible over the web. Conceptually similar applications of these technologies to related sets of languages, dialects or dictionaries (for the same language) include, for example, the OntoLex/RDF modelling of bi-dictionaries for (primarily) the languages of the Iberian peninsula (Forcada, 2021; Gracia et al., 2018), the Bavarian dialects in Austria (Declerck et al., 2016), and a vast collection of dictionaries and related resources for Latin (Passarotti et al., 2020). However, the linking provided by resources is based on previously available conceptual or lexical knowledge, which for the case of Low German, does not exist in any electronic resource we are aware of.

Instead, our linking is based on a linguistically informed mapping of forms, without considering additional information provided by the external dictionaries. We found that the FST-based approach generally yields higher coverage than Levenshtein. This is an unsurprising result, as it effectively means that an approach with (moderate) manual effort outperforms an unsupervised approach. Yet, it is noteable that the actual manual effort is indeed low, for a speaker familiar with the language, setting up a new FST, resp., the underlying mapping tables requires approximately 3-6 hours per source dictionary.

The total number of links predicted for individual dictionaries is summarized in Tab. 3 (FST linking and unrestricted confidence scores). The resulting cross-dialectal knowledge graph is provided as a RDF/Turtle dump, and consists of multiple files (RDF Graphs) representing either a dictionary (WöWö), or its linking with an external dictionary (all other dictionaries), using URIs resolving to the original pages. The knowledge graph does not contain actual information from these dictionaries, but only lemma forms, the original URL and the confidence score. We also provide an HTML view, generated from the results of a SPARQL query. Note that this uses the URLs of the lexical entries (i.e., for external dictionaries, their native URL) as the basis for hyperlinks, so that all links can be interactively explored. For a human, this HTML file (resp., for a machine, the underlying RDF data) is capable of serving as a 'digital Rosetta Stone', linking dictionaries and mapping corresponding words

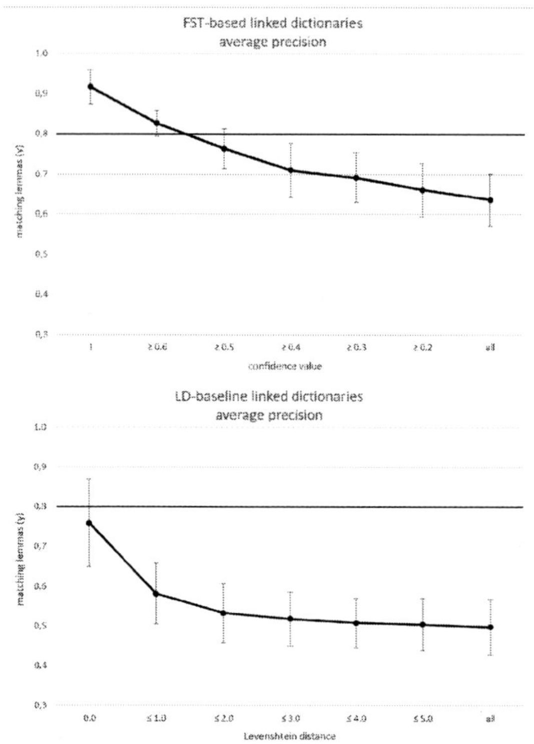

Figure 6: Average exact-match precision per source (Plattmakers, PlattWB, Reuter, Sass, WWB), computed over ≥50 WöWö links as a function of the confidence threshold for FST (top) and the distance threshold for LEV (bottom).

	linked dictionary entries		linked WöWö entries	
Plattmakers	36.30%	(2432/6700)	7.15%	(1908/26702)
PlattWB	27.81%	(6808/24479)	19.87%	(5307/26702)
Reuter	27.60%	(2834/10268)	9.60%	(2563/26702)
Sass	20.56%	(6826/33199)	22.62%	(6041/26702)
WWB	8.59%	(5841/68024)	15.76%	(4209/26702)
total			38.56%	(10295/26702)

Table 3: Resulting cross-dialectal links.

across dialects – without resorting to a standard variety or spelling.

The linking covers more than 10.000 WöWö entries. This number may appear small in comparison to the 26,702 of the WöWö in total, but to a large extent, this is due to compounds and derived forms that were included in WöWö, but not (or, at least, not as independent lemmas) in the other dictionaries because these are part of productive morphology. As such, we have 41 WöWö lemmas for *trecken* 'to pull' and its derived forms in WöWö, but only 18 of these have been linked. Further, WöWö contains a considerable number of phrasal expressions, which are not necessarily included in the other dictionaries, because these take a primary stance on documenting lexical semantics, not idiomatic expressions.

The linking method employed here primarily serves to establish a baseline for future research, our cross-dialectal dictionary serves as a testbed for a number of community standards for machine-readable dictionaries on the web in general, and for non-standardized, low-resource languages in particular. Future directions include the development of more refined methods for lexical alignment, where weights are trained on the basis of confirmed lexical link, as well as the improvement of the resources and to faciliate the further uptake of the methodologies for linking and data modelling by intensifying ties and establishing collaborations with providers of dictionaries in the realm of Low German as well as related languages and language varieties. Aside from contributing to the emerging, global network of web-accessible and interlinked lexical resources in OntoLex (Declerck et al., 2015), this also offers a possibility to improve the linking over a purely formal approach, as it then allows us to also integrate information from glosses, etc., directly, so that more traditional methods for translation inference across dictionaries (Mausam et al., 2009; Goel et al., 2022; Quadrado et al., 2023) can be used – which actually take translations and dictionary glosses into account.

Overall, we succeeded in creating an initial version of a 'Rosetta stone' for major dialects of Low German in Germany in the sense that there now is a human- and machine-readable lexical knowledge graph of (North Saxon) lemmas and their interdialectal links into other, externally hosted dictionaries. Directions for future research include using the generated links as an empirical basis for weighted Levenshtein, probabilistic FSTs and neural transliteration. Previously, these methods have not been applicable to Low German because of a general lack of parallel, cross-dialectal data.

Limitations

The WöWö dictionary is extremely rich and dense in lexicographic and linguistic information, but provided in a format tailored to human readers, which makes it virtually impossible to create an exhaustive RDF formalization. Thus, we extract and extend core aspects to include references to other dictionaries that may provide additional information, e.g., definitions. So far, we have only extracted basic information: lexical entries, written and phonetic representations, and translations. Additional details, such as usage examples, are more challenging to extract and left for future work. Another limitation is the restriction of the resulting lexical knowledge graph to WöWö lemmas for legal reasons. Nevertheless, we consider this data a valuable contribution because it can also serve as training data for future applications of statistical or neural methods of transliteration. These can then be applied to link the respective dictionaries directly and completely, if copyright clearance can be obtained.

Improvements over our experiments would be weighted Levenshtein Distance, probabilistic FSTs or supervised neural transliteration. However, we are not aware of suitable training data. In fact, the linking we produce could represent the first instance of such data. In the absence of training data, we implement a linguistically informed normalization by means of traditional symbolic methods, and generate candidate matches between normalized source language lemmas and normalized WöWö lemmas, ranked by a confidence score that captures the level of (formal) ambiguity in $n : m$ mappings. While the phonological correspondences are well understood and uncontroversial, use of solely formal criteria is prone to link formally similar but semantically unrelated lemmas.

Because of concerns regarding legal constraints for the re-usability of external resources, the resulting knowledge graph is restricted to lemmas in the WöWö dictionary. If the linking is applied into all directions, much better coverage of the vocabulary is to be expected. We refrain from incorporating sense definitions (or glosses) of these resources into the resulting knowledge graph, as this might constitute an infringement of intellectual property, but without definitions, these links can neither be validated nor provide actual lexical information. While the resulting knowledge graph is built with LLOD technology, it does not actually constitute Linguistic Linked Open Data, as our WöWö data is linked with dictionaries whose lexical entry URIs resolve to HTML, not RDF, and most of these linked data sources are not 'open' in the sense of the Open Definition. Whenever any of these sources become accessible as Linked (Open) Data, they can, however, be seamlessly integrated.

It may seem like another limitation that we did not compare with an LLM baseline. As Low German literature is relatively extensive, at least prominent authors such as Fritz Reuter (Mecklenburgian) and the Low German Wikipedias have been present in the training data of multilingual LLMs. We conducted a number of such experiments with GPT-4o and focused on Reuter, the full character inventories of Reuter and WöWö dictionaries, and a randomly selected set of lemmas from both dictionaries. Initially, our prompts were tailored towards creating SFST transducers, but as GPT-4o repeatedly returned FOMA syntax, we eventually asked for FOMA. These resulting transducers effectively performed 1:1 mappings and the removal of diacritics. To put more focus on the mapping task itself, we then changed the prompt to produce a JSON dictionary with character replacements. Again, these were effectively 1:1 replacements and diacritic removal. Without any promising result, we abandoned these experiments after two working days. For comparison, writing the Reuter FST by hand took 3 hours. It is unsurprising that LLMs largely fail at this task because even though they certainly have seen some Low German data as part of their training, they seem to have difficulties to generalize over the multitude of orthographies in a way that allows for transliteration. This may actually be different when asking the system to transliterate directly, but this clearly is an unjustifiable waste of energy in comparison to the little human effort it takes to come up with a mapping table. An alternative future direction for LLM-based techniques may include encapsulating FSTs or a cross-dialectal dictionary lookup as agentic components, so that the language capacity (implicitly normalized towards the majority dialects as represented in the literature used for training) of the model is separated from its actual transliteration capabilities (for which it lacks training data). With FSTs and an a cross-dialectal, interlinked resource, fundamental components for such a system are provided along with this paper.

Acknowledgements

We would like to thank Peter Neuber for providing us with the basis for our cross-dialectal lexical knowledge graph, as well as four anonymous reviewers for comments and feedback. The contribution of Christian Fäth has been partially supported by a travel grant by the Center for Advanced Transnational Studies (Jakob-Fugger-Zentrum) at the University of Augsburg. Janine Siewert's work was supported by the Research Council of Finland through project No. 342859 "CorCoDial – Corpus-based computational dialectology".

References

Astrid Adler and Rahel Beyer. 2017. Languages and language policies in Germany/Sprachen und Sprachenpolitik in Deutschland. In *National language institutions and national languages. Contributions to the EFNIL Conference*, pages 221–242.

Andreas Bieberstedt. 2021. Niederdeutsch als Lehrvarietät. Aspekte einer Normierung des Niederdeutschen für den Unterricht am Beispiel der Orthographie. In Birte Arendt, Robert Langhanke, and Ulrike Stern, editors, *Niederdeutschdidaktik: Ansätze–Problemfelder–Perspektiven*, pages 247–284. Peter Lang, Berlin and New York.

Christian Bizer, Tom Heath, and Tim Berners-Lee. 2009. Linked Data - The Story So Far. *International Journal on Semantic Web and Information Systems (IJSWIS)*, 5(3):1–22.

Verena Blaschke, Hinrich Schütze, and Barbara Plank. 2023. A Survey of Corpora for Germanic Low-Resource Languages and Dialect. In *Proceedings of the 24th Nordic Conference on Computational Linguistics (NoDaLiDa)*, pages 392–414.

Anneliese Bretschneider. 1951. Volkssprache der Prignitz. *Jahrbuch des Vereins für niederdeutsche Sprachforschung*, 74, p.82-98, and 75, p.62-109.

Elke Brückmann. 2025. Das Online-Wörterbuch für ostfriesisches Plattdeutsch. `https://www.platt-wb.de`. Accessed Jan 6th, 2025; based on Vries, Gernot de, Ostfriesisches Wörterbuch Hochdeutsch / Plattdeutsch. Oostfreesk Woordenbook Hoogdüütsk / Plattdüütsk, Leer 2000.

Marcus Buck. 2007-2024. Plattmakers Das Plattdeutsche Wörterbuch. `https://plattmakers.de`. Accessed Jan 15th, 2024.

Christian Chiarcos, Tabea Gröger, and Christian Fäth. 2025. Putting Low German on the map (of Linguistic Linked Open Data). In *Proceedings of the 5th Conference on Language, Data and Knowledge (LDK-2025)*, Naples, Italy.

Philipp Cimiano, Christian Chiarcos, John P McCrae, and Jorge Gracia. 2020. *Linguistic Linked Data: Representation, Generation and Applications*. Springer Nature.

Thierry Declerck, Amelie Dorn, and Eveline Wandl-Vogt. 2016. Adding Polarity Information to Entries of the Database of Bavarian Dialects in Austria. In *Proceedings of the 17th EURALEX International Congress, Ivane Javakhishvili Tbilisi University Press, Tbilisi, Georgia*, pages 654–659.

Thierry Declerck, Eveline Wandl-Vogt, and Karlheinz Mörth. 2015. Towards a pan European lexicography by means of linked (open) data. *Proceedings of eLex*, pages 342–355.

Klaas-Hinrich Ehlers. 2021. Welches Niederdeutsch unterrichten? Ein kritischer Problemaufriss vor dem Hintergrund der jüngeren Entwicklung des Niederdeutschen in Mecklenburg-Vorpommern. In Birte Arendt, Robert Langhanke, and Ulrike Stern, editors, *Niederdeutschdidaktik: Ansätze–Problemfelder–Perspektiven*, pages 29–60. Peter Lang, Berlin and New York.

Mikel L Forcada. 2021. Free/open-source machine translation for the low-resource languages of spain. In *3rd Conference on Language, Data and Knowledge (LDK 2021)*. Schloss Dagstuhl–Leibniz-Zentrum für Informatik.

Shashwat Goel, Jorge Gracia, and Mikel L Forcada. 2022. Bilingual dictionary generation and enrichment via graph exploration. *Semantic Web*, 13(6):1103–1132.

Jorge Gracia and Daniel Vila-Suero. 2015. Guidelines for linguistic linked data generation: Bilingual dictionaries. Technical report, W3C Community Group Best Practices for Multilingual Linked Open Data (BMLOD). Final Community Group Report 29 September 2015.

Jorge Gracia, Marta Villegas, Asuncion Gomez-Perez, and Nuria Bel. 2018. The apertium bilingual dictionaries on the web of data. *Semantic Web*, 9(2):231–240.

Peter Hansen. 2025. Das Fritz-Reuter-Wörterbuch. `https://www.niederdeutsche-literatur.de/dwn/index-frw.php`. Accessed Jan 6th, 2025.

Emil Mackel. 1905. *Die Mundart der Prignitz*. Soltau.

Thomas Margoni. 2016. The Harmonisation of EU Copyright Law: The Originality Standard. In Mark Perry, editor, *Global Governance of Intellectual Property in the 21st Century: Reflecting Policy Through Change*, pages 85–105. Springer International Publishing, Cham.

Peter Martens. 1979. Zum normativen Zwang der Standardsprache. Anpassung von mundartlichen Ausspracheformen und Schreibweisen an die hochdeutschen Standardsysteme. *Zeitschrift für Dialektologie und Linguistik*, pages 7–25.

Peter Martens. 2002. Zur Schreibung des Niederdeutschen. Eine Kritik der "Bremer Schreibung" in der" Niederdeutschen Grammatik" von 1998. *Zeitschrift für Dialektologie und Linguistik*, 69(H. 2):146–163.

Mausam, Stephen Soderland, Oren Etzioni, Daniel Weld, Michael Skinner, and Jeff Bilmes. 2009. Compiling a Massive, Multilingual Dictionary via Probabilistic Inference. In *Proceedings of the Joint Conference of the 47th Annual Meeting of the ACL and the 4th International Joint Conference on Natural Language Processing of the AFNLP*, pages 262–270, Suntec, Singapore. Association for Computational Linguistics.

Carl Friedrich Müller. 1904. *Reuter-Lexikon: der plattdeutsche Sprachschatz in Fritz Reuters Schriften*, volume 19. Hesse & Becker.

Peter Neuber. 2001. *Wöhrner Wöör: Niederdeutsches Wörterbuch aus Dithmarschen ; hochdeutsch - plattdeutsch*. P. Neuber, Wöhrden.

Hermann Niebaum, Hans Taubken, Paul Teepe, Felix Wortmann, and Robert Damme. 1969-2021. *Westfälisches Wörterbuch*. Kommission für Mundart- und Namenforschung des Landschaftsverbandes Westfalen-Lippe. Wachholtz Verlag Murmann Publishers, Kiel/Hamburg. 5 Vols; digitally edited by the Wörterbuchnetz of the Trier Center for Digital Humanities, Version 01/23, `https://www.woerterbuchnetz.de/WWB`, accessed 2025-03-11.

Marco Passarotti, Francesco Mambrini, Greta Franzini, Flavio Massimiliano Cecchini, Eleonora Litta, Giovanni Moretti, Paolo Ruffolo, and Rachele Sprugnoli. 2020. Interlinking through lemmas. the lexical collection of the lila knowledge base of linguistic resources for latin. *Studi e Saggi Linguistici*, 58(1):177–212.

Hermann Pfaff. 1898. *Die Vocale des mittelpommerschen Dialects*, volume 239. A. Straube.

João Pedro Quadrado, Carlos Roberto Valêncio, Adriane Orenha Ottaiano, Geraldo Francisco D Zafalon, Luís Marcello Moraes Silva, and Angelo Cesar Colombini. 2023. Generation of new bilingual dictionaries through inference techniques supported by a graph oriented database management system. In *2023 IEEE International Conference on Knowledge Graph (ICKG)*, pages 19–26. IEEE.

Gertrud Reershemius. 2010. Niederdeutsch im Internet. Möglichkeiten und Grenzen computervermittelter Kommunikation für den Spracherhalt. *Zeitschrift für Dialektologie und Linguistik*, 77(2):183–206.

Leoš Šatava. 2019. New speakers in the context of the minority languages in Europe and the revitalization efforts. *Treatises and Documents, Journal of Ethnic Studies*, 82:131–51.

Helmut Schmid. 2006. A Programming Language for Finite State Transducers. In *Finite-State Methods and Natural Language Processing: 5th International Workshop, FSMNLP 2005, Helsinki, Finland, September 1-2, 2005, Revised Papers*, volume 4002, page 308. Springer Science & Business Media.

Andrew Charles Schwenk. 2017. *Promoting and monitoring Low German: education policies and ideologies of language in the northern German Bundesländer*. Ph.D. thesis, University of Illinois at Urbana-Champaign.

Eduard Sievers. 1875. *Der Heliand und die angelsächsische Genesis*. Lippert.

Claudia Soria, Irene Russo, Valeria Quochi, Davyth Hicks, Antton Gurrutxaga, Anneli Sarhimaa, and Matti Tuomisto. 2016. Fostering digital representation of EU regional and minority languages: The digital language diversity project. In *Proceedings of the Tenth International Conference on Language Resources and Evaluation (LREC'16)*, pages 3256–3260.

Hermann Teuchert. 1907. Die Mundart von Warthe (Uckermark). *Niederdeutsches Jahrbuch*, 33:27.

Hermann Teuchert. 1914. Zur plattdeutschen Rechtschreibung. *Zeitschrift für Deutsche Mundarten*, pages 228–237.

Heinrich Thies. 2025. SASS Plattdeutsches Netzwörterbuch. `https://netz.sass-platt.de`. Accessed Jan 6th, 2025.

Kathrin Weber and Timo Schürmann. 2018. Verschriftung und Normierung–niederdeutsche WhatsApp-Kommunikation innerhalb einer geschlossenen SchreiberInnengruppe. *Networx; 82*.

Wilhelm Wisser. 1927. *Plattdeutsche Volksmärchen*. Eugen Diederichs Verlag, Jena.

A Appendix

WöWö	German translation (WöWö)	Plattmakers	PlattWb	Reuter	Sass	WWB
Dubenslağ	Taubenschlag			Duwenslag [1.0]	Duvenslag [1.0]	Düwen-slag [1.0]
Dwang	Zwang	Dwang [1.0]	Dwang [1.0]	Dwang [1.0]	Dwang [1.0]	Dwang [1.0]
Dwárgenrott	Zwergenschar				Dwargenrott [1.0]	
Dwârğ	Zwerg	Dwarg [1.0]			Dwarg [1.0]	
Dwéérbålken	Querbalken1				Dweerbalken [1.0]	
Dwēērsack	Quersack /Schultersack	Dweersack [1.0]				Dwe^{e}rs-sak [1.0]
Dwēērstock	Fenstersprosse					Dwe^{e}rs-stäke [0.67] Dwe^{e}rs-stok [0.67]
Dwēērweğ	Querweg	Dweerweg [1.0]				
Dwēēr|Quēēr	Quer durch den Garten					Kwe^{e}re [0.67]
Dårm	Darm		Darm [1.0]	Darm [1.0]	Darm [1.0]	Darm [1.0]
Dädersch|e	Täterin				Dädersche [1.0]	
Dään	Däne				Dään [0.5]	Di^{e}ne [0.67]

Figure 7: Interdialectal link index, HTML export (excerpt), columns from left to right showing WöWö, German translation (WöWö), Plattmakers, PlattWb, Reuter, Sass and WWB.

Applying an Information-theoretic Approach for Automatic Identification of German Multi-word Expressions

Sergei Bagdasarov
Saarland University, Germany
sergeiba@lst.uni-saarland.de

Elke Teich
Saarland University, Germany
e.teich@mx.uni-saarland.de

Abstract

In this study, we apply a largely information-theoretic approach to identify and extract German multi-word expressions (MWEs) from selected corpora. We analyze the register-specific use of MWEs, comparing medical scientific abstracts and newspaper articles. Our results show that the two registers vary in the use of MWEs both structurally and semantically. For instance, scientific texts exhibit more discourse-related MWEs and expressions that denote objects or phenomena, whereas in newspaper texts we observe more MWEs denoting persons or functioning as references to time or place. Furthermore, we interpret these differences in terms of the situational context, i.e. field (topic), tenor (attitude), and mode (discourse).

1 Introduction

Multi-word expressions (MWEs), formulaic sequences of at least two words that tend to cooccur together, make up a considerable proportion of language. MWEs vary greatly in their nature, ranging from highly opaque idiomatic expressions like *da liegt der Hund begraben*, complex prepositions (*in Bezug auf*) to light verb constructions (*zur Verfügung stellen*) and terminological patterns (*lokale Tumorkontrolle*). Despite their heterogeneity, MWEs seem to share a common property of being processed holistically as whole units or at least providing predictable transitions from one token to the other. This results in a processing advantage in comparison to non-formulaic sequences of comparable length (Tremblay and Baayen, 2010; Siyanova-Chanturia et al., 2017).

This processing advantage make MWEs an important factor influencing the formation of an efficient code of communication, especially within clearly distinguishable functional varieties of language, i.e., registers. However, the functional variation in the use of formulaic language, particularly in languages other than English, seems to be an under-researched topic in linguistics. Another yet unresolved question, despite more than two decades of active research, is the accurate identification, extraction, and classification of MWEs.

Our goal here is, therefore, twofold. First, we test a novel information-theoretic approach for MWE extraction (Gries, 2022a) that, to the best of our knowledge, has not been used on German data yet. Second, we aim to analyze the formulaic language in German scientific and newspaper texts and establish how the contextual differences between these two registers impact the use of MWEs.

The remainder of the paper is structured as follows. Section 2 offers an overview of related work on register variation in English and German, as well as different approaches to MWE identification. Section 3 presents our data and briefly describes the MWE identification procedure used in this study. In Sections 4 and 5 we present the MWEs extracted from our data and discuss the use of formulaic language in German scientific and newspaper texts. And finally, Section 6 summarizes the present work and outlines the potential for future research.

2 Related Work

2.1 Register Variation

Conceptually, our work is rooted in register theory, register being defined as a language variety that can be described in terms of its context of situation (field, tenor, and mode (Halliday and Hasan, 1985)). The field of discourse refers to the topic of a text as well as to the overall purpose of communication (e.g., transmit information, describe world phenomena, etc.). Thus, variation in field is especially evident at the lexical level including specific terminology in specialized texts (such as scientific texts). The tenor of discourse describes the relationship between the author and the audi-

Proceedings of the 21st Conference on Natural Language Processing (KONVENS), Volume 1: Long and Short Papers, pages 295–305, 2025

ence (e.g., professional vs. layperson) as well as the author's attitude towards the subject matter of a text. Finally, the mode refers to the channel and medium of communication (spoken vs. written) as well as to the general discourse organization of a text.

Building on this theoretical framework, Biber and Gray (2010) and Biber and Conrad (2019) conducted extensive research on English scientific writing, comparing it to other registers. There are also numerous studies that adopt a diachronic perspective showing the evolution and formation of a register. For instance, Biber and Gray (2011) show how scientific English evolved towards a more nominal style of writing. Similarly, Degaetano-Ortlieb and Teich (2022) and Degaetano-Ortlieb (2021) apply information-theoretic methods to trace how scientific English became more conventionalized and informationally denser over a period of 300+ years.

While the research on register variation is mostly focused on English, the German language has been studied from this perspective as well. For example, Neumann (2014) carried out a comprehensive study of eight registers in German and English based on a broad selection of linguistic features; or Kunz and Lapshinova-Koltunski (2015) and Krielke (2021) explore discourse-related and syntactic aspects of register variation in German, also drawing a comparison with English.

However, register-based studies on MWEs seem to be rather limited. Conrad and Biber (2005) analyze lexical bundles in different English registers. Similarly, Breeze (2013) studies the same type of MWEs in several legal subregisters. Adopting a broader perspective on MWEs, Alves et al. (2024a) and Alves et al. (2024b) conducted diachronic analyses of different MWE types in English scientific writing. However, to our knowledge, no comparative register-based study of German MWEs has been carried out yet.

2.2 MWE Identification

In MWE research, the problem of identification and extraction of MWEs is of key importance. Despite diverse and persistent efforts invested into developing extraction solutions in recent decades, this problem still remains a "pain in the neck" for linguists and NLP scholars (Sag et al., 2002).

The proposed approaches vary greatly in their conceptual basis and implementation. Some scholars rely on frequency as their criterion for MWE identification, extracting all sequences of *n* words that are more frequent than a defined threshold (lexical bundles) (Conrad and Biber, 2005; Breeze, 2013). Frequency is sometimes combined with some type of association measure such as mutual information (Simpson-Vlach and Ellis, 2010). Building on the idea of co-occurrence and association, Brunner and Steyer (2015) designed a corpus-driven MWE extraction approach based on collocation profiles. Again with a focus on German, Weller and Heid (2010) leverage syntactic relations to extract verbal MWEs by combining syntactic dependencies and association measures.

A variety of more computational extraction methods can also be found in the literature. For instance, Klyueva et al. (2017) use neural networks to extract verbal MWEs in 15 languages. In turn, Cap et al. (2013) trained a Conditional Random Fields classifier to detect light verb constructions in German. Moreover, a number of works rely on word embeddings for this task (Scherbakov et al., 2016; Loukachevitch and Parkhomenko, 2018).

While all these approaches have their advantages, they are subject to certain limitations. Methods that prioritize lexical bundles overlook less frequent MWEs or shorter word sequences that, however, might still be worthy of analysis (e.g., some named entities, terminological patterns). Syntactic approaches rely on previous parsing of texts and, therefore, are language-sensitive. Moreover, they often focus only on one specific type of MWEs. Automatic approaches are limited by the data sets used for training. For instance, systems that participated in the PARSEME shared task (Ramisch et al., 2020) only cover verbal MWEs in different languages, while works presented in the DiMSUM shared task (Schneider et al., 2016) focus only on English MWEs.

To overcome these limitations, some scholars combine different state-of-the-art methods in their MWE research (Alves et al., 2024a,b), which improves recall. Alternatively, one could apply a statistically motivated and language-independent extraction procedure that is capable of retrieving MWEs of different types. Such a procedure was developed by Gries (2022a) and will be described in the next section.

3 Data and Methods

3.1 Data

For the analysis of MWEs in German newspaper texts we use the Tiger corpus (version 2.2) (Brants et al., 2004). The Tiger corpus contains newspaper articles extracted from *Frankfurter Rundschau*, consisting of over 800,000 tokens.

To cover texts of the medical domain, we use the German part of the Springer medical corpus available through the MuchMore project.[1] The corpus was compiled using medical abstracts from 41 different domains ranging from arthroscopy to legal medicine, with the German part containing roughly 1,000,000 tokens. General corpus statistics are summarized in Table 1

Corpus	Texts	Sentences	Tokens
Tiger	2,163	50,474	843,232
Springer	7,808	54,839	1,137,843

Table 1: Corpus statistics for Tiger and Springer datasets.

3.2 Extraction Method

We use a largely information-theoretic method proposed by Gries (2022a) to automatically identify and extract MWEs. The core idea of the method boils down to splitting a corpus into bigrams, iterating through the bigrams, and selecting the best MWE candidates based on eight dimensions. The best candidates are then merged into one single unit, and the process is repeated N number of iterations.

The eight dimensions[2] involved in this method capture different aspects of formulaicity that characterize MWEs. Given a hypothetical bigram *ab*, these dimensions are as follows:

Dimension 1 (frequency): total bigram frequency; here, we apply a threshold of at least 10 occurrences.

Dimension 2 (dispersion): how well a bigram is distributed throughout the corpus, as measured by normalized Kullback-Leibler divergence (KLD):

$$\mathrm{KLD}(P \parallel Q) = \sum_x P(x) \log \frac{P(x)}{Q(x)} \quad (1)$$

$$\mathrm{KLD}_{\mathrm{norm}} = 1 - e^{-\mathrm{KLD}} \quad (2)$$

Dimensions 3 and 4 (type frequency): how many unique token types occur after *a* and before *b*.

[1]https://muchmore.dfki.de/resources1.htm

[2]Here, we just give a general overview of these dimensions. For more information on calculations and reasons for selecting the dimensions, see Gries (2022a), Gries (2020) and Gries (2022b).

Dimensions 5 and 6 (normalized entropy): how much uncertainty there is about what follows the token *a* and precedes the token *b*:

$$H_{\mathrm{norm}} = -\frac{\sum_{i=1}^{n} p_i \times \log_2 p_i}{\log_2 n} \quad (3)$$

Dimensions 7 and 8 (association): how strongly *a* is attracted to *b* and vice versa, as measured by normalized KLD (see again Equation 2).

After calculating the dimensions, they are normalized to range from 0 to 1 (if not already), creating an eight-dimensional vector. Euclidean distance (ED) is then computed to measure the distance of each bigram from the center of the eight-dimensional space and select the most suitable MWE candidate.

We implemented this extraction algorithm in Python, adding a preprocessing step in which all numbers, special characters and punctuation marks except for hyphens are removed. No lemmatization was performed during the preprocessing. For now, we limit the number of iterations to 200 due to the high computational load, with each iteration yielding 5 MWEs.

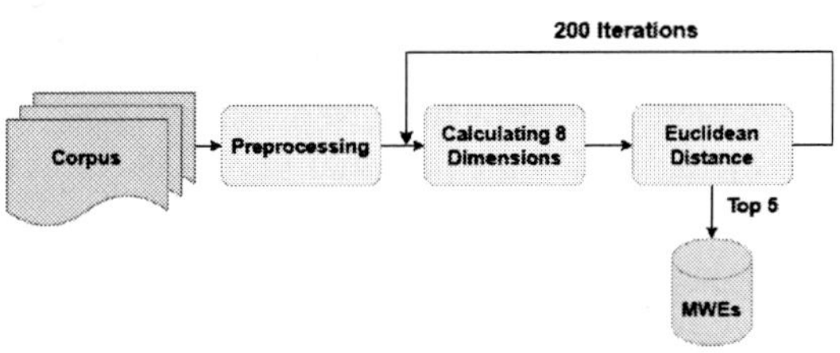

Figure 1: MWE extraction pipeline.

This extraction logic is visualized in Figure 1 and can be further illustrated with the example of the MWE *in der laufenden Periode*. First, an MWE candidate composed of tokens *laufenden* and *Periode* was ranked second by ED in iteration 29 and merged into one unit *laufenden Periode*. Then, an MWE candidate consisting of elements *der* and *laufenden Periode* was ranked third by ED in iteration 32 and merged into the unit *der laufenden Periode*. And finally, in iteration 151, an MWE candidate consisting of elements *in* and *der laufenden Periode* was ranked second by ED and merged into the final MWE *in der laufenden Periode*.

For the follow-up analysis of the extracted MWEs, we rely on the association measure again (Equations 1 and 2). However, instead of calculating the strength of the forward and backward association, we obtain one measure for the whole MWE. For instance, if an MWE consists of two elements, we calculate the association *a–>b* and *b–>a* and take the mean of both values. If an MWE has more than two elements, we calculate the association for each MWE part as described above and then take the mean of the resulting values. For example, the association strength of the MWE *in der laufenden Periode* would be the mean of the association scores of *in <–> der*, *in der <–> laufenden*, and *in der laufenden <–> Periode*.

4 Results

4.1 Extraction Results

The extraction procedure applied as described above yielded 1,000 potential MWEs for each corpus. However, thorough filtering was still required to reduce noise. First, we automatically removed all MWE candidates that were included in longer sequences. For example, *jeden Fall* was rejected because it also occurs in *auf jeden Fall*. This led to the exclusion of 194 MWE candidates from the Springer corpus and 176 MWE candidates from the Tiger corpus.

Subsequently, a human annotator with a solid linguistic background was tasked with the manual evaluation of the remaining MWE candidates. The annotator labeled the potential MWEs as successful and unsuccessful with 1s and 0s respectively according to the following criteria:

- A successful MWE consists of at least two words.
- A successful MWE constitutes a semantic unit but not necessarily a non-compositional one.
- A successful MWE does not consist only of two tokens that are grammatically or syntactically inherently bound to each other.
- A successful MWE can be allocated to one of the 10 predefined categories.[3]

The categories used for the classification of the extracted MWEs are:

Object/Phenomenon: material objects, abstract concepts, world phenomena (*der koronaren Herzkrankheit, moderne Wirtschaftspolitik*);

Person: persons' names or MWEs referring to individuals or groups and/or their function or status (*Bundestagspräsidentin Rita Süssmuth, ein Sprecher des*);

Organization: political/economic entities (*der Bundesrepublik Deutschland, der Europäischen Union*);

Action/Process/Condition: verbal or nominal MWEs denoting actions and processes or describing persons or objects (*scharf kritisiert, zur Verfügung gestellt, die statistische Auswertung*);

Discourse organizer: MWEs used to create text cohesion (*Ziel dieser Arbeit, aus diesem Grund, vor allem*);

Place: geographic locations, directions, references to places with varying degree of specificity (*in den USA, an unserer Klinik, in der Nähe*);

Time: time references with varying degree of specificity (*im nächsten Jahr, unmittelbar vor, nach Herztransplantation*);

Quantity: MWEs indicating the amount of measurable objects (*Milliarden Mark, ein paar, eine Vielzahl von*);

Attribute: characteristics or features of persons or objects (*im Alter von, Kilometer langen, statistisch signifikanten*);

Mode of Action: MWEs describing an action or process (*in vitro, immer wieder, aus Protest gegen*).

After the filtering according to these criteria, we retained 609 MWEs extracted from the Tiger corpus and 553 MWEs extracted from the Springer corpus, resulting in a precision of 60.9% and 55.3% respectively. Youssef (2024) reported a comparable precision of 48% for English data. Note that the higher precision values in our results are likely due to the exclusion of all bigrams containing symbols or punctuation during preprocessing, reducing the number of unsuccessful MWE candidates. Recall could not be calculated, as the total number of MWEs present in the corpora is unknown.

We grouped the successful MWEs into several broad syntactic patterns based on the Universal Dependencies POS tags (de Marneffe et al.) of their components (see Table 2). We found more nominal and adjectival MWEs and in the Springer corpus, structures that reflect terminology formation patterns typical of scientific language (*einer retrospektiven Studie*). Verbal MWEs are also more prominent in the Springer corpus. These are mostly expressions used for topic introduction or method description (*retrospektiv analysiert, wir untersuchten*).

In contrast, the most common MWEs extracted from the Tiger corpus are prepositional phrases,

[3]These criteria are an adapted version of the annotation guidelines used in Youssef (2024)

probably due to the need for very specific time and place references in newspaper texts (*im Ausland, am heutigen Dienstag*).

Pattern	Tiger	Springer
NP	257	279
PP	255	117
AdjP	3	23
VP	50	101
AdvP	24	15
Misc	20	18

Table 2: MWEs POS patterns. NP: noun phrase, PP: prepositional phrase, AdjP: adjectival phrase, VP: verb phrase, AdvP: adverbal phrase

Among unsuccessful MWEs, the most commonly encountered POS patterns are: determiner + noun (*der Kunde, des Parteitags*),[4] determiner + adjective (*ein neues, ein wichtiges*), reflexive pronoun + verb (*einigten sich*), and particle + infitive (*zu finanzieren*). These four patters account for 87% and 84% of rejected MWEs in Tiger and Springer corpora respectively (see Table 3 for a more detailed overview).

Pattern	Tiger	Springer
DET NOUN	102	89
DET ADJ	39	42
PART VERB	33	49
VERB PRON	14	33
Misc	27	40

Table 3: POS patterns of unsuccessful MWEs. Category "Misc" includes POS patters that correspond to less than 10 unique MWEs.

In successful MWEs, the first component tends to be more strongly connected to the second component than vice versa. The opposite trend is observed in unsuccessful MWEs. This pattern is reflected in both forward and backward association measures, as well as in the distribution of items following the first component and preceding the second component (see Figures 2 and 3). These differences are in line with the POS patterns of the excluded MWEs most of which are determiner+noun or determiner+adjective sequences. No differences in frequency and dispersion between successful and unsuccessful MWEs were observed.

[4]However, we opted to keep some cases where determiner and noun/adjective do form a fossilized construction (*ein Viertel, dieses Jahres*).

4.2 MWE Categories

The most common MWE categories in the Tiger corpus are **Place**, **Time**, **Person**, **Discourse organizer** and **Action/Process/Condition** (see Figure 4). The latter two are also prominently attested in the Springer corpus. However, **Object/Phenomenon** is the most common MWE type in scientific texts. In the following paragraphs, we will have a closer look at the most relevant MWE categories in both corpora.

Object/Phenomenon. In the Springer corpus, this MWE type is mostly represented by terminology referring to (a) diseases (*koronare Herzkrankheit*), (b) body parts (*langen Röhrenknochen, unteren Extremitäten*), (c) substances (*Vitamin E, mit Antikörpern gegen*), or (d) abstract concepts (*therapeutische Konsequenzen, ein breites Spektrum*). Many of the Springer MWEs of this type are Latin or English terms (*Ramus interventricularis anterior, Injury Severity Score*). In the Tiger corpus, this MWE type is much less frequent and consists primarily of MWEs that denote abstract concepts from the field of politics, economy or sociology (*die absolute Mehrheit, rote Zahlen, gute Chancen*).

Discourse organizers. Springer data features MWEs that (a) describe authors' scientific activity (*wir beschreiben, wir untersuchten, berichten wir über*), (b) refer to the authors' paper or study (*Ziel dieser Arbeit, der vorliegende Artikel*), or (c) present or interpret results (*legen nahe daß, sprechen dafür daß, fanden wir*). In contrast, Tiger discourse organizing MWEs contain expressions that (a) indicate the source of information (*nach offiziellen Angaben, einem Bericht der*), (b) present overall context (*angesichts des, vor diesem Hintergrund*), or (c) describe personal attitude (*er hoffe, ich denke, nach Ansicht*). Apart from that, both corpora share a number of common cohesive devices (*in der Regel, in diesem Zusammenhang, vor allem, darüber hinaus*).

Action/Process/Conditions. As mentioned in Section 4.1, MWEs of this type comprise both verbal and nominal patterns. In the Springer texts, they often refer to diagnostic and analytical methods or treatments employed in the medical field (*retrospektiv analysiert, akustisch evoziert, Entfernung des Tumors*). In newspaper articles, these MWEs describe actions commonly seen in political or economic settings (*die Abschaffung der, im Kampf gegen*). Both sets of MWEs contain light verb

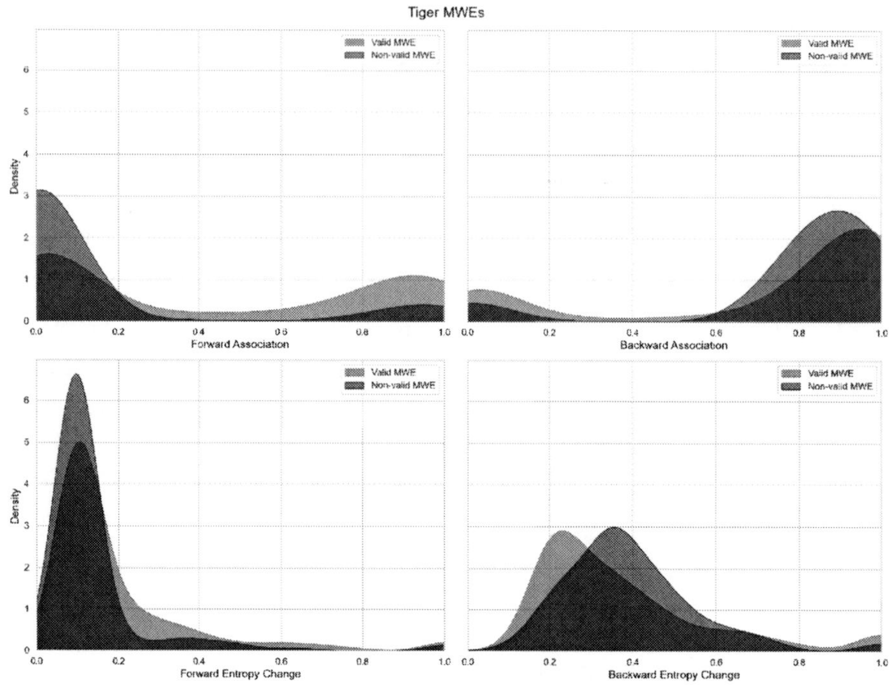

Figure 2: Comparison of successful and unsuccessful MWEs in the Tiger corpus.

constructions. However, those from the Springer corpus indicate cognitive and analytical processes (*in Betracht gezogen, in Erwägung gezogen*), while those from the Tiger corpus are more varied in their semantics (*in Frage gestellt, über die Bühne* [gehen], *ums Leben gekommen, ins Auge* [fassen]).

Place. With only seven unique expressions, MWEs of this type are not well represented in the Springer corpus. However, in the Tiger corpus this MWE type shows a wide range of realizations, with the most common being preposition + city/country/region (*in Genf, in Indien, in Afrika*). Additionally, we also found more generic and relative place reference (*im Ausland, nördlich von, im Süden*).

Time. Time MWEs in scientific texts mostly indicate the sequence of processes or events (*nach Beendigung der, nach dem Unfall, nach Abschluss der*). We also found some fixed time-related Latin expressions (*bis dato, post mortem*) and references to time periods (*in diesem Zeitraum, einen Zeitraum von*). Time MWEs in newspaper texts are especially used for comparing or presenting economic and financial statistics in different periods (*zum Jahresende, als im Vorjahr, in der laufenden Periode*). Specific time references for event contextualization are also richly attested in the Tiger corpus (*am späten, am Donnerstag Abend, der Nacht zum Freitag*). Both registers share some common MWEs used for generic time references (*in der Vergangenheit, seit langem, vor kurzem*).

Person. This type of MWEs is relatively sparsely attested in medical texts, describing mainly different groups of patients (*Patienten bei denen, Patienten mit koronarer Herzerkrankung*). In newspaper text, however, this category is primarily represented by proper names (*Bundespräsident Roman Herzog, Bundeskanzler Helmut Kohl*). References to people's social or political functions and different groups of people are also attested in our data (*ausländische Investoren, bosnische Serben, stellvertretende Vorsitzende*).

4.3 Association

In terms of association, MWEs in scientific texts tend to show stronger internal ties between the elements. Figure 5 shows that the Springer corpus contains a larger proportion of MWEs with an association score between 0.5 and 1, which shows a moderate to high association strength. In contrast, newspaper texts are more characterized by MWEs with a score between 0.2 and 0.5, indicating a rather weak association strength. Interestingly, the tendency towards higher MWE-internal ties in scientific texts also holds for 35 out of 49 MWEs that are attested in both corpora (see Table 4).

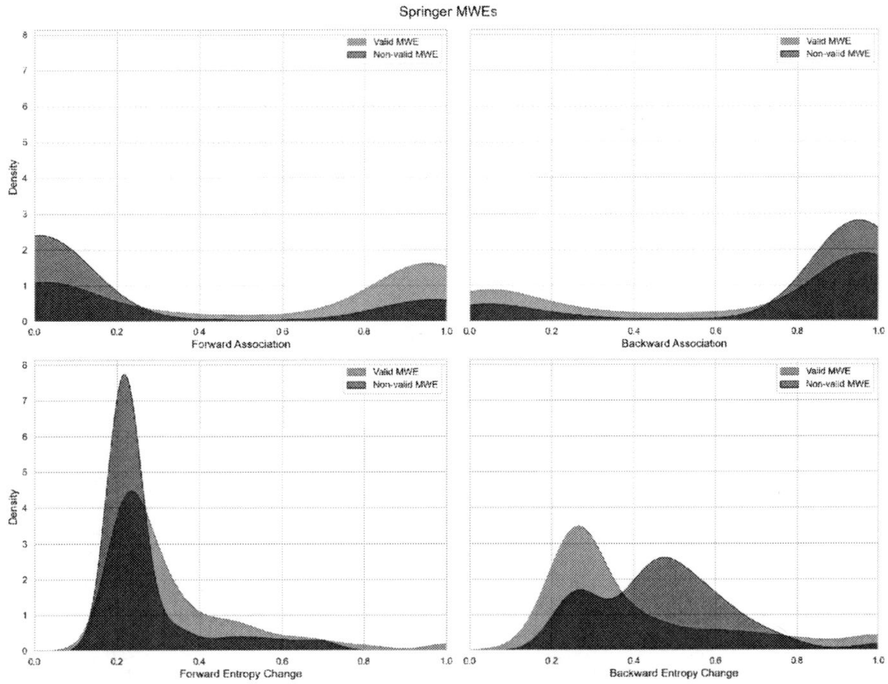

Figure 3: Comparison of successful and unsuccessful MWEs in the Springer corpus.

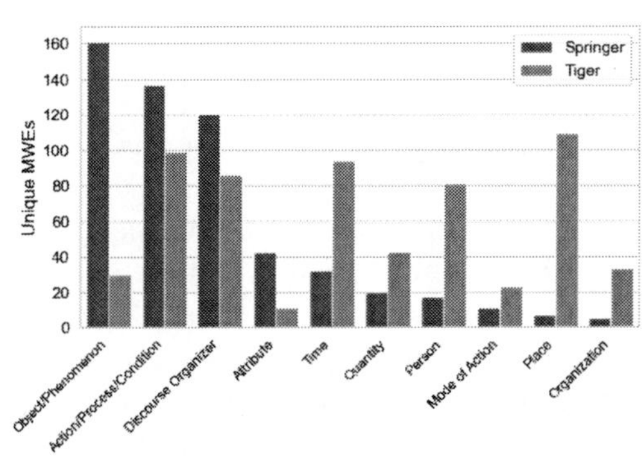

Figure 4: Comparison of MWE types in both corpora.

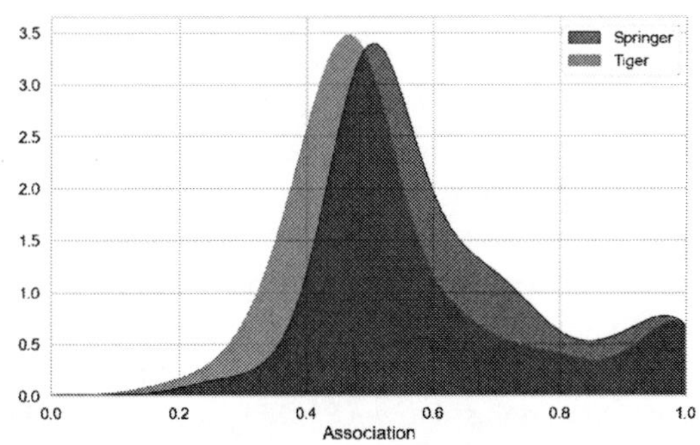

Figure 5: Comparison of mean association scores in Tiger and Springer MWEs.

MWE	Springer	Tiger
darüber hinaus	0.99	0.95
in erster Linie	0.73	0.68
doppelt so	0.59	0.52
Hinweis auf	0.52	0.46
die Tatsache daß	0.46	0.41
in der Regel	0.45	0.33

Table 4: Association scores for selected common MWEs.

Figure 6 offers a more fine-grained comparison of MWEs in different categories. **Object/Phenomenon**, **Person** and **Organization** are the categories showing the highest association strength of MWEs, while all other types show a rather moderate association strength among the elements of MWEs. The MWEs of scientific texts have a stronger association in almost all categories. The difference is by far most noticeable in the category **Object/Phenomenon**. In contrast, MWEs in the categories **Person** and **Organization** exhibit stronger word-to-word connections in newspaper texts.

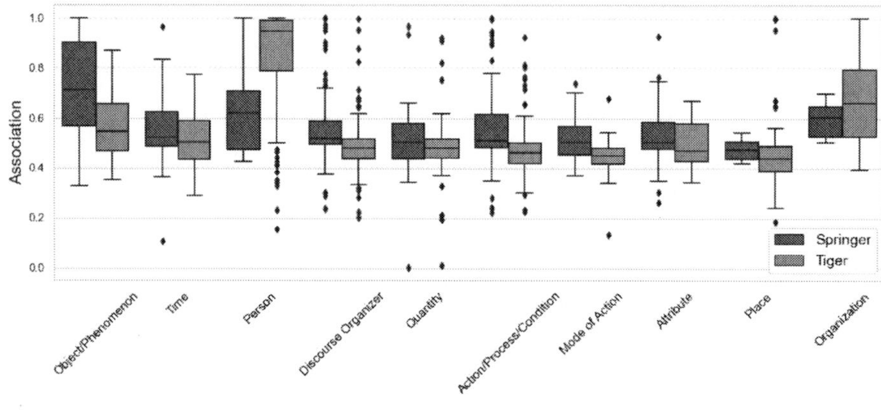

Figure 6: Strength of association across categories.

5 Discussion

As shown in Section 4.1, the output of the statistical method for MWE identification applied in this study is not perfect and still requires post-hoc filtering (see also the evaluation of the method in the original paper (Gries, 2022a, p. 14)).

Moreover, this extraction procedure, sequential in nature, sometimes struggles to cope with the variation in German syntax and morphology. For instance, some of the prepositional MWEs we encountered in the corpora are actually part of light verb constructions (e.g. *zu Buche* [schlagen], *auf der Kippe* [stehen], *zur Last* [legen], etc.). The verbs, however, were not extracted as part of the MWEs because in some of the MWE realizations they were separated from the prepositional phrase by other tokens. However, this problem could potentially be solved by increasing the number of iterations.

The flexible German syntax also led to variations of the same expression being retrieved as different MWEs, for instance, *es handelt sich* and *handelt es sich* in the Springer corpus. While this might seem redundant, we do believe that it is useful to retrieve both versions, since it allows us to further investigate the usage of MWEs. So, *handelt es sich* is more frequent and shows a slightly higher association strength than *es handelt sich*, suggesting that this expression tends to be used more in sentences with a pragmatically marked word order.

Despite its limitations, the applied extraction method has proved to be a versatile tool for MWE identification since it captures both high-frequency MWEs such as discourse organizers (*vor allem, wir berichten über, in der Regel*) and relatively rare word combinations that, however, do function as single units, for instance, proper nouns, locations, names of organizations and scientific terminology (*rheumatoider Arthritis, Bundesinnenminister Manfred Kanther, der Frankfurter Rundschau*).

The analysis of MWE types clearly reflects how the differences in the use of formulaic language are related to the contextual dimensions of register variation, i.e. field, tenor and mode.

In terms of the **field of discourse**, the main objective of scientific texts is to present new knowledge. This inevitably involves an extensive use of terminology. Consequently, we observe more nominal and adjectival MWE patters in the Springer corpus, and the MWE category Object/Phenomenon is by far more common in scientific texts compared to newspaper articles. Moreover, terminology in the scientific domain becomes more fossilized due to its repetitive use in similar contexts, indicated by a higher internal association strength between MWE components. In contrast, newspaper articles are more event-oriented than descriptive. For this reason, we see more MWEs providing local and temporal references, which are essential for establishing the context of an event, as well as MWEs referring to people and organizations who are protagonists in events.

The **tenor of discourse** can potentially explain the presence of foreign-language MWEs in scientific texts. Scientific texts are usually written by professionals in a specific field for their peers who share the same background knowledge. This shared knowledge allows them to use linguistic conventions that would not be understandable outside their community (e.g., Latin terminology). Newspaper articles, in contrast, are written for a broad audience and tend to use expressions from "general language". Even if newspaper texts touch upon topics from specialized domains such as economics or politics, they rely on general terms that can be understood by readers with no in-depth knowledge of these domains. Similarly, a scientific text intended for a broader audience (e.g., a blog entry or a plain-language summary of a scientific paper) tends to avoid specialized terminology (especially Latin terms).

In terms of the **mode of discourse**, we can see similarities and differences between scientific and newspaper texts. With the two registers using the written channel of communication, both show a high proportion of cohesive devices, especially those used for topic elaboration or cause-effect relations. However, unlike the Tiger corpus, the Springer corpus contains a considerable fraction of MWEs that include references to the authors themselves or to their texts. Such self-references play an important role in topic introduction and guide the reader's attention. Scientific texts also exhibit a number of MWEs that are used as cohesive devices for presentation and interpretation of results, which are key elements in scientific studies.

6 Conclusion and Future Work

In this study, we used a statistically motivated and language-independent method for MWE identification proposed by Gries (2022a) to extract MWEs from German texts. The method leverages both frequency-based and information-theoretic measures to better capture the essence of formulaic word sequences and enables the retrieval of different MWE types. Although the extraction output requires subsequent filtering by human experts, this method is a promising approach for MWE identification, especially in languages other than English.

Our analysis showed that the variation in the use of formulaic language in German scientific and newspaper texts can be explained in terms of field, tenor, and mode of discourse, which is in line with previous research on functional variation (see Section 2 for a brief overview).

The main focus in our future work will be on enhancing the efficiency of our Python implementation of the extraction method and increasing the number of iterations to improve the MWE recall. Additionally, we would like to explore whether the addition of further dimensions can improve the extraction precision. In this respect, surprisal should be a suitable measure to favor the retrieval of those word sequences that exhibit the most predictable transition from one token to another. Apart from that, we also plan to add more registers to our analysis.

Limitations

The Springer corpus contains only texts from medical journals, albeit covering a broad variety of medical fields. Therefore, it might fail to capture some features of language use characteristic of other scientific domains. Moreover, it is only composed of paper abstracts, which tend to be written in a more condensed way than the body of the papers. Similarly, the Tiger corpus only comprises texts coming from one newspaper – *Frankfurter Rundschau* – and may therefore be biased in terms of style.

Our research design only allowed us to evaluate the precision of the extraction method. Since it is not known how many MWEs are present in the corpora, it is not possible to calculate the recall. An additional evaluation on a dataset with gold-standard MWE annotation would provide valuable insights into the method's performance in terms of recall.

Although the annotator performed the classification of the extracted MWEs to the best of their abilities, we are aware that alternative judgments might also be possible in some cases.

Acknowledgements

This research is funded by *Deutsche Forschungsgemeinschaft* (DFG, German Research Foundation) – Project-ID 232722074 – SFB 1102.

References

Diego Alves, Stefania Degaetano-Ortlieb, Elena Schmidt, and Elke Teich. 2024a. Diachronic analysis of multi-word expression functional categories in scientific English. In *Proceedings of the Joint Workshop on Multiword Expressions and Universal Dependencies (MWE-UD) @ LREC-COLING 2024*, pages 81–87, Torino, Italia. ELRA and ICCL.

Diego Alves, Stefan Fischer, Stefania Degaetano-Ortlieb, and Elke Teich. 2024b. Multi-word expressions in English scientific writing. In *Proceedings of the 8th Joint SIGHUM Workshop on Computational Linguistics for Cultural Heritage, Social Sciences, Humanities and Literature (LaTeCH-CLfL*

2024), pages 67–76, St. Julians, Malta. Association for Computational Linguistics.

Douglas Biber and Susan Conrad. 2019. *Register, Genre, and Style*, 2nd edition. Cambridge University Press, Cambridge.

Douglas Biber and Bethany Gray. 2010. Challenging stereotypes about academic writing: Complexity, elaboration, explicitness. *Journal of English for Academic Purposes*, 9:2–20.

Douglas Biber and Bethany Gray. 2011. The historical shift of scientific academic prose in English towards less explicit styles of expression: Writing without verbs. In Vijay Bathia, Purificación Sánchez, and Pascual Pérez-Paredes, editors, *Researching specialized languages*, pages 11–24. John Benjamins, Amsterdam.

Sabine Brants, Stefanie Dipper, Peter Eisenberg, Silvia Hansen, Esther König, Wolfgang Lezius, Christian Rohrer, George Smith, and Hans Uszkoreit. 2004. Tiger: Linguistic interpretation of a german corpus. *Journal of Language and Computation*, 2:597–620.

Ruth Breeze. 2013. Lexical bundles across four legal genres. *International Journal of Corpus Linguistics*, 18(2):229–253.

Annelen Brunner and Kathrin Steyer. 2015. Corpus-driven study of multi-word expressions based on collocations from a very large corpus. In *Proceedings of the 4th Corpus Linguistics conference, Birmingham*, page 12.

Fabienne Cap, Marion Weller, and Ulrich Heid. 2013. Using a rich feature set for the identification of German MWEs. In *Proceedings of the Workshop on Multi-word Units in Machine Translation and Translation Technologies*, Nice, France.

Susan Conrad and Douglas Biber. 2005. The frequency and use of lexical bundles in conversation and academic prose. *Lexicographica*, 20(2004):56–71.

Marie-Catherine de Marneffe, Christopher D. Manning, Joakim Nivre, and Daniel Zeman. Universal Dependencies. 47(2):255–308.

Stefania Degaetano-Ortlieb. 2021. Measuring informativity: The rise of compounds as informationally dense structures in 20th century scientific English. In Elena Soave and Douglas Biber, editors, *Corpus approaches to register variation*, chapter 11, pages 291–312. John Benjamins Publishing Company.

Stefania Degaetano-Ortlieb and Elke Teich. 2022. Toward an optimal code for communication: The case of scientific English. *Corpus Linguistics and Linguistic Theory*, 18(1):175–207.

Stefan Th. Gries. 2020. Analyzing dispersion. In Magali Paquot and Stefan Th. Gries, editors, *A Practical Handbook of Corpus Linguistics*, pages 99–118. Springer, Berlin and New York.

Stefan Th. Gries. 2022a. Multi-word units (and tokenization more generally): A multi-dimensional and largely information-theoretic approach. *Lexis*, (19). Online since 26 March 2022.

Stefan Th. Gries. 2022b. What do (some of) our association measures measure (most)? association? *Journal of Second Language Studies*, 5(1):1–33.

M.A.K. Halliday and Ruqaiya Hasan. 1985. *Language, context, and text: Aspects of language in a social-semiotic perspective*. Oxford University Press, Oxford.

Natalia Klyueva, Antoine Doucet, and Milan Straka. 2017. Neural networks for multi-word expression detection. In *Proceedings of the 13th Workshop on Multiword Expressions (MWE 2017)*, pages 60–65, Valencia, Spain. Association for Computational Linguistics.

Marie-Pauline Krielke. 2021. Relativizers as markers of grammatical complexity: A diachronic, cross-register study of english and german. *Bergen Language and Linguistics Studies*, 11(1):91–120.

Kerstin Kunz and Ekaterina Lapshinova-Koltunski. 2015. Cross-linguistic analysis of discourse variation across registers. *Nordic Journal of English Studies*, 14(1):258–288.

Natalia Loukachevitch and Evgeny Parkhomenko. 2018. Recognition of multiword expressions using word embeddings. In Sergey Kuznetsov, Gennady Osipov, and Vladimir Stefanuk, editors, *Artificial Intelligence. RCAI 2018*, volume 934 of *Communications in Computer and Information Science*. Springer, Cham.

Stella Neumann. 2014. *Contrastive Register Variation: A Quantitative Approach to the Comparison of English and German*. De Gruyter Mouton, Berlin, Boston.

Carlos Ramisch, Agata Savary, Bruno Guillaume, Jakub Waszczuk, Marie Candito, Ashwini Vaidya, Verginica Barbu Mititelu, Archna Bhatia, Uxoa Iñurrieta, Voula Giouli, Tunga Güngör, Menghan Jiang, Timm Lichte, Chaya Liebeskind, Johanna Monti, Renata Ramisch, Sara Stymne, Abigail Walsh, and Hongzhi Xu. 2020. Edition 1.2 of the PARSEME shared task on semi-supervised identification of verbal multiword expressions. In *Proceedings of the Joint Workshop on Multiword Expressions and Electronic Lexicons*, pages 107–118, online. Association for Computational Linguistics.

Ivan A. Sag, Tim Baldwin, Francis Bond, Ann Copestake, and Dan Flickinger. 2002. Multiword expressions: A pain in the neck for nlp. In *International Conference on Intelligent Text Processing and Computational Linguistics*, pages 1–15, Berlin. Springer.

Andreas Scherbakov, Ekaterina Vylomova, Fei Liu, and Timothy Baldwin. 2016. Vectorweavers at semeval-2016 task 10: From incremental meaning to semantic unit (phrase by phrase). In *International Workshop on Semantic Evaluation*.

Nathan Schneider, Dirk Hovy, Anders Johannsen, and Marine Carpuat. 2016. SemEval-2016 task 10: Detecting minimal semantic units and their meanings (DiMSUM). In *Proceedings of the 10th International Workshop on Semantic Evaluation (SemEval-2016)*, pages 546–559, San Diego, California. Association for Computational Linguistics.

Rita Simpson-Vlach and Nick C. Ellis. 2010. An Academic Formulas List: New Methods in Phraseology Research. *Applied Linguistics*, 31(4):487–512.

Anna Siyanova-Chanturia, Kathy Conklin, Sendy Caffarra, Edith Kaan, and Walter J.B. van Heuven. 2017. Representation and processing of multi-word expressions in the brain. *Brain and Language*, 175:111–122.

Antoine Tremblay and Harald Baayen. 2010. Holistic processing of regular four-word sequences: A behavioral and erp study of the effects of structure, frequency, and probability on immediate free recall. In D. Wood, editor, *Perspectives on Formulaic Language: Acquisition and Communication*, page 151–173. Continuum, London.

Marion Weller and Ulrich Heid. 2010. Extraction of German multiword expressions from parsed corpora using context features. In *Proceedings of the Seventh International Conference on Language Resources and Evaluation (LREC'10)*, Valletta, Malta. European Language Resources Association (ELRA).

Chadia Ben Youssef. 2024. *mMERGE: A Corpus Driven Multiword Expressions Discovery Algorithm*. Ph.D. thesis, University of California, Santa Barbara. ProQuest ID: BenYoussef_ucsb_0035D_16720; Merritt ID: ark:/13030/m5457324.

Hit or Be Hit: Tests of (Pre)Compositional Abilities in Vision and Language Models

Mădălina Zgreabăn, Albert Gatt, Pablo Mosteiro
Utrecht University, The Netherlands
b.m.zgreaban@uu.nl, a.gatt@uu.nl, p.j.mosteiroromero@uu.nl

Abstract

Although many benchmarks have been recently proposed to test the compositional abilities of vision and language models, there has been little systematic review or comparison between them. Our study classifies such datasets, their benefits, and shortcomings. Additionally, we expand the VALSE benchmark with two large datasets of the active/passive and ditransitive/dative constructions, on which CLIP, Flava, and LiT were tested. We show models achieve roughly random-chance performance in differentiating captions from foils. We provide evidence suggesting that the linguistic constructions or the order of thematic arguments in captions or foils do not change the models' performance. However, their grammaticality, simplicity, and origin dataset seem to do so.

1 Introduction

Compositionality is constructing the meaning of a structure by its elements and their combination (Partee, 2004). General compositional abilities are important for models to generalize well on new tasks or data, especially in retrieval, text-to-image generation (Ma et al., 2023), and general artificial intelligence (Xu et al. 2022).

This definition of compositionality presupposes that models have robust representations of basic linguistic phenomena, enabling them to decode their combinations. However, Vision and Language Models (VLMs) seem to lack such robustness, as they struggle with syntax (Nikolaus et al., 2022), store less information about grammar than language models (Milewski et al., 2022), and poorly identify the correct word order of sentences (Yuksekgonul et al., 2023). They also struggle to identify primitive concepts, such as color or shape (Yun et al., 2023), attributes of objects, and the spatial relationships between them (Clark and Jaini, 2023; Lewis et al., 2023). Such results generated doubts not only about their compositional abilities (Doveh et al., 2023a; Sinha et al., 2021; Ettinger, 2020), but the possibility of developing them (Trager et al., 2024). However, other studies suggest models encode separately minimally different captions (Diwan et al., 2022), and that entity or relationship recognition is done by special attention heads, hinting at the presence of compositional abilities (Li et al., 2020).

Amid such debates, several image-to-text benchmarks testing compositional abilities of VLMs have been made available (Parcalabescu et al., 2022; Thrush et al., 2022; Yuksekgonul et al., 2023; Ma et al., 2023; Hsieh et al., 2023; Burapacheep et al., 2024; Nikolaus et al., 2022). They evaluate models on whether they can differentiate a *foil* — a caption minimally modified to no longer match the image — from the correct original caption, and, sometimes, a *hard positive* — a minimally modified caption that still correctly describes the image (Kamath et al., 2024). This assumes that compositional abilities help models differentiate sentences only similar in form (i.e., using the same words) by their meanings. These benchmarks (i) have diverse stimuli; (ii) show models score around random chance, despite their good performance in more traditional downstream vision-and-language tasks (Parcalabescu et al., 2022; Thrush et al., 2022, among others); and (iii) investigate the interaction between model size, training data, and simplicity of the captions and models' performance.

Despite the strengths mentioned above, previous benchmarks (i) have not been reviewed on the alignment of their definitions of compositionality, making it unclear if they test basic linguistic phenomena, or combinations thereof; and (ii) have not tested if grammaticality of captions or the order of their thematic arguments interact with models' performance, despite prior evidence of models leveraging grammatical cues for improved performance (Hsieh et al., 2023), and the debate about their (in)sensitivity to word order (Sinha et al., 2021;

Proceedings of the 21st Conference on Natural Language Processing (KONVENS), Volume 1: Long and Short Papers, pages 306–317, 2025

Pham et al., 2021; Ettinger, 2020; Yuksekgonul et al., 2023).

To bridge these gaps, we review previous compositional benchmarks and extend the VALSE benchmark (Parcalabescu et al., 2022) with the active/passive and the dative/ditransitive constructions. In contrast to the BLA benchmark (Chen et al., 2023), our active/passive dataset is larger, and we introduce a new ditransitive/dative dataset. Both datasets also contain simpler and complex versions of the same captions and foils. Besides these datasets, we analyzed how various factors, such as the linguistic structure, argument order, origin dataset, and grammaticality of sentences, interact with models' choices. Thus, the research question of this paper is the following:

Does linguistic structure, argument order, or origin dataset influence VLMs' choice of the correct caption?

Our main contributions and results are:

1. A categorization of VLMs benchmarks testing (pre)compositional abilities, their results, trends, and shortcomings.
2. Two datasets summing up to 9145 pairs of captions-foils.
3. Evidence showing that the linguistic structure and argument order do not influence models' results. Grammaticality, complexity, and noisiness of the origin dataset seem to do so, however.

Section 2 delves into previous literature on compositional abilities, by reviewing benchmarks and their limitations. Section 3 outlines the evaluation procedure, covering the selection of linguistic constructions and models, dataset construction, and statistical tests. Following this, Section 4 presents the results, which are then discussed in Section 5. The paper concludes with Section 6, with limitations addressed in Section 7.

2 Background

2.1 (Pre)Compositional Benchmarks

Current Benchmarks: Text-to-image benchmarks testing compositionality use compositional aspects (*compositional* benchmarks) or representations of linguistics phenomena required for them (*precompositional* benchmarks): VALSE (Parcalabescu et al., 2022), Winoground (Thrush et al., 2022), ARO (Yuksekgonul et al., 2023), CREPE (Ma et al., 2023), SugarCrepe (Hsieh et al., 2023), Colorswap (Burapacheep et al., 2024), Nikolaus et al. (2022), Kamath et al. (2024), VL-CheckList (Zhao et al., 2023), and BLA (Chen et al., 2023). We will now describe several aspects by which these benchmarks can be categorized.

Minimally Modfied Captions: Foils or *hard positives* can be created by (i) *swapping* words, e.g. going from 'a white chair and black blackboard' to 'a black chair and white blackboard' by changing attributes of objects in ColorSwap; (ii) *replacing* words with ones from other word classes; (iii) *adding* elements to the original captions, i.e. negation (see SugarCrepe); (iv) by *mixing* and combining multiple strategies systematically, e.g. using both *swap* and *replace*, such as VALSE. Their effect on whether they do or do not match the image depends on if the benchmark is intended to contain only foils, *hard positives*, or both. The column 'Minimal Differences' from Table 1 offers a complete overview of strategies for creating these captions.

Targeted phenomena: The benchmarks target visual or linguistic phenomena, where the latter are generally textual aspects reflected visually, while the former are more image-dependent, i.e., symbolic images of captions (Winoground), or relationships traced back to the image (CREPE). Concerning their coverage, linguistic phenomena can be a) specific, such as existence, plurality (VALSE), or negation (CREPE); or b) general, such as verbs, adverbs, or prepositions, named 'relations' in Winoground and 'attributes' in ColorSwap. See columns 'Type Properties' and 'Phenomena Covered' of Table 1 for an inventory of them.

Compositional property tested: The benchmarks can test (i) a *prerequisite* of compositional abilities, such as identifying the correct word order (Winoground); (ii) a compositional *ability*, such as systematicity; or (iii) an *effect* of compositionality, such as differentiating between two minimally different sentences. Note that some benchmarks might test several such aspects, see column 'Compositionality' for a full breakdown of the benchmarks' tests.

Fine-tuning: Models' performance can be negatively influenced by their training data, such as noisy, partial, or simplistic captions (Yuksekgonul et al., 2023; Doveh et al., 2023a); their training method, i.e. textual alignment, (Ossowski et al., 2024; Doveh et al., 2023a); or their textual encoder (Yuksekgonul et al., 2023; Li et al., 2023; Kamath et al., 2023; Clark and Jaini, 2023). Given compositional benchmarks have been systematically and carefully modified, they have been used for fine-tuning models, resulting in greatly improved performance, i.e. ARO, ColorSwap, or BLA (Doveh et al., 2023a). However, artifacts can influence such results, as models show smaller improvements — under 10%— on carefully controlled benchmarks such as SugarCrepe. See the column 'Tests' for an overview of benchmarks used previously for fine-tuning.

2.2 Previous results of the benchmarks

General results: Generally, results on VALSE, Winoground, SugarCrepe, ColorSwap, VL-CheckList, BLA, and ARO suggest poor compositional abilities. Specifically, models perform around or below the random chance threshold of 50%, with some exceptions, a good example being Winogrund, where model scores on text-to-image matching are as much as 70% lower than those of humans. Even though fine-tuning on foils can improve models' scores up until 70%, they still drop by 20% when confronted with another type of nominally different captions, the *hard positives* in Kamath et al. (2024).

Complexity of the caption, training datasets & model size: Models generally perform worse on longer, more complex or previously unseen captions (Winoground, CREPE). No interaction was found between the training dataset (Hsieh et al., 2023; Ma et al., 2023; Nikolaus et al., 2022) or the model size (Ma et al., 2023) and models' performance.

2.2.1 Shortcomings of evaluation benchmarks

Size: Yuksekgonul et al. (2023) argue that benchmarks that are composed of around 400 data points may not render significant statistical results. Many benchmarks, such as Winground, Colorswap, and each linguistic category from VALSE are not much bigger, with no more than 1000 data points.

Uncontrolled Artifacts: Grammaticality or plausibility artifacts (Hsieh et al., 2023) are not always controlled for, such as in ARO or CREPE, which models could exploit if fine-tuned on them, see Hsieh et al. (2023).

Inconsistent Definitions: Definitions of linguistic, visual properties, and minimal swapped units vary across studies. A phenomenon like 'pragmatics' is labeled as linguistic in Winoground and as visual in ARO. The minimal sentence elements swapped can be a singular visual concept (i.e. atom Ma et al., 2023), or a part of speech (Thrush et al., 2022). This can lead to a difficult comparison of results across studies.

Abilities tested: Current compositionality tests evaluate more effects than aspects of compositional abilities, such as systematicity (CREPE). This can lead to minimalization of the aspects tested and over/underestimation of models' abilities.

Targeted Phenomena: Visual and linguistic phenomena are arbitrarily chosen. For example, Parcalabescu et al. (2022) chose the linguistic phenomena of their benchmark based on their pervasiveness, but provided no empirical evidence to support this claim. This can lead to an over/underestimation of models' abilities, as the chosen phenomena can prove less prevalent than assumed.

3 Methodology

3.1 Datasets

VALSE: We extended VALSE due to its focus on linguistic constructions, control for unimodal collapse (Parcalabescu et al., 2022), grammaticality, and plausibility of actant swapping.

Actant Swap Category: We chose the actant swap category, which in Parcalabescu et al. (2022) was obtained by generating image captions from the SWiG dataset, and by swapping their thematic arguments to create foils. For illustration, considering the caption in (1a): its corresponding foil, shown in (2a), is obtained by swapping the subject and object, thus by *actant swapping*. Swapping might be a more difficult test than replacing/adding words (see Hsieh et al., 2023), as small syntactical changes might go unnoticed in models with less syntactic information (Milewski et al., 2022).

Added constructions: We extended the actant swap category by firstly creating passive and ditransitive versions of active captions, thereby introducing the active/passive construction, e.g. (1a) and (1b), and the dative/ditransitive construction, e.g. (1c) and (1d). Afterwards, we generate corresponding foils for them, illustrated with examples in (2), which were generated

Benchmark	Compositionality	Minimal Differences	Type Properties	Phenomena Covered	Size	Tests
VALSE (Parcalabescu et al., 2022)	Effect (Differentiation)	Mixed (*foils*)	Linguistic	Existence, Plurality, Counting, Spatial Relations, Actions, Coreference	8782	No
Winoground (Yuksekgonul et al., 2023)	Prerequisite (Word order); Effect (Differentiation)	Swap (*foils*)	Mixed	Object (l), Relation (l), Symbolic (v), Pragmatics (v), Series (v)	897	No
ColorSwap (Burapacheep et al., 2024)	Effect (Differentiation)	Swap (*foils*)	Linguistic	Color Attributes	1000	Yes
CREPE (Ma et al., 2023)	Ability (Systematicity, Productivity); Effect (Differentiation)	Mixed (*foils/hard negatives*)	Linguistic	Negatives, Atomic Swaps	100200	No
SugarCrepe (Hsieh et al., 2023)	Effect (Differentiation)	Mixed (*foils/hard negatives*)	Linguistic	Objects, Attributes, Relations	7512	Yes
ARO (Yuksekgonul et al., 2023)	Prerequisite (Word order); Effect (Differentiation)	Mixed (*foils*)	Linguistic	Relations, Attributes	52685	Yes
VL-CheckList (Zhao et al., 2023)	Effect (Differentiation)	Replace (*foils*)	Linguistic	Object, Attribute, Verb Replacements	410000	No
BLA (Chen et al., 2023)	Effect (Differentiation)	Swap (*foils*)	Linguistic	Actants, Predicates and Clauses Swaps	1939	Yes
Kamath et al. (2024)	Effect (Differentiation)	Mixed (*hard positives*)	Linguistic	Attributes, Relations and Word Order	55191	Yes

Table 1: **Overview of (Pre)Compositional Benchmarks.** *Compositionality*: (pre)compositional aspects tested, i.e. *prerequisite*, *ability* or *effect*, with phenomena specified in parenthesis; *Minimal differences*: foils/*hard positives* formed by mixed methods ('add', 'swap', 'replace'), or singular methods ('add'/'swap'/'replace'); *Type properties*: the type of properties measured, i.e. linguistic or mixed (linguistic and visual); *Phenomena Covered*: the specific phenomena covered, with types specified in parenthesis for mixed properties (*visual*, v; *linguistic*, l); *Tests*: fine-tuned models on the datasets presented in the original papers.

by swapping nouns in (1). We chose these two constructions because their variants allow isolating the effect of the construction itself from the order of thematic arguments. For example, when compared, (2a) and (1b) still have thematic arguments in similar positions in the sentence, having only the construction as the only difference between the foil and the caption. Depending if a sentence is a foil or caption it will be referred to as active caption (1a) or foil (2a), dative caption (1c) or foil (2c), and so on. See Appendix A for example images for the captions.

1. Captions
   a) A player hits a ball.
   b) A ball is hit by a player.
   c) A woman gives a book to the girl.
   d) A woman gives the girl a book.
2. Foils
   a) A ball hits a player.
   b) A player is hit by a ball.
   c) A woman gives the girl to a book.
   d) A woman gives a book the girl.

Dataset construction: We obtained each type of construction and its corresponding foils, by adapting the code of Raam (2022) to use spaCy `en_core_web_trf` parsers, chosen for its higher accuracy in part-of-speech (POS) tagging. Passive captions were obtained by changing the active verb inflections of sentences that had a subject and an object, while dative sentences were created by alternating sentences that had a subject, object, and beneficiary. Foils were obtained by swapping the object and subject in active/passive sentences, or the beneficiary and the object in ditransitive/dative ones. For each construction, only sentences that could have an alternation and an existing image were selected. Thus, each image has 2 captions and 2 foils, regardless of the linguistic construction.

We parsed (i) 1 million sentences from Conceptual Captions (CC, Sharma et al., 2018) and the actant swap dataset from VALSE for the active/passive construction; (ii) 2 million CC sentences for the ditransitive construction, double the amount of active sentences parsed given the rarity of the construction. All the code and datasets obtained will be made available upon request, similarly to Koplenig et al. (2017).

Simplified Datasets and Grammaticality: Each obtained dataset was further simplified to test potential artifacts of sentence length, by re-parsing all sentences to keep only the head of noun phrases for the thematic arguments involved in the swap. For example, we omitted extra descriptions of objects or datives containing embedded sentences (i.e. from 'the girl *whom I met yesterday*' to 'the girl'). To test the efficiency of our method of simplification, we randomly sampled 100 simplified active/passive sentences — 400 captions and foils — and observed that 12% of them were not completely simplified. See Table 2 for a complete breakdown of the numbers of each dataset.

To also statistically test if models exploit the grammaticality of sentences for their answers, we used GRUEN (Zhu and Bhat, 2020) to obtain a grammaticality score for all our sentences. Unlike Parcalabescu et al. (2022), we do not select sentences with a certain grammaticality threshold, to observe overall if more ungrammaticality has a bigger effect on models' choices.

Dataset	SWiG	CC	Total
Active/Passive	683	5450	6133
Ditransitive	0	3012	3012
Simplified Datasets			
Active/Passive	683	4737	5420
Ditransitive	0	2998	2998

Table 2: **Datasets. First table**: captions after the first round of parsing for both types of constructions; **Second table**: remaining simplified data points. Note the SWiG dataset only contained 7 ditransitive sentences, which were excluded, given they were not sufficient for the statistical analysis.

3.2 Models

For evaluation, we chose three contrastive-learning models, namely CLIP-ViT 32, Flava, and LiT-ViT B16B (Zhai et al., 2022), which have a stronger alignment between their textual and image embeddings, given their training to align the two modalities.

CLIP-ViT 32: CLIP is a dual-stream model with a vision (Dosovitskiy et al., 2021) and text (Vaswani et al., 2023) transformer as backbones, trained on WIT, a 400 million image-text pairs dataset scraped from multiple online sources. We chose CLIP given it has the best results on the actant swap category from VALSE and we wanted to investigate if this generalizes on our dataset, where actant swapping is one of the alternations made.

Flava: Flava is a dual-stream model with the same ViT image encoder and a ViT-b/16 textual encoder. It was trained on PMD, a public dataset of 70 million pairs containing, among others, CC sentences. Flava is also trained to perform well in unimodal language tasks, scoring 20% more than CLIP (Singh et al., 2022). Thus, Flava was selected for its unimodal performance, and for improved performance in multimodal (Singh et al., 2022), and even compositional tasks, such as ColorSwap, when compared to CLIP.

LiT-ViT B16B: LiT uses a ViT image encoder and a BERT textual encoder, using contrast-tuning during training. Previous studies argued for the importance of the textual modality in VLMs (Wu et al., 2023). Instead of fine-tuning both image and text encoders, LiT only fine-tunes the textual encoder, obtaining better zero-shot image classification performance than CLIP (Zhai et al., 2022). LiT is trained on a dataset containing 4 billion image-text pairs, some originating from CC.

3.3 Statistical tests

Two Linear Mixed Models (lmer, Bates et al., 2015) were conducted in RStudio (RStudio Team, 2020)[1].

The First Lmer We tested if the following factors had any significant effects on models' choices: (i) the higher grammaticality of either the caption or foil; (ii) the simplification of the caption or foil; (iii) the linguistic construction, i.e. passive or ditransitive, as opposed to the active; (iv) the origin dataset; (v) the model; (vi) and model size. Note that we ran two tests with respect to the linguistic constructions (active vs. passive or active vs. ditransitive), for all models directly, and for each model separately.

The second lmer We tested if captions or foils are chosen more by models if the order of thematic arguments in the compared sentences is different (active caption vs. active foil) or similar (passive caption vs. active foil). Grammaticality, simplification, the origin dataset, model, and model sizes were also investigated alongside word order. **Contrasts and random effects.** All tests had random effects for images, and binary or ternary orthogonal contrasts for all factors, corresponding to their levels. Note that models were introduced as fixed factors, due to the small sample of VLMs tested.

[1]For a review of linear mixed models see Gałecki and Burzykowski (2012).

4 Results

Accuracy ratios For overall visualization, Table 3 presents the accuracy ratios of models for SWiG, and Table 4 presents the accuracy ratio for models, tested on both constructions from CC.

First lmer Our results did not show any significant effect of the linguistic construction. Regardless of the model, the chances of choosing captions go down by almost half if foils are equally grammatical to captions, and slightly down if foils are more grammatical than captions. The same grammaticality value for captions and foils, and bigger foil grammaticality have a lower effect on ditransitive sentences, refer to Figure 1 for an illustration. The chance of choosing a caption is slightly increased by simplified sentences, and by their origin from SWiG, a cleaner dataset. For FLAVA or LiT, foils become more preferred, as also seen in the ratios. **Models Subsamples.** For all models captions were chosen more when comparing simplified sentences.

Second lmer No significant effect of word order was found. The trends of the first lmer test in grammaticality, models, and simplification are similar. Equally grammatical foils and captions have a smaller effect on sentences with different argument structures, while higher foil grammaticality has a bigger effect on them. For an illustration, see Figure 2. See Appendix C for detailed significance values.

Normal Captions			
Comparison	CLIP	Flava	LiT
1	69.38	46.25	64.01
2	45.17	40.11	43.12
3	64.32	56.51	62.42
4	45.96	57.64	49.08
5	52.48	43.77	45.17
Simplified Captions			
Comparison	CLIP	Flava	LiT
1	69.38	46.25	64.01
2	45.09	40.17	43.04
3	64.27	56.74	62.37
4	45.96	57.80	49.08
5	52.41	43.84	45.09

Table 3: **Ratios on SWiG.** *Comparison 1*: Active caption vs. foil; *Comparison 2*: Passive caption vs. foil; *Comparison 3*: Active vs. Passive captions; *Comparison 4*: Active vs. Passive foils; *Comparison 5*: Passive caption vs. Active foil. For each comparison, the value represents the preference of the the first term over the second.

Normal Captions			
Comparison	CLIP	Flava	LiT
Act/pass 1	64.20	24.93	52.33
Act/pass 2	54.46	42.49	44.50
Act/pass 3	64.81	29.00	59.59
Act/pass 4	44.01	56.54	46.20
Act/pass 5	48.14	53.26	35.85
Dit/Dat 1	63.44	27.22	49.71
Dit/Dat 2	55.84	35.50	41.92
Dit/Dat 3	64.87	36.35	47.12
Dit/Dat 4	45.24	52.91	46.37
Dit/Dat 5	50.31	37.04	42.12
Simplified Captions			
Comparison	CLIP	Flava	LiT
Act/pass 1	65.78	36.96	62.17
Act/pass 2	53.32	45.55	45.92
Act/pass 3	52.56	41.05	55.75
Act/pass 4	42.28	53.52	41.15
Act/pass 5	64.41	48.00	53.75
Dit/Dat 1	61.44	36.72	53.65
Dit/Dat 2	62.05	37.76	51.60
Dit/Dat 3	60.20	46.19	46.47
Dit/Dat 4	51.38	50.25	48.88
Dit/Dat 5	54.60	40.12	49.63

Table 4: **Ratios for CC**. Each 'Comparison' number indicates a different pairing of captions or foils between the active/passive construction (Act/pass) and the ditransitive one (Dit/Dat). Note that comparisons are only performed within the same construction. *Comparison 1*: Active (or Ditransitive) caption vs. foil; *Comparison 2*: Passive (or Dative) caption vs. foil; *Comparison 3*: Active (or Ditransitive) vs. Passive (or Dative) captions; *Comparison 4*: Active (or Ditransitive) vs. Passive (or Dative) foils; *Comparison 5*: Passive (or Dative) caption vs. Active (or Dative) foil. For each comparison, the value represents how much the first term of comparison is preferred over the second.

5 Discussion

General results Our overall random-chance performance indicates poor compositional abilities, in line with results obtained on VALSE, SugarCrepe, or Winoground. Our general results also provide evidence that models might be influenced by many factors, such as the simplicity, noisiness, and grammaticality of the compared sentences, where by noisiness we mean how clean the original dataset of sentences is. All aspects point to a lack of compositional ability, as such factors should not influence models' choices.

Linguistic Constructions and Argument Structure Our results do not offer evidence that specific linguistic constructions or word order of semantic arguments influence models' choices.

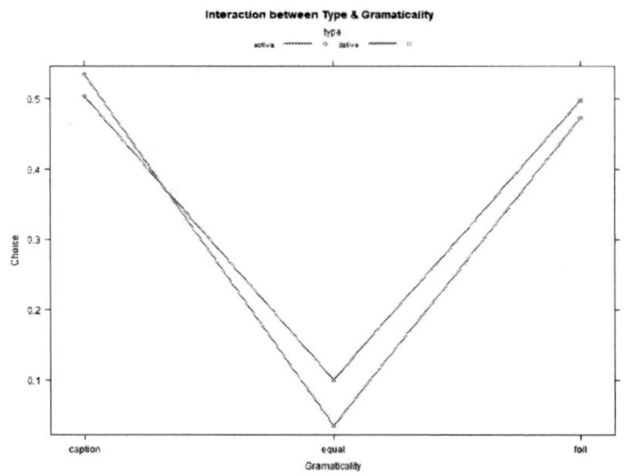

Figure 1: Plotted interaction between *Type*, with levels 'active' and 'ditransitive', and *Grammaticality*, with levels 'caption', 'foil', and 'equal'. Note that a bigger grammatical value between a *caption* or *foil* is assigned to the one with a bigger GRUEN grammaticality score. The pink line is the 'active', while the blue one is the 'ditransitive' construction.

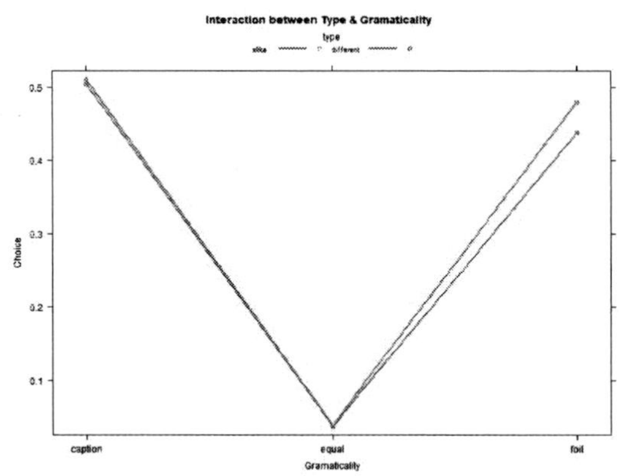

Figure 2: Plotted interaction between *Type*, with levels 'alike' and 'different', and *Grammaticality*, with levels 'caption', 'foil', and 'equal'. The pink line is 'alike', the blue one is 'different'

Grammaticality Our results suggest captions are chosen slightly less when a foil is grammatical but significantly less when captions and foils are equally grammatical. Thus, our results indicate that models favor foils, shown by the intercept of our first test (i.e. β = 0.37), but also that they might leverage grammatical cues in their decisions, in line with Hsieh et al. (2023). Tests done for each model show grammaticality affects types of constructions unevenly, i.e. passive or alternation more. This might be because our methods might introduce more ungrammaticality, or complexity to one of the structures, aspects previously shown to decrease performance (Thrush et al., 2022; Ma et al., 2023).

Simplification and Noisiness Noisier datasets lower the performance of VLMs (Thrush et al., 2022; Ma et al., 2023), which was also shown by our improved results on SWiG. Our results also show that simplifying the compared caption and foil makes models perform better (Ma et al., 2023). Simplicity and low complexity of the sentences compared might improve performance because the more complex the text is, the more actors might be in it. In such cases, models insensitive to word order will regard many more sentences as likely to match the image, thereby lowering the chance of choosing the actual caption.

Models As shown by our ratios, Flava performs the worst, followed by LiT and CLIP. All models obtain mostly chance-like performance, in line with results on ARO, Winoground, or VALSE. Note that both Flava and LiT were found previously to perform better than CLIP on other tasks. This difference in performance further reinforces the fact that traditional benchmarks do not focus on testing compositional aspects. Our results seem to suggest all models perform better on simpler sentences, unlike what was shown in Wingorund or CREPE where CLIP did better on lengthier captions. Our results could differ from those of previous studies, given that we specifically controlled for certain artifacts, for example, by comparing the same sentences in their original or simplified form, which was not previously done. All models also performed better on SWiG, a less noisy dataset, suggesting that cleaner foils and captions improve performance (Doveh et al., 2023b). This is interesting considering Flava and LiT were trained on datasets containing CC. **Flava.** Flava performs significantly worse than CLIP, unlike in benchmarks such as Winoground, and ColorSwap. This might be because Flava is worse than CLIP at recognizing good word order, as shown by ARO. **LiT.** Compared to Flava, LiT might obtain an improved performance due to its increased training dataset size, which could result in the model seeing more minimal differences in the sentences. LiT might also perform better due to its textual encoder, as Zhai et al. (2022) showed that the BERT textual encoder improves performance. **CLIP.** The performance of CLIP and its relationship to its training dataset is hard to indicate.

6 Conclusions

We reviewed previous studies about the compositional abilities of VLMs, classifying them and their downsides. The current study introduced two new VALSE datasets of 9145 pairs of captions and foils, almost doubling the VALSE benchmark.

Our tests also indicate that many aspects could influence models' performance, such as the grammaticality of the compared sentences, and their simplicity or noisiness, further reinforcing the results of previous studies. We offered evidence that these aspects affect models uniformly, unlike previous studies (Thrush et al., 2022; Ma et al., 2023). We also offered evidence that in terms of performance, CLIP is followed by LiT and then Flava. Our results indicate that Flava performs much worse than the other models.

7 Future research and limitations

One-stream models could be considered for testing in the future, given that we only evaluated dual-stream ones. One of the other shortcomings of the current paper is that it tests only three models. Thus, the methodology for the current paper could be used and easily adapted to test new models fine-tuned for better compositional performance, such as X-VLM (shown to reach the highest accuracy on relations in ARO), SigCLIP, or MosaiCLIP (Singh et al., 2023).

The current datasets could be made more balanced. For example, the SWiG dataset could be better represented, since most parsed sentences were taken from CC. A possible future research direction is to generate active constructions from captions that were originally passive. We only created passive constructions by modifying the active ones, and not the reverse. This created an imbalance, as for the ditransitive/dative construction, we created examples from both types of original constructions, i.e. ditransitive or dative. Along similar lines, one of the limitations of the current study is that we did not investigate if any of the generated foils were incorrectly generated, and whether the sentences that remained non-simplified, after simplification, influenced results. Follow-up studies could test these aspects. Generating images from the foils to see if preferences change, as in ColorSwap, could also make an interesting follow-up to the current study. We also built a parser for the 'with/against' construction that could be used for new datasets, see Appendix B, which will also be available upon request. Future studies might also consider trying to account for inconsistencies in definitions of composition ality, to enlarge the current compositional aspects tested, or to apply our methodology for languages other than English.

References

Douglas Bates, Martin Mächler, Ben Bolker, and Steve Walker. 2015. Fitting linear mixed-effects models usinglme4. *J. Stat. Softw.*, 67(1).

Jirayu Burapacheep, Ishan Gaur, Agam Bhatia, and Tristan Thrush. 2024. Colorswap: A color and word order dataset for multimodal evaluation. *Preprint*, arXiv:2402.04492.

Xinyi Chen, Raquel Fernández, and Sandro Pezzelle. 2023. The BLA benchmark: Investigating basic language abilities of pre-trained multimodal models. In *Proceedings of the 2023 Conference on Empirical Methods in Natural Language Processing*, pages 5817–5830, Singapore. Association for Computational Linguistics.

Kevin Clark and Priyank Jaini. 2023. Text-to-image diffusion models are zero-shot classifiers. *Preprint*, arXiv:2303.15233.

Anuj Diwan, Layne Berry, Eunsol Choi, David Harwath, and Kyle Mahowald. 2022. Why is winoground hard? investigating failures in visuolinguistic compositionality. *Preprint*, arXiv:2211.00768.

Alexey Dosovitskiy, Lucas Beyer, Alexander Kolesnikov, Dirk Weissenborn, Xiaohua Zhai, Thomas Unterthiner, Mostafa Dehghani, Matthias Minderer, Georg Heigold, Sylvain Gelly, Jakob Uszkoreit, and Neil Houlsby. 2021. An image is worth 16x16 words: Transformers for image recognition at scale. In *International Conference on Learning Representations*.

Sivan Doveh, Assaf Arbelle, Sivan Harary, Roei Herzig, Donghyun Kim, Paola Cascante-bonilla, Amit Alfassy, Rameswar Panda, Raja Giryes, Rogerio Feris, Shimon Ullman, and Leonid Karlinsky. 2023a. Dense and aligned captions (dac) promote compositional reasoning in vl models. *Preprint*, arXiv:2305.19595.

Sivan Doveh, Assaf Arbelle, Sivan Harary, Eli Schwartz, Roei Herzig, Raja Giryes, Rogerio Feris, Rameswar Panda, Shimon Ullman, and Leonid Karlinsky. 2023b. Teaching structured vision & language concepts to vision & language models. In *2023 IEEE/CVF Conference on Computer Vision and Pattern Recognition (CVPR)*, pages 2657–2668.

Allyson Ettinger. 2020. What bert is not: Lessons from a new suite of psycholinguistic diagnostics for language models. *Preprint*, arXiv:1907.13528.

Andrzej Gałecki and Tomasz Burzykowski. 2012. Linear mixed-effects model. In *Linear mixed-effects models using R: a step-by-step approach*, pages 245–273. Springer.

Cheng-Yu Hsieh, Jieyu Zhang, Zixian Ma, Aniruddha Kembhavi, and Ranjay Krishna. 2023. Sugarcrepe: Fixing hackable benchmarks for vision-language compositionality. In *Advances in Neural Information Processing Systems*, volume 36, pages 31096–31116. Curran Associates, Inc.

Amita Kamath, Jack Hessel, and Kai-Wei Chang. 2023. Text encoders bottleneck compositionality in contrastive vision-language models. *Preprint*, arXiv:2305.14897.

Amita Kamath, Cheng-Yu Hsieh, Kai-Wei Chang, and Ranjay Krishna. 2024. The hard positive truth about vision-language compositionality. *Preprint*, arXiv:2409.17958.

Alexander Koplenig, Peter Meyer, Sascha Wolfer, and Carolin Müller-Spitzer. 2017. The statistical trade-off between word order and word structure – Large-scale evidence for the principle of least effort. *PLOS ONE*, 12(3):1–25. Publisher: Public Library of Science.

Martha Lewis, Nihal V. Nayak, Peilin Yu, Qinan Yu, Jack Merullo, Stephen H. Bach, and Ellie Pavlick. 2023. Does clip bind concepts? probing compositionality in large image models. *Preprint*, arXiv:2212.10537.

Jie S. Li, Yow-Ting Shiue, Yong-Siang Shih, and Jonas Geiping. 2023. Augmenters at semeval-2023 task 1: Enhancing clip in handling compositionality and ambiguity for zero-shot visual wsd through prompt augmentation and text-to-image diffusion. *Preprint*, arXiv:2307.05564.

Liunian Harold Li, Mark Yatskar, Da Yin, Cho-Jui Hsieh, and Kai-Wei Chang. 2020. What does BERT with vision look at? In *Proceedings of the 58th Annual Meeting of the Association for Computational Linguistics*, pages 5265–5275, Online. Association for Computational Linguistics.

Zixian Ma, Jerry Hong, Mustafa Omer Gul, Mona Gandhi, Irena Gao, and Ranjay Krishna. 2023. Crepe: Can vision-language foundation models reason compositionally? *Preprint*, arXiv:2212.07796.

Victor Milewski, Miryam de Lhoneux, and Marie-Francine Moens. 2022. Finding structural knowledge in multimodal-bert. *Preprint*, arXiv:2203.09306.

Mitja Nikolaus, Emmanuelle Salin, Stephane Ayache, Abdellah Fourtassi, and Benoit Favre. 2022. Do vision-and-language transformers learn grounded predicate-noun dependencies? In *Proceedings of the 2022 Conference on Empirical Methods in Natural Language Processing*, pages 1538–1555, Abu Dhabi, United Arab Emirates. Association for Computational Linguistics.

Timothy Ossowski, Ming Jiang, and Junjie Hu. 2024. Prompting large vision-language models for compositional reasoning. *Preprint*, arXiv:2401.11337.

Letitia Parcalabescu, Michele Cafagna, Lilitta Muradjan, Anette Frank, Iacer Calixto, and Albert Gatt. 2022. Valse: A task-independent benchmark for vision and language models centered on linguistic phenomena. *Preprint*, arXiv:2112.07566.

Barbara H. Partee. 2004. *Compositionality in formal semantics : selected papers*. Blackwell.

Thang M. Pham, Trung Bui, Long Mai, and Anh Nguyen. 2021. Out of order: How important is the sequential order of words in a sentence in natural language understanding tasks? *Preprint*, arXiv:2012.15180.

Yannick Raam. 2022. Probing models on the active and passive voice: How far do vision and language models look beyond sentence surfaces? Unpublished BA thesis.

RStudio Team. 2020. *RStudio: Integrated Development Environment for R*. RStudio, PBC., Boston, MA.

Piyush Sharma, Nan Ding, Sebastian Goodman, and Radu Soricut. 2018. Conceptual captions: A cleaned, hypernymed, image alt-text dataset for automatic image captioning. In *Proceedings of the 56th Annual Meeting of the Association for Computational Linguistics (Volume 1: Long Papers)*, pages 2556–2565, Melbourne, Australia. Association for Computational Linguistics.

Amanpreet Singh, Ronghang Hu, Vedanuj Goswami, Guillaume Couairon, Wojciech Galuba, Marcus Rohrbach, and Douwe Kiela. 2022. Flava: A foundational language and vision alignment model. In *2022 IEEE/CVF Conference on Computer Vision and Pattern Recognition (CVPR)*, pages 15617–15629.

Harman Singh, Pengchuan Zhang, Qifan Wang, Mengjiao Wang, Wenhan Xiong, Jingfei Du, and Yu Chen. 2023. Coarse-to-fine contrastive learning in image-text-graph space for improved vision-language compositionality. *Preprint*, arXiv:2305.13812.

Koustuv Sinha, Prasanna Parthasarathi, Joelle Pineau, and Adina Williams. 2021. Unnatural language inference. *Preprint*, arXiv:2101.00010.

Tristan Thrush, Ryan Jiang, Max Bartolo, Amanpreet Singh, Adina Williams, Douwe Kiela, and Candace Ross. 2022. Winoground: Probing vision and language models for visio-linguistic compositionality. *Preprint*, arXiv:2204.03162.

Matthew Trager, Pramuditha Perera, Luca Zancato, Alessandro Achille, Parminder Bhatia, and Stefano Soatto. 2024. Linear spaces of meanings: Compositional structures in vision-language models. *Preprint*, arXiv:2302.14383.

Ashish Vaswani, Noam Shazeer, Niki Parmar, Jakob Uszkoreit, Llion Jones, Aidan N. Gomez, Lukasz Kaiser, and Illia Polosukhin. 2023. Attention is all you need. *Preprint*, arXiv:1706.03762.

Chenwei Wu, Li Erran Li, Stefano Ermon, Patrick Haffner, Rong Ge, and Zaiwei Zhang. 2023. The role of linguistic priors in measuring compositional generalization of vision-language models. *Preprint*, arXiv:2310.02777.

Zhenlin Xu, Marc Niethammer, and Colin Raffel. 2022. Compositional generalization in unsupervised compositional representation learning: A study on disentanglement and emergent language. *Preprint*, arXiv:2210.00482.

Mert Yuksekgonul, Federico Bianchi, Pratyusha Kalluri, Dan Jurafsky, and James Zou. 2023. When and why vision-language models behave like bags-of-words, and what to do about it? *Preprint*, arXiv:2210.01936.

Tian Yun, Usha Bhalla, Ellie Pavlick, and Chen Sun. 2023. Do vision-language pretrained models learn composable primitive concepts? *Preprint*, arXiv:2203.17271.

Xiaohua Zhai, Xiao Wang, Basil Mustafa, Andreas Steiner, Daniel Keysers, Alexander Kolesnikov, and Lucas Beyer. 2022. Lit: Zero-shot transfer with locked-image text tuning. In *2022 IEEE/CVF Conference on Computer Vision and Pattern Recognition (CVPR)*, pages 18102–18112.

Tiancheng Zhao, Tianqi Zhang, Mingwei Zhu, Haozhan Shen, Kyusong Lee, Xiaopeng Lu, and Jianwei Yin. 2023. Vl-checklist: Evaluating pre-trained vision-language models with objects, attributes and relations. *Preprint*, arXiv:2207.00221.

Wanzheng Zhu and Suma Bhat. 2020. Gruen for evaluating linguistic quality of generated text. *Preprint*, arXiv:2010.02498.

A Examples of captions and foils

1. Captions
    a) A player hits a ball.
    b) A ball is hit by a player.
    c) A woman gives a book to the girl.
    d) A woman gives the girl a book.
2. Foils
    a) A ball hits a player.
    b) A player is hit by a ball.
    c) A woman gives the girl to a book.
    d) A woman gives a book the girl.

Figure 3: Image for active/passive construction, obtained by Google-searching the caption. **Corresponding captions**: (1a) and (1b). **Corresponding foils**: (2a), (2b)

Figure 4: Image for the ditransitive/dative construction, obtained by Google-searching the caption. **Corresponding captions**: (1c) and (1d). **Corresponding foils**: (2c), (2d)

B With/against foil parser examples

1. Captions
    a) The boy hits the stick against the fence.
    b) The boy hits the fence with the stick.
2. Foils
    a) The boy hits the fence against the stick.
    b) The boy hits the stick with the fence.

C Statistical results

First Lmer Test Captions were coded as 1, and foils as 0, thus any positive effects of a factor on the intercept means improved performance (i.e. captions are chosen over foils). For the first lmer test, the significant values for the fixed effects are *grammaticality equal* (β = -0.43, t-score = -27.63, p-value < 0.05), *grammaticality foil* (β = -0.03, t-score = -10.08, p-value < 0.05), *complexity simplified* (β = 0.05, t-score = 18.14, p-value < 0.05), *dataset SWiG* (β = 0.04, t-score = 7.38, p-value < 0.05), *model FLAVA* (β = -0.18, t-score = -59.3, p-value < 0.05), *model LIT* (β = -0.09, t-score = -25.26, p-value < 0.05). Note that ternary factors (i.e. grammaticality, model) calculate coefficients of one level in comparison to the mean of the other two. Significant interaction values were found for *type ditransitive and grammaticality equal* (β = -0.06, t-score = -2.22, p-value < 0.05), *type ditransitive and grammaticality foil* (β = -0.05, t-score = -8.39, p-value < 0.05).

Second Lmer Test *Grammaticality equal* (β = -0.44, t-score = -19.92, p-value < 0.05), *grammaticality foil* (β = -0.03, t-score = -16.42, p-value < 0.05), *complexity simplified* (β = 0.06, t-score = 25.14, p-value < 0.05), *dataset SWiG* (β = -0.03, t-score = -3.74, p-value < 0.05), *model FLAVA* (β = -0.18, t-score = -60.17, p-value < 0.05), *model LIT* (β = -0.09, t-score = -31.54, p-value < 0.05) had significant values. The significant interaction effects were *type ditransitive and grammaticality equal* (β = -0.02, t-score = -0.49, p-value < 0.05), *type ditransitive and grammaticality foil* (β = 0.03, t-score = 6.45, p-value < 0.05).

Models subsamples The subsamples on models generally follow the trends of the first lmer model, with some exceptions, which are explained for each model. Note that simplifying captions improved performance for all models, i.e. *Flava* (β = 0.07, t-score = 15.16, p-value < 0.05), *CLIP* (β = 0.018, t-score = 3.70, p-value < 0.05), *LiT* (β = 0.06, t-score = 3.44, p-value < 0.05).

Flava Grammaticality of the foils has a significant effect only for the ditransitive construction subsample, slightly making captions more likely (β = 0.03, t-score = 3.44, p-value < 0.05). On non-subsampled data, the effect of a grammatical foil on ditransitive sentences is slightly bigger (β = 0.05, t-score = 5.11, p-value < 0.05) than on active ones.

CLIP On subsamples, only the grammaticality of the foil has a slightly lower effect on passive constructions than active ones in the active/passive subsample (β =-0.05, t-score =-3.89, p-value < 0.05).

LiT On subsampled data, a bigger grammaticality score of the foil affects less passive structures (β=0.03, t-score =-2.80, p-value < 0.05), and more ditransitive captions (β =0.06, t-score =3,36, p-value < 0.05). On both subsamples, no interactions between grammaticality and type are significant.

Hybrid Feature-Embedding Models for Robust AI Text Detection

Kasper Thomas Gartside Knudsen
IT-University of Copenhagen
Copenhagen, Denmark
kasper.knudsen@gmail.com

Christian Hardmeier
IT-University of Copenhagen
Copenhagen, Denmark
chrha@itu.dk

Abstract

Reliably detecting AI-generated text is crucial but challenged by AI evolution and evasion techniques. We introduce a set of linguistic features designed to discriminate between human and AI-generated text, and propose a hybrid detection model combining features with DistilBERT embeddings at the input level. This hybrid approach is evaluated against feature-only (XGBoost) and fine-tuned transformer (DistilBERT) methods. Furthermore, we contribute a challenging evasive test set, generated using an LLM unseen in the training data (Llama-3-8B), to evaluate performance across LLM domains and evasion techniques. While DistilBERT leads on the standard test set, our hybrid model demonstrates improved robustness against evasion, maintaining high precision on evasive texts. Hybrid feature-embedding models offer a promising approach towards building more resilient AI text detectors.

1 Introduction

Modern large language models (LLMs) generate human-like text, creating risks of misuse in academia, phishing, and disinformation, necessitating reliable AI text detection. Common classification methods include feature-based approaches, leveraging quantifiable linguistic features like term frequencies and syntactic patterns, and fine-tuned transformers, which capture deep contextual nuances. The rapid evolution of LLMs demands rigorous evaluation of detector robustness against out-of-distribution LLMs and evasive text generation.

Addressing this, we introduce novel linguistic features shown to improve the performance of feature-only classifiers in this domain. We also propose and evaluate a novel hybrid model concatenating our extensive collection of features with DistilBERT (Sanh et al., 2020) embeddings at the input level. The rationale is to combine the explicit pattern recognition of features with the deep semantic understanding of embeddings, potentially yielding a detector that is both high-performing and robust. We conduct a comparative analysis of our hybrid model against multiple baselines, including feature-only XGBoost (Chen and Guestrin, 2016) variations and a fine-tuned DistilBERT classifier. Evaluation focuses on performance against challenging texts generated by an LLM unseen during training (Llama-3-8B; Grattafiori et al., 2024), including outputs prompted to evade detection, to assess practical robustness.

2 Related Work

Research in AI text detection encompasses various approaches. Feature-based methods utilize linguistic cues, comparing strategies such as TF-IDF versus detailed handcrafted feature sets with classifiers like XGBoost (Schaaff et al., 2023; Shijaku and Canhasi, 2023). Concurrently, fine-tuned transformer models serve as powerful AI text detectors (Wang et al., 2024a). Relevant alternative techniques leverage AI model information differently, for instance through sentence-level analysis using LLM log probabilities (Wang et al., 2023) or via ensembles combining predictions from multiple detectors (Abburi et al., 2023; Zhang et al., 2024). A critical challenge across methods, however, is detector robustness against evasion; some studies develop adversarial generation techniques (Kumarage et al., 2023), while others note the limitations of current tools (Weber-Wulff et al., 2023). Our work focuses on document-level detection, investigating novel features, proposing an input-level hybrid feature-embedding model, and rigorously evaluating its robustness alongside established methods on challenging, evasive texts.

3 Methodology

This section details the dataset, the AI text detection classifiers implemented, and the methodology for evaluating robustness against evasive text.

Proceedings of the 21st Conference on Natural Language Processing (KONVENS), Volume 1: Long and Short Papers, pages 318–325, 2025

3.1 Dataset

We utilize the `ai_text_detection_pile` dataset from Hugging Face (artem9k, 2023), a large-scale collection of long-form human essays (from sources like Reddit, Q&A sites) and AI-generated texts generated by GPT models (GPT-2, GPT-3, GPT-J, ChatGPT). To ensure class balance for training and evaluation, we created a working subset of approximately 680,000 samples by sampling human texts to match the AI text count. Each sample includes the text (up to 1024 characters) and a binary *ai_generated* label.

3.2 Detection Approaches

We implement and compare three distinct detection strategies: feature-based models, a fine-tuned transformer model, and a novel hybrid model combining features and embeddings.

3.2.1 Feature-Based Detectors

We explored feature engineering using XGBoost classifiers trained on different feature sets. XGBoost models for each of these three feature configurations were independently optimized using randomized search with 3-fold cross-validation.

Baseline Features: We first established a comprehensive baseline of handcrafted features by replicating the work of Schaaff et al. (2023), excluding inapplicable dataset-specific features. This baseline includes 32 linguistic and statistical features, covering aspects like perplexity, semantics, document statistics, and readability, as well as text vector representations derived from TF-IDF (top 500 uni/bigrams) and Sentence-BERT (384-dim embeddings + average cosine distance). In total, this replicated baseline feature set comprises 917 features.

Extended Features: Our proposed contribution extends this baseline set by adding 8 new features. We hypothesized that AI text often exhibits an overly formal linguistic style that can feel distinct from typical human writing. To capture this *complexity*, we introduced these features: average dependent clauses, passive voice count, and average syntactic tree depth. Furthermore, observing AI's tendency to reuse specific words or phrases, we targeted *repetition* with the following features: n-gram entropy (uni, bi, and tri-grams), burstiness (indicates word clustering), and count of list items. A complete list of the extended features (which consists of the baseline features *and* our 8 proposed additions) is available in Appendix A, as well as mathematical definitions for select proposed features in Appendix B.

TF-IDF Model: As a much simpler baseline, we separately trained an XGBoost model using *only* the top 500 TF-IDF unigram and bigram features, replicating the work of Shijaku and Canhasi (2023).

3.2.2 Transformer-Based Detector

Representing a pure transformer approach, we fine-tuned DistilBERT (`distilbert-base-uncased`), a 66M parameter transformer, for binary text classification following guidelines from Hugging Face (2024). This approach leverages deep contextual understanding learned during pre-training. Input texts were lowercased and then tokenized to a fixed length of 512 tokens. Hyperparameters were optimized using Optuna (Akiba et al., 2019) over 10 trials based on validation performance, using mixed precision for efficiency.

3.2.3 Hybrid Feature-Embedding Detector

To investigate the synergy between linguistic patterns and contextual embeddings, we propose a hybrid model. This model combines our *extended* feature set, with sequence embeddings derived from a *pre-trained* (not fine-tuned) DistilBERT model. Specifically, we concatenate the feature vector with the embedding vector obtained via first token pooling (using the hidden state of the initial token as the sequence representation) from DistilBERT for each text sample. This combined vector feeds into a Feed-Forward Neural Network (FFNN) classifier, trained with the Adam optimizer (Kingma and Ba, 2015) and binary cross-entropy loss, and tuned using grid search.

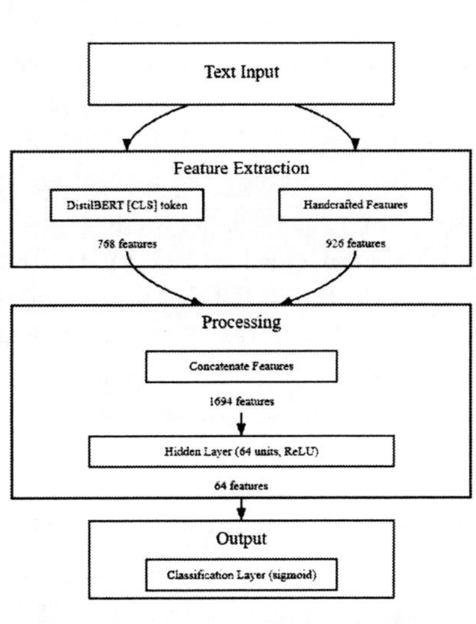

Figure 1: Hybrid FFNN Model Architecture

3.3 Evasive Text Generation

To assess practical robustness against out-of-distribution LLM behaviours and intentional evasion, we generated a challenging test set. We prompted an unseen LLM (Llama-3-8B) to rephrase 5,000 AI-generated texts from the original test set using three prompt strategies: *control* (rewrite in own style, a baseline for domain shift), *basic evasion* (rewrite to avoid detection), and *advanced evasion* (rewrite considering specific AI traits like repetition/formality to avoid detection) (see full prompts in Appendix C). Each set of 5,000 rephrased texts was combined with 5,000 human texts from the original test set, creating three balanced evasive evaluation datasets. All developed detectors were evaluated on these datasets to measure performance degradation and resilience.

4 Results

We evaluated the performance of the optimized detection models: feature-based XGBoost (baseline, extended, TF-IDF), fine-tuned DistilBERT, and our proposed hybrid FFNN. Performance was measured using accuracy, precision, recall, and F1-score on the standard test set (a 10% split of the dataset), and three evasive test sets generated using an unseen LLM (Llama-3-8B). Full result tables are available in Appendix D.

4.1 Performance on Standard Test Data

On the standard test set (Table 1), the fine-tuned DistilBERT model achieved the highest performance (98.3% F1). The baseline and extended feature-based XGBoost models also performed strongly; notably, the extended feature model achieved a small but consistent improvement of 0.1 percentage points over the baseline across all metrics (e.g., 96.6% vs. 96.5% F1). While this margin is slight, it suggests a positive contribution from our proposed linguistic features. Our hybrid FFNN model achieved a competitive 94.1% F1 score, while the TF-IDF XGBoost model lagged significantly (86.2% F1). This establishes strong performance baselines and supports the utility of feature engineering as a competitive detection strategy.

4.2 Robustness Against Evasive Texts

Evaluating models on the evasive datasets revealed varying degrees of robustness (Tables 2-4). While most detectors experienced severe performance degradation compared to the standard test set, the hybrid FFNN model demonstrated notable resilience. It exhibited comparatively slight F1 score degradation on the basic and advanced evasion texts and even improved performance on the control texts (Table 2). This observed variability across models and conditions underscores the necessity of evaluating detectors on diverse data, including outputs from unseen LLMs and text designed to evade detection, to assess practical resilience beyond potentially biased training distributions.

Regarding the feature-based detectors, the extended XGBoost consistently improved upon the baseline XGBoost across all evasive sets by at least 1% on F1-scores, further supporting the utility of the novel features against both domain shift and evasion attempts. However, both feature-based approaches showed vulnerability to the more targeted evasion strategies. Interestingly, the TF-IDF model substantially outperformed the baseline and extended XGBoost models on the basic and advanced evasion sets (e.g., 8.5% improvement on advanced evasion). This implies the handcrafted features were more susceptible to the prompt-based manipulations, while the TF-IDF representation proved more resilient, possibly due to the handcrafted set's complexity introducing noise or less robust patterns, indicating that more careful feature selection may be beneficial within such approaches.

Comparing the top-performing approaches on the evasive sets highlights the strengths of the hybrid FFNN relative to the fine-tuned DistilBERT. While DistilBERT mostly achieved higher F1 scores, the hybrid model demonstrated greater stability on evasive texts, evidenced by its significantly smaller F1 score degradation between the standard and advanced evasion test sets (a drop of only 4.9% vs. DistilBERT's 8.5%). Furthermore, the hybrid model outperformed DistilBERT on the control evasive set (F1: 94.6% vs 86.7%) and achieved F1 scores that were highly comparable on the basic and advanced evasion sets, 0.6-0.7% lower than DistilBERT. Critically, the hybrid model consistently maintained higher precision across all three evasive datasets, ranging from a 0.8% to 1.3% increase, indicating its positive classifications (AI) are more reliable against challenging and out-of-distribution text generation patterns.

4.3 Feature Importance Analysis

To interpret feature contributions, we applied SHAP (Lundberg and Lee, 2017) analysis to the

XGBoost extended feature model. Given its extensive feature space, it is significant that several of our novel handcrafted features ranked within the top 20 most impactful predictors globally (see Figure 2 in Appendix). Notably, *unigram entropy* ranked 3rd, *burstiness* ranked 11th, and *average dependent clauses* ranked 16th, with SHAP indicating higher values generally correlated with human predictions in this dataset. Their high importance confirms the contribution of these novel features to the detection model.

4.4 Impact of Evasion on Text Features

Analysis of mean values of features across labels and evasive texts (selected features shown in Table 5) reveals insights into model robustness challenges. Inherent differences existed between the training AI (GPT-family) and the unseen Llama-3 model (e.g., Llama-3 showed lower `burstiness` and `passive_voice_count`). Furthermore, evasive prompts manipulated features, reducing complexity (`dep_clauses_avg`) but sometimes yielded counter-intuitive results (e.g., reduced `error_count`, despite instructions to increase them). Averages for some novel features also appeared contradictory to model directionality learned via SHAP (Section 4.3). This discrepancy suggests that the model likely captures complex interactions or distributional nuances beyond simple averages. This combination of LLM differences and manipulated feature patterns explains the vulnerability of the feature-only XGBoost models to these challenging datasets.

5 Discussion

The performance degradation observed across all models when tested against our challenging evasive texts highlights the need for such datasets to provide a realistic assessment of resilience against evolving LLMs and adversarial tactics. The contribution of our extended features was most apparent on these challenging datasets, where they provided a clear improvement over the XGBoost baseline. Moreover, the hybrid model, which incorporates these same features, also exhibited notable robustness on these datasets. These findings demonstrate that feature engineering remains a valuable component in developing competitive and robust detection systems.

Our results also reveal a trade-off between performance on familiar data and robust generalization. While our fine-tuned transformer achieved the highest F1 scores on the standard test set, a finding consistent with similar benchmarks (Wang et al., 2024b), we argue its larger performance drop on evasive texts is the more critical result, suggesting potential sensitivity to distribution shift. In contrast, our novel hybrid FFNN model demonstrated superior resilience, evidenced by its minimal F1 degradation and consistently high precision on challenging evasive sets generated by an unseen LLM. This suggests combining linguistic features with contextual embeddings offers more stable detection against out-of-distribution patterns. The hybrid's high precision is particularly valuable for applications demanding low false positives. Although its peak performance didn't match DistilBERT here, its robustness profile suggests strong potential, possibly enhanced further via feature selection, embeddings from more powerful models, and expanded tuning.

However, even robust detectors like the hybrid model have inherent limitations and cannot serve as sole proof of misconduct (Weber-Wulff et al., 2023). We propose that practical systems, especially in academia, should integrate detection with verification techniques, for instance, analyzing a document's edit history via platform logs could reveal non-human generation patterns (e.g., large copy-pastes), though deliberate manual input might circumvent simple checks. Additionally, verifying reference validity could counteract LLM hallucination tendencies and outdated sources, providing a strong signal independent of writing style. Combining robust detectors with such verification checks, potentially programmatically, could create a more comprehensive system.

6 Conclusion

This research addressed the critical need for robust AI text detection by introducing linguistic features designed for this domain and proposing a novel hybrid model combining features with transformer embeddings. Through comparative analysis against strong feature-based (XGBoost) and fine-tuned transformer (DistilBERT) baselines, we evaluated performance on standard datasets and our challenging evasive datasets, which effectively exposed detector vulnerabilities. Our findings confirm that while fine-tuned transformers excel on in-distribution LLM data, the proposed hybrid model offers a compelling alternative, demonstrating greater robustness and stability against evasive texts while maintaining high precision. This performance is particularly advantageous for real-world scenarios requiring generalization to new text generation patterns and the minimization of costly misclassifications. Our proposed novel features also showed incremental benefits for feature-only models, particularly on evasive texts, confirming their value as discriminators of human and AI-generated text, and highlighting the necessity of robust evaluation against diverse data. Our results demonstrate that hybrid feature-embedding models serve as resilient and practically reliable AI text detection systems in the face of rapidly evolving AI capabilities.

7 Limitations

The generalizability of our findings is limited by our choice of data and models. Our training data consists of text from older AI models (GPT-2/3) and specific human genres (online essays). Similarly, our selection of DistilBERT for the fine-tuned and hybrid models constrained their potential performance. Employing larger, more contemporary transformers (such as ModernBERT (Warner et al., 2025)) was beyond our computational resources, but would likely yield stronger results and further widen the performance gap to non-transformer methods. Future work should incorporate more powerful models alongside datasets that are diverse and representative of the current AI landscape.

Furthermore, our experimental design limits the practical applicability of our findings. While this study focused on document-level detection, future work could extend our approach to incorporate sentence-level techniques for finer-grained analysis of potentially mixed human-AI texts, a common real-world scenario. Additionally, our use of a balanced dataset, while ensuring a fair comparison, does not reflect skewed distributions often found in practice. The relatively simple LLM rewriting prompts used for evasion also call for future work; more sophisticated evasive generation is needed for a thorough robustness assessment.

Finally, the proposed hybrid model has limitations regarding architecture and efficiency. The model has considerable inference overhead from dual feature extraction and embedding generation per input, contrasted with the potentially faster standalone fine-tuned model. Fast inference is particularly important for resource-constrained or real-time scenarios. Moreover, the hybrid's specific FFNN architecture, chosen feature set, and transformer embedding source represent just one possible implementation; exploration of alternative configurations may yield improved results.

8 Ethical Considerations

Our work aims to contribute positively to the challenge of identifying AI-generated text, with applications in supporting academic integrity and combating misinformation. However, we acknowledge the potential for misuse and the inherent risks of AI detection technology. As shown in our robustness evaluation, no detector is perfect, and performance can worsen on out-of-distribution or evasive text. Therefore, we argue that these tools should not be used as the sole basis for high-stakes decisions (e.g., determining academic misconduct). There is a significant risk of false positives, which could have serious negative consequences for individuals. We advocate for their use as an assistive tool for human-led evaluation, as discussed in Section 5. Finally, while the analysis of model weaknesses is necessary for improving detectors, we also recognize it could be used by adversaries to develop more effective evasion techniques.

9 Reproducibility

This study used the publicly available `ai_text_detection_pile` dataset (artem9k, 2023), which is compiled from various public online sources. To further support the reproducibility of our findings and to facilitate future research, all code and data created for this study are publicly available in a GitHub repository.[1] This includes the source code for all stages of our research, including feature extraction, model training, and evaluation, as well as the generated evasive text datasets.

The experiments were computationally intensive and conducted on high-performance computing (HPC) resources. Feature extraction and XGBoost model training were performed on multi-core CPUs (up to 64 cores), with system RAM requirements approaching 1000 GB for loading pre-computed embeddings. The fine-tuning of DistilBERT and the training of our hybrid FFNN model utilized NVIDIA A100 GPUs (40-80 GB VRAM).

[1] `https://github.com/kakn/ai-text-detection`

Acknowledgements

The authors acknowledge the IT University of Copenhagen HPC resources made available for conducting the research reported in this paper.

References

Harika Abburi, Kalyani Roy, Michael Suesserman, Nirmala Pudota, Balaji Veeramani, Edward Bowen, and Sanmitra Bhattacharya. 2023. A simple yet efficient ensemble approach for AI-generated text detection. In *Proceedings of the Third Workshop on Natural Language Generation, Evaluation, and Metrics (GEM)*, pages 413–421, Singapore. Association for Computational Linguistics.

Takuya Akiba, Shotaro Sano, Toshihiko Yanase, Takeru Ohta, and Masanori Koyama. 2019. Optuna: A Next-generation Hyperparameter Optimization Framework. In *Proceedings of the 25th ACM SIGKDD International Conference on Knowledge Discovery & Data Mining*, KDD '19, page 2623–2631, New York, NY, USA. Association for Computing Machinery.

artem9k. 2023. AI Text Detection Pile. Hugging Face Dataset. MIT License. Accessed: 2024-05-19.

Tianqi Chen and Carlos Guestrin. 2016. XGBoost: A Scalable Tree Boosting System. In *Proceedings of the 22nd ACM SIGKDD International Conference on Knowledge Discovery and Data Mining*, KDD '16, page 785–794, New York, NY, USA. Association for Computing Machinery.

Aaron Grattafiori, Abhimanyu Dubey, Abhinav Jauhri, Abhinav Pandey, Abhishek Kadian, Ahmad Al-Dahle, Aiesha Letman, Akhil Mathur, Alan Schelten, Alex Vaughan, Amy Yang, Angela Fan, Anirudh Goyal, Anthony Hartshorn, Aobo Yang, Archi Mitra, Archie Sravankumar, Artem Korenev, Arthur Hinsvark, and 181 others. 2024. The Llama 3 Herd of Models. *arXiv e-prints*, arXiv:2407.21783.

Hugging Face. 2024. Sequence Classification Guide. Accessed: 2024-05-30.

Diederik P. Kingma and Jimmy Ba. 2015. Adam: A method for stochastic optimization. In *3rd International Conference on Learning Representations, ICLR 2015, San Diego, CA, USA, May 7-9, 2015, Conference Track Proceedings*.

Tharindu Kumarage, Paras Sheth, Raha Moraffah, Joshua Garland, and Huan Liu. 2023. How reliable are AI-generated-text detectors? an assessment framework using evasive soft prompts. In *Findings of the Association for Computational Linguistics: EMNLP 2023*, pages 1337–1349, Singapore. Association for Computational Linguistics.

Scott M Lundberg and Su-In Lee. 2017. A unified approach to interpreting model predictions. In *Advances in Neural Information Processing Systems*, volume 30. Curran Associates, Inc.

Victor Sanh, Lysandre Debut, Julien Chaumond, and Thomas Wolf. 2020. DistilBERT, a distilled version of BERT: smaller, faster, cheaper and lighter. *Preprint*, arXiv:1910.01108.

Kristina Schaaff, Tim Schlippe, and Lorenz Mindner. 2023. Classification of human- and AI-generated texts for English, French, German, and Spanish. In *Proceedings of the 6th International Conference on Natural Language and Speech Processing (ICNLSP 2023)*, pages 1–10, Online. Association for Computational Linguistics.

Rexhep Shijaku and Ercan Canhasi. 2023. ChatGPT Generated Text Detection. Preprint available on ResearchGate.

Hao Wang, Jianwei Li, and Zhengyu Li. 2024a. Ai-generated text detection and classification based on bert deep learning algorithm. *Preprint*, arXiv:2405.16422.

Pengyu Wang, Linyang Li, Ke Ren, Botian Jiang, Dong Zhang, and Xipeng Qiu. 2023. SeqXGPT: Sentence-level AI-generated text detection. In *Proceedings of the 2023 Conference on Empirical Methods in Natural Language Processing*, pages 1144–1156, Singapore. Association for Computational Linguistics.

Yuxia Wang, Jonibek Mansurov, Petar Ivanov, Jinyan Su, Artem Shelmanov, Akim Tsvigun, Osama Mohammed Afzal, Tarek Mahmoud, Giovanni Puccetti, and Thomas Arnold. 2024b. SemEval-2024 task 8: Multidomain, multimodel and multilingual machine-generated text detection. In *Proceedings of the 18th International Workshop on Semantic Evaluation (SemEval-2024)*, pages 2057–2079, Mexico City, Mexico. Association for Computational Linguistics.

Benjamin Warner, Antoine Chaffin, Benjamin Clavié, Orion Weller, Oskar Hallström, Said Taghadouini, Alexis Gallagher, Raja Biswas, Faisal Ladhak, Tom Aarsen, Griffin Thomas Adams, Jeremy Howard, and Iacopo Poli. 2025. Smarter, better, faster, longer: A modern bidirectional encoder for fast, memory efficient, and long context finetuning and inference. In *Proceedings of the 63rd Annual Meeting of the Association for Computational Linguistics (Volume 1: Long Papers)*, pages 2526–2547, Vienna, Austria. Association for Computational Linguistics.

Debora Weber-Wulff, Alla Anohina-Naumeca, Sonja Bjelobaba, Tomáš Foltýnek, Jean Guerrero-Dib, Olumide Popoola, Petr Šigut, and Lorna Waddington. 2023. Testing of detection tools for AI-generated text. *International Journal for Educational Integrity*, 19(1).

Ye Zhang, Qian Leng, Mengran Zhu, Rui Ding, Yue Wu, Jintong Song, and Yulu Gong. 2024. Enhancing Text Authenticity: A Novel Hybrid Approach for AI-Generated Text Detection. In *2024 IEEE 4th International Conference on Electronic Technology, Communication and Information (ICETCI)*, pages 433–438.

A Extended Collection of Features

Group	Feature
Sentiment	Polarity
	Subjectivity
Semantics	Stop Word Count
	Special Character Count
	Punctuation Count
	Quotation Count
	Uppercase Words Relative
	Personal Pronoun Count
	Personal Pronoun Relative
	POS Per Sentence Mean
	Discourse Marker Count
Structure	Character Count
	Word Count
	Sentence Count
	Paragraph Count
	Words Per Sentence Mean
	Words Per Sentence Std
	Words Per Paragraph Mean
	Words Per Paragraph Std
	Sentences Per Paragraph Mean
	Sentences Per Paragraph Std
Lexicon	Unique Word Count
	Unique Words Per Sentence Mean
	Unique Words Per Sentence Std
	Unique Words Relative
Readability	Flesch Reading Ease
	Flesch Kincaid Grade
Complexity*	Passive Voice Count
	Syntactic Tree Depth Per Sentence Mean
	Dependent Clauses Per Sentence Mean
Repetition*	Burstiness
	Unigram Entropy
	Bigram Entropy
	Trigram Entropy
	List Item Count
Errors	Error Count
	Multi Blank Count
Text Vectors	500-dim TF-IDF Vector (Uni/Bigram)
	Sentence-BERT Vector
	Average Sentence-BERT Distance
LLM-based	Max Perplexity
	Mean Perplexity
	Zero-Shot LLM Prediction

*Groups containing our proposed features

B Formulations of Select Features

This section provides mathematical details for proposed features whose implementation is not self-evident from their names:

- **Average Syntactic Tree Depth**: The average depth of syntactic parse trees across all sentences in a text.

$$\text{ASTD} = \frac{1}{N}\sum_{i=1}^{N} d_i$$

Where N is the number of sentences and d_i is the depth of the syntactic tree for the i-th sentence.

- **N-gram Entropy**: Measures the entropy of n-gram distributions, with higher entropy indicating more variety.

$$H(X) = -\sum_{x\in X} p(x)\log p(x)$$

Where X is the set of n-grams and $p(x)$ is the probability of n-gram x, calculated from its frequency.

- **Burstiness**: Measures the variability in word frequencies, with higher values indicating more word clustering.

$$B = \frac{\sigma_w}{\mu_w}$$

Where σ_w is the standard deviation and μ_w is the mean of word frequencies.

C Evasive Text Generation Prompts

To generate the evasive text datasets, we prompted Llama-3-8B (Grattafiori et al., 2024) to rewrite AI-generated texts using the following instructions. An instruction to "Respond with only the rewritten text." followed each prompt request:

- **Control Prompt** (AI-rephrased): "Rewrite the following text in your own style and tone."
- **Basic Evasion Prompt**: "Rewrite the following text so it won't be detected by AI detection tools."
- **Advanced Evasion Prompt**: "Considering typical AI text traits like repetitive phrasing, overly formal language, and minimal errors, rewrite the following text so it won't be detected by AI detection tools."

D Classification Results

Model	Accuracy	Precision	Recall	F1
DistilBERT (Fine-tuned)	98.3%	97.0%	99.7%	98.3%
FFNN (Hybrid)	94.1%	92.8%	95.4%	94.1%
XGBoost (Baseline)	96.4%	95.6%	97.3%	96.5%
XGBoost (Extended)	96.5%	95.7%	97.4%	96.6%
XGBoost (TF-IDF)	85.7%	83.0%	89.7%	86.2%

Table 1: Performance metrics on 34,000 AI + 34,000 human texts

Model	Accuracy	Precision	Recall	F1
DistilBERT (Fine-tuned)	87.8%	95.9%	79.1%	86.7%
FFNN (Hybrid)	92.1%	97.2%	92.1%	94.6%
XGBoost (Baseline)	71.5%	63.9%	98.8%	77.6%
XGBoost (Extended)	73.2%	56.4%	98.7%	78.7%
XGBoost (TF-IDF)	72.3%	77.2%	63.2%	69.5%

Table 2: Performance metrics on 5000 AI-rephrased + 5000 human texts

Model	Accuracy	Precision	Recall	F1
DistilBERT (Fine-tuned)	91.5%	96.2%	86.4%	91.0%
FFNN (Hybrid)	86.5%	97.0%	84.5%	90.3%
XGBoost (Baseline)	68.1%	61.4%	97.6%	75.4%
XGBoost (Extended)	69.8%	62.7%	97.8%	76.4%
XGBoost (TF-IDF)	81.4%	81.3%	81.5%	81.4%

Table 3: Performance metrics on 5000 basic evasive AI + 5000 human texts

Model	Accuracy	Precision	Recall	F1
DistilBERT (Fine-tuned)	90.4%	96.1%	84.2%	89.8%
FFNN (Hybrid)	85.0%	96.9%	82.6%	89.2%
XGBoost (Baseline)	57.7%	54.2%	98.5%	70.0%
XGBoost (Extended)	60.3%	55.8%	98.5%	71.3%
XGBoost (TF-IDF)	80.0%	80.8%	78.8%	79.8%

Table 4: Performance metrics on 5000 advanced evasive AI + 5000 human texts

E SHAP Visualization

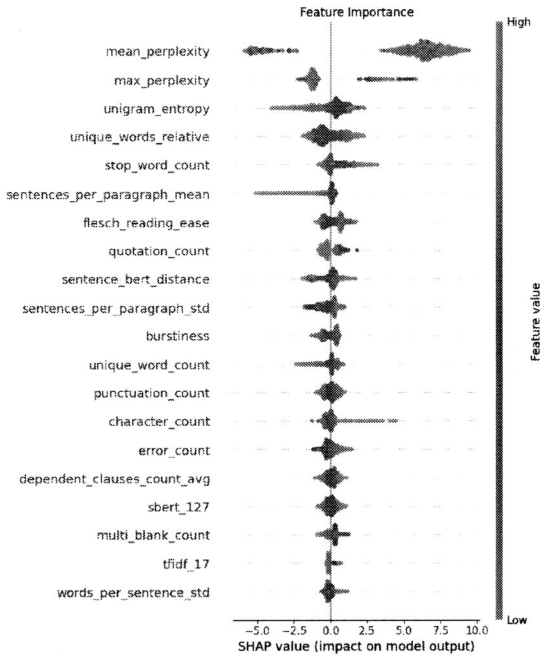

Figure 2: SHAP summary plot for the extended feature model

F Feature Means Across Labels

Feature	Human	AI	Control	Basic	Advanced
quotation_count	1.85	6.85	2.08	2.71	2.70
list_item_count	0.22	0.38	0.41	0.57	0.53
passive_voice_count	1.47	2.41	1.37	1.54	1.47
words_per_par_std	31.34	21.41	10.29	12.00	11.46
stop_word_count	128.72	184.00	104.24	102.23	99.17
discourse_count	22.70	32.30	20.63	18.85	19.27
dep_clauses_avg	1.17	1.65	1.53	1.34	1.33
error_count	8.40	6.01	1.93	2.28	2.45
burstiness	3.57	4.67	2.90	3.00	2.93
uniq_words_per_sent	17.08	21.87	21.01	20.44	20.45
syntactic_depth_avg	5.53	6.95	6.89	6.93	6.86
flesch_reading_ease	73.57	62.77	61.22	49.20	50.17
unigram_entropy	6.52	6.40	6.38	6.20	6.31

Table 5: Mean values of select features for human and AI texts (340k texts each) and various evasive texts (5k texts each, only AI label).

Using LLMs for experimental stimulus pretests in linguistics. Evidence from semantic associations between words and social gender

Christian Lang and **Franziska Kretzschmar** and **Sandra Hansen**
Department of Grammar, Leibniz Institute for the German Language, Mannheim, Germany
lang@ids-mannheim.de, kretzschmar@ids-mannheim.de, hansen@ids-mannheim.de

Abstract

Whether large language models (LLMs) can validly complement or substitute human participants in experimental research remains an open question. Focusing on language cognition, we assess the suitability of GPT-4o and LLaMA 3.1 models (70B Instruct and 8B Instruct) for performing a semantic-association task in German. LLMs labeled noun phrases by social-gender association and rated association strength, mirroring a human participant task. Overall, LLM ratings aligned with human data, but item-level analyses revealed systematic deviations in response patterns.

1 Introduction

The increasing abilities of large language models (LLMs) to generate human-like output has initiated empirical investigations on whether LLMs may be a valid experimental data source either in addition to humans or even replacing them (e.g., Aher et al., 2023; Argyle et al., 2023; Cai et al., 2024; Kuribayashi et al., 2024; Misra et al., 2020; Zhu et al., 2023). The main arguments for using LLM-generated data over human data were that LLMs do not suffer from humans' adaptations to an experimental procedure (e.g., fatigue or learning effects, cf. Digutsch and Kosinski, 2023), and, as a research-supporting tool, LLMs would mitigate monetary and time costs at preparatory stages in one's research project such as in pilot studies or item pre-tests (cf. Dillion et al., 2023; Trott, 2024).

Strikingly, the results of the existing comparisons of authentic natural and artificial datasets across varying tasks suggest that despite the qualitative similarity of LLM-based and human-based results overall, LLM-generated data often show a tendency to over- or underestimate aggregate measures of human data. As argued (and empirically tested) in detail by Trott (2024), this may lead to differences in magnitude between LLM-based and human-based results. Further research is needed to analyze the robustness of this pattern, i.e. to what extent LLM-based and human-based data diverge or converge at the (aggregated) condition and item level depending on LLMs, tasks and languages.

Here, we compare data from three LLMs and a human sample presented with the same task. Our use case is an item pre-test, a necessary step in experimental research to control stimuli for implicit biases that may have undesirable effects on the results of the main study. In its simplest form, a separate participant sample would perform some task with a set of items. Based on the aggregated pre-test results, the researcher would then select items for the main study. Our research question is to what extent different LLMs are suitable for this type of item pre-test. We analyze LLMs performance vis-à-vis human behavior in a semantic-association task involving social-gender associations in German.

We investigate the stereotypical association of the lexical meaning of a noun phrase (NP) with a person of female or male gender (i.e., social gender, see Lewis and Lupyan (2020) for an overview of its cross-linguistic influence, and Esaulova et al. (2017) for the impact of social-gender associations on sentence comprehension in German).[1] If included in a pre-test, participants would typically have to label (i.e., associate) words for social gender and/or rate the association strength – which we implemented as a task in our study.

We consider this task an ideal testing ground to compare results from LLMs with human participants, because LLMs basically act as models of distributional semantics (Enyan et al., 2024). This makes them predestined for questions of (semantic) association, or context-sensitive phenomena more

[1] A prominent example is the NP *die Flugbegleitung* [flight attendant] that is typically associated with a female person in German (Esaulova et al., 2017). However, other role descriptions for people may have associations that are less obvious to language users, e.g. *genius*, *authority* or *movie star*.

Proceedings of the 21st Conference on Natural Language Processing (KONVENS), Volume 1: Long and Short Papers, pages 326–332, 2025

generally. The extensive training data of LLMs contain data points relevant for our (or any) task. When prompted neutrally – i.e., not limited to a specific persona –, the output of the LLMs provides an aggregation of these relevant data points that is representative of the training data. We test to what extent this aggregation is comparable to human data at the condition and item level.

In general, our study adds new data from an hitherto unstudied experimental task to the literature, as well as data from a target language other than English. Moreover, unlike the pertinent prior studies with large lexical databases and mainly ChatGPT models (see Section 2), our work examines 1) a novel semantic dimension—social-gender associations, 2) a more ecologically valid item set regarding size and composition, and 3) models from different families.

2 Related Research

For English psycholinguistic databases, it has been found that LLMs and humans generate similar data when condition-based aggregations are compared (e.g., Digutsch and Kosinski, 2023; Trott, 2024). However, it has also been found that effect sizes vary, i.e. although LLMs show relative differences between conditions that are similar to humans, absolute values for the measures per condition differ (even strikingly so for some tasks, cf. Cai et al., 2024; Trott, 2024). For example, in their study on semantic-association priming, the difference in effect size led Digutsch and Kosinski (2023) to conclude that priming due to semantic similarity (overlap in number of semantic features) has a stronger impact on LLM performance than semantic association (co-occurrence of words). Similarly, Trott (2024) found in a series of regression analyses that many predictor variables show changes in effect size depending on the type of data generation, with some of them suggesting that information on semantic categories are more important to humans than to LLMs. Thus, quantitative differences across conditions suggest qualitative differences in how humans and LLMs use semantic information.

3 Data base and methodology

We provide supplementary materials including the item list, full LLM prompts, a sample workflow to generate and process the LLM data, aggregated data, and the analysis script here: `https://osf.io/ezy9p/?view_only=c72db52d721c49fb9be492bd4b914d10`.

3.1 Dataset

From the literature on grammatical gender marking and social gender in German (Thurmair, 2006; Klein, 2022; Kopf, 2022; Schoenthal, 1989), we identified NPs from each grammatical-gender category (masculine, feminine, neuter) for which social gender may vary between male, female or no clear association.[2] From the resulting list, we excluded pejoratives, animal names used as rare metaphors for humans, words for which there was a highly salient suffixed word form to indicate a female person (such as *Passagier**in*** [female passenger]), ambiguous and infrequent words. If a base word allowed several compounds, we did not use more than four (e.g., *star*: *movie star, pop star*) to match the number of experimental lists (see Section 3.2.2). To balance the distribution of grammatical gender, we added 19 NPs not covered in the cited literature. The final list included 116 NPs: 30 feminine, 47 masculine, 36 neuter, and 3 with varying grammatical gender (e.g., *der/das Balg* [annoying child]).

3.2 General experimental task

The semantic-association task consisted of two steps, which were identical for LLM prompts and task instructions for humans. First, LLMs and humans had to label NPs for their associated social gender, choosing either the label *Person männlichen Geschlechts* [person of male gender], *Person weiblichen Geschlechts* [person of female gender], or *keins von beiden* [neither]. Second, if an item was labeled as person of male or female gender, we asked the LLMs/human annotators to rate the association strength on a scale from 1 (very low) to 5 (very high). The following subsections describe the specifics of data collection for LLMs and the human sample, respectively.

3.2.1 LLM-Generated Assessments

We applied three different LLMs —GPT-4o (a widely adopted proprietary model) and LLaMA 3.1 (70B and 8B, open-source models differing in size)— to label 116 NPs for social gender using zero-shot prompting (see supplementary materials).

We accessed LLaMA models via ChatAI (Doosthosseini et al., 2024) and GPT-4o through OpenAI's commercial service, using OpenAI's chat

[2]For example, the grammatical gender of *die Aushilfe* [temporary staff] is feminine, but the associated social gender can be male, female or neither. Note that the NP selection was part in stimulus creation for a future reading study.

completion API for all models. Each labeling was initiated through a separate API call to prevent contextual carryover. The system prompt (developer role, in English) defined a neutral assistant persona and structured output for easier processing, aligning with the pre-test goal of a general, condition-level assessment. The task prompt (user role) was delivered in German and templated to ensure consistent wording across all 116 noun phrases. We chose this language combination to maximize clarity (via English system prompt) and linguistic relevance (via German task prompt).[3]

Due to the non-deterministic nature of LLMs, outputs generated with the same prompt can differ from one another.[4] Hence, and in line with previous research (Elman, 1990; Wilcox et al., 2024), we used each LLM to generate multiple labels and ratings (N = 33) per item, corresponding to the number of participant labels and ratings per NP (see Section 3.2.2). We kept the temperature at 0 to make LLM outputs as deterministic—and thus as reproducible—as possible.

3.2.2 Study with human participants

The experiment was designed to be as similar as possible to the LLM-generated assessments, with two modifications following standards in psycholinguistic experiments. First, items were allocated to 4 lists of 29 NPs each to rule out fatigue or learning effects of human participants; each participant was randomly assigned to one of the lists. The lists were compiled according to the following criteria: a) nearly even distribution of grammatical gender across lists, and b) no more than two items with the same word stem (e.g., *star* and *movie star* etc.) per list. Moreover, to prevent a list from containing a majority of items with a clear bias towards one social gender, we used the LLM ratings to allocate NPs to lists with a near-equal distribution regarding LLM-based gender labels. Second, items were presented with a unique randomized order per participant to prevent sequence effects.

The study was run on the survey platfom *Unipark* (`https://www.unipark.com`). 132 participants (52 females, 76 males, 3 diverse, 1 not specified; age range: 22-75) were recruited with *Prolific* (`https://www.prolific.com`) and received monetary compensation for their participation. There were no missing or erroneous responses, resulting in 33 data points per NP/item.

Annotator	m	n	f	unclear
Human annotators	39	65	11	1
GPT-4o	31	69	16	0
LLaMA 3.1 70B	36	67	13	0
LLaMA 3.1 8B	111	0	5	0

Table 1: Distribution of majority vote labels by annotator (LLM or human annotators)

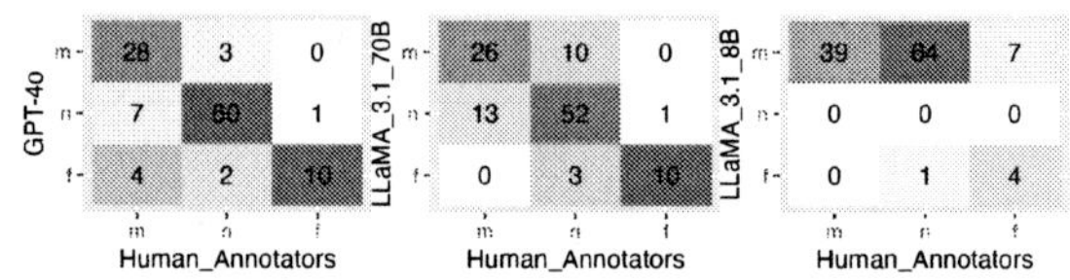

Class	Prec.	Rec.	F1
m	0.90	0.72	0.80
n	0.88	0.92	0.90
f	0.62	0.91	0.74
avg. weighted F1: 0.85			

Class	Prec.	Rec.	F1
m	0.72	0.67	0.69
n	0.79	0.80	0.79
f	0.77	0.91	0.83
avg. weighted F1: 0.76			

Class	Prec.	Rec.	F1
m	0.35	1.00	0.52
n	NA	0.00	NA
f	0.80	0.36	0.50
avg. weighted F1: NA			

Figure 1: Top: Confusion matrices with overlap of associative labeling per category, based on majority votes; N = 115 (we excluded the NP with unclear majority vote). Y-axis: LLM labels, X-axis: human labels (reference). Bottom: macro average of precision, recall and F1

4 Results

In the following, we use the human annotators as a benchmark against which the LLMs are compared. Table 1[5] shows the majority-vote distribution (most frequent label across 33 trials) for humans and LLMs. All NPs had a majority vote, except *Scheusal* [beast] with human annotators, which showed a 14–14 tie between *person of male gender* and *neither*.

The distributions are very similar, with the label *neither* being the most frequent and the label *person of female gender* being the least frequent. There appear to be only small differences between LLM-generated and human labels (e.g., the more frequent assignment of the label *person of female gender* by GPT-4o). An exception is LLaMA 3.1 8B, which deviates fundamentally in that it almost exclusively assigns the label *person of male gender* to the NPs and never assigns the label *neither*.

The confusion matrix in Figure 1 shows the alignment between the LLM labels and human-based labels, along with performance metrics per

[3]English prompts often yield better performance (cf. Schulhoff et al., 2025, p. 20), while the task required attention to German-specific features such as grammatical gender.

[4]Even with temperature 0 and a fixed seed, the OpenAI API produces varying outputs; an initial 10-run test showed noticeable variation in NP labels.

[5]Here and below: *m*: *person of (social) male gender*; *n*: *neither*; *f*: *person of (social) female gender*.

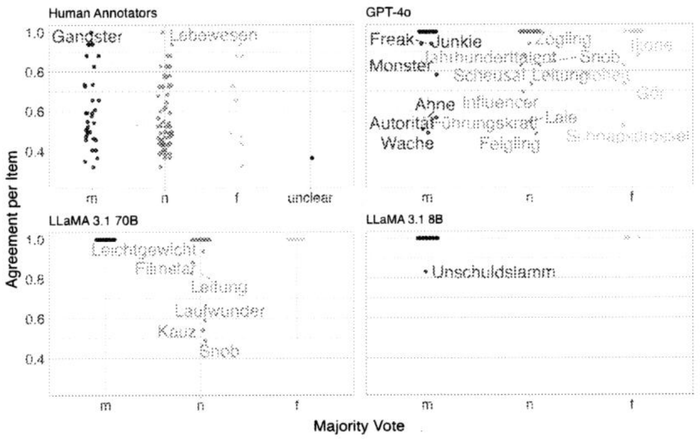

Figure 2: Agreement per item between trials/iterations (N = 116 items); NP names shown: humans agreement = 1; LLMs agreement < 1

gender category (macro average of precision, recall, and F1 score). Again, GPT-4o shows the most human-like performance, whereas LLaMA 3.1 8B deviates most from human annotations. Although Table 1 and Figure 1 suggest reasonable alignment between GPT-4o (and to a lesser extent LLaMA 3.1 70B) and human annotators, further analysis reveals a more nuanced picture.

We calculated the observed percent agreement P_i for each item i using Equation 1[6] (cf. Fleiss, 1971, p. 379):

$$P_i = \sum_{j=1}^{k} \frac{n_j(n_j - 1)}{n(n-1)} \quad (1)$$

Figure 2[7] shows the percent observed agreement for every item for humans and LLMs. Strikingly, LLMs produce perfect agreement (agreement = 1) across all 33 iterations for the majority of items, whereas only two items (*Gangster* = 'person of male gender' and *Lebewesen* [*living being*] = 'neither') show perfect agreement among humans. Within the group of LLMs, GPT-4o exhibits a greater number of items with agreement < 1 than the other models, and LLaMA 3.1 8B shows disagreement for only one item (*Unschuldslamm* [innocent lamb]).[8]

Figure 3 illustrates the distribution of LLM-generated labels for the items with an agreement

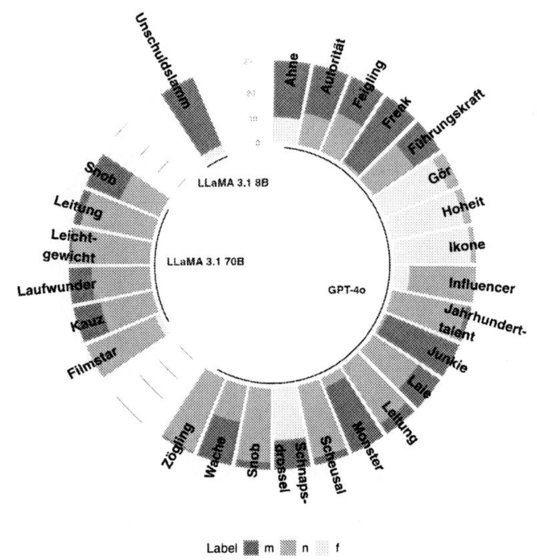

Figure 3: Distribution of labels for items with LLM agreement < 1

< 1. It is noticeable that the labels *person of male gender* and *person of female gender* were only assigned to the same item in three cases (*Ahne* [ancestor], *Schnapsdrossel* [whino], *Unschuldslamm* [innocent lamb]). In all other cases, the agreement value < 1 results from the combination of either *person of male gender* or *person of female gender* with *neither*. This does not apply to the human annotators who assigned all three labels to several items, as is visible in Figure 4.

Figure 5 shows the distribution of association-strength values 1 (very low) to 5 (very high). Both humans and LLMs rated their labels with high association strength, with a mean value of 4; this pattern was more pronounced for the male gender category. However, only humans make use of the entire scale, LLMs rarely label with (very) low association strength, as reflected in smaller standard deviation (SD) values: humans $\pm$ 1.17, GPT-4o $\pm$ 0.5; LLaMA 70B $\pm$ 0.78, LLaMA 8B $\pm$ 0.18.[9]

5 Discussion

We compared LLMs output with human behavior in a semantic-association task, where German NPs had to be labeled for their association (strength) with a social gender. The key findings are: 1) There is substantial variation between LLMs, with

[6] k represents the total number of labels (*male gender, female gender, neither*: $k = 3$), n is the total number of annotators per item ($n = 33$), and n_j denotes the number of annotators that assigned the item to label j.

[7] All images are available in higher resolution in the supplementary materials.

[8] An interactive visualization showing label distributions per item and the proximity between LLMs and human annotators is available at `https://wdsmuek.shinyapps.io/vote_viewer/`.

[9] We further analyzed the summed log-probabilities of label sub-tokens in relation to agreement and association strength. GPT-4o showed a positive correlation with agreement, and both GPT-4o and LLaMA 3.1 70B with association strength. See supplementary materials for visualizations.

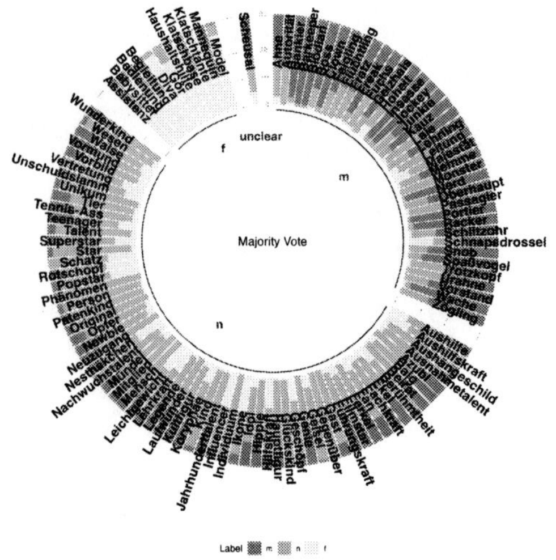

Figure 4: Distribution of labels for items with human annotator agreement < 1

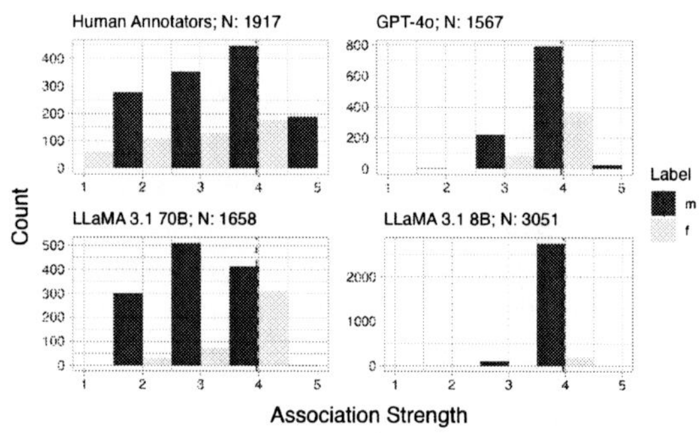

Figure 5: Distribution of association strength. Dashed lines represent the mean per gender category.

the smallest model (LlaMA 3.1 8B) showing the least human-like output. 2) In terms of social-gender labels, the two larger models produce aggregate output (majority votes) comparable to humans, hence there is aggregation/condition-level similarity (Fig. 1). 3) At the item level, the distribution of raw data points suggests differences between trials in that the human data exhibit larger variation per item compared with the non-human-like consistency of LLMs (i.e., perfect agreement, Fig. 2). This aligns with differences in scale effects, as LLMs, in contrast to humans, label NPs only with higher, but not with lower association strength (Fig. 5) – which may be plausible given LLM-internal probabilities (see footnote 9).

Our results support previous findings that associative semantic relations may be treated differently by LLMs and humans (Digutsch and Kosinski, 2023), suggesting that LLMs task performance is qualitatively different from human responses at the item level. While, across trials for NPs with an agreement < 1, human responses may include any of the three social-gender labels for an NP, LLMs use only two labels (Figs. 3 & 4). One reason may be that humans use context information based on (inter alia) differences in exposure, salience or individual significance, thereby promoting inter- and intraindividual variation. Hence, different people may have different associations for a *pop star*, for example. When prompted with the same neutral prompt as in our study, these factors cannot exert any influence for LLMs context use. Thus, neutrally prompted LLMs may capture aggregation-based tendencies of social-gender associations across varied contexts, but capturing individual variation requires at least carefully designed personas, if not other ways of data generation (see Franke et al., 2024; Murthy et al., 2025).

6 Summary

We find similar condition-level (aggregated) results for LLMs and humans, while the underlying distribution of responses differs in a semantic-association task. This supports conclusions that LLMs may not, in every task, serve as a substitute for human data beyond qualitative (condition-based) effect reports (Franke et al., 2024; Murthy et al., 2025; Trott, 2024). For our use case, experimental pre-tests, LLMs may be useful for condition-based assessments regarding item selection. Yet, when pre-test data are used with other statistical methods (e.g., power analysis, simulation), the current approach to LLMs use may not add insightful data. In such cases, substituting human data with LLM data may cause Type-M errors, affecting replicability across AI and human datasets (for discussion of Type-M error in (psycho)linguistics, cf. Vasishth, 2023).

Limitations

Our study relies on prompt-based methods and is thus subject to the limitations identified by Hu and Levy (2023). We employ a single prompt, despite evidence that minor prompt variations can significantly affect outputs (cf. Schulhoff et al., 2025). It is also an open question how individual variation can be accurately captured. Finally, the use of only three language models limits the generalizability of our findings.

References

Gati Aher, Rosa I. Arriaga, and Adam Tauman Kalai. 2023. Using large language models to simulate multiple humans and replicate human subject studies. In *Proceedings of the 40th International Conference on Machine Learning*, ICML'23. JMLR.org.

Lisa P. Argyle, Ethan C. Busby, Nancy Fulda, Joshua R. Gubler, Christopher Rytting, and David Wingate. 2023. Out of one, many: Using language models to simulate human samples. *Political Analysis*, 31(3):337–351.

Zhenguang Cai, Xufeng Duan, David Haslett, Shuqi Wang, and Martin Pickering. 2024. Do large language models resemble humans in language use? In *Proceedings of the Workshop on Cognitive Modeling and Computational Linguistics*, pages 37–56, Bangkok, Thailand. Association for Computational Linguistics.

Jan Digutsch and Michal Kosinski. 2023. Overlap in meaning is a stronger predictor of semantic activation in GPT-3 than in humans. *Scientific Reports*, 13(1):5035.

Danica Dillion, Niket Tandon, Yuling Gu, and Kurt Gray. 2023. Can AI language models replace human participants? *Trends in Cognitive Sciences*, 27(7):597–600. Publisher: Elsevier.

Ali Doosthosseini, Jonathan Decker, Hendrik Nolte, and Julian M. Kunkel. 2024. Chat ai: A seamless slurm-native solution for hpc-based services. *Preprint*, arXiv:2407.00110.

Jeffrey L. Elman. 1990. Finding structure in time. *Cognitive science*, 14(2):179–211.

Zhang Enyan, Zewei Wang, Michael A. Lepori, Ellie Pavlick, and Helena Aparicio. 2024. Are LLMs Models of Distributional Semantics? A case study on quantifiers. *Preprint*, arXiv:2410.13984.

Yulia Esaulova, Chiara Reali, and Lisa von Stockhausen. 2017. Prominence of Gender Cues in the assignment of Thematic Roles in German. *Applied Psycholinguistics*, 38(5):1132–1172.

Joseph L. Fleiss. 1971. Measuring nominal scale agreement among many raters. *Psychological Bulletin*, 76(5):378–382.

Michael Franke, Polina Tsvilodub, and Fausto Carcassi. 2024. Bayesian Statistical Modeling with predictors from LLMs. *Preprint*, arXiv:2406.09012.

Jennifer Hu and Roger Levy. 2023. Prompting is not a substitute for probability measurements in large language models. *Preprint*, arXiv:2305.13264.

Andreas Klein. 2022. Wohin mit Epikoina? – Überlegungen zur Grammatik und Pragmatik geschlechtsindefiniter Personenbezeichnungen. In Dabriele Diewald and Damaris Nübling, editors, *Genus – Sexus – Gender.*, pages 135–189. de Gruyter, Berlin.

Kristin Kopf. 2022. Ist Sharon Manager? Anglizismen und das generische Maskulinum. In Dabriele Diewald and Damaris Nübling, editors, *Genus – Sexus – Gender.*, pages 65–103. de Gruyter, Berlin.

Tatsuki Kuribayashi, Yohei Oseki, and Timothy Baldwin. 2024. Psychometric predictive power of large language models. *Preprint*, arXiv:2311.07484.

Molly Lewis and Gary Lupyan. 2020. Gender stereotypes are reflected in the distributional structure of 25 languages. *Nature Human Behaviour*, 4:1021–1028.

Kanishka Misra, Allyson Ettinger, and Julia Rayz. 2020. Exploring BERT's sensitivity to lexical cues using tests from semantic priming. In *Findings of the Association for Computational Linguistics: EMNLP 2020*, pages 4625–4635, Online. Association for Computational Linguistics.

Sonia Krishna Murthy, Tomer Ullman, and Jennifer Hu. 2025. One fish, two fish, but not the whole sea: Alignment reduces language models' conceptual diversity. In *Proceedings of the 2025 Conference of the Nations of the Americas Chapter of the Association for Computational Linguistics: Human Language Technologies (Volume 1: Long Papers)*, pages 11241–11258, Albuquerque, New Mexico. Association for Computational Linguistics.

Gisela Schoenthal. 1989. Personenbezeichnungen im Deutschen als Gegenstand feministischer Sprachkritik. *Zeitschrift für Germanistische Linguistik*, 17(3):296–314.

Sander Schulhoff, Michael Ilie, Nishant Balepur, Konstantine Kahadze, Amanda Liu, Chenglei Si, Yinheng Li, Aayush Gupta, HyoJung Han, Sevien Schulhoff, Pranav Sandeep Dulepet, Saurav Vidyadhara, Dayeon Ki, Sweta Agrawal, Chau Pham, Gerson Kroiz, Feileen Li, Hudson Tao, Ashay Srivastava, Hevander Da Costa, Saloni Gupta, Megan L. Rogers, Inna Goncearenco, Giuseppe Sarli, Igor Galynker, Denis Peskoff, Marine Carpuat, Jules White, Shyamal Anadkat, Alexander Hoyle, and Philip Resnik. 2025. The prompt report: A systematic survey of prompt engineering techniques. *Preprint*, arXiv:2406.06608.

Maria Thurmair. 2006. Das Model und ihr Prinz. Kongruenz und Texteinbettung bei Genus-Sexus-Divergenz. *Deutsche Sprache*, 34:191–220.

Sean Trott. 2024. Can Large Language Models help augment English psycholinguistic datasets? *Behavior Research Methods*, 56:6082–6100.

Shravan Vasishth. 2023. Some right ways to analyze (psycho)linguistic data. *Annual Review of Linguistics*, 9:273–291.

Ethan Gottlieb Wilcox, Richard Futrell, and Roger Levy. 2024. Using Computational Models to Test Syntactic Learnability. *Linguistic Inquiry*, 55(4):805–848.

Yiming Zhu, Peixian Zhang, Ehsan-Ul Haq, Pan Hui, and Gareth Tyson. 2023. Can ChatGPT reproduce human-generated labels? A study of social computing tasks. *Preprint*, arXiv:2304.10145.

PETapter: Leveraging PET-style classification heads for modular few-shot parameter-efficient fine-tuning

Jonas Rieger and **Mattes Ruckdeschel** and **Gregor Wiedemann**
Leibniz Institute for Media Research | Hans-Bredow-Institut (HBI)
Rothenbaumchaussee 36, 20148 Hamburg, Germany
rieger@statistik.tu-dortmund.de
{m.ruckdeschel, g.wiedemann} @leibniz-hbi.de

Abstract

Few-shot learning and parameter-efficient fine-tuning (PEFT) are crucial to overcome the challenges of data scarcity and ever growing language model sizes. This applies in particular to specialized scientific domains, where researchers might lack expertise and resources to fine-tune high-performing language models to nuanced tasks. We propose PETapter, a novel method that effectively combines PEFT methods with PET-style classification heads to boost few-shot learning capabilities without the significant computational overhead typically associated with full model training. We validate our approach on three established NLP benchmark datasets and one real-world dataset from communication research. We show that PETapter not only achieves comparable performance to full few-shot fine-tuning using pattern-exploiting training (PET), but also provides greater reliability and higher parameter efficiency while enabling higher modularity and easy sharing of the trained modules, which enables more researchers to utilize high-performing NLP-methods in their research.

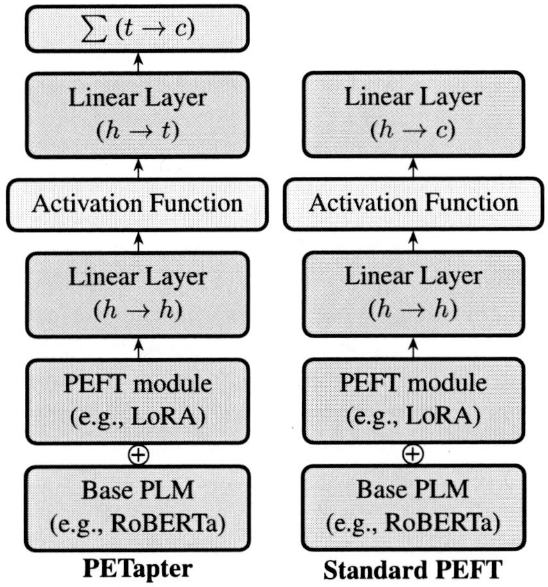

Figure 1: Schematic representation of the PETapter architecture compared to standard PEFT methods.

1 Introduction

Few-shot learning and parameter-efficient fine-tuning (PEFT) have emerged as pivotal disciplines in the realm of natural language processing (NLP), especially in applications where data scarcity poses significant challenges. Whilst for a lot of scientists from fields like communication science or political science, raw text data is available, high-quality labeled data is still scarce and the creation is time-consuming, costly and requiring trained experts. Discourse analysis in those fields makes, for instance, use of the NLP sub-task of argument mining, i.e. argument identification and stance classification. Due to the nuanced and context-dependent nature of argumentative discourse, standard fine-tuning methods for pretrained language models (PLM) with only a few labeled data points usually perform poorly in these tasks (e.g., Rieger et al., 2024). Few-shot learning, with its promise to generalize from a limited number of training samples, offers an alternative pathway towards mitigating the data scarcity problem. However, the deployment of large-scale language models (even) in a few-shot setting can be challenging, primarily due to the substantial computational resources required for training and fine-tuning, as these methods update all parameters of the model by default. PEFT methods, such as adapter modules, present a viable solution to this issue by enabling the adaptation of pretrained models to specific tasks with minimal modifications to the model architecture. Specifically, these methods freeze a large part of the model's parameters and train only small parts of the existing or few newly added layers (Poth et al., 2023). Further, PEFT methods using a standard

Proceedings of the 21st Conference on Natural Language Processing (KONVENS), Volume 1: Long and Short Papers, pages 333–348, 2025

linear layer perform significantly worse than few-shot methods when using few observations (cf. Sections 5.3 and 6.3).

For this reason, this paper aims to delve into the intersection of few-shot learning and parameter-efficient fine-tuning. By integrating few-shot learning paradigms with PEFT techniques, this paper explores how, e.g., argument mining applications can leverage the strengths of both approaches to efficiently classify text sequences, even when only little data is available. Utilizing three typical NLP benchmark datasets and a real-world argument mining dataset, we demonstrate that the combination of few-shot and PEFT methodologies can significantly reduce the reliance on extensive annotated datasets while achieving competitive performance (to full few-shot fine-tuning) with reduced computational effort. It thus combines the advantages of the two fields, few-shot learning and PEFT. This allows for the creation of small yet powerful language models that can easily be created by non-experts, opening up new qualitative and quantitative research opportunities to researchers from various backgrounds who want to leverage text data.

As our main contribution, we introduce PETapter as a combination of PET-style classification heads with PEFT methods. We show that in most scenarios PETapter is as performant as PET itself, i.e. noticeable better than PEFT with a standard classification head. PETapter additionally offers all PEFT advantages, i.e. it requires less computational resources and is easier to share in the research community due to its modularity. We also show that PETapter provides more robust predictions than PET, especially on real-world datasets. Our detailed and carefully selected study design enables reliable conclusions to be drawn about (meaningful) performance differences between the methods examined. This paper not only contributes to the theoretical advancement of NLP techniques but also offers practical insights for researchers and practitioners working on supervised text classification problems.

In Section 2, we review relevant preliminary NLP work, in Section 3, we recapitulate the definition of pattern-verbalizer pairs (PVP) for usage in our new method PETapter in Section 4. In Sections 5 and 6, we conduct intensive NLP benchmark studies and a real-world study, which we finally discuss in Section 7 and summarize in Section 8. Data and code are available in the GitHub repository `https://github.com/JonasRieger/petapter`.

2 Related Work

Recent generative LLMs such the GPT, Llama, and Qwen model family achieve surprisingly high zero-shot performance on many NLP tasks including automatic content analysis (Gilardi et al., 2023). However, due to the high demands on computing power, it is difficult to process very large amounts of data on standard hardware, and to control for the matching between the LLM-understanding of categories with detailed codebook definitions. For this reason, smaller pretrained language models (PLMs) fine-tuned on manually labeled data still serve as the basis for most classification tasks in applied settings, e.g. in communication science. A frequently compared model is RoBERTa (Liu et al., 2019) due to its strong performance even with a comparatively small number of parameters (Base: 125 million, Large: 355 million) with its multilingual alternative XLM-RoBERTa (Conneau et al., 2020) achieving good performance, at least for high resource languages. As the next best model, (m)DeBERTa (He et al., 2023) forms a promising base PLM, but with 1.5 billion parameters it already has significantly higher requirements in terms of GPU capacity and computation time.

2.1 Parameter-Efficient Fine-Tuning (PEFT)

The ever-increasing sizes of base PLMs pose a great challenge for fully fine-tuning all parameters. Rebuffi et al. (2017), as well as Houlsby et al. (2019), were among the first to tackle this problem by freezing the PLM and instead inserting and training bottleneck feed-forward layers within the pretrained architecture. Pfeiffer et al. (2020) refined this idea into a slightly more parameter-efficient and robust method, though still sequential in its basic idea, which is named Pfeiffer adapters. Techniques such as low-rank adaptation (LoRA, Hu et al., 2022) and $(IA)^3$ (Liu et al., 2022) introduce minimal updates to the model weights, while their parallel approach makes it possible to combine the newly learned parameters with the frozen ones in such a way that there is no overhead during inference. Recent innovations such as considering different ranks for each linear layer in PRILoRA (Benedek and Wolf, 2024), sharing the low-rank matrices across all layers with layer-specific learned scaling vectors in VeRA (Kopiczko et al., 2024) or LoRA-like decomposition of pretrained weights in DoRA (Liu et al., 2024) are examples of further LoRA-like advancements in the field of parameter-efficient fine-tuning.

In addition, ComPEFT (Yadav et al., 2025) and QLoRA (Dettmers et al., 2023) offer the possibility of even more effective parameter usage with condensation of information through quantization and desparsification. RoSA (Nikdan et al., 2024) combines low-rank adaptation with high sparsity training following the idea of robust principal component analysis. Several specialized approaches exist, one of which is AdaSent (Huang et al., 2023) focusing on PEFT for sentence representations.

While many implementations are often limited to the PEFT character of the methods (Mangrulkar et al., 2022; Hu et al., 2023a,b), the Python package Adapters (Poth et al., 2023) facilitates the modular use of PEFT methods, highlighting a trend towards modular deep learning (Pfeiffer et al., 2023) and holistic PEFT implementations (He et al., 2022; Sabry and Belz, 2023).

2.2 Few-Shot Text Classification

Few-shot text classification aims to maximize model performance with minimal labeled data. For this, a lot of approaches are based on a combination of prompt-based learning and meta learning. Schick and Schütze (2021) were the first to propose the utilization of so-called *prompt-based* cloze questions. In this pattern-exploiting training (PET), a masked token is predicted in a language model task style, similar to that used in pretraining. The authors show that due to the model's prior knowledge, it is able to predict these so-called verbalizers better than plain numbered class labels. Furthermore, the authors show that *meta-learning* on soft labels generated by augmentations using iterative PET (iPET) also leads to an improvement, so that a combination of prompt-based learning and meta-learning (Zhang et al., 2022) is proposed. Chen and Shu (2023) use such an approach and propose the use of label-guided data augmentation methods for prompt-based few-shot tuning.

Ling et al. (2023) demonstrate the possibility of an optimized automated search for verbalizers in prompt-based learning, while Karimi Mahabadi et al. (2022) suggest an approach without the need for prompts. Complementary to this, SetFit (Tunstall et al., 2022) form triplets of positive and negative examples and use contrastive learning to effectively train on few training samples. The recipe T-Few (Liu et al., 2022) as an additional dedicated few-shot model is based on the zero-shot model T0 (Sanh et al., 2022) and enriches it with a combination of losses, the PEFT method $(IA)^3$ and a pretraining of it using out-of-domain data, which can be quite expensive with regard to the training time needed. PET, Setfit and T-Few represent key developments in the few-shot field and produce comparable performances on the RAFT benchmark dataset (Alex et al., 2021), each with strengths and weaknesses on different datasets.

2.3 Argument Mining

In the field of argument mining, the following works are related to our idea of using PETapter to identify argumentative sentences from news media: Hüning et al. (2022) classify whether user-generated chat messages contain an argument using machine learning techniques utilizing sentence embeddings as features. For simplicity, they categorize claims as *no argument* in their setting. Jurkschat et al. (2022) consider the possibility of few-shot methods for classifying aspects of argumentative sentences and show that PET performs best among the methods considered. Likewise, PET is used by Rieger et al. (2024) and compared with the use of PEFT methods for the identification of claims and arguments from news media articles. The authors find that the task is challenging even for humans, so that only moderate inter-coder agreements are achieved.

In the following, we present the PETapter model, which combines few-shot and PEFT methods to achieve great performance, in particular in real-world data scarce argument mining settings.

3 Pattern-Verbalizer-Pair (PVP)

The term Pattern-Verbalizer-Pairs (PVPs) was introduced in Schick and Schütze (2021) and refers to the combination of two elements: the transformation of an input into a cloze-style input (pattern), and the set of options (verbalizer) for filling in the gap in the text. The latter is typically derived from the class labels. In the following we define how we use PVPs for PETapter.

We consider a pretrained language model (PLM) M with an underlying vocabulary V, where [MASK] $\in V$, i.e. we assume a mask token to be contained in the vocabulary. In addition, let $\mathcal{L}$ be a set of target labels for a classification task and $x \in V^n$ an input (possibly consisting of several segments) that contains a total of n tokens from the vocabulary V. We define a pattern as a function $P^m : V^n \rightarrow V^{n+p}$, where $m \leq p$ is the number of

[MASK] tokens contained in the pattern and p is the total number of vocabulary items added to the input x by the pattern function.

Furthermore, let $v^m : \mathcal{L} \rightarrow V^m$ be a verbalizer function that assigns m tokens from the vocabulary V to each label $\ell \in \mathcal{L}$. As the inventors of PET (Schick and Schütze, 2021) suggest, we refer to the combination (P^m, v^m) as a pattern-verbalizer pair (PVP). The pattern function P^m is used to transform the input x into a kind of cloze question and the verbalizer function v^m provides for each label the "speaking" and representative fill-in words for the corresponding cloze question, which are to be predicted by the model M. All PVPs used in this paper can be found in the Appendices A and B. An example PVP for the Yelp dataset (cf. Section 5) is given by:

Pattern [text]* [SEP] Question: What does the customer think of this restaurant? Answer: [MASK].

Verbalizers

class label	verbalizer
1 star	terrible
2 stars	bad
3 stars	okay
4 stars	good
5 stars	great

4 PETapter

PETapter can be seen as a modular classification head which can be added flexibly to a PEFT framework as an alternative to a classical linear layer classification head[1], cf. Figure 1. Here, the last (purple) linear layer of the classification head does not reduce the dimension directly to the number of classes c, but to the size t of the sub-vocabulary T of the verbalizer function used. If we again consider the example verbalizer from Section 3, this results in the word set {bad, good, great, okay, terrible}. Depending on the tokenizer used, this set is identical to the sub-vocabulary T (if each word above is composed of exactly one token) or T is composed of the set of corresponding tokens. Thus, each dimension of the output embedding represents a token from the reduced verbalizer vocabulary (instead of the full tokenizer vocabulary), similar to and motivated by the pattern-exploiting training (PET) by Schick and Schütze (2021). Then, the logits for the verbalizers (possibly composed of several tokens) can be calculated as a sum of the logits of the masked tokens in the pattern (cf. Equation 1).

In general, PETapter can be combined with any PEFT method (cf. the blue segment in Figure 1), i.e. it also features all its advantages over full fine-tuning: faster training, less resource requirements, better sharability and reusability due to modularity as well as robustification (at least) with regard to the elimination of catastrophic forgetting. Specifically, PETapter implements all these advantages over PET, which uses full fine-tuning, while performing on par (cf. Sections 5.3 and 6.3).

Let $\mathcal{L}$ be a set of target labels for a classification task with $|\mathcal{L}| = c$, let $P^m(x)$ be a pattern function inserting m [MASK] tokens to an input x, and let $v^m(\ell)$ be an injective function that maps each of the labels $\ell \in \mathcal{L}$ to m vocabulary tokens. Then, we obtain the subset of the vocabulary relevant for the verbalizers as $T = \bigcup_{\ell \in \mathcal{L}} \bigcup_{i=1}^{m} v^m(\ell)_i$ with $T \subset V$ and $t = |T|$ the corresponding number of relevant tokens, i.e. we can refine $v^m : \mathcal{L} \rightarrow T^m$.

Moreover, let $M(v^m(\ell) \mid P^m(x)) \in \mathbb{R}^m$ denote the logits for the m [MASK] tokens, the output of the top linear layer (purple) in Figure 1 on the left. The final score for each of the label candidates ℓ for a given input text x is then given as

$$s(\ell \mid x) = \sum_{i=1}^{m} M(v^m(\ell) \mid P^m(x))_i \qquad (1)$$

and the corresponding pseudo-probability as

$$q(\ell \mid x) = \frac{\exp(s(\ell \mid x))}{\sum_{\ell' \in \mathcal{L}} \exp(s(\ell' \mid x))}. \qquad (2)$$

Using this, we can calculate the cross-entropy loss over all observations as

$$\begin{aligned} L_{\text{CE}} &= - \sum_{(x,\ell^*)} \sum_{\ell \in \mathcal{L}} \mathbb{1}_{\{\ell = \ell^*\}}(x, \ell^*) \log[q(\ell \mid x)] \\ &= - \sum_{(x,\ell^*)} \log[q(\ell^* \mid x)] \qquad (3) \end{aligned}$$

if we consider $\ell^* \in \mathcal{L}$ to be the true label of x.

5 Benchmark Study

To evaluate how well our model performs in comparison to existing state-of-the-art methods, we consider three established NLP datasets in a first

[1]A classical linear layer classification head maps the last embedding with hidden size h to logits or pseudo-probabilities of the size of the number of classes c.

	n	Data	Prompt Pattern PETapter (IA)^3	Prompt Pattern PETapter LoRA	Prompt Pattern PETapter Pfeif.	Prompt Pattern PET	Q&A Pattern PETapter (IA)^3	Q&A Pattern PETapter LoRA	Q&A Pattern PETapter Pfeif.	Q&A Pattern PET	Linear Layer (IA)^3	Linear Layer LoRA	Linear Layer Pfeif.
RoBERTa Base	10	AG	0.668 ±.092	0.681 ±.080	0.683 ±.078	**0.804 ±.036**	0.596 ±.077	0.672 ±.077	0.680 ±.088	0.800 ±.028	0.297 ±.053	0.293 ±.045	0.316 ±.059
RoBERTa Base	10	Yahoo	0.236 ±.016	0.292 ±.033	0.271 ±.042	**0.545 ±.040**	0.274 ±.026	0.295 ±.041	0.285 ±.036	0.515 ±.036	0.105 ±.009	0.116 ±.020	0.123 ±.016
RoBERTa Base	10	Yelp	0.403 ±.037	0.434 ±.035	0.423 ±.038	0.441 ±.017	0.359 ±.037	0.412 ±.042	0.390 ±.047	**0.442 ±.025**	0.215 ±.017	0.219 ±.023	0.224 ±.027
RoBERTa Base	100	AG	0.856 ±.012	0.861 ±.012	0.860 ±.012	**0.875 ±.007**	0.863 ±.006	0.861 ±.010	0.862 ±.011	0.871 ±.008	0.837 ±.007	0.862 ±.008	0.864 ±.008
RoBERTa Base	100	Yahoo	0.622 ±.018	0.642 ±.009	0.642 ±.011	**0.666 ±.007**	0.622 ±.005	0.637 ±.007	0.633 ±.008	0.659 ±.007	0.418 ±.034	0.636 ±.013	0.633 ±.012
RoBERTa Base	100	Yelp	0.541 ±.010	0.553 ±.018	0.551 ±.016	0.552 ±.014	0.536 ±.014	0.553 ±.015	0.548 ±.014	**0.554 ±.015**	0.354 ±.022	0.538 ±.018	0.535 ±.020
RoBERTa Large	10	AG	0.641 ±.100	0.714 ±.070	0.702 ±.081	**0.842 ±.025**	0.611 ±.073	0.746 ±.054	0.738 ±.060	0.836 ±.032	0.305 ±.030	0.373 ±.049	0.443 ±.104
RoBERTa Large	10	Yahoo	0.242 ±.027	0.331 ±.040	0.290 ±.056	**0.574 ±.030**	0.323 ±.049	0.365 ±.049	0.346 ±.054	0.550 ±.040	0.124 ±.012	0.150 ±.027	0.169 ±.041
RoBERTa Large	10	Yelp	0.442 ±.040	0.470 ±.041	0.479 ±.035	0.475 ±.026	0.440 ±.049	0.472 ±.049	**0.490 ±.046**	0.486 ±.041	0.211 ±.010	0.221 ±.012	0.216 ±.014
RoBERTa Large	100	AG	0.868 ±.011	0.873 ±.010	0.875 ±.010	**0.877 ±.009**	0.876 ±.009	0.870 ±.010	0.873 ±.010	0.874 ±.009	0.833 ±.011	0.875 ±.008	0.875 ±.008
RoBERTa Large	100	Yahoo	0.654 ±.020	0.662 ±.014	0.661 ±.017	**0.680 ±.013**	0.655 ±.010	0.654 ±.008	0.656 ±.012	0.675 ±.013	0.364 ±.043	0.648 ±.016	0.647 ±.015
RoBERTa Large	100	Yelp	0.611 ±.011	0.613 ±.014	0.614 ±.010	0.593 ±.014	**0.626 ±.008**	0.622 ±.013	0.620 ±.013	0.595 ±.016	0.347 ±.019	0.551 ±.019	0.512 ±.043

Table 1: Mean accuracies (± standard deviation) of the experiments in the benchmark study.

RoBERTa	Architecture	AG	Yahoo	Yelp
Base	PETapter	0.33	0.33	0.32
Base	PET	0.38	0.39	0.39
Large	PETapter	0.65	0.64	0.65
Large	PET	1.00	1.00	1.00
Large	PET	6.1s	6.2s	6.2s

Table 2: Comparison of training times per iteration of $n = 100$ observations in the benchmark study. The last row shows the time for PET using RoBERTa Large. The other rows indicate the time relative to it. The times for using PETapter or a linear layer are identical, as are for the three architectures (IA)^3, LoRA, and Pfeiffer.

benchmark study. These have quite a laboratory character, as the distribution of the class labels is pretty much balanced. Furthermore, it is not finally clear to what extent (possibly implicit) information about the test data of such publicly available datasets is contained in PLMs (Li and Flanigan, 2024). Nevertheless, such datasets with predefined train-test splits offer the possibility of comparing methods across studies without the need of rerunning all the experiments.

5.1 Datasets: AG, Yahoo, Yelp

We follow the study by Schick and Schütze (2022) and use the three established NLP datasets *AG's News* (AG), *Yahoo Questions* (Yahoo), and *Yelp Full* (Yelp), which are presented by Zhang et al. (2015). In Appendix A, further information on the three datasets is given.

For the training, we create 5 stratified datasets with $n = 10$ randomly drawn observations and 5 datasets with $n = 100$ observations each for the problems AG, Yahoo, and Yelp. We evaluate all experiments with the corresponding entire test dataset from the predefined split.

5.2 Experimental Setup

As PLM, we use RoBERTa Base and Large. For fine-tuning methods, we consider the few-shot method PET, PEFT methods with a (standard) linear layer as classification head, and our method PETapter, i.e. PEFT methods in combination with a PET-style classification head. In both cases, we consider the methods (IA)^3, LoRA and a Pfeiffer adapter as PEFT methods. For PET and PETapter, we compare the use of *prompt* or *Q&A* pattern, following Schick and Schütze (2022). While *prompt* patterns tend to be rather minimalistic (e.g., "[text]* [SEP] All in all, it was [MASK]." for the Yelp dataset), *Q&A* patterns are based on a classic question-answer structure for language models (cf., e.g., the example PVP in Section 3). In each dataset, we measure the difference in using $n = 10$ or 100 observations. Moreover, we repeat each experiment five times, i.e. in Table 1 each cell corresponds to 25 experiments (5 repetitions $\times$ 5 datasets). In Appendix A, further information on all parameters as well as the used patterns is given.

5.3 Results

Table 1 shows the average accuracy of the settings and the standard deviation across the 25 experiments per cell. Overall, it can be seen that the best performance is achieved by PET using the prompt pattern, while PETapter achieves the best values in two scenarios and the linear layer classification head never performs best. As expected, RoBERTa Large consistently yields better results than the Base variant, although the PEFT methods generally benefit somewhat more from the use of the larger model. The accuracy achieved by PETapter is usually very close to that of PET. Merely in the setting $n = 10$ for Yahoo the values are significantly worse. On the other hand, for $n = 100$ on Yelp, all three PEFT architectures combined with our PETapter method are noticeably better than PET itself. $(IA)^3$ with Q&A pattern even leads to the best global performance in this case, while it produces rather low scores in most scenarios. Our explanation for this is that $(IA)^3$ is just one component of the generally in benchmarks competitively performing T-Few. Overall, prompt and Q&A pattern perform similarly. Thus, we can confirm these findings from Schick and Schütze (2022) regarding PET and show that they generally hold for PETapter as well. Basically, it can be seen that the linear layer rarely comes close to the performance of PETapter; using linear layer classification heads in combination with $(IA)^3$ leads to the worst results overall.

As a result, it is evident that PETapter is to be preferred over the use of a classical linear layer as a classification head in use cases where the benefits of PEFT methods are desired. At the same time, PETapter achieves comparable performance to PET in most cases.

In addition, as a PEFT method (cf. Section 2.1), PETapter can be trained more effectively than standard PET. In Table 2 the training times of the models are displayed. According to this, for RoBERTa Large, PETapter (no matter the fine-tuning architecture) requires $\approx 65\%$ of the time of regular PET per iteration. Compared to a regular PEFT approach using a linear layer, PETapter does not result in any overhead regarding training time.

6 Real-World Study

As indicated in Section 5, the evaluation based on AG, Yahoo, and Yelp represents a lab situation, e.g., because of their balancedness and (potential) inclusion in the pretraining of language models. Complementary to this, in a second study, we compare the performance of the methods on a (so far unpublished) dataset with real-world challenges. It is a dataset in the context of argument mining with argumentative sentences on the topic of *arms deliveries to Ukraine* with a total of 7301 thematically relevant articles in 2022 from 22 German media outlets. For further reading, a detailed explanation of the creation and composition can be found in the study of Rieger et al. (2024). Here, we consider a version of the dataset consisting of 1766 labeled data with the four possible labels claim/argument for/against, with non-relevant sentences already removed.

6.1 Dataset: Ukraine Arms Deliveries

The German language Ukraine dataset consists of 766 train (294 articles) and 1000 test (369 articles) observations. Using a two-stage sampling (first article, then sentence) we intend to tackle the problem that including very related sentences from the same article in both splits could lead to an overoptimistic estimation of the error. Here, a single observation consists of a target sentence to be classified as well as two contextual sentences before and after it. Based on the 766 observations, we draw training sets of sizes $n = 10, 100, 250$ according to three different sampling strategies.

Label	Train				Test
	10*	100*	250*	All	
argumentagainst	1.2	11.8	29.4	92	118
argumentfor	1.9	19.4	48.6	152	162
claimagainst	2.4	23.5	58.8	184	248
claimfor	4.6	45.2	113.2	354	456

Table 3: Label distribution in the train and test data split of the Ukraine dataset. *Expected distribution for random selection.

We draw the same number of observations from the subsets of the four labels in *equal* sampling, i.e. 25 observations each in the scenario of $n = 100$. Using *random* sampling, we make a simple random selection from the total number of all possible training examples and with *stratified* sampling we ensure that the label distribution of the entire training set is replicated as accurately as

n	Sampling	PETapter (IA)^3	PETapter LoRA	PETapter Pfeiffer	PET	Linear Layer (IA)^3	Linear Layer LoRA	Linear Layer Pfeiffer
10	Equal	0.28 ±.046	0.31 ±.043	**0.33 ±.057**	0.33 ±.080	0.14 ±.039	0.13 ±.042	0.15 ±.041
10	Stratified	0.19 ±.023	0.27 ±.039	0.33 ±.027	**0.40 ±.055**	0.16 ±.000	0.16 ±.001	0.17 ±.021
100	Equal	0.49 ±.023	0.57 ±.020	0.57 ±.028	**0.59 ±.027**	0.23 ±.041	0.26 ±.029	0.29 ±.030
100	Random	0.41 ±.036	**0.56 ±.036**	0.55 ±.036	0.56 ±.053	0.16 ±.000	0.20 ±.041	0.26 ±.037
100	Stratified	0.40 ±.029	0.58 ±.042	0.57 ±.035	**0.59 ±.054**	0.16 ±.000	0.20 ±.030	0.26 ±.035
250	Equal	0.57 ±.015	0.67 ±.014	0.68 ±.018	**0.70 ±.025**	0.28 ±.027	0.46 ±.050	0.49 ±.075
250	Random	0.50 ±.031	**0.67 ±.021**	0.67 ±.024	0.67 ±.109	0.16 ±.000	0.38 ±.031	0.45 ±.086
250	Stratified	0.48 ±.036	0.67 ±.019	**0.67 ±.018**	0.67 ±.109	0.16 ±.003	0.37 ±.040	0.46 ±.082

Table 4: Mean macro-F1 scores (± standard deviation) of the experiments in the real-world study (Ukraine).

	Label	Equal Sampling PETapter	Equal Sampling PET	Equal Sampling Lin. Layer	Stratified Sampling PETapter	Stratified Sampling PET	Stratified Sampling Lin. Layer
Precision	argumentagainst	0.50 ±.031	0.51 ±.040	0.34 ±.068	**0.54 ±.037**	0.54 ±.122	0.39 ±.092
	argumentfor	0.58 ±.045	0.63 ±.064	0.45 ±.075	0.64 ±.032	**0.66 ±.145**	0.47 ±.135
	claimagainst	0.70 ±.033	**0.71 ±.045**	0.50 ±.078	0.68 ±.036	0.66 ±.143	0.49 ±.065
	claimfor	0.87 ±.022	**0.90 ±.023**	0.69 ±.076	0.84 ±.022	0.83 ±.080	0.65 ±.064
Recall	argumentagainst	0.75 ±.043	**0.81 ±.061**	0.46 ±.113	0.53 ±.064	0.57 ±.140	0.16 ±.098
	argumentfor	0.66 ±.048	**0.70 ±.047**	0.65 ±.060	0.63 ±.053	0.61 ±.138	0.42 ±.147
	claimagainst	0.75 ±.026	0.76 ±.051	0.51 ±.090	**0.78 ±.028**	0.75 ±.161	0.54 ±.121
	claimfor	0.67 ±.034	0.67 ±.047	0.48 ±.121	0.78 ±.022	**0.80 ±.051**	0.74 ±.051
Macro-F1	argumentagainst	0.60 ±.029	**0.62 ±.031**	0.38 ±.082	0.53 ±.045	0.55 ±.123	0.22 ±.100
	argumentfor	0.62 ±.026	**0.66 ±.040**	0.53 ±.061	0.63 ±.024	0.63 ±.134	0.44 ±.138
	claimagainst	0.72 ±.019	**0.73 ±.025**	0.50 ±.072	0.72 ±.028	0.70 ±.148	0.51 ±.084
	claimfor	0.76 ±.018	0.77 ±.031	0.56 ±.105	**0.81 ±.012**	0.81 ±.040	0.69 ±.049

Table 5: Mean precision, recall, and macro-F1 scores per label (each ± standard deviation) of the experiments in the real-world study (Ukraine). We consider the Pfeiffer adapter as the PEFT method of PETapter and $n = 250$. We omit the results using random sampling as they are quite similar to those of the stratified datasets, cf. Table 8.

possible even in smaller samples. We create 5 datasets for each combination of sampling strategy (Equal, Random, Stratified) and number of shots ($n = 10, 100, 250$). Table 3 provides the label distributions of the training and test dataset and the corresponding expected numbers under random sampling with $n = 100, 250$. Even though the numbers are given in the table, we do not consider to random sample only 10 observations in order to ensure a minimum of one observation per label in all training sets.

6.2 Experimental Setup

For the comparison of our PETapter model to PET and PEFT with a linear layer as classification head, we use the XLM-RoBERTa Large model due to the German dataset. In addition to the different architectures (cf. Section 5.2), we compare the effect of different sampling strategies and the number of training observations $n = 10, 100, 250$. We again repeat each experiment five times. Thus, a single cell in Table 4 corresponds to 25 experiments (5 repetitions × 5 datasets). In the PET(apter) models, we use the English[2] natural language class labels as verbalizers and make use of the pattern

> This sentence contains [MASK] [MASK] arms deliveries to Ukraine: {[target_sentence] [SEP] [context_before] [SEP] [context_after]}*

Further, we conduct experiments with varying patterns and verbalizers, particularly ones that can be generated automatically (without human assistance) as well as ones that were selected to be as counterintuitive as possible, cf. Section 6.4.

In Appendix B, further information on all parameters as well as the used patterns is given.

6.3 Results

Table 4 shows the macro-F1 scores[3] from the real-world study. According to this, there is no significant difference between the performance of PET and PETapter. The scores using the linear layer, on the other hand, are significantly worse in all scenarios and combinations. The classification task appears to be so hard that for $n = 10$ neither any

[2]Note: German PVPs lead to worse results.

[3]Due to the unbalanced distribution of class labels in the dataset (cf. Table 3), we use macro-F1 instead of accuracy as the performance measure for a more reliable comparison of the models.

n	Sampling	No Pattern Alpha	 Normal	 Shuffle	Pattern Alpha	 Normal	 Shuffle
10	Equal	0.22 ±.039	0.25 ±.040	0.22 ±.039	0.23 ±.039	0.31 ±.043	0.28 ±.043
10	Stratified	0.20 ±.025	0.22 ±.031	0.22 ±.033	0.23 ±.067	0.27 ±.039	0.27 ±.043
100	Equal	0.47 ±.026	0.43 ±.041	0.41 ±.037	0.57 ±.041	0.57 ±.020	0.56 ±.033
100	Random	0.43 ±.046	0.39 ±.040	0.39 ±.043	0.53 ±.035	0.56 ±.036	0.54 ±.044
100	Stratified	0.40 ±.027	0.38 ±.035	0.37 ±.027	0.52 ±.051	0.58 ±.042	0.54 ±.048
250	Equal	0.62 ±.022	0.61 ±.024	0.60 ±.022	0.67 ±.021	0.67 ±.014	0.68 ±.019
250	Random	0.58 ±.035	0.57 ±.054	0.56 ±.054	0.65 ±.029	0.67 ±.021	0.66 ±.020
250	Stratified	0.60 ±.025	0.59 ±.030	0.58 ±.032	0.65 ±.019	0.67 ±.019	0.66 ±.017

Table 6: Mean macro-F1 scores (± standard deviation) of the PVP-experiments in the real-world study (Ukraine) using LoRA as PEFT method and PETapter as classification head.

scenario nor any model could achieve meaningful performance. For $n = 100, 250$, it can be seen that PET benefits greatly from the use of a balanced training set (equal sampling); this can be seen in a strong reduction of uncertainty measured by the standard deviation. In principle, however, PETapter produces consistently more reliable performances in the sense that the standard deviation of the scores is consistently lower for all settings. It can be seen that even for $n = 100$ random and stratified sampling lead to similar results.

In Table 5, we also present label-specific performance scores (precision, recall, macro-F1) for each of the four classes in the dataset. Here, we focus on the presentation of the results for $n = 250$ and the Pfeiffer adapters as PEFT method. The results of the random sampling are shown in Table 8 in the Appendix. It is of little surprise that the rarest class *argumentagainst* generates the worst precision, recall, and macro-F1 scores in the stratified sampling. In the case of equal sampling, this remains true only for the precision; the recall can be increased through the oversampling for PET from previously 51% to the then highest value of the four classes of 81%. The fact that an equal sampling in the training set leads to higher overall macro-F1 scores and lower uncertainty than a stratified sampling can be explained by the fact that the corresponding recall values of otherwise rarely occurring classes can be increased in this way.

In general, PETapter provides the best overall performance in this real-world study. While it yields a similar level of performance, it produces more reliable performance values overall. Thus, PETapter makes the idea of PET easily accessible in PEFT settings without loss of performance. While PET on our system[4] processes 7 observations per second (obs/s) during training and 8 obs/s during testing, PETapter processes 25 obs/s during training and 51 obs/s ((IA)^3/LoRA) or 42 obs/s (Pfeiffer) during testing. This shows a meaningful speed-up of PETapter compared to PET for the training as well as the inference phase.

[4]48 GB NVIDIA RTX 6000 Ada, Intel Xeon W7-3445 20×2.6 GHz, 256 GB ECC DDR5-4800 RAM

6.4 PVP-Experiments

A major criticism of PET-like models is the need for manual generation of patterns and verbalizers. To address this, we tested the use of automated PVPs (*No Pattern* as the most minimalistic version of a prompt pattern and *Alpha* verbalizers, which only use the letters "a" to "e") and badly chosen verbalizers (*Shuffle*, i.e., mixing up the verbalizers, e.g., "argument against" and "claim for"). The specific patterns and verbalizers that we use are given in Appendix B. For reasons of complexity, we limit the experiment to the combination of LoRA and PETapter, which seems to produce rather robust predictions (cf. Sections 5.3 and 6.3).

As a result from Table 6, it can be concluded that the pattern should at best be chosen manually, as there are notable differences between the performances in all scenarios. However, the choice of verbalizer in our task has hardly any influence on the performance already for $n = 100$. In fact, when using *No Pattern*, *Alpha* mostly performs better than the manually selected verbalizers, which may be because *Alpha* consists of only one token each, while the other two scenarios require two tokens per verbalizer. Moreover, we found that the *Shuffle* verbalizers do not result in any noteworthy differences in label-specific performance values compared to the *Normal* verbalizers (table not included due to space constraints).

As an extension, Table 7 indicates that a combination of the five repetitions using a majority vote leads to superior and more stable results. In particular in the scenario of limited human resources, this offers the possibility of boosting the performance

Data	n	PVP	Mean	Majority
AG	10	Manual	0.71 ±.080	0.71 ±.071
AG	100	Manual	0.87 ±.010	0.87 ±.009
Yahoo	10	Manual	0.30 ±.044	0.32 ±.034
Yahoo	100	Manual	0.66 ±.013	0.66 ±.012
Yelp	10	Manual	0.45 ±.055	0.45 ±.053
Yelp	100	Manual	0.61 ±.013	0.62 ±.009
Ukraine	10	Manual	0.27 ±.039	0.27 ±.029
Ukraine	100	Manual	0.58 ±.042	0.59 ±.025
Ukraine	250	Manual	0.67 ±.019	0.69 ±.018
Ukraine	10	Autom.	0.20 ±.025	0.20 ±.021
Ukraine	100	Autom.	0.40 ±.027	0.41 ±.018
Ukraine	250	Autom.	0.60 ±.025	0.62 ±.025

Table 7: Mean (majority) macro-F1 scores (± standard deviation) using LoRA and PETapter. For Ukraine, we present the results using the *Stratified* sampling. *Manual* PVP means *Prompt* pattern for AG, Yahoo, and Yelp; for Ukraine, it represents the combination of *Pattern* using the *Normal* verbalizers, *Autom.* represents the combination of *No Pattern* and *Alpha*.

of automatically selected PVPs by simply stacking independent repetitions.

7 Discussion

The results show that PET benefits greatly from equal sampling with unbalanced data. We were not able to achieve this gain to the same extent using PETapter. Therefore, even though equal sampling is not a realistic scenario in (few-shot) real-world settings, it could be promising to develop PEFT methods in such a way that they benefit from balanced data as much as PET.

Following the mathematical definition of PETapter (cf. Equation 1), it is recommended to always use the same number of verbalizer tokens for each class. We also recommend using as simple patterns as possible. Initial experiments have shown that PET in particular leads to poor results with small n if the pattern is too complex. PETapter was slightly more robust against the choice of pattern in these experiments. In addition, although grammatical correctness of the pattern is desirable, it is not essential to achieve satisfactory results.

8 Conclusion

We show that our novel method PETapter combines the advantages of few-shot learning and parameter-efficient fine-tuning (PEFT). PETapter combines PEFT methods with PET-style classification heads. This way it makes the idea of PET easily accessible in PEFT settings. As a result, it achieves PET performance and increased reliability of the results while offering all the advantages of PEFT. It can be trained faster with higher parameter efficiency and without catastrophic forgetting. Furthermore, it offers a modularity that makes it easier to share models because the newly learned parameters require, e.g., only 16 MB compared to 2.1 GB of disk space. Due to the implementation in the Adapters (Poth et al., 2023) framework, it allows easy execution and combination with existing/new PEFT methods like QLoRA (Dettmers et al., 2023), mixture of experts models (Zadouri et al., 2024), or others (cf. Section 2.1). Our method makes high-performing text classification in scarce label situations feasible for more researchers by lowering the technological boundaries to fine-tuning petrained language models.

Acknowledgements

This work was funded by the Bundesministerium für Bildung und Forschung (BMBF) as part of the project *FLACA: Few-shot learning for automated content analysis in communication science* (project no. 16DKWN064B) and by the Deutsche Forschungsgemeinschaft (DFG) as part of the project *FAME: A framework for argument mining and evaluation* (project no. 406289255). In addition, we acknowledge the computation resources facilitated by seed funding from the Research Center Trustworthy Data Science and Security as part of the project *Trustworthy performance evaluation of large language models*.

Limitations

As mentioned in Sections 7 and 8, not all promising models and combinations of model ingredients can be evaluated. Therefore, it is expected that better performance scores can be achieved by optimizing the combination of all mentioned ingredients, cf. Section 2. Instead, we show that the PETapter idea is a promising method overall, if the underlying task is possible to be formulated as a classification task. In addition, our analyses are limited to four data sets (also for reasons of sustainable NLP), which are restricted to the languages English and German. In return, we pay a lot of attention to a reliable evaluation through 5 repetitions × 5 sampled datasets for each of the considered scenarios in Sections 5 and 6, which makes the resulting performance scores very reliable for the analyzed settings.

References

Neel Alex, Eli Lifland, Lewis Tunstall, Abhishek Thakur, Pegah Maham, C. Jess Riedel, Emmie Hine, Carolyn Ashurst, Paul Sedille, Alexis Carlier, Michael Noetel, and Andreas Stuhlmüller. 2021. RAFT: A real-world few-shot text classification benchmark. In *Thirty-fifth Conference on Neural Information Processing Systems Datasets and Benchmarks Track (Round 2)*.

Nadav Benedek and Lior Wolf. 2024. PRILoRA: Pruned and rank-increasing low-rank adaptation. In *Findings of the Association for Computational Linguistics: EACL 2024*, pages 252–263, St. Julian's, Malta. Association for Computational Linguistics.

Canyu Chen and Kai Shu. 2023. PromptDA: Label-guided data augmentation for prompt-based few shot learners. In *Proceedings of the 17th Conference of the European Chapter of the Association for Computational Linguistics*, pages 562–574, Dubrovnik, Croatia. Association for Computational Linguistics.

Alexis Conneau, Kartikay Khandelwal, Naman Goyal, Vishrav Chaudhary, Guillaume Wenzek, Francisco Guzmán, Edouard Grave, Myle Ott, Luke Zettlemoyer, and Veselin Stoyanov. 2020. Unsupervised cross-lingual representation learning at scale. In *Proceedings of the 58th Annual Meeting of the Association for Computational Linguistics*, pages 8440–8451, Online. Association for Computational Linguistics.

Tim Dettmers, Artidoro Pagnoni, Ari Holtzman, and Luke Zettlemoyer. 2023. QLoRA: Efficient finetuning of quantized LLMs. In *Thirty-seventh Conference on Neural Information Processing Systems*.

Fabrizio Gilardi, Meysam Alizadeh, and Maël Kubli. 2023. ChatGPT outperforms crowd workers for text-annotation tasks. *Proceedings of the National Academy of Sciences*, 120(30).

Junxian He, Chunting Zhou, Xuezhe Ma, Taylor Berg-Kirkpatrick, and Graham Neubig. 2022. Towards a unified view of parameter-efficient transfer learning. In *International Conference on Learning Representations*.

Pengcheng He, Jianfeng Gao, and Weizhu Chen. 2023. DeBERTav3: Improving DeBERTa using ELECTRA-style pre-training with gradient-disentangled embedding sharing. In *The Eleventh International Conference on Learning Representations*.

Neil Houlsby, Andrei Giurgiu, Stanislaw Jastrzebski, Bruna Morrone, Quentin De Laroussilhe, Andrea Gesmundo, Mona Attariyan, and Sylvain Gelly. 2019. Parameter-efficient transfer learning for NLP. In *Proceedings of the 36th International Conference on Machine Learning*, volume 97 of *Proceedings of Machine Learning Research*, pages 2790–2799. PMLR.

Edward J. Hu, Yelong Shen, Phillip Wallis, Zeyuan Allen-Zhu, Yuanzhi Li, Shean Wang, Lu Wang, and Weizhu Chen. 2022. LoRA: Low-rank adaptation of large language models. In *International Conference on Learning Representations*.

Shengding Hu, Ning Ding, Weilin Zhao, Xingtai Lv, Zhen Zhang, Zhiyuan Liu, and Maosong Sun. 2023a. OpenDelta: A plug-and-play library for parameter-efficient adaptation of pre-trained models. In *Proceedings of the 61st Annual Meeting of the Association for Computational Linguistics (Volume 3: System Demonstrations)*, pages 274–281, Toronto, Canada. Association for Computational Linguistics.

Zhiqiang Hu, Lei Wang, Yihuai Lan, Wanyu Xu, Ee-Peng Lim, Lidong Bing, Xing Xu, Soujanya Poria, and Roy Lee. 2023b. LLM-adapters: An adapter family for parameter-efficient fine-tuning of large language models. In *Proceedings of the 2023 Conference on Empirical Methods in Natural Language Processing*, pages 5254–5276, Singapore. Association for Computational Linguistics.

Yongxin Huang, Kexin Wang, Sourav Dutta, Raj Patel, Goran Glavaš, and Iryna Gurevych. 2023. AdaSent: Efficient domain-adapted sentence embeddings for few-shot classification. In *Proceedings of the 2023 Conference on Empirical Methods in Natural Language Processing*, pages 3420–3434, Singapore. Association for Computational Linguistics.

Hendrik Hüning, Lydia Mechtenberg, and Stephanie Wang. 2022. Detecting arguments and their positions in experimental communication data. Available at SSRN.

Lena Jurkschat, Gregor Wiedemann, Maximilian Heinrich, Mattes Ruckdeschel, and Sunna Torge. 2022. Few-shot learning for argument aspects of the nuclear energy debate. In *Proceedings of the Thirteenth Language Resources and Evaluation Conference*, pages 663–672, Marseille, France. European Language Resources Association.

Rabeeh Karimi Mahabadi, Luke Zettlemoyer, James Henderson, Lambert Mathias, Marzieh Saeidi, Veselin Stoyanov, and Majid Yazdani. 2022. Prompt-free and efficient few-shot learning with language models. In *Proceedings of the 60th Annual Meeting of the Association for Computational Linguistics (Volume 1: Long Papers)*, pages 3638–3652, Dublin, Ireland. Association for Computational Linguistics.

Dawid Jan Kopiczko, Tijmen Blankevoort, and Yuki M Asano. 2024. VeRA: Vector-based random matrix adaptation. In *The Twelfth International Conference on Learning Representations*.

Changmao Li and Jeffrey Flanigan. 2024. Task contamination: Language models may not be few-shot anymore. *Proceedings of the AAAI Conference on Artificial Intelligence*, 38(16):18471–18480.

Tongtao Ling, Lei Chen, Yutao Lai, and Hai-Lin Liu. 2023. Evolutionary verbalizer search for prompt-based few shot text classification. In *Knowledge Science, Engineering and Management*, pages 279–290, Cham. Springer Nature Switzerland.

Haokun Liu, Derek Tam, Mohammed Muqeeth, Jay Mohta, Tenghao Huang, Mohit Bansal, and Colin A Raffel. 2022. Few-shot parameter-efficient fine-tuning is better and cheaper than in-context learning. In *Advances in Neural Information Processing Systems*, volume 35, pages 1950–1965. Curran Associates, Inc.

Shih-Yang Liu, Chien-Yi Wang, Hongxu Yin, Pavlo Molchanov, Yu-Chiang Frank Wang, Kwang-Ting Cheng, and Min-Hung Chen. 2024. DoRA: Weight-decomposed low-rank adaptation. In *Proceedings of the 41st International Conference on Machine Learning*, Proceedings of Machine Learning Research. PMLR.

Yinhan Liu, Myle Ott, Naman Goyal, Jingfei Du, Mandar Joshi, Danqi Chen, Omer Levy, Mike Lewis, Luke Zettlemoyer, and Veselin Stoyanov. 2019. RoBERTa: A robustly optimized bert pretraining approach.

Sourab Mangrulkar, Sylvain Gugger, Lysandre Debut, Younes Belkada, Sayak Paul, and Benjamin Bossan. 2022. PEFT: State-of-the-art parameter-efficient fine-tuning methods. `https://github.com/huggingface/peft`.

Mahdi Nikdan, Soroush Tabesh, Elvir Crnčević, and Dan Alistarh. 2024. RoSA: Accurate parameter-efficient fine-tuning via robust adaptation. In *Proceedings of the 41st International Conference on Machine Learning*, Proceedings of Machine Learning Research. PMLR.

Jonas Pfeiffer, Andreas Rücklé, Clifton Poth, Aishwarya Kamath, Ivan Vulić, Sebastian Ruder, Kyunghyun Cho, and Iryna Gurevych. 2020. AdapterHub: A framework for adapting transformers. In *Proceedings of the 2020 Conference on Empirical Methods in Natural Language Processing: System Demonstrations*, pages 46–54, Online. Association for Computational Linguistics.

Jonas Pfeiffer, Sebastian Ruder, Ivan Vulić, and Edoardo Maria Ponti. 2023. Modular deep learning. *Transactions on Machine Learning Research*. Survey Certification.

Clifton Poth, Hannah Sterz, Indraneil Paul, Sukannya Purkayastha, Leon Engländer, Timo Imhof, Ivan Vulić, Sebastian Ruder, Iryna Gurevych, and Jonas Pfeiffer. 2023. Adapters: A unified library for parameter-efficient and modular transfer learning. In *Proceedings of the 2023 Conference on Empirical Methods in Natural Language Processing: System Demonstrations*, pages 149–160, Singapore. Association for Computational Linguistics.

Sylvestre-Alvise Rebuffi, Hakan Bilen, and Andrea Vedaldi. 2017. Learning multiple visual domains with residual adapters. In *Advances in Neural Information Processing Systems*, volume 30. Curran Associates, Inc.

Jonas Rieger, Kostiantyn Yanchenko, Mattes Ruckdeschel, Gerret von Nordheim, Katharina Kleinen-von Königslöw, and Gregor Wiedemann. 2023. Few-shot learning for automated content analysis (FLACA) in the German media debate on arms deliveries to Ukraine. In *Digital Total*, page 19.

Jonas Rieger, Kostiantyn Yanchenko, Mattes Ruckdeschel, Gerret von Nordheim, Katharina Kleinen-von Königslöw, and Gregor Wiedemann. 2024. Few-shot learning for automated content analysis: Efficient coding of arguments and claims in the debate on arms deliveries to Ukraine. *Studies in Communication and Media*, 13:72–100.

Mohammed Sabry and Anya Belz. 2023. PEFT-Ref: A modular reference architecture and typology for parameter-efficient finetuning techniques.

Victor Sanh, Albert Webson, Colin Raffel, Stephen Bach, Lintang Sutawika, Zaid Alyafeai, Antoine Chaffin, Arnaud Stiegler, Arun Raja, Manan Dey, M Saiful Bari, Canwen Xu, Urmish Thakker, Shanya Sharma Sharma, Eliza Szczechla, Taewoon Kim, Gunjan Chhablani, Nihal Nayak, Debajyoti Datta, Jonathan Chang, Mike Tian-Jian Jiang, Han Wang, Matteo Manica, Sheng Shen, Zheng Xin Yong, Harshit Pandey, Rachel Bawden, Thomas Wang, Trishala Neeraj, Jos Rozen, Abheesht Sharma, Andrea Santilli, Thibault Fevry, Jason Alan Fries, Ryan Teehan, Teven Le Scao, Stella Biderman, Leo Gao, Thomas Wolf, and Alexander M Rush. 2022. Multitask prompted training enables zero-shot task generalization. In *International Conference on Learning Representations*.

Timo Schick and Hinrich Schütze. 2021. Exploiting cloze-questions for few-shot text classification and natural language inference. In *Proceedings of the 16th Conference of the European Chapter of the Association for Computational Linguistics: Main Volume*, pages 255–269, Online. Association for Computational Linguistics.

Timo Schick and Hinrich Schütze. 2022. True few-shot learning with Prompts—A real-world perspective. *Transactions of the Association for Computational Linguistics*, 10:716–731.

Lewis Tunstall, Nils Reimers, Unso Eun Seo Jo, Luke Bates, Daniel Korat, Moshe Wasserblat, and Oren Pereg. 2022. Efficient few-shot learning without prompts.

Thomas Wolf, Lysandre Debut, Victor Sanh, Julien Chaumond, Clement Delangue, Anthony Moi, Pierric Cistac, Tim Rault, Remi Louf, Morgan Funtowicz, Joe Davison, Sam Shleifer, Patrick von Platen, Clara Ma, Yacine Jernite, Julien Plu, Canwen Xu,

Teven Le Scao, Sylvain Gugger, Mariama Drame, Quentin Lhoest, and Alexander Rush. 2020. Transformers: State-of-the-art natural language processing. In *Proceedings of the 2020 Conference on Empirical Methods in Natural Language Processing: System Demonstrations*, pages 38–45, Online. Association for Computational Linguistics.

Prateek Yadav, Leshem Choshen, Colin Raffel, and Mohit Bansal. 2025. ComPEFT: Compression for communicating parameter efficient updates via sparsification and quantization. *Transactions on Machine Learning Research*.

Ted Zadouri, Ahmet Üstün, Arash Ahmadian, Beyza Ermis, Acyr Locatelli, and Sara Hooker. 2024. Pushing mixture of experts to the limit: Extremely parameter efficient moe for instruction tuning. In *The Twelfth International Conference on Learning Representations*.

Haoxing Zhang, Xiaofeng Zhang, Haibo Huang, and Lei Yu. 2022. Prompt-based meta-learning for few-shot text classification. In *Proceedings of the 2022 Conference on Empirical Methods in Natural Language Processing*, pages 1342–1357, Abu Dhabi, United Arab Emirates. Association for Computational Linguistics.

Xiang Zhang, Junbo Jake Zhao, and Yann LeCun. 2015. Character-level convolutional networks for text classification. In *NIPS*.

A Details of Benchmark Study

For the benchmark study, we compare the use of "roberta-base" and "roberta-large" from HuggingFace's Transformers (Wolf et al., 2020). For PET (https://github.com/timoschick/pet), we use the two parameters pet_num_train_epochs=10 and pet_per_gpu_train_batch_size=1 that differ from the default. For all experiments using the package Adapter (Poth et al., 2023), we use the parameters

- c_rate=16 (Pfeiffer),
- r=8 (LoRA),
- alpha=16 (LoRA),
- learning_rate=5.0e-5,
- max_epochs=30,
- per_device_train_batch_size=2

and alternate arch with ia3, lora, and pfeiffer. The patterns in the following subsections are motivated by the results of the study of Schick and Schütze (2022). Due to the limited input length of PLMs, potential truncations of the input elements in the pattern are indicated with *, potentially as group within { } brackets.

A.1 AG's News

This English language dataset is available at https://huggingface.co/datasets/ag_news (Zhang et al., 2015) and consists of 120 thousand training and 7.6 thousand test observations.

Prompt Pattern [MASK] News: [text]*

Q&A Pattern [text]* [SEP] Question: What is the topic of this article? Answer: [MASK].

Verbalizers

World World
Sports Sports
Business Business
Sci/Tech Tech

A.2 Yahoo Questions

This English language dataset is available at https://huggingface.co/datasets/yahoo_answers_topics (Zhang et al., 2015) and consists of 1.4 million training and 60 thousand test observations.

Prompt Pattern [MASK] Question: {[question_title] [question_content] [best_answer]}*

Q&A Pattern {[question_title] [question_content] [best_answer]}* [SEP] Question: What is the topic of this question? Answer: [MASK].

Verbalizers

Society & Culture Society
Science & Mathematics Science
Health Health
Education & Reference Education
Computers & Internet Computer
Sports Sports
Business & Finance Business
Entertainment & Music Entertainment
Family & Relationships Relationship
Politics & Government Politics

A.3 Yelp Full

This English language dataset is available at https://huggingface.co/datasets/yelp_review_full (Zhang et al., 2015) and consists of 650 thousand training and 50 thousand test observations.

Prompt Pattern [text]* [SEP] All in all, it was [MASK].

Q&A Pattern [text]* [SEP] Question: What does the customer think of this restaurant? Answer: [MASK].

Verbalizers

1 star terrible
2 stars bad
3 stars okay
4 stars good
5 stars great

B Details of the Real-World Study

This dataset is available in the GitHub repository https://github.com/JonasRieger/petapter. Since this dataset is in German language, we use "xlm-roberta-large" from HuggingFace's Transformers (Wolf et al., 2020). For PET (https://github.com/timoschick/pet), we use the two parameters pet_num_train_epochs=10 and pet_per_gpu_train_batch_size=1 (for a fair training time comparison in Table 2, we use pet_per_gpu_train_batch_size=2) that differ from the default. For all experiments using the

	Label	Random Sampling PETapter	Random Sampling PET	Random Sampling Lin. Layer	Stratified Sampling PETapter	Stratified Sampling PET	Stratified Sampling Lin. Layer
Precision	argumentagainst	0.57 ±.042	0.57 ±.126	0.37 ±.228	0.54 ±.037	0.54 ±.122	0.39 ±.092
	argumentfor	0.64 ±.050	0.66 ±.141	0.45 ±.117	0.64 ±.032	0.66 ±.145	0.47 ±.135
	claimagainst	0.68 ±.030	0.66 ±.141	0.52 ±.063	0.68 ±.036	0.66 ±.143	0.49 ±.065
	claimfor	0.81 ±.027	0.81 ±.077	0.65 ±.065	0.84 ±.022	0.83 ±.080	0.65 ±.064
Recall	argumentagainst	0.51 ±.059	0.53 ±.147	0.12 ±.093	0.53 ±.064	0.57 ±.140	0.16 ±.098
	argumentfor	0.61 ±.056	0.61 ±.140	0.42 ±.169	0.63 ±.053	0.61 ±.138	0.42 ±.147
	claimagainst	0.75 ±.039	0.74 ±.157	0.54 ±.175	0.78 ±.028	0.75 ±.161	0.54 ±.121
	claimfor	0.80 ±.029	0.82 ±.047	0.76 ±.054	0.78 ±.022	0.80 ±.051	0.74 ±.051
Macro-F1	argumentagainst	0.53 ±.037	0.55 ±.128	0.16 ±.109	0.53 ±.045	0.55 ±.123	0.22 ±.100
	argumentfor	0.62 ±.046	0.63 ±.134	0.43 ±.142	0.63 ±.024	0.63 ±.134	0.44 ±.138
	claimagainst	0.71 ±.025	0.70 ±.146	0.52 ±.124	0.72 ±.028	0.70 ±.148	0.51 ±.084
	claimfor	0.81 ±.016	0.81 ±.039	0.70 ±.036	0.81 ±.012	0.81 ±.040	0.69 ±.049

Table 8: Mean precision, recall, and macro-F1 scores per label (each ± standard deviation) of the experiments in the real-world study (Ukraine). We consider the Pfeiffer adapter as the PEFT method of PETapter and $n = 250$. In addition to the results from Table 5, we present the results of random sampling in comparison to stratified sampling.

package Adapter (Poth et al., 2023), we use the parameters

- `c_rate=16` (Pfeiffer),
- `r=8` (LoRA),
- `alpha=16` (LoRA),
- `learning_rate=5.0e-5`,
- `max_epochs=30`,
- `per_device_train_batch_size=2`

and alternate `arch` with `ia3`, `lora`, and `pfeiffer`.

Due to the limited input length of PLMs, potential truncations of the input elements in the pattern are indicated with *, potentially as group within {} brackets. We place the target sentence at the beginning to ensure that it is never truncated due to restrictions regarding the model's input length of 512 tokens. Experiments with target_sentence in the middle returned slightly worse results. In the same way, experiments with an equivalent German pattern yield slightly worse results.

Pattern This sentence contains [MASK] [MASK] arms deliveries to Ukraine: {[target_sentence] [SEP] [context_before] [SEP] [context_after]}*

No Pattern [MASK] [MASK]: {[target_sentence] [SEP] [context_before] [SEP] [context_after]}*

Alpha Verbalizers

The alphanumeric verbalizers only consist of one token each, so that in this case the used pattern is reduced to one [MASK] token only.

argumentagainst a
argumentfor b
claimagainst c
claimfor d
nostance e

Normal Verbalizers

argumentagainst argument against
argumentfor argument for
claimagainst claim against
claimfor claim for
nostance nothing regarding

Shuffle Verbalizers

argumentagainst claim for
argumentfor claim against
claimagainst nothing regarding
claimfor argument against
nostance argument for

C RAFT Benchmark

The RAFT Leaderboard (Alex et al., 2021, `https://raft.elicit.org/`) has been under maintenance for some time now. We made a submission a while ago, but unfortunately still got no score. If the scores are published in the future, we will include a table with comparative values for T-Few (Liu et al., 2022), Setfit (Tunstall et al., 2022), PET (Schick and Schütze, 2021) and the human baseline in the GitHub repository `https://github.com/JonasRieger/petapter`.

The 11 datasets of RAFT are in English language and available at `https://huggingface.co/datasets/ought/raft`. We use the model "microsoft/deberta-v2-xxlarge" from HuggingFace's Transformers (Wolf et al., 2020) and for all 11 datasets the parameters

- arch=lora,
- r=8,
- alpha=16,
- learning_rate=5.0e-5,
- max_epochs=30,
- per_device_train_batch_size=2,
- number_of_runs=5,

where we select the majority vote out of the five runs as the final submission.

The patterns in the following subsections are motivated by the results of the study of Schick and Schütze (2022). Due to the limited input length of PLMs, potential truncations of the input elements in the patterns are indicated with *, potentially as group within { } brackets.

C.1 ade_corpus_v2

Pattern [Sentence]* [SEP] Question: Is this sentence related to an adverse drug effect (ADE)? Answer: [MASK].

Verbalizers

not ADE-related No
ADE-related Yes

C.2 banking_77

For the processing of the *banking_77* dataset, some preprocessing is necessary. As there are only 50 observations in each of the training sets of the RAFT setting, but at the same time there are 77 different classes in this specific dataset, the model misses 27 of the classes in the training set. To overcome this, we augment the training data such that each of the 50 observations is combined with all 77 classes using the yes/no pattern below. As a result, the 27 classes that were previously not included in the training data now become part it each 50 times in combination with the label *no*.

Pattern The following is a banking customer service query. [SEP] {[Query] [SEP] Is [Label]}* the correct category for this query? Answer: [MASK].

Verbalizers

No No
Yes Yes

C.3 neurips_impact_statement_risks

Pattern {Title: [Paper title] [SEP] Statement: [Impact statement]}* [SEP] Question: Does this impact statement mention a harmful application? Answer: [MASK].

Verbalizers

doesn't mention a harmful application No
mentions a harmful application Yes

C.4 one_stop_english

Pattern [Article]* [SEP] Question: Is the level of this article 'elementary', 'intermediate' or 'advanced'? Answer: [MASK].

Verbalizers

elementary elementary
intermediate intermediate
advanced advanced

C.5 overruling

Pattern In law, an overruling sentence is a statement that nullifies a previous case decision as a precedent. [SEP] [Sentence]* [SEP] Question: Is this sentence overruling? Answer: [MASK].

Verbalizers

not overruling No
overruling Yes

C.6 semiconductor_org_types

Pattern {Title: [Paper title] [SEP] Organization name: [Organization name]}* [SEP] Question: What is the category of this institution? Answer: [MASK].

Verbalizers

company Company
research institute Institute
university University

C.7 systematic_review_inclusion

Pattern {Journal: [Journal] [SEP] Title: [Title] [SEP] Abstract: [Abstract]}* [SEP] Question: Should this paper be included in a meta-review which includes the findings of systematic reviews on interventions designed to promote charitable donations? Answer: [MASK].

Verbalizers

not included No
included Yes

C.8 tai_safety_research

Pattern Transformative AI (TAI) is defined as AI that precipitates a transition comparable to (or more significant than) the agricultural or industrial revolution [SEP] {Journal: [Publication Title] [SEP] Title: [Title] [SEP] Abstract: [Abstract Note]}* [SEP] Question: Is this paper a TAI safety research paper? Answer: [MASK].

Verbalizers

not TAI safety research No
TAI safety research Yes

C.9 terms_of_service

Pattern The following sentence is from a Terms of Service. [SEP] [Sentence]* [SEP] Question: Is this sentence potentially unfair? Answer: [MASK].

Verbalizers

not potentially unfair No
potentially unfair Yes

C.10 tweet_eval_hate

Pattern [Tweet]* [SEP] Question: Does this tweet contain hate speech against either immigrants or women? Answer: [MASK].

Verbalizers

not hate speech No
hate speech Yes

C.11 twitter_complaints

Pattern [Tweet text]* [SEP] Question: Does this tweet contain a complaint? Answer: [MASK].

Verbalizers

no complaint No
complaint Yes

D GPT Comparison

A different version of the Ukraine dataset, in which not only the four classes outlined in this paper are considered, but also *irrelevant* sentences are contained, is studied by Rieger et al. (2023) in a comparison between full fine-tuning methods, PET and PEFT methods. The authors show that PETapter already with only 272 observations outperforms zero-shot GPT-4. The authors further observe that GPT-4 performs better on this real-world and unpublished dataset in a zero-shot manner than using an in-context learning prompt with few (up to 10) examples. Moreover, they found out that GPT-3.5 performs significantly worse than GPT-4 on this task.

Large Language Model Data Generation for Enhanced Intent Recognition in German Speech

Theresa Pekarek Rosin and **Burak Can Kaplan** and **Stefan Wermter**
University of Hamburg - Knowledge Technology
Vogt-Koelln-Strasse 30, 22527 Hamburg - Germany
www.knowledge-technology.info
Correspondence: theresa.pekarek-rosin@uni-hamburg.de

Abstract

Intent recognition (IR) for speech commands is essential for artificial intelligence (AI) assistant systems; however, most existing approaches are limited to short commands and are predominantly developed for English. This paper addresses these limitations by focusing on IR from speech by elderly German speakers. We propose a novel approach that combines an adapted Whisper ASR model, fine-tuned on elderly German speech (SVC-de), with Transformer-based language models trained on synthetic text datasets generated by three well-known large language models (LLMs): LeoLM, Llama3, and ChatGPT. To evaluate the robustness of our approach, we generate synthetic speech with a text-to-speech model and conduct extensive cross-dataset testing. Our results show that synthetic LLM-generated data significantly boosts classification performance and robustness to different speaking styles and unseen vocabulary. Notably, we find that LeoLM, a smaller, domain-specific 13B LLM, surpasses the much larger ChatGPT (175B) in dataset quality for German intent recognition. Our approach demonstrates that generative AI can effectively bridge data gaps in low-resource domains. We provide detailed documentation of our data generation and training process to ensure transparency and reproducibility.

1 Introduction

Speech command recognition is essential for natural interaction with artificial agents in everyday life, especially for elderly or handicapped users (Fronemann et al., 2021). Commercial solutions have seen vast improvements and increased usage over the last few years. However, their cloud-based models not only struggle with speech from user groups that would benefit from a voice assistant the most (Moro-Velazquez et al., 2019; Ngueajio and Washington, 2022), but they also introduce privacy issues because the processing of speech input usually does not happen locally.

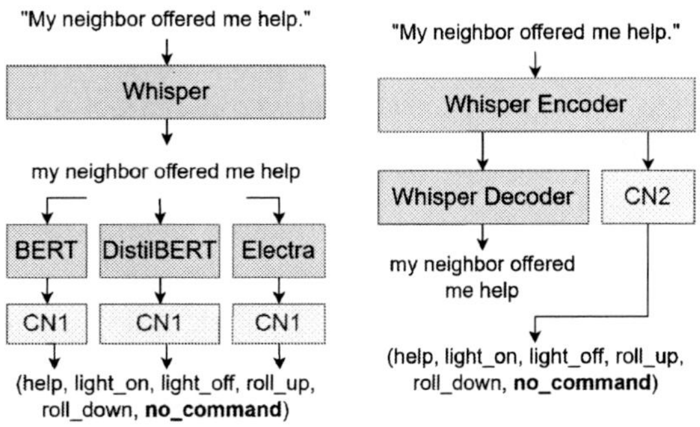

Figure 1: An overview of our model setup (left) and a traditional baseline (right). The speech is transcribed with a Whisper ASR model, the transcript is then classified with a transformer-based LM (BERT, DistilBERT, Electra) trained on a generated text dataset and a one-layer classification network (CN1). For the baseline, we use the output of the Whisper encoder to classify the intent with a two-layer classification network (CN2).

Additionally, traditional speech command recognition is usually restricted to short phrases and words (Warden, 2018), which requires the user to adapt to the system and change their way of speaking. That is usually not as intuitive for older people who might not have the same experience with recent technologies as younger users (Pekarek Rosin et al., 2025). Therefore, we argue that to create a more natural interaction with speech-based assistant systems, we need to move away from one-word command recognition to unconstrained utterance-based intent recognition.

However, the lack of large-scale datasets for languages besides English makes it difficult to implement such a change by retraining open-source speech models for intent recognition on different domains (e.g., elderly voices). Collecting new speech data on a larger scale for any speech recognition or classification task is not only an incredible effort for researchers and participants but also ultimately inefficient, since the process would need to be repeated every time new functionalities become available. This issue is amplified by the amount of training data that Transformer-based, state-of-the-art models require to be trained in their entirety.

We suggest two potential solutions to these issues: 1) through the use of layer-specific fine-tuning (Shor et al., 2019; Pekarek Rosin and Wermter, 2023) pretrained foundation models can be adapted to other domains with small amounts of speech data while preserving existing knowledge, 2) through the generation of additional domain-focused data with large language models (LLMs), we can increase the generalization abilities of the model to different linguistic patterns.

We combine a state-of-the-art automatic speech recognition (ASR) model, Whisper (Radford et al., 2023), with three transformer-based pretrained language models, BERT (Devlin et al., 2019), DistilBERT (Sanh et al., 2019), and Electra (Clark et al., 2020) for German speech intent recognition. We utilize three LLMs to generate additional training data for these language models, and we synthesize speech samples based on this data with a text-to-speech model to evaluate our approach.

2 Related Work

Speech command recognition typically involves accurately identifying words or short phrases as commands linked to functionalities in an underlying system. This classification can be performed on either the audio feature representations or the transcript produced by the ASR model. In contrast, intent recognition requires a larger context, such as complete sentences, to discern user intent. For English-language tasks, the Speech Command Dataset (Warden, 2018) is a commonly used resource for training and evaluating models in speech command recognition or keyword spotting.

Diverse strategies have been proposed for speech command recognition, with a recent approach by Sadovsky et al. (2023) exploring the use of spiking neural networks for this task, and achieving a maximum accuracy of 72% on the Speech Command Dataset. Other baselines mentioned in their paper reach 79% accuracy using Gated Recurrent Units.

Berg et al. (2021) propose the Keyword Transformer model. They train their model on the Speech Command Dataset for approximately 100 episodes and achieve between 97.49% and 98.56% accuracy using knowledge distillation with only minimal improvements over the baseline.

In low-resource settings, Kumar Nayak et al. (2023) explore speech command recognition in the Kui language using a small dataset of 7,090 utterances covering just seven words. Their convolutional neural network (CNN) baseline was the only model to exceed 90% accuracy after 300 training episodes, highlighting the challenges of limited data. Similarly, Hernández et al. (2024) investigate intent recognition in Spanish and Nahuatl by training models on a manually collected dataset of 383 natural language navigation commands. Their results show that transformer-based models outperform traditional baselines, especially for longer and more complex utterances.

Despite these advances, most approaches often rely on extensive training, large-scale datasets, or costly real-world data collection. Notably, the lack of recent work examining this research topic for German speech suggests that the absence of datasets deters research in that direction.

LLMs have emerged as powerful tools for synthetic dataset generation (Kaplan et al., 2025), enabling the creation of task-specific training data and offering a solution to data scarcity. Additionally, their capabilities in common-sense reasoning (Li et al., 2022) and their strong performance in natural language understanding make them well-suited for tasks such as intent recognition. Transformer-based language models have shown value in both data augmentation for intent classification (Kumar et al., 2020) and in intent classification itself (Chen et al., 2019).

Additionally, the use of more powerful LLMs for intent recognition has increased significantly (Dighe et al., 2024; Dzeparoska et al., 2024; Wang et al., 2024), and LLMs have been widely studied for their ability to assist people through multimodal applications with speech (Wagner et al., 2024; Padmanabha et al., 2024). However, the majority of the work has been conducted in English, leaving considerable room for exploration in other languages. While some recent work explores German-language applications of LLMs (Irrgang et al., 2024; Volk et al., 2024), they have primarily focused on other tasks. The release of German LLMs, such as LeoLM [1], has demonstrated the potential of LLMs for the German language and motivates our work, which explores the use of LLM-generated datasets to create robust intent recognition systems for German speakers.

[1] `https://laion.ai/blog/leo-lm/`

3 Methodology

3.1 Senior Voice Commands Dataset

The German Senior Voice Commands (SVC-de) is a dataset collected by Pekarek Rosin and Wermter (2023) for the development of speech-based interaction with a home assistant system for German senior citizens. The dataset contains recordings from 30 native German speakers (21 female, 9 male) between the ages of 50 and 99, of 52 sentence-based speech commands. Per speaker, approximately 6-7 minutes of audio from two different microphones is available, which leads to a total of 3 hours and 9 minutes of speech data. The recorded sentences can be separated into 6 classes: "help", "light_on", "light_off", "roll_up", "roll_down", and "no_command". The class "no_command" essentially serves to catch common false positives in command classification to decrease wrong triggers, while keeping the interaction natural without the involvement of wake-words or restriction of the user's speech.

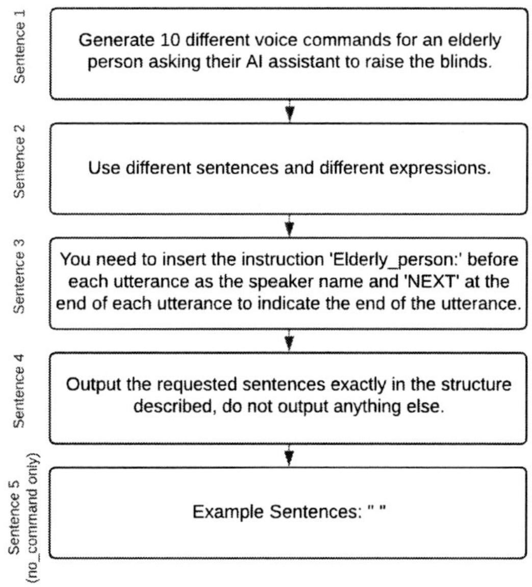

Figure 2: An example for the structure of our prompts. The original prompts are in German and can be found in Appendix A in Table 5.

3.2 Intent Recognition Dataset

For our intent recognition task, we generated sentences for the same six classes, with three different large language models (LLMs): LeoLM-13b[1], Llama3-8b[2], and ChatGPT by OpenAI. Llama3 is a well-known recent option for local LLMs, while LeoLM was developed specifically for the German language. We included ChatGPT as an assumed upper baseline, since it outperforms most LLMs on a large number of tasks, even though its lack of transparency makes results hard to reproduce. We generated approximately 2500 samples for each LLM.

3.2.1 Prompt Engineering

We tailored specific prompts for each label to maintain consistency and aimed to keep these prompts as similar as possible. Figure 2 illustrates a general example of the prompt structure. Every prompt, except for the "no_command" label, is comprised of four sentences, each targeting different sub-tasks. The initial sentence typically clearly outlines the scenario and initiates the task generation. The second sentence aims to enhance diversity by suggesting the LLM should incorporate various situations. The third sentence helps with the structuring of the outputs, making it easier to parse them for data collection. The parsing script is employed post-generation and utilizes the shown keywords to extract the necessary data. Moreover, those keywords provide additional clues and structure to the LLM by clearly indicating the start and end points of the sentences. The final sentence, inspired by Amin et al. (2023), is designed specifically to minimize unwanted outputs that usually happen due to the nature of the pre-training of LLMs and their initial underlying prompts. After parsing, each dataset is checked manually to remove sentences with grammatical issues, nonsense content, or ones unrelated to the command they were labeled as.

The "no_command" label required more prompt engineering than the others, since the concept of false positive sentences does not seem to be easily graspable for LLMs. It often caused the LLM to hallucinate or generate data better suited to other labels. However, we managed to address this issue by employing a few-shot prompting approach with additional example sentences to enrich the existing prompt structure. To further enhance the diversity of the responses, we split the "help" label into two distinct prompts. In addition to the standard prompt, we also requested short calls for help (1-2 words) to account for emergencies, where the user might not be able to speak in full sentences. Additionally, for the "no_command" label, we tailored three different prompts that correspond to false pos-

[2]https://huggingface.co/meta-llama/Llama-3.1-8B

seed	top_p	top_k	RP	typ. p	temp.
0	1	10000	1	0.995	0.7

Table 1: The parameters used for the local LLMs. RP: Repetition Penalty

itive sentences for "help", "light_on" or "light_off", and "roll_up" or "roll_down", respectively. A few examples of false positive sentences would be: "My assistant turns on the lights as soon as it gets dark.", for control of the lights, "Every morning I open the blinds.", for control of the blinds, and "I should call my doctor later.", for help.

3.2.2 LLM Parameters

We utilized the local LLMs, LeoLM and Llama3, by integrating the TextgenWebUI Chat API [3] and Ollama[4], which offer similar functionalities as OpenAI's Chat API, but also allow access to the full range of LLM parameters. Table 1 contains all the parameters we used for the dataset generation for the local LLMs. The seeds were initialized randomly with 0 and then selected from the range $(0, 2^{35})$. They remained fixed during the generation to ensure the generated data would be diverse and reproducible. In our specific setup, the temperature setting was not as critical due to the stabilized seed; thus, we maintained it at the default value of 0.7. We selected high values for top_p, top_k, and $typical\_p$ to enrich the context diversity and expand the array of potential utterances. Additionally, we reduced the repetition penalty (RP) to prevent constriction of the LLM with the tokens it previously generated.

3.2.3 Speech Synthesis

Since our model is based on speech input, we utilize XTTS-v2[5], which is a multilingual text-to-speech model that generates high-quality speech, in its German language configuration. XTTS-v2 is an extension of the XTTS model by Casanova et al. (2024), which builds on the Tortoise model (Betker, 2023) to enable multilingual training, faster inference, and voice cloning.

We randomly select four speakers (two male, two female) between 70 and 80 years of age from the Common Voice DE 10.0 dataset (Ardila et al., 2020), and create short audio files as a reference for the generation of synthetic speech. We generate audio from these reference files for each LLM-generated text dataset and use the resulting synthetic speech for the complete evaluation of our approach.

3.3 Architecture

The task of intent recognition requires reliable speech recognition, not only to enable the use of language models to perform classification on the transcript but also to increase the transparency of the entire model in case of misclassification. Considering these conditions, we use the state-of-the-art Whisper model developed by Radford et al. (2023) in our setup. Whisper follows an encoder-decoder structure, which allows us to neatly utilize the same model for both the baseline and our approach. Specifically, we use a pretrained Whisper-small model that has already been fine-tuned for the German language[6] and adapt it to the domain of elderly German speech with the SVC-de dataset, following the approach by Pekarek Rosin and Wermter (2023). We continually train only the encoder part of the architecture with Experience Replay (Rolnick et al., 2019) on 10% of the Common Voice DE 10.0 dataset, to avoid overfitting the model on the limited vocabulary of the SVC-de dataset.

In our approach, we combine the domain-adapted Whisper model with a Transformer language model (LM) trained on synthetic text data to perform the task of intent recognition on the transcript provided by the Whisper model (Figure 1). We utilize three pretrained Transformer LMs: BERT (Devlin et al., 2019), DistilBERT (Sanh et al., 2019), and Electra (Clark et al., 2020). BERT was one of the first transformer-based LMs that allowed the adaptation to specific tasks without retraining the entire model, due to the pretrained bi-directional representations in each layer. This property makes BERT and other models like it uniquely suited for low-resource tasks. Additionally, these models have proven reliable on a variety of tasks, and pretrained German versions are readily available in the Hugging Face model repository[7].
DistilBERT reduces BERT's size by 40% through knowledge distillation, and Electra replaces BERT's masked language modeling task for pre-training with a more sample-efficient one. Since

[3] https://github.com/oobabooga/text-generation-webui

[4] https://ollama.com/

[5] https://huggingface.co/coqui/XTTS-v2

[6] https://huggingface.co/bofenghuang/whisper-small-cv11-german

[7] https://huggingface.co/

	train/test	ChatGPT	LeoLM	Llama3	Combined
	ChatGPT	95.59 ± 0.90	79.43 ± 1.79	71.00 ± 1.40	81.83 ± 1.09
BERT	LeoLM	82.91 ± 2.06	94.35 ± 0.76	76.75 ± 1.45	$\mathbf{84.26 \pm 0.40}$
	Llama3	80.00 ± 2.68	76.31 ± 1.00	92.01 ± 1.23	82.41 ± 0.44
	Combined	98.16 ± 0.92	97.43 ± 0.55	95.40 ± 0.76	96.98 ± 0.24
	train/test	ChatGPT	LeoLM	Llama3	**Combined**
	ChatGPT	92.99 ± 1.08	78.29 ± 2.17	71.75 ± 1.58	80.25 ± 0.69
DistilBERT	LeoLM	81.19 ± 1.44	93.71 ± 0.63	70.32 ± 1.42	$\mathbf{82.58 \pm 0.61}$
	Llama3	76.76 ± 2.76	74.59 ± 1.38	89.25 ± 1.40	79.67 ± 0.40
	Combined	97.70 ± 0.37	96.89 ± 0.55	94.40 ± 0.61	96.51 ± 0.36
	train/test	ChatGPT	LeoLM	Llama3	**Combined**
	ChatGPT	84.80 ± 1.79	68.89 ± 2.33	67.71 ± 1.81	72.86 ± 1.03
Electra	LeoLM	72.05 ± 2.32	87.24 ± 1.07	66.31 ± 1.72	$\mathbf{75.06 \pm 0.83}$
	Llama3	66.43 ± 1.14	71.04 ± 1.09	81.94 ± 2.92	72.35 ± 1.23
	Combined	94.88 ± 1.01	94.35 ± 0.81	93.85 ± 0.67	94.33 ± 0.36

Table 2: Results for intent recognition from text with all transformer models on all synthetic text datasets. Results are averaged over 5 runs, each model was trained for 5 epochs. We show the mean accuracy (%) on the test dataset, averaged over 5 checkpoints, and the standard deviation.

the application context of our approach is real-time interaction with the user, and we want to create a model that could be used locally without access to GPU resources, we utilize these comparatively smaller Transformer models instead of LLMs.

3.4 Experimental Setup

In our experimental setup, we take a pretrained BERT (bert-base-german-cased), DistilBERT (distilbert-base-german-cased), and Electra (german-nlp-group/electra-base-german-uncased) model from the Hugging Face model repository[7]. We equip each model with a fully connected output layer for classification and keep the pretrained model frozen. We train the models with a learning rate of 3e-4 and a dropout of 0.1 over 5 epochs, on the ChatGPT-, LeoLM-, and Llama3-generated text datasets, with a split of 70-20-10 for training, validation, and testing. We selected these hyperparameters empirically, since the models converged after approximately 4 epochs.

Afterward, we perform a cross-evaluation between datasets and also evaluate each model on a combination of all generated datasets, to examine whether there are noticeable differences in quality within the LLM-generated data. This also allows us to assess whether there are LLM-specific patterns in the data and if one of the datasets allows a higher level of generalization to unseen sentences.

We then combine the domain-adapted Whisper-small model with the trained LMs and evaluate our architecture on the generated speech datasets. The goal is to compare its performance with the accuracy achieved by the text transformers. We also examine the word error rate (WER) and character error rate (CER) of Whisper on the generated speech datasets and compare them with its performance on SVC-de, to assess the quality of the synthetic speech.

As a baseline, we use the output of the encoder part of the Whisper model to train a two-layer classification network for intent recognition on the SVC-de dataset only. This baseline represents traditional approaches and their limitations in low-resource domains.

4 Results

We train and evaluate BERT, DistilBERT, and Electra on each synthetic dataset to examine how well they generalize to different semantic structures and syntax. As seen in Table 2, the transformer models trained with data generated by LeoLM show the best generalization abilities across all datasets. While BERT and DistilBERT perform similarly,

Dataset	WER (%) ↓	CER (%) ↓
ChatGPT	12.14	6.16
LeoLM	15.01	8.41
Llama3	9.56	4.94
SVC-de	5.65	5.42

Table 3: The word error rate (WER) and the character error rate (CER) of the domain-adapted Whisper-small on the real-world SVC-de dataset and the synthetic speech datasets.

Electra's accuracy is on average 10% lower. We also trained the LMs on the SVC-de transcripts and found that the results of the evaluation matched the baseline results in Table 4, with low accuracies (35-40%) across all synthetic datasets.

The confusion matrices in Figure 3 show that models trained on the LeoLM data generally show a more stable performance, even for unseen samples generated by other models. All models exhibit some level of confusion with the differentiation of "light_on" and "roll_up" from their counterparts and "no_command". However, BERT outperforms both Electra and DistilBERT. Electra seems to have more issues overall with the separation of different classes, which is also reflected in the previously discussed lower accuracies. A notable, positive result is the fact that all models across all datasets seem to be able to distinguish real calls for help reliably from the false positives introduced in the data for "no_command".

We continue the evaluation of our approach and the baseline with synthetic speech, as discussed in Section 3.2. As can be seen in Table 3, the quality of the generated speech is within an acceptable range, considering the domain-adapted ASR model was not trained on the synthetic speech. We observe word error rates (WERs) of 12.14% for ChatGPT, 15.01% for LeoLM, and 9.56% for Llama3. Meanwhile, the real speech from the SVC-de dataset achieves a WER as low as 5.65%, which is in line with the results by Pekarek Rosin and Wermter (2023).

The results in Table 4 show that pre-training the LMs on the data generated by the LLMs increases the overall models' robustness against unseen sentences. This is supported by the significantly lower performance of the baseline on the synthetic data, with around a 50% difference in accuracy. The LeoLM data proves to be especially useful for pre-training, with Whisper+DistilBERT(LeoLM) achieving the highest accuracy with 83.01% on SVC-de compared to the baseline result of 95.05%. It even outperforms the models trained on a combination of the synthetic text data. The same patterns that can be observed in the evaluation of the text data (Table 2) are present here as well, with a performance drop for Electra-based models. Overall, we observe that adding a language model trained on a supplementary synthetic text dataset vastly improves generalization to new data, compared to the baseline results.

5 Discussion

In our approach, we equip a Whisper ASR model with a Transformer LM for intent recognition, to allow LLM-generated text data to supplement the small-scale speech dataset available for the task (SVC-de). Our results show that training the LM on the synthetic text data increases the overall model's ability to generalize across various semantic structures and syntax, and previously unseen sentences.

LeoLM, a local LLM specifically created for the German language, outperforms both ChatGPT and Llama3 in terms of generalization to unseen data (Table 2) and demonstrates a more stable performance overall (Figure 3). This shows the potential of language-specific fine-tuning for local LLMs, which offer more transparency of their parameters and therefore higher control of the output and reproducibility. Notably, models trained only on the Llama3 data do not trail behind the ones trained on LeoLM or ChatGPT, even though Llama3 is a smaller model. For the BERT models in particular, performance differences are minimal, and BERT(Llama3) even outperforms BERT(ChatGPT) on the dataset combination.

The confusion matrices in Figure 3 show that the distinction between "help" and the false positives contained in "no_command" seems to be straightforward for all models, which is great for real-life applications, since calls for help should ideally not be misclassified at all. All models seem to struggle to varying degrees with differentiating between "light_on" or "light_off" and "roll_up" or "roll_down", which is to be expected due to the high similarity of the generated sentences. The Electra models seem to have more issues with this differentiation overall, especially the model trained on the ChatGPT data. In a real home assistant system, this would ideally be alleviated by introducing

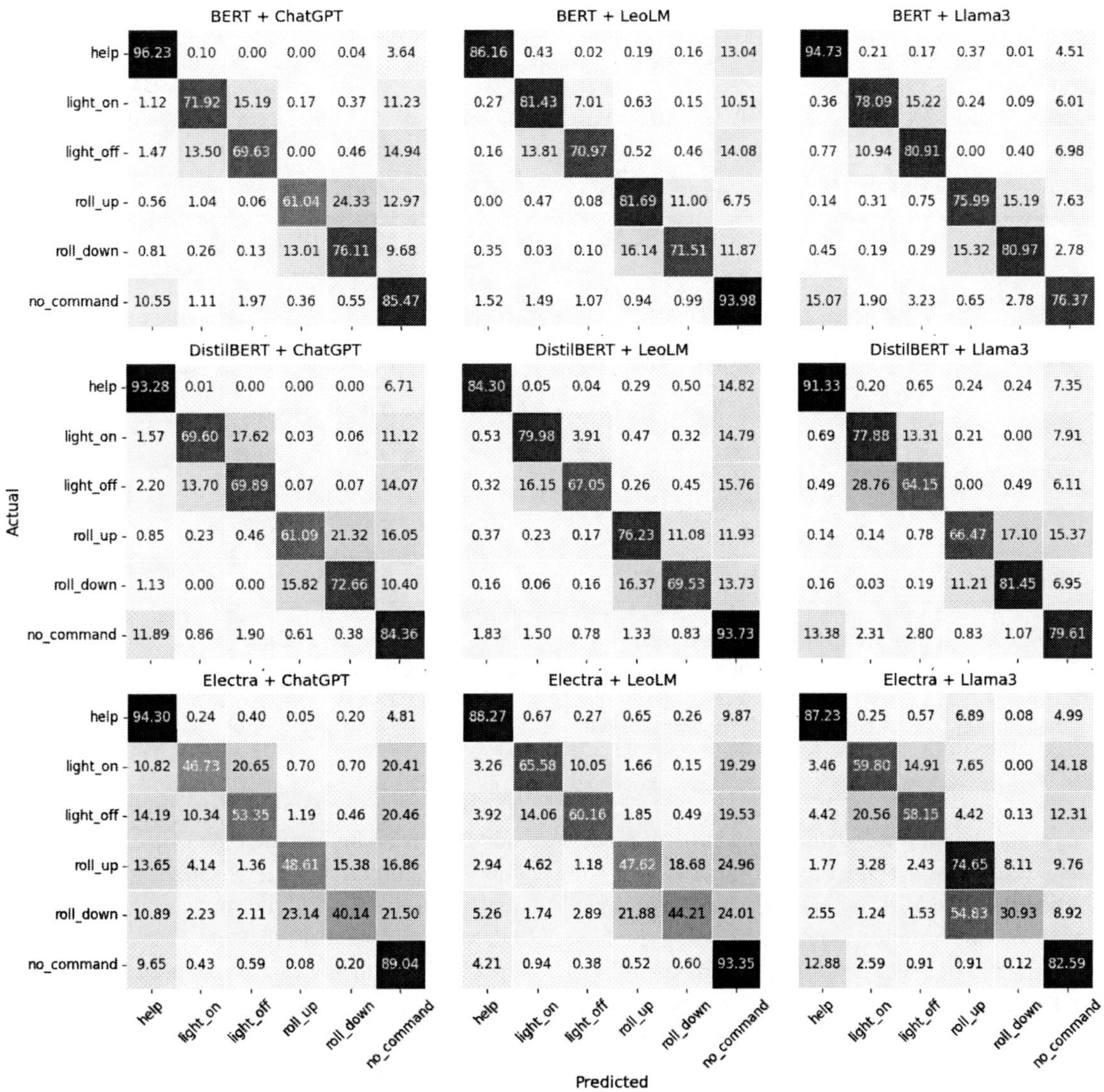

Figure 3: Confusion matrices for all LM+dataset variations, evaluated on the combination of all generated datasets.

context information to help reduce uncertainty, e.g., by checking the state of the lights or blinds.

The word error rates (WERs) of the synthetic speech datasets (Table 3) are comparable to the ones measured by Pekarek Rosin and Wermter (2023) for Whisper-small-de on the Common Voice DE test split (11.2%). This indicates that the quality of the synthetic speech approximates real speech. As can be seen in Table 4, the evaluation results on the synthetic speech datasets and SVC-de show that BERT and DistilBERT can keep the classification performance high for unseen speech data. The performance for the speech-based evaluation drops slightly across all models compared to the text-only evaluations, which is expected since ASR models usually create noisy transcriptions (Table 3), and some information might be lost. We also observe that supplementing with data from a single LLM (LeoLM) seems to be more beneficial than combining the data from all LLMs for training.

The low performance of the baseline Whisper-Encoder+CN on the synthetic datasets highlights how fine-tuning on small-scale speech data can significantly affect pretrained model generalizability and emphasizes the advantage of our approach. Since the WER of the synthetic speech is comparable to real speech, the limited vocabulary of the real dataset likely explains the baseline's low accuracy. Additionally, while SVC-de was used for domain adaptation of the Whisper encoder,

	train/test	ChatGPT-s	LeoLM-s	Llama3-s	SVC-de
Whisper+BERT	ChatGPT	91.49 ± 0.95	77.51 ± 1.44	71.35 ± 1.54	65.91 ± 3.86
	LeoLM	78.28 ± 0.46	89.95 ± 0.43	72.88 ± 1.06	$\mathbf{73.51 \pm 2.65}$
	Llama3	76.04 ± 1.11	71.99 ± 0.88	91.09 ± 0.70	63.44 ± 6.63
	Combined	93.63 ± 0.44	92.32 ± 0.26	94.23 ± 0.37	74.37 ± 2.87
Whisper+DistilBERT	ChatGPT	87.50 ± 1.60	73.93 ± 0.83	68.11 ± 2.23	75.58 ± 3.80
	LeoLM	74.29 ± 1.37	86.69 ± 1.42	67.43 ± 1.80	$\mathbf{83.01 \pm 1.54}$
	Llama3	75.04 ± 1.06	71.93 ± 0.83	87.04 ± 1.07	71.47 ± 1.89
	Combined	94.35 ± 0.11	92.13 ± 0.21	92.12 ± 0.42	72.28 ± 1.35
Whisper+Electra	ChatGPT	74.16 ± 1.34	65.50 ± 0.42	64.48 ± 0.84	61.67 ± 0.96
	LeoLM	65.94 ± 0.63	80.97 ± 0.36	63.35 ± 0.74	$\mathbf{71.42 \pm 2.27}$
	Llama3	67.16 ± 1.01	69.05 ± 1.64	81.76 ± 1.73	51.52 ± 4.53
	Combined	87.32 ± 0.65	86.48 ± 0.67	90.10 ± 0.32	68.61 ± 1.09
Whisper-Encoder+CN	SVC-de	34.72 ± 0.61	38.40 ± 0.65	36.36 ± 0.75	95.05 ± 0.39

Table 4: Results of the evaluation on the synthetic speech datasets (-s), and on the SVC-de dataset of all combinations of Whisper+LM models, trained on the text datasets generated by ChatGPT, LeoLM, and Llama3. Whisper-Encoder+CN is the baseline trained only on the real speech dataset, SVC-de. We show the mean accuracy (%), averaged over 5 checkpoints, and the standard deviation.

none of the Whisper+LM variations were explicitly trained on it for classification. Still, all models achieved above-average accuracy on SVC-de, with Whisper+DistilBERT(LeoLM) outperforming all other model variations and approaching the baseline trained on SVC-de (Whisper-Encoder+CN).

Finally, all our models require only 5 epochs to be trained sufficiently, which can be done in a fraction of the time needed for other approaches (Section 2), since each training run on the generated text data takes only 1-2 minutes.

6 Conclusion

In this paper, we present a novel approach for intent recognition (IR) in the domain of elderly German speakers using a home assistant system. We leverage a pretrained Whisper model and adapt it to the domain through layer-specific fine-tuning and continual learning on the SVC-de dataset. To address the limitations of the dataset, we generate supplementary classification datasets with three large language models (LLMs): LeoLM, Llama3, and ChatGPT. These datasets are then used to train transformer-based language models (LMs) for IR.

Our results show that a pretrained ASR model combined with an LM trained on synthetic text data displays increased robustness to diverse linguistic patterns and unseen vocabulary. Evaluating our models on high-quality synthetic speech shows that they outperform the baseline trained only on real-world data (SVC-de), indicating improved robustness to different speakers. This adaptability is critical for reducing user strain in real-world applications. We find that training Transformer LMs on synthetic text data is more efficient than continued ASR fine-tuning in terms of resources and generalizability of the model. Additionally, our models are reliably able to differentiate calls for help from false alarms, which is essential for a home-assistant system for elderly speakers.

This work is an exploration of LLMs and generative AI for the generation of German speech and language processing datasets. We show that (1) a domain-specific, smaller LLM like LeoLM (13B) can surpass larger models like ChatGPT (175B) in dataset quality, while offering transparency and reproducibility; (2) supplementing an ASR model with a language model trained on synthetic text data can enhance model performance and robustness; and (3) our method offers a fast and efficient way to adapt existing speech systems for IR tasks. As such, our approach offers a practical and scalable solution for deploying reliable home-assistant systems in real-world speaker environments.

Ethical Considerations

No experiments with human participants or additional recordings were conducted during this research. We chose to use local LLMs as well as ChatGPT for the dataset generation to explore their performance, since local LLMs allow for greater control of their parameters. For the sake of transparency, we have shared every parameter (Table 1) and prompt (Appendix A) we used. The generated data can be fully reproduced using the same LLMs, prompts, and parameters, provided that the same seed is used.

Limitations

In this research, we have encountered a couple of limitations associated with the use of smaller LLMs. It was observed that the LLM may truncate its outputs. To address this issue, we implemented a check during the parsing phase to verify the completeness of each utterance in terms of starting and ending keywords. If incomplete, the parser excludes that utterance, ensuring that the parsed data does not contain missing values. We also observed instances where recurrent utterances appear in more than one output. This issue is resolved by eliminating duplicate utterances during parsing and selecting the more diverse ones during manual filtering. For the ASR model, we chose one model to simplify the experimental setup, but ideally, we would have examined the performance of different versions of Whisper as well. The approach we follow for domain adaptation does an extensive evaluation with the same dataset, so we did not repeat a similar evaluation.

Acknowledgments

The authors gratefully acknowledge funding from Horizon Europe under the MSCA grant agreement No 101072488 (TRAIL), the German BMWK (SIDIMO), and the Study Abroad Graduate Scholarship by the Ministry of National Education of Türkiye.

References

Mostafa M. Amin, Erik Cambria, and Björn W. Schuller. 2023. Will affective computing emerge from foundation models and general artificial intelligence? a first evaluation of ChatGPT. *IEEE Intelligent Systems*, 38(02):15–23.

Rosana Ardila, Megan Branson, Kelly Davis, Michael Kohler, Josh Meyer, Michael Henretty, Reuben Morais, Lindsay Saunders, Francis Tyers, and Gregor Weber. 2020. Common voice: A massively-multilingual speech corpus. In *Proceedings of the 12th Language Resources and Evaluation Conference*, Marseille, France. European Language Resources Association.

Axel Berg, Mark O'Connor, and Miguel Tairum Cruz. 2021. Keyword transformer: A self-attention model for keyword spotting. In *Proceedings of Interspeech 2021*, pages 4249–4253. ISCA.

James Betker. 2023. Better speech synthesis through scaling. *ArXiv*.

Edresson Casanova, Kelly Davis, Eren Gölge, Görkem Göknar, Iulian Gulea, Logan Hart, Aya Aljafari, Joshua Meyer, Reuben Morais, Samuel Olayemi, and Julian Weber. 2024. Xtts: a massively multilingual zero-shot text-to-speech model. In *Interspeech 2024*, pages 4978–4982.

Qian Chen, Zhu Zhuo, and Wen Wang. 2019. BERT for joint intent classification and slot filling. *arXiv*.

Kevin Clark, Minh-Thang Luong, Quoc V. Le, and Christopher D. Manning. 2020. ELECTRA: Pre-training text encoders as discriminators rather than generators. In *Proceedings of ICLR 2020*.

Jacob Devlin, Ming-Wei Chang, Kenton Lee, and Kristina Toutanova. 2019. BERT: Pre-training of Deep Bidirectional Transformers for Language Understanding. In *Proceedings of NAACL-HLT 2019*, page 4171–4186.

Pranay Dighe, Yi Su, Shangshang Zheng, Yunshu Liu, Vineet Garg, Xiaochuan Niu, and Ahmed Tewfik. 2024. Leveraging large language models for exploiting ASR uncertainty. In *Proceedings of 2024 IEEE International Conference on Acoustics, Speech and Signal Processing (ICASSP)*, pages 12231–12235.

Kristina Dzeparoska, Ali Tizghadam, and Alberto Leon-Garcia. 2024. Intent assurance using LLMs guided by intent drift. *arXiv*.

Nora Fronemann, Kathrin Pollmann, and Wulf Loh. 2021. Should my robot know what's best for me? Human–robot interaction between user experience and ethical design. *AI & SOCIETY*, 37:517 – 533.

Amadeo Hernández, Rosa María Ortega-Mendoza, Esaú Villatoro-Tello, César Joel Camacho-Bello, and Obed Pérez-Cortés. 2024. Natural language understanding for navigation of service robots in low-resource domains and languages: Scenarios in spanish and nahuatl. *Mathematics*, 12.

Verena Irrgang, Veronika Solopova, Steffen Zeiler, Robert M. Nickel, and Dorothea Kolossa. 2024. Features and detectability of German texts generated with large language models. In *Proceedings of the 20th Conference on Natural Language Processing*

(KONVENS 2024), pages 264–280, Vienna, Austria. Association for Computational Linguistics.

Burak Can Kaplan, Hugo Cesar De Castro Carneiro, and Stefan Wermter. 2025. Can large language models generate effective datasets for emotion recognition in conversations? *ArXiv*.

Varun Kumar, Ashutosh Choudhary, and Eunah Cho. 2020. Data augmentation using pre-trained transformer models. In *Proceedings of the 2nd Workshop on Life-long Learning for Spoken Language Systems*, pages 18–26, Suzhou, China. Association for Computational Linguistics.

Subrat Kumar Nayak, Ajit Kumar Nayak, Smitaprava Mishra, and Prithviraj Mohanty. 2023. Deep learning approaches for speech command recognition in a low resource kui language. *International Journal of Intelligent Systems and Applications in Engineering*, 11(2):377–386.

Xiang Lorraine Li, Adhiguna Kuncoro, Jordan Hoffmann, Cyprien de Masson d'Autume, Phil Blunsom, and Aida Nematzadeh. 2022. A systematic investigation of commonsense knowledge in large language models. In *Proceedings of the 2022 Conference on Empirical Methods in Natural Language Processing*, pages 11838–11855, Abu Dhabi, United Arab Emirates. Association for Computational Linguistics.

Laureano Moro-Velazquez, Jaejin Cho, Shinji Watanabe, Mark A. Hasegawa-Johnson, Odette Scharenborg, Heejin Kim, and Najim Dehak. 2019. Study of the performance of automatic speech recognition systems in speakers with parkinson's disease. In *Proceedings of INTERSPEECH 2019*, pages 3875–3879, Graz, Austria. ISCA.

Mikel K. Ngueajio and Gloria Washington. 2022. Hey ASR system! why aren't you more inclusive? automatic speech recognition systems' bias and proposed bias mitigation techniques. a literature review. In *Proceedings of 24th International Conference on Human-Computer Interaction (HCI 2022)*, page 421–440. Springer-Verlag.

Akhil Padmanabha, Jessie Yuan, Janavi Gupta, Zulekha Karachiwalla, Carmel Majidi, Henny Admoni, and Zackory Erickson. 2024. Voicepilot: Harnessing LLMs as speech interfaces for physically assistive robots. *arXiv*.

Theresa Pekarek Rosin, Vanessa Hassouna, Xiaowen Sun, Luca Krohm, Henri-Leon Kordt, Michael Beetz, and Stefan Wermter. 2025. A framework for adapting human-robot interaction to diverse user groups. In *Social Robotics*, pages 24–38, Singapore. Springer Nature Singapore.

Theresa Pekarek Rosin and Stefan Wermter. 2023. Replay to remember: Continual layer-specific fine-tuning for german speech recognition. In *Artificial Neural Networks and Machine Learning–ICANN 2023*, pages 489–500.

Alec Radford, Jong Wook Kim, Tao Xu, Greg Brockman, Christine McLeavey, and Ilya Sutskever. 2023. Robust speech recognition via large-scale weak supervision. In *Proceedings of the 40th International Conference on Machine Learning*, ICML'23. JMLR.org.

David Rolnick, Arun Ahuja, Jonathan Schwarz, Timothy Lillicrap, and Gregory Wayne. 2019. Experience replay for continual learning. In *Proceedings of the 33rd International Conference on Neural Information Processing Systems (NeurIPS)*, pages 348–358, Vancouver, BC, Canada. Curran Associates, Inc.

Erik Sadovsky, Maros Jakubec, and Roman Jarina. 2023. Speech command recognition based on convolutional spiking neural networks. In *Proceedings of the 33rd International Conference Radioelektronika (RADIOELEKTRONIKA)*, pages 1–5.

Victor Sanh, Lysandre Debut, Julien Chaumond, and Thomas Wolf. 2019. DistilBERT, a distilled version of BERT: smaller, faster, cheaper and lighter. In *5th Workshop on Energy Efficient Machine Learning and Cognitive Computing (EMC^2) - NeurIPS 2019*.

Joel Shor, Dotan Emanuel, Oran Lang, Omry Tuval, Michael Brenner, Julie Cattiau, Fernando Vieira, Maeve McNally, Taylor Charbonneau, Melissa Nollstadt, Avinatan Hassidim, and Yossi Matias. 2019. Personalizing ASR for dysarthric and accented speech with limited data. In *Proceedings of INTERSPEECH 2019*, pages 784–788, Graz, Austria. ISCA.

Martin Volk, Dominic P. Fischer, Patricia Scheurer, Raphael Schwitter, and Phillip B. Ströbel. 2024. LLM-based translation across 500 years. the case for early New High German. In *Proceedings of the 20th Conference on Natural Language Processing (KONVENS 2024)*, pages 368–375, Vienna, Austria. Association for Computational Linguistics.

Dominik Wagner, Alexander Churchill, Siddharth Sigtia, Panayiotis Georgiou, Matt Mirsamadi, Aarshee Mishra, and Erik Marchi. 2024. A multimodal approach to device-directed speech detection with large language models. In *Proceedings of 2024 IEEE International Conference on Acoustics, Speech and Signal Processing (ICASSP)*, pages 10451–10455.

Pei Wang, Keqing He, Yejie Wang, Xiaoshuai Song, Yutao Mou, Jingang Wang, Yunsen Xian, Xunliang Cai, and Weiran Xu. 2024. Beyond the known: Investigating LLMs performance on out-of-domain intent detection. *arXiv*.

P. Warden. 2018. Speech commands: A dataset for limited-vocabulary speech recognition. *ArXiv*.

A Prompts

Label	Prompt
help	Generieren Sie 10 verschiedene Sprachbefehle, mit denen ein älterer Mensch seinen KI-Assistenten in gefährlichen Situationen um Hilfe bitten kann, ohne jedes Mal explizit um Hilfe zu bitten. Verwenden Sie verschiedene Sätze und unterschiedliche Gesundheitssituationen. Sie müssen vor jeder Äußerung die Anweisung 'Ältere_Person:' als Sprechername einfügen und 'NÄCHSTES' am Ende jeder Äußerung, um das Ende der Äußerung zu kennzeichnen. Geben Sie die angeforderten Sätze genau in der beschriebenen Struktur aus, geben Sie nichts anderes aus.
	Generieren Sie 10 verschiedene sehr kurze Sprachbefehle, mit denen eine ältere Person ihren KI-Assistenten in gefährlichen Situationen um Hilfe bitten kann, ohne jedes Mal explizit um Hilfe zu bitten. Verwenden Sie verschiedene, kurze Sätze, die aus ein bis zwei Wörtern bestehen und verschiedene Gesundheitssituationen beschreiben. Fügen Sie vor jeder Äußerung die Anweisung 'Ältere_Person:' als Sprechername ein und am Ende jeder Äußerung 'NÄCHSTES', um das Ende der Äußerung zu markieren. Geben Sie die geforderten Sätze genau in der beschriebenen Struktur aus, geben Sie nichts anderes aus.
roll	Generieren Sie 10 verschiedene Sprachbefehle für eine ältere Person, die ihren KI-Assistenten bittet, die Rollläden hochzufahren. Verwenden Sie verschiedene Sätze und unterschiedliche Ausdrücke. Sie müssen vor jeder Äußerung die Anweisung 'Ältere_Person:' als Sprechername einfügen und 'NÄCHSTES' am Ende jeder Äußerung, um das Ende der Äußerung zu kennzeichnen. Geben Sie die angeforderten Sätze genau in der beschriebenen Struktur aus, geben Sie nichts anderes aus.
	Generieren Sie 10 verschiedene Sprachbefehle für eine ältere Person, die ihren KI-Assistenten bittet, die Rollläden herunterzufahren. Verwenden Sie verschiedene Sätze und unterschiedliche Ausdrücke. Sie müssen vor jeder Äußerung die Anweisung 'Ältere_Person:' als Sprechername einfügen und 'NÄCHSTES' am Ende jeder Äußerung, um das Ende der Äußerung zu kennzeichnen. Geben Sie die angeforderten Sätze genau in der beschriebenen Struktur aus, geben Sie nichts anderes aus.
lights	Generieren Sie 10 verschiedene Sprachbefehle für eine ältere Person, die ihren KI-Assistenten bittet, das Licht einzuschalten. Verwenden Sie verschiedene Sätze und unterschiedliche Ausdrücke. Sie müssen vor jeder Äußerung die Anweisung 'Ältere_Person:' als Sprechername einfügen und 'NÄCHSTES' am Ende jeder Äußerung, um das Ende der Äußerung zu kennzeichnen. Geben Sie die angeforderten Sätze genau in der beschriebenen Struktur aus, geben Sie nichts anderes aus.
	Generieren Sie 10 verschiedene Sprachbefehle für eine ältere Person, die ihren KI-Assistenten bittet, das Licht auszuschalten. Verwenden Sie verschiedene Sätze und unterschiedliche Ausdrücke. Sie müssen vor jeder Äußerung die Anweisung 'Ältere_Person:' als Sprechername einfügen und 'NÄCHSTES' am Ende jeder Äußerung, um das Ende der Äußerung zu kennzeichnen. Geben Sie die angeforderten Sätze genau in der beschriebenen Struktur aus, geben Sie nichts anderes aus.
no_command	Generieren Sie 10 Sätze von einer älteren Person, die von einer Spracherkennung fälschlicherweise als 'Bitte um Hilfe' klassifiziert werden können, aber in Wirklichkeit als 'kein Befehl' für einen KI-Assistenten verwendet werden. Der Assistent benutzt dafür eine Keyword Detection. Verwenden Sie verschiedene Sätze und verschiedene Ausdrücke. Sie müssen vor jeder Äußerung als Sprechernamen die Anweisung 'Ältere_Person:' und am Ende jeder Äußerung 'NÄCHSTES' einfügen, um das Ende der Äußerung anzuzeigen. Ein paar Beispiele: Ältere_Person: Kannst du mir bitte helfen, mein Handy zu finden? NÄCHSTES Ältere_Person: Mein Sohn hat mir gestern mit dem Garten geholfen. NÄCHSTES Ältere_Person: Manchmal muss ich um Hilfe bitten. NÄCHSTES Ältere_Person: Diese neuen Geräte sind ohne Hilfe gar nicht zu bedienen. NÄCHSTES Ältere_Person: Früher konnte ich alles alleine, ohne um Hilfe zu bitten. NÄCHSTES
	Generieren Sie 10 Sätze von einer älteren Person, die von einer Spracherkennung fälschlicherweise als 'Rollläden hoch- oder runterfahren' klassifiziert werden können, aber in Wirklichkeit als 'kein Befehl' für einen KI-Assistenten verwendet werden. Der Assistent benutzt dafür eine Keyword Detection. Verwenden Sie verschiedene Sätze und verschiedene Ausdrücke. Sie müssen vor jeder Äußerung als Sprechernamen die Anweisung 'Ältere_Person:' und am Ende jeder Äußerung 'NÄCHSTES' einfügen, um das Ende der Äußerung anzuzeigen. Ein paar Beispiele: Ältere_Person: Mein Assistent fährt die Rollläden jeden Abend pünktlich um 18:00 herunter. NÄCHSTES Ältere_Person: Im Sommer habe ich die Jalousien gerne den ganzen Tag unten. NÄCHSTES Ältere_Person: Es ist sehr praktisch, dass mein Sprachassistent die Rollläden steuern kann. NÄCHSTES Ältere_Person: Meine Rollläden sind beim letzten Sturm kaputtgegangen. NÄCHSTES Ältere_Person: Sobald meine Jalousien oben sind, kann ich meinen Tag beginnen. NÄCHSTES
	Generieren Sie 10 Sätze von einer älteren Person, die von einer Spracherkennung fälschlicherweise als 'Licht ein- oder ausschalten' klassifiziert werden können, aber in Wirklichkeit als 'kein Befehl' für einen KI-Assistenten verwendet werden. Der Assistent benutzt dafür eine Keyword Detection. Verwenden Sie verschiedene Sätze und verschiedene Ausdrücke. Sie müssen vor jeder Äußerung als Sprechernamen die Anweisung 'Ältere_Person:' und am Ende jeder Äußerung 'NÄCHSTES' einfügen, um das Ende der Äußerung anzuzeigen. Ein paar Beispiele: Ältere_Person: Mein Assistent schaltet mir jeden morgen die Lichter an. NÄCHSTES Ältere_Person: Gestern hatten wir schon sehr früh kein Licht mehr im Raum. NÄCHSTES Ältere_Person: Die Tatsache, dass mein Sprachassistent das Licht an- und ausschalten kann ist sehr praktisch. NÄCHSTES Ältere_Person: Da ist mir ein Licht aufgegangen. NÄCHSTES Ältere_Person: Manchmal ist es hier ziemlich dunkel ohne Licht. NÄCHSTES

Table 5: All the prompts used for the different classes in the datasets.

Detecting Sexism and Its Severity in German Online Comments: Modeling Annotation Subjectivity with BERT and mBERT

Melanie Woodrow and Margot Mieskes
University of Applied Sciences, Darmstadt, Germany
melanie.woodrow@stud.h-da.de
margot.mieskes@h-da.de

Abstract

This study is based on the GermEval 2024 GerMS-Detect Shared Task[1], which collected user comments from an Austrian news platform and manually annotated them to reflect the presence and intensity of sexism. Its aim is to improve the detection of misogyny and sexism in German-speaking online forums. To address this task, we employed multiple classification strategies, including majority voting, the presence of annotator disagreement, and predicting the most frequent label. We fine-tuned BERT and its multilingual variant, mBERT, on the annotated dataset and evaluated their performance using precision, recall, and F1-score. In addition, we explored label distribution prediction to model annotator disagreement, using metrics such as Mean Squared Error, Kullback-Leibler divergence, and Jensen-Shannon divergence. This paper discusses challenges such as class imbalance and overfitting. Despite these, our results show that mBERT slightly outperforms BERT in binary classification tasks, though it faces difficulties with more complex distributional predictions. The findings highlight both the potential and limitations of pre-trained language models for detecting sexism in online discourse.

Content Warning: This paper includes examples of harmful and offensive language that do not reflect our opinions in any way.

1 Introduction

Sexist statements are found both in real life (Pingree et al., 1976) and in online environments (Plakoyiannaki et al., 2008). The European Institute for Gender Equality[2] defines sexism as a "hierarchical [way of thinking] that can be conscious and hostile, or it can be unconscious, manifesting itself as unconscious bias. Sexism can touch everyone, but women are particularly affected". The anonymity afforded by online platforms such as forums often facilitates and amplifies sexist behavior (Fox et al., 2015), leading to consequences that extend beyond the digital space (Skinner, 2022).

As the prevalence of online communication increases, so does the spread of discriminatory content. Identifying and moderating such content is critical to fostering respectful digital interactions. However, research shows that even recent large language models exhibit gender bias and are not reliably equipped to detect sexism (Mehrabi et al., 2021; Sheng et al., 2019). This emphasizes the need for dedicated models and datasets tailored for sexism detection.

In our work, we investigate the prediction of sexist content and its severity in German comments from an Austrian online news portal. We base our work on the GermEval 2024 GerMS-Detect Shared Task[3], provided by the Austrian Research Institute for Artificial Intelligence (OFAI), which includes two classification subtasks and an annotated dataset (GERMS-AT) (Krenn et al., 2024). The main goal of the annotations was to identify comments that make it difficult for women to participate in forum discussions and thus feel unwelcome.

We fine-tune the pre-trained BERT (Devlin et al., 2019) and mBERT models, which have not been explicitly fine-tuned for detecting sexism, on a set of binary, multi-class, and distributional classification tasks. To achieve this, we define multiple labeling strategies, such as majority voting, annotator disagreement, and distribution-based supervision. These strategies are detailed in Section 3 and reflect different ways to interpret subjective annotations. The trained models are evaluated on a test set without ground-truth labels, and results are reported us-

[1] https://ofai.github.io/GermEval2024-GerMS/
[2] https://eige.europa.eu/publications-resources/toolkits-guides/sexism-at-work-handbook/part-1-understand/what-sexism?language_content_entity=en
[3] https://ofai.github.io/GermEval2024-GerMS/

Proceedings of the 21st Conference on Natural Language Processing (KONVENS), Volume 1: Long and Short Papers, pages 360–370, 2025

ing a range of classification and divergence-based metrics.

In addition, the distribution of labels should be predicted in order to reflect the diversity of opinions among the annotators. This study highlights the strengths and weaknesses of pre-trained language models in dealing with subjective and culturally nuanced social issues such as sexism.

The main contributions of this work are:

- We explore a variety of labeling strategies that capture different levels of subjectivity and disagreement in human annotations.
- We fine-tune and evaluate BERT and mBERT for both classification and label distribution prediction on German comments.
- We compare the performance of binary, ordinal, and distributional prediction tasks and analyze the impact of model choice and task complexity.
- We highlight the potential and limitations of pre-trained transformer models for detecting sexism and subjective language in online discourse.

The remainder of this paper is structured as follows: Section 2 presents relevant related work on sexism detection and subjective annotation strategies. Section 3 describes the dataset, labeling strategies, and model setup. In Section 4, we report experimental results across the multiple subtasks and strategies. Section 5 discusses the findings in the context of subjectivity and model performance, followed by Section 6 which concludes the paper and outlines directions for future research. Finally, we also outline the limitations and ethical considerations of this work at the very end of the paper.

2 Related Work

Early approaches to text classification relied on manual features such as bag-of-words, TF-IDF, and n-grams, and commonly used algorithms like Support Vector Machines, Decision Trees, or k-Nearest Neighbors (Joachims, 1998). While effective to a degree, these methods often struggle to capture contextual or implicit meaning in language. With the rise of transformer-based models such as BERT (Devlin et al., 2019), classification performance significantly improved across various NLP tasks. The following presented works highlight the success of using BERT and its variants for classifying different types of hate speech.

Das et al. (2023) demonstrated the effectiveness of fine-tuning RoBERTa for explainable sexism detection across multiple subtasks, including binary and fine-grained classification, as part of the SemEval-2023 EDOS task. Furthermore, Belbachir et al. (2024) explored integrating sentiment analysis with transformer models such as RoBERTa and LSTM for the SemEval-2023 Task, achieving higher F1-scores in sexism classification compared to other tested models. Additionally, Saleh et al. (2023) evaluated the performance of BERT against domain-specific embeddings for hate speech detection, further confirming BERT's effectiveness for binary classification in socially sensitive domains such as social media.

Sexism detection is inherently subjective, and different annotators may interpret content in varying ways (Almanea and Poesio, 2022). Several studies have therefore explored how to model disagreement and perspective in annotations (Almanea and Poesio, 2022; Akhtar et al., 2020). Label aggregation strategies, such as majority vote, union, or distribution modeling, are commonly used to approximate ground truth. Jiang et al. (2024) investigated how annotator attitudes influence automated classification of sexist content and showed that incorporating annotator metadata can improve the performance of large language models on Gender-Based Violence (GBV) related tasks.

Furthermore, sexism detection presents challenges distinct from general hate speech detection, as previous work shows higher false positive rates and less consistent performance when models are trained on counterfactual augmented data (Sen et al., 2022). Sexist language often manifests implicitly, through sarcasm or cultural slang, making it difficult for models to detect without contextual understanding and further complication classification (Belbachir et al., 2024).

These challenges highlight the need for models and evaluation frameworks that account for ambiguity, subjectivity, and disagreement, factors which are especially critical in the detection of nuanced social biases such as sexism.

3 Methods and Data

The following sections describe the dataset and annotation framework used in this study, along with the labeling strategies applied for both classification and distributional modeling (Section 3.1). In Section 3.2 we then describe the pre-processing steps and model architectures (Section 3.3) used for fine-tuning BERT and mBERT, followed by our training setup, hyperparameter choices, and methods for addressing class imbalance (Section 3.4). Finally, in Section 3.5, we explain the evaluation metrics used to assess model performance across both subtasks.

3.1 Dataset and Labeling Strategies

As mentioned in Section 1, this work is based on the dataset and task definitions provided for the GermEval 2024 GerMS-Detect Shared Task (Krenn et al., 2024), which focuses on detecting sexism in user-generated comments from an Austrian online news portal. Each comment was annotated by up to ten annotators with an average of five, who assigned a label on a scale ranging from 0 ("no sexism") to 4 ("extreme sexism"). The training dataset contains approximately 4,500 comments and includes the annotations, specifically the labels given by annotators. The dataset also includes a unique ID for each comment and each annotator involved in the labeling process.

Due to the subjective nature of the task, no single "ground truth" label is provided. Instead, the dataset supports multiple labeling strategies derived from the annotation distributions.[4] We use the following five strategies:

bin_one : Label is 1 if at least one annotator selected a value greater than 0.
bin_all : Label is 1 only if all annotators assigned a value greater than 0.
bin_maj : Label is 1 if the majority of annotators selected any value above 0; 0 if the majority selected 0.
disagree_bin : Label is 1 if annotators disagreed on whether the comment was sexist (i.e., mix of 0 and >0).
multi_maj : Predict the majority label among the five ordinal values. In case of ties, any of the tied labels is considered correct.

The use of multiple labeling strategies enables a deeper understanding of how models handle different types of subjectivity in sexist content detection.

Strategies such as `bin_one`, which labels a comment as sexist if any annotator perceives it as such, are highly sensitive but may increase false positives. Conversely, `bin_all` demands full agreement among annotators, resulting in a stricter but potentially more conservative model.

Majority-based strategies like `bin_maj` aim to balance sensitivity and precision by reflecting the predominant perception. The `disagree_bin` strategy explicitly models cases of annotator disagreement, capturing instances where the presence of sexism is ambiguous or culturally interpreted differently.

Finally, `multi_maj` preserves ordinal information about the severity of sexism but poses challenges due to class imbalance and the subtle gradations between label values.

Our results show that models trained with looser strategies (e.g., `bin_one`) generally achieve higher recall, whereas stricter or distributional strategies (e.g., `multi_maj`) are more difficult for the models to optimize (see Table 3 and Table 4).

In addition to these single-label tasks, the shared task includes a second subtask: predicting the full distribution of labels assigned by annotators. Instead of training the model to predict a single "correct" label, this approach requires the model to output a probability distribution that matches the normalized annotation frequencies for each comment. This subtask captures the nuances and subjectivity of annotator perspectives more accurately. This approach better reflects the inherent subjectivity of sexism detection. We consider two distributional strategies: `dist_bin` collapses the ordinal annotations into a binary distribution (sexist vs. non-sexist), simplifying the task and reducing sparsity. In contrast, `dist_multi` preserves the full five-point ordinal scale, allowing the model to learn finer distinctions in perceived severity. We implement two strategies for this subtask:

dist_bin : Predict the normalized binary distribution by collapsing all values >0 into class 1. For example, [0, 0, 1, 1, 1] becomes [0.4, 0.6].
dist_multi : Predict the full five-class ordinal distribution, preserving all individual annotations.

The GERMS-AT training dataset consists of 4,486 user-generated comments from an Austrian online news platform. Each comment is annotated by an average of five annotators, with an average comment length of 33 tokens. Most comments are relatively short and show typical signs of informal forum communication.

[4]For details on the annotation see `https://ofai.github.io/GermEval2024-GerMS/guidelines.html`

Examples 1–3

Example 1
Comment: "Was soll das depperte Sternderl? *?"
Translation: "What's with the dumb little star? *?"
Explanation: The asterisk (*) is often used in German to signal gender inclusivity (e.g., "Leser*innen" for "readers of all genders"). The comment expresses ridicule toward this usage.
Label distribution: 0: 4, 1: 3, 2: 3, 3: 0, 4: 0
Derived labels: `bin_maj = 1`, `bin_one = 1`, `bin_all = 0`, `disagree_bin = 1`, `multi_maj = 0`

Example 2
Comment: "Im Chaos zuzeln sie heimlich den Staat aus..."
Translation: "In the chaos, they're secretly sucking the state dry..."
Explanation: "Turquoise" refers to the Austrian People's Party (VP), implying political critique rather than sexist content.
Label distribution: 0: 5, 1–4: 0
Derived labels: `bin_maj = 0`, `bin_one = 0`, `bin_all = 0`, `disagree_bin = 0`, `multi_maj = 0`

Example 3
Comment: "Mit der Fotze hat er sich keinen Gefallen getan..."
Translation: "He did himself no favor with that cunt..."
Explanation: The comment uses a strongly offensive gendered slur, contributing to its classification as severe sexism.
Label distribution: 0: 0, 1: 0, 2: 2, 3: 3, 4: 6
Derived labels: `bin_maj = 1`, `bin_one = 1`, `bin_all = 1`, `disagree_bin = 0`, `multi_maj = 4`

Figure 1: Illustrative examples (1–3) showing comment content, interpretation, and derived labels.

Statistic	Value
Total comments	4,486
Average comment length	33.0 tokens
Longest comment	366 tokens
Average annotations per comment	5.0

Table 1: Statistics of the GERMS-AT training dataset.

Statistic	Value
Total comments	1,512
Average comment length	32.51
Longest comment	146 tokens

Table 2: Statistics of the GERMS-AT test dataset.

In addition to the training data, the test set contains a total of 1,512 comments. The average token length per comment is similar to the training set at approximately 32.5 tokens. However, the longest comment in the test set is notably shorter, with a maximum of 146 tokens compared to 366 in the training data.

The examples in Figure 1 illustrate how different annotation strategies affect the interpretation of sexist content. These comments were taken from the provided training data set. A rough English translation and explanation (where appropriate) are provided for each example.[5]

3.2 Pre-processing and Tokenization

Minimal pre-processing is applied to preserve the original structure and expressions in the comments,

[5]All comment translations were produced by the authors for the benefit of non-German-speaking readers. The views expressed in the comments are those of the comment authors and do not reflect the views of the authors of this paper.

including colloquial language and informal punctuation. All text is lowercased and tokenization is performed using the standard BERT WordPiece tokenizer from the Hugging Face Transformers library (Wolf et al., 2020)[6]. Stopword removal or stemming is not used, based on previous findings that such steps may harm performance in contextual models (Alzahrani and Jololian, 2021).

To determine an appropriate maximum sequence length for input truncation, we analyzed the token length distribution of all comments in the training data. As shown in Figure 2, most comments are relatively short, with the majority containing fewer than 100 tokens. However, some comments are significantly longer. To preserve as much information as possible while avoiding excessive padding and memory usage, we set the maximum token length to 276, which covers about 99% of all comments in the training dataset.

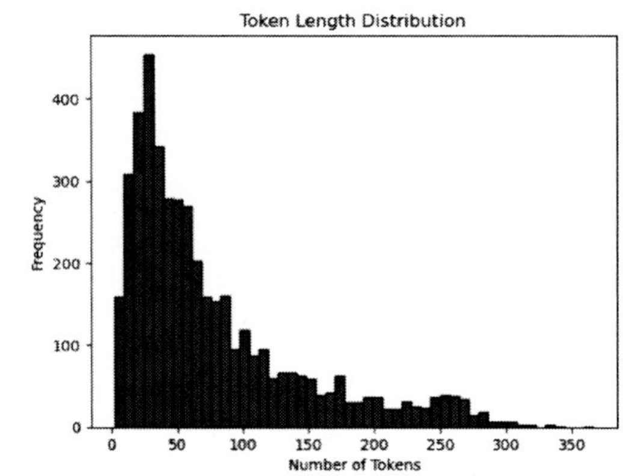

Figure 2: Distribution of comment lengths measured in BERT WordPiece tokens.

3.3 Model Architectures and Training

Although the dataset consists of German texts, `bert-base-uncased` was included as a baseline because uncased models can be more robust to inconsistent capitalization, which frequently occurs in user-generated content such as online comments. This helps mitigate noise from typos, informal writing, or inconsistent use of uppercase letters. Conversely, `bert-base-multilingual-cased` was chosen to preserve capitalization information in the multilingual setting, as German capitalization (especially for nouns) can carry important syntactic and semantic cues. This combination allows us to investigate whether retaining case information in multilingual training benefits performance compared to an uncased approach. For each classification task, a task-specific linear head is added to the [CLS] token output, followed by a softmax activation in the binary and multi-class cases.

For the distribution prediction task (Subtask 2), the model also outputs a five-class softmax probability distribution. This is compared to the gold label distribution using Kullback-Leibler (KL) divergence. This design allows the model to learn both the primary perception of sexism and the uncertainty or disagreement present in the annotations.

We decided to train using 5-fold stratified cross-validation. In each fold, 80% of the data is used for training and 20% for validation. The final evaluation is performed on a test set. All models are trained using the AdamW optimizer[7] with a linear learning rate schedule and warm-up steps.

3.4 Hyperparameters and Class Imbalance

We perform initial hyperparameter tuning using a validation split from one fold and keep the settings consistent across tasks to ensure comparability. We set the learning rate to $2e^{-5}$, batch size to 16, and use early stopping based on validation loss. Dropout is applied with a rate of 0.3.

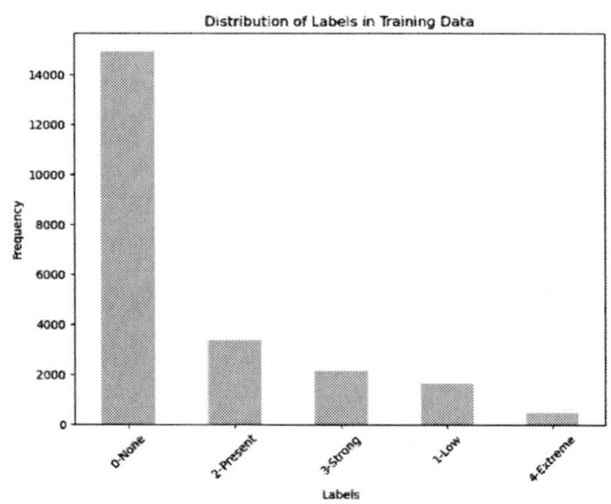

Figure 3: Distribution of the labels in the training dataset.

Some of the binary classification strategies (especially `bin_maj` and `bin_all`) exhibit class imbalance. Figure 3 shows the extent of the label distribution imbalance in the training data set which ultimately accounts for the class imbalance. This

[6] https://huggingface.co/docs/transformers/en/model_doc/bert

[7] https://pytorch.org/docs/stable/generated/torch.optim.AdamW.html

imbalance poses challenges for model training, particularly in the multi-class and distribution prediction tasks, where rarer categories may be underrepresented during learning. For this reason, we apply class weighting in the loss function or oversample the minority class during training. In the case of `multi_maj`, where the class distribution is skewed toward label 0, oversampling of rare labels is applied to each training fold individually.

In Subtask 2, distributional diversity is also limited by the frequency of certain label combinations. To address this, we increase the sampling rate for comments with rare or highly varied annotation patterns, improving the model's ability to generalize across different types of subjectivity.

3.5 Evaluation Metrics

Binary and multi-class tasks are evaluated using precision, recall, and macro-averaged F1-score. For the distributional prediction task, we compute the Kullback-Leibler divergence, Jensen-Shannon divergence and Mean-Squared-Error between the predicted and true annotation distributions. In the case of `multi_maj`, evaluation accounts for ties by treating any of the tied majority labels as correct.

4 Experiments and Results

We conducted experiments using the GERMS-AT dataset to evaluate the performance of BERT and mBERT on two of the subtasks introduced in Section 3.1: binary/multi-class classification and label distribution prediction. Hyperparameters were kept consistent for each subtask, as described in Section 3.3.

For the first subtask, we evaluated the models across five different labeling strategies: `bin_one`, `bin_all`, `bin_maj`, `disagree_bin`, and `multi_maj`. The models were assessed using precision, recall, and F1-score.

Strategy	Precision	Recall	F1-Score
bin_one	0.71	0.71	0.71
bin_all	0.74	0.83	0.77
bin_maj	0.69	0.67	0.67
disagree_bin	0.64	0.61	0.62
multi_maj	0.59	0.59	0.58

Table 3: Evaluation results for BERT (Subtask 1)

Overall, mBERT slightly outperforms BERT in binary classification tasks, particularly for `bin_one` and `bin_maj`. However, BERT achieves higher F1-scores in more complex multi-class tasks like `multi_maj`. Confusion matrices for all strategies of Subtask 1 can be found in Section A of the Appendix.

Strategy	Precision	Recall	F1-Score
bin_one	0.74	0.74	0.74
bin_all	0.77	0.67	0.71
bin_maj	0.74	0.73	0.73
disagree_bin	0.64	0.64	0.64
multi_maj	0.67	0.45	0.52

Table 4: Evaluation results for mBERT (Subtask 1)

In the second subtask, the goal was to predict the full label distribution of annotations using `dist_bin` and `dist_multi`. Table 5 presents the results using Mean Squared Error (MSE), Kullback-Leibler (KL) divergence, and Jensen-Shannon divergence (JSD).

Model	Type	MSE	KL	JSD
BERT	dist_bin	0.14	0.4	0.11
BERT	dist_multi	0.05	0.59	0.15
mBERT	dist_bin	0.12	0.36	0.09
mBERT	dist_multi	0.04	0.56	0.14

Table 5: Evaluation results for distribution prediction (Subtask 2)

It is important to note that Subtask 1 and Subtask 2 use different evaluation paradigms: while higher values of F1-score and accuracy in Subtask 1 reflect better performance, Subtask 2 employs distance- and divergence-based metrics (KL, JSD, MSE), where lower values correspond to better alignment between predicted and true distributions. The results indicate that mBERT consistently achieves lower error and divergence values across both distribution types. While the improvements over BERT are modest, they suggest mBERT is better suited to capture the subtle differences in perceived sexism among annotators. Modeling full distributions (`dist_multi`) is more challenging due to increased label complexity and class imbalance, but it offers a richer representation of annotator disagreement. Our results confirm that predicting multi-class distributions yields higher divergence values than binary ones, indicating greater difficulty for the models.

Despite these challenges, distribution prediction provides a valuable framework for capturing uncertainty and subjective variance in socially sensitive classification tasks.

5 Discussion

The experimental results demonstrate that both BERT and mBERT can be effectively fine-tuned to detect sexist content in German-language online comments. mBERT generally achieves slightly higher performance in binary classification tasks, particularly under strategies like `bin_one` and `bin_maj`, which focus on detecting the presence of any sexist expression. However, when faced with more complex tasks such as predicting label distributions or modeling fine-grained severity (`multi_maj`), BERT shows more stable and balanced performance.

The difficulty of the distribution prediction task is reflected in higher divergence scores for both models, especially for `dist_multi`. This suggests that capturing nuanced, subjective differences between annotators remains a substantial challenge for current pre-trained models. Our findings support previous observations in the literature that socially sensitive language tasks, particularly those involving subjective judgments, are inherently harder to model.

Moreover, the choice of labeling strategy has a notable impact on model behavior. Strategies prioritizing sensitivity (`bin_one`) lead to higher recall but lower precision, while more conservative strategies (`bin_all`) yield the opposite trend. This trade-off is important when considering real-world applications: systems prioritizing inclusivity might prefer high-recall models, while moderation systems aiming to minimize false positives might favor high-precision models.

Although mBERT performs slightly better in general, the differences are not dramatic. Expanding the dataset, incorporating additional contextual features (e.g., thread structure or user metadata), or using newer architectures like RoBERTa could further improve performance.

To better illustrate the model behavior and the role of annotation subjectivity, we selected three representative examples from the test dataset and their respective true labels from the targets dataset for the `bin_maj` strategy.

For the example in Figure 4 the model correctly identifies the absence of sexism, aligning it with the majority annotation. Figure 5 shows a false positive. The sarcastic tone may have led the model to misclassify the comment, despite the absence of explicitly sexist content. The statement shown in Figure 6 contains a gender-related stereotype but may not be universally interpreted as sexist. The disagreement among annotators illustrates the subjectivity of labeling and highlights the potential value of modeling label distributions instead of relying solely on single-label predictions.

Successful Prediction

Kämpferischer ... das heisst erzwingen ...
Das bedeutet, ihr wollt Leute zwingen euch ein sorgenfreies Leben zu finanzieren.
Alles klar ...

(Translation: Militant... that means to force...
That means you want to force people to finance you a carefree life.
All right then...)

Prediction: 0 **True Label:** 0

Figure 4: Example of a successful prediction

Failed Prediction

Wieso "nett"? Ist Dummheit ident mit "nett"?

(Translation: Why "nice"? Is stupidity identical with "nice"?)

Prediction: 1 **True Label:** 0

Figure 5: Example of a failed prediction (false positive).

Ambiguous Case

Das sind Schätzungen, denn Männer sind ja zu feig, sowas anzuzeigen, nicht wahr?

(Translation: Those are just estimates, because men are too cowardly to report things like that, right?)

Prediction: 0 **True Label:** 1

Figure 6: Example of an ambiguous case with subjective interpretation.

The statement shown in Figure 6 contains a gender-related stereotype but may not be universally interpreted as sexist. The disagreement among annotators illustrates the subjectivity of labeling and highlights the potential value of modeling label distributions instead of relying solely on single-label predictions.

To contextualize our results, we compare them to the scores reported by teams participating in the GermEval 2024 GerMS-Detect Shared Task[8]. Table 6 lists the average F1-scores and Jensen-Shannon divergences (JSD) of all teams who submitted a paper, along with our average scores which represent the average performance across all evaluated labeling strategies and both model variants (BERT and mBERT).

Team	F1-Score	JSD
THAugs	0.642	–
FICODE	0.641	0.354
Quabynar	0.611	0.292
GDA	0.597	0.301
pd2904	0.483	0.388
Ours	**0.669**	**0.123**

Table 6: Comparison with submitted systems from the GermEval 2024 GerMS-Detect Shared Task. Our models outperform all other teams in both classification and distribution tasks.

Our models achieved an F1-score of 0.669 and a JSD of 0.123, outperforming all teams that submitted a publication. While several teams explored advanced architectures and ensembles, such as training a separate model on each annotator, our results show that precise fine-tuning can yield strong performance using standard BERT-based models.

While our model achieved higher F1-scores and lower divergence values than all teams who submitted their publication, these comparisons are based on single evaluations on the test set.

6 Conclusion

In this paper, we investigated the detection of sexist content in German-language online comments using pre-trained transformer models. Based on the GermEval 2024 GerMS-Detect Shared Task, we explored various labeling strategies to account for the subjectivity of human annotations and fine-tuned BERT and mBERT for both classification and distributional prediction tasks.

Our results show that mBERT slightly outperforms the original BERT model in binary classification tasks, while BERT demonstrates more stable performance in distribution tasks. Additionally, we found that modeling annotation disagreement explicitly, using both binary and full distribution predictions, allows models to better capture the nuances of perceived sexism.

These findings highlight both the potential and limitations of using large language models for socially sensitive tasks. Future work could explore the use of more advanced transformer architectures, interpretability methods to explain predictions, or active learning strategies to better deal with subjective annotations.

Limitations

While our findings show that pre-trained language models such as BERT and mBERT can be fine-tuned to detect sexist content in online comments, this study has several limitations.

First, the dataset used is relatively small compared to other large-scale NLP benchmarks such as GLUE (Wang et al., 2018) or XNLI (Conneau et al., 2018). Although we used cross-validation and oversampling to improve robustness, the limited size and source diversity of the data may affect generalizability to other platforms, languages, or domains.

Second, the annotation process is inherently subjective. Although we modeled disagreement and used distributional labels, the presence of annotator bias or cultural interpretation of sexism may still affect the quality of the labels.

Third, we fine-tuned existing models without applying extensive hyperparameter optimization or exploring more recent architectures such as RoBERTa or DeBERTa. More advanced models or training strategies might improve performance, especially in the distributional prediction task.

Finally, our approach is not immediately interpretable. Understanding why a comment was classified as sexist or how the model interprets annotator disagreement remains an open question, which is especially relevant for sensitive applications like moderation. For this purpose, a label for the type of sexist content is required.

[8]Results are published in the proceedings section at `https://ofai.github.io/GermEval2024-GerMS/workshop`

Ethics Statement

This paper addresses the detection of sexism in online comments, a task that involves sensitive and subjective social judgments. We recognize that both the annotations and the model predictions reflect human interpretations of what constitutes sexist language, which may vary across cultures, identities, and personal experiences. To account for this, we explicitly model annotator disagreement and examine multiple labeling strategies, including distributional predictions.

The dataset used in this study and its annotations were provided as part of the GermEval 2024 Shared Task, which we used as is.

Our models are trained and evaluated for research purposes and are not intended for immediate deployment in real-world moderation systems without further validation. While we aim to contribute toward safer and more inclusive online environments, we also advise against the blind application of such models, especially without considering fairness, interpretability, and the potential for unintended consequences in automated content moderation.

References

S. Akhtar, V. Basile, and V. Patti. 2020. Modeling annotator perspective and polarized opinions to improve hate speech detection. In *In Proceedings of the AAAI conference on human computation and crowdsourcing*, pages 151–154.

D. Almanea and M. Poesio. 2022. Armis-the arabic misogyny and sexism corpus with annotator subjective disagreements. *In Proceedings of the Thirteenth Language Resources and Evaluation Conference*, pages 2282–2291.

E. Alzahrani and L. Jololian. 2021. How different text-preprocessing techniques using the BERT model affect the gender profiling of authors. *arXiv preprint arXiv:2109.13890.*

F. Belbachir, T. Roustan, and A. Soukane. 2024. Detecting online sexism: Integrating sentiment analysis with contextual language models. *AI*, 5(4):2852–2863.

A. Conneau, R. Rinott, G. Lample, A. Williams, S. Bowman, H. Schwenk, and V. Stoyanov. 2018. Xnli: Evaluating cross-lingual sentence representations. In *Proceedings of the 2018 Conference on EMNLP.*

A. Das, N. Raychawdhary, T. Bhattacharya, Ge. Dozier, and C. D. Seals. 2023. Au_nlp at semeval-2023 task 10: Explainable detection of online sexism using finetuned roberta. In *Proceedings of the 17th International Workshop on Semantic Evaluation (SemEval-2023)*, pages 707–717.

J. Devlin, M. W. Chang, K. Lee, and K. Toutanova. 2019. Bert: Pre-training of deep bidirectional transformers for language understanding. *NAACL-HLT.*

J. Fox, C. Cruz, and J. Y. Lee. 2015. Perpetuating online sexism offline: Anonymity, interactivity, and the effects of sexist hashtags on social media. *Computers in Human Behavior.*

A. Jiang, N. Vitsakis, T. Dinkar, G. Abercrombie, and I. Konstas. 2024. Re-examining sexism and misogyny classification with annotator attitudes. *arXiv preprint arXiv:2410.03543.*

T. Joachims. 1998. Text categorization with support vector machines: Learning with many relevant features. In *Machine Learning: ECML-98*, pages 137–142. Springer.

B. Krenn, J. Petrak, M. Kubina, and C. Burger. 2024. Germs-at: A sexism/misogyny dataset. In *Proceedings of LREC-COLING 2024.*

Ninareh Mehrabi, Fred Morstatter, Nripsuta Saxena, Kristina Lerman, and Aram Galstyan. 2021. A survey on bias and fairness in machine learning. *ACM computing surveys (CSUR)*, 54(6):1–35.

S. Pingree, R. Hawkins, M. Butler, and W. Paisley. 1976. A scale for sexism. *Journal of Communication.*

E. Plakoyiannaki, P. Mathioudaki, K.and Dimitratos, and Y. Zotos. 2008. Images of women in online advertisements of global products: Does sexism exist? *Journal of Business Ethics.*

H. Saleh, A. Alhothali, and K. Moria. 2023. Detection of hate speech using bert and hate speech word embedding with deep model. *AAI*, 37(1):2166719.

I. Sen, M. Samory, C. Wagner, and I. Augenstein. 2022. Counterfactually augmented data and unintended bias: The case of sexism and hate speech detection. *arXiv preprint arXiv:2205.04238.*

E. Sheng, K. Chang, P. Natarajan, and N. Peng. 2019. The woman worked as a babysitter: On biases in language generation. *EMNLP.*

C. Skinner. 2022. The consequences of online misogyny. *Feminist Media Studies.*

A. Wang, A. Singh, J. Michael, F. Hill, O. Levy, and S. R. Bowman. 2018. Glue: A multi-task benchmark and analysis platform for natural language understanding. In *Proceedings of the 2018 EMNLP Workshop BlackboxNLP.*

T. Wolf, L. Debut, V. Sanh, J. Chaumond, C. Delangue, A. Moi, P. Cistac, T. Rault, R. Louf, M. Funtowicz, and J. Davison. 2020. Transformers: State-of-the-art natural language processing. In *Proceedings of the 2020 conference on EMNLP: system demonstrations*, pages 38–45.

Appendix

A Confusion Matrices

To provide deeper insight into the classification behavior of our models, we include the confusion matrices for both BERT and mBERT on all labeling strategies in Subtask 1.

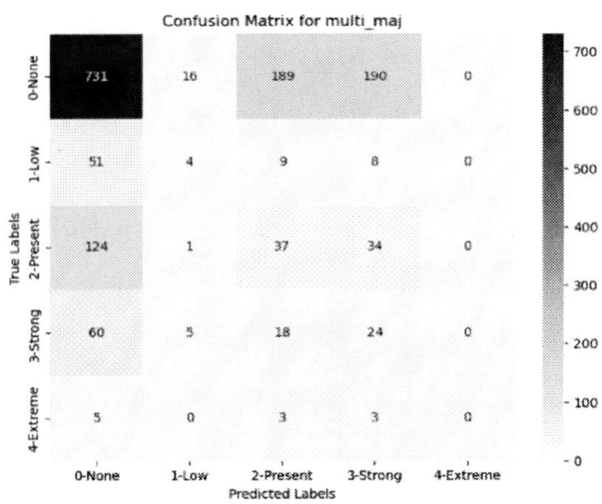

Figure 7: Confusion matrix for multi_maj (BERT)

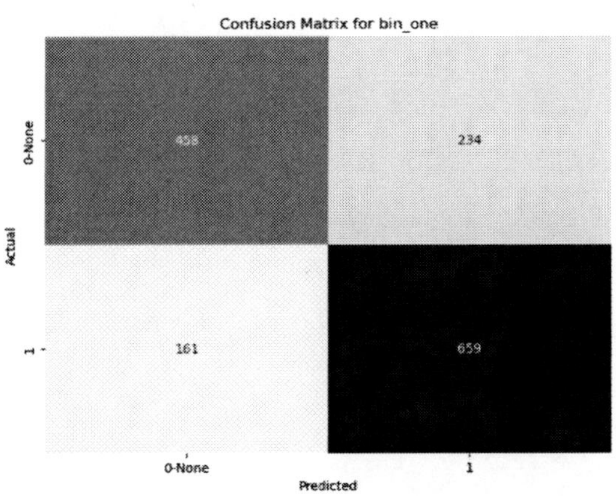

Figure 8: Confusion matrix for bin_one (BERT)

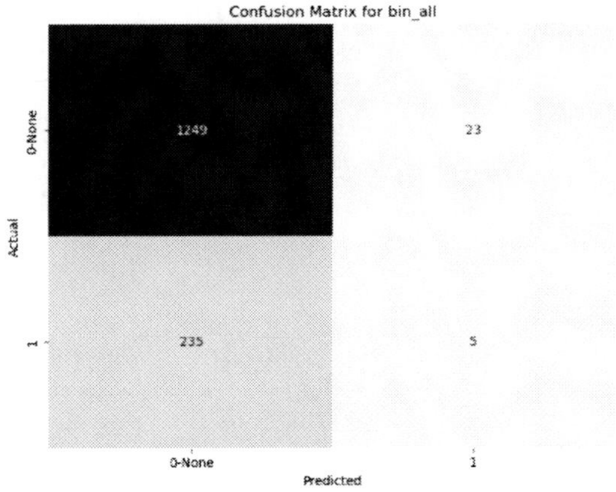

Figure 9: Confusion matrix for bin_all (BERT)

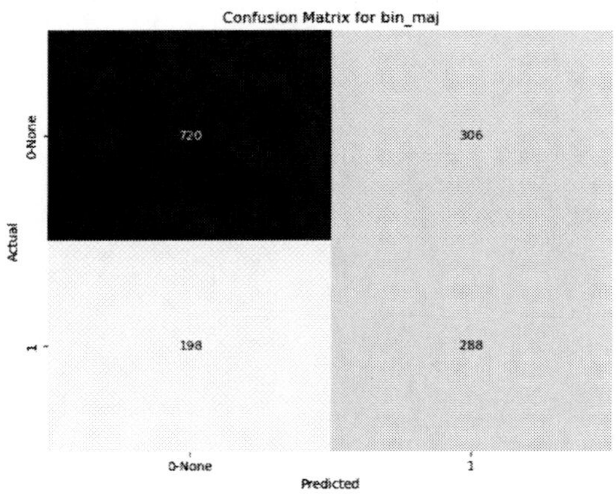

Figure 10: Confusion matrix for bin_maj (BERT)

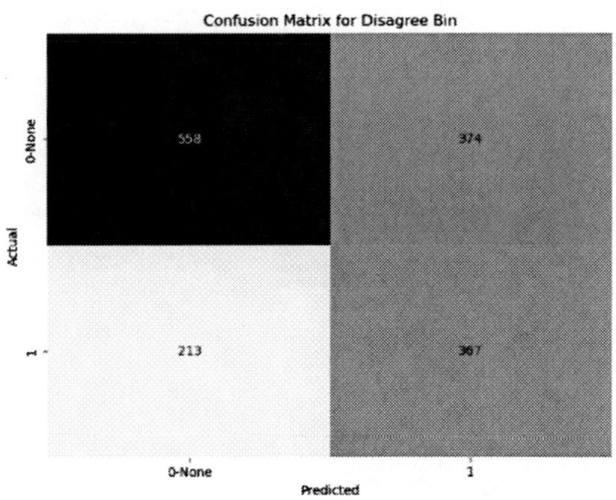

Figure 11: Confusion matrix for disagree_bin (BERT)

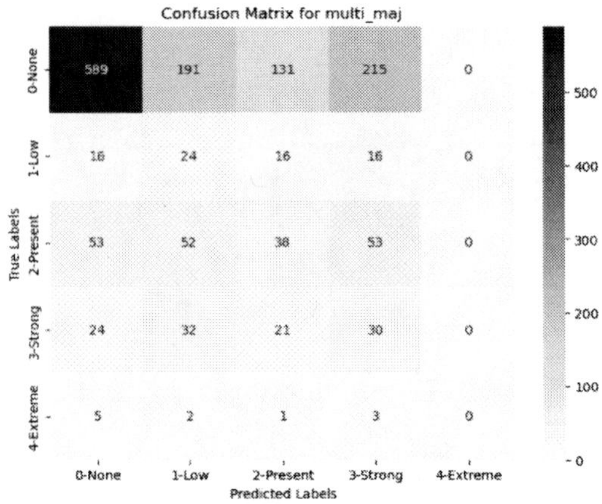

Figure 12: Confusion matrix for multi_maj (mBERT)

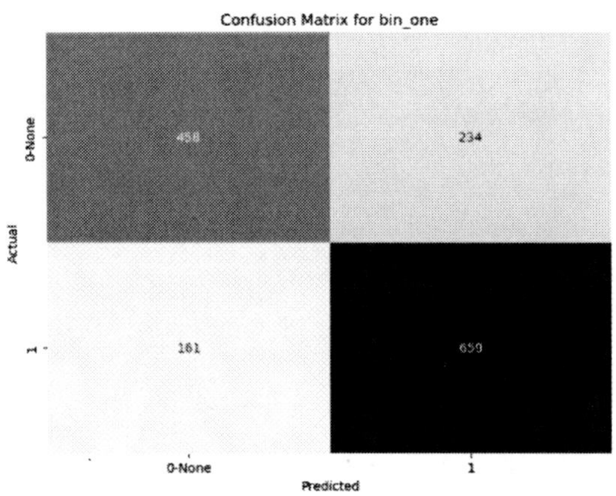

Figure 13: Confusion matrix for bin_one (mBERT)

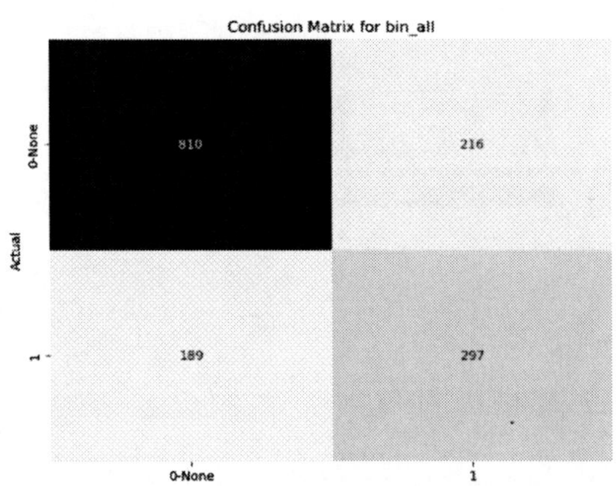

Figure 14: Confusion matrix for bin_all (mBERT)

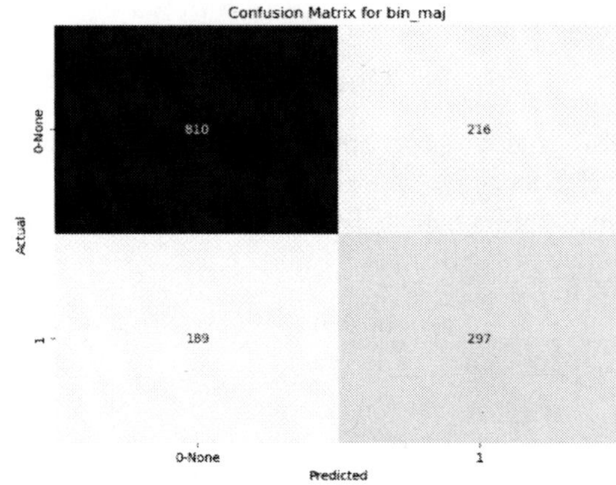

Figure 15: Confusion matrix for bin_maj (mBERT)

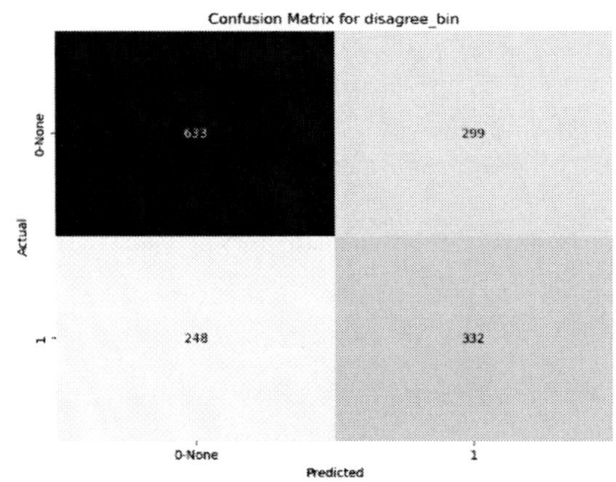

Figure 16: Confusion matrix for disagree_bin (mBERT)

Association for Computational Linguistics
209 N. Eighth Street
Stroudsburg, Pennsylvania 18360

ISBN 979-8-3313-2674-6

CURRAN ASSOCIATES INC.
proceedings.com